Victoria Crosses on the Western Front
April 1915–June 1916

Victoria Crosses on the Western Front April 1915–June 1916

Second Ypres to the Eve of the Somme

Paul Oldfield

Pen & Sword
MILITARY

First published in Great Britain in 2015 by
Pen & Sword Military
an imprint of
Pen & Sword Books Ltd
47 Church Street
Barnsley
South Yorkshire
S70 2AS

Copyright © Paul Oldfield 2015

ISBN 978 1 47382 553 6

The right of Paul Oldfield to be identified as the Author of this Work has been asserted by him in accordance with the Copyright, Designs and Patents Act 1988.

A CIP catalogue record for this book is available from the British Library

All rights reserved. No part of this book may be reproduced or transmitted in any form or by any means, electronic or mechanical including photocopying, recording or by any information storage and retrieval system, without permission from the Publisher in writing.

Typeset in Ehrhardt by
Mac Style Ltd, Bridlington, East Yorkshire
Printed and bound in the UK by CPI Group (UK) Ltd, Croydon, CR0 4YY

Pen & Sword Books Ltd incorporates the imprints of Pen & Sword Archaeology, Atlas, Aviation, Battleground, Discovery, Family History, History, Maritime, Military, Naval, Politics, Railways, Select, Social History, Transport, True Crime, and Claymore Press, Frontline Books, Leo Cooper, Praetorian Press, Remember When, Seaforth Publishing and Wharncliffe.

For a complete list of Pen & Sword titles please contact
PEN & SWORD BOOKS LIMITED
47 Church Street, Barnsley, South Yorkshire, S70 2AS, England
E-mail: enquiries@pen-and-sword.co.uk
Website: www.pen-and-sword.co.uk

Contents

Master Maps	ix
Abbreviations	xvi
Introduction	xx

Chapter 1: Second Battle of Ypres 1915   1

Battle of Gravenstafel Ridge (**Master Map 1**)   1
  60. LCpl Frederick Fisher, 13 Battalion (Royal Highlanders), CEF, 22–23 April 1915, St Julien, Belgium

Battle of St Julien (**Master Map 1**)   13
  61. CSM Frederick Hall, 8 Battalion (90 Rifles), CEF, 24 April 1915, Gravenstafel, Ypres, Belgium
  62. Lt Edward Bellew, 7 Battalion (1 British Columbia), CEF, 24 April 1915, Keerselaere, Belgium
  63. Capt Francis Scrimger, RCAMC att'd 14 Battalion (Royal Montreal), CEF, 25 April 1915, St Julien, Belgium
  64. Cpl Issy Smith, 1 Manchester, 26 April 1915, St Julien, Belgium
  65. Jemadar Mir Dast, 55th Coke's Rifles att'd 57th Wilde's Rifles, 26 April 1915, Wieltje, Belgium
  66. Pte Edward Warner, 1 Bedfordshire, 1 May 1915, Zwarteleen, Belgium
  67. Pte John Lynn, 2 Lancashire Fusiliers, 2 May 1915, St Julien, Belgium

Battle of Frezenberg Ridge (**Master Map 1**)   32
  72. LSgt Douglas Belcher, 1/5 London, 13 May 1915, South of Wieltje-St Julien Road, Belgium

Chapter 2: Aubers and Festubert   37

Battle of Aubers Ridge (**Master Maps 2 & 3**)   37
  68. Cpl John Ripley, 1 Black Watch, 9 May 1915, Rue du Bois, France
  69. LCpl David Finlay, 2 Black Watch, 9 May 1915, Near Rue du Bois, France
  70. Pte James Upton, 1 Sherwood Foresters, 9 May 1915, Rouges Bancs, France
  71. Cpl Charles Sharpe, 2 Lincolnshire, 9 May 1915, Rouges Bancs, France

Battle of Festubert (**Master Maps 3 & 4**) 48
73. LCpl Joseph Tombs, 1 King's, (Liverpool), 16 May 1915, Rue du Bois, France
74. CSM Frederick Barter, 1 Royal Welch Fusiliers, 16 May 1915, Festubert, France
75. Lt John Smyth, 15 Ludhiana Sikhs, 18 May 1915, Richebourg L'Avoué, France
76. Rfn William Mariner, 2 King's Royal Rifle Corps, 22 May 1915, Cambrin, France
77. LCpl Leonard Keyworth, 24 London, 25–26 May 1915, Givenchy, France

Chapter 3: Local Operations Summer 1915 66

Second Action of Givenchy 1915 (**Master Map 3**) 66
78. LCpl William Angus, 8 Highland Light Infantry, (att'd 8 Royal Scots), 12 June 1915, Givenchy, France
79. Lt Frederick Campbell, 1 Battalion (Ontario), CEF, 15 June 1915, Givenchy, France

Actions of Hooge (**Master Map 1**) 72
80. 2Lt Sydney Woodroffe, 8 Rifle Brigade, 30 July 1915, Hooge, Belgium

Other Operations (**Master Map 4**) 79
81. 2Lt George Boyd-Rochfort, 1 Scots Guards, 3 August 1915, Between Cambrin and La Bassée, France

Action of Pietre (**Master Map 3**) 80
82. Rfn Kulbir Thapa, 2/3 Gurkha Rifles, 25 September 1915, South of Fauquissart, France
83. Lt George Maling, 61 Field Ambulance RAMC att'd 12 Rifle Brigade, 25 September 1915, Near Fauquissart, France

Second Attack on Bellewaarde (**Master Map 1**) 85
84. 2Lt Rupert Hallowes, 4 Middlesex, 25–30 September 1915, Hooge, Belgium

Chapter 4: Loos 90

Battle of Loos (**Master Map 4**) 90
85. Piper Daniel Laidlaw, 7 King's Own Scottish Borderers, 25 September 1915, Loos and Hill 70, Loos, France
86. 2Lt Frederick Johnson, 73 Field Company RE, 25 September 1915, Hill 70, Loos, France
87. Lt Col Angus Douglas-Hamilton, 6 Cameron Highlanders, 25–26 September 1915, Hill 70, Loos, France
88. Pte Robert Dunsire, 13 Royal Scots, 25–26 September 1915, Hill 70, Loos, France

Contents   vii

89. Pte George Peachment, 2 King's Royal Rifle Corps, 25 September 1915, Hulluch, France
90. Sgt Harry Wells, 2 Royal Sussex, 25 September 1915, Hulluch, France
91. Capt Anketell Read, 1 Northamptonshire, 25 September 1915, Hulluch, France
92. Pte Henry Kenny, 1 Loyal North Lancashire, 25 September 1915, Loos, France
93. Pte Arthur Vickers, 2 Royal Warwickshire, 25 September 1915, Hulluch, France
94. Capt Arthur Kilby, 2 South Staffordshire, 25 September 1915, South of La Bassée Canal, near Auchy, France
95. Sgt Arthur Saunders, 9 Suffolk, 26 September 1915, Loos, France
96. Cpl James Pollock, 5 Cameron Highlanders, 27 September 1915, Hohenzollern Redoubt, France
97. Cpl Alfred Burt, 1 Hertfordshire, 27 September 1915, Cuinchy, France
98. 2Lt Alexander Turner, 3 att'd 1 Royal Berkshire, 28 September 1915, Fosse 8, near Vermelles, France
99. 2Lt Alfred Fleming-Sandes, 2 East Surrey, 29 September 1915, Hohenzollern Redoubt, France
100. Pte Samuel Harvey, 1 York and Lancaster, 29 September 1915, Hohenzollern Redoubt, France
101. LSgt Oliver Brooks, 3 Coldstream Guards, 8 October 1915, Hohenzollern Redoubt, France
102. Sgt John Raynes, A/LXXI Brigade RFA, 11 October 1915, Fosse 7 de Béthune, France

Actions of the Hohenzollern Redoubt **(Master Map 4)**   127
103. Cpl James Dawson, 187 (Special) Company RE, 13 October 1915, Hohenzollern Redoubt, France
104. Capt Charles Vickers, 1/7 Sherwood Foresters, 14 October 1915, Hohenzollern Redoubt, France
105. Pte Harry Christian, 2 King's Own (Royal Lancaster), 18 October 1915, Cuinchy, France

Chapter 5: Local Operations Winter 1915–16   132

(Master Maps 1, 2 & 6)
106. Pte Thomas Kenny, 13 Durham Light Infantry, 4 November 191, La Houssoie, France
107. Pte John Caffrey, 2 York and Lancaster, 16 November 1915, La Brique, Belgium
108. Cpl Samuel Meekosha, 1/6 West Yorkshire, 19 November 1915, Near the Yser, Belgium
109. Cpl Alfred Drake, 8 Rifle Brigade, 23 November 1915, La Brique, Belgium

viii   Victoria Crosses on the Western Front August 1914–April 1915

110. Pte William Young, 8 East Lancashire, 22 December 1915, Trench 51, east of Fonquevillers, France
111. Lt Eric McNair, 9 Royal Sussex, 14 February 1916, Hooge, Belgium

Chapter 6: Local Operations Spring 1916   143
(Master Maps 1, 4, 5 & 6)
112. Cpl William Cotter, 6 East Kent, 6 March 1916, Hohenzollern Redoubt, France
113. Capt Rev'd Edward Mellish, RAChD att'd 4 Royal Fusiliers, 27–29 March 1916, St Eloi, Belgium
114. 2Lt Edward Baxter, 1/8 King's (Liverpool), 17–18 April 1916, Near Blairville, France
115. Lt Richard Jones, 8 Loyal North Lancashire, 21 May 1916, Broadmarsh Crater, Vimy Ridge, France

Chapter 7: Prelude to the Somme   160
(Master Maps 2, 3, 5 , 6 & 7)
116. Pte George Chafer, 1 East Yorkshire, 3–4 June 1916, East of Meulte, France
117. Pte Arthur Procter, 1/5 King's (Liverpool), 4 June 1916, Near Ficheux, France
118. LCpl John Erskine, 5/6 Cameronians, 22 June 1916, Givenchy, France
119. Spr William Hackett, 254 Tunnelling Company RE, 22–23 June 1916, Givenchy, France
120. Capt Arthur Batten-Pooll, 3 att'd 2 Royal Munster Fusiliers, 25 June 1916, Near Calonne, France
121. Pte William Jackson, 17 Battalion, AIF, 25–26 June 1916, Near Armentieres, France
122. Pte James Hutchinson, 2/5 Lancashire Fusiliers, 28 June 1916, Opposite Ficheux, France
123. CSM Nelson Carter, 12 Royal Sussex, 30 June 1916, Richebourg L'Avoue, France

Biographies   184

Sources   438
Useful Information   448
Index   452

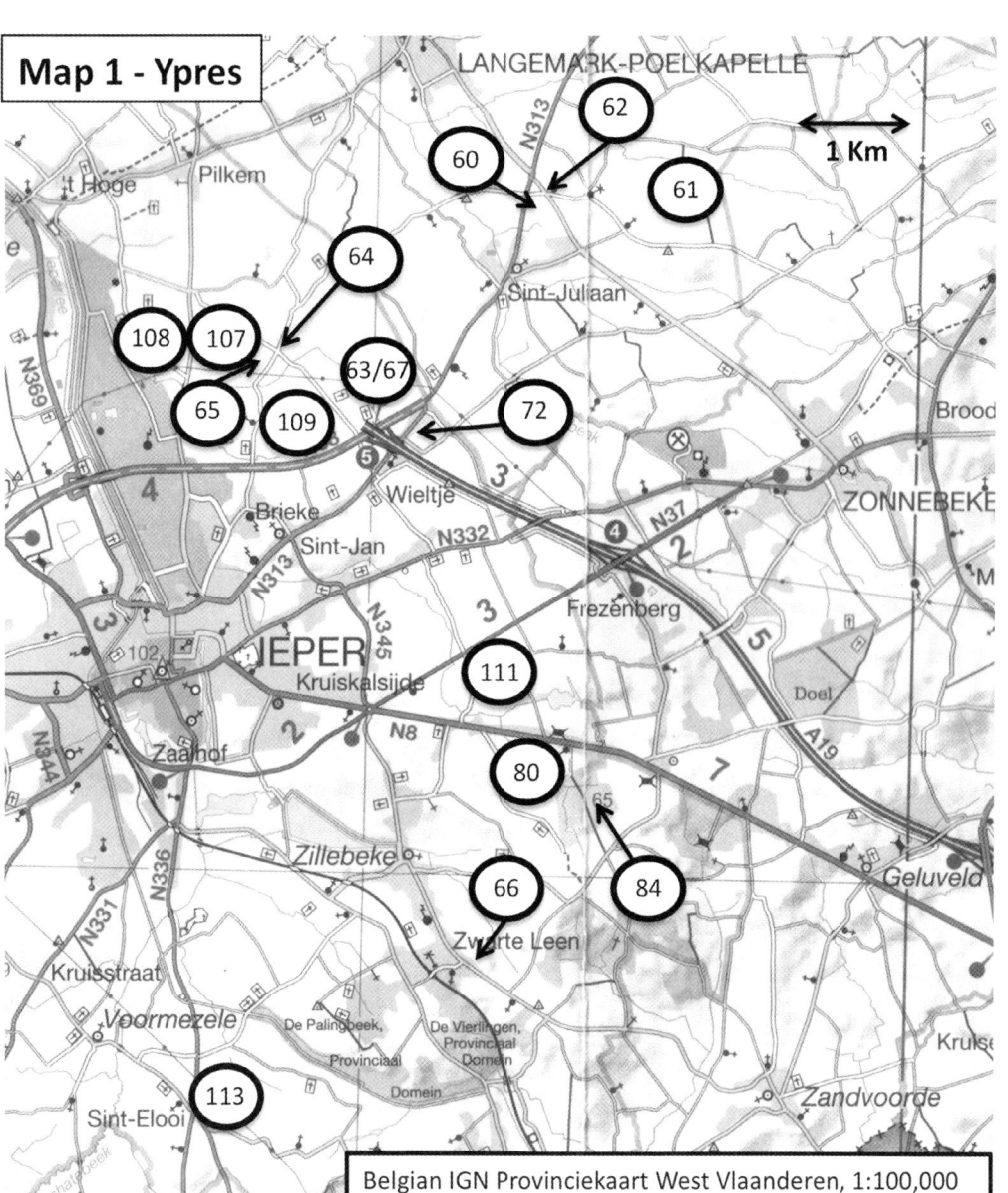

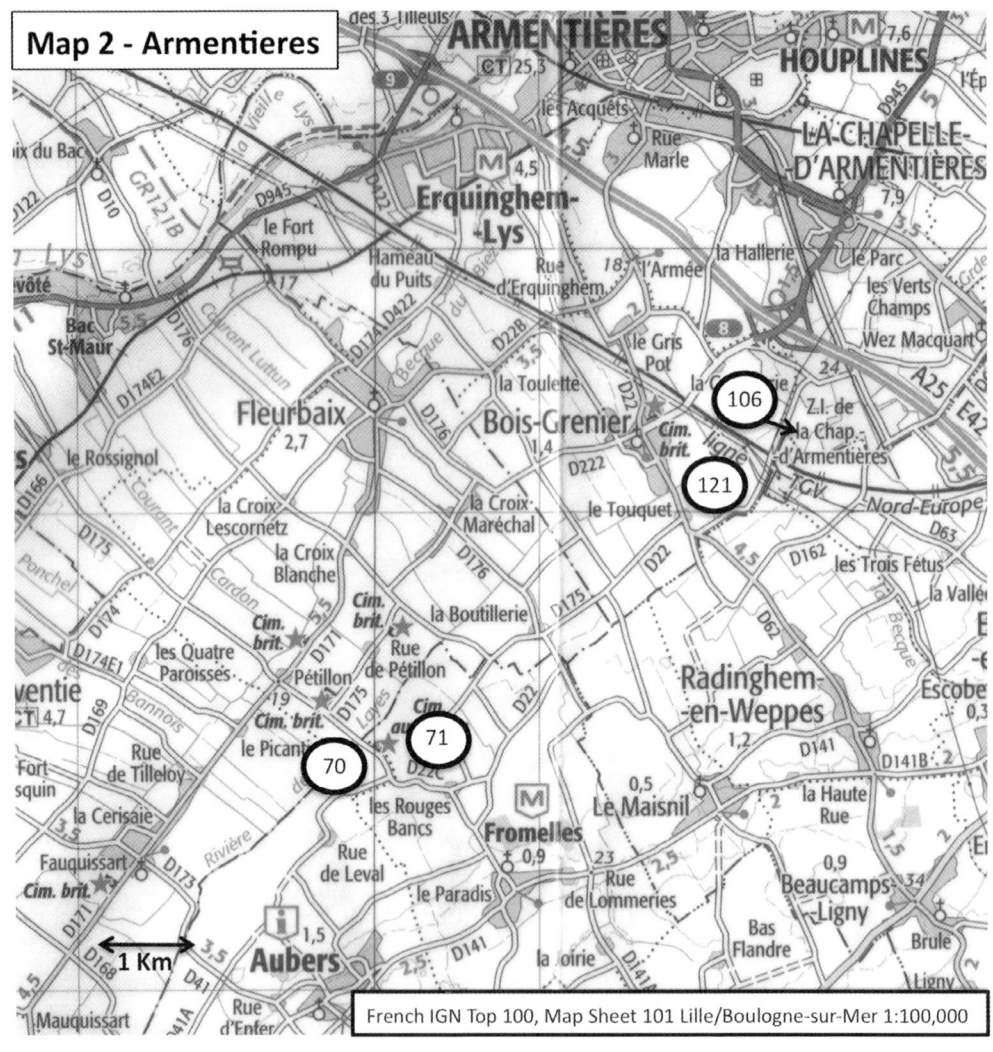

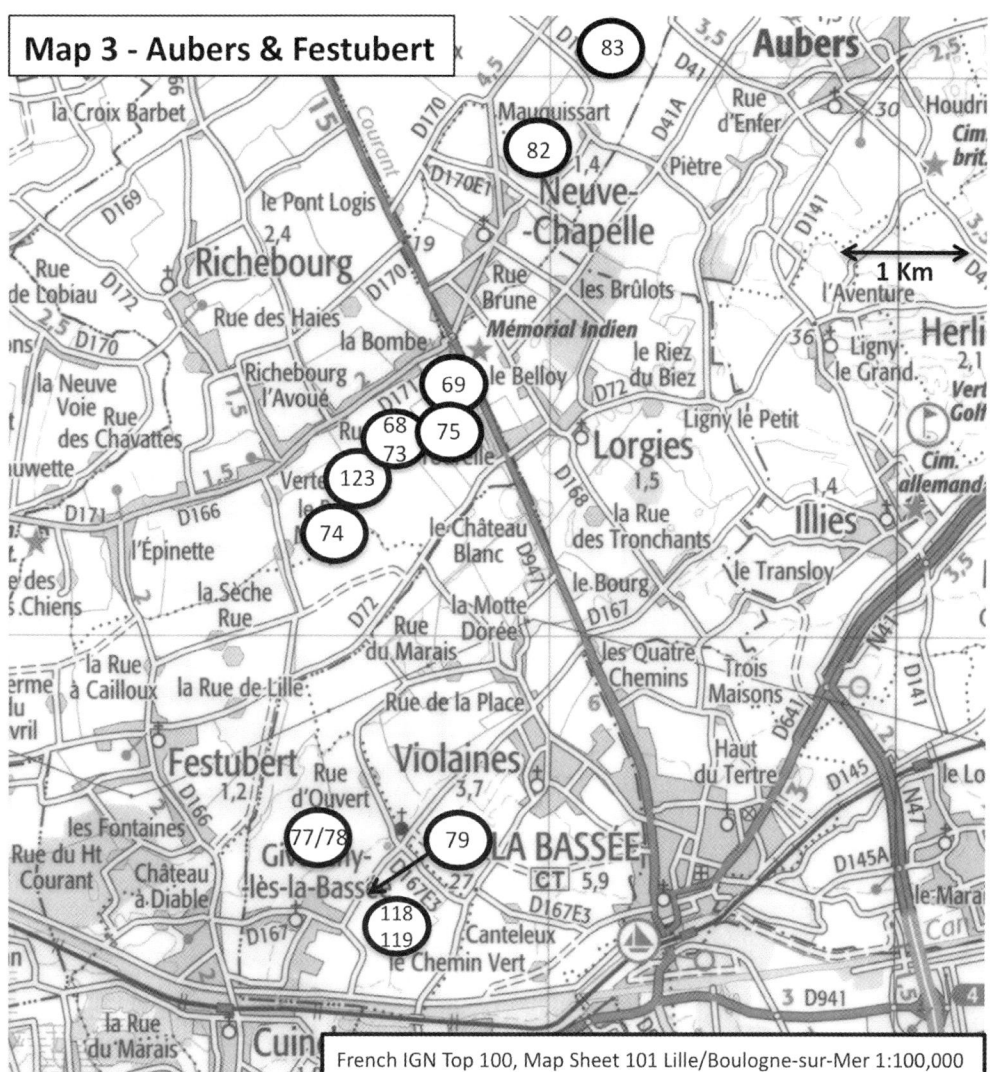

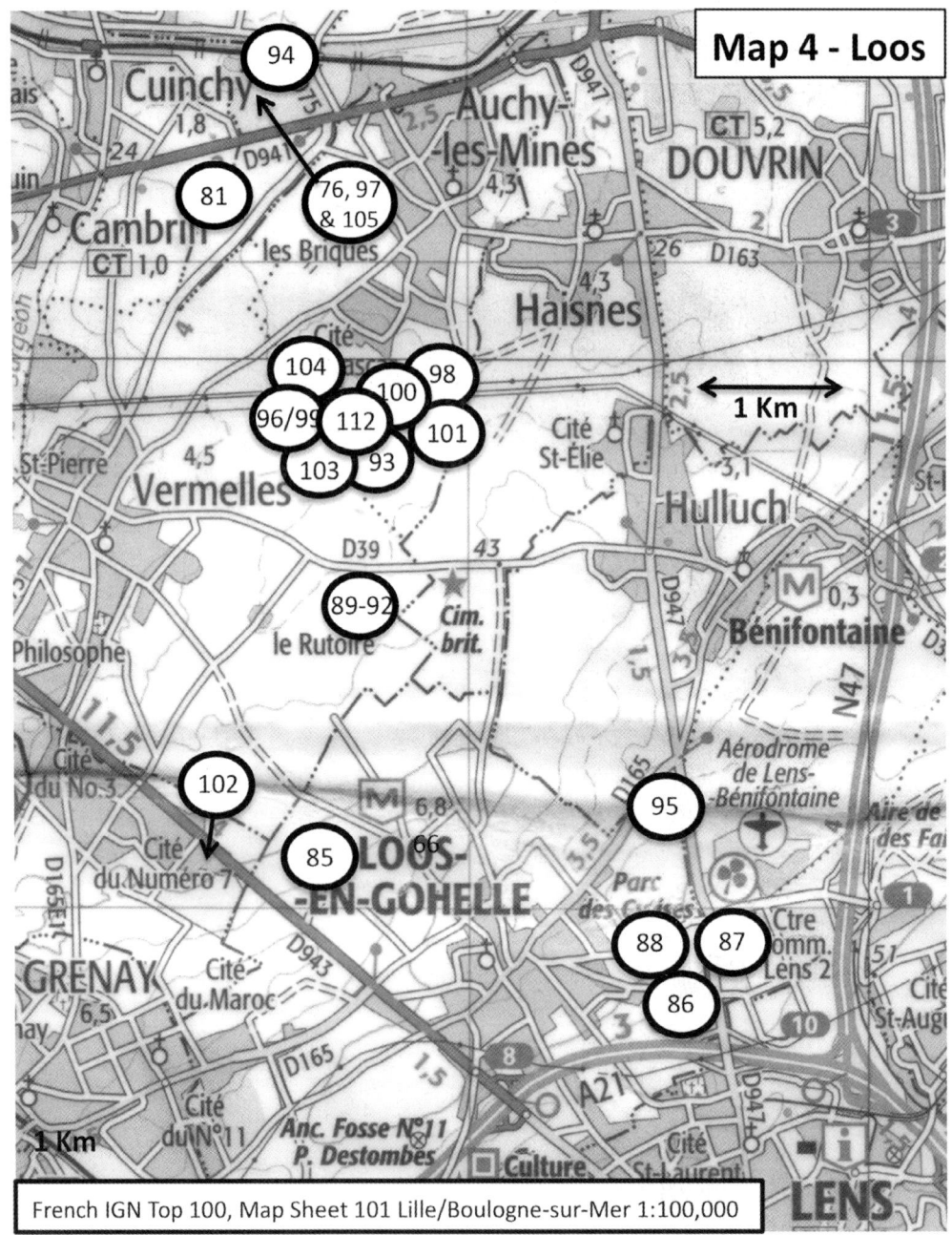

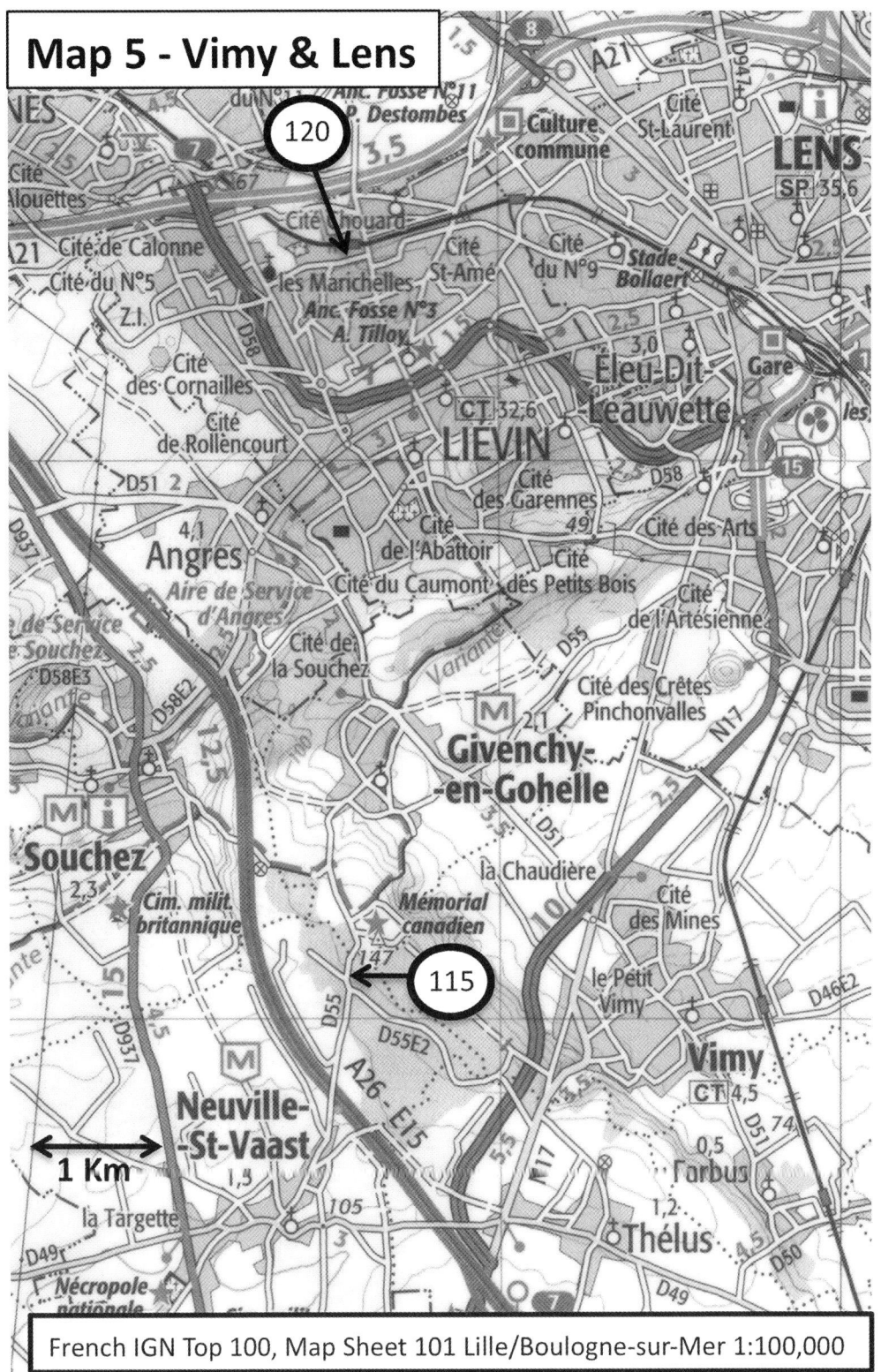

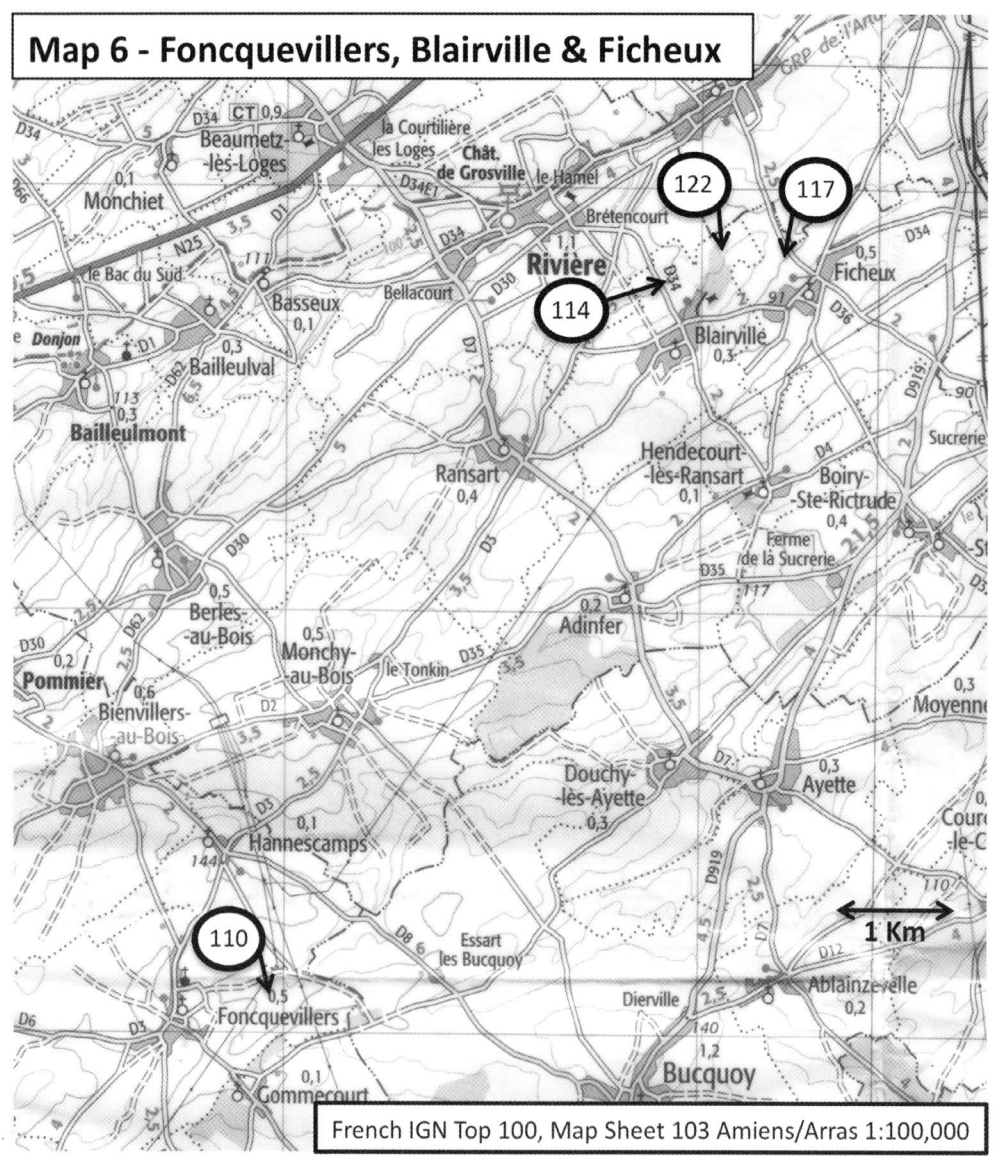

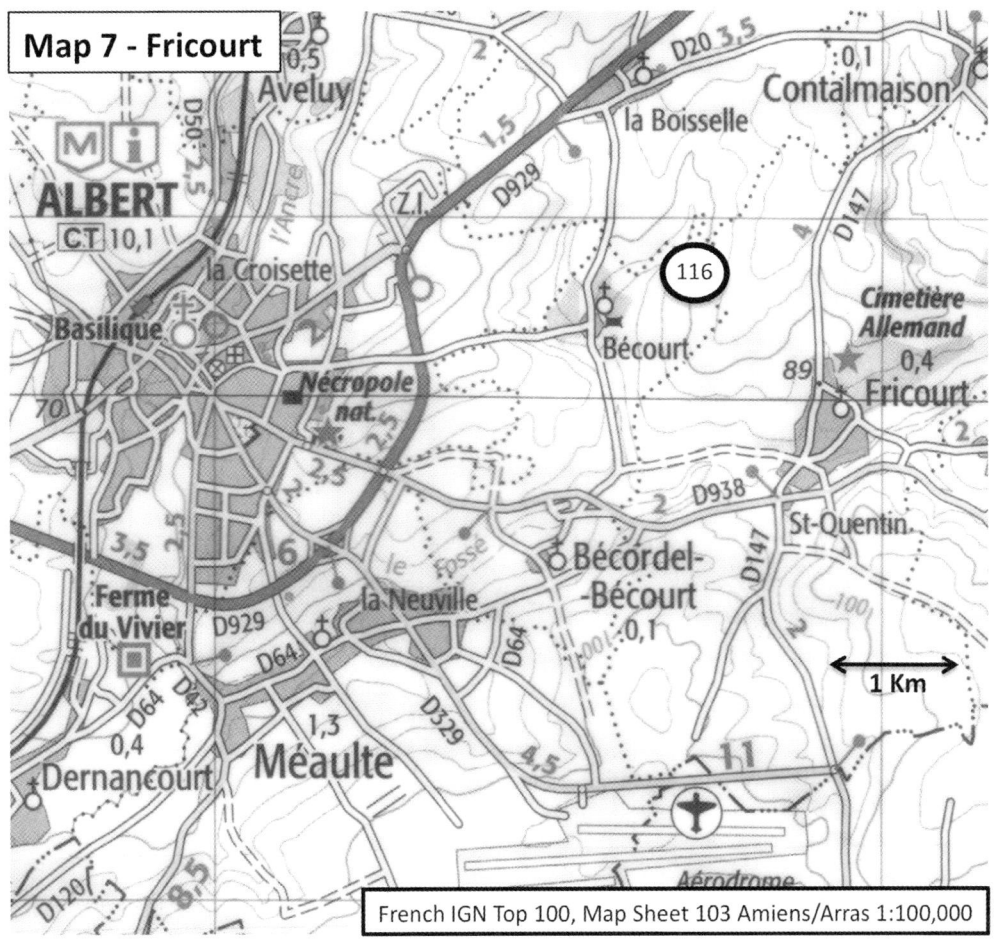

Abbreviations

AA	Anti-aircraft
ADC	Aide-de-Camp
ADS	Advanced Dressing Station
AIF	Australian Imperial Force
ARP	Air Raid Precautions
ASC	Army Service Corps
ATS	Auxiliary Territorial Service
Att'd	Attached
BA	Bachelor of Arts
BCh or ChB	Bachelor of Surgery
BEF	British Expeditionary Force
BMA	British Medical Association
Brig-Gen	Brigadier General
BS	Bachelor of Surgery
BSM	Battery Sergeant Major
BSc	Bachelor of Science
Bty	Battery (artillery unit of 4–8 guns)
CAMC	Canadian Army Medical Corps
Capt	Captain
CB	Companion of the Order of the Bath
CB	Confined to Barracks
CBE	Commander of the Order of the British Empire
CE	Canadian Engineers
CEF	Canadian Expeditionary Force
CERA	Chief Engine Room Artificer
CFA	Canadian Field Artillery
CGA	Canadian Garrison Artillery
C-in-C	Commander-in-Chief
CMG	Companion of the Order of St Michael & St George
CO	Commanding Officer
Col	Colonel
Cpl	Corporal
CQMS	Company Quartermaster Sergeant
CSgt	Colour Sergeant

CSM	Company Sergeant Major
CStJ	Commander of the Most Venerable Order of the Hospital of Saint John of Jerusalem
Cty	Cemetery
CVO	Commander of the Royal Victorian Order
CWGC	Commonwealth War Graves Commission
DAAG	Deputy Assistant Adjutant General
DCLI	Duke of Cornwall's Light Infantry
DCM	Distinguished Conduct Medal
DD	Doctor of Divinity
DJStJ	Dame of Justice of the Most Venerable Order of the Hospital of Saint John of Jerusalem
DL	Deputy Lieutenant
DLI	Durham Light Infantry
DSO	Distinguished Service Order
Dvr	Driver
FM	Field Marshal
FRCS	Fellow of the Royal College of Surgeons
GCB	Knight Grand Cross of the Order of the Bath
GCMG	Knight Grand Cross of the Order of St Michael & St George
Gen	General
GOC	General Officer Commanding
GOC-in-C	General Officer Commanding in Chief
GSO1, 2 or 3	General Staff Officer Grade 1 (Lt Col), 2 (Maj) or 3 (Capt)
HLI	Highland Light Infantry
HMHS	Her/His Majesty's Hospital Ship
HMS	Her/His Majesty's Ship
HMT	Her/His Majesty's Transport/Troopship
HRH	His/Her Royal Highness
IAOC	Indian Army Ordnance Corps
JP	Justice of the Peace
KBE	Knight Commander of the Most Excellent Order of the British
KCB	Knight Commander of the Order of the Bath
KCVO	Knight Commander of the Royal Victorian Order
KGStJ	Knight of Grace of the Most Venerable Order of the Hospital of Saint John of Jerusalem
KJStJ	Knight of Justice of the Most Venerable Order of the Hospital of Saint John of Jerusalem
Kms	Kilometres
KOSB	King's Own Scottish Borderers
KOYLI	King's Own Yorkshire Light Infantry
KRRC	King's Royal Rifle Corps

KSLI	King's Shropshire Light Infantry
LCpl	Lance Corporal
LDV	Local Defence Volunteers (predecessor of Home Guard)
LG	London Gazette
LRCP	Licentiate of the Royal College of Physicians
LSA	Licentiate of the Society of Apothecaries
Lt	Lieutenant
Lt Col	Lieutenant Colonel
Lt Gen	Lieutenant General
Maj	Major
Maj Gen	Major General
MA	Master of Arts
MB	Bachelor of Medicine
MBE	Member of the Order of the British Empire
MC	Military Cross
MGC	Machine Gun Corps
MID	Mentioned in Despatches
MM	Military Medal
MO	Medical Officer
MP	Member of Parliament
MRCP	Member of the Royal College of Physicians
MRCS	Member of the Royal College of Surgeons
MSM	Meritorious Service Medal
MT	Motor Transport
MVO	Member of the Royal Victorian Order
NSW	New South Wales
OBE	Officer of the Order of the British Empire
OP	Observation Post
OStJ	Officer of the Most Venerable Order of the Hospital of Saint John of Jerusalem
OTC	Officers' Training Corps
PC	Police Constable
PPCLI	Princess Patricia's Canadian Light Infantry
Pte	Private
QAINSR	Queen Alexandra's Imperial Nursing Service Reserve
RA	Royal Artillery
RAF	Royal Air Force
RAFVR	Royal Air Force Volunteer Reserve
RAAF	Royal Auxiliiary Air Force
RAMC	Royal Army Medical Corps
RCAF	Royal Canadian Air Force
RCAMC	Royal Canadian Army Medical Corps

RE	Royal Engineers
RFA	Royal Field Artillery
RFC	Royal Flying Corps
RGA	Royal Garrison Artillery
RHA	Royal Horse Artillery
RMS	Royal Mail Ship/Steamer
RN	Royal Navy
RNR	Royal Naval Reserve
RSL	Returned Services League
RSM	Regimental Sergeant Major
RTO	Railway Transport Officer
Sgt	Sergeant
SMLE	Short Magazine Lee Enfield
Spr	Sapper
TA	Territorial Army
TD	Territorial Decoration
TF	Territorial Force
TSS	Twin Screw Steamer
VAD	Voluntary Aid Detachment
VD	Volunteer Decoration
VC	Victoria Cross
VTC	Volunteer Training Corps
WO1 or 2	Warrant Officer Class 1 or 2
YMCA	Young Men's Christian Association

Introduction

This is the second in a series of nine books covering all 492 Western Front land forces Victoria Crosses during the First World War. It is written for the battlefield visitor as well as the armchair reader. Each account provides background information to explain the broad strategic and tactical situation, before examining the VC action in detail. Each is supported by a map to allow a visitor to stand on, or close to, the spot and at least one photograph of the site. Detailed biographies help to understand the man behind the Cross.

As far as possible chapters and sections within them follow the titles of battles, actions and affairs as decided by the post-war Battle Nomenclature Committee. VCs are numbered chronologically 60, 61, 62 … 123 from 22nd April 1915–30th June 1916. As far as possible they are described in the same order, but when a number of actions were fought simultaneously, the VCs are covered out of sequence on a geographical basis.

Refer to the master maps to find the general area for each VC. If visiting the battlefields it is advisable to purchase maps from the respective French and Belgian 'Institut Géographique National'. The French IGN Top 100 and Belgian IGN Provinciekaart at 1:100,000 scale are ideal for motoring, but 1:50,000, 1:25,000 or 1:20,000 scale maps are necessary for more detailed work, e.g. French IGN Serie Bleue and Belgian IGN Topografische Kaart. They are obtainable from the respective IGN or through reputable map suppliers on-line.

Ranks are as used on the day. Grave references have been shortened, e.g. 'Plot II, Row A, Grave 10' will appear as 'II A 10'. There are some abbreviations, many in common usage, but if unsure refer to the list provided.

Thanks are due to too many people and organizations to mention here. They are acknowledged in 'Sources' and any omissions are my fault and not intentional. However, I will single out my fellow researchers in the 'Victoria Cross Database Users Group', who provided information and other assistance selflessly over many years – Doug and Richard Arman, Vic Tambling and Alan Jordan, assisted by Alasdair Macintyre. I would also like to acknowledge the continuing support of my family.

Paul Oldfield
Wiltshire
September 2014

Chapter One

Second Battle of Ypres 1915

Battle of Gravenstafel Ridge, 22nd–23rd April 1915

> 60 LCpl Frederick Fisher, 13th Battalion (Royal Highlanders), CEF (3rd Canadian Brigade, 1st Canadian Division), Keerselaere, Belgium

By early 1915, the Germans realised that they could not force a decision on the Western Front that year. As a result, they decided to concentrate on knocking Russia out of the war. If they were successful, the western allies would then have to face the entire German might in the west, so they had to relieve pressure on the Russians. Plans were hatched for operations in other theatres and for offensive action on the Western Front. Although the Germans were going to concentrate their main efforts in the east, small attacks would be launched in the west in order to retain some initiative and to pin down Allied forces.

The BEF had suffered crippling casualties in 1914 (60,000 at Ypres alone), and as a result was short of men and materiel. Despite these problems, the BEF took over more of the front from the French. Ypres was the only significant town in Belgium still held by the Allies. Fighting around it in the First Battle of Ypres in late 1914 had resulted in a dangerous salient to the east, stretching for 27 kms from Steenstraat in the north to St Eloi in the south. V Corps was formed under Lieutenant General Plumer to take over the eastern part of the Salient from the French.

The German 4th Army (General-Oberst Duke Albrecht von Württemberg) held the front from the Belgian coast to the Lys, southeast of Ypres. Duke Albrecht planned to reduce the Ypres Salient and shorten the line. He intended holding the south of the Salient with two corps, while the main attack by XXVI and XXIII Corps from the north swept over Pilckem Ridge towards Ypres. General Erich von Falkenhayn, German Chief of the General Staff, added other aims; to test the effectiveness of poisonous gas and divert attention from an offensive in the East.

The point of attack gave the Germans a number of advantages. It was at the junction of the French and British sectors, a natural weak point, and there was no unified command over the Belgian, French and British forces (and wouldn't be until spring 1918). In addition, two of the three Allied divisions (45th Algerian and 1st Canadian) were new to the area.

German research into chemical munitions began in 1887, but negative results and the Hague Conventions of 1899 and 1907, forbidding the use of poisonous

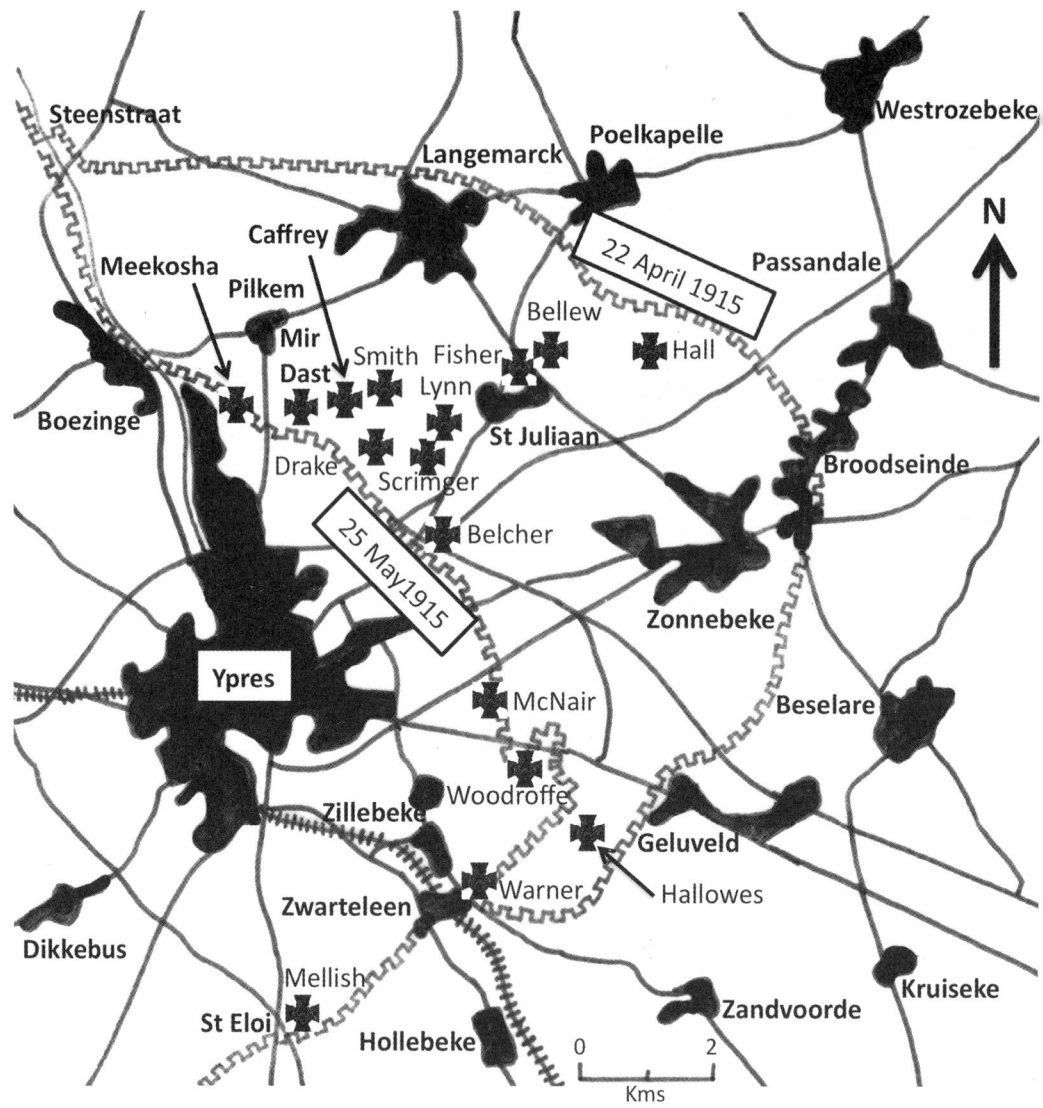

The front lines before and after the Second Battle of Ypres. 22nd April–25th May 1915. The line held by late May remained largely unchanged until the opening of the Third Battle of Ypres on 31st July 1917. The shrunken Salient proved more arduous and costly to hold, but hold it did. Also shown are the sixteen VCs in this book in the Ypres area from late April 1915 to March 1916.

gas, halted the work. Von Falkenhayn directed it to resume in September 1914. He envisaged using gas to force the enemy to leave the protection of their trenches, thereby breaking the trench stalemate and recreating a war of movement.

Chemical weapons had been used before. An irritant powder added to shrapnel shells fired at British troops at Neuve Chapelle on 27th October 1914 appeared to have had no ill effects. Explosive shells containing a liquid irritant were tried unsuccessfully against the Russians at Bolimov on 30th January 1915. Fritz Haber, Director of the Kaiser Wilhelm Institute for Physical Chemistry and Electrochemistry at Berlin-Dahlem, proposed using chlorine gas released from pressurised cylinders

Fritz Haber (1868–1934), of Jewish origin, was a brilliant chemist, whose involvement in the development of chemical weapons has overshadowed his other work. While at the University of Karlsruhe 1894–1911, he and Carl Bosch developed the Haber-Bosch process; the catalytic formation of ammonia from hydrogen and atmospheric nitrogen. He received the 1918 Nobel Prize for Chemistry for this work. Half the world's food production still depends upon this process to produce fertilisers. He carried out much of his work from 1911 at the Kaiser Wilhelm Institute in Berlin, which in 1953 was named after him.

dug into the front line and blown along by a favourable wind. Attacking troops could follow closely behind the gas cloud with little risk. Chlorine gas was available commercially and could be manufactured without the need for secrecy.

Some German commanders were disgusted by the concept and were dubious about its reliability, but they realised it might lead to a decisive breakthrough. Oberst Peterson trained a special unit, Pioneer-Regiment 35, to operate the gas cylinders and by 11th April 5,730 gas cylinders in groups of twenty were in position.

The use of gas should not have come as a surprise to the Allies. In early February, German soldiers captured by the French spoke of gas cylinders in bombproof shelters. On 28th March, a British raid at Zillebeke found cylinders in front of the German trenches. On 9th April, 'The Times' reported the Germans, "... *propose to asphyxiate our men ... by means of poisonous gas ...*" On 13th April, Private August Jaeger (51st Reserve Division) deserted to the French 11th Division (General Ferry), near Langemarck. Jaeger told of an impending attack involving asphyxiating gas carried by the wind and even provided the attack frontage – Langemarck to the Poelcapelle-Wieltje road. Ferry informed the British 28th Division and 2nd Canadian Brigade and passed the report up his chain of command, but it was received with scepticism. The French also learned from a Belgian agent that the Germans had placed an urgent order for 20,000 mouth-protectors at a factory in Ghent. Allied HQs paid little attention to the warnings; it was assumed that if gas was used it would cause minor irritation and have only a localised effect.

Duke Albrecht ordered the attack to take place on 16th April. A Belgian agent reported the move forward of German reserves and the intention to use gas when the wind was favourable. HQ V Corps was warned and instructed medical units to expect 1,000 casualties, but no arrangements were made to deal with gas. On the morning of 16th April, 6 Squadron RFC saw no gas cylinders and the roads behind the enemy lines were clear. Because there was no wind, the German assault troops had returned to the rear areas before daylight.

On 17th April, V Corps completed taking over the front from the Menin Road northwards to the Ypres-Poelcapelle road. 27th Division was on the right,

28th Division in the centre and 1st Canadian Division (Lieutenant General Edwin Alderson) continued the line for four kilometres to just beyond the Ypres-Poelcapelle road and the junction with the French 45th Algerian Division.

The Canadians found the trenches filthy, with numerous dead in shallow graves. Most trenches were breastworks, some only waist high, and were not continuous. They set to work to strengthen the front line, putting out wire, setting up strong points and joining sections into a continuous line. Two to five kilometres behind the front line, there already existed a well-wired GHQ Line consisting of a series of redoubts 350–450m apart.

When the British attacked at Hill 60 on 17th April, German commanders feared the gas cylinders would be discovered and furious counterattacks took place. German reconnaissance flights increased and shelling of Ypres and Poperinghe intensified to distract Allied attention.

The Krupps L/12, 42 cms Type M-Gerät 14 Kurze Marine-Kanone, otherwise known as 'Dicke (Big) Bertha'. The Allies tended to refer to any large German gun as Big Bertha, but the Germans restricted the name to this 42 cms howitzer. Although commonly held that it was named after Bertha Krupp, heiress and owner of the Krupps industrial empire, this may not be so. If it was named after her, one wonders what she thought of the honour!

A second attempt to launch the attack on 19th April was cancelled due to unfavourable wind and the troops withdrew covered by thick mist. That day, a 42cm howitzer (Big Bertha) sited near Houthulst Forest, joined the bombardment of Ypres. It fired up to ten 816 kgs shells per hour and heralded the start of the systematic destruction of the town. Refugees left the city, heading west for Poperinghe.

The weather improved a few days later and Duke Albrecht ordered the attack for 22nd April. During the night German troops packed into the front line and gas pipes were laid over the parapet. However, as dawn broke the wind was not favourable and the attack was postponed until 4 p.m. The left of 1st Canadian Division reported pipes projecting through the German parapet. At 4 p.m. the wind was blowing from the

Bertha Krupp 1886–1957.

An enormous shell hole at Ypres, possibly caused by Big Bertha (Australian official photograph).

north at seven kilometres per hour. The commanders of XXIII Reserve and XXVI Reserve Corps were unhappy about attacking in broad daylight, but 4th Army issued the order.

1st Canadian Division's front was held by 2nd and 3rd Canadian Brigades. 2nd Canadian Brigade (Brigadier General Currie) on the right had 8th Canadian Battalion on its left, 5th Canadian Battalion on its right and 7th Canadian Battalion in reserve on the St Julien Fortuin road, at Bombarded Cross Roads and in Wieltje. 3rd Canadian Brigade (Brigadier General Turner VC) on the left, in contact with the French, had 13th Canadian Battalion on the left, 15th Canadian Battalion on the right

German pioneers in Poland attending to gas cylinders in a sandbagged emplacement. The pipes that will discharge the gas into no man's land disappear over the parapet in front.

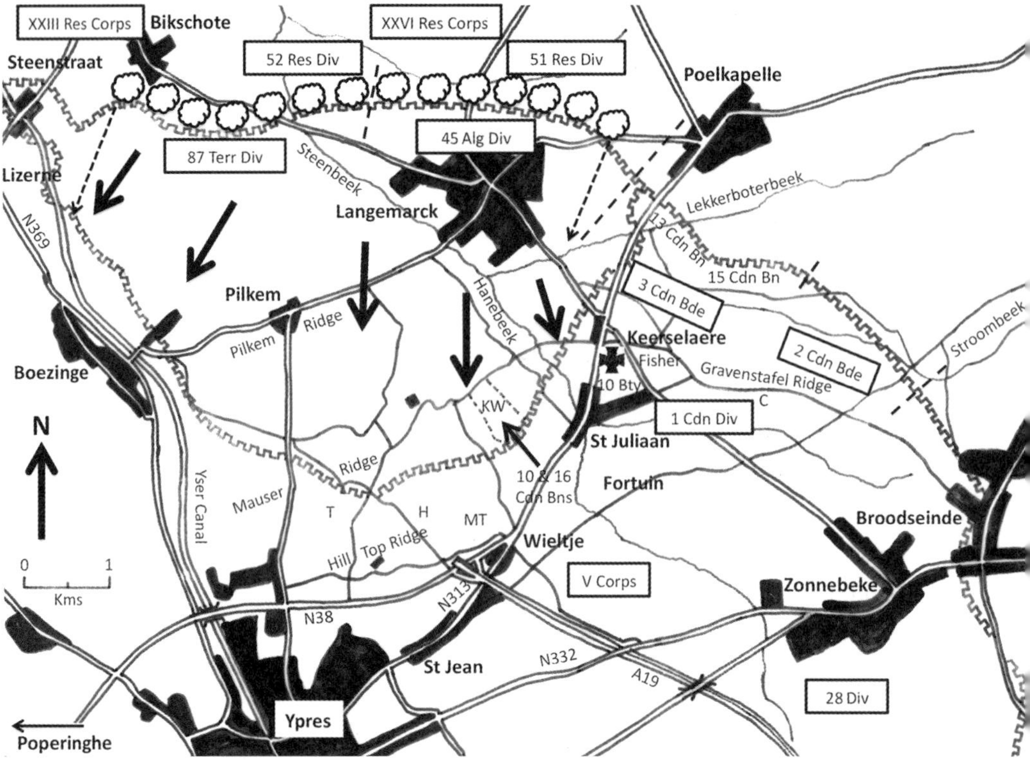

The area of the gas attack on 22nd April 1915. The front lines before and after are shown. The Germans punched an enormous hole in the Allied line, threatening Ypres and the whole of the BEF. A number of locations are shown by letters – T = Turco Farm, H = Hampshire Farm, MT = Mouse (Shell) Trap Farm, KW = Kitcheners' Wood and C = Locality C. From Ypres drive northeast on the N313 towards Poelcapelle. Go through St Juliaan and park somewhere convenient and safe on the right where the buildings run out. The fields on the right are where 10th Battery CFA was located on 22nd April 1915.

This is a French gas attack on the Somme in 1917, but it illustrates what would have happened on 22nd April 1915 near Langemarck (Canadian Military History Vol 8).

and 14th Canadian Battalion in reserve at St Jean. A battalion from each brigade (10th and 16th) formed the Divisional reserve, while 1st Canadian Brigade was the Second Army Reserve at Vlamertinghe, five kilometres west of Ypres.

The afternoon of 22nd April was sunny and the sound of fighting at Hill 60 could be heard in the north of the Salient. A furious bombardment of Ypres by Big Bertha and other heavy howitzers opened, but the German field artillery was silent. At 5 p.m. the gas cylinder valves were opened and 168 tons of chlorine gas were discharged in ten minutes along the front held by the French between Steenstraat and Langemarck.

It took ten minutes for the thick yellow-green cloud to reach the French trenches. The French assumed that the Germans were advancing behind a smoke screen but when the cloud arrived soldiers developed severe chest pains and a burning sensation in the throat. Many died within minutes, primarily from asphyxiation. Others were blinded by hydrochloric acid forming in the eyes when the chlorine combined with water. The gas was denser than air and filled the trenches, forcing the defenders to climb out into heavy enemy fire. Captain Hugh Pollard was a witness, *"… in a moment death had them by the throat. One cannot blame them that they broke and fled … Hundreds of them fell and died; others lay helpless, froth upon their agonized lips …"*.

The cloud rolled through the French 87th Territorial and 45th Algerian Divisions. Only a few men remained to fight, leaving a gap of six kilometres in the front. The main effect was in a rectangular area bounded by Steenstraat, Boesinghe, Keerselare and Langemarck, but it was noticed further behind the lines. French troops passed through V Corps' rear area, but it was impossible to understand what they were saying. However, it was clear that something serious had happened.

German assault troops advanced behind the cloud, wearing gauze and cotton masks. In XXIII Reserve Corps, 46th Reserve Division with some troops of 45th

German troops with early cotton and gauze gas masks.

Reserve Division advanced towards the Yser Canal and Steenstraat, where the gas did not have such a significant effect; the advance here made slow progress against the French and Belgians. XXVI Reserve Corps headed for Langemarck and Pilckem Ridge. In this area the gas devastated 87th Territorial Division and the German 51st and 52nd Reserve Divisions pushed through almost unhindered towards Pilckem Ridge.

The Colt-Browning M1895/14 machine-gun in service with Canadian forces early in WW1 fired 450 rounds per minute. It was the first successful gas operated machine-gun to enter service, but had a strange external cocking lever that was apt to dig into the ground if fired from a low position, hence its nickname, 'Potato Digger'. As it was air-cooled, it was lighter than the water-cooled machine-guns in use with other armies, but if fired for prolonged periods tended to overheat. It also operated from a closed-bolt, making it prone to cook-offs. The Canadians adopted the Vickers soon after.

By 5.30 p.m., the Germans had broken through, creating a gap between Steenstraat and the left of 3rd Canadian Brigade; the way to Ypres appeared to be open. The French right, held by 1st Tirailleurs, had not been badly affected by the gas and remained in position, supported by 2nd bis Zouaves (half battalion) to the north of Kitcheners' Wood.

1 Company (Major DR McCuaig – DSO for this action) was on the left of 13th Canadian Battalion. There was a 100m gap on its right, through which flowed a stream, before 2 Company in the centre and on the right flank was 4 Company. 3 Company (Major EC Norsworthy) was in support, with two platoons 350m behind 1 Company and the other two platoons were with Battalion HQ in St Julien. A mile of road to the north of St Julien was left unguarded except for 10th Battery CFA south of Keerselaare.

At 5.30 p.m., 3rd Canadian Brigade reported its area was quiet, but a cloud of green vapour was seen in the French area from where there was heavy firing. Alderson returned to his HQ at 5.50 p.m. after inspecting the forward brigades. At 6 p.m., he ordered HQ 3rd Canadian Brigade to render any help possible to the French. 14th Canadian Battalion in reserve was ordered by Brigadier General Turner to report to Brigade HQ at Mouse (Shell) Trap Farm. On arrival the Battalion (less No.2 Company at St Julien under 13th Canadian Battalion) was deployed in the GHQ Line north of the Wieltje-St Julien road, together with 3rd Field Company CE and the Brigade Grenade Company. From there, 500 Zouaves extended the line to Hampshire Farm. Patrols went forward to establish contact with 13th Canadian Battalion and about 200 Algerians from 1st and 2nd Tirailleurs (45th Algerian Division) joined the Canadians. The two Colt machine-guns of 14th Canadian Battalion were mounted in the ruins of the village.

On the left of 13th Canadian Battalion, Major McCuaig led one of the 1 Company platoons across the St Julien-Poelcapelle road into the trenches of 1st Tirailleurs.

They held a breastwork 75m from the road and exchanged fire with Germans occupying a hedge 100m away. Lack of cover prevented them from extending the French line to the rear, so half the Canadian platoon took up positions in the ditch of the St Julien-Poelcapelle road, where it was joined by another platoon and a machine-gun team. A dozen casualties were caused when this position was hit from behind by a friendly battery. Several hundred metres behind the left of 13th Canadian Battalion, two supporting platoons of 3 Company lined the road ditch around the culvert carrying the Lekkerboterbeek, supported by some Tirailleurs. They came under extreme pressure from the attacking Germans.

Half an hour after the launch of the attack, 52nd Reserve Division had advanced three kilometres. 51st Reserve Division's progress had been slower, having encountered opposition at Langemarck and on the Canadian left. Without the full support of 51st Reserve Division on its left, 52nd Reserve Division halted on Pilckem Ridge, only a few hundred metres west of HQ 3rd Canadian Brigade.

Canadian units began moving to meet the threat. 1st Canadian Division Engineers were having their evening meal prior to working in the trenches. 3rd Field Company moved to the GHQ Line east of Mouse (Shell) Trap Farm, covering the Wieltje-St Julien road, while the other companies prepared the Canal bridges for demolition. 1st Brigade CFA moved to positions near the Canal. The doctor, Major John McCrae, witnessed French stragglers and Belgian refugees steaming past. As shells roared overhead into Ypres, he did what he could to assist the injured. A week later, McCrae wrote the poem *In Flanders Fields*.

10th Canadian Battalion in divisional reserve was ordered to Wieltje. At 6.08 p.m., Brigadier General Turner ordered 2 Company, 14th Canadian Battalion, to support the French at Keerselaere. 27th and 28th Divisions also began moving reserves.

French troops around Langemarck put up stubborn resistance until 6 p.m. Once it fell, 51st Reserve Division was ordered to continue. The German success at Langemarck, the withdrawal of French troops and the renewed German advance towards St Julien, increased the threat to the left of 1st Canadian Division. The defensive flank thrown back along the St Julien-Poelcapelle road stopped the German advance at that point, but a further advance would allow them to swing northeast into the Division's rear.

By 7 p.m., 52nd Reserve Division had captured Kitcheners' Wood, including four 4.7″ guns of 2nd London Battery RGA. As darkness fell, 1 Company, 13th Canadian Battalion, on the left of the Division, was forced to withdraw across the St Julien-Poelcapelle road. There it was at right angles to the front line and had little protection against enemy fire. Alderson placed one of his reserves, 16th Canadian Battalion, at the disposal of 3rd Canadian Brigade and impressed upon the Brigade HQ that it must hold. At 7.55 p.m., HQ 3rd Canadian Brigade reported it had no troops between Mouse (Shell) Trap Farm and St Julien and asked 2nd Canadian Brigade to occupy this line. 1 Company, 7th Canadian Battalion had already moved forward from Wieltje to the southeast of Kitcheners' Wood, but HQ 3rd Canadian Brigade did not know this.

At 8 p.m., General Smith-Dorrien released 1st Canadian Brigade (1st, 2nd, 3rd and 4th Canadian Battalions) to V Corps from Second Army Reserve. 2nd and 3rd Canadian Battalions were sent immediately to 1st Canadian Division and Alderson ordered them to 3rd Canadian Brigade. HQ V Corps released 2nd East Yorkshire from 28th Division's reserve to Alderson's command; it was the first of thirty-three British battalions to come under Alderson before the crisis was over. By 8.45 p.m., 10th Canadian Battalion had occupied the GHQ Line and 7th Canadian Battalion was moving to Locality C, on the western part of Gravenstafel Ridge, to protect 2nd Canadian Brigade's left in contact with 8th Canadian Battalion on the right.

The German 51st and 52nd Reserve Divisions were only seven kilometres from Hill 60. A determined thrust could have cut off 50,000 British troops and 150 guns in the Salient and spelled disaster for the BEF; the situation was bleak. With a few exceptions on their left and right flanks, the French had retired from their first and second lines.

Just before 9 p.m., 51st Reserve Division attacked 1st Tirailleurs on the left of the Canadians. The French gave way, but 200 joined the platoons of 13th Canadian Battalion holding the new flank along the St Julien-Poelcapelle road. A platoon each from 2 and 4 Companies joined the roadside garrison. The Machine-gun Section under Lieutenant JG Ross sited its two guns (Sergeant Trainor and Lance Corporal Parkes) along the road, using pried up cobbles to form rudimentary defensive positions. Enemy pressure was constant and Major McCuaig organised a new line 250m to the rear in case he had to fall back.

3rd Brigade CFA (9th, 10th 11th and 12th Batteries) had fired continuously into the advancing Germans. 10th Battery (Major WBM King) was in an orchard south of Keerselaere, 100m east of the St Julien-Poelcapelle road. The Battery had assisted 13th Canadian Battalion to halt the German advance towards St Julien, but was threatened as German pressure increased along the St Julien-Poelcapelle road.

About 7 p.m., German heads were seen bobbing above a hedge as they advanced only 200m from the Battery position. Major King swung two guns round to face west and continued firing. Leaves and branches fell on the gun crews as machine-guns were directed against the orchard. The ammunition wagon teams were destroyed west of St Julien, but with the help of fifty-five men from 7th and 15th Canadian Battalions, the ammunition was carried 500m by hand to the guns.

When the machine-gun fire died down and the Germans withdrew a little, Major King requested infantry protection for the Battery. **Lance Corporal Fred Fisher**, in charge of one of 13th Canadian Battalion's Colt machine-guns, was with two platoons of 3 Company in reserve at St Julien. With sixty other men under Lieutenant GW Stairs (killed 24th April – Ypres (Menin Gate) Memorial) of 14th Canadian Battalion, he moved into position in advance of 10th Battery's guns.

At 9 p.m., Major King was ordered to withdraw, but was unsure if the limbers would be able to reach him, so he ordered two transport wagons to pull two guns to a rendezvous southwest of Mouse (Shell) Trap Farm. King was going to recover the remaining two guns with transport wagons, but at 11 p.m. the limbers arrived

Second Battle of Ypres 1915   11

The guns of 10th Battery CFA were in these fields just east of the tree lined St Julien – Poelcapelle road on the left. The prominent poplars beyond the buildings in the distance are close to Vancouver Corner. The German advance came towards the camera position, but was held by the Canadians to the right of the road about 1,600m beyond Vancouver Corner. To the left, where the French had been forced back, German troops threatened the guns and also the rear of 1st Canadian Division. Fred Fisher was in action in the vicinity of the buildings, firing across the road into the German advance. St Julien, where he went to collect reinforcements, is 500m behind the camera. There is a café there opposite the war memorial.

and the guns and remaining wagons were removed. By the early hours of 23rd April all four guns had been moved across the Yser Canal.

During the protracted withdrawal of the guns, Fisher came under heavy fire and four of his six men became casualties. He returned to St Julien and collected four 14th Canadian Battalion men, but during the hazardous return journey he lost them. Fisher managed to get back and brought his machine-gun into action to clear a section of wood of Germans. He also took charge of an abandoned French machine-gun and got it working again. His actions allowed the guns to get away and he eventually reported to Lieutenant Ross, the Machine-Gun Officer.

Earlier the French requested support for a counterattack by 45th Algerian Division towards Pilckem. At 8.52 p.m., 3rd Canadian Brigade was ordered to support the French by attacking towards Kitcheners' Wood. 2nd and 3rd Canadian Battalions (1st Canadian Brigade) and 2nd East Kent (28th Division) were expected, but had not arrived by 10.47 p.m., when Brigadier General Turner ordered 10th and 16th Canadian Battalions and 3rd Brigade CFA to counterattack. They were to clear the Wood on a two-company frontage with 10th Canadian Battalion leading and 16th Canadian Battalion in support, starting from 450m northeast of Mouse (Shell) Trap Farm.

Another view northwards over the 10th Battery CFA position. The large greenhouse in the right distance is where Lieutenant Edward Bellew won his VC on 24th April.

The attack began in silence at 11.48 p.m. with Kitcheners' Wood silhouetted in the dim moonlight. As the leading companies forced their way through a hedge halfway to the Wood, the enemy opened fire. There were many casualties, but the men burst through and charged. In fierce fighting, 10th Canadian Battalion reached the northern end of Kitcheners' Wood while 16th Canadian Battalion swung right to exit the Wood on the northeast side. The French counterattack did not materialise.

10th Canadian Battalion was fired on from the rear as a redoubt in the southwest corner of the Wood had been overlooked. The Germans also held part of the northwest. Another attack was driven off and by then both battalions had suffered at least 50% casualties. With insufficient strength to dislodge the Germans, the forward positions were evacuated, the 4.7″ gun ammunition destroyed and a new line was established on the southern edge of the Wood. 2nd and 3rd Canadian Battalions arrived to help extend the line.

By the end of 22nd April, the German XXIII Reserve Corps had pushed the French over the Yser Canal between Steenstraat and Het Sas and established a stronghold at Lizerne. However, stiff resistance by the Belgians and French denied the Germans crossings opposite Boesinghe. XXVI Reserve Corps had broken through as far as a line from the south of Pilckem to the northwest of St Julien.

At midnight, Colonel AD Geddes, 2nd East Kent, was put in command of 'Geddes Detachment', consisting of two battalions each from 27th and 28th Divisions (4th Rifle Brigade, 2nd KSLI, 2nd East Kent and 3rd Middlesex) at the disposal of 1st Canadian Division. At 3 a.m., Geddes received the order to fill the gap between the Canadian left and the French right. Meanwhile Alderson moved 1st and 4th Canadian Battalions to cooperate with a French attack against Pilckem at 5 a.m.

1st and 4th Canadian Battalions deployed below the crest of Hill Top Ridge with two companies of 3rd Middlesex on the right. At dawn they could see the Germans digging in on Mauser Ridge, 1,400m to the north. There was no sign of the French but, at 5.25 a.m., the advance began. They came under heavy small arms and artillery fire. 3rd Middlesex and a company of 1st Canadian Battalion reached Turco Farm, 300m from the German positions, but were shelled out by their own artillery. The attack was pinned down and the battalions began to dig in. It was not until midday that a battalion of Zouaves moved up on the left.

By the early hours of 23rd April, the platoons of 13th Canadian Battalion in the defensive flank along the St Julien-Poelcapelle road at the Lekkerboterbeek had been all but wiped out (Major Norsworthy is buried in Tyne Cot Cemetery – LIX B 24). No reinforcements arrived, so at daybreak the left of 13th Canadian Battalion fell back in good order to the line prepared during the night. The withdrawal was just about complete when Captain Tomlinson's 2nd East Kent company and two platoons of 3 Company arrived to restore the original line. Later the Germans tried to get along the road, shouting that they were French, but the ruse failed. Fire was received from three sides and eventually the roadside positions had to be abandoned to avoid more casualties. They pulled back into trenches, which gave a little more cover.

When it was decided to abandon the roadside position, Lieutenant Ross' machine-guns made a determined effort to reduce the enfilade fire that was causing so many casualties. Ross and Lance Corporal Fred Fisher crawled out of a shallow trench to set up Fisher's machine-gun. Fisher was dangerously exposed and was about to open fire when he was shot in the chest and died instantly. Sergeant McLeod took Fisher's place, but was also hit. Ross crawled to the other gun, as it was better placed to engage the enemy. The situation improved a little, but the rest of the day was spent cut off under heavy fire and with little food, water or ammunition. When orders came to pull back to the line occupied in the morning, Ross and others buried Fisher in the trench before leaving.

By dawn on 23rd April the gap in the Allied line had been plugged by ten battalions under Brigadier General Turner and Colonel Geddes. Three and a half battalions of 27th Division were in a second line. They faced forty-two German battalions and were outnumbered five-to-one in guns. The line was tenuous, but it was continuous except for the 1,400m gap from Keerselaare northwards to the original left of 1st Canadian Division.

The French were ready to counterattack at 3 p.m. and a general advance was ordered from Kitcheners' Wood to the Canal. 13th Brigade (5th Division), commanded by Brigadier General R Wanless O'Gowan, just out of the action at Hill 60, was given command of the operation. Delays in positioning troops caused a postponement until 4.15 p.m. Geddes received no order placing him under 13th Brigade's command and acted independently.

On the right were 2nd DCLI and two companies of 9th Royal Scots under Lieutenant Colonel Tuson. In the centre, Geddes Detachment was to pass through 1st and 4th Canadian Battalions and 3rd Middlesex and on the left was 13th Brigade. The attack was up an open slope, with little cover and in broad daylight. It ran into a storm of enemy fire from Mauser Ridge and was held 200m short of the enemy line. Other units joined in the attack, but by 7 p.m. it was over and after dark the British dug in 550m from the enemy on a line from Kitcheners' Wood to the junction with the French on the Canal.

The battle was by no means over, but by nightfall the front had been patched up, although it had taken every battalion in division and corps reserve plus two from the Army reserve. Losses had been severe; the Canadians alone had 687 fatalities on 22nd and 23rd April. Sir John French wrote, *"… the Canadians held their ground with a magnificent display of tenacity and courage; … these splendid troops averted a disaster …"*.

Battle of St Julien, 24th April–4th May 1915

61 CSM Frederick Hall, 8th Battalion (90th Rifles), CEF (2nd Canadian Brigade, 1st Canadian Division), Gravenstafel, Belgium
62 Lt Edward Bellew, 7th Battalion (1st British Columbia), CEF (2nd Canadian Brigade, 1st Canadian Division), Keerselaere, Belgium
63 Capt Francis Scrimger, RCAMC att'd 14th Battalion (Royal Montreal), CEF (3rd Canadian Brigade, 1st Canadian Division), St Julien, Belgium
64 Cpl Issy Smith, 1st Manchester (Jullundur Brigade, 3rd (Lahore) Division), St Julien, Belgium
65 Jemadar Mir Dast, 55th Coke's Rifles att'd 57th Wilde's Rifles (Ferozepore Brigade, 3rd (Lahore) Division), Wieltje, Belgium
66 Pte Edward Warner, 1st Bedfordshire (15th Brigade, 5th Division), Zwarteleen, Belgium
67 Pte John Lynn, 2nd Lancashire Fusiliers (12th Brigade, 4th Division), St Julien, Belgium

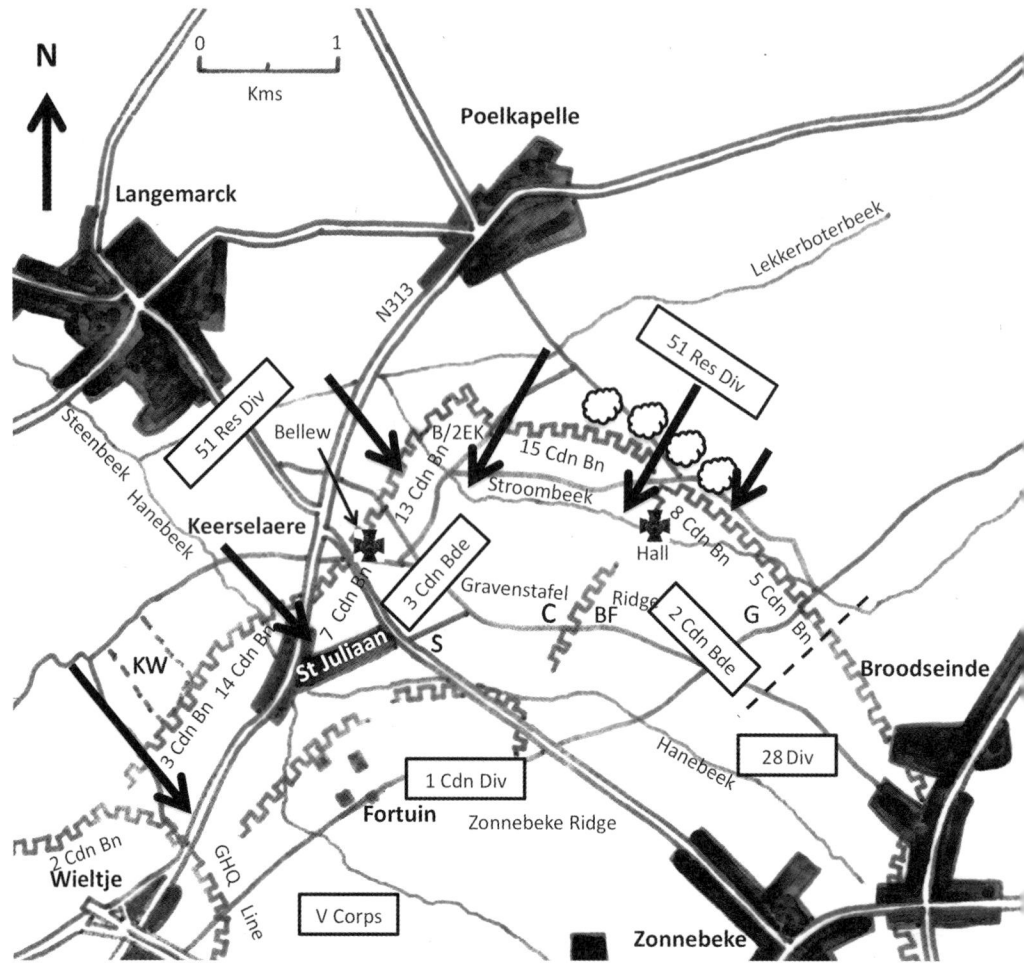

Continue 700m from the Fisher VC site and stop in the car park at the St Julien Canadian Vancouver Corner Memorial on the right. Having looked at the memorial, turn left out of the car park towards Zonnebeke. After 200m go beyond the crossroads and park at the side of the road. Look back towards Vancouver Corner. This is the high ground where Edward Bellew sited his machine-guns on 24th April 1915 to resist the German onslaught coming from the northwest. From the site of Bellew's VC action continue 700m and turn left in Sebastopol. The road is straight and goes uphill for 500m. At the T-junction turn right and drive for one kilometre along the top of Gravenstafel Ridge to reach Boetleer's Farm. On the way you will pass a memorial to 15th Canadian Battalion on the left at Locality C. Park the car in the trackway on the left just before Boetleer's Farm and walk north along it for 200m to overlook the area where 15th and 8th Canadian Battalions fought on 24th April 1915. A number of locations are shown by letters – S = Sebastopol, KW = Kitcheners' Wood, G = Gravenstafel, BF = Boetleer's Farm and C = Locality C.

The German intention on 24th April was to cut off retreat from the Salient. While they stood fast from the Canal to Mauser Ridge, the apex of the Canadian front would be attacked from three sides. Then, following an advance through St Julien and Fortuin, they would seize Zonnebeke Ridge. 51st Reserve Division was reinforced by 2nd Reserve Ersatz Brigade. XXVI Reserve Corps had an ad hoc brigade waiting to exploit success. XXIII Reserve Corps was to continue along the Canal with the intention of cutting off any retreat at Vlamertinghe, west of Ypres.

The Canadian front had been shortened by 13th Canadian Battalion and B Company, 2nd East Kent pulling back to a line running southwest from the left of 15th Canadian Battalion to 7th Canadian Battalion east of Keerselaere. The Canadian front was then held by eight battalions, from right to left – 5th, 8th and 15th Canadian Battalions holding the original front, then B Company, 2nd East Kent and 13th, 7th, 14th, 3rd and 2nd Canadian Battalions. They faced three times that number of German battalions.

7th Canadian Battalion had moved at 2 a.m. to support 13th Canadian Battalion in the vicinity of the crossroads near Keerselaere, leaving 1 Company under Captain Warden to defend Locality C. The Battalion deployed 2 Company on the left, with Sgt Weeks' machine-gun, 4 Company in the centre and two platoons of 3 Company on the right and the other two in support. The Battalion was in contact with 13th Canadian Battalion on the right and 14th Canadian Battalion on the left. **Lieutenant Edward Bellew** was with two more machine-guns at the crossroads with 4 Company.

At 3.30 a.m., two red and a green rockets rose above the Canadian lines. Thirty minutes later the Germans opened a heavy bombardment and released a cloud of chlorine gas on a frontage of 1,100m towards the Canadian lines northeast of St Julien, held by 8th (right) and 15th (left) Canadian Battalions. On seeing the cloud, word was passed among the Canadian troops to urinate on cotton wadding or handkerchiefs or dip them in water and place them over their noses and mouths. Although not totally effective, this simple expedient saved numerous lives. It may have been **Captain Francis Scrimger** RCAMC of 2nd Canadian Field Ambulance, who passed the order to use urine.

A five metres high cloud of gas rolled over the defenders, engulfing the right of 15th Canadian Battalion and the left of 8th Canadian Battalion. The latter, supported by an effective shrapnel barrage, poured heavy enfilade fire from its right forward company into the attackers. Those surviving in the centre and left, with their eyes and lungs filling with water, desperately resisted the advance, but were hampered by their unreliable Ross rifles jamming. Many men collapsed, but there was no panic, indeed in one section of 8th Canadian Battalion's line the men had to be restrained from attacking the Germans! Visibility was down to ten metres at times, but they hung on. The gas was upon them for about ten minutes, during which bayonets changed to the colour of copper. The troops on the left had to be replaced twice during the morning, but their fierce resistance held up the German advance.

The right of 15th Canadian Battalion was less successful. It could not be supported from the left, as the companies there were unable to see the area under attack. In addition, the guns of 3rd Battery CFA had been moved back too far to support the Battalion. The survivors fell back to the Stroombeek and the Germans broke through in two platoon locations and advanced 650m into the Canadian lines. They overcame the survivors at the Stroombeek and pressed on to 300m from Locality C.

The Battalion had to pull back to the reserve line, but two platoons and B Company, 2nd East Kent clung on at the apex.

Due to the wind direction, the attack against the northwest face of the apex was not supported by gas. Having passed over 8th and 15th Canadian Battalions, the cloud mainly missed 2nd East Kent and 13th, 7th and 14th Canadian Battalions. The attack here was repelled initially by small arms fire, assisted by 122nd Heavy Battery RGA at Frezenberg. Then the German artillery systematically shelled the trenches. At 8.30 a.m., when there was a lull in the barrage, 13th Canadian Battalion, which was threatened from front and rear due to 15th Canadian Battalion being forced back, had to retire to Gravenstafel Ridge. However, B Company, 2nd East Kent and two platoons of 15th Canadian Battalion did not get the message and were overwhelmed; the survivors surrendered at about 9 a.m.

Brigadier General Turner (3rd Canadian Brigade) initially believed the left of 2nd Canadian Brigade had been overwhelmed. He was short of reserves and had to use the badly depleted 10th and 16th Canadian Battalions. The remnants of 10th Canadian Battalion moved from Kitcheners' Wood to hold the vital ground of Locality C, while 16th Canadian Battalion took up positions in the GHQ Line.

Around the same time, Brigadier General Currie (2nd Canadian Brigade) reinforced 8th Canadian Battalion with a company each from 5th and 7th Canadian Battalions. 8th Canadian Battalion's reserve company was moved to the left to help 15th Canadian Battalion and to seal the open flank. Two platoons sent north of Boetleer's Farm had to cross a stretch of open ground illuminated by German flares while under heavy fire. When they reached the trenches, **CSM Frederick Hall** discovered two of the men were missing. Without hesitating, he twice crawled out of the trench to carry them to safety.

About 9 a.m., a wounded man was heard calling for help. Hall gathered two volunteers, Corporal Payne and Private Rogerson, and climbed over the parados, instantly drawing heavy fire. Payne and Rogerson were wounded within minutes and required Hall's assistance to get back to the safety of their own lines. After a few minutes' rest, Hall set off alone to bring in the wounded man. Enemy fire intensified, but he reached the soldier, who was so badly injured he was unable to move. Hall wriggled under the man's body and managed to hoist him onto his back. He then

A sweeping view from northwest through to northeast from Boetleer's Farm on Gravenstafel Ridge. The Stroombeek runs along the low ground right to left. The front line held by 8th Canadian Battalion was about 500m beyond the Stroombeek on the next ridge. CSM Frederick Hall's daring rescues took place between here and 8th Canadian Battalion's lines.

began to crawl towards the trench but, when he looked up to check his direction, he was hit in the head by a bullet and killed instantly. The wounded man was also killed.

A gap of 1,350m had opened in the line of 3rd Canadian Brigade, but the Germans had suffered heavy losses and there was a lull. Just before noon another barrage fell and the German advance resumed between Kitcheners' Wood and Locality C. The COs of 7th, 14th and 15th Canadian Battalions met just after 11 a.m. They were out of contact with HQ 3rd Canadian Brigade and decided to pull back about 300m from the exposed Gravenstafel Ridge to a new line to the south from St Julien (left) to Locality C (right). In the withdrawal the right fell back without many losses, but the advancing Germans pressed the left closely and the majority of two companies of 7th Canadian Battalion were overrun 450m northeast of St Julien. The position remained critical, for the Germans were able to sweep the south side of Gravenstafel Ridge with fire. About midday the German assault recommenced, following a heavy bombardment of the entire Canadian front. At 12.30 p.m. the three COs agreed on a further withdrawal of 900m to north of the Gravenstafel-Wieltje road. It was conducted in contact with the enemy throughout.

The German attack had opened a gap between the right of 7th Canadian Battalion and 8th Canadian Battalion. Sgt Weeks' machine-gun was put out of action by rifle fire. Near Keerselaere, **Lieutenant Edward Bellew**, Machine-Gun Officer of 7th Canadian Battalion, was wounded. One of his guns jammed and could not be coaxed back into action. He was cut off from the Battalion, but kept his last machine-gun in action on high ground to engage the advancing 51st Reserve Division. When the ammunition was expended, he fired rifles in relays loaded by other men. Gradually casualties mounted leaving only Bellew and Sergeant Hugh Nisbet Pearless (DCM for this action). They continued firing until a shell killed Pearless (Ypres (Menin Gate) Memorial) and wounded Bellew. He used a rifle to smash the machine-gun and prevent the Germans from using it, before he was taken prisoner. The Germans were going to shoot him because he continued to resist after part of his unit surrendered, but at the last minute he was reprieved.

4th East Yorkshire and 4th Green Howards (150th Brigade) had been sent up as reserves in the GHQ Line in front of Wieltje and Fortuin, while 1st Royal Irish Regiment moved to stop the enemy at Fortuin. These battalions received a series of contradictory orders throughout the day. There was confusion between Alderson and Turner; he told Turner to use the former two battalions to strengthen his line and hold on. Turner took this to mean the GHQ Line and at 1.40 p.m. ordered the

The crossroads east of Keerselaere. Edward Bellew sited his machine-guns on this slightly higher ground in order to resist the German onslaught. Much of the view from the crossroads is now obscured by the huge glasshouse on the right. The top of the St Julien Canadian Vancouver Corner Memorial is behind the trees in the centre.

six Canadian and two British battalions under 3rd Canadian Brigade to hold the GHQ Line from the Wieltje-Poelcapelle road southwards.

Near Kitcheners' Wood, the hard-pressed 2nd and 3rd Canadian Battalions held the Germans advancing up the Steenbeek. When the order to retire to the GHQ Line came, only 2nd Canadian Battalion on the left was able to get away. Part of its right company and two companies of 3rd Canadian Battalion were pinned down in their positions and could not move, but continued to resist.

The retirement of 7th, 14th and 15th Canadian Battalions had exposed the right flank of the defences of St Julien and 51st Reserve Division forced its way into the village from three sides, but it held on until 4 p.m. Throughout this time 5th and 8th Canadian Battalions conducted a robust defence of 2nd Canadian Brigade's line on the right.

With the situation critical between St Julien and Fortuin, at 9 a.m. General Plumer put all V Corps reserves under GOC 27th Division, Major General TD'O Snow. At midday, Snow sent 1st Royal Irish Regiment to a position north of Fortuin. He then sent the reserves of 28th Division (1st Suffolk and 12th London from 84th Brigade and two companies of 1/8th Middlesex from 85th Brigade) from near Zonnebeke to join 1st Royal Irish Regiment and directed Brigadier General Turner to drive the enemy northeast. Turner was unaware of Snow's appointment and, satisfied that he was complying with Alderson's instructions, ignored Snow.

Brigadier General Currie was concerned about his left flank where 5th and 8th Canadian Battalions were holding the original line. On the left, a company of 5th Canadian Battalion at Boetleer's Farm and a weak 7th Canadian Battalion company at Locality C held the only remaining positions on Gravenstafel Ridge. At 1 p.m., when a counter-attack by 150th Brigade had not materialised, Currie went back. He learned from Brigadier General Bush, commanding 150th Brigade, that Alderson had cancelled the counterattack. Currie saw Snow about 3.30 p.m., but Snow had no forces to allocate to him. However, the situation of 2nd Canadian Brigade was improved by the arrival of 1st Suffolk and 12th London. Struggling forward under heavy fire, they halted along the Zonnebeke-Keerselare road just south of the

Looking west along Gravenstafel Ridge, with Boetleer's Farm behind the camera. The buildings are on the site of Locality C. There is a memorial to 15th Canadian Battalion on the roadside to the left of the buildings below the telegraph post.

Hanebeek and began to dig in facing Locality C, which had fallen to the Germans. After dark, two companies of 1st Suffolk were sent to reinforce the small force at Boetleer's Farm by occupying the crest to the west. After midnight they were joined by the remnants of 7th and 10th Canadian Battalions, each only 150 strong, led forward personally by Currie. A tenuous line was re-established on 2nd Canadian Brigade's left flank.

Meanwhile 4th East Yorkshire and 4th Green Howards arrived at Fortuin and came under fire from Germans advancing south from St Julien. They changed direction to counterattack, joined by 1st Royal Irish Regiment. Assisted by Canadian artillery, they drove the Germans back to St Julien and there were no further German attacks in this area that day. However, their action came too late to save the remnants of 2nd and 3rd Canadian Battalions between St Julien and Kitcheners' Wood who, having

The 15th Canadian Battalion memorial on the roadside on Gravenstafel Ridge, with Poelcapelle church in the background.

held the Germans for hours, were overwhelmed. After dark the three attacking battalions withdrew to Potijze and reopened a gap, which fortunately the Germans were unable to exploit that night.

Despite the confusion and misunderstandings caused by broken communications and the fog of war, the arrival of five British battalions had ensured 3rd Canadian Brigade was not overwhelmed and 2nd Canadian Brigade and 28th Division were not isolated and attacked from the rear. The Canadians asked 28th Division for help towards evening between Gravenstafel and Fortuin. One and a half companies of 2nd Northumberland Fusiliers, two companies of 2nd Cheshire and a company of 1/1st Monmouthshire (all 84th Brigade) moved off at 8.30 p.m. and joined 1st Suffolk and two half companies of 1/8th Middlesex near Boetleer's Farm.

The French launched counterattacks at 8.30 a.m. and 2 p.m. and eventually managed to retake Lizerne, but attacks against Het Sas made no progress. Foch assured Sir John French that fresh divisions were being brought up, but the British realised, despite the best of intentions, that they could not rely on the French.

At 6.30 p.m., Plumer ordered Alderson to counterattack on the morning of the 25th to retake St Julien, using 10th and 150th Brigades and six other battalions (2nd KOYLI and 9th London in 13th Brigade, 4th Canadian Battalion, 1st Royal Irish Regiment from 27th Division and 12th London and 1st Suffolk from 28th Division). Alderson nominated Brigadier General Hull (10th Brigade) to command the attack. He had fifteen battalions in total, but only five took part. The first objective was Fortuin, then St Julien and Kitcheners' Wood.

Alderson allowed the maximum possible time for preparations prior to the attack when he issued orders at 8 p.m. on the 24th. The attack was set for 3.30 a.m., but warning orders took time to find the scattered units and at 9 p.m. only one CO had arrived to be briefed. Alderson delayed the attack to 4.30 a.m. Hull moved his HQ to Mouse (Shell) Trap Farm, but traffic congestion and only two narrow gaps in the wire of the GHQ Line slowed the move to the start positions and the attack was slipped to 5.30 a.m., by when it was daylight.

There was no time for reconnaissance and it was a wet and dark night. Hull struggled to find the attacking battalions and his intelligence was out of date – he did not know that the Germans were not in St Julien or Fortuin. The artillery was not informed about the change of start time and opened fire at the original time, leaving little support for the real attack.

Hull was not in communication with the other units, so ordered the four battalions of his own Brigade to attack. 1st Royal Irish Fusiliers and 2nd Royal Dublin Fusiliers, right and left of the Hanebeek at Fortuin, were directed on St Julien. 1st Royal Warwickshire, with 7th Argyll & Sutherland Highlanders, in support was to attack Kitcheners' Wood and 2nd Seaforth Highlanders was between the two attacks to connect them.

The Germans had begun to reoccupy St Julien and when Hull's force attacked, the lines were swept with heavy fire. All battalions were stopped short of their objectives and 50% casualties were suffered in some cases. Supports came up and a line was established curving left and right from Vanheule Farm, south of St Julien, to the Hanebeek and Mouse (Shell) Trap Farm. Although 10th Brigade lost 2,400 men in this attack, it was not entirely in vain as it blocked the enemy at St Julien and this line held until 4th May, when there was a deliberately withdrawal.

Duke Albrecht ordered actions against the French to be halted and the gains consolidated while XXVI Reserve Corps renewed its attacks to cut off the British in the Salient. The Germans attacked unsuccessfully at 5 a.m. against 28th Division and at 3.30 p.m. against 2nd Canadian Brigade around Boetleer's Farm.

3rd Canadian Brigade was relieved. 8th Canadian Battalion's left flank, which had been exposed the previous day when 15th Canadian Battalion was forced back, was reinforced and after two days continuous fighting went into reserve, having been relieved by 8th DLI; it had suffered 570 casualties. Brigadier General Currie ordered 2nd Canadian Brigade to retire on the right and as a result the left flank of 85th Brigade (28th Division) conformed.

Plumer decided to reorganize V Corps' front. 11th Brigade and the Lahore Division began to arrive. 28th Division (Major General Bulfin) took over 2nd Canadian Brigade and other Canadian units up to the Fortuin-St Julien road, leaving 1st Canadian Division responsible for the line westwards to the junction with the French. Within these two commands, Plumer ordered as many troops as possible to revert to their proper commanders and a great deal of night activity was necessary to effect the changes.

Co-located with HQ 3rd Canadian Brigade at Mouse (Shell) Trap Farm was an Advanced Dressing Station of 2nd Canadian Field Ambulance, to which **Captain Frank Scrimger** RCAMC was attached from 19th April. From when the German offensive started, Scrimger had hardly any rest while tending the wounded under heavy fire. He was assisted by Sergeant Berthell and a section of stretcher-bearers. They initially treated the French victims of the first gas attack and that night attended to the casualties from the counterattack on Kitcheners' Wood. During one afternoon and evening alone more than 400 wounded passed through the ADS.

On the 24th, Scrimger was in the GHQ Line trenches occupied by 1, 3 and 4 Companies, 14th Canadian Battalion, where he dressed the wounds of five badly injured men. During 25th April, HQ 3rd Canadian Brigade and the ADS at Mouse (Shell) Trap Farm came under very heavy shellfire and a nearby small arms ammunition store was ignited, setting the buildings alight. The HQ and the ADS had to be moved to safer locations. All but fifteen badly wounded men were removed before the intensity of the enemy shelling increased. Under heavy fire, Scrimger and his staff carried the remaining casualties on their backs, assisted by volunteers. Captain Harold F MacDonald, who was already wounded, received more serious wounds to his neck and shoulder and collapsed. Scrimger dragged him into the remains of the ADS and dressed the new wounds. He then carried MacDonald to a ditch 15m in front, where they lay half in the water. Scrimger curled himself

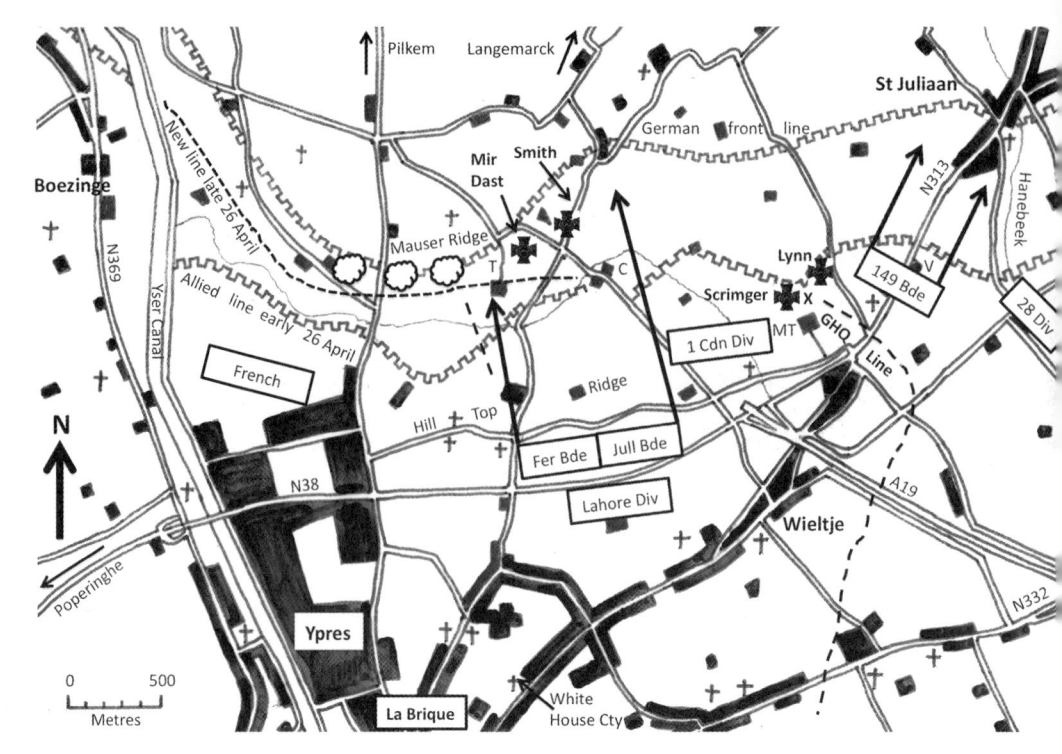

A number of locations are shown by letters – T = Turco Farm, C = Canadian Farm, MT = Mouse (Shell) Trap Farm, X = original site of Mouse (Shell) Trap Farm and V = Vanheule Farm.

Drive south from St Juliaan on the N313, passing Seaforth Cemetery on the right after 800m. Take the next right after 150m and drive north for 600m to park at a clump of trees on the right. Avoid blocking the passing place. Look back down the road. The rebuilt Mouse (Shell) Trap Farm is to the right of the road some 500m away. The original was 150m to the north and a remnant of the moat that surrounded it survives in the fields. This is where Francis Scrimger sheltered the wounded Captain Macdonald on 25th April 1915. This is also the area in which John Lynn manned his machine-gun throughout a gas attack on 2nd May. Look directly from where you are parked towards the site of the old farm. This is the line of the short leg of the 'L' formed by 2nd Lancashire Fusiliers' front. Contemporary maps show a number of field boundaries joining the road at right angles here and it seems likely that it was one of these that Lynn used to position his machine-gun and gain some extra height.

To reach the sites of Issy Smith's and Mir Dast's VC actions, approach from St Juliaan on the N313 but do not turn right until 350m after Seaforth Cemetery, opposite the left turn signed for St Jan. Drive 800m west, passing the entrance lane to Mouse (Shell) Trap Farm on the right. At the crossroads turn right and drive northwest for 1,100m to the crossroads and turn right. Park on the right at a track entrance after 150m. Look across the road. The higher ground is Mauser Ridge where the Germans were entrenched. Look south over the shallow valley and beyond to a slight rise, which is Hill Top Ridge. 1st Manchester attacked towards you and where you are is about as far as Issy Smith reached. Return to the crossroads and turn right. The road bends left and after 350m there is a left turn to what was Turco Farm. Park at the junction and look back the way you have just driven. There are good views to the top of Mauser Ridge to the left and to the right all the way to Hill Top Ridge and beyond. Mir Dast was stopped just east of here.

round MacDonald's wounded head and shoulder to protect him from the shellfire. Seventy-five 6″ shells exploded around them, five within five metres. They were dazed by the explosions and covered in mud but, when the shelling slackened, Scrimger staggered with MacDonald to safety. He summoned some stretcher-bearers and had MacDonald carried to another dressing station.

Thus far Allied efforts in countering the German offensive had been isolated and lacked artillery support. If the enemy was to be thrown back, a more comprehensive

Part of the moat that surrounded Mouse (Shell) Trap Farm in 1915. The rebuilt farm is beyond. This is where Francis Scrimger sheltered Captain Macdonald prior to getting him away on 25th April 1915.

and coordinated approach was required. At a conference on the afternoon of 25th April, the French declared they were preparing a counter-offensive to recapture Lizerne, Steenstraat and Het Sas and drive the Germans back over the Canal. Sir John French authorised General Smith-Dorrien to cooperate. The Lahore Division would attack east of the Ypres-Langemarck road, but not before it had marched over thirty miles through the night from Neuve Chapelle to get there. It came under the direct command of Second Army, with V Corps on the right cooperating with artillery and a supporting attack by 149th Brigade towards St Julien. A battalion of 10th Brigade was to advance between the two thrusts as they diverged. Geddes Detachment was in support in the GHQ Line. The Canadians were to stand fast and support the attack with artillery.

The French attack was planned for 5 p.m. on 26th April, but they brought it forward to 2 p.m., limiting the preparation time for the newly arrived Lahore Division. However, by 1 p.m. the two assault brigades had moved forward under artillery fire and were on the start line west of Wieltje, behind Hill Top Ridge. The objective, Mauser Ridge, was the same as for Geddes Detachment a few days previously, but the precise location of the enemy was unclear.

On the left, the Ferozepore Brigade attacked with 129th Baluchis (right), 57th Wilde's Rifles (centre) and 1st Connaught Rangers (left). On the right was the Jullundur Brigade. Its leading units from the right were 1st Manchester, 40th Pathans and 47th Sikhs, with 59th Rifles and 4th Suffolk forming a second line some 360m behind. 1st Manchester had been in billets at L'Epinette when it was roused on the afternoon of 24th April. It marched twenty-three miles before midnight and continued for a further twelve miles at 6 a.m., arriving near Vlamertinghe at 10.30 a.m., where twelve men in **Corporal Issy Smith's** platoon were killed by a single enemy shell.

The earlier zero hour meant the move to the start line was in full view of the enemy. The artillery had insufficient ammunition for an effective barrage and poor visibility precluded accurate observation; there was no prospect of accurate wire cutting or close support. The Jullundur Brigade was spotted in its assembly area by

This is the approximate area on Mauser Ridge that Issy Smith reached on 26th April 1915. The cottage on the right is at the crossroads. Centre and left on the tree-lined skyline is Hill Top Ridge. It is easy to appreciate how exposed the Lahore Division troops were during their advance.

an enemy aircraft and from 11 a.m. onwards was under artillery fire. At 12.30 p.m. both brigades moved up to their assault positions and when the bombardment started at 1.20 p.m. they advanced as far forward as possible before it ceased. Some German shells fired in retaliation contained a tear agent.

1st Manchester formed up in four lines with two companies leading on a frontage of 135m; it had 1,500m to cover to its objective. It, and all the other battalions, came under heavy fire crossing Hill Top Ridge from artillery and small arms; whole platoons were knocked out by German 5.9″ howitzer shells. The attack continued across a gentle valley and up the slopes of Mauser Ridge towards the Germans trenches.

Fire from northeast of Canadian Farm forced the Jullundur Brigade to veer left, which in turn forced the Ferozepore Brigade over the boundary with the French. Units became intermingled, but they pressed on through 13th Brigade's line towards the objective. The whole attack bogged down about 100m from the enemy front line. 1st Manchester pressed on until stopped only 50m from the enemy trench and sought what scant cover was available.

Although pinned down with the rest of the Battalion, Issy Smith left cover and dashed forward to the aid of a severely wounded man. Having applied a field dressing, Smith carried him 250m to the safety of the aid post, despite being under a hail of fire. He then went out to collect Sergeant Rooke and carried him on his back away from the enemy line. Lieutenant Shipster told Smith to put Rooke down while he got help for him. Shipster was then shot through the neck and Smith bandaged him before carrying him to the trenches occupied by 4th Suffolk. He returned with a stretcher to collect Rooke and got him to the 4th Suffolk aid post, before again returning to bring more wounded to safety, all from the most exposed positions in full view of the enemy. At one time he was offered a brandy flask by an officer but, despite his exhaustion, refused. The attack cost 1st Manchester 287 casualties, including Lieutenant Colonel HWE Hitchins, who had only been promoted to command the Battalion a few days previously (White House Cemetery, St Jean-les-Ypres – III A 1).

57th Wilde's Rifles had only a very short time to issue orders to the companies, and collect shovels, picks and bombs, before moving to the assembly area. It formed in columns of platoons with three companies in line (from the right 4, 3 and 1), on a frontage of 170m. 2 Company was about 70m behind the centre. The objective was 1,350m away and the Battalion suffered heavy losses crossing the open ground. The supporting barrage was almost non-existent. The Battalion reported some enemy shells were filled with asphyxiating gas. Men sought any scrap of cover to protect them while they advanced and the units on the right closed in, causing formation to be lost. By the time that they were 70m from the German trenches most officers had been killed and wounded, and the advance stalled. Only two British officers were uninjured. The gas affected the men badly and many fell back, hardly able to understand what was happening to them. Captain Mahon, assisted by Lieutenants Mein and Deedes, collected about sixty men in a trench and they were joined after dark by isolated parties.

The Quartermaster, Lieutenant Mein (MC for this action), took some tins of chloride of lime to the front. He instructed the men to dip the end of their pagris (turban) in it, before tying it over their mouth and nose to counter the gas. Mein also brought up rations and ammunition under heavy shellfire, supported the two remaining British officers in the front line and took part in an attack the following day.

Jemadar Mir Dast of 55th Coke's Rifles, attached to 57th Wilde's Rifles, led his platoon during the attack. Afterwards, when no British officers were left, he

Mauser Ridge on the left sweeping round to the south through the crossroads cottage in the centre to the tree-lined Hill Top Ridge, with Turco Farm on the extreme right. Mir Dast's VC action was between here and the crossroads.

collected various parties of the Battalion and rallied them. Many of the men had been gassed, but he kept them together until retirement was ordered after dusk. As they fell back, he collected various detachments from a number of trenches and brought them in safely. Later he helped recover eight wounded British and Indian officers to safety, whilst exposed to very heavy fire, during which he was wounded. One of those rescued by Mir Dast was Havildar Mangal Singh, who was unconscious due to gas poisoning. When he recovered sufficiently, he also went out to bring in the wounded and was awarded the Indian Order of Merit, 2nd Class.

The Battalion dug in and held its ground until relieved on 29th April, having suffered considerable casualties. Forty-four were killed or died of wounds according to the regimental history, but only twenty-four could be traced in CWGC records. There were also 277 wounded and gassed and seven missing from the 580 who went into the line on the 24th. Although the Battalion remained in France until December, this was its last major engagement; thereafter it was only employed in line holding.

The French made some progress on the left and recaptured most of Lizerne but, at 2.20 p.m., the Germans released chlorine gas northwest of Turco Farm, the first time it was used defensively. The French were stopped in their tracks. The gas caused many casualties and much confusion in the Lahore Division, particularly in the Ferozepore Brigade, and most troops fell back, suffering more casualties from German fire as they crossed the Ridge again.

Plans to renew the advance in the early evening came to nothing and the Sirhind Brigade, in reserve, took over the front line. It relieved the assault troops, whose six assault battalions had suffered 1,829 casualties, including five of the COs.

V Corps formations failed to make progress. There had been little opportunity to coordinate with the Lahore Division. Detailed orders for 149th Brigade and the artillery did not arrive until 1.10 p.m., less than an hour before the attack began. With no time for reconnaissance, the assault troops were hampered by the narrow gap in the GHQ Line, where they came under heavy fire and lost the limited artillery support. Advancing astride the Wieltje-St Julien road they were devastated by machine-guns to the front and left. One of the casualties was the Brigade commander, Brigadier General James Riddell (Tyne Cot Cemetery – XXXIV H 14). This was the first time a Territorial Force brigade had attacked as a complete brigade. 10th Brigade also received its orders too late (1.25 p.m.) to commit a battalion between the Lahore Division and 149th Brigade. At 7.30 p.m., 149th Brigade was ordered back to Wieltje, having suffered 1,200 casualties.

Despite the huge effort and massive casualties, the British situation in the Salient remained critical. The trenches were everywhere overlooked and the German artillery was dominant. With First Army's offensive in the south approaching, there was unlikely to be many reinforcements, but during the night 2nd Cavalry Division arrived to reinforce V Corps.

On the 27th a combined British and French offensive was ordered with the same plan, objectives and boundaries as 26th April. Smith-Dorrien ordered the Lahore Division not to advance until the French had made significant progress. For some reason the Lahore Division ignored this and when it attacked at 1.30 p.m. it came under the same fire as the previous day. It was stopped well short of Mauser Ridge.

A composite brigade of 1,290 men from four battalions was formed under Lieutenant Colonel Tuson. Following a further bombardment, the attack was to be resumed in contact with the Sirhind Brigade. The French set off before the British were ready and failed to make any progress. The Sirhind and Ferozepore Brigades and Tuson's force set off at 5.30 p.m. and made little progress. They had to fall back when the French withdrew under gas attack. By nightfall the lines of the morning had been re-established. The only gain of the day was the French completing the recapture of Lizerne, regaining Het Sas and the line of the Canal north of Steenstraat. The Indian brigades were brought back behind Hill Top Ridge. This was the last attempt by the British to retake the losses of 22nd April.

General Smith-Dorrien wrote to Sir John French's Chief of General Staff, Lieutenant General Sir William Robertson, proposing a withdrawal of four kilometres in stages to the GHQ Line to shorten the British front. There was no love lost between French and Smith-Dorrien and the letter was just the excuse French needed. At 4.35 p.m., he dismissed Smith-Dorrien, one of the most competent commanders in the BEF at the time. Robertson gave the news to Smith-Dorrien in soldierly fashion, *"Orace you're for 'ome!"* He handed over to Plumer, who took command of all troops in the Salient. Plumer's Force consisted of:

V Corps – 2nd Cavalry, 1st Canadian, 27th, 28th and Lahore Divisions.
50th Division.
10th & 11th Brigades (4th Division).
13th Brigade (5th Division).
54th & 55th Field Companies RE (7th Division).

Plumer was to consolidate the line and make it more secure, while preparing a line east of Ypres in case it became necessary to fall back. The French seemed unable to make any progress on the left, but Foch was unwilling to withdraw to better positions. Ironically, when Plumer recommended a general withdrawal to a new line, Sir John French accepted it, but first wanted to give counterattacks a chance to succeed.

On 28th April, French met Foch, who asked him to delay withdrawing until after one more French attack. It achieved almost nothing. Next day French met Foch again. They agreed on a joint attack on the 30th, but if it were unsuccessful, the British would withdraw. The French attack was to be between the Canal and the Ypres-Langemarck road. They made a preliminary attack on Steenstraat at 6 p.m., and got into the village, but could not drive the Germans off the west bank of the Canal.

In the joint attack on 30th April, the Sirhind Brigade was to attack with the French at 8 a.m., but thick fog forced a postponement until 11.15 a.m. The French left made some progress, but the right failed to advance and the Sirhind Brigade remained in its trenches behind Hill Top Ridge. The French requested assistance with an attack next day and Plumer agreed to provide artillery support, but no troops unless it was part of a general offensive. That night French gave Foch one more day before the British began the withdrawal. During the night, 12th Brigade (4th Division) took over the line held by the left of 10th Brigade and 13th Brigade.

Drive east from Ypres on the N8 towards Menen, i.e. the Menin Road. At the major roundabout take the right turn for Zillebeke. Go straight through the village and on towards Zwarteleen. Go past the turning to Hill 60 (there is a café/restaurant there) on the right and park immediately after on the right side. 100m on from the Hill 60 turning is a left turn. It is a minor road leading to a few houses. Walk 40m along it and stop. The British front line was a few metres left of this road. Trench 46 ran into the British front line at this point coming through the field behind the first house on the left. Walk another 100m down the track to the gates of the private house. Trench 46 ran diagonally across this field, which is where Edward Warner earned his VC. Look back up the way you came. Hill 60 is 250m beyond the houses alongside the main road.

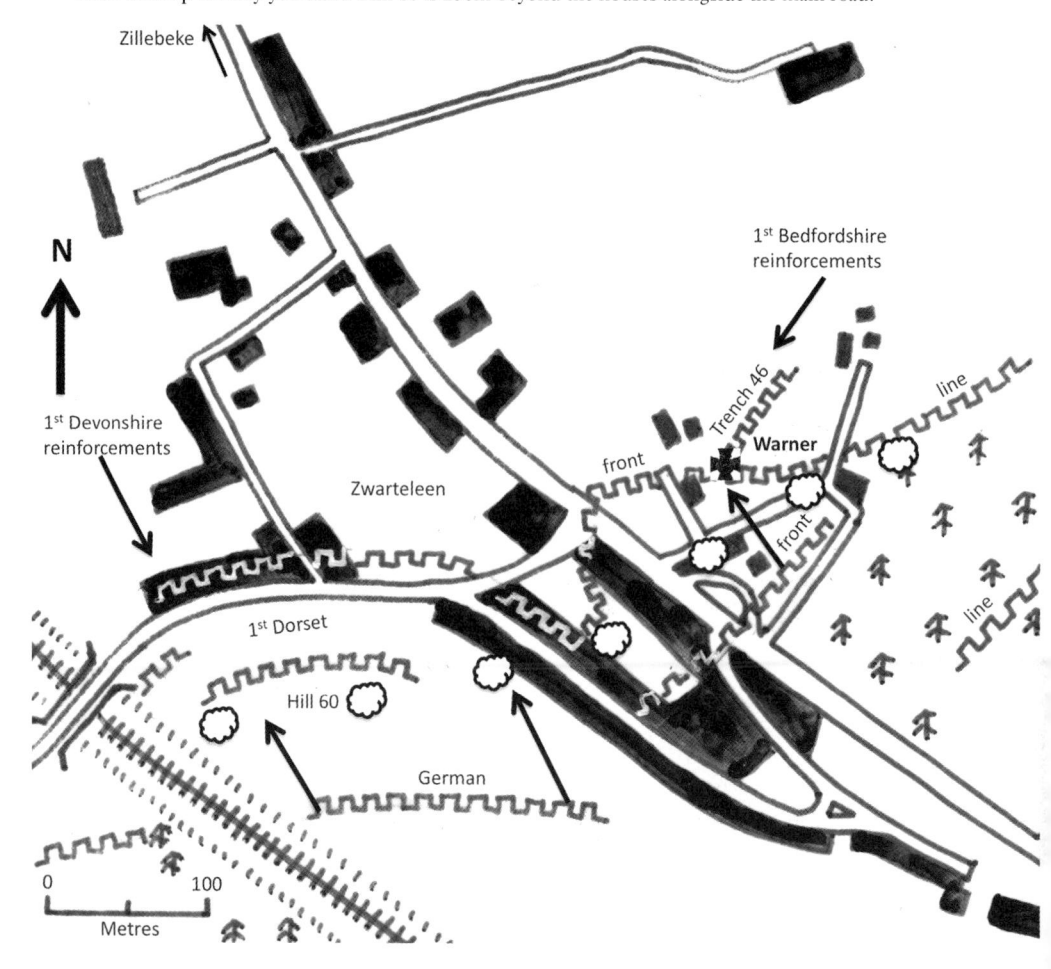

The French attack on 1st May was scheduled for 3.10 p.m., with support from the Sirhind Brigade if progress was made. The barrage fell, but the French did not leave their trenches and a second attempt at 4.40 p.m. also failed to develop. The French were exhausted and their priority was a forthcoming operation around Arras. Foch decided to go onto the defensive around Ypres and the British were then able to withdraw from the tip of the Salient. Plumer issued orders for the withdrawal to commence that night.

As the withdrawal was about to begin, the Germans attacked at Hill 60, held by 1st Dorset (15th Brigade). At 7 p.m., after a short but severe bombardment, the Germans released gas less than 100m from the British trenches. The wind carried it so quickly that few managed to don their improvised respirators before the cloud was upon them. The German infantry opened fire, bombing parties moved forward against the flanks and artillery screened off the approaches to the Hill.

1st Dorset rallied sufficient men to halt the initial attack, allowing time for reinforcements to arrive. Elements of 1st Devonshire (14th Brigade) and 1st Bedfordshire raced to the rescue, but had virtually no protection against gas. Despite this they pressed on to occupy the front line before the enemy could gain a foothold.

1st Bedfordshire was in the line to the left of 1st Dorset. Captain Gledstanes led some men to the right to help cover the gap caused by the gas attack. **Private Edward Warner** single-handedly occupied a deserted portion of Trench 46, but the gas was so concentrated that other men sent to help him were driven back. Warner went and fetched the reinforcements himself. However, the exertion completely exhausted him. He eventually collapsed and died shortly afterwards, but his action undoubtedly saved the trench.

Psychologically this action was important for the British; it was the first occasion in which the Germans launched a gas attack without gaining an advantage. However, the cost to 1st Dorset was high; ninety men died in the trenches from gas poisoning and another fifty-eight succumbed later in hospital.

The first stage of the withdrawal was the relief of the Lahore Division, which had suffered 3,889 casualties. Before the next phase began the Germans attacked the five

The British front line ran from here to the right of the left cottage and on towards Hill 60, which is out of sight beyond the far houses along the main road. Trench 46 crossed this field diagonally from right to left to join the front line just this side of the left cottage. The German attack came from the left. Right of centre in the far distance are the spires of Ypres, emphasising the importance of the slightly higher ground around Hill 60.

kilometres of front held by 4th Division from Berlin Wood to Turco Farm. A heavy bombardment opened at noon, followed by gas shells in the afternoon. At 4.30 p.m. gas cylinders were opened and the cloud was followed by 51st and 53rd Reserve Divisions between St Julien and Berlin Wood.

The gas took a few minutes to pass over no man's land and a further fifteen minutes to clear the British trenches. The right of the French, the whole of 12th Brigade and the left of 10th Brigade were affected. 2nd Lancashire Fusiliers' front was 'L' shaped, centred on Mouse (Shell) Trap Farm. The short arm of the L, running northeast to southwest, was held by B Company, with 10th Brigade on its right. D and A Companies held the long east to west arm, with 1st King's Own Royal Lancaster to the left of A Company. C Company was in reserve in a communications trench just behind and between D and A Companies. There were no lateral communications and the men had worked hard since taking over on 1st May to improve the parlous state of the trenches, which were little more than holes in hedged banks. Three machine-guns were allocated to B Company and one of these was commanded by **Private John Lynn** at 'Suicide Corner' (not located).

B Company's sentries observed the gas issuing from the enemy trenches in long jets. With no means of lateral communications, they could not raise the alarm and the rest of the Battalion could not see the cloud approaching because of the shape of the ground. B Company had a few minutes to don improvised respirators, consisting of a cotton wool pad soaked in sodium hypochlorite. For some reason not every man had been issued with one, so the MO, Lieutenant Tyrell (later Air Vice Marshall Sir William Tyrell KBE DSO MC), told those around him to soak a piece of fabric in their own urine (the ammonia in urine neutralises chlorine) and tie it over their mouth and nose. Due to the lack of warning, many men in A and D Companies were late donning their respirators and, despite the efforts of their officers to stem the withdrawal, many fled. The Battalion suffered 449 hospitalised gas casualties and many more had minor poisoning. By contrast only nine men were killed and forty wounded in this action.

Mouse (Shell) Trap Farm from the northeast, looking along the line of the short arm of 2nd Lancashire Fusiliers' 'L' shaped front. Wieltje is in the left background. The site of Mouse (Shell) Trap Farm in 1915 is on the right, marked by a faint dark line in the field below the copse and right of the pylon.

From the site of the original Mouse (Shell) Trap Farm looking northeast along the short arm of 2nd Lancashire Fusiliers' 'L' shaped front. It was between here and the clump of trees that John Lynn won his VC.

As soon as B Company had their respirators on, they opened fire into the gas cloud. Lynn had no respirator, but manned his machine-gun and raked no man's land with continuous fire. As the gas rolled over the trenches many men were overcome and the remainder were unable to see what was going on. In order to get a better field of view, Lynn dismantled the machine-gun and moved it onto a tree stump on top of a bank, from where he could see the Germans advancing behind the gas cloud. The combined weight of fire from Lynn's machine-gun, his comrades' rifle fire and the British artillery succeeded in halting the attack.

Lynn refused to give up firing until every sign of the attack had died down. Throughout the whole time it took the gas to cross the trenches, Lynn was exposed to it without any form of protection. Once the attack had been driven off, he turned his attention to helping those suffering from gas poisoning. By this time his own face was black and he was coughing up blood. Inevitably he collapsed and was carried to a dugout, but he had to be restrained from returning to his machine-gun when another attack was reported imminent. An hour later, he was carried to hospital where he died in great agony. About ninety men returned to the trenches later, all that was left of the Battalion.

The French held and so did 1st King's Own Royal Lancaster, but a gap opened where 2nd Lancashire Fusiliers retired. A King's Own Royal Lancaster platoon occupied a building in no man's land to cover the gap, while 10th Brigade sent 7th Argyll & Sutherland Highlanders and a company of 5th South Lancashire was sent from 12th Brigade's reserve. Soon afterwards, 4th Hussars and 5th Lancers also arrived. By 8 p.m. the front was quiet again and the withdrawal went ahead that night as planned.

On the morning of 3rd May, another German attack appeared imminent, but when it did not materialise, orders went out for the final stage of the withdrawal. The Germans attacked near Berlin Wood in the afternoon, but all was quiet again by 9 p.m. During the night the divisions pulled back to the new line covered by mist.

The relief of the Canadians by 4th Division was completed. The Canadians had suffered 6,036 casualties since 22nd April, but had established their reputation as second to none in their first major action of the war. The Canadian artillery remained to cover the front from Mouse (Shell) Trap to Turco Farms until finally relieved on 19th May.

Battle of Frezenberg, 8th–13th May 1915

> 72 LSgt Douglas Belcher, 1/5th London (London Rifle Brigade) (11th Brigade, 4th Division), South of Wieltje-St Julien road, Belgium

The period 5th-7th May was less frantic than the previous days, but it was never inactive. The Germans recaptured Hill 60 on the 5th after a heavy gas attack, but the following day the British regained some of the trenches. Meanwhile the Germans moved their artillery forward and massed three corps opposite Frezenberg Ridge. The British trenches in that area were unfinished; some were less than a metre deep. Some positions, on the forward slope and around Bellewaarde Lake, were very exposed to direct artillery and small arms fire.

On 8th May, 4th Division was holding the northern end of the British line in the Salient, with 28th Division on the right and the French on the left. At 5.30 a.m., the Germans opened a new phase in the Second Battle of Ypres with a massive bombardment. It severely disrupted 83rd Brigade holding the forward slope of Frezenberg Ridge. However, the first and second German attacks were repelled, but the third, directed at the flanks of Frezenberg village, pushed the defenders back 400m. The right of 83rd Brigade and its neighbour, 80th Brigade, managed to stop the advance; 4th KRRC and PPCLI only held on by using their signalers, pioneers and batmen.

However, on the left, 84th Brigade's left flank was exposed. 12th London (Rangers), 2nd East Yorkshire and 5th King's Own Royal Lancaster attacked to check the enemy and suffered enormous casualties. The Germans pressed on, opening a gap of three kilometres in the line. Of the six British battalions engaged, only 1,400 men were available next day, but 28th Division's front held. On the right, 80th Brigade formed a defensive flank and the Germans consolidated in expectation of a British counterattack.

85th Brigade's counterattack on the right was broken up by artillery before it got into its attacking positions. 10th Brigade swept in overnight to stabilise the position and forced the Germans out of the gap. The British dug in 1,200m behind the original front on the reverse slope of Verlorenhoek Ridge, where they were less exposed to German artillery.

9th May saw the opening of the French offensive in Artois and the British supporting attack on Aubers Ridge, but there was no reduction in the pressure east of Ypres. Following a heavy bombardment, the Germans attacked 27th Division along the Menin Road, supported by heavy artillery concentrations, but they failed to make significant progress. The same day, Brigadier General Prowse, commanding 11th Brigade, took command of all 4th Division troops east of the Yser Canal. During the following nights working parties dug a new Divisional Support line.

On 11th May, 1/5th London (11th Brigade) was ordered from its billets in dugouts west of the Yser Canal to take over forward positions east of Wieltje, with 1st East Lancashire on the left and 1st Cavalry Division on the right. On arrival at 9 p.m., 150 men from 1 Company and a platoon of 2 Company occupied the front line. 3 Company provided three parties, each of twenty men, to man posts at key points around the village, while the rest of the Company occupied a system of old trenches north of Wieltje. 4 Company and Battalion HQ occupied the line between Essex Farm (later renamed Wieltje Farm and is not to be confused with the famous

Drive south from St Juliaan on the N313. Pass Seaforth Cemetery on the right and after 350m take the next left for St Jan. Drive 500m southwest and park under the A19 Autoroute bridge, avoiding blocking the cycle lane. Walk back and turn immediately right and left into Kattestraat. The fields on the right are where Belcher held his post on 23rd May 1915.

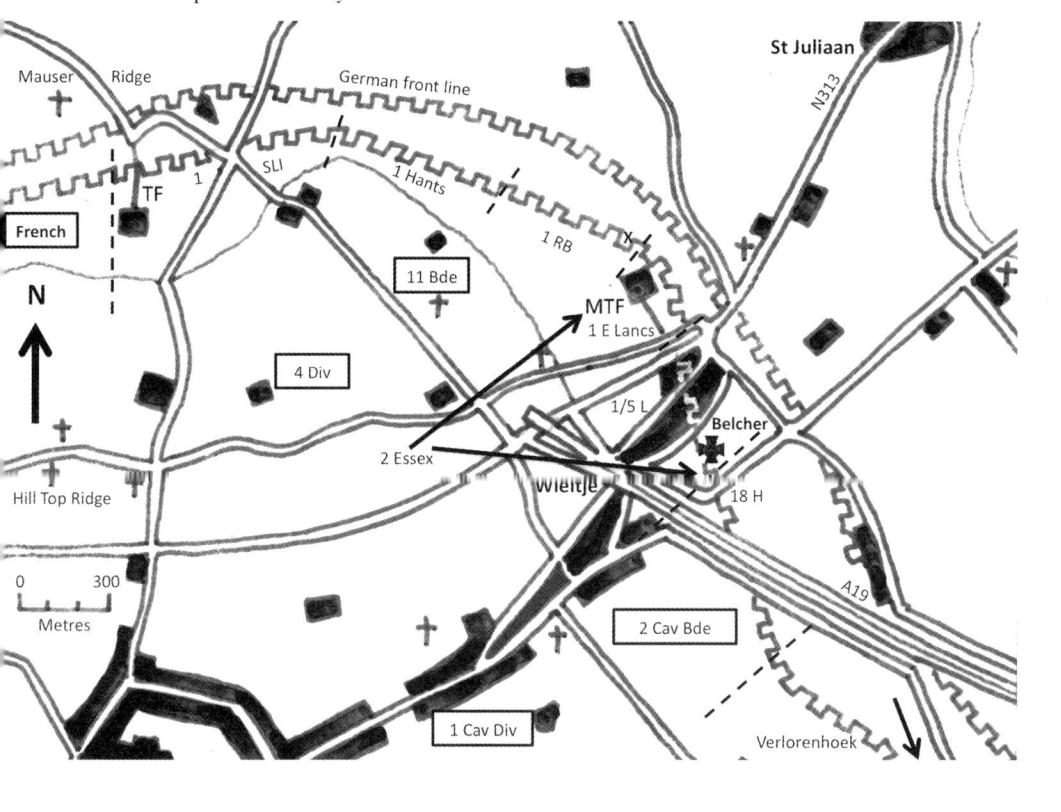

Essex Farm on the Yser Canal north of Ypres) and the Wieltje-St Jean road, west of the village. The front line trench was found to be a narrow and shallow ditch, badly battered by shellfire and hardly worthy of the title. To add to the discomfort it rained all night and the next day.

That night, 1st and 3rd Cavalry Divisions relieved 28th Division, holding the front from Bellewaarde Lake northwards to 550m southeast of Mouse (Shell) Trap Farm. The trenches here were also inadequate, with little protective wire and the ground had been churned into a quagmire by shells and rain.

Early on 13th May the line was held from left to right by 1st Somerset Light Infantry, 1st Hampshire, 1st Rifle Brigade, 1st East Lancashire and 1/5th London joining the Cavalry on the right. 2nd Essex (12th Brigade) and the rest of 1/5th London were in the Divisional Support Line. 1st King's Own was at La Brique with 1/2nd Monmouthshire and 1/5th South Lancashire at Canal Bank; all three battalions were in 12th Brigade.

At 3.30 a.m. on 13th May, the Germans opened a heavy bombardment on the British trenches and rear areas between Hooge and the Ypres-St Julien road. At one time over 150 shells per minute were landing around Mouse (Shell) Trap Farm. The British had little with which to respond, due to artillery ammunition being diverted to the Aubers attack and to Gallipoli.

At 8 a.m., an attack by the German 39th Division broke into the trenches south of Verlorenhoek and 7th Cavalry Brigade was forced to withdraw. Reinforcements and counterattacks restored the front, but at heavy cost. The gap was filled by 8th Cavalry Brigade and settled on a line of shell holes, 900m behind the original front. Part of the front was also taken over by 4th and 27th Divisions.

To the north, at 6.15 a.m., Prowse received a report from 2nd Essex that a wounded NCO of 18th Hussars (right of 1/5th London) had reported that his captain had ordered a retirement. Other messages from 2nd Essex and 1/5th London indicated that the cavalry had indeed retired. Prowse immediately sent orders to 2nd Cavalry Brigade that their trenches must be reoccupied at all costs. 1st King's Own stood two companies to in readiness to move up to Wieltje and patrols were sent to ascertain 2nd Cavalry Brigade's situation.

At 7 a.m. the enemy was seen massing in front of 1st Hampshire and 1st Rifle Brigade from Mouse (Shell) Trap Farm to the St Julien-Wieltje road. Shelling of Prowse's centre and right intensified and the situation was unclear to the right of Shell (Monte) Trap Farm. At 7.45 a.m., CO 2nd Essex sent a company forward to clear it up. Five minutes later, Prowse ordered 2nd Essex to counterattack at once, supported by 1st King's Own, while 1/5th South Lancashire moved forward to the Divisional Support Line and 1/2nd Monmouthshire to the Divisional Second Line. 4th Division was asked to send reserve battalions to Canal Bank and La Brique.

The 2nd Essex reserve company found the Germans had taken Mouse (Shell) Trap Farm and trenches south of it, but managed to drive them out. Part of 2nd Essex diverted right and retook some trenches abandoned by the cavalry at the junction with 1/5th London, while 1st King's Own moved two companies up to Wieltje. Gradually the situation at Mouse (Shell) Trap Farm was restored.

At 7.35 a.m., 4 Company, 1/5th London and three platoons of 2 Company reinforced the front line and were ordered to hold it at all costs. It was impossible to fit all the men into the remains of the shallow front line trench, which had been flattened by the bombardment, and most of 4 Company had to shelter in shell holes. Enemy shelling was concentrated on the Wieltje-St Julien road and it was feared an attempt to break through would be made there. The machine-gun covering this approach was knocked out, along with its crew, leaving a 30m gap between the right of 1/5th London's line and **Sergeant Belcher's** breastwork post south of the road.

By early afternoon another machine-gun team was in position and an attack was repulsed, but not without sustaining further heavy casualties. No more attacks were made against 1/5th London, but on the flanks the situation remained critical. To the left, Mouse (Shell) Trap Farm was lost and regained several times, but the right flank caused the greatest concern, where the left of 2nd Cavalry Brigade had been forced to retire. This left a gap of about 270m in the line, exposing 11th Brigade's right flank. Visibility was severely limited due to smoke and trees. All that was left to cover this area was Belcher's post, manned by only eight men.

Belcher was not deterred by the odds. Realising the importance of his position, he conducted an energetic defence, which convinced the enemy that his post was held in considerable strength. Devastatingly accurate fire raked the Germans every time they threatened the position. However, the breastworks were gradually worn away and the party was forced to occupy a vacant trench on the right.

During the afternoon, the rest of 1/5th London improved its positions and a new line was dug to connect an isolated platoon on the extreme left. The Battalion was relieved by 1st King's Own around midnight and moved into Second Line trenches

Kattestraat looking northeast, with the A19 embankment behind the camera. Belcher's Post was 200m into the field on the right.

Reverse view of the previous picture with Kattestraat on the right. The British line crossed diagonally across this field from right to left, approximately following the line of maize. The row of trees in the centre distance is alongside the A19. Douglas Belcher held this section of the line against numerous attacks from the right.

to the right of Essex Farm. Belcher's action had lasted for nine hours, during which one of his men was killed and three were wounded, but the bluff was maintained until the post was relieved. In addition to Belcher's VC, Lance Corporal Rowe and Rifleman Buck received the Military Medal.

After the Battle of Frezenberg; there was a lull of ten days. On 24th May, the comparative peace was shattered when the Germans attacked with gas on a front of six kilometres from south of Hooge to Turco Farm. The British left was threatened by the loss of Mouse (Shell) Trap Farm in the first wave of the attack and, despite heroic efforts, they were unable to recover it. That night a counterattack got to within a few metres of the German trenches, but with heavy losses. It was decided to evacuate the triangle of ground behind Mouse (Shell) Trap Farm and organise a fresh line along the west side of the Wieltje-Turco Farm road.

The month's fighting in the Second Battle of Ypres resulted in 59,000 BEF casualties; the French suffered another 10,000 and the Germans 35,000. The Ypres Salient had been reduced to a maximum depth of only five kilometres, making it even more difficult to defend. However, the line remained almost unchanged until the Third Battle of Ypres commenced on 31st July 1917.

The Battle highlighted significant shortcomings in intelligence and communications, rendering senior commanders ineffective for long periods. However, at lower levels the initiative and boldness of commanders and troops had saved the day, albeit at enormous cost. Both sides went on to develop more sophisticated gas weapons and countermeasures, but the use of gas in the future was neither a surprise nor particularly effective. By mid-1916, gas clouds had been replaced by gas shells.

Chapter Two

Aubers and Festubert

Battle of Aubers Ridge, 9th May 1915

> 68 Cpl John Ripley, 1st Black Watch (1st (Guards) Brigade, 1st Division), Rue du Bois, France
> 69 LCpl David Finlay, 2nd Black Watch (Bareilly Brigade, Meerut Division), Near Rue du Bois, France
> 70 Pte James Upton, 1st Nottinghamshire and Derbyshire (Sherwood Foresters) (24th Brigade, 8th Division), Rouges Bancs, France
> 71 Cpl Charles Sharpe, 2nd Lincolnshire (25th Brigade, 8th Division), Rouges Bancs, France

Despite being pre-empted by the German attack at Ypres on 22nd April, the Allied commanders were determined to press ahead with a joint offensive between Arras and Armentières in early May. The concept was for the French to punch a hole in the German defences and for the British to continue the rupture northwards. First Army (Haig) launched the British offensive from two separate areas along nine and a half kilometres of front, extending from Chocolat Menier Corner in the south, to La Cordonnerie Farm in the north.

In the southern sector, I Corps (right) and the Indian Corps (left) attacked south of Neuve Chapelle, while in the northern sector IV Corps attacked at Rouges Bancs. The intention was for the two thrusts to link up at La Cliqueterie Farm, a mile south of Aubers. 2nd Cavalry Division was held in readiness to exploit a breakthrough. The ultimate objective was the La Bassée-Fournes road.

At 5 a.m. on 9th May, 600 guns commenced the heaviest British bombardment to date. Half an hour later, the artillery increased its rate of fire and the guns assigned to wire cutting lifted onto the enemy front line. At the same time the assault troops left their trenches, negotiated gaps cut in their own wire the previous night and crossed pre-laid bridges over the many drainage ditches. Ten minutes later the guns lifted a further 550m and the assault began.

1st Division carried out I Corps' attack, with 2nd and 3rd Brigades leading on the right and left respectively. The previous night the assault troops had moved into specially constructed breastworks behind the front line. As they left their trenches during the final bombardment, they were met by heavy fire but, in spite of losses, a rough assault line was formed in no man's land to await the artillery lift. The attack ran into devastating fire from the enemy trenches and from emplacements in front

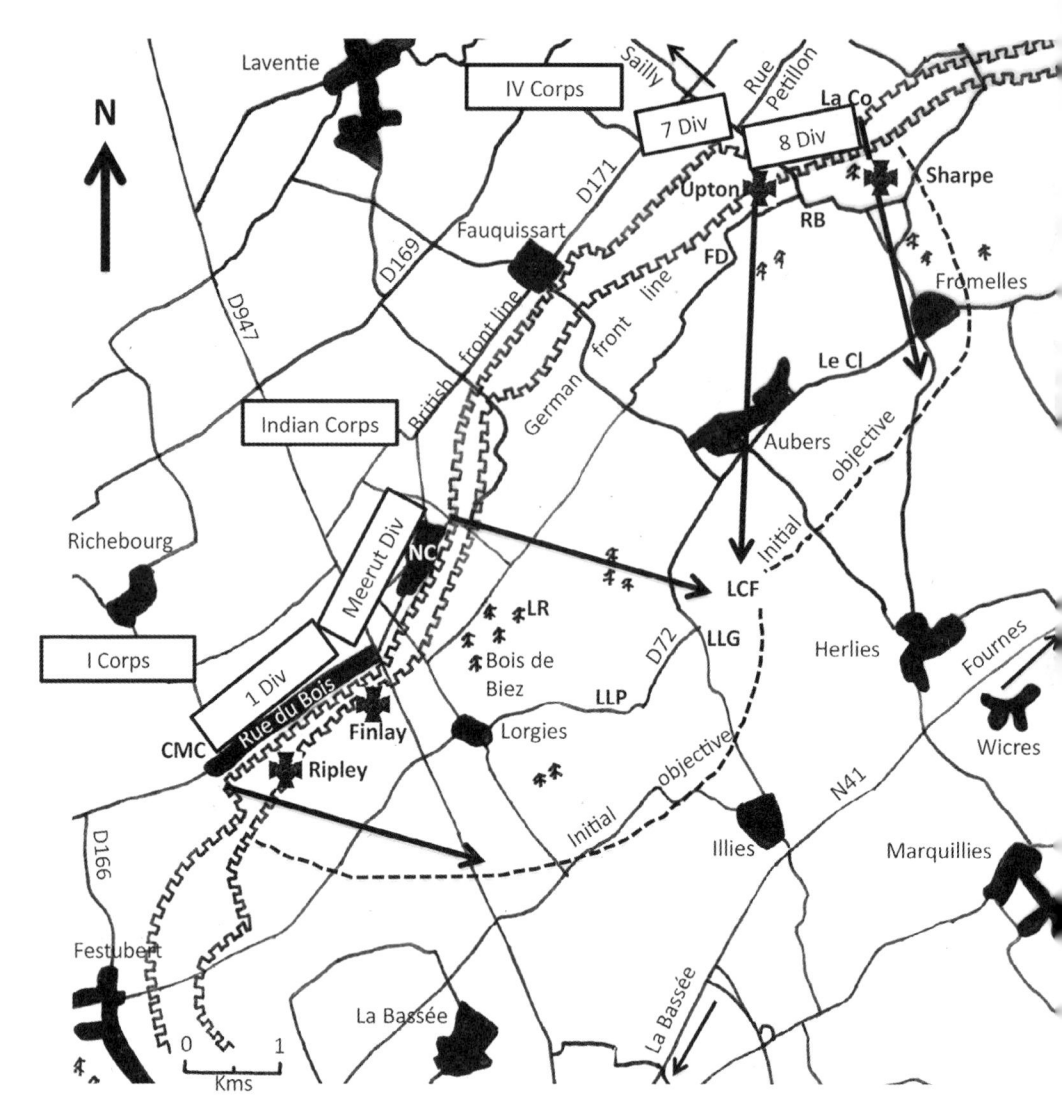

The plan for the Battle of Aubers Ridge on 9th May 1915. A number of locations are shown by letters – CMC = Chocolat Menier Corner, NC = Neuve Chapelle, LR = La Russie, LLP = Ligny le Petit, LLG = Ligny le Grand, LCF = La Cliqueterie Farm, Le Cl = Le Clercq Farm, FD = Farm Delaval, RB = Rouges Bancs and La Co = La Cordonnerie.

of the almost intact wire. Few men reached the enemy parapet. Those who did were soon destroyed there and the survivors were pinned down in no man's land. An ineffectual bombardment from 6.15 a.m. to 7 a.m. was followed by a second assault, which was also a complete failure. Another bombardment from 7.45 a.m. to 8.45 a.m. merely attracted heavy German retaliatory fire.

1st (Guards) Brigade moved forward after the failure of the morning attack. 1st Black Watch moved from Chocolat Menier Corner to occupy the front line at Rue du Bois, in case of an enemy counterattack. Its left rested on the cinder track and the right on Albert Road (not identified). By 8.50 a.m., A, B and D Companies were

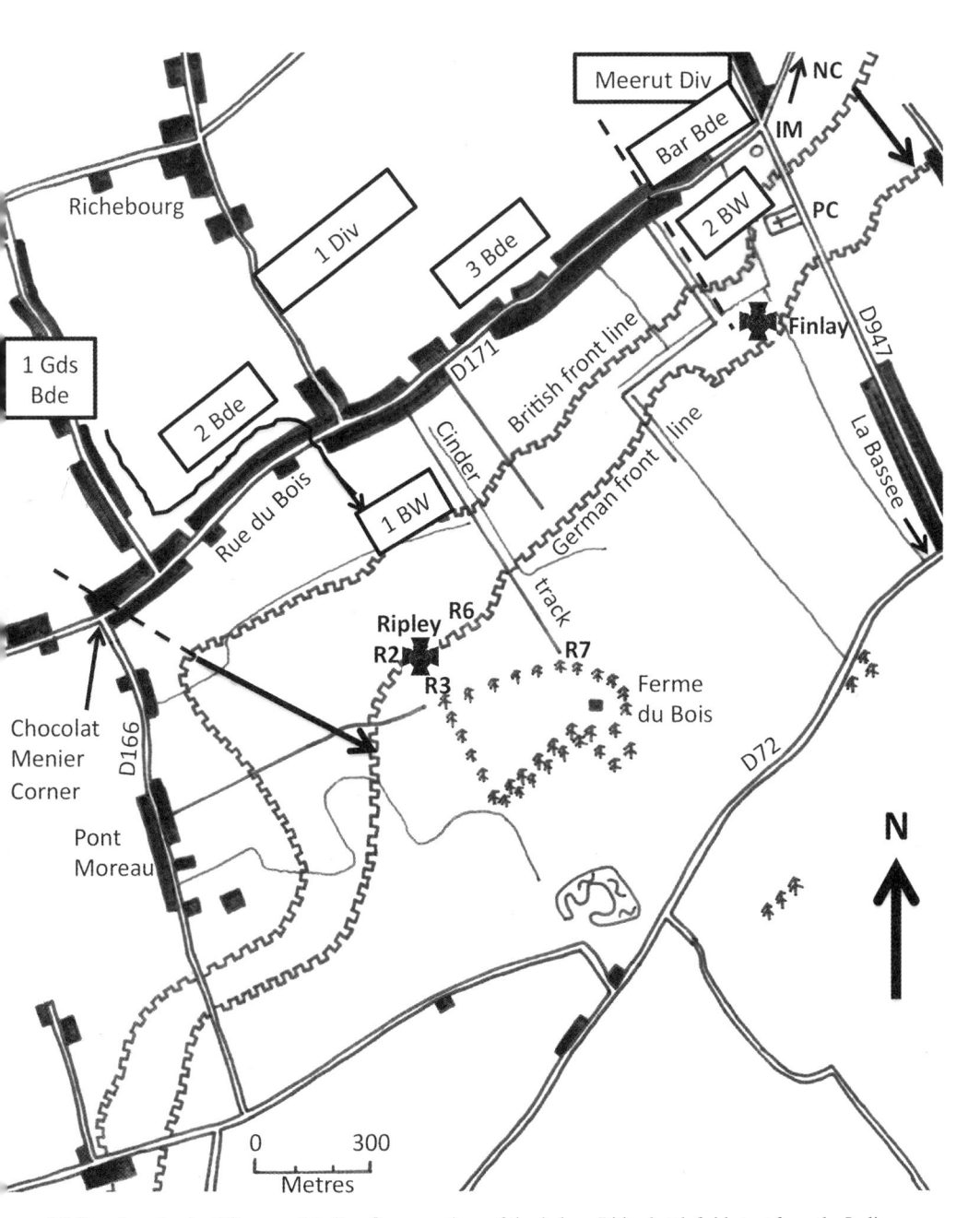

All directions for the I Corps and Indian Corps sections of the Aubers Ridge battlefield start from the Indian Memorial at La Bombe crossroads, where the main north-south D947 La Bassée – Estaires road is crossed by the D171. A number of locations in the northeast corner are shown by letters – NC = Neuve Chapelle, IM = Indian Memorial and PC = Portuguese Cemetery.

From the Indian Memorial drive southwest along the D171 Rue du Bois road. After 2.2 kms turn left onto the D166 heading south towards Festubert. After 550m there is a track on the left, at Pont Moreau. Park here and walk along the track to the east for 600m, where there is a slight right bend. The German front line is about 60m in front. The site of **John Ripley's VC** action is about 200m northeast of here.

From the Indian Memorial drive southwest along the D171 Rue du Bois road. After 400m turn left onto a metalled minor road. It soon gives way to a farm track with a reasonable surface at first, but do not be tempted to drive further as it soon degenerates. Walk 350m southeast along the track to the right turn where a deep ditch runs across. The British front line was 20m behind you and the ditch is the one crossed by **David Finlay** during the attack on 9th May 1915.

in the front line (A Line) with C Company and two companies of 1st Coldstream Guards in the support line (B Line). The remainder of 1st Coldstream Guards was behind (C Line) with two companies of 1/14th London (London Scottish).

Another attack was ordered for 12.40 p.m., but it was postponed to 2.40 p.m., and further delayed until 4 p.m. to conform to the Indian Corps. 2nd Brigade was relieved after suffering heavy casualties during the morning. Two battalions each from 1st (Guards) and 3rd Brigades (right and left respectively) mounted the renewed attack, supported by the remainder of 1st (Guards) Brigade. If a breakthrough was achieved, 2nd Brigade was to advance once again from the reserve line.

1st Black Watch (right) and 1st Cameron Highlanders (left) led 1st (Guards) Brigade. 1st Black Watch was to occupy the front line breastworks from R2 to R6 with the final objective being the trench R3 to R7. A Company on the right and D Company on the left made the attack, supported by B and C Companies respectively. If successful, 1st Coldstream Guards, 1st Scots Guards and 1/14th London were to follow.

1st Cameron Highlanders was delayed moving into its assault positions, but 1st Black Watch was ordered to go ahead with the attack, despite having no support on its left. The bombardment was more effective than previously and some gaps were cut in the wire. At 3.57 p.m., A and D Companies, supported by two platoons each from B and C Companies, surged over the parapet with pipes playing and rushed over the 300m of no man's land. A Company and two platoons of 1st Cameron Highlanders managed to start on time and reached the enemy parapet just as the barrage lifted. The German front line fell in many places and on the right about fifty men managed to reach the second line.

Corporal John Ripley, in Lieutenant Lyles's platoon on the right of A Company, led the right hand section on the extreme right of the attack. He managed to get through the wire and was the first man to reach the parapet, where he remained fully exposed until he had directed those following through the gap. When he had assembled his men, he led them through a gap in the parapet to the second trench. Despite his initial success, Ripley could not hope to sustain his position with only eight men. However, he set his party to work, blocking the trenches on the flanks, but the Germans were quick to recover. Ripley's party was soon surrounded and support from the front line was cut off by enemy machine-gun fire. Every man was hit in the ensuing action, including Ripley who received a serious head wound. The party was eventually overrun and the survivors made their way back.

The attacks by 1st Cameron Highlanders and 3rd Brigade failed completely. The commanders of 1st (Guards) and 3rd Brigades realised that nothing could be gained and the attack was halted. The troops in no man's land were withdrawn under cover of a fresh bombardment in the late afternoon. 1st (Guards) Brigade was relieved during the evening and pulled back to billets at Hinges. The Brigade incurred 838 casualties, of which 469 were in 1st Black Watch.

The Meerut Division launched the Indian Corps' attack. The objective was the line Bois de Biez – Ligny le Petit – Ligny le Grand – La Cliqueterie. The Dehra Dun Brigade was to lead, with the Bareilly Brigade in support. Two battalions of the Garhwal Brigade were to secure the eastern edge of the Bois de Biez and capture La Russie.

The Germans in this area had survived the bombardment almost unscathed and even manned machine-gun posts forward of their own wire. Despite suffering heavy casualties, the infantry rushed forward as one when the artillery lifted. However, the shrapnel barrage had been insufficient to cut lanes in the wire and the troops were forced to take cover about half way across no man's land. The Dehra Dun Brigade suffered nearly 900 casualties.

A repetition of the morning's attack at 2.40 p.m., following a forty minutes bombardment, was delayed until 4 p.m. to allow time for the Bareilly Brigade to take over the lead. Many casualties were suffered as the relief was completed in daylight. The Bareilly Brigade formed up with 2nd Black Watch on the right, 58th Rifles in the centre and 41st Dogras on the left. 1/4th Black Watch and 125th Rifles' machine-guns were to occupy the front trench when the assault battalions advanced.

2nd Black Watch took over from 2/2nd Gurkha Rifles (Dehra Dun Brigade), having moved forward through a nightmare of blocked trenches under constant artillery fire. The relief was completed just before zero hour. Despite protests that the Germans had been unaffected by the bombardment, the Corps Commander ordered the attack to go ahead at all costs. Accordingly, at 3.20 p.m., the British bombardment began and five minutes before zero, 2 and 4 Companies, 2nd Black Watch left their trenches and lay down in no man's land.

When the attack commenced, 2nd Black Watch and the right company of 58th Rifles were hit by well-directed rifle and machine-gun fire from the front and left flank. The

From the bend in the track east of Pont Moreau. The houses on the left are along Rue du Bois. The white structures amongst the trees in the centre distance are part of the Portuguese Cemetery. The bend in the track is on the right with Ferme du Bois in the distance beyond. John Ripley's VC action was just beyond the clump of bushes, right of centre.

left of 58th Rifles was plastered by the British artillery and could not get through. 41st Dogras was hit by the German artillery and heavy and accurate small arms fire. The British artillery was so ineffective that Germans stood behind their parados to gain better fire positions. COs ordered their reserve companies to remain in the trenches.

In 2nd Black Watch, **Lance Corporal David Finlay** led a party of twelve bombers in this attack. He intended to get as close as possible to the enemy trenches before the bombardment lifted. There was a four metres wide ditch, 20m forward of the front line and then 250m of open ground to cover to the enemy front line. As they crossed a bridge over the ditch, the Germans opened fire, killing two men. The remainder made it over, but eight more were killed on the far side. Finlay and the two others rushed on and had covered 75m before a shell exploded close to them. Finlay was not injured, but was knocked unconscious for ten minutes. On coming round, he saw one of his comrades lying wounded close by. Having ordered the other survivor to make his way back, Finlay crawled to the injured man, dressed his wounds and, in full view of the enemy and under very heavy fire, carried and dragged his comrade over 100m to safety.

By 6 p.m., the Bareilly Brigade's front had been reorganised to resist a German counterattack, which did not materialise. That night the Garhwal Brigade relieved the Bareilly Brigade. 2nd Black Watch was relieved by 1/3rd London and moved back to the reserve trenches. The Bareilly Brigade had suffered 1,101 casualties, of which 274 were in 2nd Black Watch.

IV Corps attacked on a frontage of 1,370m astride the Sailly-Fromelles road at Rouges Bancs, five kilometres northeast of the Indian Corps. The initial breach was to be made by 8th Division, with 24th Brigade on the right and 25th Brigade on the left; the boundary between them was the Sailly-Fromelles road. 23rd Brigade was in reserve. Then, while 8th Division protected the left flank, 7th Division was to swing right to link up with the Indian Corps at La Cliqueterie Farm. The assault troops took up positions in no man's land during the final bombardment. Only fifteen minutes were allowed for wire cutting and forty minutes to bombard the enemy trenches.

The impressive Indian Memorial at La Bombe corner is on the left, with the Portuguese Cemetery to the right. In the centre is the ditch crossed by 2nd Black Watch on 9th May 1915. The British front line was about 20m behind the ditch and parallel with it. The German lines were on the right of picture.

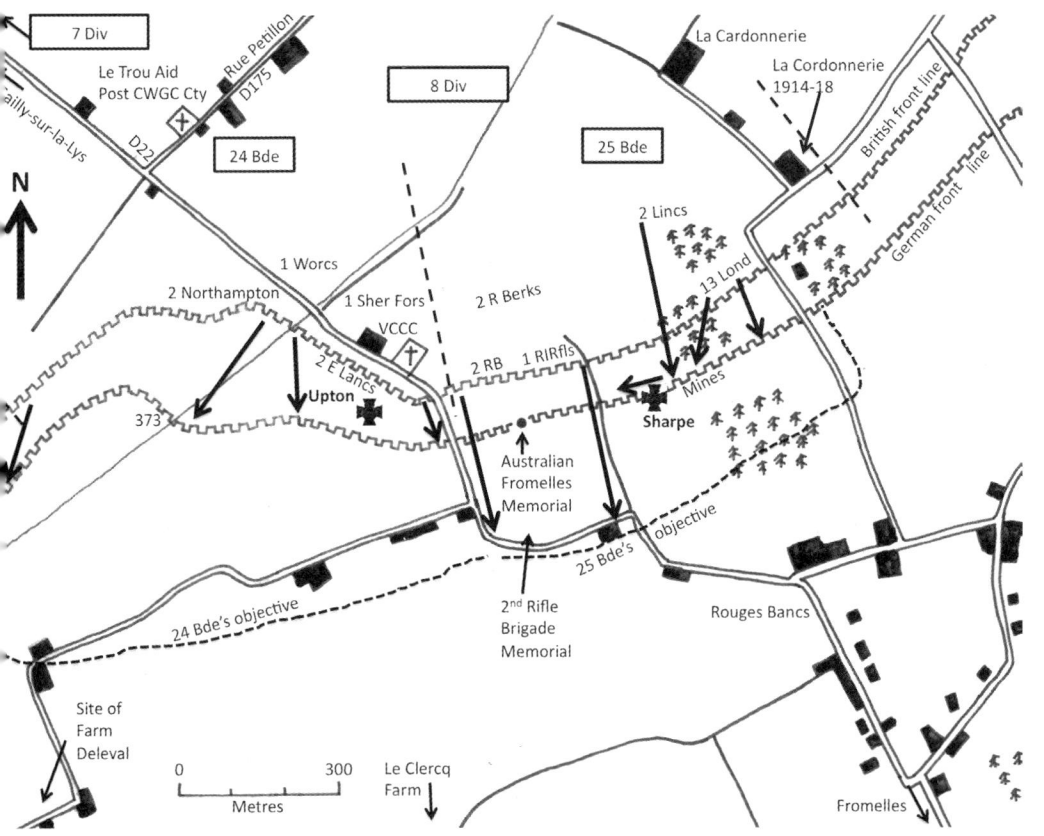

Approach the IV Corps battle area from the northwest along the D175 Sailly-sur-la-Lys – Fromelles road and stop at VC Corner CWGC Cemetery, which is marked as VCCC. From the Cemetery there is a good view across the whole of the 24th Brigade front on 9th May 1915. This is an ideal place from which to consider **James Upton's** VC action. Continue 400m southeast along the D175 and park at the 2nd Rifle Brigade memorial on the left. Walk on 200m and turn left along a rough track and follow it northwards for 200m. Look right between the copses. You are looking down the German front line towards the mine craters. This is the trench bombed by **Charles Sharpe**.

24th Brigade's attack on the right was made against a wide salient in the enemy line, each side of which was attacked by one battalion; 2nd Northamptonshire on the right and 2nd East Lancashire on the left. 1st Worcestershire and 1st Sherwood Foresters followed behind, with 1/5th Black Watch in reserve. Having passed over the German front line, 1st Sherwood Foresters was to bear right. In the second phase, 2nd Northamptonshire was to continue the advance, while 1st Sherwood Foresters seized a group of houses at Farm Delaval and extended to the left. 1st Worcestershire was to pass through 2nd East Lancashire to take Le Clercq Farm.

The night before the attack, two field guns were brought into the front line and the right gun appeared to be successful in cutting several lanes in the enemy wire. However, the emplacement for the gun on the left collapsed, making accurate fire impossible.

When the attack commenced at 5.40 a.m., 2nd East Lancashire was halted about 20m into no man's land by machine-gun fire. Only a few of 2nd Northamptonshire

From VC Corner Cemetery. Fromelles church is above the bend in the road on the left. The British front line ran from left to right in the foreground and the German lines were 100–170m beyond, in front of the buildings, which are on the road leading to Farm Deleval. James Upton's VC was won between the two lines in this field.

breached the enemy breastworks. D Company, 1st Sherwood Foresters set off at 6.10 a.m. and immediately came under fire from five machine-guns. The advance veered to the right, towards Point 373, but the enemy was just as strong there and no entry was made into their lines. B Company got to within 40m of the wire, where it was stopped with heavy casualties. Survivors reported a single four metres wide gap in the wire. The other gaps were incomplete, because they were in dead ground and could not be seen by the artillery observers.

Another attack was launched at 7.35 a.m. 2nd East Lancashire was supported this time by A and C Companies, 1st Sherwood Foresters. The impetus was lost almost immediately in the face of intense fire and the survivors sought what little cover was available. German shelling forced 1st Sherwood Foresters to withdraw into the breastworks at 1.15 p.m.

When 1st Sherwood Foresters' attack broke down, **Corporal Upton** took shelter in a shallow trench, 30m in front of the British front line. The wounded were lying all around and their cries of anguish and pain stirred him into action. Crawling out of the trench, he made his way towards the enemy lines. He came upon a sergeant

Reverse view of the previous picture. The white walls of VC Corner Cemetery are left of centre. On the right, a number of concrete bunkers and flag poles mark the German front line, with the Australian Fromelles Memorial beyond. Behind the Memorial is a copse in the southwest corner of which are the remains of the mine craters from 9th May 1915.

from 1st Worcestershire with a broken thigh. Having bandaged the wound and fitted a splint to the leg, Upton carried the man back to the trench and left him in the care of a comrade. Despite the enemy fire, he then discarded his equipment and went out again. He found a very large man with a serious stomach wound, who was too heavy to carry. So instead he manhandled the wounded man onto a waterproof sheet and dragged him back. The third man rescued had both legs shattered. When only ten metres from the trench, a shell exploded a few yards away killing the injured man outright. Upton was not harmed seriously, but he had to rest for a while to recover from the shock. He eventually rescued another ten men under heavy small arms and artillery fire. That night the Battalion was relieved by 1st Worcestershire and marched back to bivouacs at Rouge de Bout, having suffered 359 casualties.

The 25th Brigade attack was led by 2nd Rifle Brigade (right) and 1st Royal Irish Rifles (left), supported by 2nd Royal Berkshires and 2nd Lincolnshire respectively. On the extreme left, 1/13th London was to rush two mine craters, which were to be fired at 5.40 a.m. 1st London was in reserve, to move into the trenches vacated by 2nd Royal Berkshires and 2nd Lincolnshire. In the second and third phases, 2nd Royal Berkshires and 2nd Lincolnshire would pass through the leading battalions and continue the advance. Finally, 2nd Rifle Brigade and 1st Royal Irish Rifles would take up the lead again to the final objective.

On the left of 25th Brigade, the wire had been well cut, but British shells falling short caused a number of casualties. When the attack commenced, no man's land was crossed quickly, despite heavy losses from small arms and artillery fire. The German breastworks were captured and the assault troops pressed on to the bend in the Fromelles road 200m further on. The support battalions suffered badly as they struggled forward through intense fire and units became intermingled. 2nd Lincolnshire, led by A and B Companies, left its assembly trenches near Rue Petillon to follow 1st Royal Irish Rifles. They reached the first line of German trenches, but could get no further due to heavy small arms fire from both flanks and enemy artillery fire. C and D Companies were held in the British front line to avoid further unnecessary casualties.

The brigade commander, Brigadier General Arthur Lowry Cole, arrived in the front line at 6.25 a.m. He ordered Captain BJ Thruston (later DSO & Legion d'Honneur; died November 1918, attached to West African Frontier Force, buried in Freetown (King Tom) Cemetery – 2 D 5), commanding C Company, 2nd Lincolnshire, with 150 men of his own and D Companies, to push down a sap on the left. They were to reach the mine craters held by 1/13th London and then fight westwards to link up with the left of 2nd Rifle Brigade.

A bombing and blocking party, under 2nd Lieutenant Eric Black (Ploegsteert Memorial), was sent ahead by Thruston. This party reached the enemy trench and bombed its way for 270m westwards, before running out of bombs. It was then forced back under intense fire from right and left. Meanwhile 2nd Scottish Rifles' bombers (23rd Brigade) cleared the trench to the east of the craters. From 9 a.m. onwards men were sent forward to occupy the captured trenches, but few got through, despite Thruston organising five machine-guns to silence the enemy machine-guns beyond the craters. By 10.30 a.m., although well established in the trench to the west of the craters, Thruston's party was cut off by fire sweeping no man's land behind them. 1/13th London was forced back and by 2.15 p.m. had abandoned its gains and was back in the British lines. Under pressure from three sides, Thruston was forced to abandon his position at 8 p.m. and, under cover of darkness, brought his men back.

From just behind the German front line looking northeast. Behind the telegraph pole on the right, on the edge of the copse, is where the mines were fired. Charles Sharpe cleared the German front line trench from there towards the bush on the left.

Corporal Sharpe commanded a blocking party in the advance towards the craters. He was sent forward to take and hold a portion of trench and was the first to reach the enemy position. Although the rest of his party was hit, he set off immediately to bomb along a 50m stretch of trench. Having been joined by four other men (three received the DCM – Privates D Bills, W Dunderdale and J F Leeman), he continued the attack and cleared another 230m of trench with great determination. Despite considerable enemy pressure, they held the trench all day.

The 2nd Rifle Brigade memorial on the north side of the D175, 400m southeast of VC Corner Cemetery. There is space to park here. The copse with the mine craters is in the background.

Meanwhile elsewhere in 25th Brigade's area there was chaos. About 6.45 a.m., a considerable rearward movement by British troops was seen from the Germans lines. It is understood that an unauthorised order was given to retire and the assault troops began falling back. Germans prisoners, mixed in with the retiring British, gave the impression of a counterattack. Brigadier General Lowry Cole stood on the parapet to encourage the men to carry on advancing. He was mortally wounded (Le Trou Aid Post Cemetery, Fleurbaix – E 22) and Lieutenant Colonel RB Stephens, CO 2nd Rifle Brigade, was informed that command of the Brigade had devolved to him. By the time the mess had been sorted out, the German fire had increased in intensity and heroic efforts to renew the offensive and reinforce the lodgements in the German lines came to nothing.

By 8 a.m., 2nd Rifle Brigade was being forced back from its advanced position, but a mixed force of 2nd Rifle Brigade and 1st Royal Irish Rifles was still holding out in the German front line at 1.10 p.m. During the night all the gains had to be given up. 23rd Brigade relieved 25th Brigade; the latter had 2,331 casualties. 2nd Lincolnshire was relieved at 11 p.m., having suffered almost 300 casualties.

Next morning, Haig closed down the offensive. The results were disappointing, considering that the French had met with considerable success. There were many reasons why the offensive failed, but chief amongst them was the weakness of the British artillery and the shortage of high explosive shells. Over 11,500 casualties were suffered for no gain whatsoever.

Battle of Festubert, 15th–25th May 1915

73 LCpl Joseph Tombs, 1st King's (Liverpool) Regiment (6th Brigade, 2nd Division), Rue du Bois, France
74 CSM Frederick Barter, 1st Royal Welsh Fusiliers (22nd Brigade, 7th Division), Festubert, France
75 Lt John Smyth, 15th Ludhiana Sikhs (9th (Sirhind) Brigade, 3rd (Lahore) Division), Richebourg L'Avoué, France
76 Rfn William Mariner, 2nd King's Royal Rifle Corps (2nd Brigade, 1st Division), Cambrin, France
77 LCpl Leonard Keyworth, 24th London (The Queen's) (142nd Brigade, 47th Division), Givenchy, France

Despite the failure of the Aubers attack on 9th May, another offensive was launched in the same area a week later to assist the French Tenth Army's attack on Vimy Ridge to the south. The Meerut, 2nd and 7th Divisions were to make the initial assault, on a frontage of 4,800m.

As a result of lessons learned at Aubers, tactics were changed. Rather than a short hurricane bombardment followed by an infantry advance with unlimited objectives, this attack would follow the more attritional French practice of a deliberate preparatory barrage over a number of days, before the infantry attacked limited objectives.

The objective was the line of La Quinque Rue, the Festubert – La Tourelle road, involving an average advance of 900m. The plan called for the Meerut and 2nd Divisions in the north to attack between Chocolat Menier Corner and Port Arthur and a few hours later for 7th Division to join the advance some 600m to the south from the northeast of Festubert. The intention was to pinch out a strong enemy position by avoiding a frontal assault.

The preparatory bombardment by 433 guns opened on the morning of 13th May. Although over 100,000 shells were fired, the British artillery lacked heavy explosive shells and much of the shrapnel barrage was ineffective. The weather also played a part, with heavy rain softening the ground and many shells failing to explode. It was clear the bombardment was not achieving its aims and there was a postponement of 24 hours.

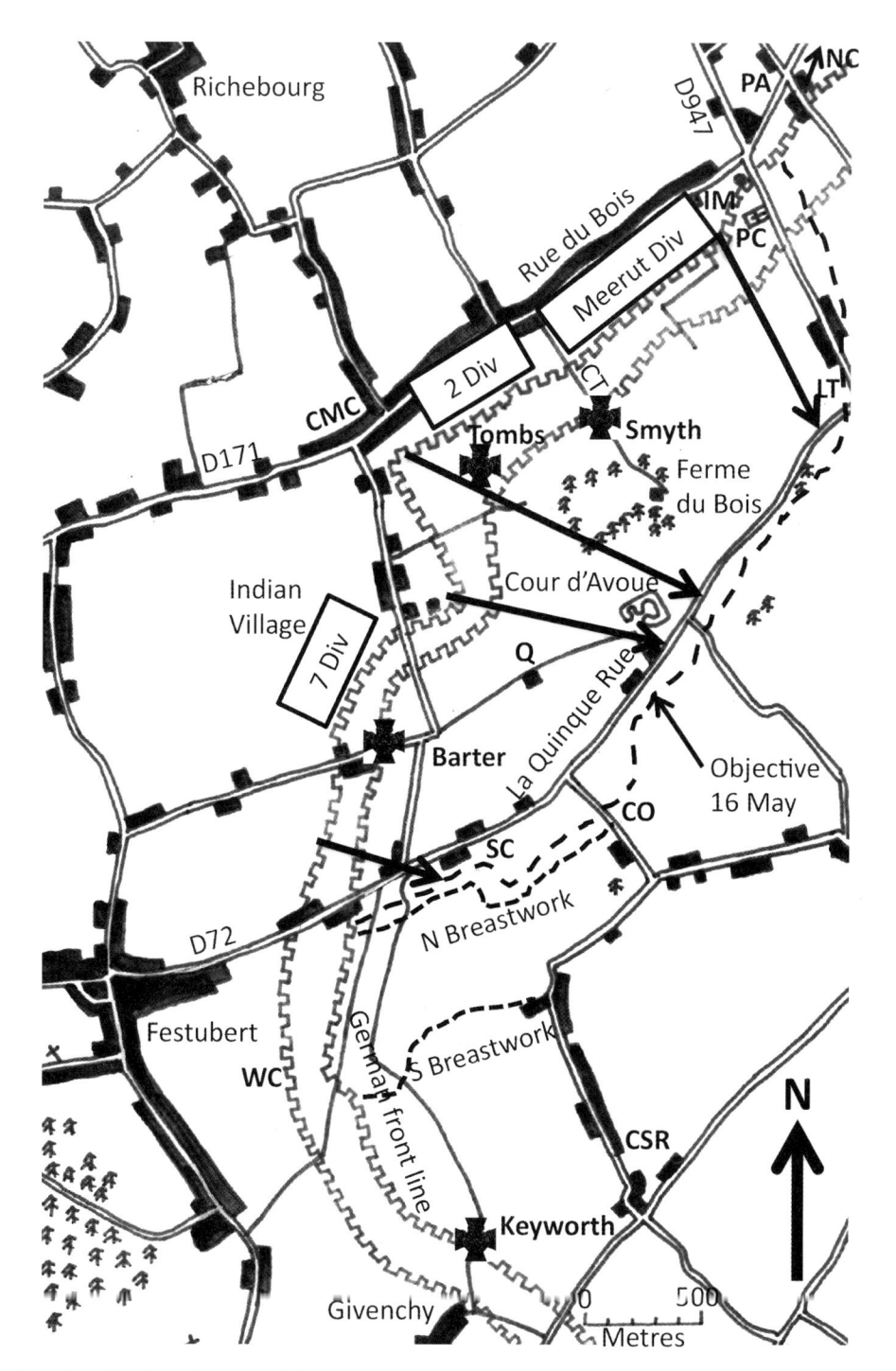

Overview of the Festubert battlefield. A number of locations on this and the other Festubert maps are shown by letters – CMC = Chocolat Menier Corner, CO = Canadian Orchard, CSR = Chapelle St Roch, CT = cinder track, IM = Indian Memorial, LT = La Tourelle, NC = Neuve Chapelle, PA = Port Arthur, PC = Portuguese Cemetery, Q = Quadrilateral and SC = Stafford Corner. There are cafés near the churches in Richebourg and Neuve Chapelle.

By 10 p.m. on 15th May, the assault units were in position. In the Meerut Division, the Garwhal Brigade was to make the initial attack with 2nd Leicestershire on the right and 39th Garwhal Rifles on the left. Both battalions were allocated six machine-guns each. 3rd London and two companies of 2/3rd Gurkhas were in support and the rest of the latter Battalion was in reserve. Portable bridges were placed in advance over ditches; not an easy task with an alert enemy sending up flares. As the Dehra Dun Brigade was in Corps reserve, the Sirhind Brigade (Lahore Division) was made available to support the Garwhal Brigade.

As the assault neared, men went forward of the ditches with following waves lying down behind. At 11.30 p.m., the barrage lifted and the leading platoons set off in the first British night attack of the war. The wire was reasonably well cut in this area and the attack initially swept over no man's land almost unhindered. It was then met by concentrated machine-gun and rifle fire, accompanied by mortars and shrapnel. The Germans illuminated no man's land with numerous flares and a searchlight, which turned night into day. The Germans were also reported to have employed some form of fireball, which burst into flames on striking the ground. The bridges became blocked and shell holes and fallen trees also impeded progress. The forward troops were quickly cut off from support. The impression was that the Germans knew the time and place of the offensive precisely. By midnight it was clear that the Garwhal Brigade attack had failed and the two leading battalions were withdrawn, having lost about 400 men.

The Meerut Division tried to renew its attack at 3.15 a.m. on 16th May after a thirty minutes bombardment. Before the attack commenced, the Germans were pouring heavy fire over no man's land. 3rd London and 2/3rd Gurkhas went forward and some parties got over the bridges by advancing in short rushes, but 180 men were lost with little gained.

It was clear no progress would be made in this area and, at 5.40 a.m., further attacks by the Meerut Division were halted. The Sirhind Brigade was placed under 2nd Division on the right and took over part of the line held by 5th Brigade. The relief was conducted in extremely difficult conditions along flooded and blocked trenches and was not completed until the 18th.

2nd Division attacked with 5th Brigade on the left, 6th Brigade on the right and 4th (Guards) Brigade in reserve. 5th Brigade was led by 2nd Royal Inniskilling Fusiliers and 2nd Worcestershire, with 2nd Oxfordshire & Buckinghamshire Light Infantry in support. It was hit by heavy machine-gun fire, but some of 2nd Royal Inniskilling Fusiliers on the right reached the German front line. 2nd Oxfordshire & Buckinghamshire Light Infantry was sent up in support.

6th Brigade, to the west of the cinder track from Rue du Bois to Ferme du Bois, attacked with 1/7th King's (right), 1st Royal Berkshire (centre) and 1st KRRC (left). It almost reached the enemy positions between R1 and R6 before being seen. Consequently the front and support trenches fell quickly. However, during the advance, 1/7th King's drifted to the left and, although it seized a portion of the

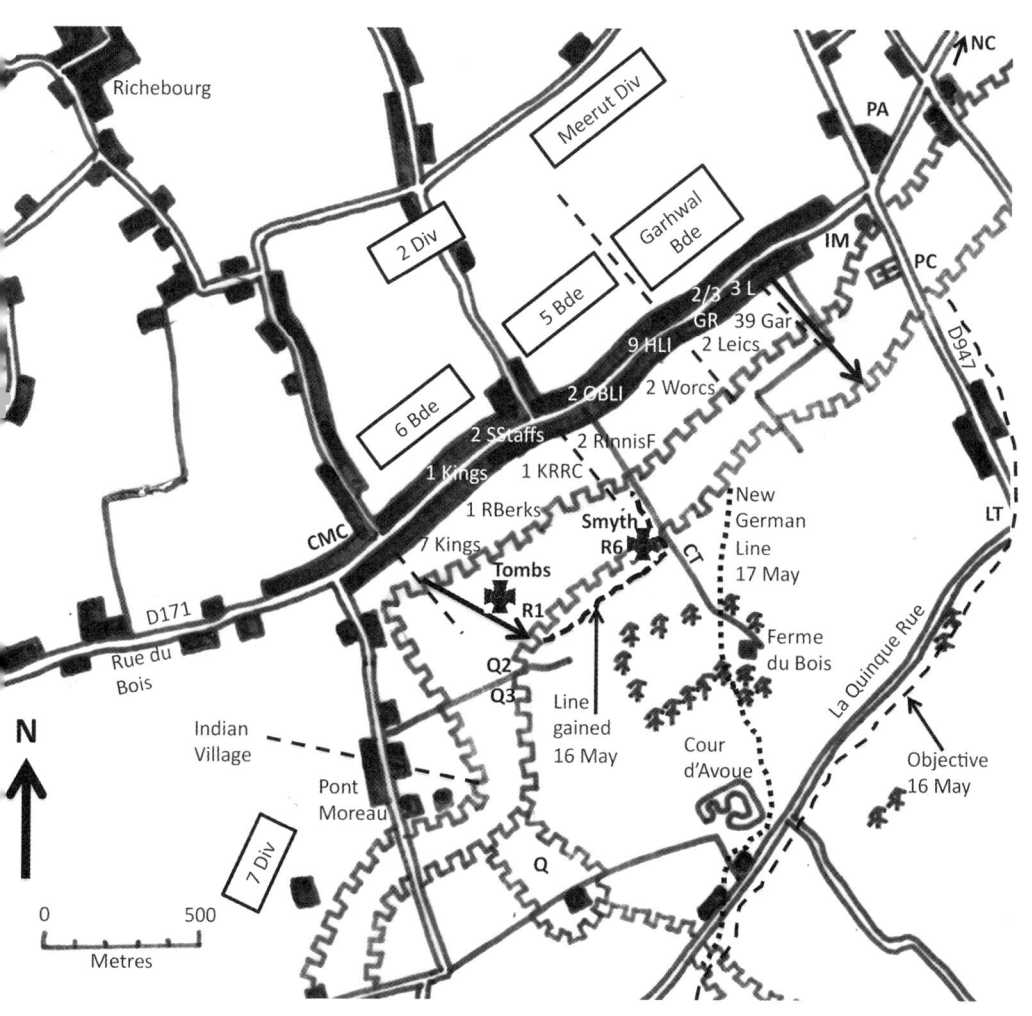

The Meerut and 2nd Divisions' area of the Festubert battlefield in more detail. The only gains made on 16th May were by 6th Brigade.

front line, it failed to take R1. Despite 6th Brigade's success, the failure of most of 5th Brigade enabled the Germans to sweep no man's land with enfilade fire as the support battalions (1st King's and 2nd South Staffordshire) followed. Efforts to dig new communications trenches across no man's land came to nothing in the heavy fire.

Before the attack, C and D Companies, 1st King's had formed up in assembly trenches (C and D Lines) 450m behind 1/7th King's. When the attack commenced, the Companies moved forward into the trenches vacated by 1/7th King's (A and B Lines) and were replaced by A and B Companies in the assembly trenches. At 12.30 a.m., D Company moved across no man's land to reinforce 1st Royal Berkshire and C Company followed at 1 a.m., while A and B Companies moved into the front line with 2nd South Staffordshire on the left. The plan was for C and D Companies to pass through 1st Royal Berkshire to take Cour d'Avoué Farm, but they were too scattered to be organised for an assault.

There was great urgency to get on and B Company was ordered forward. The first platoon was mown down by a machine-gun at Q2 on the right. Before the second could be halted it suffered the same fate. The third platoon was stopped before it too was wiped out. As the light grew snipers began picking off survivors in no man's land, but many managed to crawl back to the front line.

To all intents and purposes, 2nd Division's attack had ended and it was too disorganised to support 7th Division to the south at dawn. The Germans shelled the area throughout the day, wrecking communications trenches and causing over a hundred casualties to 1st King's alone. An attempt to push to the right to seize Q2 and Q3 at 9.30 a.m. had to be abandoned in the face of overwhelming firepower. Renewed attacks between 11.30 a.m. and 1 p.m. also came to nothing and attention turned to consolidating the gains. At 3 p.m., parties from A Company dashed 300m over no man's land to resupply ammunition. During the night the Battalion relieved 1st Royal Berkshires in the forward part of the captured enemy trench. Next day 1st King's attempted to press on to Cour d'Avoué Farm, but was forced back due to lack of flank support.

Lance Corporal Joseph Tombs was one of those stuck in no man's land in front of A Line after the attack on the 16th. He crawled back to the front line dragging a badly wounded man with him. There he sheltered from the heavy fire, but was unable to ignore the cries of the wounded and obtained permission to try to rescue some of them. Climbing over the parapet he was momentarily frozen by the scene of carnage, but recovered quickly and dashed into no man's land. He fell and it was feared that he had been hit, but a few minutes later he was seen crawling back with a wounded man. As he neared the trench he lifted the man onto his back and

The best view over Joseph Tombs' VC site is from the same position as for John Ripley during the Battle of Aubers Ridge a few days before Festubert. At Pont Moreau, south of Chocolat Menier Corner, park on the roadside and walk east along the track for 550m to where it bends slightly right. This is about where Q2 and Q3 were located. Look due north and Joseph Tombs' VC site is approximately half way between you and Rue du Bois, i.e. the line of houses.

made a run for it. He went out again and returned supporting another man at the waist, as he crawled back on his hands and knees. The fourth man he brought in was so badly wounded that Tombs had to drag him using an improvised harness made of rifle slings around the man's neck and under his arms. It is alleged that he even resorted to dragging him with his teeth! Shortly after bringing in this man, Tombs was wounded by shrapnel in the stomach. A report in the Birmingham Gazette on 11th October 1915, states that while rescuing the fourth man, Tombs had to shelter the injured man in a shell hole. They were approached by a German. The wounded man was unconscious and Tombs, who was unarmed, feigned death until the German turned him over and he dispached him with a kukri given to him by a Gurkha.

7th Division's attack at 3.15 a.m. on 16th May was preceded by an intensification of the bombardment from 2.45 a.m. The attack was made by 20th and 22nd Brigades, left and right respectively, with 21st Brigade in reserve. Having gained the German front line the main objective was the North Breastwork communication trench, running from 'M5' to Canadian Orchard. Six field guns were brought into the front line to open gaps in the German breastworks. Their fire had to be very carefully coordinated to avoid hitting the British troops as they formed up.

20th Brigade, astride Princes Road, faced roughly southeast. At 3.10 a.m., the leading platoons of 2nd Scots Guards and 2nd Border left the front line to get close to the German trenches before the barrage lifted. A considerable number of casualties were caused when some of the men advanced into the British shelling. Five minutes later the attack went in. It was slowed by a deep ditch and heavy crossfire from the Quadrilateral on the left front, which was untouched by the bombardment. The German front line was gained despite the lack of support from 2nd Division on the left flank, but the Brigade made little progress beyond.

22nd Brigade, straddling Rue de Cailloux, was led by 2nd Royal West Surrey on the right and 1st Royal Welsh Fusiliers on the left, with 1st South Staffordshire and 2nd Royal Warwickshire in support. On the left flank was a gap of 350m before 2nd Scots Guards (20th Brigade).

1st Royal Welsh Fusiliers was to attack in line of companies on a frontage of 300m, with A Company leading, followed successively by B, C and D Companies. Its initial objective was the German second line. Having secured it, the Battalion was to swing southeast and occupy the Northern Breastwork communications trench, with the line being prolonged to the right by 2nd Royal Warwickshire and 2nd Royal West Surrey. A Company's ultimate objective was Canadian Orchard, about 1,100m from the British lines, with the other Companies echeloned to the right rear.

The night before the attack 1st Royal Welsh Fusiliers moved into the line via Indian Village, with its right resting on Rue des Cailloux. Work parties laid bridges over a large ditch in no man's land and patrols reported that the wire was well cut, but the enemy breastworks were not much damaged. At 2.45 a.m., the final

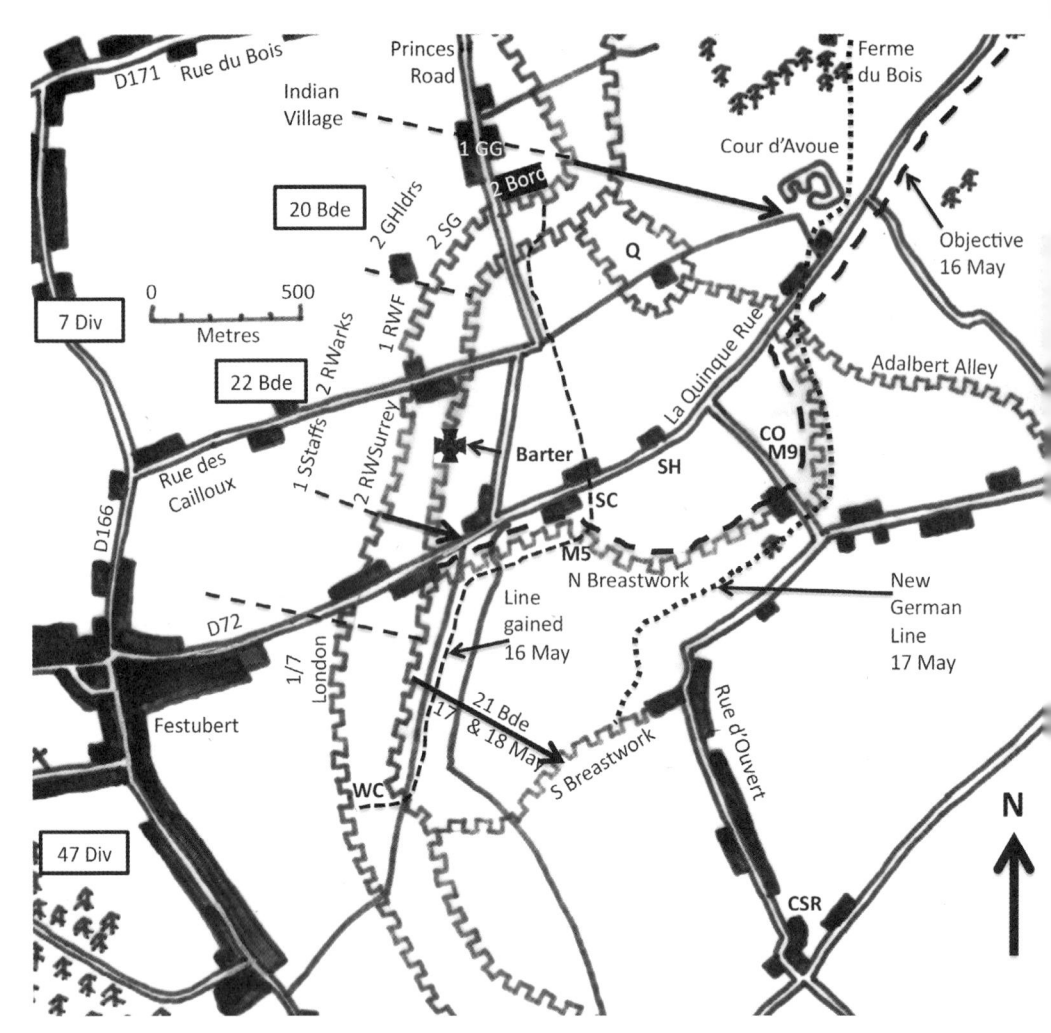

From Festubert church drive east on the D72 towards Lorgies. After 1,350m turn left and 550m further on turn right and park on the right after 100m where there is plenty of space for other vehicles to pass. Walk back to the junction and 100m beyond to look south along the line of trench cleared by CSM Barter.

bombardment began, with many shells falling short. Twenty minutes later the German artillery joined in. At 3.15 a.m., the artillery lifted and 22nd Brigade moved off into heavy machine-gun fire. The advance halted for fifteen minutes for more shelling, but at 3.45 a.m. it resumed, supported by 1st South Staffordshire on the right. Despite casualties, the German front line was reached and bombing parties begin working along it.

In the attack, A Company, 1st Royal Welsh Fusiliers crossed the ditch quickly before coming under heavy artillery and small arms fire from the right. The enemy breastworks were reached and scaled with the use of ladders. After half an hour of intense hand-to-hand fighting, the position was secured. However, the rear companies suffered heavily as they crossed no man's land.

Looking south along the line of the trench cleared by Frederick Barter and his party. The trench was parallel with the lane on the left. Festubert is in the right distance.

On reaching the front line **Sergeant Major Frederick Barter** called for volunteer bombers to follow him. He collected a party of eight, including an extraordinary 2nd Royal West Surrey soldier; Captain Hugh Sale Smart, 2/53rd Sikhs (Frontier Force) was on sick leave in England when war broke out and enlisted as G/4034 Private Thomas Hardy to ensure he got to the front.

Barter led the volunteers in a bombing attack along the front line to the south. The enemy was caught unawares and three officers and 102 soldiers surrendered. Barter's party eventually cleared 450m of trench and greatly assisted the Brigade in achieving its initial objectives. They also cut the leads connected to eleven mines before the Germans could detonate them. Smart was killed in this action, having performed numerous acts of bravery for which he was never honoured; he is commemorated on the Le Touret Memorial.

By 6.00 a.m., 2nd Royal West Surrey and 1st South Staffordshire had reached the Northern Breastwork, which they secured from Stafford Corner to the old German front line. At 6.30 a.m., about eighty men of 1st Royal Welsh Fusiliers under Captain Stockwell, intermingled with elements of 2nd Royal Warwickshire and 2nd Scots Guards (20th Brigade), joined 2nd Royal West Surrey near the Orchard at 'M9' and a house was captured. 2nd Scots Guards had to withdraw a little; it was caught by the British artillery firing off the map and also by German fire from Adalbert Alley.

Stockwell's party set up a German machine-gun and prevented the enemy withdrawing some field guns 350m away. They also repulsed a counterattack, but

Captain Hugh Sale Smart, 2/53rd Sikhs (Frontier Force) served as G/4034 Private Thomas Hardy.

further attempts to take the Orchard and other buildings at the northeast end of the North Breastwork failed, despite the support of 100 men from 1/7th London (47th Division). By 9 a.m., the attack had ground to a halt. The position held by the mixed force offered little protection from enemy shelling, which grew in intensity during the day.

At 10.00 a.m., General Monro (I Corps) directed that renewed attacks be made on the inner flanks to close the gap between 7th and 2nd Divisions. They were to converge on Cour d'Avoué Farm. In 7th Division, 1st Grenadier Guards, on the left of 20th Brigade, managed to cross no man's land using a new trench being dug by 1/6th Gordon Highlanders. They bombed along 300m of enemy trench, but were unable to advance in the open due to intense enemy fire every time they showed themselves. 2nd Division was in no position to make another attack and Monro's initiative came to nothing.

On 22nd Brigade's right flank, specialist Brigade bombers and others from 1st South Staffordshire continued to advance south through the German trenches. They reached Willow Corner on the front of 47th Division, a distance of 800m, and took 190 prisoners. During the rest of the day, 7th Division's situation did not change appreciably. Gradually support on 22nd Brigade's flanks was whittled away and 1st Royal Welsh Fusiliers became separated from the rest of the Brigade. It held on until 7.30 p.m. against a number of German counterattacks before being pulled back. It had incurred 578 casualties.

During the night the remnants of 2nd Royal West Surrey and 2nd Border were also withdrawn. The British front was then held by 1/7th London (attached to 22nd Brigade) from Willow Corner, then 1st South Staffordshire holding the Northern Breastwork to Stafford Corner. There the line turned north, held by 2nd Scots Guards, to the junction of Princes Road and Rue des Cailloux to join the original front line.

At 11.45 p.m., First Army decided to continue with the offensive in I Corps' area. The first priority was to close the gap between the two divisions, before pressing on towards Chapelle St Roch.

During 17th May, German units between Ferme du Bois and the Southern Breastwork began to withdraw to a new line, 1,100m to the rear. The British shelled the Quadrilateral in the early hours, which stopped part of the German garrison from withdrawing. They were then hit by their own as well as the British artillery. About 450 reached the British lines where they surrendered. Reports reaching HQ I Corps indicated that the German line might be collapsing, but it was not immediately clear which British units were capable of advancing to take advantage. It was not until 9.30 a.m. that 21st Brigade began to advance into the gap, with 2nd Royal Scots Fusiliers and 2nd Yorkshire leading. By 10.15 a.m. the Quadrilateral and some ground to the left had been cleared.

At 10.00 a.m., 6th Brigade also advanced, led by 2nd South Staffordshire and 1st King's, with 2nd Highland Light Infantry on the left. They ran into heavy machine-gun fire from the left and, when the British artillery fired in support, it hit 2nd Royal Scots Fusiliers in the Quadrilateral. Around midday, First Army brought 3rd Canadian Brigade to readiness and extended the front of the Indian Corps to release 5th Brigade (2nd Division) for a further advance. In the afternoon attempts to capture the Orchard and the section of the Northern Breastwork nearby were halted by machine-gun and artillery fire. Reserves coming forward were held up on congested roads, while the wet weather worsened ground conditions.

At 7.30 p.m., 21st Brigade attacked with 2nd Bedfordshire and 1/4th Cameron Highlanders on the extreme right to seize the Southern Breastwork some 360m away. They stumbled upon a number of hidden ditches in which some men drowned, but a few of 1/4th Cameron Highlanders got into the Breastwork. During the rest of the day and that night, the Germans continued to pull back to the new line from Rue d'Ouvert to the cinder track near Ferme du Bois. This went unnoticed by the British.

That night the Sirhind Brigade was ordered forward from reserve to relieve 5th Brigade. 3 Company, 15th Sikhs under Captain K Hyde-Cates, relieved two companies of 2nd Highland Light Infantry in a section of captured trench in front of Ferme du Bois known as the 'Glory Hole'. Two more companies took up support positions behind and the fourth was held in reserve. Progress was slow through partially flooded trenches packed with wounded and the Germans sent up flares repeatedly, making movement over the open hazardous. Only a barricade separated the two sides and there were numerous casualties.

About 4 a.m. on the 18th, Hyde-Cates realised that the Germans were reinforcing their line and rapid fire was opened in the dim light. By dawn it was clear that the enemy trench was packed with men and an attack seemed inevitable. Soon after, the Germans started bombing and the Sikhs responded strongly until noon, when all the dry bombs had been expended. The situation was critical; without bombs it was not possible to hold the position. Communication with Hyde-Cates' isolated position was maintained most courageously by two signalers, who laid a telephone line over the open.

Early in the afternoon new plans were laid for the Guards Brigade to advance on the right on Cour d'Avoue. The Sirhind Brigade would cooperate with 15th Sikhs and 1st Highland Light Infantry bombing along the German trenches to establish a line from which 4th Kings could make a flank attack on Ferme du Bois and connect with the Guards Brigade. However, many of the Sirhind Brigade troops were not even in the line when the initial orders were issued. The barrage fell at 3.45 p.m. and the detailed orders did not arrive until 4 p.m., with the attack scheduled to go in thirty minutes later. It was an impossible task. Two attempts were made by 2nd Highland Light Infantry to get into position and reinforce Hyde-Cates, but on both occasions the party was almost wiped out. The attack by 4th King's never took place.

Despite this, at 3.30 p.m., **Lieutenant John Smyth** was ordered to take a bombing party from the support line to the front line in front of Rue du Bois. They

The Le Touret Memorial, where Captain Hugh Sale Smart (served as Private Thomas Hardy) is commemorated. The Memorial commemorates over 13,400 British soldiers who were killed between Estaires and Grenay from October 1914 to 24th September 1915 who have no known grave.

had 225m to cover over open ground, except for a shallow communications trench, half full of water and corpses. Smyth had ten bombers from 4 Company and two boxes of bombs (96 bombs in total). They had cover for the first 50m, but thereafter were enfiladed by field guns from the left, which forced them to veer right and dive for cover into a chest-deep stream. They lost one man severely wounded there. When the shelling slackened they returned to the trench and attempted to get forward again, but man after man was hit. The survivors crawled over the bodies of their comrades and others, but continued to be exposed by gaps in the trench walls. All the while the Germans fired at them furiously and as they continued towards their objective, they lost more men. Thirty metres from the forward trench, Smyth had only three men left and any attempt to rise up was met with a hail of bullets.

With so few men, they were unable to push or pull the bomb boxes along. Accounts vary at this point. In one version they wriggled forward with one box of bombs until reaching a stream, which was too deep to wade. They crawled along the bank until they found a place that was just fordable and struggled across under heavy fire, but were then covered by their comrades and reached the safety of the trench to deliver the box of bombs. In another, more likely, version, Smyth ordered the survivors to take a bomb in each hand, but while opening a box Sepoy Harnam Singh was shot through the head and killed. Smyth had no choice but to leave the boxes and hope to retrieve them after dark. The three survivors, Smyth, Lance Naik

Ferme du Bois

Drive along Rue du Bois (D171) northeasterly towards Neuve Chapelle. Pass the D166 turning to Richebourg Centre on the left and continue for 600m where there is a turning on the left. Go on another 130m and there is a track on the right. Pull in here and park. Walk south along what was the cinder track in 1915. After 750m the track runs into private land. The cinder track in the foreground leads to Ferme du Bois in the trees in the centre distance. The field on the right is the southeasterly point of the gains made on 16th May. The front line ran parallel with and to the right of the track and followed the line of the wheat field round to the right. John Smyth's party brought up the bombs to sustain Captain K Hyde-Cates' 3 Company, 15th Sikhs through the field from the right rear.

Mangal Singh and Sepoy Lal Singh then crawled into the forward trench. They failed to deliver the bombs, but nevertheless it was a hugely courageous attempt. Smyth had several bullet holes through his tunic and cap and his cane had been struck four times. Shortly after setting the box down, Lal Singh was struck by a bullet and killed. Stretcher-bearers went out later to recover the wounded.

In addition to Smyth's VC, Lance Naik Mangal Singh was awarded the Indian Order of Merit 2nd Class and the others received the Indian Distinguished Service Medal (Sepoys Lal Singh (Neuve-Chapelle Memorial), Sucha Singh, Sapuram Singh of 15th Sikhs; Sepoys Sarain Singh, Sundur Singh, Ganda Singh, Harnam Singh (Neuve-Chapelle Memorial) of 19th Punjabis; and Sepoys Fateh Singh and Ujagar Singh of 45th Sikhs).

Whenever Smyth went on a dangerous mission, his men insisted he wore the pagri, the Sikh headdress, to make him less conspicuous. In this instance there was no time so he went with his service cap. As he was the only member of the party to escape death or serious injury, he never wore the pagri again. The only member of his Regiment who thought he would return was his batman, Ishar Singh. He refused food and drink and remained on the parapet, holding Smyth's British warm greatcoat for his return. Smyth was totally drained by the action. The CO gave him a tot of rum, wrapped him in a blanket and let him sleep under the orderly room table until midday the following day.

On 18th May, it rained for most of the morning. At 3.00 a.m., 21st Brigade repeated its attack of the previous day, but was repulsed. The small party of 1/4th Cameron Highlanders in the Southern Breastwork was forced to withdraw due to lack of bombs.

First Army ordered a renewal of the attack in the afternoon, but stocks of 4.5" Howitzer ammunition were dangerously low and none was available for the attack. Orders reached units with little time for preparation, but at 3.00 p.m., the bombardment opened. The attack was to be carried out by 3rd Canadian Brigade, making its way forward from reserve to be attached to 7th Division, and 4th (Guards) Brigade (2nd Division), between the School House and Cour d'Avoué Farm. To the north, a subsidiary attack by the Sirhind Brigade near Ferme du Bois did not take place due to heavy enemy shelling, although there was some supporting bombing.

The British artillery had no effect on the new German line, which had not then been discovered. At 4.30 p.m., 4th (Guards) Brigade moved off, but was cut to pieces in a few minutes by machine-guns. A few hours later 2nd Division broke off the attack. It was not until 5.20 p.m. that 3rd Canadian Brigade arrived, having been hampered by the late arrival of orders and slow progress on the roads. It was ordered to relieve 21st Brigade.

By this time 2nd and 7th Divisions were exhausted and weakened by casualties. In the afternoon First Army ordered their relief by the Canadian and 51st (Highland) Divisions. With fresh troops, the intention was to continue towards Violaines and Chapelle St Roch.

During 19th-20th May, the Germans continued to strengthen their new line, while the British reliefs went ahead. 3rd Canadian Brigade gradually pushed forward and occupied the Orchard (renamed Canadian Orchard). Early on 22nd May, the Sirhind Brigade tried to take Ferme du Bois, but was halted by a combination of mud, ditches and heavy fire.

On the night of 22nd May, 2nd King's Royal Rifle Corps (2nd Brigade, 1st Division) was holding the front line near Cuinchy/Cambrin south of the Canal. Numerous casualties resulted from a German machine-gun shooting-up the parapet and harassing working parties. **Rifleman William Mariner** in B Company volunteered to silence the machine-gun.

Covered by the noise of a violent thunderstorm, Mariner crawled into no man's land alone and managed to reach the emplacement undetected. Crawling on top, he threw a grenade under the roof. Those inside the emplacement not seriously injured beat a hasty retreat. About fifteen minutes later, Mariner heard the Germans returning along the trench. Climbing back onto the emplacement he threw another grenade. The Germans opened fire on their own wire where they expected the attacker to be sheltering. Mariner avoided the enemy fire and was also lucky not to be hit by his comrades' return fire. After lying still for an hour under the enemy parapet, he crawled back to his own trench and narrowly avoided being bayoneted by a sentry by mistake.

Renewal of the offensive commenced on 24th May with a preliminary operation by a brigade each of 47th (its first major action) and Canadian Divisions astride the South Breastwork. The artillery bombardment began the previous evening. At 2.30 a.m., 140th and 2nd Canadian Brigades attacked along the Southern Breastwork. The Canadians advanced about 150m before being halted by machine-gun fire, but

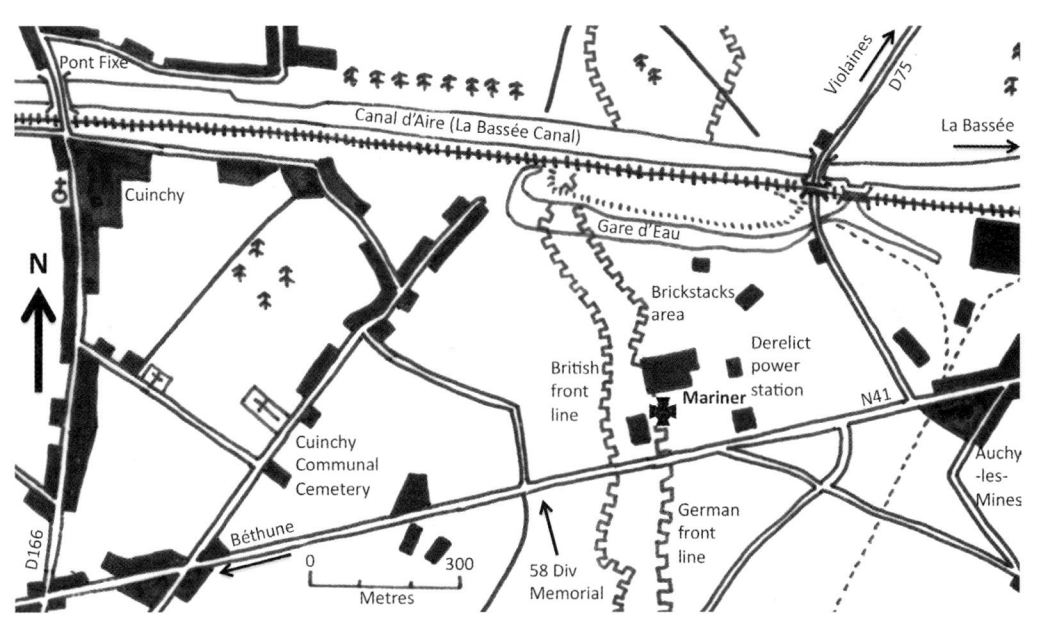

Drive west along the N41 from Auchy-les-Mines towards Béthune. You will pass the derelict power station on the right, but look out for the French 58th Division memorial set back 100m from the road on the left. Turn right on a minor road towards Cuinchy and stop at the next corner. The area to the right is the derelict power station and the site of the Brickstacks. The area is walled/fenced off and contains lots of post-industrial dangers. In any case, the landscape has been altered completely since WW1 and is completely overgrown in places. It is not worth going inside.

140th Brigade made little progress. That night the Canadians attempted to seize the fortified house south of the Orchard without success.

The main attack by 47th Division came at 6.30 p.m. on 25th May, following the artillery preparation which commenced at 2 p.m. The attack was made by 142nd Brigade at the 'S' Bend, north of the Givenchy – Chapelle St Roch road. 23rd (left) and 24th (right) London were to capture the enemy front line between 'J7' and 'I4'. 23rd London was to seize 'J7' and push 200m south along the front line trench. 24th London was to seize 'I4' and bomb south for 200m to 'I2'. Both Battalions were then to press on; 23rd London to 'J11' via 'J8' and 'I6' and 24th London to 'I9' and 'I8'.

The leading companies of 23rd and 24th London took their first objectives and between 6.45 a.m. and 9 a.m. the position was consolidated. Half of the leading company of 24th London was lost in the initial advance and all the bombers were killed except for **Lance Corporal Leonard Keyworth** in A Company. He reached the enemy parapet, where he rained bombs on the Germans from point blank range, stopping only when his supply was exhausted to retrieve grenade bags from

The French 58th Division Memorial, situated 100m south of the N41.

Looking south along no man's land from the railway embankment east of Cuinchy. Mariner attacked the machine-gun post in the dense vegetation on the other side of the Gare d'Eau.

his dead comrades. He threw 150 bombs over the next two hours, by which time the enemy trench was totally wrecked and full of dead and dying, but the Battalion was unable to press on to seize 'I2' or the other objectives of 'I8' and 'I9' on the higher ground.

Despite being exposed throughout, Keyworth escaped with a cut on his ear and the mirror in his breast pocket was hit without injuring him. A bullet went through his pack and another struck his mess tin. Fifty-eight of the seventy-five bombers who took part in the assault with him became casualties. During the attack, 2nd Lieutenant Frank Meryon Chance (Le Touret Memorial) was mortally wounded as he reached the enemy parapet. Once the initial assault had succeeded, Keyworth and others tried to get to him. However, the enemy fire was too fierce and the dying officer gallantly waved them back.

24th London was assisted by a party of 47th Divisional Cyclist Company under Lieutenant KG Gunn to continue the advance. Only 40m separated the attackers from 'I2', but the ground was so badly broken by shellfire that progress was very

From 24th London's front line looking in the direction of the attack on 25th May 1915. Givenchy village is on the right and the British front line came down the hill on the right of the track towards the camera position. 'I4' was at the left end of the trees in the centre, below the farm with the mast in the distance.

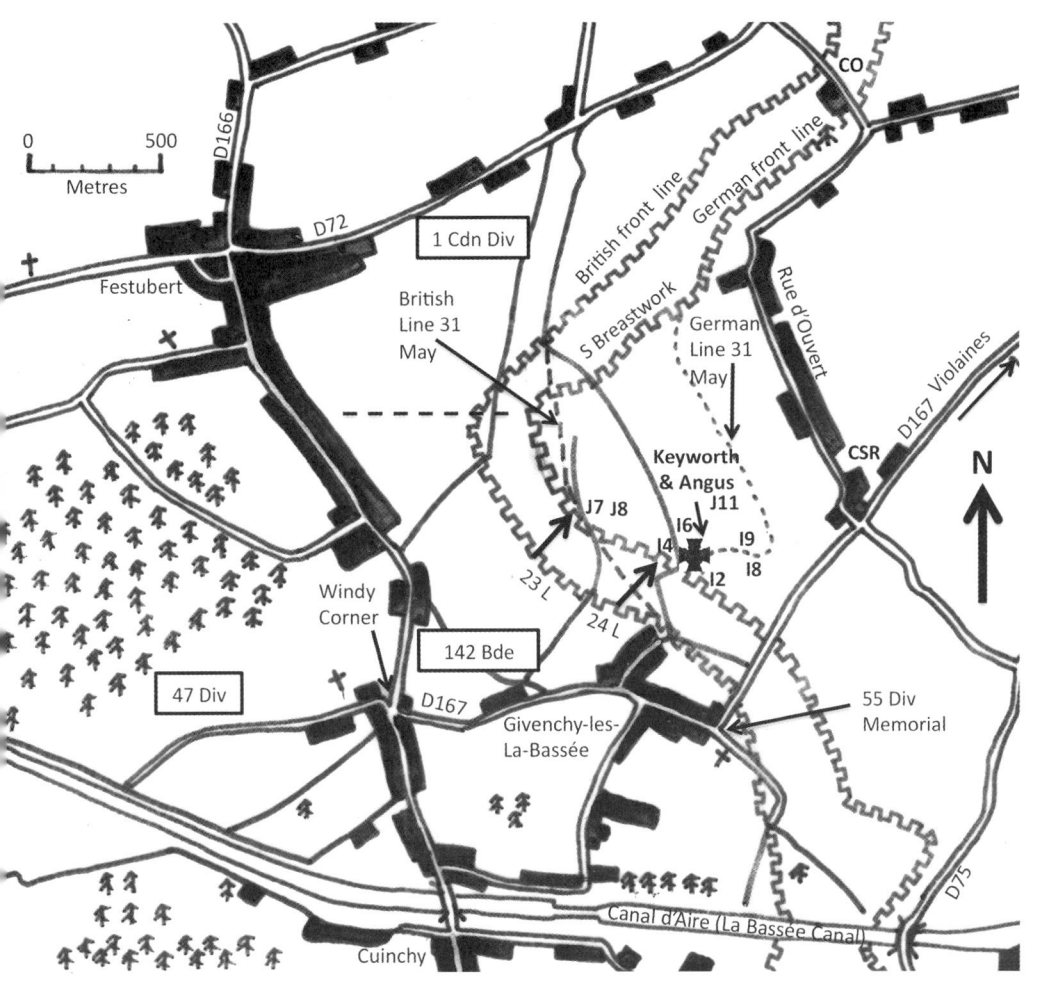

From the 55th Division memorial on the D167 Givenchy-Violaines road, drive north for 250m and turn left onto a minor road. Follow it for 300m to the first buildings. Park here without blocking any of the narrow routes and walk down the lane to the north. After 200m it swings right. The next left bend is the site of 'I4', where Leonard Keyworth was in action on 25th-26th May 1915. William Angus' VC action was in the same area on 12th June.

slow. There was stiff resistance and the Brigade was subjected to enfilade artillery fire from the south. Although heavy casualties were sustained, the position was held against determined German counterattacks, including two particularly strong ones between 9 p.m. and 10 p.m. By then all four 24th London companies were in the

Almost a reversal of the previous view. The German front line ran through the field on the left to the track corner and then up the hill into the distance. 24th London attacked from the right. Givenchy village is in the distance, right of the trees.

captured trench. By 11.09 p.m., 23rd London was in contact with the Canadians, but there was a 50m stretch of destroyed trench between them.

A company of 20th London sent to support 24th London added to the congestion and the flanks were constantly sniped. In the early hours of the 26th, twenty Germans were captured in a mine by 2nd Lieutenants Morland (3rd Field Company RE) and CG Davies (24th London). Communications trenches were dug across no man's land. 24th London supported by the Divisional Cyclists and a platoon of 20th London gained a few yards along the trench towards 'I2'.

The Canadian attack on the left at 9 p.m. along South Breastwork by Seely's Detachment of dismounted cavalrymen managed to advance within 200m of the new enemy line. Failure to make more progress was mainly due to a shortage of artillery ammunition.

Shelling, bombing and sniping, particularly from the flanks, continued throughout the night and the situation remained precarious. Enemy guns south of the Canal, near Auchy-les-la-Bassée, were the most troublesome, as they were out of range of the British guns. From midday until 5 p.m. on the 26th, the Germans shelled the captured trenches, but made no attempt to recapture them. There were hundreds of casualties from this shelling, but the Brigade held its position. At 3.30 p.m., 23rd London was withdrawn into Divisional reserve and at 8.30 p.m., 20th London began relieving 22nd and 24th London, which went into Brigade reserve around Windy Corner. By the time 24th London was relieved, it had suffered 408 casualties.

On 25th May, General Foch requested that the British take over another divisional front south of the La Bassée Canal, to enable the French attacks to continue at Vimy. 2nd Division was ordered from rest and completed the relief by 31st May.

However, the decision also caused Sir John French to order Haig to close down the Festubert offensive. Ammunition stocks were very low and it was clear by then that the Germans held their new line in considerable strength. The British suffered 16,648 casualties in the period 15th-25th May at Festubert. The German defenders had about 5,000 casualties, including 800 taken prisoner. Casualties during the Second Battle of Artois were 102,533 French and 73,072 Germans.

Although the British achieved a small tactical success at Festubert, the results overall were once again disappointing and with no strategic impact. There were a number of reasons for this, including poor weather, lack of surprise, congestion in the trenches delaying the deployment of reserves, woefully inadequate British bombs and poor intelligence failing to detect the new German line. Despite the offensive being launched jointly with the French, the Germans were still able to shift their reserves relatively freely.

However, the most serious problem was the British artillery. Its guns were worn out through overuse. Ammunition was in short supply and of poor quality due to faulty manufacture; there were numerous duds. There were far too few heavy guns firing the high explosive shells needed to destroy enemy defences. The field artillery's mainly shrapnel shells were incapable of achieving this. The issue burst into the news on 15th May 1915 in an article in 'The Times' by Colonel Repington. The public was outraged to learn that British troops were dying unnecessarily because they could not be properly supplied. It led to the downfall of Asquith's Liberal Government and the formation of a Coalition, with David Lloyd George as its first Minister of Munitions.

Chapter Three

Local Operations Summer 1915

Second Action of Givenchy, 12th June 1915

78 LCpl William Angus, 8th (Lanark) Battalion, The Highland Light Infantry (att'd 8th Battalion, The Royal Scots) (22nd Brigade, 7th Division)

79 Lt Frederick Campbell, 1st Battalion (Ontario), Canadian Expeditionary Force (1st Canadian Brigade, 1st Canadian Division)

Following the Battle of Festubert, the summer of 1915 was characterised by a series of minor engagements and localised actions. On the night of 3rd/4th June a mine was exploded under the German salient southwest of Chapelle St Roch at Point 'I4'. 1/6th Gordon Highlanders occupied the crater, but the Battalion was driven out later. Skirmishing continued in the area while plans were made for a much larger attack later in the month.

In the meantime, 22nd Brigade attempted to improve the line around 'I4'. On the night of 9th/10th June, 2nd Royal West Surrey's attack failed. 8th Royal Scots relieved the West Surreys on 10th June and made two unsuccessful attempts to rush the enemy crater on the nights of 10th/11th and 11th/12th June. The main problem was thick belts of barbed wire, which could only be breached by heavy artillery fire. Attempts by the Royal Scots' bombers to blast a way into the enemy lines were defeated by German bombers, whose grenades were superior to the British home made devices.

From 'I4'. The German trenches were on the slightly higher ground. The remains of mine warfare are within the trees. William Angus came from the right to rescue James Martin, who was stuck on this bank. The southern part of Festubert is in the right background.

Local Operations Summer 1915   67

One of the mine craters near 'I4'. They are very overgrown, having been used as dumps for decades and are consequently difficult to make out.

The second Royal Scots attack, by thirty-five men of A Company, including fifteen bombers, was led by Lieutenant James Martin. During it the Germans fired a small mine, causing the raiders to beat a hasty retreat back to their own trenches. There it was discovered that Martin was missing. Several men searched no man's land to no avail, but early next morning he was spotted lying very close to the enemy parapet. Slight movements indicated he was alive. The mine explosion had stunned Martin and when he recovered consciousness he found that his left arm was buried in the debris. Only the steep bank of the German parapet separated him from the enemy. As it grew light, a periscope in the German trench was seen concentrating on the area where Martin lay. Well-aimed shots from a British rifle smashed the periscope and others that were raised later. Martin freed himself and tried to crawl away, but was hit twice in the attempt.

Many men volunteered to attempt a rescue, but the CO would only allow one man to try. **Lance Corporal Angus** was chosen. He came from Carluke, the same town as Martin, and both had joined 8th Royal Scots from the same company of 8th Highland Light Infantry. At 2 p.m., despite warnings that it was certain death, Angus slipped out into no man's land. The British front line was filled with the best marksmen to give covering fire and a machine-gun was set up just behind. By skilful use of ground, Angus covered the 60m to where Martin lay. He cleared the return route as he went, without drawing any German fire. While giving the officer a drink from a brandy flask, they were seen by the Germans, who opened fire from as little as two metres away. Fortunately the parapet was much higher than the surrounding land and the covering fire from the Royal Scots trenches helped to disturb the enemy's aim.

The Germans then threw a grenade at the pair and Angus realised they must make a dash for safety. Martin staggered to his feet and, directed by Angus, made a rush for the British lines. After covering twenty metres he collapsed, but managed to crawl and drag himself back, despite being wounded on the way. The Germans threw so many grenades that the smoke and dust made it impossible for their marksmen to shoot accurately. Angus took a slightly different route to draw the enemy fire and had a dozen or more grenades thrown at him. By the time he reached safety, he had been hit by about forty fragments and was seriously wounded, but both he and Martin recovered from their ordeal.

15th June 1915

By the middle of June, 1st Canadian Division was holding the line on the right of IV Corps, in the centre of the First Army front. The La Bassée Canal formed the Division's right flank, with I Corps beyond. 7th Division was on the left. Opposite was the German 134th (Saxon) Infantry Regiment. There was a brief respite at this time and the narrowness of the front held (only 900m) meant that 1st Canadian Division needed only a single brigade in the line.

The trenches were slightly higher than at Festubert and were consequently relatively dry. The shape of the ground allowed the forward trenches to be approached from cover. No man's land varied from 70m to 450m wide and the narrowest point was where the 'Duck's Bill' protruded towards the German lines.

There was insufficient artillery ammunition to conduct a simultaneous attack on both sides of the Canal. The revised scheme was for IV Corps to attack alone on a narrow front north of the Canal towards Violaines. There were a few postponements in order to coordinate the attack with a renewal of the French offensive, but it was finally set for 15th June. 7th and 51st Divisions were to attack the line Chapelle St Roch – Rue d'Ouvert, while 1st Canadian Division to the south secured the right flank, *"... giving such assistance as may be possible without actually assaulting the enemy's trench line"*. However, the Canadians could not protect the right flank of the attack without breaking into the German lines.

Lieutenant General Alderson planned a limited assault on two strongpoints by 1st Canadian Brigade; 'H2' opposite the 'Duck's Bill' ('Dorchester') and 'H3', 135m north of a feature known to the Canadians as 'Stony Mountain'. Five artillery groups were to cover the attack under the Division's artillery commander, Brigadier-General HE Borstall. In addition to the normal complement of guns, he also had eight 4.5" Howitzers, eight 6" Howitzers, a group of French 75mm guns and 2nd and 3rd Brigades CFA. The Division's 18 Pounders were to cut the enemy wire. Delays in launching the attack meant the Germans had time to repair gaps in their wire and these had to be cut again. As a result, more ammunition was expended than was intended, but the wire was well cut (six shells for every metre of front).

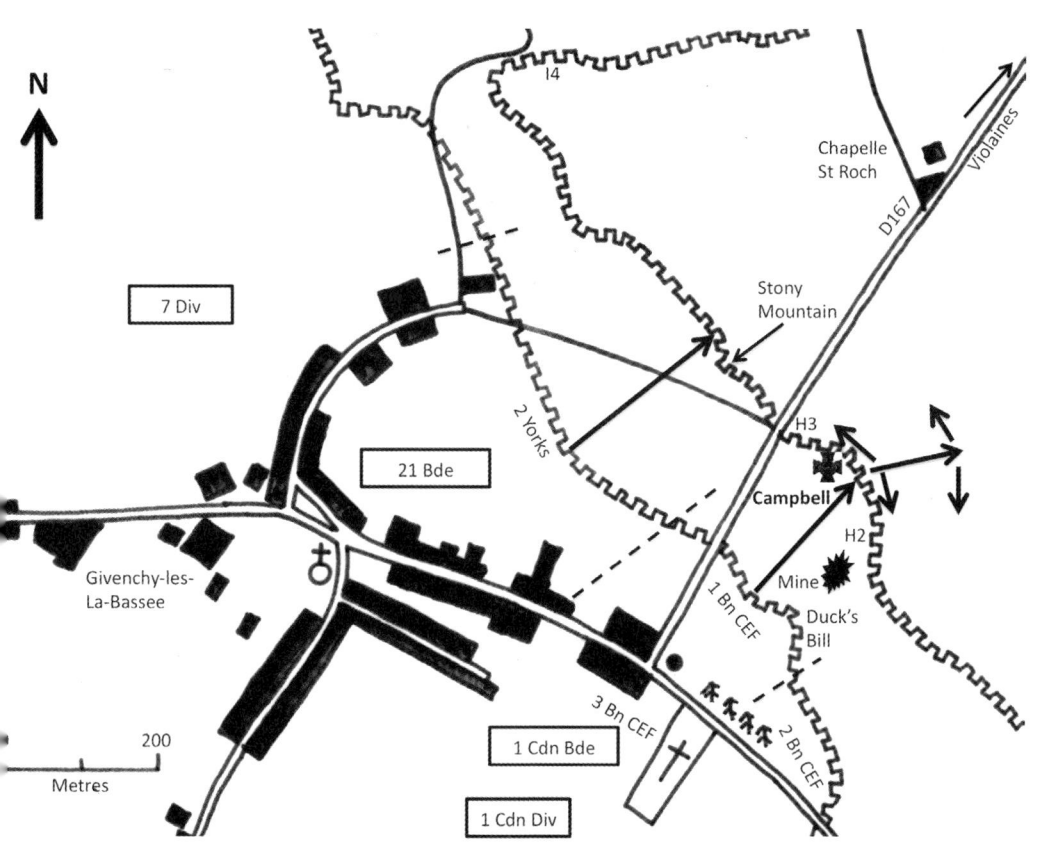

Drive east through Givenchy-les-la-Bassée on the D167 towards Violaines. At the 55th Division Memorial turn right and park at the cemetery. There are a number of May-June 1940 CWGC graves within and, intriguingly, one Soviet soldier from September 1944. Walk back to the memorial, where there are some information boards about the action at Red Dragon Crater in June 1916 (see 118 & 119). Walk north along the road towards Violaines. After 100m you are on the British front line. Continue to a left turn. Just before it on the left are the remains of a German concrete pillbox at 'H3'. Look back down the road. A slight depression to the left is all that remains of Red Dragon Crater, but with crops high in the summer it is often difficult to make out. The Canadian attack in which Frederick Campbell won his VC was launched from the front line to the right of Red Dragon Crater northwards, parallel with the road. The nearest reliable café to Frederick Campbell's VC action is in the centre of Richebourg, opposite the church.

The night before the attack, three modified 18 Pounders were brought into the front line to neutralise or destroy enemy machine-gun positions. They had heavily armoured shields and the wheels were covered in rubber to reduce noise as they were manhandled into position behind sandbag walls. Two guns from 4th Battery CFA were near the 'Duck's Bill', 70m from the German front line trench and the other gun, from 6th Battery CFA, was in a ruined farmhouse within 270m of 'H3'.

Behind the Canadian lines assembly trenches were constructed and by midafternoon on 15th June, 1st Canadian Brigade was in position. 1st Battalion CEF (Lieutenant Colonel Hill) was to make the attack, newly armed with the SMLE rifle, which officially replaced the hated Ross rifle a few days before. In support, parties of 2nd and 3rd Battalions CEF were to secure the enemy front line and connect it to the Canadian lines.

The artillery bombarded the German trenches steadily for two days. At 6 a.m. on the 15th the rate of fire was increased for the next twelve hours. By 3 p.m., 2nd Battalion had shifted to the right to allow 1st Battalion to take up its assault positions. 4th Battalion CEF was further to the right, on the Canal, and 3rd Battalion was in support. The assault troops waited in the trenches, singing popular but unprintable songs.

At 5.45 p.m., the three forward 18 Pounders were unmasked by knocking down the sandbag walls and began blasting the German parapet. However, one gun did not fire for fear of hitting troops in the front trenches. As a result, machine-guns in the twin redoubt at 'H3' were not engaged. The extent of the wire cutting told the Germans precisely where the attack would occur and their first reaction was to pour heavy artillery fire into the Givenchy area. The infantry crowded in the forward trenches suffered casualties and two 18 Pounders were put out of action after firing 120 rounds. However, they accounted for three to six machine-guns, depending on accounts. A number of 18 Pounder crewmen were killed and wounded, but the guns were recovered successfully the following night.

At 5.58 p.m., 176 Tunnelling Company RE exploded a mine close to the German front line. It had been intended to destroy 'H2', but flooding meant the tunnel had to stop short. In compensation the size of the charge was increased to 3,000 lbs of ammonal. The crater, almost 40m across, did not destroy the strongpoint, but it did cause some casualties amongst bombing parties of 1st Battalion and set off or buried bomb reserve stores. As soon as the debris settled, 4 Company, under Major GJL Smith, was on its way, closely followed by 3 Company, under Captain GL Wilkinson, with two machine-guns under **Lieutenant Frederick Campbell**. One gun crew was wiped out in the advance, but the other reached the enemy front line south of 'H3', moved along it to the left and set up.

'Dorchester' was seized successfully, but machine-gun fire from 'Stony Mountain' halted that part of the attack with many killed and wounded. The artillery lifted and both companies continued the advance to the second German line and began bombing left and right to establish blocks, assisted by eight sappers of 1st Field Company CE.

From the German support line near Chapelle St Roch on the D167 Violaines road looking south towards Givenchy. 1st Battalion CEF attacked from just in front of the tree line in the centre towards the camera. Givenchy church is on the extreme right.

Prisoners were sent back, some being killed by their own machine-gun fire from 'Stony Mountain'. Lieutenant CA James, commanding the right bombing party, was killed at the time of the mine explosion (Beuvry Communal Cemetery – 50), but his men went on. The left bombing party, under Lieutenant GN Gordon, advanced on 'Stony Mountain', but most were hit, including Gordon, having exhausted their supply of bombs. Most of the sappers were also killed or wounded, except for Sapper Harmon. He was unable to block the trench alone, but collected bombs and continued the fight until he was forced to retire, having been wounded ten times.

At 6.10 p.m., 2 Company, under Lieutenant TC Sims (Captain FW Robinson had been killed – Beuvry Communal Cemetery – 48), crossed no man's land and occupied the German front line. At 7 p.m., 1 Company, under Lieutenant Tranter (Captain Delamere was wounded), also crossed over. Tranter was wounded and CSM C Owen took over. Work commenced to reverse the trench.

To the north, reports from 7th and 51st Divisions indicated the enemy front line had been seized along the entire attack frontage, but soon after it was clear they still held 'H3'. From there northwards to the crater at 'I4', fired twelve days earlier, the German machine-guns were able to sweep no man's land as far south as the 'Duck's Bill' and caused casualties to the third and fourth waves. 1st Battalion attempted to bomb northwards to 'H3', but was halted by counterattacks and a shortage of grenades. The men in the second position were poorly placed, as 7th Division on the left had not advanced beyond the enemy front line and this left the flank open.

A counterattack developed and maintaining communications between the British and German front lines was extremely hazardous for the runners and ammunition carriers. As a consequence it was some time before it was known that 4 Company was under extreme pressure. Conditions in the crowded trenches also slowed response times. By this time Campbell had only Private Harold Vincent and one Colt machine-gun with him; the tripod was broken crossing no man's land. The rifle company survivors had run out of grenades and Campbell ordered them to retire while he covered them, resting the machine-gun on Vincent's back. Campbell fired over 1,000 rounds covering the retirement until his right femur was fractured close to the hip by an enemy bullet.

Campbell ordered Vincent, who had been badly burned by the machine-gun, to retire. Vincent cut off the belt and managed to drag the machine-gun back to his own lines; he was awarded the DCM. Campbell was able to crawl some distance before he was rescued and carried back for treatment by CSM Owen.

2 Company tried to get forward but met the survivors of the two forward companies coming back. 2nd Battalion's bombers and two platoons of 3rd Battalion carried on the fight for the mine crater. Private Smith, buried in the mine explosion, dug himself out and gathered grenades from the dead and wounded. He delivered them to the front line twice on his hands and knees but when the fire became too hot he resorted to tossing the bombs to his comrades in the trench (with the pins still in!). His clothing was shot to rags, but he survived unharmed.

From the German front line at 'H3' looking southeast. Givenchy is on the far right. The British front line ran just in front of the tree line on the right. The German front line ran away from the camera beyond the junction in the foreground. Frederick Campbell's VC action was about 75m into the field in line with the sign. To the right of the junction in the foreground in the roadside ditch are the remains of a concrete pillbox, but it is not visible from this angle.

A company of 3rd Battalion, sent forward just before 9 p.m. (the order was issued at 7.30 p.m.), was stopped by enemy fire at the Canadian front line. The survivors of 1st Battalion were cut off and began erecting barriers south of 'Stony Mountain'. They were forced to pull back to the German front line, but Captain Smith decided by 10 p.m. that due to pressure on the flanks and from the front that this too had to be abandoned. He was killed as he reached the original front line (Beuvry Communal Cemetery – 47). The attack resulted in 366 casualties. Of the twenty-three officers in 1st Battalion who went into the attack, only three were unharmed.

3rd Battalion was ordered to renew the attack, but there were a number of postponements while the situation elsewhere along the attack frontage was clarified and a fresh bombardment was organised. At 4.45 p.m. on 16th June, the attack was launched after two hours of bombardment. The Germans were ready and met 3rd Battalion with a hail of small arms fire. No permanent lodgments were made and a further attack by Royal Canadian Dragoons at 9 p.m. was cancelled. By 19th June the French Artois offensive was over and Sir John French instructed Haig to shut down First Army's attacks.

Actions of Hooge, 30th July 1915

80 2Lt Sydney Woodroffe, 8th Battalion, The Rifle Brigade (41st Brigade, 14th Division)

Hooge was the site of a number of small but significant actions in July and August 1915. On 19th July, the British exploded a mine, laid by 175 Tunnelling Company RE, but the crater was not occupied due to constant mortaring, bombing and sniping. Both sides dug their trenches up to the lip. Attempts on the 22nd to seize other parts of the enemy line failed.

The German retaliation came on 30th July. That morning the Hooge front was held by 41st Brigade, with 8th Rifle Brigade straddling the crater and 7th KRRC to the right. These Battalions had gone into the line the previous night, completing the relief around 2 a.m. 8th Rifle Brigade's front line was held by two platoons of A Company to the left of the crater in 'G10' and three platoons of C Company to

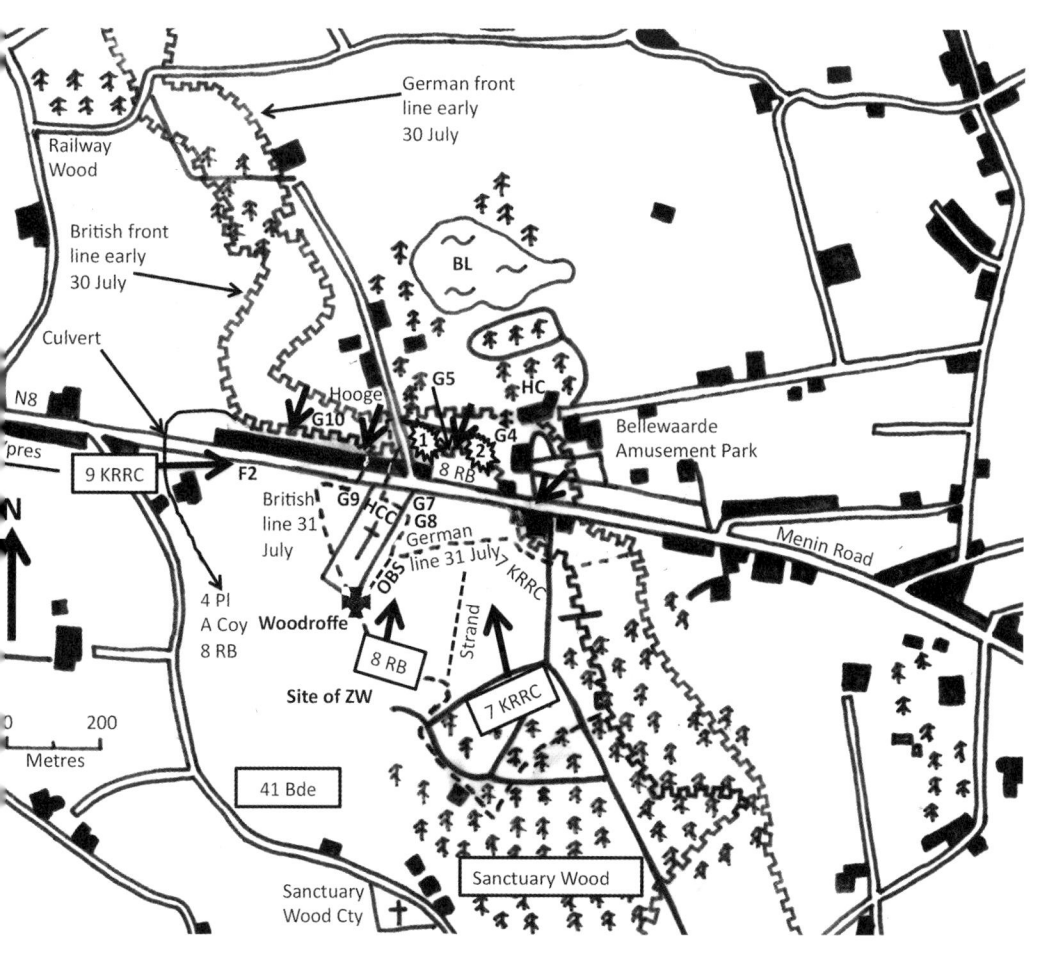

Leave Ypres on the N8 (Menin Road) towards Menen. Just over a kilometre after the major roundabout, turn right, signed for Hill 62. Follow this for 900m until the road bends left. Pull over, there are a few places to park a car, and look across the fields to the left up the rise towards Hooge Crater Cemetery and the Menin Road. The whole of the ground in front of you was involved in the battle here on 30th July 1915. When finished considering this action, continue to Sanctuary Wood Cemetery and beyond to Hill 62 if time permits. There is a café on the right just as you return to the main N8 road or continue east towards Menen and the café at Hooge Crater. The museum there is also worth a visit if time permits.

Some abbreviations have been used on this map – 1 = 19th July mine crater, 2 = 30th July mine crater, BL = Bellewaarde Lake, HC = Hooge Chateau, HCC = Hooge Chateau Cemetery, OBS = Old Bond Street communications trench and ZW = Zouave Wood.

the right in 'G4' and 'G5'. Two platoons of A Company in 'F2' and a platoon of C Company in 'G7' were in support. B and D Companies, left and right respectively, were in reserve in Zouave Wood with a B Company platoon in a supporting position 100m south of the Wood with one machine-gun. Four other machine-guns were in the front line. It was a poor position. The crater split the front line, with no lateral communications to left or right. The wire was inadequate and, although the trenches were deep, they were narrow, making movement difficult.

A terrifying, but not altogether effective, jet of liquid fire.

The relief was unusual as the Germans made no attempt to interfere with it. The silence continued throughout the night, even when bombs were thrown into the German trenches, in places only five metres away. At 3.15 a.m., the peace was shattered when the remains of Hooge Chateau stables were blown up by a mine. The troops on either side of the crater then heard a strange hissing sound. Suddenly the sky turned red as 30m long tongues of liquid flame and billowing clouds of black smoke were projected into the trenches from seven large static canisters. This was the first time flamethrowers had been used against the British.

Although terrifying, the effectiveness of the flamethrowers is often exaggerated. The supporting medical units dealt with few burns cases, although some casualties may have died before being evacuated. Most men instinctively threw themselves to the bottom of their trenches, and the majority of the heat and flames went upwards. The Germans still had to clear the positions with grenade and bayonet.

Hooge and the Menin Road from the south, near Sanctuary Wood Cemetery. Hooge is in the centre and the line of houses is aligned with the Menin Road. Ypres is off to the left. The building resembling a chapel is Hooge Crater Museum. In the far distance on the left is Railway Wood with the culvert under the Menin Road south of it. Old Bond Street, where Sydney Woodroffe was killed, ran along the right side of Hooge Crater Cemetery. Zouave Wood stood between the camera and the Cemetery. Even with its limited cover, it was still a daunting prospect to advance from here against the German line on the higher ground.

Some posts, such as 'G5', were fully manned when the assaulting troops reached them.

At the same time the Germans opened up with every form of supporting fire available. The front line, and as far back as Ypres, was subjected to the most savage bombardment. Most of those in the front line were overwhelmed, but the survivors made a well-ordered retirement to the support line. The attack, by five companies of 126th Infantry Regiment, achieved complete surprise. Having broken in at the crater, they fanned out to roll up the trenches on either side, including part of 7th KRRC's line. While they established themselves in the Hooge ruins, their bombers advanced along two communication trenches, Old Bond Street and the Strand. A counterattack by B Company, 8th Rifle Brigade failed to recover the lost ground, but did succeed in halting the German advance and allowing the remnants of two platoons of A Company to get away. B Company then established a block halfway along Old Bond Street.

The flanks resisted strongly and on the right 7th KRRC held its forward posts all day before withdrawing. However, by 4.30 a.m. the Germans had regained all their losses from 19th July and more, putting the British into a severely disadvantaged position.

2nd Lieutenant Sydney Woodroffe, commanding 4 Platoon in A Company, held the extreme left of the front line in 'G10'. When the attack came, 4 Platoon avoided the liquid fire, which was directed mainly against the sides of the crater, but was heavily attacked by bombers, initially from the right flank, but eventually from all directions. Woodroffe defended the post until his bombs were exhausted and he was almost surrounded. He then led an orderly and skilful withdrawal to the west, along the road to the culvert. Having got his men into a secure position, Woodroffe reported to the CO.

About 8 a.m., a company of 8th KRRC arrived as reinforcements from 41st Brigade, but the situation remained serious. The enemy bombers in Old Bond Street and the Strand kept up constant pressure, but were eventually stopped 200m short of Zouave Wood, which had been heavily bombarded and all communications were knocked out. Despite this, 8th Rifle Brigade continued to hold its northern edge.

A counterattack was ordered for 2.45 p.m. On the left, 8th Rifle Brigade was to advance with its right on the Strand, supported by 7th Rifle Brigade. On the right was 7th KRRC, supported by 8th KRRC. In 8th Rifle Brigade, while D Company on the right concentrated on recapturing 'G8' and 'G7' on the Menin Road, the remnants of A and B Companies were ordered to attack 'G9', with their centre on Old Bond Street. Simultaneously, bombing parties were to attack along the communication trenches. On the left flank, 9th KRRC, supported by 9th Rifle Brigade (42nd Brigade), were to launch a subsidiary attack from the area of the culvert on the Menin Road. 6th SLI (43rd Brigade) was in reserve in Zouave Wood. 46th Division on the far right and 6th Division on the far left provided fire support.

This appears to be a strong counterattack force, but the troops were those just ousted from the forward trenches or those who had been relieved the night before after ten hard days in the line. All were exhausted, hungry and inexperienced in counterattack tactics. There was little time to prepare and only a short forty-five minutes bombardment was possible. No thought was given to how to counter German counterattacks if the attack succeeded.

Sydney Woodroffe withdrew 4 Platoon towards the camera on the left of the pathway leading to Hooge in the distance. He used the culvert in the foreground to cross the Menin Road and get his men to safety.

The plan for the attacking infantry was suicidal. The forward battalions were to advance, cut gaps in the wire in full view of the enemy positions and then attack uphill against Germans who had had the best part of twelve hours to prepare to meet them.

As they struggled into position, the troops suffered casualties from German artillery fire. British shelling caused lots of dust, making it impossible to ascertain the effect it was having. Many shells went over the forward Germans trenches, which were largely unaffected. Before the bombardment finished, German troops could be seen manning the parapet and heavy machine-gun fire was being received. Major FM Crum of 8th KRRC wrote, "… *I for one honestly felt there was no fraction of a chance of success; 800–900 yards across the open, up a glacis held by trenches, with*

Leslie Woodroffe, Sydney's brother, was seriously wounded in the counterattack on 30th July 1915 and was awarded the MC. Leslie returned to the front to rejoin 8th Rifle Brigade on 1st June 1916 and was wounded the same day. He died on 4th June and is buried in Barlin Communal Cemetery Extension, France.

Billy Grenfell, son of Lord Desborough, brother of Julian Grenfell, the war poet and cousin of Francis Grenfell, VC. He was killed in the counterattack and is commemorated on the Ypres (Menin Gate) Memorial.

no covering guns, and under an unholy bombardment from every kind of German gun, fired from every side into our salient ... It certainly seemed a case of goodbye to this world ... It made it harder because I knew our Brigadier had personally protested, and yet had received a peremptory order to counterattack."

The officers attempted to reduce the risks. Sydney's brother, Captain Leslie Woodroffe, commanding D Company, 8th Rifle Brigade moved his men along a communications trench until they were beyond the wire. They cut through the wall of the trench and doubled along the enemy side of the wire for 150m to establish an assault line, under heavy small arms fire throughout. Leslie Woodroffe was hit in the thigh and knee and a bullet hit his boot heel, while another went through a pocket. His whistle was passed to Lieutenant Gerald William 'Billy' Grenfell (son of Lord Desborough, brother of Julian Grenfell, the war poet and cousin of Francis Grenfell VC). Leslie lay in no man's land until 9 p.m. when he crawled back to the lines.

The attack was met with a hail of concentrated machine-gun fire. Grenfell led his Company with his glasses hanging half off, sprinting forward with his fists clenched until he was hit in the head by a bullet. In A Company to the left, Sydney Woodroffe advanced with a cheek wound covered in a bandage. He charged up the hill, but was hit three times before being killed trying to cut the wire. A witness saw him, *"He staggers, wounded ... recovers, walks on ... he is hit again, but staggers forward – right up to the enemy's wire and begins to cut it. He falls, but struggles up ... he is cutting now with his one remaining hand ... he dies on the wire ... At last it ends – this terrible slaughter. No one has faltered, but all are fallen. The attack is held. The dusk comes on. The wood is filled with wounded, dying, dead. They are everywhere."*

Also lost in this attack was Lieutenant Gilbert Talbot of 7th Rifle Brigade. He arrived on the edge of Zouave Wood with only sixteen men unwounded. When the whistle blew, he leapt up and rushed forward shouting, *"Come on my lads, this is our day!"* As he was cutting through the wire, he was hit in the neck and fell over the wire. He died soon after. Talbot House at Poperinghe was named after him.

There was some progress at the culvert by 9th KRRC, but at heavy cost, and the Battalion had to be reinforced by 9th Rifle Brigade to withstand a German counterattack. At 3.15 p.m., Brigadier-General O Nugent DSO called off the attack. Some COs had already held back their support companies to avoid further unnecessary losses. A new line was formed along the northern edge of Zouave and Sanctuary Woods. Early the next morning the Germans attempted another flamethrower attack, but it was repelled.

Gilbert Talbot, after whom Talbot House at Poperinghe was named.

About 2 a.m., 8th Rifle Brigade was relieved by 7th Rifle Brigade and 6th Duke of Cornwall's Light Infantry (43rd Brigade). It had suffered 488 casualties out of the 769 men who went into the line. The rest of 41st and 42nd Brigades suffered 818 and 346 casualties respectively. 41st Brigade's young officers were mainly from Oxford and Cambridge OTCs. The cream of the nation was squandered senselessly in this ill-conceived counterattack.

Diversionary feints by 49th Division and the French XXXVI Corps on the left and 46th Division on the right followed. The Germans were misled after seven days of systematic bombardment into assuming this was routine 'hate' and sheltered in their dugouts. On 9th August, 18th and 16th Brigades (6th Division), with sappers and trench mortars, supported by a RFC squadron, attacked again. They recaptured the losses quickly and another 450m of enemy territory.

Looking along the length of Old Bond Street from the north. 8th Rifle Brigade counter-attacked towards the camera. Hooge Crater Cemetery is on the right, with the author's sons and father-in-law visiting a relative's grave. The line of trees in the centre middle distance is along the road to Sanctuary Wood Cemetery, from where the opposite battlefield panorama was taken.

Other Operations, 3rd August 1915

> 81 2Lt George Boyd-Rochfort, 1st Battalion Scots Guards (1st (Guards) Brigade, 1st Division)

No specific action was being fought in the Cambrin area when **2nd Lieutenant George Boyd-Rochfort** won his VC. His Battalion took over the trenches south of the Béthune-La Bassée road on 31st July. The Brigade war diary records almost

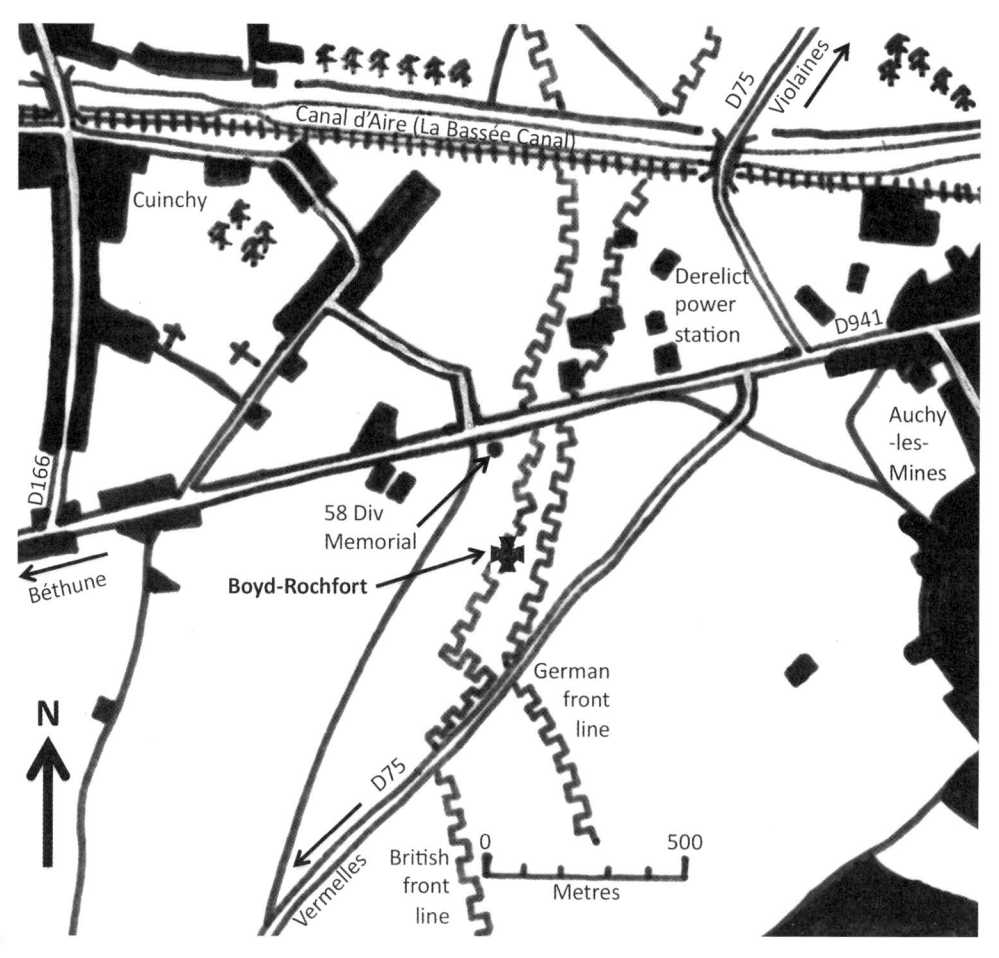

Drive east along the D941 Béthune-La Bassée road. Pass the D166 turning to Cuinchy on the left and 1,100m further on is a grassy area in front of a memorial to the French 58th Division. Park off the road carefully. Walk 130m eastwards alongside the road, but beware, as this stretch can be a racetrack. Look slightly west of south from the roadside. You are looking along the line of the British front line in August 1915. The small knoll upon which the memorial stands was in an angle of the front line and is marked on contemporary trench maps. The Scots Guards front extended at least 750m south of where you are standing and there were a number of communications trenches leading to the rear, i.e. to the right of the front line. Which one Boyd-Rochfort was in when he threw the trench mortar bomb over the parapet is not known.

Looking south along the British front Line from the N41 Béthune-La Bassée road. The French 58th Division memorial in the centre was just behind the front line.

no incidents over the next few days; it was extraordinarily quiet. At 2 a.m. on the morning of 3rd August 1915 he was supervising a working party of about forty men in a communications trench. A trench mortar bomb landed on the parapet close to him and toppled into the trench. He could easily have stepped around a traverse into relative safety, but instead shouted a warning, caught the bomb before it hit the ground and hurled it back over the parapet. The bomb exploded immediately, burying him and another man, but without injuring either of them. His presence of mind and outstanding courage saved many lives and countless injuries.

Action of Pietre, 25th September 1915

> 82 Rfn Kulbir Thapa, 2/3rd Gurkha Rifles (20th Garhwal Brigade, 7th Meerut Division)
> 83 Lt George Maling, 61st Field Ambulance RAMC (att'd 12th Battalion, The Rifle Brigade) (60th Brigade, 20th Division)

Three subsidiary operations were launched in support of the September 1915 Anglo-French offensive in Champagne and at Loos; the Second Attack on Bellewaarde, the Action of Bois Grenier and the Action of Pietre. The latter, launched by the Indian Corps north of Neuve Chapelle, was to seize the salient west of Moulin du Pietre at Mauquissart. The aim was to prevent enemy reserves from being moved to the main attack areas and to sow the seeds of doubt in the minds of the Germans about where the main blow would fall. Three objectives were laid down:

- Establish a line along the road from Mauquissart to the 'Duck's Bill'.
- Press on, with the left leading, to gain a hold on Aubers Ridge between Haut Pommereau and la Cliqueterie Farm.
- Continue southeast to assist the main offensive around Loos by turning the La Bassée defences from the north.

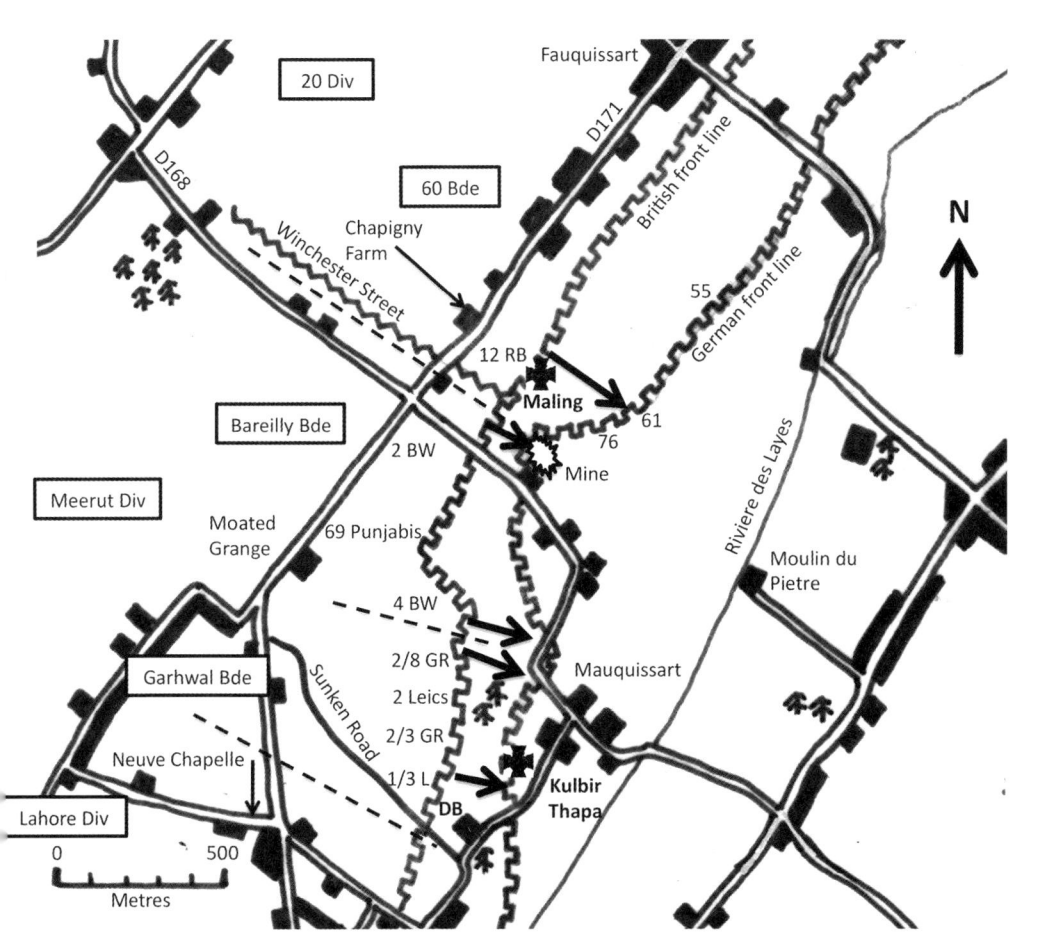

Drive northeast through Neuve Chapelle (there is a café near the church) on the D171 towards Fleurbaix. As the main road bends left, take the road on the right. After 300m at the T-junction turn right, then left after 150m. After 400m park at the side of the narrow road keeping well over. There is a field entrance on the left, from where you can overlook the area where 2/3rd Gurkhas attacked on 25th September 1915 and where Kulbir Thapa won his VC.

Continue into Marquissart and turn left. Follow the road round a right then a left hand bend and continue to the main crossroads. Turn right onto the D171. Drive slowly, as there is a turning into a track on the right after 150m. Park here and walk along the track for 100m. Look back towards the main road. The prominent group of buildings is Chapigny Farm, advanced HQ of 60th Brigade HQ and Battalion HQ of 12th Rifle Brigade at the start of the battle. Look southeast towards a clump of trees. About 150m in this direction was the head of Chaplin Street, where the Battalion HQ and RAP were blown up and where George Maling performed his deeds. The attack by 12th Rifle Brigade was in roughly the same direction towards Moulin de Pietre. The abbreviation DB on the map is for 'Duck's Bill'.

Gas was to be used for the first time by the British, but there were serious misgivings about its utility and reliability. As a result, two schemes were drawn up – 'A' with gas and 'B' without. An enormous effort was required to install 1,100 gas cylinders, but by 6th September the shelters had been constructed. Later it was learned that only 160 cylinders were available for this front and the whole gas plan had to be recast to make best use of the limited supplies. By the night of 23rd-24th September, Lieutenant Kent's men in 189th Company RE had them all in position.

The attack was to be made by the Meerut Division at 6 a.m. on 25th September, with 20th Division cooperating with the Lahore Division to cover the Meerut Division's flanks. The bombardment commenced four days before the attack and the Germans were subjected to vigorous small arms fire and numerous bombs to prevent them making repairs by night. A mine was to be exploded on the left, two minutes before the gas and smoke were released. The assaulting troops would follow close behind, while the flanks were masked off with smoke from a variety of devices – smoke candles, phosphorus smoke bombs hurled by catapults out to 300m and trench mortars. Field guns were brought into the front line to destroy enemy machine-guns just before the attack began.

The Garhwal Brigade was on the right and the Bareilly Brigade on the left, with the Dehra Dun Brigade in reserve. Each forward brigade had three assault battalions in line and two in reserve. The Garhwal Brigade's assault battalions from right to left were: 2/3rd Gurkhas, 2nd Leicestershire and 2/8th Gurkhas. On the right was 1/3rd London holding the 'Duck's Bill'. In support was 39th Garhwal Rifles in Home Counties Trench. The Bareilly Brigade on the left was similarly disposed.

The bombardment was conducted in poor visibility, making it difficult to ascertain the results, although the wire was reportedly well cut. On 22nd September, the Lahore Division made a feint attack, firing an artillery barrage for five minutes on the front line then five minutes on the support line, while bayonets were shown over the parapet and dummy heads were raised accompanied by much shouting. The Germans were not drawn into retaliating, but may have suffered casualties when the guns returned to the front line. 19th Division did the same next day. As the attack drew nearer, the weather deteriorated and the trenches began to fill with water.

2/3rd Gurkhas left its billets at 7.30 p.m. on 24th September and moved into the line past the north side of the Moated Grange. 2nd Leicestershire was in front and congestion in the trenches meant the Battalion did not reach its allotted positions until 10.10 p.m. Orders were issued to attack using Plan A, but this was rescinded and Plan B was adopted and vice versa again during the night as the wind direction changed.

In the early hours of 25th September the wind was from the west again. At 4.40 a.m. on the right flank, 1/3rd London in the 'Duck's Bill' was shelled and

Taken from just behind the German front line, with the Moated Grange in the distance on the left. 2/3rd Gurkha Rifles attacked from that direction just this side of the copse towards Mauquissart on the right of the picture. This is the area in which Kulbir Thapa rescued the 2nd Leicestershire soldier.

the tops of several gas cylinders were blown off, immediately filling the front and support trenches with heavy concentrations of gas. Nineteen men were knocked out, as well as a Manchester Regiment bombing party. The officer in charge of the gas was one of the casualties and the SNCO gave orders that no gas was to be released because the wind had changed direction and was blowing more into the British trenches than away from them. The damaged cylinders were buried quickly. The gas alarm spread through the trenches, reaching 2/3rd Gurkhas at 4.45 a.m. Several men were gassed and final preparations had to be carried out in gas masks.

The mine exploded at 5.48 a.m., creating a crater almost 30m across. Two minutes later an intense bombardment opened. Two field guns and a Hotchkiss machine-gun in the front line were unmasked. One gun was damaged, but they fired 123 rounds between them in just over four minutes and much damage was caused to the enemy front line. The smoke barrage masked off enemy observers successfully.

The wind was too light and much of the gas ended up in the British trenches. Gas detachments were forced to use their initiative; some released their gas and others did not. Those that did soon found the wind changed direction and blew it back into the British lines.

At 6 a.m., when the guns lifted, the attackers set off and were almost immediately lost in the smoke and gas. 2/3rd Gurkhas had been warned that the wire on its front had probably not been destroyed. As a result it attacked on a narrower front with 4 Company under Lieutenants Bagot-Chester and Wood leading. 3 Company followed under Lieutenant Colonel Brakspear (the Battalion was commanded by Colonel Ormsby).

Visibility was only a few metres and at first there was no opposing fire. The Battalion had under 200m to cover, but after 70m emerged from the smoke and ran into a hail of small arms fire. Men fell everywhere and those who reached the uncut wire had to run up and down trying to find gaps. The survivors were forced into cover, some within 15m of the enemy lines, where they lay completely still all day. 2 Company tried to get forward but met a similar fate. Lieutenant Wood and four men got into the enemy trench, but this party was destroyed there. A gap between the left flank and 2nd Leicestershire opened and a party under Subadar Bhim Sing was sent to fill it at 7.30 a.m. The Dehra Dun Brigade was scheduled to advance at 10.30 a.m., but due to congestion did not get into position until 2.15 p.m., when its advance was cancelled.

84   Victoria Crosses on the Western Front April 1915–June 1916

It began to rain heavily at 3 p.m. and this seems to have reduced the enemy fire. After dark the survivors came in. The Battalion's casualties were 241, including 86 out of 120 in 4 Company. 2nd Leicestershire suffered 447 casualties and 2/8th Gurkhas a further 481.

Rifleman Kulbir Thapa was one of those who got into the German trench with Lieutenant Wood; he was the only one who came back alive. He was wounded, but charged straight over the German trench. Behind it he found a wounded 2nd Leicestershire soldier who begged him to get away and save himself. Kulbir refused and stayed with him for the rest of that day and the following night. In thick mist next morning, Kulbir managed to bring the man out through the German wire unobserved, although there were a number of narrow escapes. He got the man into a shell hole and then went back twice to rescue two wounded Gurkhas in broad daylight, carrying them back under fire. He was most fortunate to survive because the Germans left their trenches in the mist to shoot or bayonet the wounded in no man's land. The Battalion was not relieved until 29th September. This was its last offensive action in France. On 8th November it left for Egypt.

Although the attack faltered on the right due to uncut wire, on the left the support trench was taken by the Bareilly Brigade and the advance continued, albeit at some cost. The Moulin was reached, although the buildings remained in German hands. Before the reserve brigade could deploy, the Germans counterattacked vigorously and regained all their losses. By 4 p.m., the last British troops had been withdrawn. Total casualties in the Indian Corps were 3,973.

12th Rifle Brigade was to the left of the Bareilly Brigade, about 180m northeast of Winchester Street. It was ordered to attack at 7.30 a.m. between Points 76 and 61. However, due to communications problems the advance did not begin until 8.25 a.m. By then enemy resistance had stiffened and heavy casualties were suffered, particularly from fire directed from around Point 55 on the left. Despite this, D Company reached the enemy third line and almost got to the Moulin. When the Bareilly Brigade, on the left of the Meerut Division, was forced to pull back at 11 a.m., D Company was left exposed. In the face of open flanks and heavy counterattacks, it was forced to withdraw. By 12.30 p.m., all 12th Rifle Brigade companies were back in the British lines and were sent to hold the support line between Winchester Street and Erith Street communications trench, 600m to the northeast, while 6th KSLI and 12th KRRC held the front line.

Chapigny Farm from 12th Rifle Brigade's front line. The D171 Neuve Chapelle – Fleurbaix road runs in front of it.

From 12th Rifle Brigade's front line looking southeast. This is where George Maling's aid post was blown up, but he continued to treat the wounded. In the left distance is Aubers church. The ditch in the centre points towards Moulin du Pietre in the trees in the distance. The buildings on the right are on the German front line where the mine was fired.

During this action, Battalion HQ had started off in the advanced brigade HQ dugouts at Chapigny Farm, but at 8.45 a.m. moved into the front line trench at the head of Chaplin Street communications trench. At about 11 a.m., Battalion HQ was hit by a large shell, which killed the whole HQ party except for the CO and Adjutant. The same shell wrecked the Regimental Aid Post, killing the corporal in charge and causing many other casualties. **Lieutenant George Maling**, the Battalion MO, who had been tending the wounded since 6.25 a.m., was knocked senseless by the explosion. However, he recovered quickly and returned to work. A few minutes later, another shell landed on the parapet and he was hurled into the air. This time the Aid Post was completely destroyed and the only other medical orderly was wounded. Maling returned to his work once again, disregarding the danger around him. He carried on alone until relieved at 8 a.m. on the 26th, during which time he treated over 300 casualties.

Second Attack on Bellewaarde, 25th–30th September 1915

84 2Lt Rupert Hallowes, 4th Battalion, The Middlesex Regiment (8th Brigade, 3rd Division)

The British launched three subsidiary attacks on 25th September 1915 to distract German attention away from the offensive at Loos. The most extensive of these diversions was made by two divisions on a frontage of 1,800m at Hooge and Bellewaarde near Ypres. 3rd Division (V Corps) on the right, made the main attack, while 14th Division (VI Corps) made a smaller attack on the left against Bellewaarde Farm. There was insufficient artillery ammunition to support these diversions properly.

In 3rd Division's area, 7th Brigade committed two battalions against Hooge Chateau, while three battalions of 8th Brigade attacked through Sanctuary Wood opposite Stirling Castle, south of the Menin Road. One company from 9th Brigade

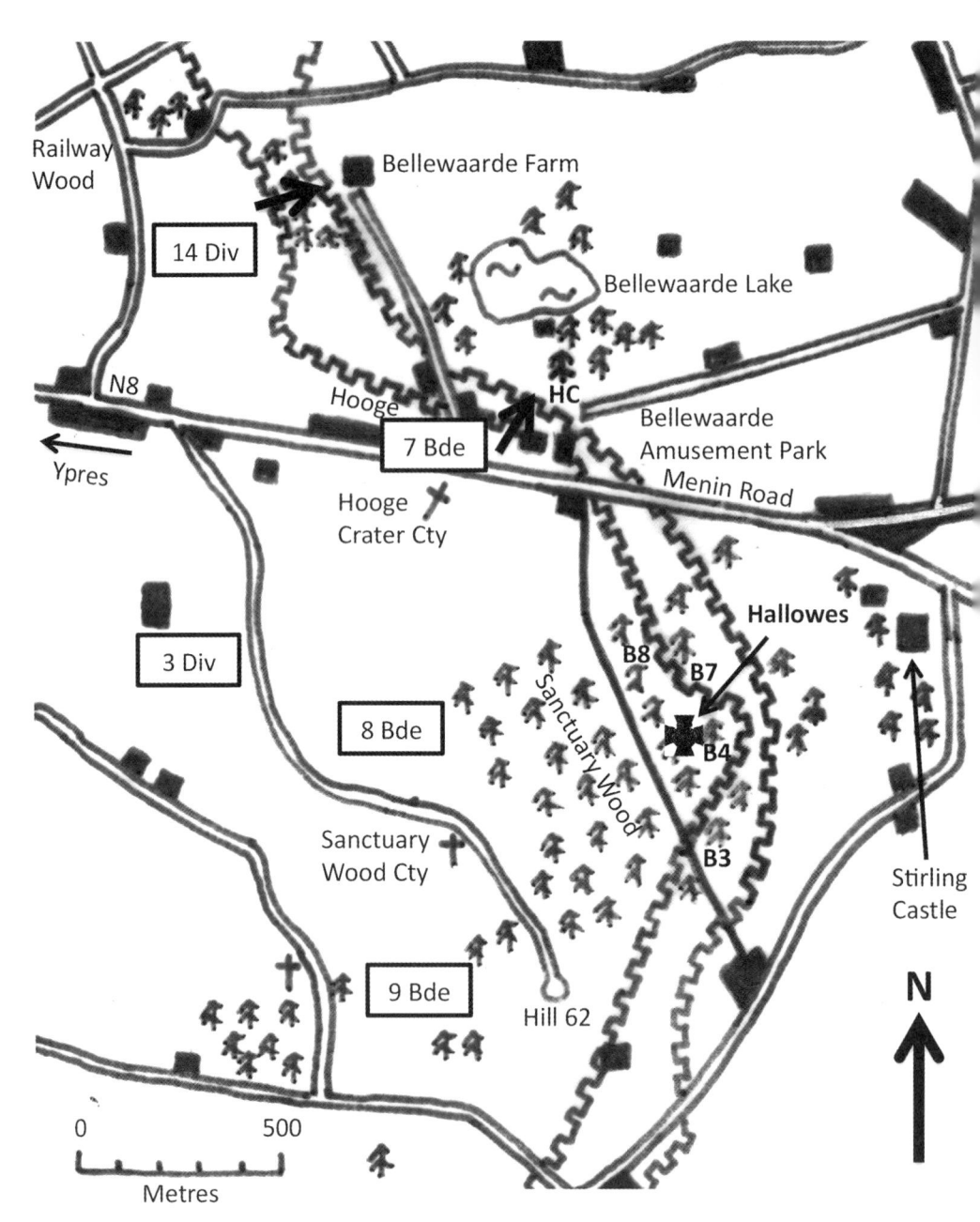

Leave Ypres on the N8 (Menin Road) towards Menen. Go past Bellewaarde Park and the road bends to the right, where there is a left turn to Becelaere. Continue another 200m and turn right at the 18th Division Memorial. After 400m the road bends right and after another 700m there is a large farm on the right. Park here. Walk 400m along the track northeast into Sanctuary Wood. You should enter the wood at a right angle bend with trees to your left and fields on the right. The internal corner here is the area of 'B3'. Continue 130m and there is a firebreak on the right. Walk 50m along it uphill. On the right, under the trees, the remains of a concrete bunker mark the German front line. Turn around and face back down the break. 'B4' was directly in front of you.

attacked to the right of 8th Brigade. The leading battalions in 8th Brigade were 2nd Royal Scots (left), 1st Gordon Highlanders (centre) and 4th Gordon Highlanders (right), with 2nd Suffolk and 4th Middlesex in reserve. A preparatory bombardment was fired over the days before the attack, but most heavy guns had been sent south to Loos and there was a shortage of ammunition for the guns that remained. There were also shortages of grenades and wire cutters; 8th Brigade had to give up ninety pairs of the latter to 7th and 9th Brigades. During the night of 24th/25th September, the 18 Pounders fired shrapnel to prevent the Germans repairing the gaps in their wire that had been cut the previous day.

The assault battalions moved into the advanced trenches on the night of 23rd September. The final bombardment began at 3.50 a.m. on the 25th. Although 112 guns fired on 8th Brigade's front, many were 18 Pounders firing shrapnel and had little effect on the enemy trenches. Three minutes later the German artillery retaliated. At 4.19 a.m., two mines were exploded in front of 2nd Royal Scots and two more thirty seconds later.

At 4.20 a.m., the assault troops set off into the rain and mist. Initially there was success in every sector and prisoners were making their way back by 5.45 a.m. However, a shortage of bombs soon began to tell and by 10 a.m. the forward troops were under pressure and heavy artillery fire. All the gains were lost gradually to determined German counterattacks.

Two companies of 4th Middlesex were sent forward at 2.20 p.m. Two platoons of D Company bombed up a communication trench leading to 'Fort 13' (precise

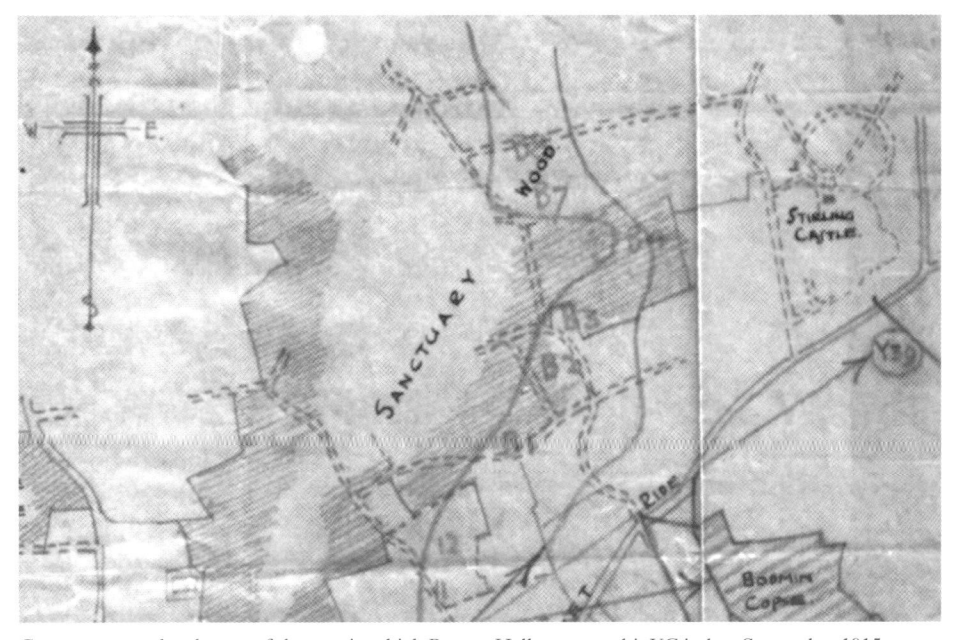

Contemporary sketch map of the area in which Rupert Hallowes won his VC in late September 1915.

location unknown) to assist 4th Gordon Highlanders, which had already taken and lost this position. The other platoons of D Company went to relieve pressure on the rest of 4th Gordon Highlanders.

By 2.40 p.m., only a company of 2nd Royal Scots was still hanging on in the German lines and it was in a dangerous salient, under heavy artillery and mortar fire. A counterattack was expected and at 3 p.m. C Company, 4th Middlesex and some bombers reinforced 2nd Royal Scots, which was in danger of being outflanked, as the Germans had infiltrated between it and 1st Gordon Highlanders. Heavy fire and the counterattack made it impossible for supports to approach the salient from about 4.15 p.m. Meanwhile, B Company, 4th Middlesex was sent over the open through heavy shellfire to garrison 'B8' and the 'B8' support trenches at the northern edge of Sanctuary Wood, as all the communication trenches had been blown in by this time.

At 4.30 p.m., 2nd Royal Scots was pushed out of the enemy trenches and was later relieved by 4th Middlesex in 'B3', 'B4' and half of 'B7'. By 7.30 p.m. the shelling had stopped and the evacuation of the wounded commenced. 8th Brigade had suffered almost 1,000 casualties, but 167 prisoners were taken.

That night and the next few days were spent making a continuous firing line and rebuilding the trenches. Frequent short but sharp encounters with the enemy followed. **2nd Lieutenant Rupert Hallowes** was not awarded his VC for one particular deed, but rather for his sustained courage and inspiration over six days. During four very heavy bombardments, he climbed onto the parapet and encouraged the soldiers to stick it out. He also conducted a number of hazardous reconnaissance missions on the German positions. On the night of 26th/27th September, he saw two wounded Royal Scots soldiers in no man's land. Leaving the trench, he personally organised the rescue of these men while exposed to heavy rifle fire. The German artillery then opened a furious and accurate bombardment. To put heart into the men, Hallowes again climbed onto the parapet and calmly walked up and down, giving encouragement to everyone.

At 4.30 p.m. on 29th September, the Germans exploded a mine under 'B4' occupied by 4th Middlesex. Heavy artillery and mortar fire followed and infantry rushed in with bombs to occupy the crater. Some appeared to be dressed in Royal Scots uniforms taken from the dead on 25th September. The mine destroyed an important observation position and gave the Germans a considerable advantage. About eighty men were missing after the explosion because a relief was taking place at the time. 4th Middlesex suffered a total of 149 casualties that day. Lack of bombs delayed a counterattack.

On 30th September, a counterattack was carried out against the 'B4' salient by three companies; one each from 4th Middlesex (right), 2nd Royal Scots (centre) and 2nd Suffolk (left). Bombers were attached from the Honourable Artillery Company (7th Brigade) and 10th Liverpool (9th Brigade), although the former did not arrive in time. The artillery opened up at 3 p.m. and was effective against the enemy

Remains of the concrete bunker in Sanctuary Wood near 'B4'.

trenches, but the wire was not well cut. The Germans held commanding ground around the mine crater and seemed to have limitless supplies of bombs. They also had a number of well sited machine-guns.

The flanks of the attack made some progress, but in the centre the troops could not get beyond wire blocks in the trenches. A shortage of bombs held up progress and at 4.30 p.m., the attack was halted and the gains consolidated. Hallowes went back under heavy shellfire to get more bombs. Early on 1st October a carrying party from another unit dropped a bomb into his trench accidentally and he was mortally wounded. He went on encouraging his men until the end, but eventually died of his wounds.

Chapter Four

Loos

Battle of Loos, 25th–26th September 1915

85 Piper Daniel Laidlaw, 7th Battalion, The King's Own Scottish Borderers (46th Brigade, 15th (Scottish) Division) Loos and Hill 70, France
86 2Lt Frederick Johnson, 73rd Field Company RE (15th (Scottish) Division) Hill 70, France
87 Lt Col Angus Douglas-Hamilton, 6th Battalion, The Queen's Own Cameron Highlanders (45th Brigade, 15th (Scottish) Division) Hill 70, France
88 Pte Robert Dunsire, 13th Battalion, The Royal Scots (45th Brigade, 15th (Scottish) Division) Hill 70, France
89 Pte George Peachment, 2nd Battalion, The King's Royal Rifle Corps (2nd Brigade, 1st Division) Le Rutoire, France
90 Sgt Harry Wells, 2nd Battalion, The Royal Sussex Regiment (2nd Brigade, 1st Division) Le Rutoire, France
91 Capt Anketell Read, 1st Battalion, The Northamptonshire Regiment (2nd Brigade, 1st Division) Le Rutoire, France
92 Pte Henry Kenny, 1st Battalion, The Loyal North Lancashire Regiment (2nd Brigade, 1st Division) Le Rutoire, France
93 Pte Arthur Vickers, 2nd Battalion, The Royal Warwickshire Regiment (22nd Brigade, 7th Division) Hulluch, France
94 Capt Arthur Kilby, 2nd Battalion, The South Staffordshire Regiment (6th Brigade, 2nd Division) Auchy, France
95 Sgt Arthur Saunders, 9th Battalion, The Suffolk Regiment (71st Brigade, 24th Division) Loos, France

In late September 1915, Anglo–French forces launched simultaneous offensives in Champagne and Artois. In Artois the British cooperated with the French Tenth Army between Arras and the La Bassée Canal. The British were responsible for the front from the Canal southwards to Loos. Between the British and the French Tenth Army a gap of 3,600m opposite Liévin and Lens was not attacked. The two thrusts were intended to link up, having bypassed these locations. Six British infantry divisions were committed to the opening attack, with a further three infantry and three cavalry divisions in reserve. The BEF was unable to commit more forces as it had recently taken over an extra thirty-five kilometres of front from the French on the Somme.

The French had 420 heavy guns to support seventeen assault divisions. The British had seventy heavy guns supporting six divisions; only half the concentration. To compensate for the lack of guns and ammunition, the BEF decided to use chlorine gas for the first time and to employ smoke to cover the initial advance. Gas was to be released for twelve minutes, followed by smoke for eight minutes, then gas for another twelve minutes, followed by smoke again for eight minutes before the assault.

The ground was not ideal, being generally open with no hedges or fences and few ditches. There were numerous mine works and colliery villages. The area was

Leave Loos centre on the D165 heading southwest and 300m before reaching the N43 turn left onto a minor road. Cross the N43 and go over the A21 Autoroute towards Liévin. Pass under a green footbridge (remember it). Pass a car park and café on the right and continue with a high wall and fence on top on the left. When the wall ends, turn immediate left into 'Base 11/19'. It does not matter if you miss this turning as the next left goes to the same place. 'Base 11/19' consists of preserved mining buildings (Fosse 11). Coming from Liévin it is signed, but not from Loos for some obscure reason! Most of the mine buildings are fenced off, but you can walk around them and see the concrete pithead alongside the older iron girder winding gear. Park and find your way to the green bridge you passed under previously. Cross the bridge towards the two enormous spoil heaps on the site of the Double Crassier. Bear left with the track to join a metalled roadway. Follow it round to the right between the two spoil heaps until you see the remains of the tramway climbing the spoil heap on the right. For the best view, follow the tramway to the top; it is easier walking to the side of the sleepers. The view from the top encompasses the whole Loos battlefield (on a clear day). Those who prefer the Dress Circle to the Gods should continue along the metalled road until it emerges onto a plateau. Head for the northern edge to overlook the battlefield. The view is not as spectacular, but still worth the effort. The other spoil heap has an easier climb, but part of the battlefield is obscured by the spoil heap in front.

Base 11/19 from the top of the spoil heap.

crossed by two spurs running southwest to northeast across the line of advance. To the east was Cité Spur, with Hill 70 towards its northern end. Grenay (Lone Tree) Spur lay to the west, with Loos in the valley between the two. The lie of the land and fortified villages gave the Germans considerable advantages. The main pitheads (Fosses) and auxiliary shafts (Puits) were topped by towers up to 30m high, offering the defenders excellent observation, as did the mine dumps (Crassiers). Conversely, the British could see little of the German support lines. There were also a number of significant man made features:

- Double Crassier – a slagheap southwest of Loos commanding the Loos valley.
- Tower Bridge – double winding towers at Loos overlooking most of the area.
- Puits 14 bis – mine buildings commanding the area between Loos and the Dump.
- Dump – a large slagheap at Fosse 8 overlooking Loos and the British rear areas.

The British artillery could not be moved forward until these features and Hill 70 had been taken; but, if the initial attack was successful, the wire in front of the second German position was out of range. While the guns were being brought forward, the Germans would have plenty of time to bring up reinforcements.

First Army under General Sir Douglas Haig, committed two corps to the initial assault north of Lens; I Corps (2nd, 9th, and 7th Divisions) in the north and IV Corps (1st, 15th and 47th Divisions) in the south. XI Corps (Guards, 21st and

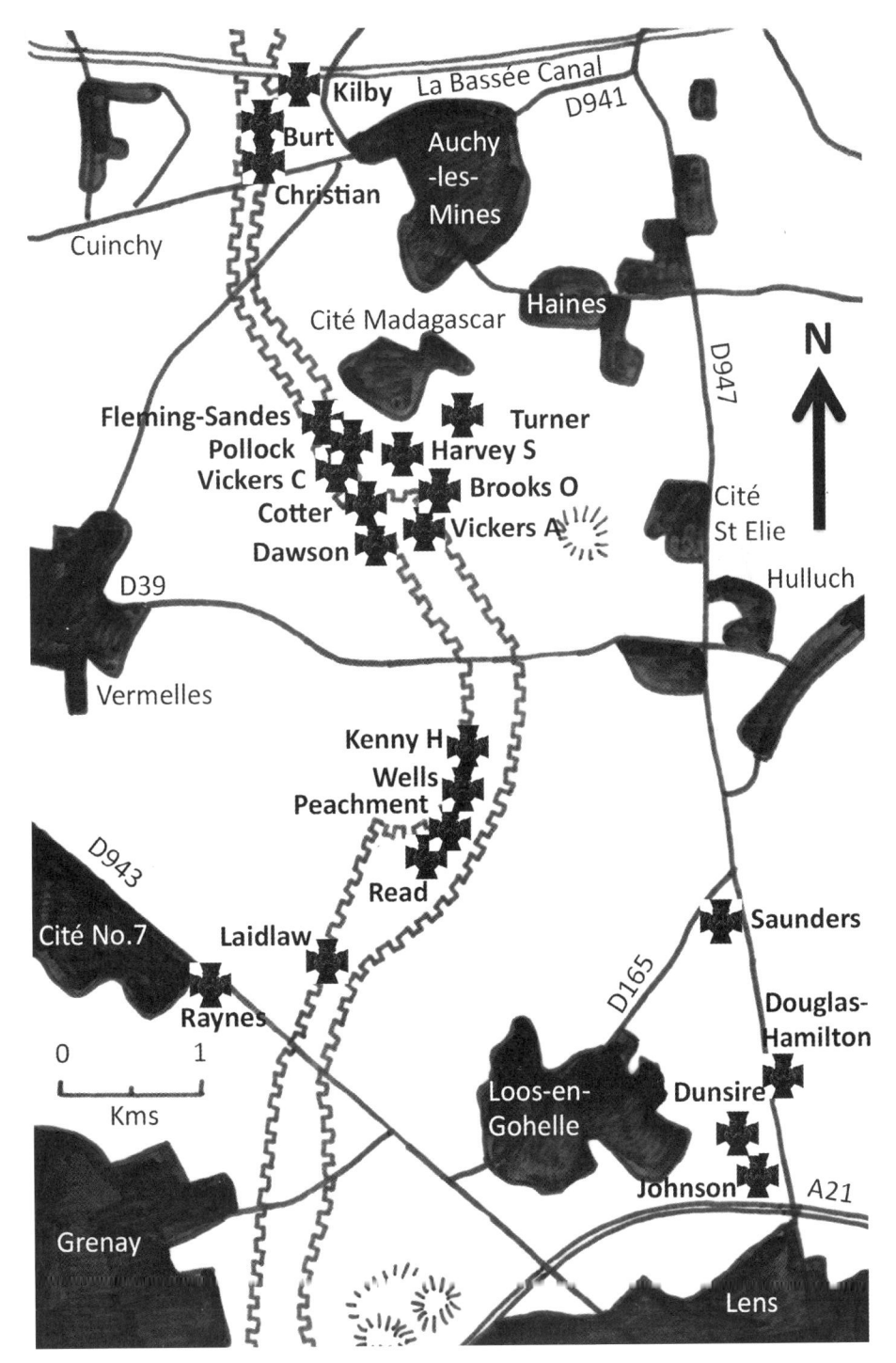

The front lines on 25th September 1915 before the opening of the Battle of Loos. Twenty-two VCs were awarded for actions in this area. The majority were for the Battle of Loos (25th September – 8th October) and the Actions of the Hohenzollern Redoubt (13th-19th October). Two others, Harry Christian and William Cotter, were either outside the formal area of these battles or after they had finished, but are shown for completeness.

24th Divisions) was in reserve, in addition to the Cavalry Corps. 21st and 24th Divisions had not been in the line before and were moved forward in a series of long exhausting marches.

Maintaining security was impossible. Britain was full of talk about the coming 'Big Push' and preparations at the front were obvious. The Germans knew where the attack would fall, only the date and time were unknown, but when the bombardment opened it was clearly not far away.

An enormous amount of preparation work was required. Communications trenches and bomb stores were dug. Signal cables were buried deeply. Gas cylinders had to be brought into the line and dug in at night; 15th Division alone moved 1,500 of them, each weighing 140 lbs. There were also advanced HQs, dressing stations, dugouts and other structures to complete as well as bringing forward trench bridges, water, rations and ammunition, all by hand.

On 21st September the bombardment commenced. Ironically, artillery observers were hampered by fine weather, which resulted in the exploding shells throwing up clouds of dust. Conversely on the 23rd and 24th, it was mist and rain that obscured their view. As a result much of the German wire remained intact. Each night heavy small arms fire was maintained on the enemy lines to dissuade him from coming out to repair any damage. A number of feint attacks were carried out during the bombardment in an attempt to make the Germans man their lines and incur casualties from the shelling. The Germans made little response.

Late on the 24th the weather was predicted to be favourable for releasing gas. The assault troops moved into their positions by 2.30 a.m. on 25th September. Every man had two smoke helmets, one rolled on top of his head ready for immediate use. At 4.00 a.m. the bombardment increased in intensity and at 5.50 a.m. stepped up another gear. At the same time the gas was released. A 10–15m high wall of gas moved very slowly forwards, with holes being punched in it by shrapnel shells. By 6.30 a.m., when the attack commenced, the cloud in most places had not reached the German lines. In some places it stood still over the British trenches. The assault troops left the front line and moved steadily across no man's land as the artillery lifted. Eleven VCs were awarded for the first two days of the Loos battle and these will be described from south to north.

In 47th Division's area, the gas moved forward as expected. Covered by thick smoke, the leading units took the defenders by surprise. Counterattacks threatened the positions taken, but a line from the Double Crassier to Loos cemetery was secured and the open flank to the south was covered. The advance continued into the south of Loos and there was a certain amount of intermingling with units of 15th Division.

In the centre of IV Corps, 15th Division attacked Loos on a frontage of 1,350m. 46th Brigade on the left and 44th Brigade on the right were to advance in five columns (each of an infantry battalion, engineer section and pioneer platoon), to take the Lens and Loos Road Redoubts and Loos village. The first brigade to reach

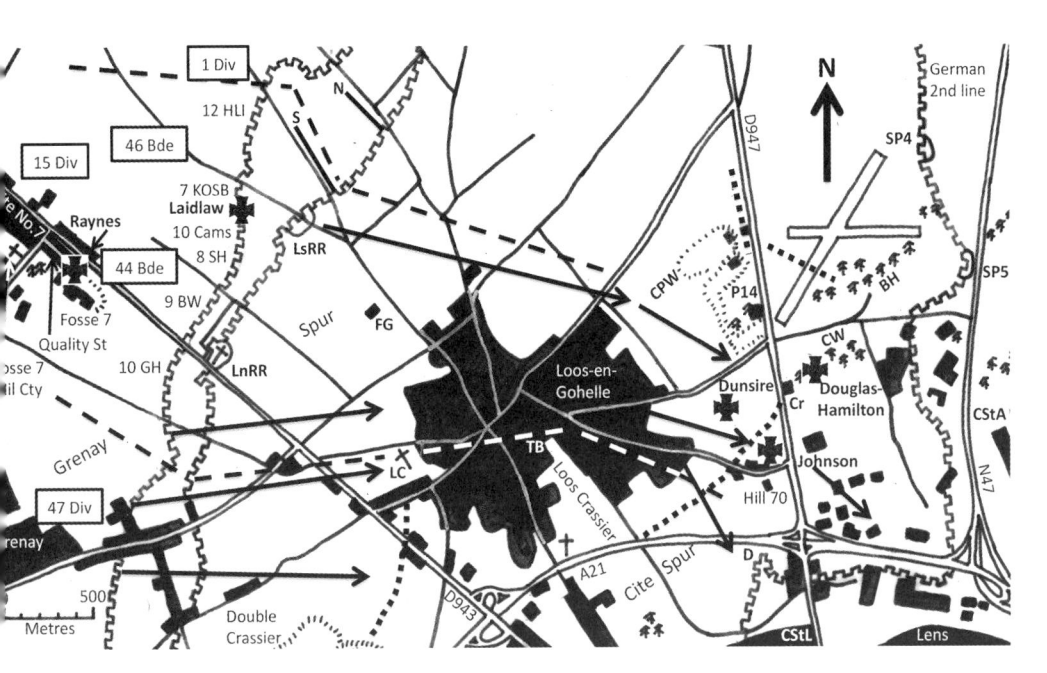

The 15th Division area on 25th September 1915. Dashed lines mark divisional boundaries and the heavy dotted lines are the limit of the British advance at dawn on 26th September. Some abbreviations are used – BH = Bois Hugo, CW = Chalet Wood, CPW = Chalk Pit Wood, CStA = Cité St Auguste, CStL = Cité St Laurent, Cr = Crematorium, D = Dynamitière, FG = Fort Glatz, LC = Loos Cemetery, LnRR = Lens Road Redoubt, LsRR = Loos Road Redoubt, N = Northern Sap, P14 = Puits 14 bis, S = Southern Sap, SP = Stutzpunkt, TB = Tower Bridge.

Hill 70 was to hold it, while the other continued to Cité St Auguste and beyond. The 5th Column, on the northern flank, was to bomb along Southern Sap to clear the German front line northwards and link up with 1st Division.

The leading battalions set off at 6.30 a.m. but were badly affected by gas, which in this area hardly moved. They had 200m to cover to the German trenches, but after 40m emerged from the gas and smoke, where two machine-guns, well supported by artillery, took a heavy toll before bombing parties managed to destroy the positions. However, because the wire was well cut, the first trench line was taken. The 5th Column found only a shallow ditch at Southern Sap. It suffered casualties in the open and also because 2nd Brigade on the left was delayed by uncut wire.

7th KOSB was in the centre of 46th Brigade, with two companies of 12th HLI on the left and 10th Cameronians on the right. 7th KOSB was led by a platoon each from A and B Companies on a frontage of 400m. While waiting for the attack to start, Lieutenant MCdeB Young (died of wounds next day – Noeux-les-Mines Communal Cemetery, I A 29), was aware that many men were distressed by the gas and enemy artillery. When the order came to attack, many were reluctant to move and Young realised that something had to be done quickly to make them go

96 Victoria Crosses on the Western Front April 1915–June 1916

From Loos Road Redoubt looking west. 7th KOSB attacked uphill towards the camera. In the background are the mine dumps at Grenay. To reach the site of Daniel Laidlaw's VC action, approach Loos from the northwest along the N43. Pass Dud Corner Cemetery and the Loos Memorial on the left. Continue down the hill to the roundabout and turn left along a narrow metalled road. After 900m at the crossroads turn left. This road is a little bumpy in places. Pass the farm buildings on the left (Fort Glatz) and continue to the irregular track junction at the top of the hill. Park here and walk along the left fork for 250–300m to the site of the Loos Road Redoubt. The track marks 7th KOSB's northern (right as you look at it) boundary. The Battalion attacked towards you up the hill from its front line positions about 100–150m beyond the Redoubt. From here you appreciate the open nature of the Loos battlefield, as devoid of cover now as it was then.

forward. He called on **Piper Daniel Laidlaw** to play. Disregarding the heavy fire and gas, Laidlaw climbed out of the trench and marched along the parapet while piping to encourage his comrades. They surged over the top and charged forward with Laidlaw keeping up as best he could, playing *'Blue Bonnets over the Border'*. Casualties were heavy, but there were few checks to the advance. As he arrived at the German front line, Laidlaw was hit by shrapnel in the ankle and leg, but he hobbled

Having advanced to this point on the top of Grenay Spur, the troops of 15th Scottish Division got their first sight of Loos village, previously hidden in dead ground, and beyond. Hill 70 is just left of Loos church in the far distance. On the right is the Double Crassier. The views over the Loos battlefield from the top of these former mine dumps is unsurpassed, particularly the one on the left.

Hill 70

Double Crassier   Dud Corner Cemetery/Loos Redoubt

From behind 7th KOSB's front line looking south. Dud Corner Cemetery/Loos Memorial is on the right, on the site of the Lens Road Redoubt and dominates the ground all around it. In the left background is the Double Crassier, much larger than in 1915. Daniel Laidlaw advanced with pipes playing to the left of picture.

after the Battalion changing tunes to *'The Standard of the Braes o' Mar'*. Only when he was sure that the enemy trenches on Hill 70 had been carried did he make his way back to the old front line. Without Laidlaw's pipes to stir the blood it is possible the initial attack in this area might never have got underway.

After capturing the first system of trenches, the leading battalions continued down the slope towards Loos. There were delays as uncut wire was negotiated and machine-guns near the cemetery and in Fort Glatz were silenced by bombing parties. Fierce hand-to-hand and house-to-house fighting followed but the village was secured by 8 a.m. Shortly afterwards the remnants of the units involved emerged from the eastern end of Loos and advanced up Hill 70. They were well ahead of the flanking units.

Most of the officers were already casualties and no reorganisation had taken place before the advance continued. 47th Division to the south had not advanced as quickly and this caused a southwards drift as the advancing troops tried to make contact on the open right flank. Despite these problems, the attackers seized Hill 70 and the Redoubt by about 9 a.m. Drunk with success, and thinking Cité St Auguste had been taken, 800–900 soldiers set off in utter confusion to pursue the fleeing Germans. They were hit by heavy cross-fire from Bois Hugo, Cité St Laurent, Cité St Auguste and the Dynamitière. Despite this, they were only 80m from the enemy positions when they were halted by uncut wire. The mob could neither go on nor back up the exposed slopes of Hill 70. Most tried to dig-in, but a few attempted to fall back. Taking this to be a general retirement, the whole German line counterattacked north of Cité St Laurent and retook Hill 70 Redoubt. Fortunately a few officers managed to bring 300–400 men under control behind the crest and prevented the whole of the Hill being lost.

When the French Tenth Army attack commenced south of Lens at 12.45 a.m., the Germans were forced to prepare their reserves to meet this new threat. Further counterattacks against the British were temporarily halted, giving the attackers some breathing room.

73rd Field Company RE had been attached to 44th Brigade for the assault. Most men in 1 and 2 Sections leading had fallen during the fight for Loos, but some made it to the top of Hill 70 with the infantry. 3 and 4 Sections, in reserve, had waited at Fosse 7, where 4 Section lost eleven men while constructing a bridge over a trench crossing the Lens Road. 3 and 4 Sections were ordered to follow 10th Gordon Highlanders to a point between Tower Bridge and the Windmill (between Loos and Hill 70 but not marked on contemporary maps). On reaching Loos, the CO of 10th Gordon

The top of Hill 70 from the line held by the British late on 25th September. Loos is behind the camera. In the far left distance is the Crematorium, with Chalet Wood behind. To reach this position, drive northeast on the D165 towards Hulluch from the square in the centre of Loos, where there are a couple of cafés. After 150m turn right on Rue Kleber signed 'Halle de Tennis'. Continue 200m and turn left signed 'Stade Eric Sikorsa'. Take the right fork after 100m signed 'Ecole O Leroy' and continue 850m. Turn right on Chemin de la Voie Perdue and park on the hard standing on the right. This is the western edge of the Hill 70 Redoubt held by Frederick Johnson and others.

Highlanders ordered Captain Cardew to advance up Hill 70, which was reached at 9.30 a.m. The sappers assisted the infantry at the Keep area of the Redoubt, but initially they were forced back by heavy fire. Captain Cardew and **2nd Lieutenant Frederick Johnson** found a machine-gun and with ten sappers made for the Redoubt again. They succeeded in taking it and Johnson was instrumental in organising its defence.

Shortly afterwards they were driven out and Cardew was severely wounded. Although Johnson had been hit in the leg, he took command and, refusing all aid, led several charges. He repeatedly rallied his men, but despite his gallantry the enemy remained firmly in control of the Keep. At midnight, seeing that nothing further could be gained, the remaining sappers retired and helped the infantry to prepare a new defensive line a little down the Hill. Only then did Johnson go for medical assistance.

The reverse view of the previous picture from the western edge of Hill 70 Redoubt. Trees obscure the view to the southwest, but the complete domination of the ground to the northwest (right) is evident. Frederick Johnson was in action in and around the Redoubt.

At 10.15 a.m., 45th Brigade was committed to reinforce the leading brigades. 6th Cameron Highlanders had moved into the vacated British front line at 6.30 a.m. and parties began digging communication trenches towards the German lines. At 10.35 a.m., the Battalion's grenadiers were placed under command of 46th Brigade to cover a gap to the north caused by the initial failure of 1st Division. They bombed northwards along the German front line from Southern Sap towards Lone Tree, where 2nd Brigade was held up. After 60m they were stopped by a barrier manned by Germans bombers with a machine-gun. At 11.30 a.m., the rest of the Battalion began moving forward on the left, with A and B Companies leading. They reached the vicinity of Puis 14 bis, where C and D Companies joined them at 1 p.m. The Battalion formed a line from the northwest corner of Chalet Wood to Chalk Pit Wood, with Battalion HQ in the Chalk Pit. At 4.30 p.m., contact was eventually made with 1st Division.

At nightfall 15th Division held from Loos Crassier to Puits 14 bis, where it joined 2nd Brigade of 1st Division. A mixture of units from 44th, 45th and 46th Brigades held the line just below the crest of Hill 70.

At the northern end of IV Corps, 1st Division was allocated a frontage of 1,260m south of the Vermelles – Hulluch road. Its objective was the Haute Deûle Canal. 1st Brigade on the left attacked due east. 2nd Brigade on the right, having secured the enemy front and support lines between Lone Tree (a solitary cherry tree in no man's land) and Northern Sap, was to swing southeast. It was to seize

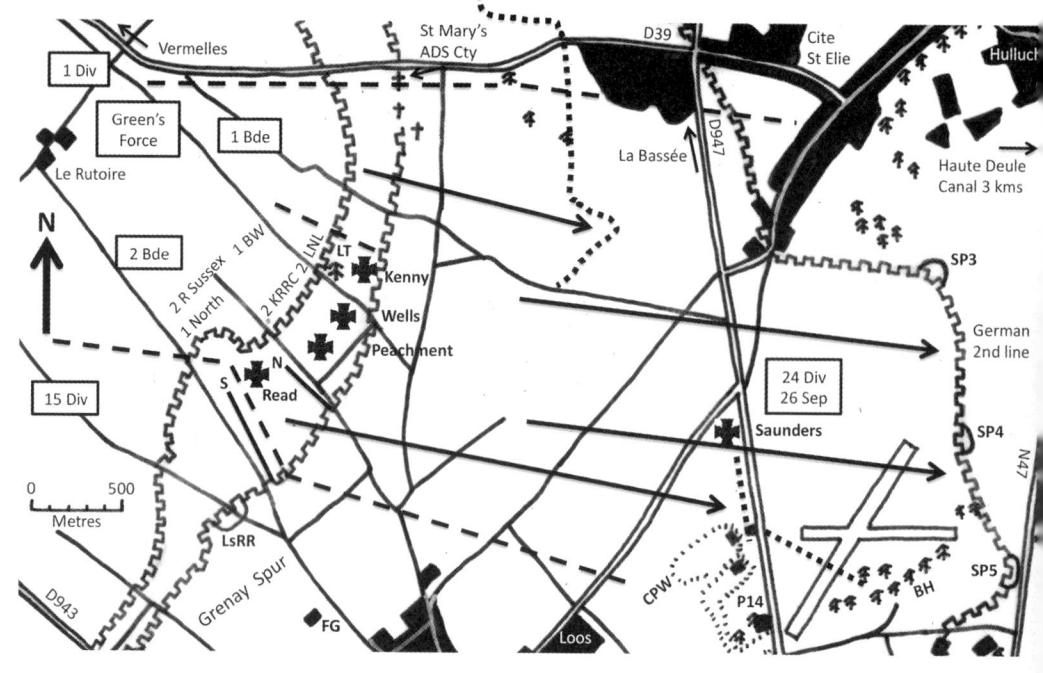

The 1st Division area on 25th September 1915. Dashed lines mark divisional boundaries and the heavy dotted lines are the limit of the British advance at dawn on 26th September. Some abbreviations are used – BH = Bois Hugo, CPW = Chalk Pit Wood, FG = Fort Glatz, LsRR = Loos Road Redoubt, LT = Lone Tree, N = Northern Sap, P14 = Puits 14 bis, S = Southern Sap, SP = Stutzpunkt.

Bois Hugo and the Chalk Pit and link up with 15th Division on the right flank. The gap opening between the two brigades was to be filled by Green's Force, consisting of the fifth battalions from 1st and 2nd Brigades (1/14th London and 1/9th King's), commanded by the CO of 2nd Royal Sussex. 3rd Brigade was in reserve to support the advance to the German second position and onwards to the Haute Deûle Canal.

The sites of all four 2nd Brigade VCs on 25th September 1915 can be viewed from one location. From the irregular track junction close to Laidlaw's VC site, turn 90° right and head northeast along the top of the spur. After 400m at the T-junction turn left and 500m further on turn right on the gravel track; it is perfectly adequate for normal cars if driven slowly. 300m on at the T-junction stop and park well over to one side to allow farm vehicles to pass. Walk along the rough track to the left/northwest for about 450m to the replanted Lone Tree. The German front line is about 100m behind you and the British lines are to your front, varying in distance from about 200m on the right to over 600m on the left. Kenny's VC site is about 200m north of Lone Tree and the other three are to the southwest; about 100m for Wells, 250m for Peachment and 400m

1st Brigade advanced 1,100m and halted in front of Hulluch, but 2nd Brigade ran into problems immediately. The assault battalions, 1st Loyal North Lancashire on the left and 2nd KRRC on the right, were badly affected by the gas released at 5.50 a.m. Over 400 soldiers were overcome and had to be replaced by men from later waves. The wind then changed direction and the attack was delayed until 6.34 a.m. while more gas was released. The German wire was in dead ground and was consequently uncut. Two machine guns and heavy rifle fire hit the advancing troops as they attempted desperately to cut through the wire. The lines of infantry following could not move forward and took cover just below the crest line. By 7.30 a.m. the gas and smoke had cleared, exposing the troops pinned-down in no man's land.

2nd KRRC suffered particularly badly in the attack. Having failed to break into the enemy positions, it was ordered to reorganise in the front line. As **Rifleman George Peachment** retired he saw his company commander, Captain GR Dubs, lying wounded. The enemy fire was intense, but Peachment crawled to the officer's

The replanted Lone Tree in no man's land from the former German front line.

for Read. There is little to see in the immediate area. This is one of the most featureless parts of the Loos battlefield.

A panoramic view from the former German front line over the front attacked by 1st Division. On the far right is St Mary's ADS Cemetery, where John Kipling, son of Rudyard, has a headstone. In the centre is the Lone Tree in the middle of no man's land with the British front line beyond it parallel with the sweep of the picture. On the far left is Grenay with its mine dumps. The VC actions of Anketell Read, George Peachment and Harry Wells were to the left of the track running away from the camera past Lone Tree. Henry Kenny's action was to the right of the track roughly in line with St Mary's ADS Cemetery.

St Mary's ADS Cemetery

assistance. Ignoring the danger, he knelt over Dubs to attend to his wounds. Despite being wounded by a bomb splinter, Peachment continued his work, even though he could have sheltered in nearby shell holes. A minute later he was wounded fatally by a rifle bullet. This was a remarkably unselfish act by one of the youngest soldiers in the Battalion. Dubs survived the war and was later awarded the MC, French Croix de Guerre and was Mentioned three times.

When 2nd Brigade's leading battalions attacked at 6.30 a.m., 2nd Royal Sussex moved into the vacated front line between 'B2' and 'A5' and prepared to follow. However, due to the thick smoke and gas, it was not possible to keep a check on the progress of the attack. From about 6.45 a.m., companies went forward on their own initiative and became entangled with the leading battalions as they attempted to get through the enemy wire. The whole attack bogged down. 2nd Royal Sussex, together with C, D and part of B Companies, 1st Northamptonshire and the survivors of 1st Loyal North Lancashire, were ordered to make a second attack at 9 a.m.

Sergeant Harry Wells' took command of his platoon when the officer was killed. Pressing on despite heavy casualties, he got to within 15m of the wire, but by then over half the platoon was dead or
wounded and the rest badly shaken. However, Wells refused to give in and twice more led his men forward. He was killed as he stood up to rally the few survivors for another attempt.

Captain Anketell Read and one hundred men in 1st Northamptonshire were badly affected by gas before the first attack. After the second attack he saw a party of about sixty men from various battalions retiring towards him and he willed himself to get out of the front line trench and rally them. Under his leadership they returned to the firing line south of Lone Tree. Read took no cover whatsoever, moving about freely to encourage the men, and inevitably he was hit by a sniper and mortally wounded.

Private Henry Kenny in 1st Loyal North Lancashire retired with the rest of his unit after the failure of the second attack. Having regained the relative safety of the front line he went back into no man's land, despite the heavy fire, and rescued six

Reverse view of the previous panorama from the former British front line looking towards the top of Grenay Spur. The Double Crassier on the right is almost the only discernable feature.

wounded men. On the last occasion he was wounded in the neck as he passed the rescued man over the parapet.

To the north and south, 1st Brigade and 15th Division respectively, had been successful, but if the gap in front of 2nd Brigade were not filled then failure was inevitable. At 9.10 a.m., HQ 1st Division ordered Green's Force to advance in support, but all the runners were hit and the orders were not received until 10.55 a.m. The attack by 1/14th London and 1/9th King's at Lone Tree met with a hail of bullets and many men went down. 2nd Royal Munster Fusiliers in support was forced to advance above ground because the trenches near Le Rutoire were choked with dead and wounded. As a result the Battalion suffered massive casualties. The whole attack ground to a halt.

Green's Force made another frontal assault, but failed to break the weakened German garrison. 1st Gloucestershire (3rd Brigade) attached to 2nd Brigade was ordered to outflank the opposition by approaching through 15th Division's area to the south, while other elements of 3rd Brigade assisted 1st Brigade in holding its gains on the Lens – La Bassée road. Around 1.15 p.m., HQ 1st Division decided to hold most of the front with a screen while the remaining men in 2nd Brigade shifted south to exploit 15th Division's success. The Germans in that area were almost surrounded and threatened from the rear, resulting in 400 of them opposite 2nd Brigade surrendering. 2nd Brigade and Green's Force, by then only 1,500 strong, swept forward to secure the enemy trenches at 3.40 p.m. They reached the Lens – La Bassée road north of Chalk Pit Wood at 5.20 p.m., where they were in contact with 15th Division.

By nightfall, 2nd Brigade was in touch with 15th Division on the right and 1st Brigade was in touch with 7th Division (I Corps) on the left, but there was a gap of 1,350m between them. There were insufficient men left within 1st Division to fill the gap due to the heavy losses. In any case the extent of the gap was not appreciated by the divisional staff; it would have serious implications next day.

At the southern end of I Corps, 7th Division attacked between the Vermelles – Hulluch road and the Hohenzollern Redoubt, with the objective of advancing to the enemy second position between Hulluch and Cité St Elie. The Germans here were well dug in and the preparatory bombardment was largely ineffective. The assault was carried out by 22nd Brigade on the left and 20th Brigade on the right, with 21st Brigade in reserve. As 20th Brigade struggled forward, many men ripped off their

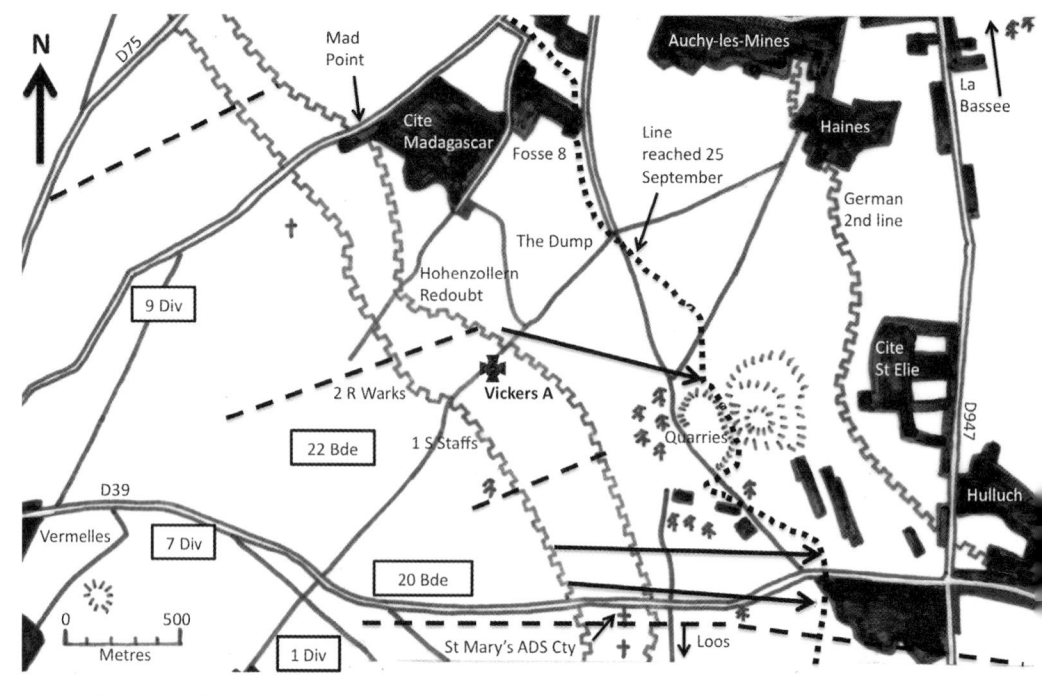

In Auchy-les-Mines drive southeast along the D163 towards Haisnes. Where the road swings left/east, turn right, signed for the cemetery. Follow this road for 1,100m southwards. Just after the Dump, on the right is a right turn onto a rough track. Park here and walk almost 1,100m along this track to the southwest. Turn round and look back. You are on the British front line on the axis of 2nd Royal Warwickshire's attack. The large thicket on the left is the Hohenzollern Redoubt. Retrace your steps for 400m. This is where the German front line ran from the Hohenzollern Redoubt and crossed the track.

gas helmets to breath and were gassed. Heavy losses were incurred from German shelling and machine-guns caused more casualties. The wire was only partially cleared, but the German front line was crossed towards Gun Trench and Hulluch and the support battalions came up. Another attack was halted by heavy fire.

22nd Brigade's attack at 6.30 a.m. was made by 2nd Royal Warwickshire on the left and 1st South Staffordshire on the right. Before the assault, both battalions were badly affected by gas. Smoke covered the advance but, firing blind, the German

From the centre of 2nd Royal Warwickshire's front line looking towards the German positions. The Hohenzollern Redoubt is the scrubby area on the left. The Dump is right of centre with Haines beyond in the distance. Arthur Vickers cut through the wire to the right of the track in the foreground, in line with the double topped pylon in front of the Dump.

artillery still caused many casualties. As the attackers emerged from the smoke, they found themselves 30m from a belt of uncut wire hidden in long grass. They were met by very heavy small arms fire. Undeterred, the leading battalions literally threw themselves into the wire and crawled over it. **Private Arthur Vickers** in 2nd Royal Warwickshire dashed forward in full view of the enemy. Standing upright, he cut two paths through the wire. Miraculously he was not hit and due to his heroism, and others like him, the enemy front and support lines were taken by 7.30 a.m.

By 8.45 a.m., 22nd Brigade had crossed the Loos – La Bassée Road south of the Vermelles – Hulluch road. There it caused heavy losses to German reinforcements moving into Cité St Elie. The Quarries were captured around 9.30 a.m. and patrols reached the edge of Cité St Elie, but further advance was not possible without support. 21st Brigade moving up from reserve was stopped by uncut wire in front of Hulluch and the positions captured previously by 22nd Brigade were consolidated. The cost had been horrific; at the end of the day, 2nd Royal Warwickshire was officerless and only 140 men remained of the 648 who had gone into action.

9th Division faced the formidable Hohenzollern Redoubt and Fosse 8. 26th Brigade advanced through well-cut wire to take the front face of the Redoubt. Fosse Trench at the rear of the Redoubt fell just after 7.00 a.m. The troops pressed on towards Fosse 8 and after thirty minutes were in Corons Trench, where they reorganised. South of the Dump, the German second line at Pekin Trench was reached at 8.05 a.m., but these troops were 900m ahead of those consolidating the Redoubt. 27th Brigade was ordered to move up in support, but encountered numerous problems and suffered casualties on the way. In 28th Brigade's area on the left, the gas drifted behind the front line and gave no cover as the men crossed no man's land. German artillery also hit the front line when it was packed with men. Some gas cylinders were destroyed, releasing more gas into the trenches. The wire was uncut and the survivors were forced to seek whatever cover was available. At 12.15 p.m., the attack was renewed, but the bombardment was too weak and the troops lost heavily again; most did not even reach the German wire. Further attacks were halted at 1.30 p.m. and the survivors reorganised to defend their original line.

Despite heavy casualties and checks in some places, I Corps' 7th and 9th Divisions had performed well. The advance had broken into the German defences in some areas and the timely commitment of a fresh division had every chance of breaching the German second position. If advantage was to be taken of this situation, the reserve division needed to be moving as early as 9.00 a.m.; but it was not until 1.00 p.m. that 73rd Brigade of 24th Division was ordered to reinforce Fosse 8. It was too late. During the afternoon, Pekin Trench came under heavy shellfire and the Germans bombed from the Haisnes – Auchy road southwards while others worked north from Cité Trench. By 5.00 p.m. half the position had been lost and the survivors were ordered to withdraw after dark.

2nd Division was to create a protective flank. 5th Brigade made a subsidiary attack to the north of the La Bassée Canal at 6 a.m. It failed, but did succeed in diverting some attention from the main attack. South of the Canal, 6th Brigade was on the left and 19th Brigade on the right. Ten minutes before zero hour, two large mines were blown by 173 Tunnelling Company RE opposite 19th Brigade. When the attack came, the enemy was fully alert. The gas blew back into the British trenches causing casualties. As the infantry advanced, they bunched to avoid the craters and these choke points were the targets for concentrated machine-gun fire. The Germans were seen standing on their parapet to take advantage of such easy targets. By 9.00 a.m. it was clear that no progress was going to be made and orders came to withdraw to the original front line.

The ground in front of 6th Brigade had already been devastated by mine craters. A Royal Engineers officer believed the wind conditions were unsuitable for gas to be released and refused to take responsibility. Brigade HQ ordered him to continue, but the release was delayed by ten minutes. Two mines exploded by 170 Tunnelling Company RE added to the confusion. 2nd South Staffordshire was the left assault battalion from the Canal to Ridley Walk, which included the Brickstacks area. 1st King's was on the right. When the gas was released there was almost no wind and it hung over the British trenches, giving the Germans time to light fires on their parapets to disperse any poisonous fumes that reached them.

The leading waves of 1st King's found the wire uncut and the advance petered out at the far lip of the new craters. 2nd South Staffordshire's area was also badly cut up by mine craters and the gas cloud was so concentrated that it incapacitated 130 men before the advance began. A and B Companies on the right faced the Brickstacks, while C Company on the left had the task of rushing Embankment Redoubt. Despite every man being affected by gas, the attack commenced on time. The craters channelled the attackers into predictable approaches. A and B Companies were halted almost immediately on the edge of a crater by murderous machine-gun fire. C Company was hit from both sides of the Canal, but managed to reach the enemy wire led by **Captain Arthur Kilby**. He was hit in the hand as soon as the attack began and on reaching the wire his foot was blown off. Although he was unable to move, he continued to encourage his men and returned the enemy fire with a rifle. After the attack, there were only twenty men left in C Company.

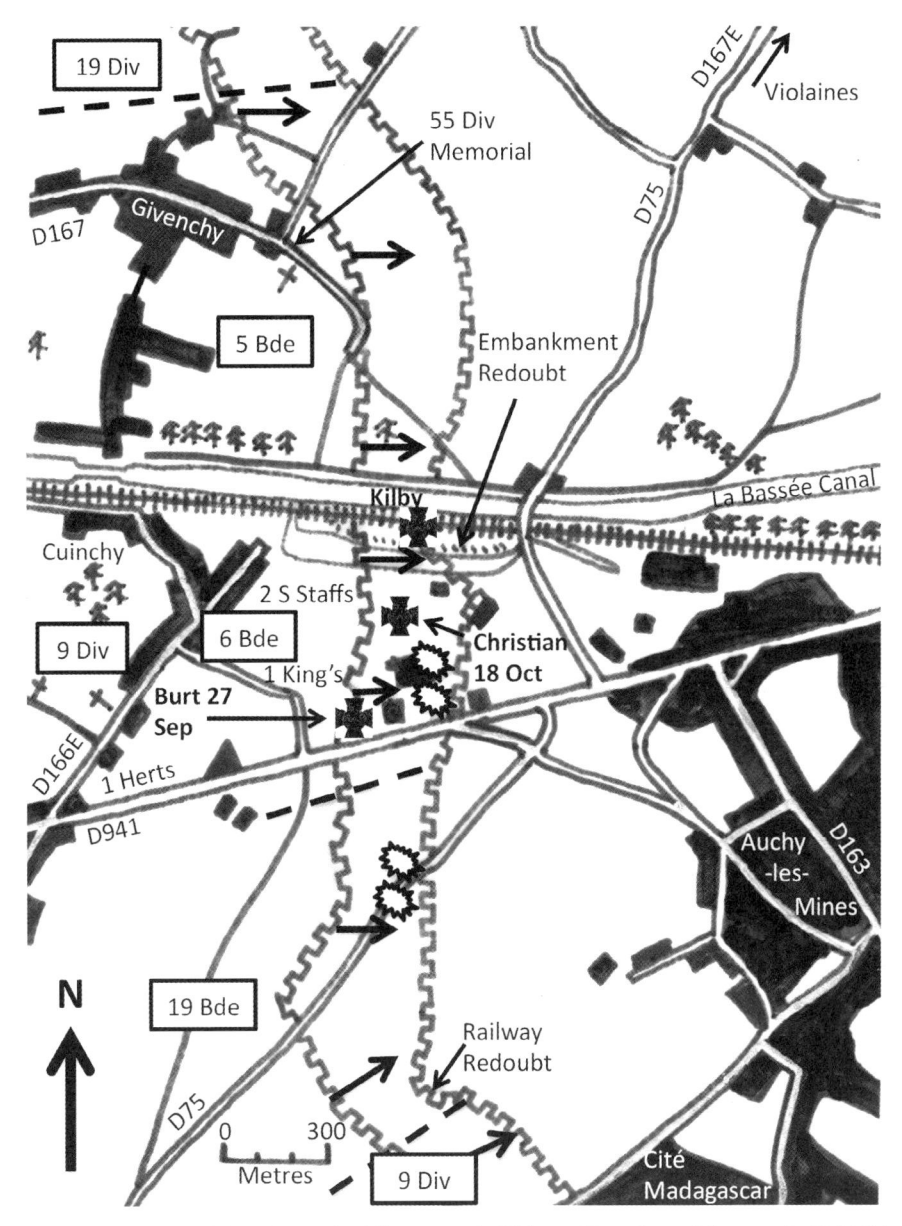

Drive west along the N41 from Auchy-les-Mines towards Béthune. Turn sharp right onto the D166E into Cuinchy and continue one kilometre until the road runs out. There is a railway embankment in front and the La Bassée Canal is just beyond it, out of sight. On the right, across the reservoir, is Embankment Redoubt where Arthur Kilby won his VC on 25th September 1915 and where he lay buried until 1929. It is not recommended trying to get onto the Redoubt. Look further right, i.e. south of the reservoir, where there is a glider tower. To the right of it is where Alfred Burt's (27th September) and Harry Christian's (18th October) VC actions took place. It is on the site of a disused post-WW1 power station, itself on the site of the Brickstacks. The area is walled/fenced off and contains lots of post-industrial dangers. The landscape has been altered completely since WW1 and it is completely overgrown in places. It is not worth going inside.

A good view of the Redoubt can be gained from the other side of the Canal. Cross the La Bassée Canal on the D166 Cuinchy – Festubert road. 550m after the Canal turn right onto the D167 into Givenchy-les-la-Bassée. Go through the village, passing the church on the right. At the 55th Division Memorial turn right and park at the village cemetery. Continue on foot and follow the track round to the right/south until reaching the canal towpath. In front is the culvert under the railway leading to the old power station reservoir. It is in the same place as in 1915 and featured in Michael O'Leary's VC action earlier in 1915 (see *Victoria Crosses on the Western Front, August 1914–April 1915, Mons to Hill 60*). Left of the culvert and beyond the railway is the higher ground where Embankment Redoubt was located in 1915.

The Battalion withdrew at 8 a.m. to allow for another bombardment prior to a second assault. This attack was clearly not going to achieve anything and was cancelled later. Around midday the Battalion was relieved by 1st Royal Berkshire. By 9.45 a.m. all efforts to move forward by 2nd Division had come to an end.

After dark volunteers went into no man's land to recover the wounded, but Kilby was not found, although some of his men searched for the next two nights. A few days later the Germans displayed a wreath of flowers above their parapet bearing the inscription, *For King and Fatherland. In memory of Captain Kilby, Williams and 13 men of the South Staffords, who died as heroes.* Lieutenant David Marmaduke Williams had accompanied Kilby during the action and charged to within 20m of the German trenches before he was shot down (Cabaret-Rouge British Cemetery, Souchez – XVI K 5). The Germans also placed a cross over Kilby's grave on the towpath near the Redoubt inscribed *The Kilby family may think of their son with pride, as we remember him with respect.* His remains were not rediscovered until 1929. Kilby had already been noted for his work on a very dangerous reconnaissance of the enemy positions along the Canal towpath on the night of 5th/6th September, during which he was accompanied by Lieutenant Thompson of 1st King's.

From the north bank of the La Bassée Canal looking across to Embankment Redoubt beyond the railway line. The bridge on the far left carries the D65 Auchy – Violaines road.

Initial reports had been optimistic and by 8.45 a.m. all the Corps' reserves had been committed. Haig asked Sir John French to release XI Corps to maintain the advance. French issued the orders to move forward at 9.30 a.m., but did not immediately place XI Corps at First Army's disposal. Meanwhile, First Army ordered 3rd Cavalry Division forward to Corons de Rutoire in readiness to move forward as soon as Cité St Auguste fell. XI Corps was still far to the rear when it received the order. 21st and 24th Divisions commenced the march at 11.15 a.m., but the roads were choked with traffic and progress was slow.

Despite heavy casualties and disappointment over the use of gas, there was some optimism at noon. The enemy line had been broken into in places. 47th and 15th Divisions had captured Loos and there were signs of German withdrawal in panic in Lens. 7th Division had reached the outskirts of Hulluch and 9th Division had made some headway against the immensely strong Hohenzollern Redoubt and Fosse 8. There had been failures elsewhere, but there was everything to play for, provided the reserves arrived in time to take advantage of the situation.

At 2.35 p.m., Haig ordered 21st and 24th Divisions to push forward between Hulluch and Cité St Auguste to secure passages over the Haute Deûle Canal. These

Divisions had no indication that the enemy had not been defeated and was broken and retreating. The orders did not reach the forward brigades until 5.00 p.m. and they were still struggling through the congestion at 6 p.m. when they should have been on the start line. Haig was acutely aware of an opportunity slipping away and was forced to deploy the two divisions piecemeal as they arrived to support the units already in action. The advance therefore had to be limited to the line of the Lens – La Bassée road, but this still meant committing two new, untried and exhausted divisions to a night attack in torrential rain and without a clue where the enemy were.

However, by dawn on 26th September some headway had been made. Units of 62nd Brigade (21st Division) had reinforced 15th Division, but not without sustaining heavy casualties. 63rd Brigade (21st Division) on the right reached the Lens – La Bassée road and 64th Brigade was in support north of Loos. On the left of 24th Division, 72nd Brigade (24th Division) was in an old German communications trench east of the Haisnes – Loos road, while 71st Brigade was west of the road.

Elsewhere the line had altered little from the previous afternoon, despite German counterattacks throughout the night. HQ First Army did not have an accurate picture of the situation. It was unaware of the scale of loss or that the Germans had reinforced their positions. Believing there had been a breakthrough south of Hulluch, plans were made to continue the offensive. Haig sent out orders at 11.30 p.m. for a general attack for 11 a.m. along the whole front from Hill 70 to Cité St Elie. The main assault was to be made by 21st and 24th Divisions against the German second position in the centre, while 15th and 1st Divisions secured the right and left flanks respectively.

A preliminary attack at 9 a.m. to capture Hill 70 and secure the right flank for the main assault by 45th and 62nd Brigades was a shambles. Units were still split up

From the D947 Lens (left) to Hulluch (right) road looking east. Hill 70 is on the left with the Double Crassier beyond. Loos is on the right with the Grenay Spur rising above it. The mine dumps at Grenay are in the far distance. The initial attack by 15th Division on 25th September came over Grenay Spur through the village towards the camera position. The preliminary attack by elements of 45th and 62nd Brigades on the morning of the 26th headed for Hill 70 and towards the camera. The open ground beyond the D947 is where Robert Dunsire carried out two daring rescues of wounded men.

110 Victoria Crosses on the Western Front April 1915–June 1916

and disorganised from the previous day's fighting. Many men were not briefed until the last minute and the artillery preparation was hopelessly inadequate. The outer perimeter trench of Hill 70 Redoubt was taken, but little else was achieved and the Keep defied all efforts to take it.

6th Cameron Highlanders was on the extreme left flank of this attack, its objective being the western end of Chalet Wood. The CO, **Lieutenant Colonel Angus Douglas-Hamilton,** led his men forward. Having been repulsed in the initial assault, he attacked three more times. There was desperate hand-to-hand fighting in Chalet Wood and each attack was made with fewer and fewer men. Leading fifty men in the final attack at 10.30 a.m., Douglas-Hamilton was hit and fell. Two officers bandaged his wounds, but he still attempted to press on with the attack. He died about twenty minutes later with the words, *I must get up*. Despite being unable to take Chalet Wood, the survivors hung on that night and, when they were relieved next morning, marched out of the line only 130 strong.

The previous evening 13th Royal Scots had gone forward to take part in an attack that was subsequently cancelled. During the night, the companies filled gaps in the line at Hill 70 and on the Lens – La Bassée road. However, by morning they had been regrouped to take part in the preliminary attack at 8.30 a.m. The Battalion was on the left of 45th Brigade, with its right on the sunken road leading to Loos. 11th Argyll & Sutherland Highlanders was in the centre and 7th Royal Scots Fusiliers was on the right. 13th Royal Scots had A, B and C Companies in line with D Company in reserve. Having been shelled by the British artillery

Drive north on the D947 from Hill 70 towards Hulluch. 700m north of the Hill 70 roundabout there is a pull-in on the right where you can stop for a short time. The picture looks north along the D947 towards Hulluch. The trees to the left of the road are at Puits 14 bis and the road was the line reached on 25th September. On 26th September, 6th Cameron Highlanders attacked across it to the right into Chalet Wood, which now has a crematorium at its western end. This is where Angus Douglas-Hamilton led repeated attacks and was finally killed. His remains may still be there.

From the same parking position below Hill 70 as for Frederick Johnson, looking north. 13th Royal Scots attacked from the low ground on the left across this field towards the top of Hill 70 just out of view on the right.

before the attack, B Company was unable to take part at all. A Company ran into uncut wire and was forced back to its own trenches. C Company hardly got out of its trenches before being forced back by machine-gun fire. D Company and the Battalion machine-guns were sent to assist on the right flank, where a breakthrough was threatened. An attempt by a platoon to take Chalet Wood after the failure of the 6th Cameron Highlanders attack also ended in disaster. The Battalion suffered 325 casualties in this fiasco.

From Hill 70, return towards Loos and after 850m turn sharp right. Pass the school on the right and after 600m turn left into a 30 kph zone. There are places to turn and park for a short time on the left. Look east and tracking from left to right you will see an area of scrubby bushes where Chalk Pit Wood used to stand, then the old industrial buildings at Puits 14 bis, the crematorium at the western end of Chalet Wood and finally Hill 70 on the right. This picture looks along the axis of 13th Royal Scots' attack towards the top of Hill 70 to the left of the prominent white house. Robert Dunsire made his rescues in the field in front of it.

After the failure of the attack **Private Robert Dunsire** in D Company saw a wounded man moving in no man's land. The area was swept by heavy fire, but he left the cover of his trench and went to the rescue. Having brought the man to safety, Dunsire heard another man shout for assistance and went out to rescue him as well. Bullets constantly kicked up the ground around him, but he returned unhurt.

At 11.00 a.m. a heavy German bombardment fell on the forward positions. Almost leaderless, the exhausted troops of 21st Division began falling back on Loos village, leaving 45th Brigade's left flank exposed. By 3.30 p.m. a general retirement from Hill 70 was in progress due to confused orders, while other units were still moving to reinforce the Hill. How this came about has never been resolved satisfactorily. A counterattack against Loos Crassier was held by 1/20th London. By 8.00 p.m., 3rd Dragoon Guards and 1st Royal Dragoons of 6th Cavalry Brigade had rallied the remnants of 45th and 46th Brigades retiring from Loos and re-established the position on the lower slopes of Hill 70.

Further north in the early hours of 26th September, the Germans retook the Quarries, but were held at Fosse 8. A hastily arranged counterattack to retake the Quarries at 6.45 a.m. failed. At 10.50 a.m., orders reached units of 21st (right) and 24th (left) Divisions to attack without specific objectives. The troops were exhausted and because of piecemeal deployments overnight the available force had been reduced from twenty-four to just six battalions.

72nd Brigade in 24th Division attacked on time and in good order with two battalions of 71st Brigade in support (11th Essex on the left and 9th Suffolk on the right). The objective was a 900m section of the German second line between Stutzpunkts III and IV, southeast of Hulluch. This advance steadied the retreating 63rd Brigade in 21st Division and, although terribly disorganised, it turned and joined the attack. However, a short time later it lost direction and moved towards Hill 70, exposing it to fire from Chalet Wood and Bois Hugo. It began to withdraw again. 72nd Brigade came under enfilade and frontal fire and some British shells fell short. Only a thin line reached the virtually undamaged German wire about 1.00 p.m. The survivors took cover in long grass but, as they tried to retire, many were hit by machine-gun fire. By midday, 1st Division's attack against Hulluch had also failed, leaving 24th Division with both flanks unprotected and engaged on three sides.

The order to attack had reached 9th Suffolk very late and consequently the men set off with little time for briefing or orientation. At 11.25 a.m. 71st Brigade's units began to move forward to assist 72nd Brigade. Despite the problems on the flanks, by

Looking north along the D947 with Hulluch on the right of the road. Arthur Saunders' VC action was in the field left of the road. On the far right the line of bushes is approximately on the German second position.

1 p.m. the leading battalions of 72nd Brigade were within 50m of the enemy trenches, but could progress no further because of a thick belt of uncut wire. Meanwhile 71st Brigade had been halted 150–200m beyond the Lens – La Bassée road.

The battle raged on into the late afternoon and, although the centre held, the flanks eventually gave way, having retired and advanced twice in the meantime. At about 7 p.m., a steady and orderly retirement began to the old German front line, with some 500 men remaining to cover the withdrawal. **Sergeant Arthur Saunders** had advanced with 9th Suffolks. When his officer was wounded he took command of two machine-guns and kept up with the battalion in front, giving every assistance despite a serious thigh wound. When the retreat began, Saunders picked up one of his Lewis Guns and crawled to where Lieutenant AFP Christison (6th Cameron Highlanders) was taking cover in a shell-hole with another Lewis Gun. Saunders made to crawl to another shell hole when a shell almost blew off his left leg below the knee. Christison dressed and applied a tourniquet to the wound and gave Saunders his water bottle. A few minutes later they saw about 150 Germans advancing and both opened fire causing many casualties. The attack was broken up, enabling the rest of the troops in the area to withdraw and occupy the old German second line against possible counterattacks.

During the night the Guards Division relieved the battered 21st and 24th Divisions. Christison and Saunders were eventually picked up by Scots Guards stretcher-bearers and evacuated. Saunders' leg was very badly shattered, but was saved from amputation. Christison also survived, ending his military career as Lieutenant General Sir AFP Christison Bt KBE CB DSO MC.

Men straggling rearward were eventually brought under control in the old British and German front lines. Sir John French finally placed the Guards Division under First Army to restore the situation. By nightfall the remnants of 15th, 21st and 24th Divisions were being relieved by 3rd Cavalry and Guards Divisions. HQ First Army issued orders at 11.30 p.m. to consolidate the line held, while a new reserve was created and plans were made to recapture Hill 70.

27th–28th September 1915

96 Cpl James Pollock, 5th Battalion, The Cameron Highlanders (26th Brigade, 9th Division) Hohenzollern Redoubt, France
97 Cpl Alfred Burt, 1st Battalion, The Hertfordshire Regiment (6th Brigade, 2nd Division) Cuinchy, France
98 2Lt Alexander Turner, 3rd (att'd 1st) Battalion, The Royal Berkshire Regiment (6th Brigade, 2nd Division) Fosse 8, near Vermelles, France

By 27th September the impetus of the British offensive at Loos had been lost. The Germans had retaken Hill 70 and efforts by the British to retake the Quarries were unsuccessful. However, the Guards Division, Cavalry Corps and Carter Force had

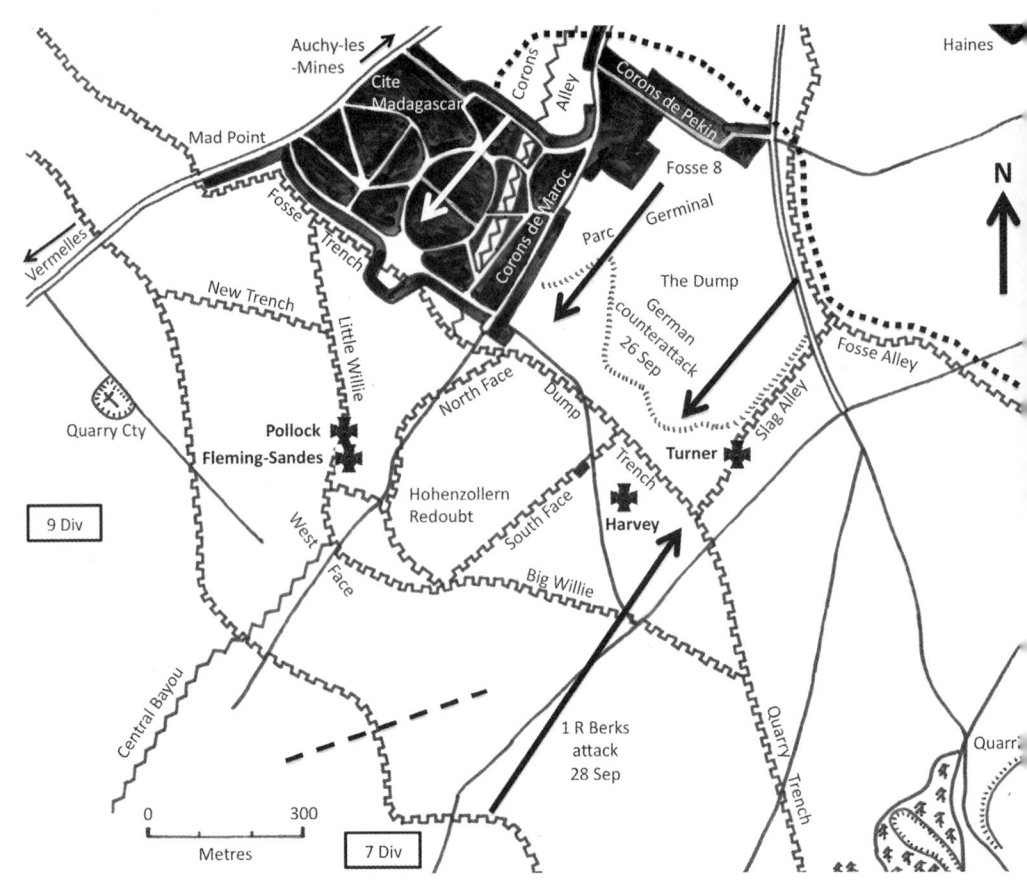

Drive southeast on the main road through Auchy-les-Mines, where there are a number of cafes and shops. At the 'Flash' café turn right signed 'Cite de 8' on a minor road. After 500m turn left signed 'Cite de 8' and follow round to the right. Go straight on for 800m, until the buildings run out and there is a farm on the left fronted by four prominent poplars. Park close into the edge here. Sometimes there is an interesting collection of unexploded ordnance under these trees; look but leave well alone. The 46th Division Memorial is a few metres along the track to the southwest on the left. The scrub covered rise either side of the track in front marks the Hohenzollern Redoubt. Walk along the track for 700m to beyond the overhead power lines and turn round. You are approximately on the British front line on 25th September 1915. Little Willie hugged the slightly higher ground on the left, heading north towards the first buildings of Cite Madagascar (Mad Point). This mound was formed by post-war dumping, but the slight rise upon which it sits was still a significant position in the trench lines. This is where James Pollock, Alfred Fleming-Sandes and Charles Vickers won their VCs. Right of the track, the undergrowth is much thicker and it can be very close and claustrophobic. This is where some of the mine craters can be seen, but it takes a little determination.

managed to stabilise the front, except at Fosse 8 where the beleaguered garrison was without food and water for two days.

At dawn on the 27th, the Germans bombarded the British trenches east of the Dump and shortly afterwards launched a feint attack against Stone Alley, southwest of Cité St Elie. Between 600 and 1,000 Germans rushed the Dump and forced the defenders back to the eastern face of the Hohenzollern Redoubt. The situation was confused, with units intermingled and soldiers separated from their leaders. The Germans maintained constant pressure by bombarding the position and sniping from the Dump and the Corons. They also worked their way around either side

Loos 115

The iron harvest of unexploded shells, mortar bombs and barbed wire pickets in the farmyard near the Hohenzollern Redoubt.

The 46th Division Memorial near the Hohenzollern Redoubt.

of the Redoubt with strong bombing parties fighting along North Face and South Face. However, the main threat was from Little Willie Trench north of the Redoubt, where British bombers only just held the German bombers from behind barricades. The situation was critical; if Little Willie Trench fell, the rest of the Redoubt would follow. Accordingly, at 8 a.m., 26th Brigade sent 100 men to reinforce 73rd Brigade in the Redoubt, including an officer and thirty men from 5th Cameron Highlanders.

As the German bombers approached the neck of the Redoubt, **Corporal James Pollock** (C Company, 5th Cameron Highlanders) gained permission to try to take

West Face of the Hohenzollern Redoubt from the British front line on 25th September 1915. The Quarries area is in the far right distance. The track leads to Cité Madagascar. Little Willie Trench ran from the base of the grassy mound with the bushy topped tree towards Mad Point, the houses on the extreme left. It was along this section of trench that James Pollock (27th September), Alfred Fleming-Sandes (29th September) and Charles Vickers (15th October) won their VCs.

A closer view along the line of Little Willie.

the enemy in the flank. He and Private Lyon stripped off their equipment and made off, carrying only bombs. Lyon was hit as he left the trench, but Pollock covered 35m of open ground under heavy fire and caught the Germans unaware. He rained bombs down upon them and the survivors abandoned a barricade and fled. Pollock was exposed to enemy fire for an hour and was wounded twice before he took cover in Little Willie. His actions undoubtedly saved the Redoubt.

26th Brigade was ordered to charge Dump Trench at 3 p.m., but had only 600 men available. Advancing from the old British front line, the Brigade immediately ran into trouble and instead of attacking the Dump was forced into the cover of the Redoubt, which by then was severely overcrowded. At midnight 26th Brigade was withdrawn.

Also on the 27th, Haig ordered XI Corps to recapture Hill 70. 2nd Guards Brigade was to attack through Chalk Pit Wood and Bois Hugo to secure the southern edge of Chalet Wood. From there it was to launch the final assault simultaneously with a 3rd Guards Brigade frontal attack from the west. There were two diversionary attacks. In the south, 47th Division renewed its efforts to capture the whole of Chalk Pit Copse, while at Cuinchy in the north 1st King's and 1st Hertfordshire (2nd Division) were to attack if the prospects for success seemed favourable. The latter attack was to be supported by a release of gas between the Canal and the Vermelles – La Basseé road.

From the centre of the old power station site at Auchy-les-Mines in September 1999. This area has since become very overgrown and there are numerous post-industrial hazards, so it is not advisable to try to gain the same view now. In the far left distance is Loos. The prominent poplar trees left of centre are on the D941 Auchy – Cambrin road. Alfred Burt's VC action on 27th September was to the left of these trees. Harry Christian's action on 18th October was beyond and slightly left of the building in the centre foreground. Cuinchy church is just right of the tower in the centre. On the right, over the reservoir is Embankment Redoubt where Arthur Kilby won his VC on 25th September. The railway and Canal are beyond in dead ground. William Mariner's action in May 1915 and Michael O'Leary's in February 1915 were also in this area.

The Guards attack failed to secure Hill 70, although some progress was made. At 4.40 p.m., covered by a smoke screen, 2nd Guards Brigade advanced to Chalk Pit Wood and the Chalk Pit, but a further advance to Puits 14 bis was halted by machine-gun fire from Bois Hugo. During another attack on Puits 14 bis the following afternoon, 2nd Guards Brigade again suffered heavy casualties and was halted. It was during this period that 2nd Lieutenant John Kipling, 2nd Irish Guards, son of Rudyard Kipling, was wounded and listed missing.

On the right, 47th Division was entirely successful in securing Chalk Pit Copse and the line remained there for almost three years. At Cuinchy only half the gas could be released due to the variable wind direction. The Germans lit fires along their parapet to force the small amount of gas that reached it upwards. Half an hour later, at 5.30 p.m., fighting patrols were met by heavy German small arms fire and the attack was cancelled.

Corporal Alfred Burt's company of 1st Hertfordshire had been detailed to take part in this attack. While waiting to go over the top, a minenwerfer bomb landed in the trench. Burt was well aware of its destructive power and could easily have taken cover around a traverse. Instead he put his foot against the bomb, wrenched out the fuse and threw it over the parapet. His quick thinking and courageous action rendered the bomb harmless and saved many lives.

By the end of 27th September the British were clinging on to their few remaining gains. The troops who attacked on the 25th and the reserves thrown in piecemeal thereafter were exhausted. The three vital positions of Fosse 8, the Quarries and Hill 70 had been lost and the French Tenth Army attack had also failed, allowing the Germans to redirect reserves to Loos.

85th Brigade (28th Division), assisted by some other units, was ordered to retake the Dump and Fosse 8 early on the morning of 28th September. The Brigade was held up in the congestion behind the lines and by 6 a.m. only two battalions had made it to the start line, too late to launch the attack. However, at 2.30 a.m., 1st Royal Berkshire (Carter Force – a composite brigade of 2nd Division) did make the attempt. The Battalion had just over 700m to cover over badly cut up and unknown ground. At least two lines of trenches occupied by British troops and two belts of barbed wire had to be negotiated before reaching the start line. Setting off in bright moonlight, the Battalion was spotted by the Germans half way to the objective and came under heavy fire. A, B and part of C Companies and the bombers got to within

In Auchy-les-Mines drive southeast along the D163 towards Haisnes. Where the road swings left/east, turn right, signed for the cemetery. Follow this road for 1,100m southwards. Just after the Dump on the right, is a right turn onto a rough track. Park here and walk 350m along this track to the southwest with the Dump on your right. This view is from where Dump Trench crossed the track. The junction with Slag Alley was about 60m north of the track, about midway between the pylon on the left and the edge of the Dump in the centre of the picture. Slag Alley ran northeast from that junction towards Haines, parallel with the edge of the Dump and the track. Alexander Turner cleared 125m of Slag Alley northeast from the junction with Dump Trench.

60m of the Dump, where they were halted, mainly due to a large German bombing party in Slag Alley. The remainder of C Company and D Company occupied the old British front line.

2nd Lieutenant Alexander Turner volunteered to lead another attack. He set off down Slag Alley, throwing bombs one after another and driving all before him. Although the enemy constantly threw bombs back at him, he cleared 125m of trench in this manner until he was badly wounded by a rifle bullet in the abdomen. The CO had been wounded and the Second in Command killed, so Captain Frizeyell, commanding D Company, assumed command and launched another attack. This swept half way up the Dump before being driven back by bombers. The withdrawal to the British front line, about 125m behind, was carried out with little loss due to Turner's determined action, which relieved pressure on the right flank in Slag Alley. At daylight the Battalion was back in the old British trenches, having suffered 289 casualties. Turner was helped back to the dressing station and was eventually taken to No.1 Casualty Clearing Station at Chocques, where he died on 1st October.

During the 28th it was agreed that the French Tenth Army would relieve 47th Division to enable the British First Army to create a reserve. First Army would then secure Hill 70, following which the French would extend their front to the left to include this position. Having achieved that, the British would continue the offensive towards Pont à Vendin. 12th and 46th Divisions from the Ypres area were sent to replace the exhausted 21st and 24th Divisions. Preparations for the renewal of the offensive were almost as elaborate as those for 25th September.

Photo labels: Slag Alley, Haines

29th September 1915

> 99 2Lt Alfred Fleming-Sandes, 2nd Battalion, The East Surrey Regiment (85th Brigade, 28th Division) Hohenzollern Redoubt, France
>
> 100 Private Samuel Harvey, 1st Battalion, The York and Lancaster Regiment (83rd Brigade, 28th Division) Hohenzollern Redoubt, France

While plans were being developed to renew the Loos offensive, a number of small operations were carried out to recapture the Dump and Fosse 8; all failed. Meanwhile the Germans battered away incessantly at the Hohenzollern Redoubt, gaining footholds in Big Willie and Little Willie trenches.

At 1.30 p.m. on 27th September, two companies of 2nd East Kent and 3rd Royal Fusiliers in 85th Brigade set off to make good the Hohenzollern Redoubt, prior to an attack by the whole Brigade to take Fosse Trench and Dump Trench. The rest of 85th Brigade followed. When the 2nd East Kent companies arrived they found the Redoubt choked with men of 26th, 27th and 73rd Brigades.

2nd East Surrey did not reach Brigade HQ, 450m southwest of the Hohenzollern Redoubt, until 7.30 p.m., due to congestion in the trenches caused mainly by wounded being brought back. The Battalion was ordered to take over the line from New Trench to the old British line, clear up the situation there and then attack Little Willie. It struggled forward under heavy shellfire along Central Bayou communication trench and by 1.30 a.m. on 28th September was in position. A Company was in the northwest of the Redoubt, while B Company held New Trench, connecting the old British front line with Little Willie. C and D Companies remained in the old British front line trench from where the 25th September offensive had been launched. 3rd Royal Fusiliers was on the right.

The previous evening, HQ 28th Division had ordered Corons Alley and Corons de Maroc to be retaken. The attack was due to be launched by 2nd East Kent and

3rd Middlesex at 5 a.m., but it had to be postponed until 9.30 a.m. because the troops were still moving forward. Meanwhile the two forward battalions probed ahead. 3rd Royal Fusiliers in Big Willie bombed along North Face and South Face to the junctions with Dump Trench and at 6.30 a.m. took over Dump Trench. A Company, 2nd East Surrey advanced along Little Willie but, having reached the end of the Redoubt, was halted by German bombers. B Company attempted to get into Little Willie from New Trench, but was halted by a barricade. There was a lull in the fighting after 9 a.m. when 2nd East Surrey ran out of bombs.

At 9.30 a.m., 2nd East Kent and 3rd Middlesex attacked after a short artillery barrage. 3rd Middlesex advanced through D Company, 2nd East Surrey, to reinforce 2nd East Kent in the right of the Redoubt. The casualties from this advance choked the already crowded Central Bayou. Some progress was made initially, but the attacking battalions were forced to withdraw to South Face in mid-afternoon. As they withdrew the Germans counterattacked into Dump Trench. Throughout the rest of the day the Germans maintained the pressure, but during the night it was comparatively quiet and consolidation work was carried out with the sappers.

At 6.30 p.m. 2nd East Surrey was ordered to bomb the enemy out of Little Willie and consolidate on the line New Trench – Little Willie – Redoubt. At the same time 3rd Royal Fusiliers was to bomb up North Face and South Face to reach Dump Trench between the two. Meanwhile 3rd Middlesex was to hold Big Willie from the Hohenzollern Redoubt until gaining touch with 22nd Brigade (7th Division) on the right. 2nd East Kent was to hold Dump Trench from the junction with South Face

From the farm at the southern edge of Cité Madagascar, walk back towards Auchy-les-Mines for 70m. Turn right along a track. After 20m, on the left is the entrance to Parc Germinal, which is the landscaped part of the Dump. For those feeling energetic and determined it is possible to reach the top of the Dump on the southwest side, but it is difficult. Once through the gate, follow tracks and your nose in a generally southeasterly direction. After a while you have to commit to pushing through the trees on the right. If you get it right you will emerge onto a sunken trackway with a locked gate on the right. Turn left and get as far as you can along the trackway, then push up the slope half right in a generally southerly direction. From the top you can see over the site of Dump Trench, Big Willie and all the way to Loos. It is hard work, particularly through the summer growth, but it amply rewards the effort.

This view is from the top of the Dump with the Quarries on the extreme left, the Double Crassiers at Loos in the centre and the Hohenzollern Redoubt beyond the trees on the extreme right. Sam Harvey brought up the grenade boxes towards you from the rough direction of the Double Crassier on 29th September 1915. Oliver Brooks' VC action in clearing Big Willie on 8th October 1915 took place under the power lines.

to the junction with Big Willie. Overnight it became clear that offensive action was going to be limited by the inadequate supply of bombs.

The situation early on 29th September found 2nd East Surrey in New Trench and a small portion of Little Willie north and south of it, with its supports in the old British front line. 3rd Royal Fusiliers held the Redoubt and had bombed up a portion of both North and South Faces. 2nd East Kent was in Big Willie to the right of 3rd Royal Fusiliers and 3rd Middlesex continued the line in Big Willie to Quarry Trench in touch with 7th Division.

Heavy fighting broke out again at the Redoubt at 8.30 a.m. when enemy bombers, supported by artillery, attacked 2nd East Surrey. Fighting in A Company's area went on all morning, with neither side gaining advantage. At 1 p.m. the Germans gained the upper hand when 2nd East Surrey ran short of bombs and was forced to retire to a barricade just inside the Redoubt. After one attempt to regain the lost section had failed, a line was established in a communications trench at right angles to Little Willie. From there 2nd East Surrey was able to enfilade the advancing Germans and halt them, but the position was exposed and many casualties were sustained. Soon afterwards the right of the Redoubt began to give way and the centre of the position was also unsteady.

At this critical moment, **2nd Lieutenant Alfred Fleming-Sandes** arrived with a supply of bombs from the rear. As the unit on the right began to give way, the men around Fleming-Sandes wanted to pull back. He rallied them and then left the cover of the trench with a bag of grenades. He caught the enemy in Little Willie unawares and bombed them from the parapet in full view of their machine-gunners. His right arm was broken by a rifle bullet, but he continued to throw bombs with his left until he was shot in the face. His decisive action drove the Germans back and saved the left of the Redoubt. With the right flank in the air, two platoons of D Company were sent up in support. The Battalion held on throughout the 30th without losing any ground and was relieved on the morning of 1st October.

While Fleming-Sandes was saving the left of the Redoubt, 1st York and Lancaster (83rd Brigade) was securing the right. The Battalion had been called forward on the morning of 28th September to hold the Redoubt, but failed to reach it due to the congestion in Central Bayou. After dark, A and B Companies went forward and reached the Redoubt about 5 a.m. on the 29th. They pushed down Big Willie to relieve 2nd East Kent about 10.00 a.m. and held Dump Trench from South Face to the junction with Big Willie. C and D Companies remained in the old British trenches.

On arrival in Dump Trench, the leading elements of A Company found 2nd East Kent severely weakened. The defences on the right of the Redoubt were crumbling and the enemy was in possession of much of the Trench. The Germans saw the relief taking place from the top of the Dump and their bombers attacked along every possible approach. A Company's bombers were at the back and, due to the congestion in the trenches, could not get forward. The situation was desperate, with the enemy on the verge of overrunning the position.

Seeing what was happening, Captain Buckley led B Company's bombers over the top and delivered a crushing counterattack. At about the same time, A Company and the remnants of 2nd East Kent hurled themselves at the Germans in a desperate bayonet charge. The counterattack threw the Germans back and also succeeded in capturing another portion of Dump Trench, but the cost was enormous. In A Company only the Sergeant Major and twenty-two men were left standing at the end of the day.

At one point during this attack bombs were urgently needed to keep up the momentum and **Private Samuel Harvey** volunteered to fetch some. He tried to get back along the communication trench, but found it impossible to press through the mass of dead, wounded and reinforcements. He therefore resorted to making

If you do not want to take the energetic option, continue along the track southeast from the entrance to Parc Germinal for 225m. Where it swings right, almost due south is where Dump Trench crossed the track. The picture is taken from this point with the Dump on the extreme left, the Quarries in the centre distance and the Double Crassier above the track on the right. Sam Harvey crossed the field in front from right to left to bring up the grenade boxes.

frequent trips over the open and managed to bring up thirty boxes of grenades under intense fire before being wounded in the head.

For the rest of the day the Germans probed for weak spots and at one time a strong bombing party made progress down Big Willie. B Company, assisted by 2nd East Yorkshire's bombers, fought them back bay-by-bay for over six hours. The situation was restored when D Company eventually came up and took the Germans in the rear.

After the furious activity of the 29th, the next day was much quieter and that night 84th Brigade began relieving 85th Brigade. Fighting continued throughout 1st and 2nd October and in the early hours of the 3rd, the Redoubt was lost. However, the British managed to hold on to Big Willie. Haig was so worried about the situation there that he cancelled the renewal of the offensive set for 6th October and instead ordered attacks against Fosse 8, the Hohenzollern Redoubt and the Quarries.

8th October 1915

> 101 LSgt Oliver Brooks, 3rd Battalion, Coldstream Guards (1st (Guards) Brigade, Guards Division) Big Willie Trench, Hohenzollern Redoubt, France

On 30th September, the French offensive in Champagne came to an end, but Haig intended renewing the Loos offensive on 4th October. Preparations were almost as elaborate as for 25th September, with advanced trenches being dug and hundreds of gas cylinders manhandled into the front line. The French began to relieve British units on the right flank, but were two days late due to bad weather and traffic congestion. By 3rd October, the Hohenzollern Redoubt had been lost except for Big Willie Trench. The offensive was delayed to allow time for preparatory attacks on Fosse 8 and Hill 70.

On 8th October, the arrangements were interrupted by a German counter-offensive. German artillery bombarded the whole Loos front between the La Bassée Canal and Lens for about three hours. At 4.00 p.m. the infantry attacked. On the right the shelling failed to damage the French wire and the attack was halted. Despite heavy casualties, 1st Division's machine-guns stopped the attack within 40m of the front line between the Loos – Puits 14 bis track and the Chalk Pit.

However, further north, in the area of the Hohenzollern Redoubt, the situation was more serious. The Germans had previously dug saps around the last 100m of Big Willie, thereby isolating it into a narrow salient. At 4 p.m., German bombers attacked from the Quarries and Fosse 8 against Quarry Trench and Big Willie, with the intention of bombing north and south simultaneously to meet in the middle. A three-sided attack developed on Big Willie Trench in the area of the Le Rutoire – Haisnes track.

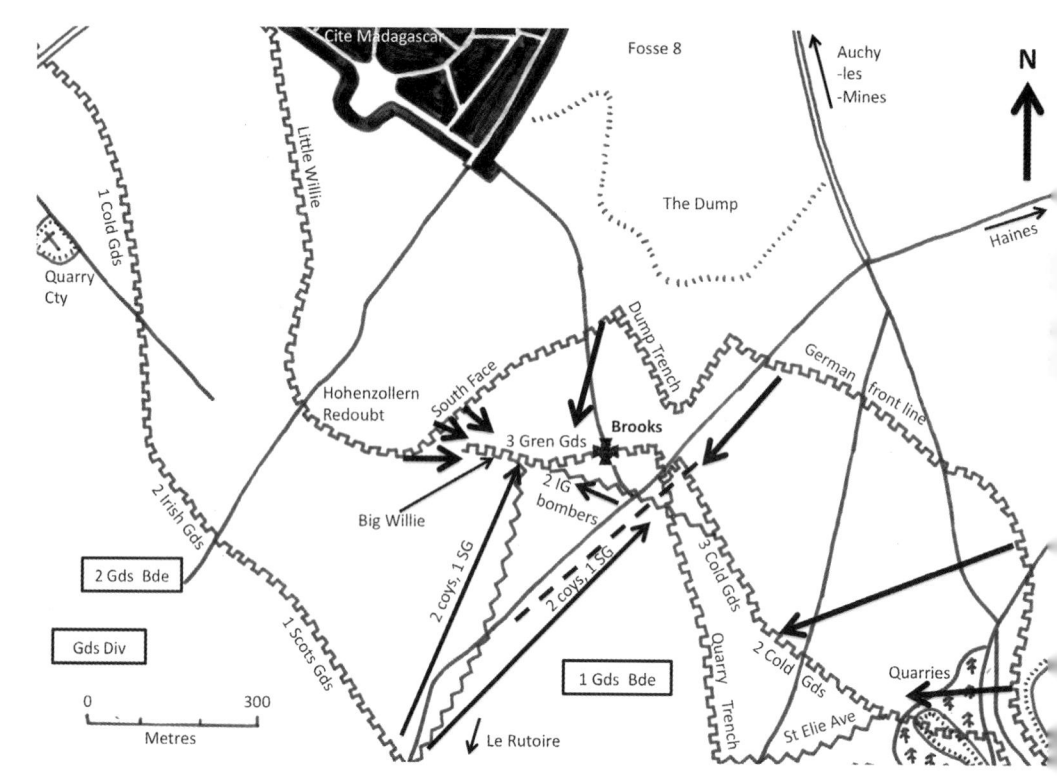

From the farm at the southern edge of Cité Madagascar, walk back towards Auchy-les-Mines for 70m. Turn right along a track and continue southeast for 250m. The track swings right, almost due south. Continue 300m to the T-junction. Turn left for 150m then turn round. This is where Big Willie crossed the track and headed towards the southern edge of the Hohenzollern Redoubt.

The front here was held by 1st (Guards) Brigade, with 2nd Coldstream Guards on the right and 3rd Coldstream Guards on the left. 2nd Coldstream Guards was attacked about 4 p.m. A saphead at the end of St Elie Avenue was almost lost and ten minutes later another between Points 78 & 90 (not identified), but the Battalion managed to hold off all attacks, mainly due to a plentiful supply of Mills grenades. On the left, 3rd Coldstream Guards was bombarded from 12.15 p.m. At 3.15 p.m. the Battalion was attacked and some Germans got into the most northerly sap, but they were bombed out and three prisoners were taken.

3rd Grenadier Guards (2nd Guards Brigade) was to the north of 3rd Coldstream Guards in Big Willie. It was assaulted by three battalions and was forced back 180m along Big Willie to the junction with Dump Trench, where a block was formed by 3rd Coldstream Guards. This Battalion was also hard pressed and a sap was lost, but a counterattack by two companies of 1st Scots Guards (2nd Guards Brigade) recovered it. Then a party of seven bombers from 3rd Coldstream Guards, led by **Lance Sergeant Oliver Brooks**, began to bomb its way back along the lost section of Big Willie, followed by a company of 3rd Grenadier Guards and two companies of 1st Scots Guards. Bombers from 2nd Irish Guards (2nd Guards Brigade) also got into Big Willie from a communications trench and took the enemy in the flank. Brooks was under constant fire and survived a hail of enemy bombs. He threw

From the Haines–Le Rutoire track. The Hohenzollern Redoubt is the area of scrubby bushes below the pylons right of centre. Le Rutoire is in the distance on the left below the mine dump. The left hand line of overhead power cables is above the section of Big Willie cleared by Oliver Brooks and his team of bombers on 8th October 1915.

numerous bombs himself, almost as quickly as his men could pass them forward to him. He was always quick to follow up explosions, often rounding a traverse before the last bomb had gone off. Two companies of 1st Irish Guards (1st Guards Brigade reserve) were also committed and by about 7 p.m. the combined force had recaptured Big Willie and 3rd Grenadier Guards was back in control.

The Germans later made another attack over the open, but it was repulsed by machine-gun fire. Bombing continued until nightfall, but the danger had passed and the situation was restored. The other bombers with Brooks were awarded the DCM. The Brigade war diary estimated 3rd Coldstream Guards expended 5,000 grenades that day.

11th October 1915

> 102 Sgt John Crawshaw, Raynes A Battery, LXXI Brigade, Royal Field Artillery (15th (Scottish) Division) Fosse 7 de Béthune, France

Although there was no major action on 11th and 12th October, the artillery was active, particularly with counter-battery fire. **Sergeant John Raynes'** Battery (A/LXXI) came under very heavy high explosive and gas shellfire on the 11th at Fosse 7 de Béthune. One of the guns was out of action. At one point the shelling was so intense that the Battery was ordered to stop firing and to take cover. Raynes then went forward 10m to where 9708 Sergeant John Ayres and six men from his gun had been wounded and buried by exploding shells. Still under fire, Raynes bandaged Ayres' wounds before returning to his own gun. A few minutes later another lull in the firing allowed Raynes to go back to Ayres' assistance. With two other gunners, both of whom were killed shortly afterwards, he carried Ayres to a dugout. Just as they got inside, a gas shell exploded in the entrance. Ayres did not have his gas helmet and Raynes put his own on the injured man. Although badly affected by

126 Victoria Crosses on the Western Front April 1915–June 1916

Quality Street from the southeast. The houses appear to be contemporary.

From Dud Corner Cemetery (Lens Road Redoubt on 25th September 1915) looking northwest towards Mazingarbe. Fosse 7 is the copse on the left of the picture and Quality Street is hidden in the trees just left of the road. Drive northwest along the N43 from here towards Mazingarbe and Vermelles. After 850m take the minor left turn. The factory buildings at the end of this short road are on the site of Fosse 7. Take the first right. This is Quality Street and most of the houses appear to be original. Go to the end of Quality Street and at the junction turn left and park at Fosse 7 Cemetery on the right after 150m. The five dead from A/71 Battery on 11th–12th October 1915 are buried together along the back wall.

the gas, Raynes returned to serve his gun once again. Ayres died later in the day and is buried in Fosse 7 Military Cemetery at Mazingarbe (Collective Grave II G 2a).

At 10 a.m. the following day at Quality Street, the Germans shelled the Battery again. The fire was so accurate that at one time the Battery Commander sent every man still standing to a nearby dressing station for attention. Later two guns received direct hits and a house used as the Battery kitchen was hit by a shell, burying sixteen men. Raynes managed to extricate himself from the rubble, but he was bleeding profusely from the head and also had a leg wound. Despite his injuries, he dug out Battery Sergeant Major Austin and carried him unassisted to the dressing station. Returning to the ruined house, Raynes helped to rescue the others trapped under the fallen masonry. As soon as his own wounds had been dressed, he reported back to his gun, which was still under heavy shellfire.

Over the two days, A/LXXI Battery suffered twenty-two casualties and two guns were put out of action. In addition

The five members of A/LXXI Battery killed on 11th/12th October 1915 are buried in Fosse 7 Military Cemetery, Mazingarbe, a few hundred metres from Quality Street. Their graves are along the back wall. Sergeant Ayres' grave is second from the left.

to Serjeant Ayres, four other members of the Battery were killed and are also buried in Fosse 7 Military Cemetery, Mazingarbe (Collective Grave II G 2a) – 9322 Bombardier Thomas William Dathan, 9154 Gunner Leonard Bean, 73853 Gunner Nicholas Houghton and 78682 Gunner William Humphreys.

Actions of the Hohenzollern Redoubt, 13th–18th October 1915

> 103 Cpl James Dawson, 187th (Special) Company, Royal Engineers Hohenzollern Redoubt, France
> 104 Capt Charles Vickers, 1/7th Battalion, The Nottinghamshire and Derbyshire Regiment (Sherwood Foresters) (139th Brigade, 46th (North Midlands) Division) Hohenzollern Redoubt, France
> 105 Pte Harry Christian, 2nd Battalion The King's Own (Royal Lancaster) Regiment (83rd Brigade, 28th Division) Cuinchy, France

The German counterattack on 8th October delayed British offensive preparations. The attack was eventually set for 2 p.m. on 13th October. In the intervening period there was constant low level fighting. On 11th October, the French Tenth Army attack on Vimy Ridge failed, with heavy casualties. A British attempt to recover some trenches at the Double Crassier, lost on 8th October, did not even reach the German wire.

First Army's distant objectives, stipulated in the original offensive orders for 25th September, were no longer achievable. For the next stage, closer objectives were selected to establish a more advantageous line from which to launch further offensive operations in the future. IV Corps was to consolidate the Lens – La Bassée road between Chalk Pit Wood and the Vermelles – Hulluch road, while XI Corps was to recover the Hohenzollern Redoubt, the Quarries and Fosse 8.

At midday on 13th October, the British bombardment commenced, but it was not heavy enough to cause significant damage to the enemy positions. At 1.00 p.m., gas and smoke was released for an hour, following which the infantry attacked. In IV Corps, 1st Division's attack on the Lens – La Bassée road between Loos and Hulluch was hit by intense fire. There were few gaps in the wire and the attack was halted. The survivors withdrew after dark, having suffered 1,200 casualties. 12th Division attacked between Gun Trench and the Quarries. Gun Trench was reached and a foothold was gained in the Quarries, but an unexpected enemy trench and a thin smoke screen meant there were no more gains.

The recapture of the Hohenzollern Redoubt and Fosse 8 was entrusted to 46th Division, which had taken over the front from the Guards Division the previous night. The relief was not completed until 6 a.m. and consequently the officers had insufficient time to familiarise themselves with the ground.

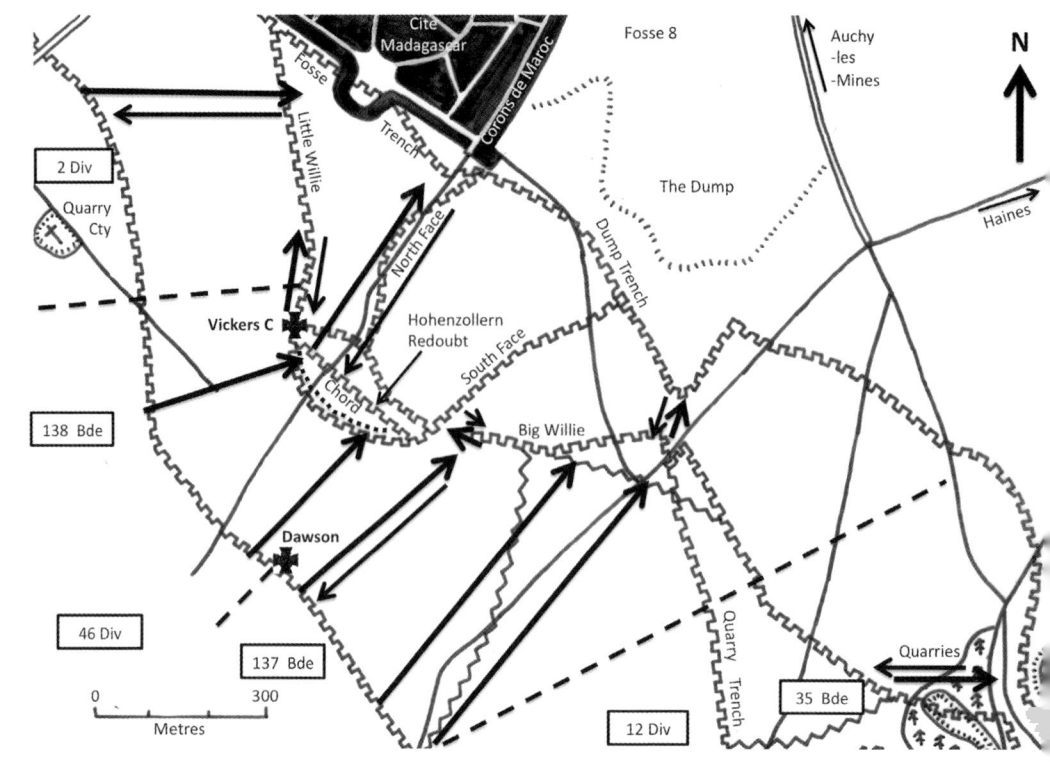

From the farm at the southern edge of Cité Madagascar, walk southwest 350m to the start of the scrubby bushes on the site of the Hohenzollern Redoubt. Turn left, keeping the bushes on your right, and follow them round to the southwest. Where they run out, look south towards the Double Crassiers at Loos; 200m along this line is approximately where James Dawson pushed the leaking gas cylinders out of the front line trench. To visit the site of Charles Vickers' VC action, follow the directions for James Pollock and Alfred Fleming-Sandes on 27th and 29th September 1915 respectively. The dashed line around the southwest of the Hohenzollern Redoubt was the only gain still held at the end of 13th October 1915.

From the British front line, on the boundary between 137th and 138th Brigades. The precise position on the front line where James Dawson disposed of the gas cylinders is not known, but it was close to the Hohenzollern Redoubt, which is on the left of picture. The Dump is in the centre and the Quarries area is on the right.

On the right, 137th Brigade was to cross Big Willie and Dump Trenches to occupy Fosse Alley. On the left, 138th Brigade was to pass through the Hohenzollern Redoubt to the Fosse 8 Corons north of the Dump, which was not to be attacked. The gas released in this area was not effective; most of it settled in no man's land and very little reached the enemy lines. However, it warned the Germans that an attack was coming and they laid down a heavy counter-bombardment.

During the gas release, **Corporal James Dawson** noticed a lot of gas collecting in the British trenches. He climbed out of the trench and, although fully exposed to enemy fire, calmly walked along the parados, directing his men in releasing the gas and advising the infantry on which sections of the trench to avoid. He then came upon three leaking cylinders. One at a time he rolled them about fifteen metres out of harm's way and then fired his rifle into them to allow the gas to escape and disperse quickly. His coolness saved many casualties before the main attack got underway.

As the leading battalions of 137th Brigade emerged from their trenches they were met with a terrific fusillade of fire from the Dump and Corons. Very few men even reached the British held sections of Big Willie. 138th Brigade's attack began ten minutes later and had a shorter distance to cover. The troops were to some extent sheltered from machine-guns at the Dump by the Hohenzollern Redoubt and reached the first objectives. However, when the advance resumed towards Fosse Trench, heavy fire from the Dump and Mad Point caused heavy losses and the attack was halted within ten minutes. By nightfall the attackers had been forced back to the Redoubt. 2nd Division to the north tried to assist by sending bombing parties towards Little Willie. They were hit by heavy fire and just about all involved became casualties.

At 2.45 p.m., A and B Companies, 1/7th Sherwood Foresters (139th Brigade in reserve, attached to 138th Brigade), were sent to the northern end of the Redoubt to support an attack. A Company was sent along South Face and B Company along North Face. They were unable to progress any further and lay down behind the forward trench, where they were joined by half of C Company, while the remainder of the Battalion held the old front line trench.

The Dump   Quarries

Half a company under Captain Warren occupied the northwest corner of the Redoubt and the southern end of Little Willie, where the Battalion bombers under Captain HH Walton were slowly driving the Germans back. Walton was killed about 4.30 p.m. and the Germans drove the bombing party back behind a barricade at the southern end of Little Willie. A retirement on the right of the Redoubt about 5 p.m. allowed the Germans to get behind Warren's party. He held on until 8 p.m., then pulled his men back over the open into the Redoubt, where they took up positions behind a barricade at the northwest corner. The battle had degenerated into a series of bombing actions in which 1/7th Sherwood Foresters was at a severe disadvantage, being poorly supplied with grenades.

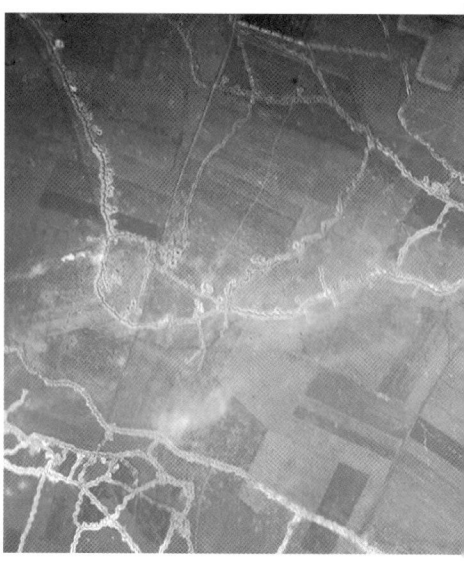

Aerial photograph of the Hohenzollern Redoubt before the commencement of the Battle of Loos.

In the evening, HQ XI Corps decided to evacuate the eastern face of the Hohenzollern Redoubt and a new trench, The Chord, was dug during the night. Elements of all battalions in 139th Brigade were sent forward as reinforcements, although the majority of the Redoubt's garrison was from 1/7th Sherwood Foresters. 1/8th Sherwood Foresters sent its grenadiers and one company to assist 1/7th Sherwood Foresters. They constructed a new communications trench linking the Redoubt at West Face with the old British front line, the previous one having been completely levelled.

At 4 a.m. on the 14th the Germans counterattacked across the open after bombing and bombarding for most of the night. By 5 a.m., the enemy pressure necessitated sending fifty men of D Company to reinforce the Redoubt. Seven men were sent to the southern-most point of Little Willie, where they held the barricade until one of their own bombs exploded amongst them. Everyone was injured, but one man managed to get back and reported the incident to **Captain Charles Vickers**, who immediately went to the scene and took control.

Vickers threw bomb after bomb at the enemy, while directing the other bombers as well. The Germans attacked from all directions, but for some hours Vickers' team kept them out. It was clear that the barricade would eventually be taken and Vickers ordered another to be built behind him, while he continued to hold the position, assisted by a few other men. Vickers had been wounded many times and was becoming weak and giddy, but he refused to give in and continued to call for more bombs. Eventually he was the only man left. Bombs continued to drop into the trench and he was wounded again, this time severely. Fortunately A Company,

1/5th Sherwood Foresters and some bombers from the Welsh Guards arrived at this time and rescued Vickers, carrying him over the second barricade on a door. The German attack was eventually halted and 1/7th Sherwood Foresters returned to the old British front line.

46th Division lost 3,763 men in this action, mostly in the first ten minutes of the attack on 13th October. For this terrible loss, the Division only managed to secure the western portion of the Hohenzollern Redoubt.

Joffre closed down the Artois offensive on 15th October. The Loos offensive was also shut down. It cost the British 61,000 casualties in the main offensive and the subsidiary attacks, including almost 7,800 killed. Heavy losses had been suffered amongst the remaining pre-war regulars and in the New Army divisions.

Although the main fighting around Loos had ended by the middle of October, a number of small actions were fought as both sides jockeyed to gain local advantage. On 17th October, 83rd Brigade took over the line from the La Bassée Canal south to the Béthune – La Bassée road. This area had already been the scene of a number of engagements and was noted for its maze of trenches, shell holes, saps, brickstacks and mine craters. 2nd King's Own held the line from the Canal south to Hanover Street. On 18th October, a party of 2nd King's Own, including **Private Harry Christian**, occupied one of the craters and the Germans retaliated with a heavy minenwerfer bombardment. The fire was so intense that the party had to withdraw in some haste.

As he reached safety, Christian realised that three men were missing. He immediately returned to the crater, where he discovered that the men had been buried by the explosions. One by one Christian dug them out, despite the crater lip receiving direct hits, and carried them back to safety. He then placed himself in an exposed position from where he could observe the minenwerfer bombs in flight and warn his comrades which way to go to avoid them. During the course of this action eight men were killed, but there would undoubtedly have been more if it had not been for Christian's actions.

Loos demonstrated that a determined assault force, prepared to suffer heavy casualties, could break into strongly defended positions. Sir Douglas Haig believed that a fleeting opportunity to break through had been missed because reserves controlled by HQ BEF were held too far to the rear. As a result they arrived too late to maintain the momentum and force a way through. This proved to be the final straw in Sir John French's performance as commander of the BEF. By the end of the year he had gone home. Haig became Commander-in-Chief of the BEF for the rest of the war.

Chapter Five

Local Operations Winter 1915–16

La Houssoie, France, 4th November 1915

106 Pte Thomas Kenny, 13th Battalion, The Durham Light Infantry (68th Brigade, 23rd Division)

From the church in Bois Grenier drive northeast on the D222 towards Armentières. Go under the TGV railway and stop 750m further on at Ration Farm Military Cemetery on the left. This is where Lieutenant Brown is buried, the officer rescued by Thomas Kenny. Another 300m on turn right, signed 'Zone Industrielle la Houssoye'. After 700m look for a minor road on the right, just after the turning to the 'Dechetterie' on the left. Follow this minor road southwards; you should have overhead power lines to your right running parallel. After 620m there is a small kink in the road. Park and look left 50m into the field to the point in the British front line where Brown and Kenny went out into no man's land. Their general direction was towards the iron girder tower.

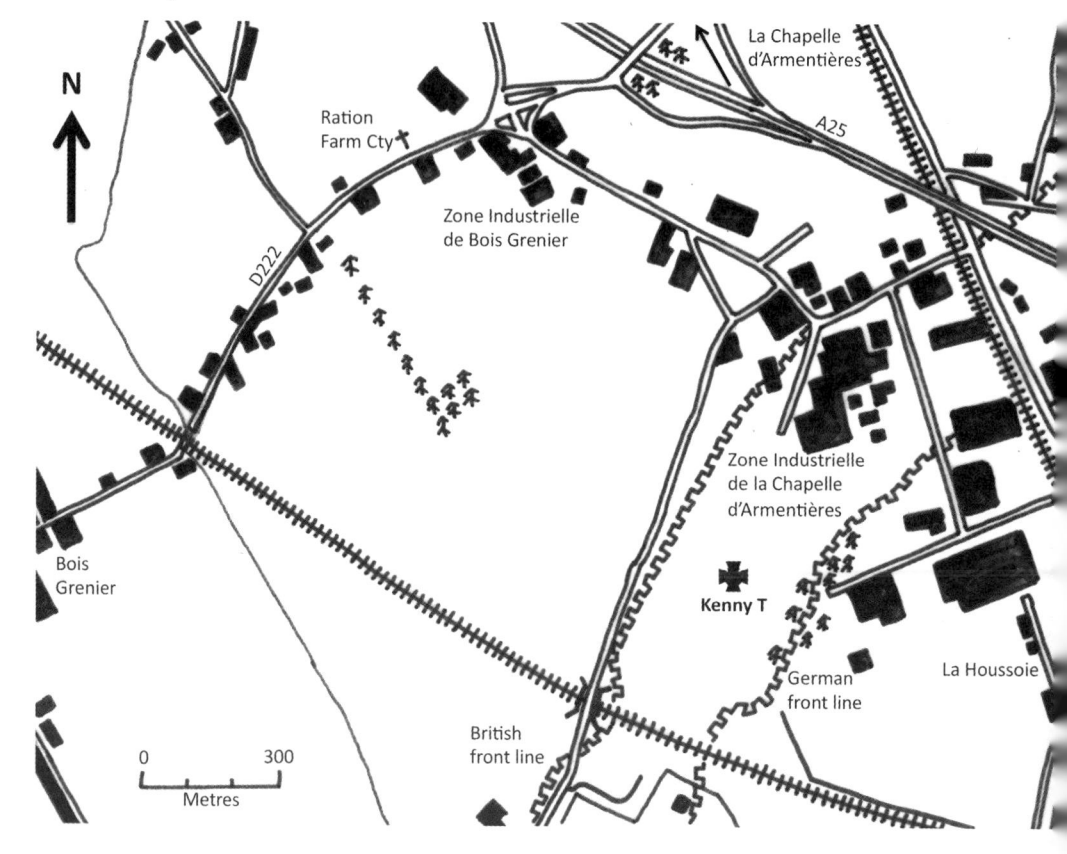

Local Operations Winter 1915–16   133

The British front line ran parallel with the road in the foreground, about 50m into the field. This is where Thomas Kenny and Lieutenant Philip Brown left the trenches and headed towards the tower in the distance.

Ration Farm Cemetery, where Lieutenant Philip Brown is buried.

At the beginning of November 1915 in the Armentières – Bois Grenier area, patrols from both sides vied with each other constantly for control of no man's land. At 9 p.m. on 4th November, Lieutenant Philip Brown left the front line trench accompanied by **Private Thomas Kenny** to visit his men on a wiring party. It was a thick foggy night and they missed the wire completely, overrunning it by some distance. After wandering about lost for a while they sat down to listen to the noises of the night in the hope that this would give them a clue as to which way to go. At 9.45 p.m., as they got up, a German patrol lying in a ditch close by opened fire and Brown fell, shot through both thighs.

With German bullets whistling all round, Kenny managed to manhandle Brown onto his back and crawled away into the fog. He crawled for about an hour, occasionally taking cover from the heavy enemy fire. Brown ordered Kenny to go on alone and save himself, but he refused to leave the officer. When he was just

From the bridge over the TGV railway south of the industrial area. The British front line ran parallel with and to the right of the road. Kenny and Brown left the front line indicated by the arrow and headed towards the buildings on the right.

about exhausted he came upon a ditch, that he recognised. Leaving Brown there in cover, he went off to find his bearings and at about 11 p.m. stumbled upon Captain G White and two men in a listening post. Stretcher-bearers were called for and Privates Thomas Kerr and Michael Brough came forward. Kenny was at the very limits of his physical endurance, but led them to where he had left Brown.

The rescue was very hazardous, with the enemy pouring heavy rifle fire into the area and showers of grenades were exploding within 30m. The party made it back safely, covered by White. Brown was very weak from loss of blood, but recovered consciousness long enough to say, *Well Kenny you're a hero*, before being carried back to a dressing station. Their efforts were in vain; Brown died before he arrived and he is buried in Ration Farm Military Cemetery, La Chapelle-d'Armentières (I F 5). Privates Kerr and Brough were recommended for, but did not receive, the DCM. However, later in the war 17750 Sergeant Michael Brough was awarded the DCM and MM and Bar.

La Brique, Belgium, 16th November 1915

107 Pte John Caffrey, 2nd Battalion, The York and Lancaster Regiment (16th Brigade, 6th Division)

There are few details of the circumstances under which **Private John Caffrey** won the VC, except for the citation in the London Gazette. At the time, 6th Division was involved in routine line holding in the Ypres salient. No major actions were taking place, but continuous low-level activity produced a steady stream of casualties. 2nd York and Lancaster (16th Brigade) entered the line on 13th November, relieving 8th West Yorkshire (49th Division) in the Morteldje salient at 10.50 p.m.

Communications trenches were under water and many collapsed. Fire trenches were also mainly flooded and there were no lateral communications trenches between platoons. Because conditions were so bad, the companies had to be rotated in the front line every 24 hours. Efforts to improve the trenches were made, but movement in daylight was impossible.

At 9 a.m. on the 16th a badly wounded West Yorkshire soldier was observed lying in no man's land in full view of the enemy. 2167 Corporal Albert James Stirk RAMC and Caffrey immediately went out to rescue the man, but they were forced back by heavy shrapnel fire. However, on the second attempt they managed to reach him, in spite of heavy sniping and machine-gun fire. Having bandaged the wounded man, Stirk lifted him onto Caffrey's back, but was then shot in the head. Caffrey made the West Yorkshire soldier as comfortable as possible, bandaged Stirk's wound and helped him back to safety. Once Stirk had been delivered to the front line trench, Caffrey returned for the other man and brought him in as well.

Albert Stirk survived and was awarded the DCM (LG 21st January 1916) and was MID (LG 31st December 1915). He served in the RAMC 18th November 1908–17th

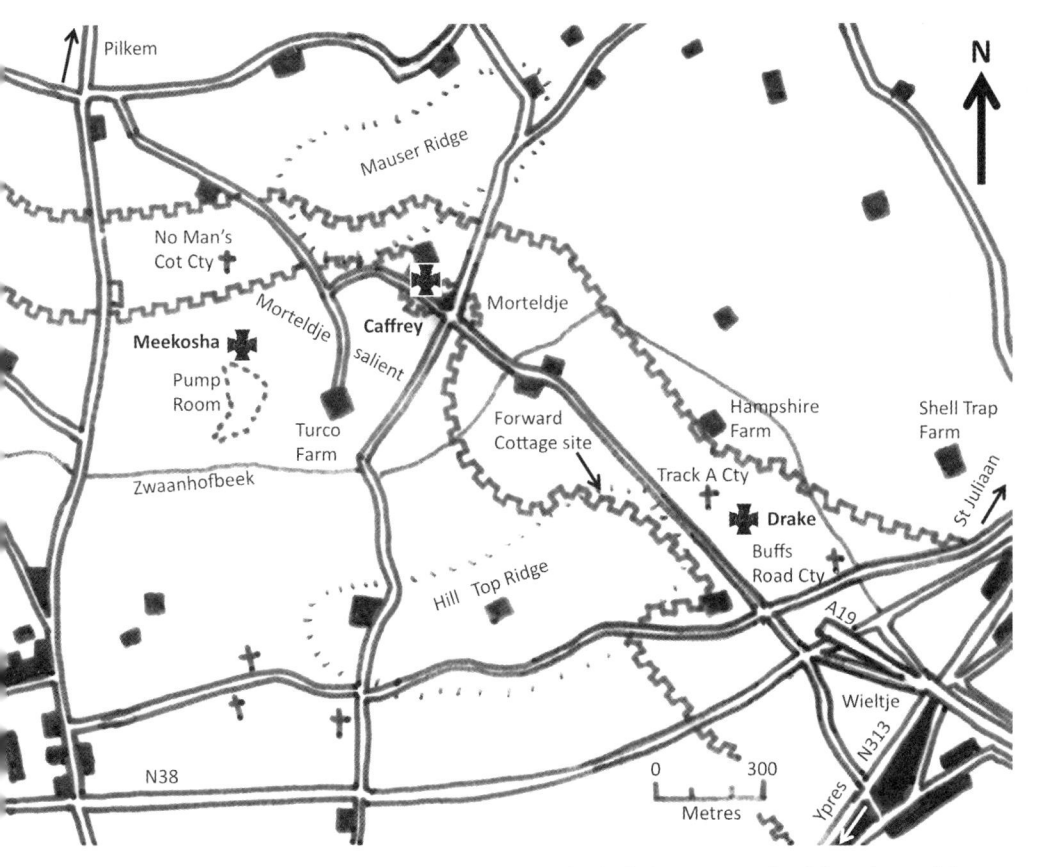

Drive south from St Juliaan on the N313. After 800m pass Seaforth Cemetery on the right and turn right after 350m opposite the left turn for St Jan. Drive on 800m west, passing the entrance lane to Mouse (Shell) Trap Farm on the right. At the crossroads turn right and after 1,100m there is a crossroads with a cottage on the right on the site of Morteldje Estaminet. This is where John Caffrey won his VC. Continue northwest and the road bends left. After 350m there is a left turn to what was Turco Farm in 1915. Park at this junction. The Pump Room where Samuel Meekosha won his VC was in the low ground in front of you. No Man's Cot Cemetery is to the right of it. Return the way you came, passing Morteldje on the left. Continue for 800m southeast and stop on the left at the entrance to Track X Cemetery. This was about midway between the lines on 23rd November 1915 and Drake's VC action took place about 150m southeast of it.

Morteldje crossroads from the entrance to Turco Farm. John Caffrey's VC action was to the left of the house in the centre, which is on the site of Morteldje Estaminet.

November 1911 and 18th September 1912–18th September 1913. Having been mobilised on 6th August 1914, he went to France on 20th August and was promoted corporal on 20th January 1915. He was wounded by shrapnel on 28th July and received a gunshot wound on 18th August. The wound he received while helping John Caffrey on 16th November 1915 resulted in him being discharged on 21st January 1916. He was issued Silver War Badge No.187425 on 31st July 1917.

From just behind the British front line looking westwards into the rear areas. Turco Farm is on the left and No Man's Cot Cemetery on the right. The Pump Room, where Samuel Meekosha won his VC, was in the low ground in the centre.

Near the Yser, Belgium, 19th November 1915

108 Cpl Samuel Meekosha, 1/6th Battalion, The West Yorkshire Regiment (146th Brigade, 49th (West Riding) Division)

On 15th November 1915, 1/6th West Yorkshire went into the front line two miles north-northeast of Ypres to relieve 1/8th West Yorkshire. Shelling and sniping were routine hazards, but heavy frosts and the wet conditions added considerably to the discomfort. On the 19th, **Corporal Samuel Meekosha**'s platoon of about twenty men was in an isolated position, the Pump Room, on the right of the Battalion. At 4.15 p.m. it came under very heavy artillery fire, with about eighty shells landing in a few seconds. Six men were killed, seven injured and many of the remainder were buried.

Meekosha took command and sent three newly arrived recruits to HQ to get help. He then began to dig out those who had been buried, standing in full view of

Looking northeast along no man's land from the end of the A19 Autoroute embankment. The British lines were just to the left of the road running into the centre distance from the crossroads on the left. The Cross in Track A Cemetery is slightly left of centre alongside a lone bushy tree. Hampshire Farm is right of centre. Alfred Drake's VC action was in the maize field between the camera position and the Cemetery.

[Panoramic photo labels: Pump Room; No Man's Cot Cemetery]

the enemy only a short distance away. He was assisted by 3225 Private F Johnson, 2626 Private J Sayers and 1266 Private EJ Wilkinson. During this time another ten large calibre shells landed within 20m. By his efforts he saved at least four men from certain death. The Battalion was relieved later the same day by 1/5th West Yorkshire and went into divisional reserve at Poperinghe.

Johnson, Sayers and Wilkinson were awarded the DCM for their part in this action, LG 22nd January 1916. Sayers was killed as a sergeant on 15th July 1916 and is commemorated on the Thiepval Memorial, France. As a lance corporal, Wilkinson was killed on 11th August 1916 and is buried in Authuille Military Cemetery, France (G 15).

La Brique, Belgium, 23rd November 1915

> 109 Cpl Alfred George Drake, 8th Battalion, The Rifle Brigade (41st Brigade, 14th (Light) Division)

On 22nd November, 8th Rifle Brigade relieved 7th King's Royal Rifle Corps in the front line in thick fog. The line held extended from Forward Cottages on the left to Liverpool Street (not identified) on the right. It was comparatively quiet on the 23rd, with steady shelling and machine-gun fire after dusk.

[Panoramic photo label: Hampshire Farm]

That night, Lieutenant Tryon led a four-man patrol into no man's land in front of 'B14'. When they were 135m out from the British lines, close to the enemy trenches, they were surprised in the light of a flare. Tryon and another man were hit. **Corporal Alfred Drake** ordered the fourth man, B/3121 Rifleman JE Beazley, to get the injured soldier back to safety, while he remained with the officer. Tryon was wounded in the neck and was too seriously injured to be moved without help.

Drake was hit repeatedly as he knelt over the officer to bandage his wounds. When the patrol did not return at the appointed time, two search parties went out, but returned having found no trace of it. A third party, consisting of Lieutenants Backus and Gorell-Barnes (the Adjutant), B1652 Corporal W Hobday and Rifleman Beazley then went out. Beazley had already been in one of the other search parties. By the time they found Tryon, Drake was dead. However, his self-sacrifice undoubtedly saved Tryon's life and he was brought in under heavy machine-gun fire. Corporal Hobday (LG 14th January & 15th March 1916) and Rifleman Beazley (LG 22nd January 1916) were awarded the DCM for their part in this incident.

Trench 51, east of Foncquevillers, France, 22nd December 1915

110 Pte William Young, 8th Battalion, The East Lancashire Regiment (112th Brigade, 37th Division)

8th East Lancashire had been in the Foncquevillers area for some months when winter set in, making the dreadful conditions in the trenches even worse. The situation was described in the Regimental history as, *The usual trench routine, the usual shelling, the usual patrols, the usual rain and discomfort.* In the front line, conditions were so bad that platoons could not be left there for more than twenty-four hours at a time.

Private William Young returned to the Battalion in December 1915, having recovered from the effects of gas in his eyes. At stand-to on the morning of

From the centre of no man's land looking over the German lines east of Foncquevillers. The 'Little Z' is right of centre at the end of the copse with a pylon beyond it. William Young approached from the higher ground on the right, beyond which in the distance is Bois de Sartel. This was attacked by 46th Division on 1st July 1916. Gommecourt village is out of sight behind the wood.

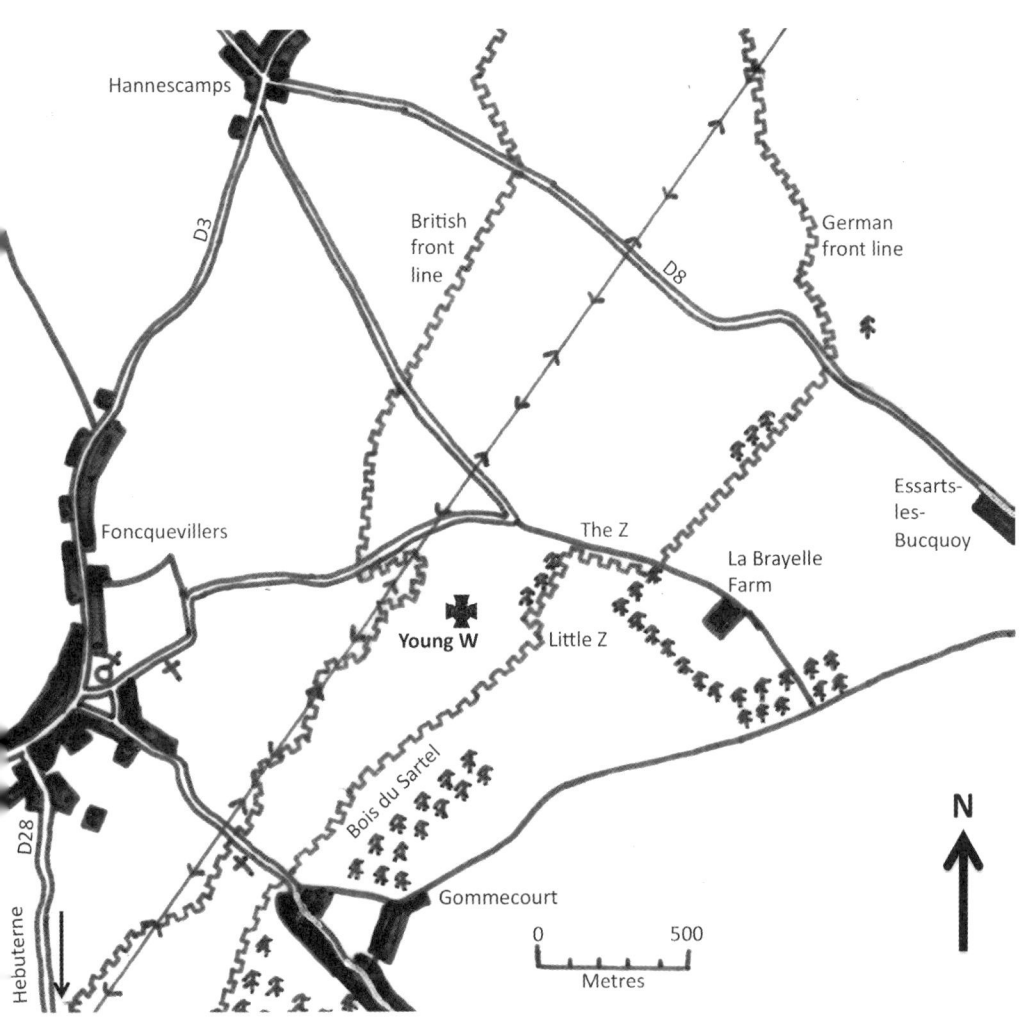

On the south side of Foncquevillers church there is a memorial to a Canadian Halifax crew in WW2. Drive northeast on a minor road, do not head southeast towards Gommecourt. Pass the village cemetery on the right after 250m. At the T-junction turn left and after 150m turn right onto a metalled track. It tends to have a muddy surface so drive with care, as it can be slippery. Go under the power lines and turn left uphill at the next junction. Stop after 100m in the middle of no man's land. Look south. The track to the east towards la Brayelle Farm marks the middle leg of the 'Z' on the German front line. Follow the line of trees with the pylon in front to the right until it runs out. That is the 'Little Z'. Young's VC action was in front of it in the shallow re-entrant. You can return the way you came or continue north to the D8 in Hannescamp. There is a café in Hébuterne.

22nd December the Battalion was in the line east of Foncquevillers and north of Gommecourt. Young was manning the B Company parapet when he saw Sergeant Allen lying in front of the wire, having been wounded the previous night on a patrol. Young jumped out of the trench, disregarded the heavy enemy fire and dashed forward to assist Allen. The Sergeant tried to make Young take cover, but he refused and was almost immediately hit in the lower jaw by a rifle bullet and was seriously wounded in the chest.

Private Green dashed out to join Young and together they managed to bring Allen back to the British lines. Despite his wounds, Young walked to the dressing station unaided, from where he was eventually evacuated to England. Green received the DCM for his part in this incident.

Hooge, Belgium, 14th February 1916

> 111 Lt Eric Archibald McNair, 9th Battalion, The Royal Sussex Regiment (73rd Brigade, 24th Division)

Prior to launching their massive offensive at Verdun, the Germans made a series of diversionary attacks in the Ypres salient. Some of these actions amounted to little more than a heavy artillery bombardment, but on occasions the opportunity was taken to make small gains. On St Valentine's Day, there were two such attacks; one against the Bluff and the other against 24th Division at Hooge and Sanctuary Wood. This is where the first Western Front VC of 1916 was won.

On 13th February, the line held by 73rd Brigade at Railway Wood was bombarded from 8.30 a.m. until 4.15 p.m. On the right, 17th Brigade was also bombarded and three front trenches were made untenable. HQ 24th Division sent 73rd Brigade two Maxims to cover the gap. During the night parties of both brigades made repairs, hampered by frequent enemy shelling, but 17th Brigade was able to re-establish some posts on its former front line.

A Company, 9th Royal Sussex suffered thirty casualties during the bombardment and was relieved by D Company in the front line. Next day both sides shelled each other and occasionally these exchanges were very heavy. At 7.45 a.m., the British artillery succeeded in collapsing an enemy trench. At 12.45 p.m., the Germans

From the Menin Road looking north. Railway Wood is on the left. The copse centre right is where Eric McNair won his VC.

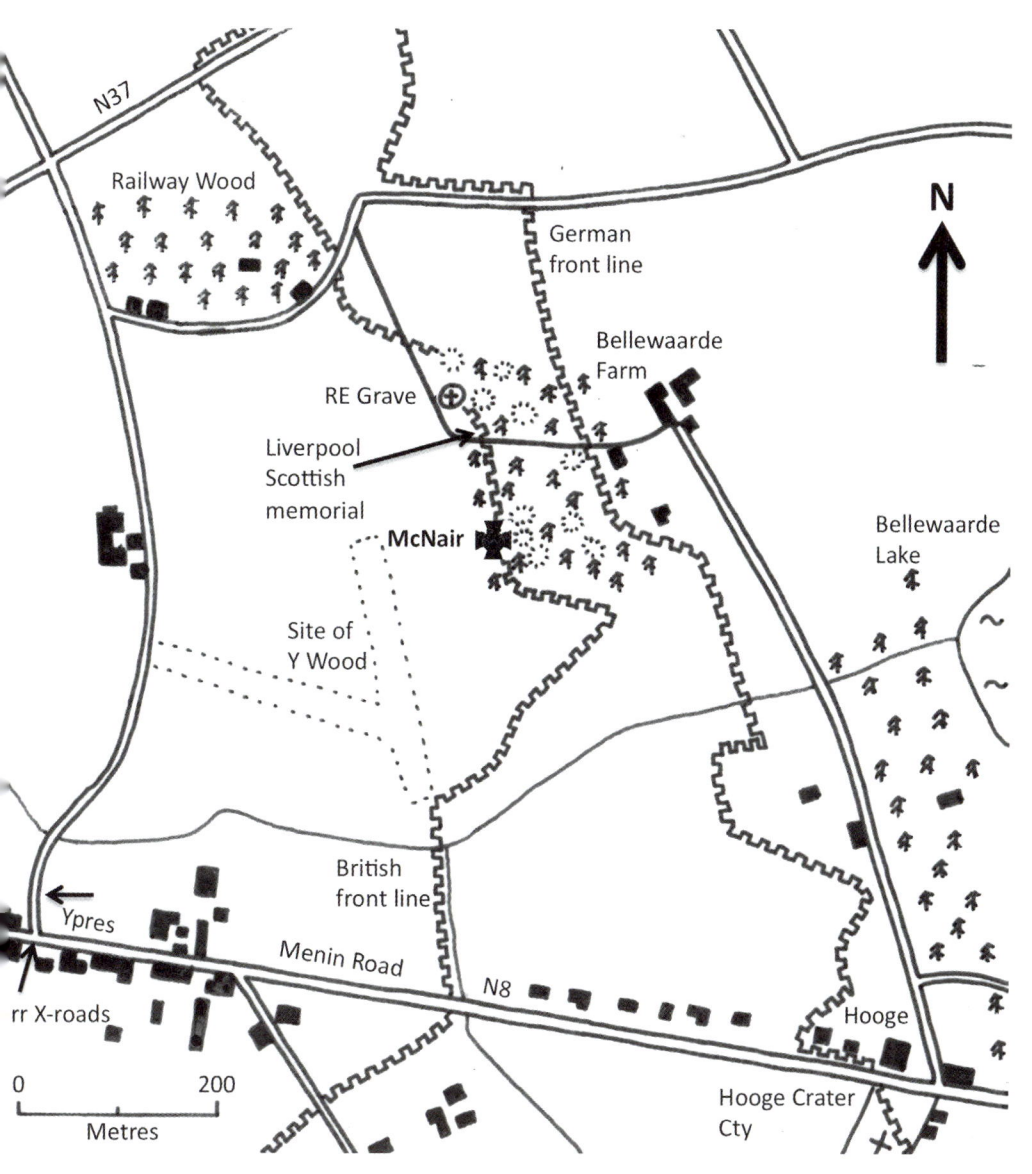

Leave Ypres on the N8 (Menin Road) towards Menen. One kilometre after the major roundabout take the left turn. After 650m turn right and park in the track entrance on the right after 200m. The trees on the other side of the road are Railway Wood. The railway ran on the far side of it and is now a major road (N37). Walk southeast along the track to the RE Grave. The track swings left through the wood towards Bellewaarde Farm. This is private. On the corner is a memorial to the Liverpool Scottish; Noel Chavasse VC and Bar was the MO of that Battalion. Continue south on the public footpath keeping the wood on your left. The British front line ran parallel with the track just inside the trees. Occasionally through the trees you will see the mine craters within. This is the area where Eric McNair was active in February 1916.

shelled a section of trench held by 9th Royal Sussex ('H13–19') and also against Hooge. At 4 p.m., the Germans shelled the Bluff heavily. However, the main action of the day came in the evening when 73rd Brigade was stood to. At about 5.30 p.m., the British artillery opened fire in response to an SOS signal from Hooge and at

From the RE Grave looking south. Buildings along the Menin Road can be seen beyond the maize. The British front line ran along the edge of the trees on the left.

6.30 p.m. the Germans fired two mines under 73rd Brigade's front, including one in front of 9th Royal Sussex's front line at 'H16'. The crater touched the front line trench and there were heavy losses, including one of D Company's platoons buried alive. However, before the enemy could follow up the explosions, B and D Companies had seized the crater.

Lieutenant Eric McNair was in the front line when the mines went off. Although he was badly shaken, he pulled himself together and organised the defence of the crater. By the time the Germans attacked, he had set up a machine-gun on the near edge and they were driven off with heavy losses. When the immediate crisis was over, McNair ran back to bring up reinforcements. The communications trench was blocked and he had to resort to running over open ground in full view of the enemy and under heavy fire. He led the reinforcements back the same way. His quick thinking and decisive action saved this section of the line from being overrun.

The survivors spent the night digging new positions around the craters, including a new trench connecting the crater with the main position. They were relieved next day by 13th Middlesex, having suffered 139 casualties.

One of the many mine craters in the copse west of Bellewaarde Farm. This is where Eric McNair held off the German attack on 14th February 1916.

Chapter Six

Local Operations Spring 1916

Hohenzollern Redoubt, France, 6th March 1916

112 Cpl William Reginald Cotter, 6th Battalion, The East Kent Regiment (Buffs) (37th Brigade, 12th (Eastern) Division)

When the Battle of Loos came to an end in October 1915, British gains in the Hohenzollern Redoubt had been reduced to the extreme western sector. In the following months the Germans launched a number of attacks, which nibbled away at the British defences. Eventually the Chord, the trench connecting the north and south of the Redoubt, was lost, but the British were not prepared to leave the situation as it was. By the end of February 1916, three deep mines, the largest yet prepared by the British, had been completed under the German front line by 170 Tunnelling Company. These were known as A, B and C from south to north. A fourth mine was placed under the existing No.2 Crater.

At 5.45 p.m. on 2nd March, the mines were fired and as soon as the debris settled the artillery opened fire. Two battalions of 36th Brigade attacked and the three new craters were captured, along with five old ones (Nos 1 to 5). Triangle Crater, at the junction of the Chord and Big Willie, was also taken, but the northern part of the Chord remained in German hands. The capture of Triangle Crater was a significant bonus, as it proved to be the entry point to most of the German mines in the area. Major Neville Elliot-Cooper, 8th Royal Fusiliers (destined to win the VC in 1917), commanded a company in the seizure of Craters 1, 2 and A, for which he was awarded the MC.

The Germans made repeated counterattacks over the next few days and on 4th March recovered Triangle Crater. The British line held firm elsewhere, although heavy casualties were incurred and next day 36th Brigade had to be relieved by 37th Brigade. 6th East Kent relieved 11th Middlesex on the right of the Brigade's sector in Kaiserin Trench, Crater A and Nos 1 and 2 Craters. On the left was 7th East Surrey, with 6th Royal West Kent in support. The relief was completed by 1.30 p.m., expect for A Crater, which had to be carried out in darkness, due to enemy snipers. The trenches were in very poor condition due to the weather and

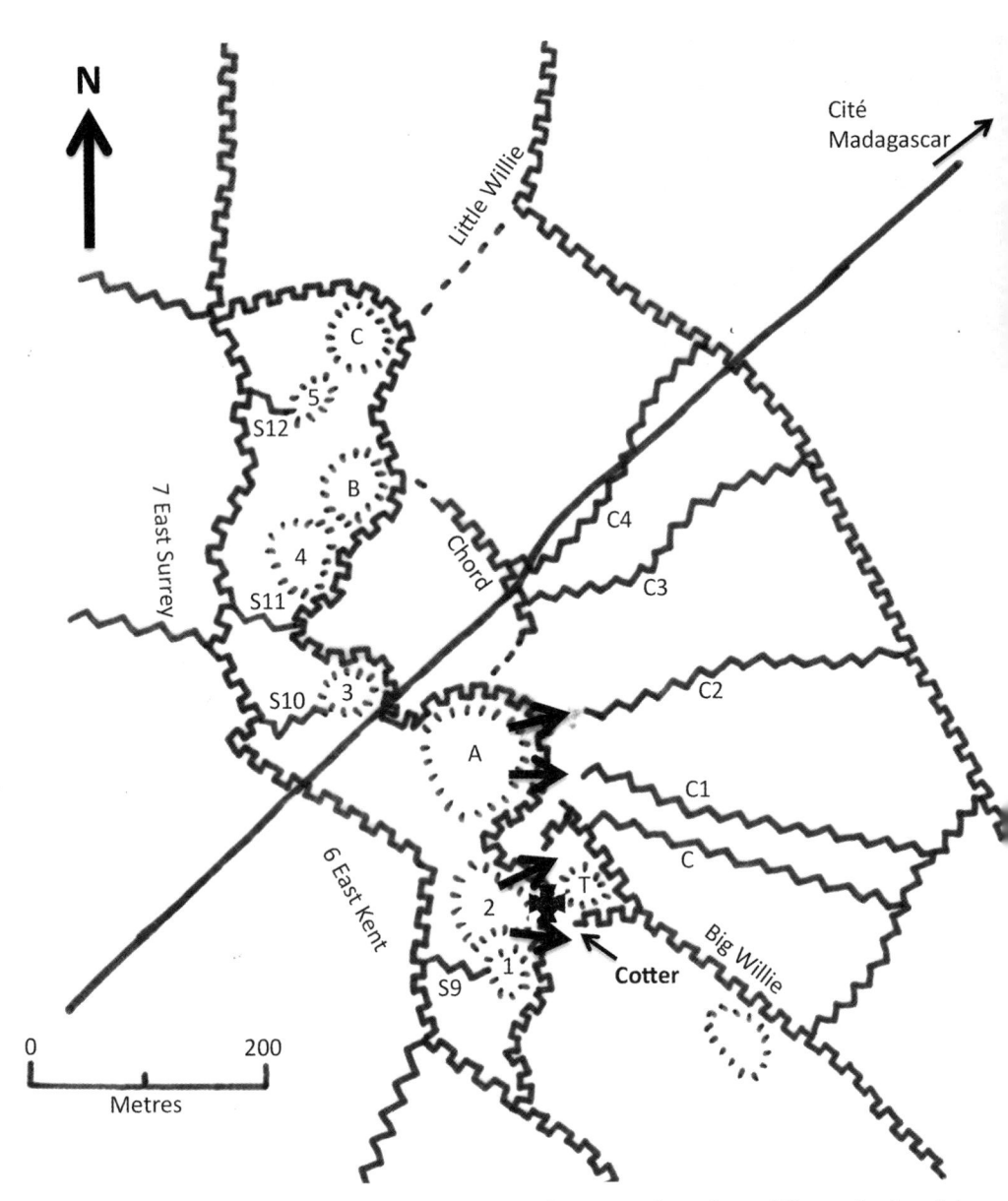

144   Victoria Crosses on the Western Front April 1915–June 1916

From the farm at the southeastern corner of Cité Madagascar, walk southwest 350m to the site of the Hohenzollern Redoubt. At the start of the thick vegetation turn left (south) along it. After 100m turn right into the vegetation. It is almost secondary jungle in there, so full leg and arm coverage is essential. A compass is also useful to maintain direction. With care you can pick your way through the scrub. Find the large crater to the north; this is understood to be Crater A. South of it and separated by a narrow causeway, is No.2 Crater, which Cotter held. To the east of No. 2 Crater are the shallow remnants of Triangle Crater (marked 'T'). No.1 Crater is south of No.2 Crater, just within the thick vegetation, which has been omitted from the map for the sake of clarity. The craters marked north of the track have long since been filled in. Saps are shown as 'S9', 'S10' etc.

From Triangle Crater looking west towards the lip of No.2 Crater.

the continuous shelling. The Germans were also very active with continuous bombing, particularly against No.1 Crater.

At 4.30 a.m. on 6th March a mine was fired just south of Sap 6, close to the German front line, to blow in a hostile gallery; no attempt was made by either side to occupy the crater. At 5.10 a.m., the Germans blew a small mine near Sap 2. No damage was caused and neither side occupied the crater. At 9 a.m., the Germans fired another mine close to Sap 6, about 20m in front of the British parapet. It caused Saps 5 and 6 to be partially filled, but there was no other damage and work parties were soon clearing them up to the lip of the crater. Finally, at 4 p.m., the Germans exploded another mine in front of Alexander Trench near Sap 6, accompanied by a heavy barrage. Slight damage was caused to the front line and there were sixteen casualties caused by the shock of the explosion.

C Company, 6th East Kents, under Captain Ward, was ordered to retake Triangle Crater and consolidate on the line of the Chord – Big Willie, supported by two platoons of D Company as carriers. The attack was scheduled for 6 a.m., but this was subsequently delayed until 6 p.m. Three parties, each of one platoon, were to attack simultaneously:

- No.1 Party on the left was to attack from A Crater, gain the Chord and block off communications trenches 'C1' and 'C2' leading into the German lines.
- No.2 Party was to start from No.2 Crater, then attack along the northern face of Triangle Crater to seize and consolidate the Chord. It was then to double block Communications Trench 'C' and gain contact with No.1 Party on the left. Contact was also to be made with No.3 Party at the junction of Big Willie and the Chord.
- No.3 Party was also to start from No.2 Crater, attack along the southern face of Triangle Crater and block Big Willie south of a hostile mineshaft. It was also to clear the eastern lip of Triangle Crater and consolidate it.

In addition there was a party of sappers to deal with the mineshaft. A party of A Company bombers was to protect the left flank of C Company.

No.3 Party, attacking through mud up to its knees, was caught by enemy machine-guns and bombers and driven back into No.2 Crater. The other two parties met successfully in the Chord, but there came up against a German bombing force of about a hundred, who seemed to have limitless supplies of bombs. When their bombs ran out, they were also compelled to fall back. At 6.55 p.m., the attack was reported to have failed and the front was under such pressure that reinforcements had to be sent up to hold back German counterattacks.

During the initial attack **Corporal William Cotter** led his party along the north of Triangle Crater, but they became cut off due to heavy casualties on their right. He returned under heavy fire to report this and then went back with a supply of bombs to enable his men to fight their way back to No.2 Crater. While directing operations, he lost his right leg below the knee and was also wounded in both arms. Despite these horrific wounds, he crawled almost 50m to reach the lip of No.2 Crater. On the way he met Lance Corporal Newman, whose section was bombing to the right. Cotter directed him to bomb towards the left, where his efforts would be of more use. Reaching No.2 Crater, Cotter discovered that he was the senior rank as the Germans began to counterattack. The situation was chaotic, with men hurling bombs in all directions and causing casualties to themselves. Taking up a position on the side of the crater, he took control, steadied the men around him and altered their dispositions to meet the next counterattack. He continued to issue fire orders for two hours until the attacks were finally repulsed, controlling the supply of bombs and ammunition throughout. Only then did he allow his wounds to be dressed. Although he could not be evacuated from the crater for fourteen hours in freezing conditions, he remained cheerful throughout. His actions saved the Crater and halted what could have been a disastrous enemy incursion.

The eastern lip of No.2 Crater held by William Cotter on 6th March 1916.

Although Cotter did not live to receive the honour he so richly deserved, he was told he had been recommended for the VC before he lapsed into unconsciousness and died at a Casualty Clearing Station at Lillers. Before he died, he recounted the action to Nursing Sister Katherine 'Kate' Evelyn Luard QAINSR (1872–1962). He told her he was leading a bombing attack when he made a wrong turn and came up against strong enemy forces. *It was dark, and I did not know my leg was gone – so I kept on throwing bombs and little Wood* (probably L/9182 Private Robert William Wood, 6th East Kent, died 7th March 1916, buried in Vermelles British Cemetery – II H 5) *he kept by me and took out the pins for me.* Kate Luard was awarded the Royal Red Cross and Bar for her services during the Great War.

By 12.50 a.m. on the 7th the situation was relative quiet, but more mine explosions followed later in the day. That afternoon, 6th East Kent was relieved by 6th Royal West Kent.

St Eloi, Belgium, 27th–29th March 1916

> 113 Capt Rev'd Edward Noel Mellish, Royal Army Chaplains Department attached 4th Battalion, The Royal Fusiliers (9th Brigade, 3rd Division)

In late March 1916 the British carried out a small operation at St Eloi to pinch out a salient in the line around the Mound, an artificial earth bank that gave the Germans excellent observation over the British lines. In February, three deep mines,

Leave Ypres southwards on the N336 towards Messines. At the St Eloi roundabout stay on the N336 towards Armentières, passing an artillery piece on your right. Park after 150m on the left. Opposite is a green gate leading to the 1917 St Eloi crater. It is worth a visit if you have time. The gate has a key pad. Ring the Ypres Tourist Office (+32 (0) 57 239 220), give your name and phone number and they will give you the key pad code. It is open 1st April – 15th November, 10 a.m. to 5 p.m. However, the action involving Padre Mellish was on the left of this road. It is difficult to access because of private land and the growth of trees over the decades. A few metres south of the green gate is a left turn, which forks immediately. Walk a little way along the left fork to see Crater No.4 on the right with Crater No.5 just out of sight through the trees in front. The gate at the end of the road leads to Shelley Farm, but it is private and this is as far as you can go. Return to the fork and notice the electricity distribution tower with WW2 shrapnel damage. Take the right fork (Eekhofstraat) and follow round the corner. This used to be a straight road, but it has been diverted to pass around the craters. Just beyond the farm buildings on the left is Shelley Farm, which is private. On the way back peer through the gate on the right to look over Crater No.5.

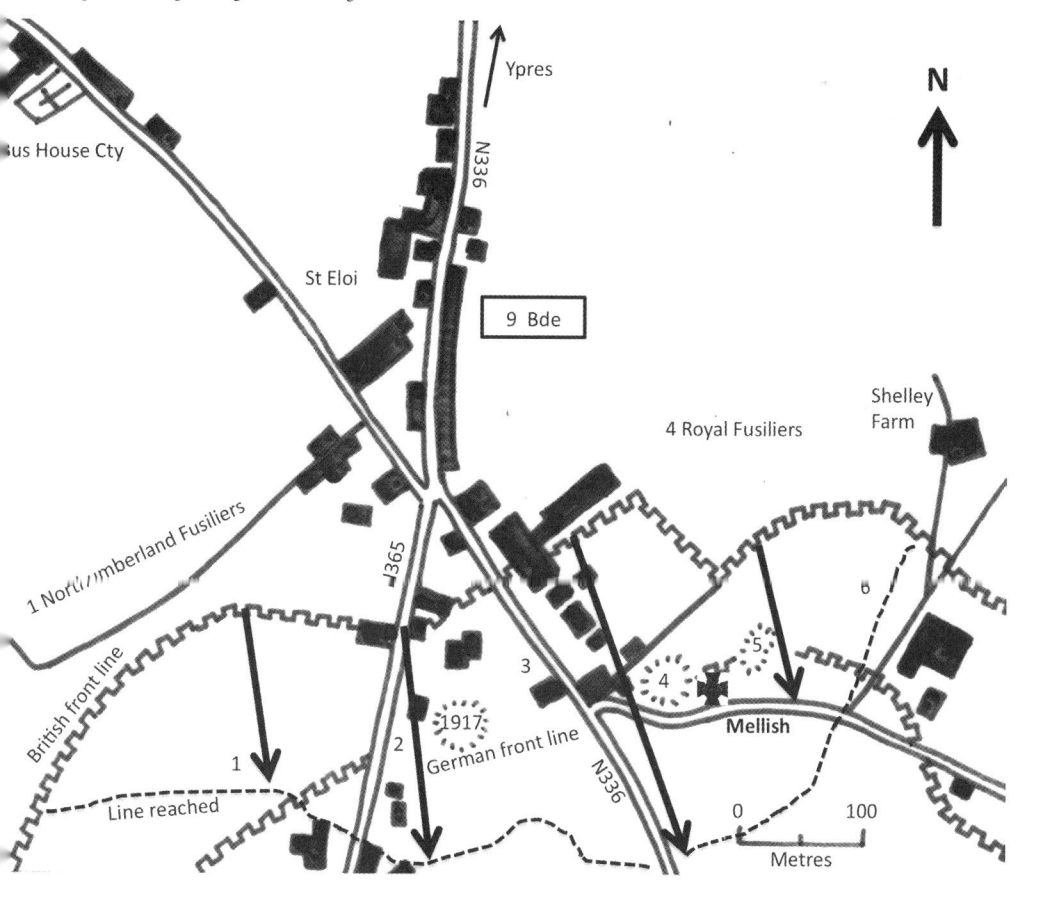

commenced the previous August, were completed beneath the German positions. These branched into six chambers packed with explosives, which were to be fired immediately prior to a pre-dawn attack by 9th Brigade. In order to achieve surprise there was no artillery preparation or wire cutting prior to the attack, which was limited to a narrow frontage of 550m.

1st Northumberland Fusiliers (right) and 4th Royal Fusiliers (left) were selected to make the attack from the flanks of the salient, thirty seconds after the mines exploded. The objective was the German third line, some 200m beyond the line of mine craters. The night preceding the attack was cold and wet and the assault troops suffered terribly as they lay in the mud waiting for zero hour. Between 3.40 and 4.05 a.m. scaling ladders and trench bridges were positioned and lanes were cut through the British wire. The holding battalions evacuated the forward trenches to avoid casualties from the mine explosions. Everything was conducted in complete silence and the Germans suspected nothing. At the first signs of dawn at 4.15 a.m., the first mine blew with the remainder following in the next few seconds. Mines 2, 3, 4, and 5 destroyed completely the German forward defences, while Mines 1 and 6 formed defensive works on the flanks. The artillery opened fire simultaneously and sealed off the area.

The infantry sprang forward into the attack as soon as the mine debris landed. 1st Northumberland Fusiliers crossed no man's land very quickly and reached its objectives with almost no casualties. 4th Royal Fusiliers, attacking with all four companies in line (from left to right – W, X, Y and Z), was less fortunate. The Battalion was caught by enfilade machine-gun fire from the left flank and suffered 261 casualties. The loss of many officers (only the CO, Adjutant and one other officer were not hit) caused confusion and a gap opened on the left of the line. The mines also rendered large sections of the attack frontage impassable.

The Germans were quick to react and their first shells landed only forty seconds after the British assault troops left their trenches. 4th Royal Fusiliers' objective was not taken on the left, but the trenches on the right were occupied and contact was made with 1st Northumberland Fusiliers. A platoon each from Y and Z Companies

Crater No.4 with Crater No.5 beyond the trees on the right. On the extreme left is the electricity distribution tower on the N336. 4th Royal Fusiliers attacked towards the camera from the centre of the picture.

Local Operations Spring 1916   149

Reverse view of the previous picture taken from behind 4th Royal Fusiliers' front line in March 2000. The electricity distribution tower is in the centre with Crater No.4 in the open area to the left. Crater No.5 is under the tall trees on the far left.

managed to get around the east side of No.5 Crater and consolidated an enemy trench on the south side. Other platoons of Y and Z Companies passed between No.4 and No.5 Craters to occupy an enemy trench south of No.4 Crater. This line was intended to be the new second line, but because the attack had failed to reach its objective it became the new front line instead.

Throughout the day artillery and machine-guns swept continuously across the open ground between the old front line and the new line, making it extremely hazardous to reach the wounded lying in the open. The Germans counterattacked at 8.15 a.m., but it achieved little and they lost heavily. About 200 Germans were taken prisoner in the initial attack and after the counterattack. The German artillery was particularly intense from 8.30 p.m. until midnight and this delayed the relief of 4th Royal Fusiliers by 2nd Royal Scots, which was not completed until 6 a.m. on the 28th. 1st Northumberland Fusiliers was relieved by 13th King's about the same time. Savage fighting continued until 19th April, by which time most of the captured ground had been lost.

During the attack **Padre Edward Mellish** began taking the wounded back to safety even before the stretcher-bearers were in action. He eventually brought in ten badly wounded men, but such was the intensity of the enemy fire that three men were killed while he was actually dressing their wounds. For the rest of the day he walked about calmly with a prayer book under his arm while 142nd Field

Looking north towards Crater No.5 in the dip to the left of the chalet. This is private property and can only be glimpsed through the gateway.

A later German photograph of Crater No.3.

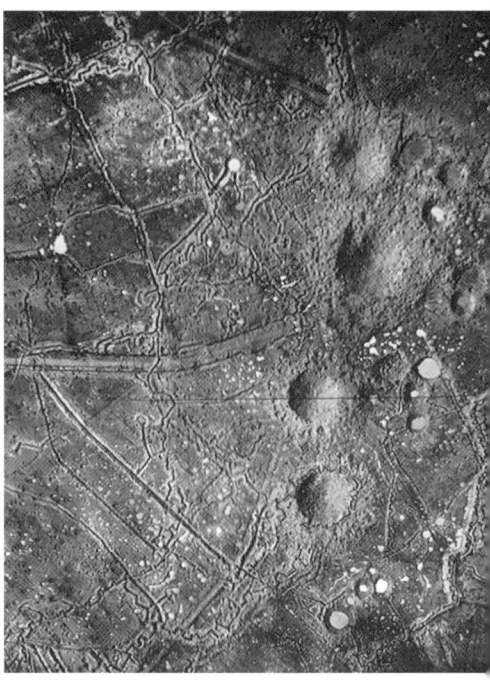

Air photograph of the four main St Eloi craters. The remains of the roads are also visible.

Ambulance personnel continued the recovery operation. Mellish did not give up searching until 6 a.m. the following morning.

Next day Mellish was in no man's land again, despite his unit being relieved, and rescued another twelve men. On one occasion his batman, Robins, had to pull him out of the mud on the edge of a crater, the mines having destroyed the drainage system installed by the Germans. Ground conditions were so poor that the rescuers laid canvas mats over the mud in order to help move the wounded. On the night of the third day, Mellish went out with the Field Ambulance and a party of six volunteer officers' servants and grooms from 2nd Suffolk (3/4699 Private W Sterry and 3/8446 Private W Thompson of Y Company and 3/7582 Private A Corville, 6932 Private G Reed, 13204 Private M Titch and 3/5661 Private S Parmenter of Z Company) to rescue the remainder of the wounded. Later a noted irreligious soldier was in hospital telling his companions how the Padre had rescued him. Another man asked what religion the Padre was and the soldier, who clearly had no idea, replied, *Well, I'm the same as 'im now and the bloke as sez a word agin our church will 'ave 'is .... 'ead bashed in!"*. Muscular Christianity indeed!

Near Blairville, France, 17th–18th April 1916

> 114 2Lt Edward Baxter, 1/8th Battalion, The King's (Liverpool Regiment (Liverpool Irish) (164th Brigade, 55th Division)

55th Division took over the Blairville – Ficheux area from the French in February 1916 and remained there until being thrown into the Somme battles in July. The first in a series of raids was launched by 1/8th King's on the night of 17th/18th April. Meticulous preparations commenced on 3rd April, while the Battalion was out of the line at Bretencourt. Volunteers were drawn from each company and three officers and forty-three other ranks were selected. The raiding party trained in wire cutting and trench entry techniques on specially constructed practice trenches. Captain Mahon was chosen to lead the raid and the other officers were 2nd Lieutenants Limerick and **Edward Baxter**. The force was divided into a number of smaller parties:

- Right and left storming parties, each of an officer and ten men, including bayonet men, bombers and carriers. They were to enter the enemy trench and work their way right and left, taking prisoners, bombing dugouts and cutting telephone wires. They were not to proceed more than four traverses and were to block communications trenches. Some wore chest shields.
- Parapet party of eight men with ladders and spare bombs were to assist the storming parties to get out of the trench at the end of the raid and deal with any prisoners and wounded.
- Covering party of fifteen men, including telephonists. They were to lay a white tape to the German parapet and a telephone line to the wire. Its task was to prevent the storming parties being surprised from the flanks and to cover them. It would be the last element to pull back. These men were taught various German phrases, but had forgotten them by the time the raid was launched!

The Battalion went into the line on 10th April and five of the six following nights were spent reconnoitring entry points into the enemy trenches. The sixth night was cancelled due to a full moon and little cloud. A point equidistant between two saps, 215m apart, was chosen close to the Blairville – Rivière road. Having made all the preparations, they had to wait for a cloudy night to cover the moon.

At midnight on 16th April Limerick led the wire cutters and covering party into no man's land, while long-range machine-gun fire helped to cover any noise. Having reached a disused German trench about 470m from the British lines, they had to lie low for an hour due to the close proximity of a German working party. Meanwhile the rest of the raiders followed and prepared to launch the raid as soon as the wire was breached.

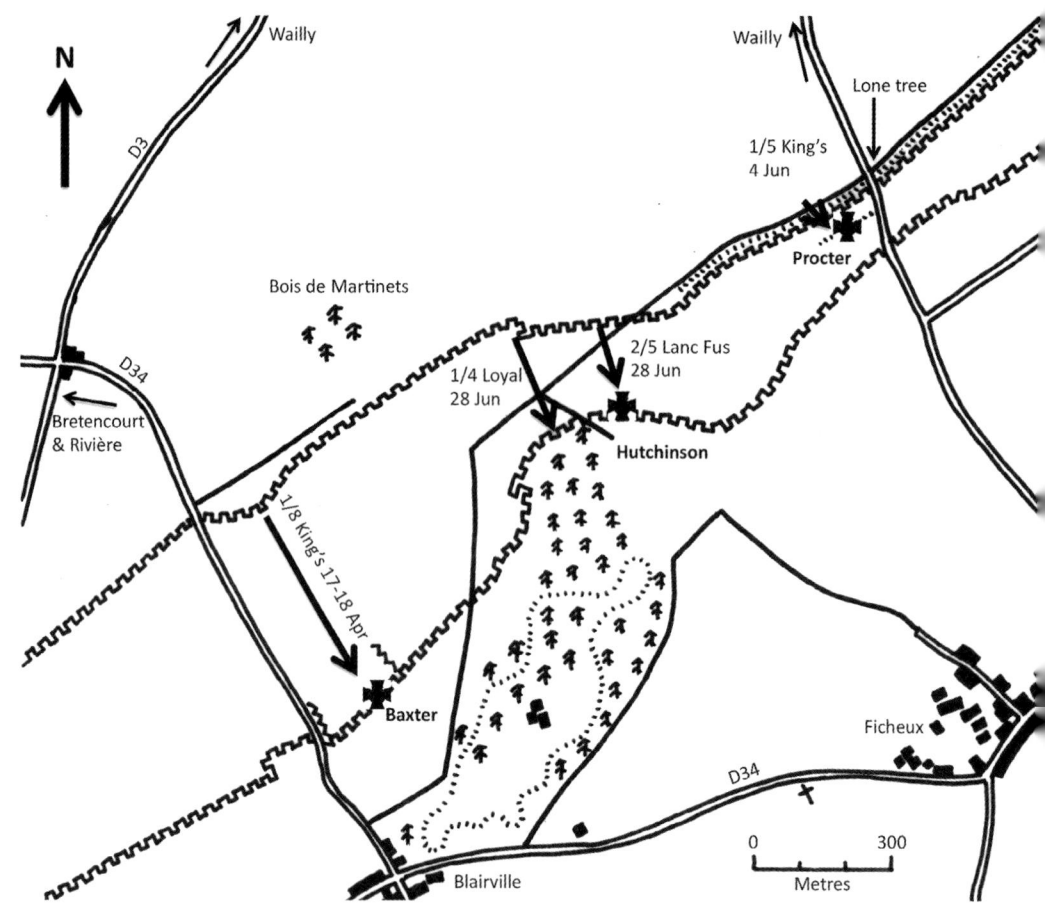

From the church in Blairville, drive east for 150m and turn left towards Rivière on the D34. After 150m stop at the staggered junction and turn left and immediately right towards Rivière. After another 800m turn right onto a track and park. The British front line was a few metres south of and parallel with this track. Look south towards Blairville, the church is very prominent. You are looking in the direction taken by Edward Baxter and the 1/8th King's raiding party in April 1916. About 300m in front of you and 100m east of the road is a telegraph pole. This is about where the entry through the German wire was made, with the enemy trenches beyond.

Return to the D34 and turn right. After 450m turn right onto the D3 and follow it into Wailly. Leave Wailly south on the minor road to Ficheux. After 1,300m there is a cross track with a prominent lone tree on the left. Park in the track on the left, where there is room to fit a car and still allow access. Be careful exiting as the tree obscures the road to the left. Look west across the road; the British front line ran just to the left of and parallel with the track. This is where the 1/5th King's raid was launched on 4th June 1916. The low earth bank where Arthur Procter earned his VC is about 70m to the left of the track. It has been eroded by almost a century of ploughing and can be difficult to see, particularly in summer when the crops are high.

Having considered the 1/5th King's raid, walk 700m along the rough track to the west, almost to the corner of Blairville Wood to see the site where James Hutchinson won his VC. The original track came out of the sunken section and headed for the southeast face of the Wood, but today passes it to the north. A fence marks the line of the original track and 100m short of the Wood is the entry point for the raid by 2/5th Lancashire Fusiliers on 28th June 1916. There was another simultaneous raid 250m to the southwest.

As soon as the Germans disappeared at about 1 a.m., the wire cutters set to work. After an hour they had cut through thirteen rows of wire and realised they had insufficient time to finish the job and carry out the raid that night. Baxter went forward with a relief cutting party in an attempt to make up the lost time. However, at 3.25 a.m., with two belts of wire remaining and dawn almost breaking, the cutters were recalled. By 3.45 a.m. everyone was back in the British trenches.

Wire cutting in close proximity to the enemy was always an extremely tense experience. In this instance, German sentries could be heard talking just beyond the parapet. While Baxter's party was working, a warning bell fell off the wire. Everyone froze expecting to be discovered, but for some reason the Germans did not hear it. Baxter had extracted the pin from a grenade in readiness for the expected fight. Somehow he let the grenade slip and the fuse started to burn. It would have been natural for him to have simply rolled into cover. However, this would have compromised the whole raid and put many lives in jeopardy. Instead he calmly but swiftly picked up the grenade, unscrewed the base plug, pulled out the detonator and smothered it into the earth before it went off. This was a remarkably cool act in the circumstances.

It was decided to try again next night if the Germans had not noticed the gaps cut in their wire. Once the moon had clouded over around midnight, a patrol confirmed that the enemy had made no attempt to mend the wire. The cutting party of two officers and two NCOs, supported by the covering party, deployed

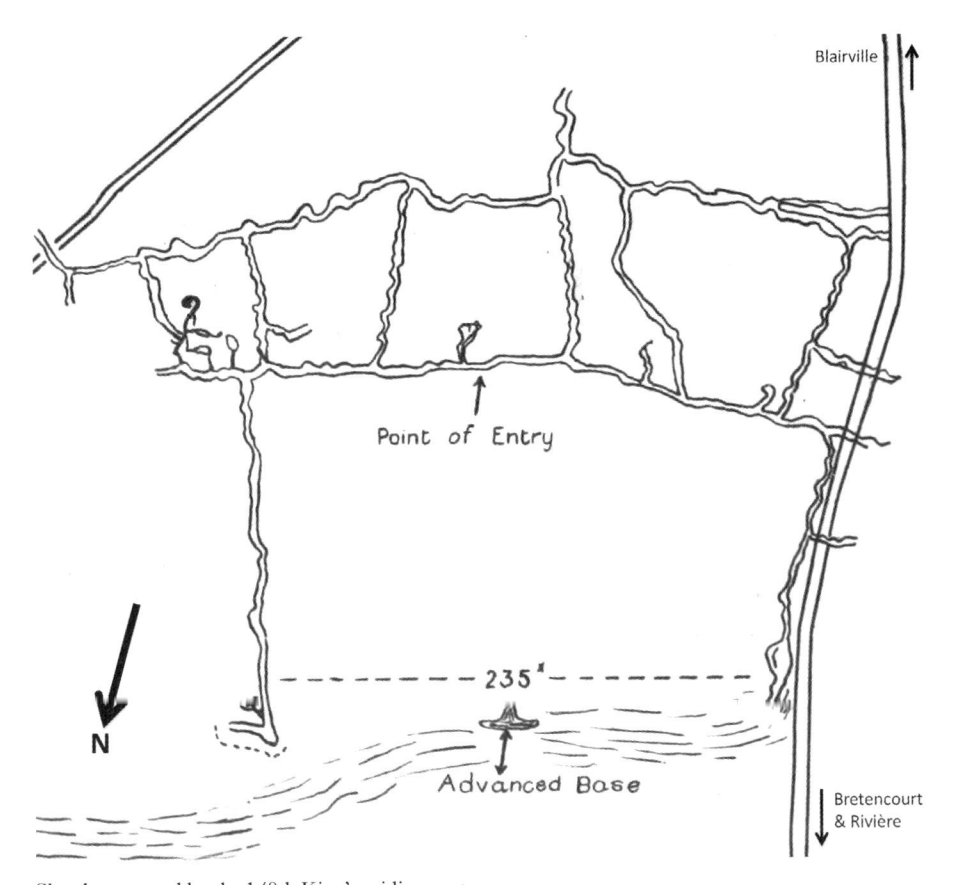

Sketch map used by the 1/8th King's raiding party.

154   Victoria Crosses on the Western Front April 1915–June 1916

at 12.30 a.m. and finished their task by 2.20 a.m. Meanwhile the rest of the raiders had been guided forward along the white tape. At 2.25 a.m., the two storming parties rushed forward. At the same time, the telephonist sent back the message, *Slow*. This was the signal for the artillery to fire a slow box barrage to isolate the assault area and for supporting machine-guns to open fire on the flanking trenches.

Baxter led the left storming party. He was first into the trench, shooting the sentry with his revolver. His men then fanned out, bombed two dugouts and killed four Germans in the trench. The right storming party had a similar experience, killing three Germans in the trench and bombing a deep dugout.

From the point where the 1/8th King's raiding party left the British front line, looking south towards the site of the raid on 17th-18th April 1916. The church in Blairville is on the right with the D34 road to Bretencourt and Rivière below it. The entry point into the German lines was in the area of the telegraph pole in the field on the left.

The German trench was found to be around four metres deep, with wooden sides and the floor lined with bricks or concrete. The short ladders taken by the raiders only just reached the fire-step, which was reached from the bottom of the trench by steps. This made it almost impossible to take back a prisoner, but two helmets were recovered, one marked 'LJR77', which identified the unit as Landwehr Infanterie Regiment 77. Although three deep dugouts were bombed and there were many shouts and screams from below, the depth of these shelters made it impossible to get inside and take prisoners. A grenade store was destroyed and telephone wires

Section through the German trench as reported by the 1/8th King's raiding party.

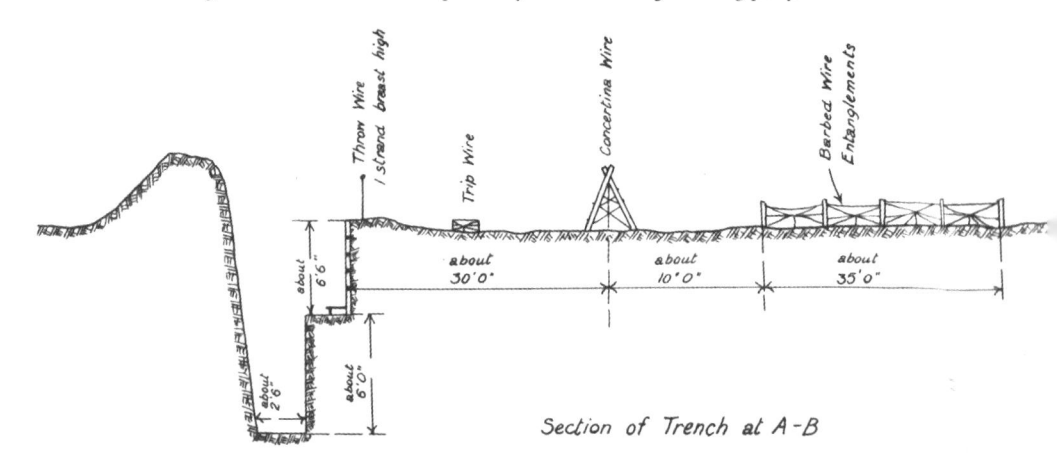

were cut. This may have delayed the German response, which was quite feeble, just a few shells, some grenades, but almost no small arms fire.

When the order came to retire after ten minutes (three whistle blasts), Baxter positioned himself on the parapet and counted every man out. He was seen assisting the last man out of the enemy trench. On hearing the whistle the telephonists sent the message, *'Fast'*, and the artillery fire increased and lowered to cover the retirement. The party followed the white tape back through the wire and reassembled in the British trenches. Baxter was the only man missing and Limerick immediately took a search party to the German wire, but no trace of him was found. It was assumed he went back into the enemy trench for an unknown purpose and met his end when the Germans returned or he was hit and fell into the trench. It was estimated that fifty-seven enemy were killed in the raid. In addition to Baxter's VC, the raiders earned a DCM and three MMs.

Broadmarsh Crater, Vimy Ridge, France, 21st May 1916

115 Lt Richard Jones, 8th Battalion, The Loyal North Lancashire Regiment (7th Brigade, 25th Division)

In March 1916, the British took over the comparatively quiet Vimy sector from the French. The Germans held almost all nine miles of the top of Vimy Ridge, but of more immediate concern was the advanced state of German mining in the area. A three-month long underground battle commenced, drawing in ten British and five French tunnelling companies. Gradually, but not without sacrifice, the British gained the upper hand. The Germans realised they were losing the war underground and decided that they must capture the entrances to the British tunnel systems.

Apart from continuous mortar fire, there were no other signs that an attack was imminent. Reserve divisions were therefore withdrawn to the south for the forthcoming Somme offensive. On the night of 18th/19th May, the Germans captured the area around Broadmarsh Crater. However, the situation did not concern the high command unduly and a reorganisation of Army, Corps, and Divisional boundaries went ahead on the night of 19th/20th May. That night, 8th Loyal North Lancashire retook the lost ground.

The line was then held by 1st Wiltshire on the right and 10th Cheshire on the left, with the boundary between them being Grange communication trench. 8th Loyal North Lancashire was in reserve in Pylones and on Béthune Road. A single platoon of 8th Loyal North Lancashire under **Lieutenant Richard Jones** held Broadmarsh Crater. Two companies of 7th Rifle Brigade employed on mine fatigues were available in an emergency and 3rd Worcestershire was held back in divisional reserve.

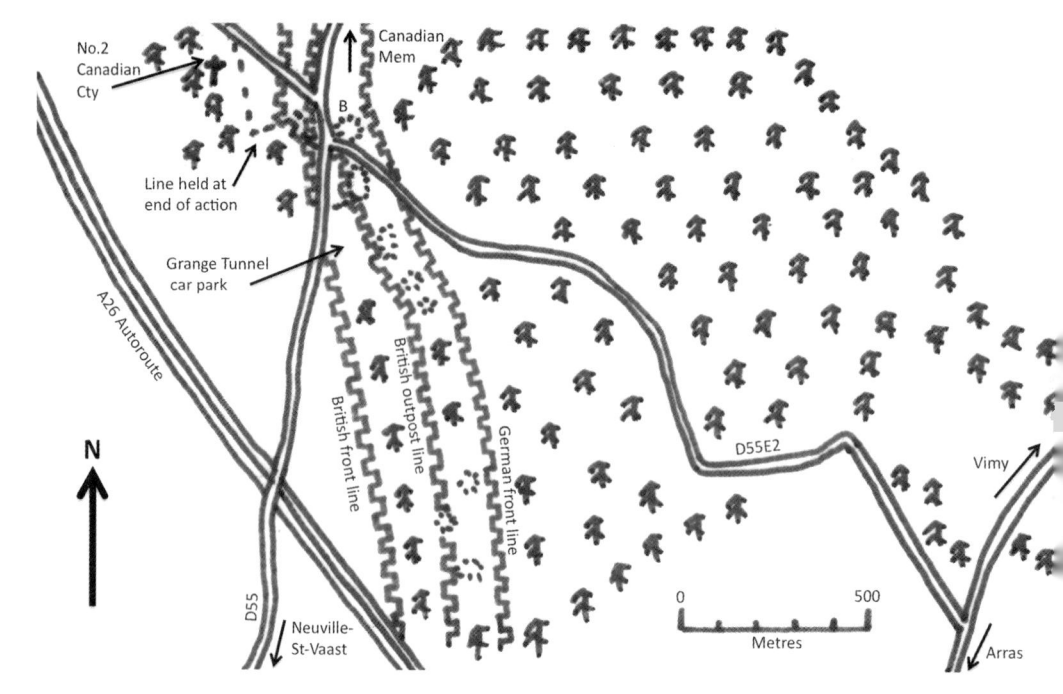

Follow signs for the Canadian Memorial on Vimy Ridge. Park at the Grange Tunnel car park (free). A visit is recommended if time permits, but it is best to book ahead at busy times of the year (it can be done online). Walk north on the D55 towards the Memorial. After 150m there is a right turn onto the D55E2 to Vimy. Continue on the D55 for another 100m to the left turn to No.2 Canadian Cemetery. On the other side of the D55 is Broadmarsh Crater, marked with a 'B' on the map. Look back along the D55. About 30m south of Broadmarsh Crater is where the mine was exploded on 21st May 1916. There is nothing to see now as it lies beneath the road. Jones was in action all round Broadmarsh Crater, but was particularly noted for his actions between Broadmarsh and the new crater. This map is designed purely to set Richard Jones' VC action into the main features of the surrounding terrain.

At 3.45 a.m. on 21st May, the Germans commenced a bombardment by eighty batteries, including minenwerfer, on 1,600m of front. It was particularly heavy on the sector from 'P77' to 'P79'. Except for a lull from 11 a.m. until 3 p.m., the shelling went on all day and 70,000 shells were fired. The forward British defences almost ceased to exist and all telephone lines forward of Brigade HQ were cut. The Germans also used gas and lachrymatory shells, which further hampered communications. As an attack seemed likely, C Company, 8th Loyal North Lancashire was moved forward to Cross Street. The platoon in Broadmarsh Crater was cut off by a curtain of gas shells behind. The communication trench leading to the Crater was obliterated in the bombardment and a dump of bombs was blown up and a Lewis Gun destroyed.

At 7.45 p.m., a mine was exploded 30m south of Broadmarsh Crater, the guns lifted and the Germans attacked the front from Broadmarsh Crater in the south to Momber Crater in the north. 140th Brigade (47th Division) bore the brunt of the assault and its front and support lines were overrun. However, the Germans made less impression upon 141st Brigade to the north of 140th Brigade and 7th Brigade (25th Division) to the south. These two formations turned their flanks inwards to prevent the breakthrough spreading.

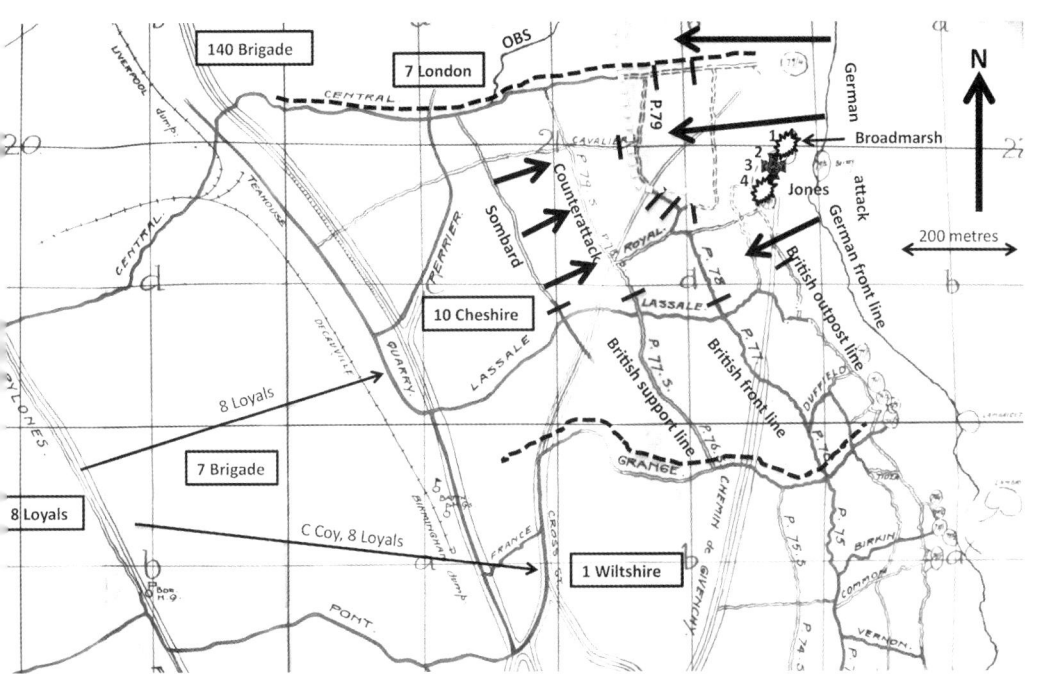

The left sector of 7th Brigade's front on 21st May 1916, based on a sketch map used at the time. The approximate position of the current Grange Tunnel car park is shown for orientation. Short black lines across trenches mark the blocks established to limit the German advance. The approximate position of the four posts held by Richard Jones' platoon are shown around Broadmarsh Crater. The curved dashed white line in the top right of the map denotes the area finally given up by the British. OBS = Old Boot Street.

On the left of 7th Brigade's area, the enemy attacked in lines, coming on steadily in files at irregular intervals. In the second line men were seen throwing up lights and it was believed they were showing their artillery where they had reached. 2nd Lieutenant Oates and a dozen men of 10th Cheshire with two machine-guns inflicted heavy losses on the Germans. They took cover in the remnants of the British trenches and began bombing down Central Trench, preceded by a minenwerfer barrage, which knocked out both machine-guns. Oates' party ran out of bombs and retired towards Lassale, where they established a block. The Germans got into the left of the support line, but were blocked by Oates' party in Central and by a party of 7th London in Old Boot Street. 8th Loyal North Lancashire moved forward to the Quarry to prepare a counterattack. Efforts were hampered by the whole of 10th Cheshire's HQ becoming casualties. More blocks were established by 1st Wiltshire on the right.

From the site of the small mine on the D55 looking north towards Broadmarsh Crater on the other side of the road. Richard Jones was particularly active between the two craters.

Out in front, Lieutenant Richard Jones' platoon occupied four bombing posts in an isolated position around Broadmarsh Crater. One post was on the lip of the crater and the others were spread along the defence trench leading back to the British lines. Jones expected to be attacked from the north but, just before the main attack commenced, the Germans exploded a mine 30m to the south of Broadmarsh Crater at the end of Royal Avenue. Shortly afterwards German infantry came on in three lines. The first line was spaced with about three metres between each man, but succeeding lines were more densely packed, with men carrying stores to rebuild trenches and lay new belts of wire.

Jones was determined to hold on and positioned himself close to No.2 Post, from where he could observe the ground between the two craters. This Post accounted for a German machine-gun team before it could bring its weapon into use. Meanwhile, Nos 3 and 4 Posts managed to keep the enemy out of the new crater for fifteen minutes. Private Regan, a particularly good bomb thrower, was able to reach the far edge of the new crater and threw fifteen boxes of bombs. The lip of the new crater was denied to the enemy for half an hour, but the supply of bombs ran out and the platoon had only their rifles.

Jones constantly rallied his men and kept them firing. He personally accounted for at least fifteen Germans coming on between the two craters, shouting out his score as he went on. Eventually he ran out of rifle ammunition, but saw some grenades close by. As he rose to throw one, he was shot through the head and died instantly.

Inspired by Jones' example, the platoon fought on, led by Corporal Coates, because the platoon sergeant had been killed before Jones. The men even resorted to throwing rocks and grenade boxes when their ammunition ran out. At about

From the D55E2 looking towards the junction with the D55 on the left where the small mine was exploded. Broadmarsh Crater is right of centre. The German attack came out of the trees on the far right.

10 p.m., the platoon was down to only nine men, all wounded, and was forced to give up the Crater. As they pulled back, the survivors of No.1 Post found a box of grenades and used them all before dashing back to the line held by 10th Cheshire. Coates was wounded four times, but continued to urge the men on. The survivors assisted 10th Cheshire in constructing trench blocks. Coates received the MM for this action and one wonders why he did not receive a significantly higher award. Two DCMs and a further two MMs were awarded to the platoon.

By 2 a.m. on the 22nd the counterattack was ready. Three companies of 8th Loyal North Lancashire began crawling forward from Sombard, a disused trench. When they were about 100m from the enemy, two machine-guns opened up. They charged and the enemy fled from the support line. With no sign of a supporting counterattack on the left, a halt was called and blocks were established along Cavalier and Central Trenches. Touch was maintained with 7th London in Old Boot Street. At 2.45 a.m., green flares went up from the German lines, followed by a very heavy shrapnel barrage. Fortunately casualties were light. There was some shelling during the rest of the day and after dark the whole front was taken over by 3rd Worcestershire.

Poorly coordinated counterattacks failed to evict the Germans fully. Fierce fighting went on for a few days, during which the British recovered some lost ground, although the Germans retained the mineshafts. Because of the impending Somme offensive, and the desire to husband limited resources, the British suspended further counterattacks and the front remained much as it was until the major battle in this area in April 1917. The actions cost 7th Brigade about 650 casualties.

Chapter Seven

Prelude to the Somme

East of Meaulte, France, 3rd/4th June 1916

> 116 Pte George Chafer, 1st Battalion, The East Yorkshire Regiment (64th Brigade, 21st Division)

June 1916 saw the final preparations for the 'Big Push'. In common with many other units, 1st East Yorkshire had moved to the Somme area at the end of March and had spent the intervening period either training for the coming offensive or holding the line. The Fricourt sector was comparatively quiet until early June, when the Germans suddenly became very aggressive. 1st East Yorkshire went into the Brigade left sub-section on 1st June, relieving 13th Northumberland Fusiliers in the front line. 9th KOYLI was on the right and 15th DLI in support, with 10th KOYLI in reserve in Meaulte.

At 11 p.m. on 3rd June, the enemy artillery and trench mortars opened a heavy bombardment, which struck the British lines on 1st East Yorkshire's (C Company) left boundary with 21st Northumberland Fusiliers (102nd Brigade, 34th Division). The front line trench was almost levelled and the whole area was swept by machine-guns. However, in the early stages there were no casualties. The bombardment resumed at 12.45 a.m. and at 1.15 a.m. the enemy launched a strong raid, entering the trenches at the junction between the two battalions. To make matters worse the air was thick with gas. A 1st East Yorkshire listening post was captured, but all the men managed to escape. Although most of the fighting took place in 21st Northumberland Fusiliers' lines, 1st East Yorkshires lost heavily, with twenty-two killed or died of wounds (most are buried in Norfolk Cemetery, Becordel-Becourt) and forty-two wounded. Unusually there is only passing reference to this action in the Brigade war diary.

Looking southeast from the track south of the Lochnagar Crater on the boundary between 102nd and 64th Brigades. The front line of C Company, 1st East Yorkshire straddled this track, with the German attack being launched from their lines along the high ground on the far left. George Chafer's VC action was on the hillside to the left of the bushes at the bottom of the re-entrant.

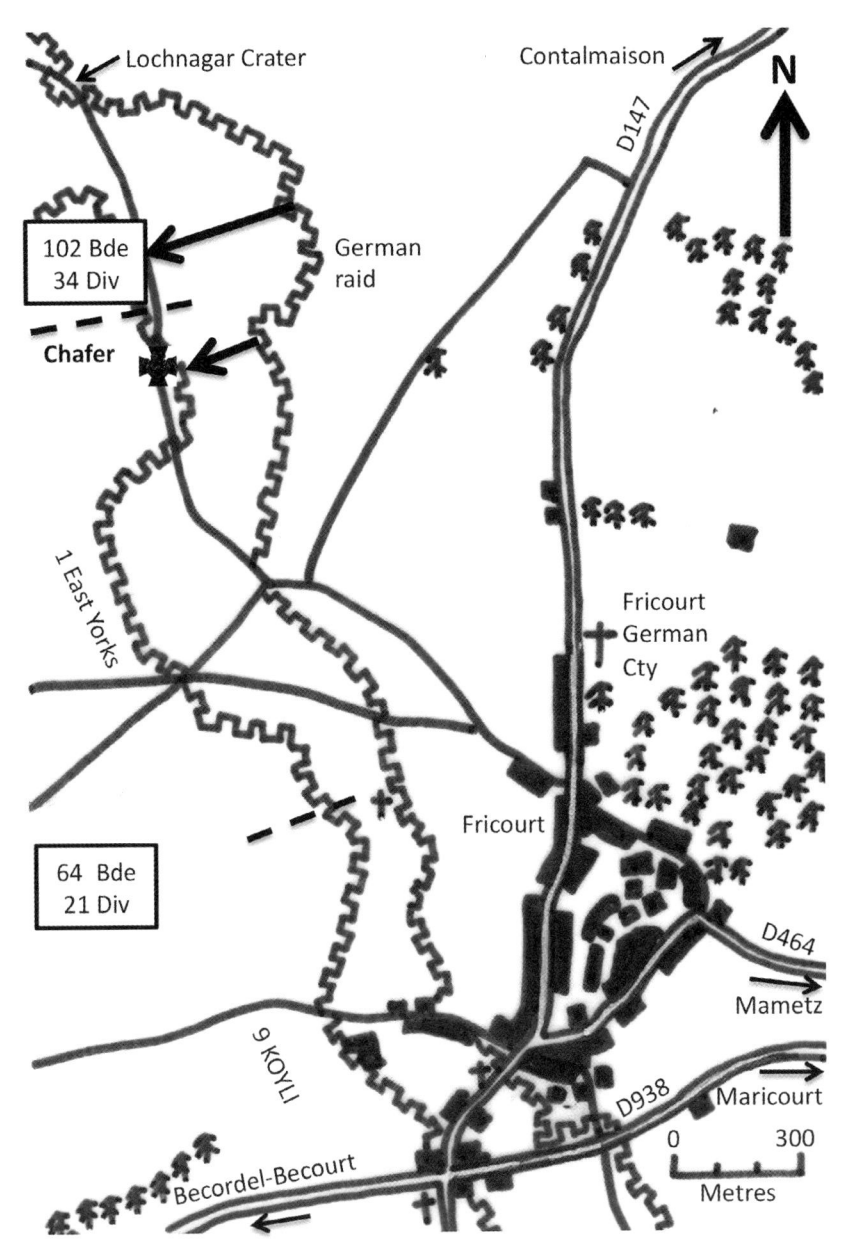

There are two options to approach the site of Chafer's VC action. The closest is from the north. Park at the Lochnagar Crater at La Boisselle and walk south on the metalled track. After 300m the tarmac runs out and it becomes rougher; it's fine for 4WD but not normal cars. The bottom of the re-entrant can be very muddy, even in summer. 700m from the Crater, as the track gradually bends left/eastwards and upwards, is where George Chafer won his VC on 3rd/4th June 1916. Continue to a track heading off to the right/south. This is where the German front line ran across the track.

Another approach is to drive south on the D147 from Contalmaison. Pass Fricourt German Cemetery on the left and 250m further on turn right onto a single track metalled road. After 200m a track on the left goes to Fricourt New Military Cemetery, but keep right for another 500m until the track bends round to the left/west. Stop on the right where there is plenty of space to park and turn. Walk on 100m and stop at the track junction on the left, i.e. on the German front line. Walk northwest along the track for another 550m. This is where the German attack struck the front held by C Company, 1st East Yorkshire, from the right side of the track.

From the German front line at the track junction looking northeast. The British front line ran across the picture along the line of the darker vegetation in the left middle ground. In the left distance is Bécourt Wood. Bushes around the Lochnagar Crater can be seen on the right with the track leading into the reentrant where George Chafer was in action.

Private George Chafer was badly wounded and concussed in the attack. He had a hole through his left hand, one leg was badly torn open by a shell splinter and he was choked and blinded by gas. A runner passing close to Chafer was partially buried by an exploding shell. He cried out for someone to take a message from him and deliver it to the company commander. Despite being in terrible pain, Chafer crawled to the runner and took the message from his pocket. Then, in spite of the hail of fire, he climbed out of the trench into the open where he could move more quickly. He crawled along until he reached the forward trench and met an unwounded corporal. Having explained the situation to him, Chafer handed over the message just before collapsing from loss of blood.

Near Ficheux, France, 4th June 1916

117 Pte Arthur Procter, 1/5th Battalion, The King's (Liverpool Regiment) (165th Brigade, 55th Division)

On 28th May, Sir Douglas Haig issued orders for First, Second and Third Armies to *take steps to deceive the enemy as to the real front of attack*, in the forthcoming offensive to be launched by Fourth Army on the Somme. Measures were to include:

- Overt preparations for assault, such as the construction of advanced trenches, dummy assembly trenches and gun positions.
- Wire cutting to force the enemy to man his defences, cause fatigue and prevent reserves being moved.

- Gas and smoke discharges to force the enemy to wear respirators and man their defences, followed by barrages on the enemy lines to cause fatigue and casualties.
- Barrages on communications and rest billets.
- Raids by night in company strength upwards supported by heavy artillery and mortar concentrations.

On the night of 3rd/4th June, 1/5th King's mounted a raid on the enemy trenches, following six days of meticulously detailed training at Beaumetz. The raiding party of eighty-nine all ranks (seventy-nine according to the Brigade war diary) reported to Battalion HQ at Calvaire at 4 p.m. on the 3rd for final preparations. Faces were blackened and all identifying items removed. At 12.15 a.m. they slipped over the parapet and took up positions along a low ridge about 70m into no man's land and about 100m from the enemy lines. At 12.35 a.m. they signalled that they were in position and five minutes later the artillery barrage on the enemy front and support trenches fell along a frontage of 2,250m.

The intense bombardment consisted of field and heavy artillery and several batteries of trench mortars – four 8" Howitzers, two 6" Howitzers, two 60 Pounders, ten 4.5" Howitzers, seven batteries of 18 Pounders, two batteries of 2" Mortars, three batteries of Stokes Mortars and a battery of 3.7" Mortars. One of the artillery units involved was 7th Lancashire (Howitzer) Battery of 4th West Lancashire Brigade RFA, in which Bombardier Cyril Edward Gourley (VC 1917) was serving. Some shells fell short amongst the raiding party and messages were sent back. The firing ceased at 12.55 a.m., but by then fifty-seven men had been hit, of whom ten were killed. CWGC records indicate that nine men were killed and five more succumbed to their wounds within a few days. They are buried in Wailly Orchard Cemetery, Avesnes-le-Comte Communal

The British front line crossed the road at this point. The low ridge is within the maize in the centre. The German front line ran along the top of the hill.

Reverse of the previous picture from the German front line looking over the British lines, which crossed the road at the lone tree on the right and ran across the picture to the left. Wailly is in the background. The low ridge where Arthur Procter won his VC is in the maize to the left of the road.

The area of the 1/5th King's raid on 4th June 1916 from the British front line to the west. The sunken and overgrown track on the left is just behind and parallel with the British front line. The low ridge is in the maize in the centre, beyond which a van can be seen on the Wailly – Ficheux road. The German front line ran parallel with the darker vegetation at the top of the hill on the right. For a map of this action, see the account for Edward Baxter on 17/18th April 1916.

Cemetery Extension and Bellacourt Military Cemetery. The raid could not go on and the party withdrew, bringing in thirty-nine wounded. On returning to the British lines, it was realised that eight men were missing.

Around noon next day, **Private Arthur Procter**, a stretcher-bearer, very carefully looked over the parapet. He saw two bodies, which were thought to be dead, move slightly, one of whom was 2333 Private William Wilfred Jones. They were lying 70m away, in full view of the enemy, but without hesitation he went out and immediately came under fire. By a combination of short dashes and crawling, he reached the two men and managed to drag them into the cover of the low ridge used by the raiding party. Procter bandaged their wounds and made them as comfortable as possible, even stripping off his cardigan because one of the men felt cold. Before leaving, Procter promised they would be rescued after dark and then dashed back, again under intense fire. Later that day the Battalion was relieved by 1/6th King's, but before departing arrangements were made to bring in the wounded men that night. This was done, but William Jones died of wounds on 8th June and was buried at Avesnes-le-Comte Communal Cemetery Extension (II A 10). Procter met his mother in England in August 1916.

Givenchy, France, 22nd/23rd June 1916

118 LCpl John Erskine, 5th/6th Battalion, The Cameronians (Scottish Rifles) (19th Brigade, 33rd Division)
119 Spr William Hackett, 254 Tunnelling Company, Royal Engineers

On 22nd June 1916, 33rd Division was holding the line in the Givenchy sector astride the La Bassée Canal, one of the most active mining areas on the Western Front. At 1.55 a.m., following a two hours bombardment, the German 295 Pioneer

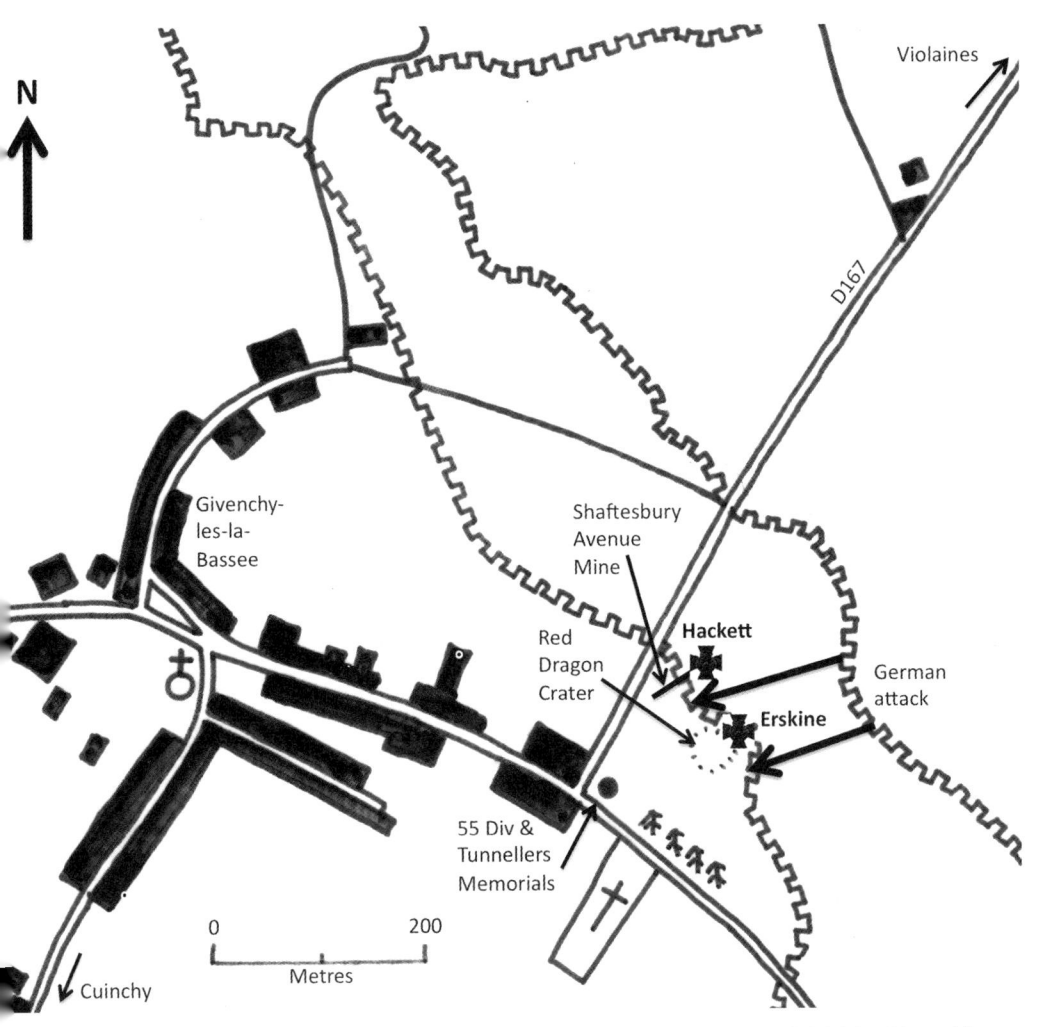

Drive east through Givenchy-les-la-Bassée on the D167 towards Violaines. At the 55th Division Memorial turn right and park at the cemetery. There are a number of May–June 1940 CWGC graves within and, intriguingly, one Soviet soldier from September 1944. Walk back to the Memorial to see the information boards about tunnellers and the action at Red Dragon Crater. Walk north along the road towards Violaines. After 100m you are on the British front line in June 1916. Continue to a left turn. Just before it on the left roadside are the remains of a German concrete pillbox on the German front line. Look back down the road. A slight depression to the left of the road is all that remains of Red Dragon Crater, but crops make it difficult to see in the summer. The nearest reliable café in this area is in the centre of Richebourg, opposite the church.

Mining Company exploded a large mine under a salient in the lines known to the British as the 'Duck's Bill'. It completely obliterated the British saps in the area and blew in the front line. A minute of heavy artillery fire followed. Then about 200 German infantry attacked each side of the crater and gained a footing in the trenches held by 2nd Royal Welsh Fusiliers.

The flanks of the attack held firm and an immediate counterattack drove out the raiders, leaving behind a dozen dead and a wounded prisoner. However, the area around the newly formed Red Dragon Crater (named in honour of the RWF) was a complete shambles and a great deal of consolidation work was required to dig out

1916 photograph of the Red Dragon Crater area looking east from Givenchy.

the trenches and establish a post on the near lip of the crater. The Germans made two attempts to occupy their side of the crater, but were forced back by Lewis guns. They were then active with rifle grenades and there was a barrage on the trenches from 11.45 p.m. to 1.45 a.m., which caused considerable damage. The Brigade sapping platoon from 5th/6th Cameronians, commanded by 2nd Lieutenant David James Stevenson, was sent forward to assist in clearing up and repairing the damage. Amongst the platoon was **Lance Corporal John Erskine**.

On reaching the crater, Erskine saw many wounded lying in the open. Disregarding the heavy and continuous fire, he dashed forward and rescued Sergeant Weir and later Private Archibald Ogg. Stevenson was hit by a sniper while directing the consolidation work on the lip of the crater. Erskine saw him fall and thought he was dead until he saw the officer move. At this Erskine climbed over the lip of the crater, exposing himself to the intense enemy fire and for an hour used his own body to shield Stevenson while help was being arranged. Eventually a shallow trench was dug to their exposed position and Erskine was able to help carry Stevenson to

From the German front line looking southeast over the British lines, with Givenchy on the right. The road is the D167 to Violaines. Red Dragon Crater is the slight depression in the field. William Hackett and Thomas Collins lie entombed a few metres into the field on the left.

Red Dragon Crater

Prelude to the Somme   167

safety. Despite these heroic efforts, Stevenson died shortly afterwards and is buried in Gorre British and Indian Cemetery (I B 22).

Meanwhile another drama was being enacted below ground. Five men were working in the main drive off Shaftesbury Avenue Mine Shaft when the German mine exploded. The shock wave caused the tunnel to collapse, trapping five men near the face. Relays of sappers began digging towards them and after twenty hours a small opening was made through the broken timbers and fallen clay.

Three men were able to scramble to safety through the narrow hole. One of the two remaining, Private Thomas Collins (14th Welsh) was a large man who was also badly injured. He could not be passed through the small hole, but the other man, **Sapper William Hackett**, could have reached safety. The tunnel was in danger of collapsing again and Hackett was ordered to get out. He refused to leave saying, *I'm a tunneller. I must look after my mate*. Seconds later the opening was swallowed up by a fall and the two men were lost. The rescue party dug for four more days, but failed to reach them. Of all the tales of bravery associated with the Victoria Cross, this must rank as the most outstanding example of deliberate self-sacrifice.

254th Tunnelling Company's War Diary does not commence until July 1916 and there is no mention of Shaftesbury Avenue Mine in it, although New Shaftesbury in the Givenchy South sector is mentioned. There is also mention of an enemy mine destroying a gallery for thirty-six feet and trapping two men at the face, whom it proved impossible to rescue. This mine is named as No.1 Half Moon in the Givenchy North sector and seems to refer to the same incident in which Hackett won his VC, but it is not entirely clear. For their part in the rescue attempt, Sappers 132930 H

The Tunnellers Memorial next to the 55th Division Memorial. The T-shaped window looks directly to the spot above the collapsed Shaftesbury Mine where William Hackett and Thomas Collins remain buried.

A similar view to the previous picture from March 2000, taken in July 2014. With crops growing it is even more difficult to see the remains of Red Dragon Crater.

Pooley, brothers 132671 George Smith and 132670 James Smith and 132931 Joseph Thornton were awarded the Military Medal (LG 10th August 1916).

Thomas Collins is commemorated on the Thiepval Memorial and his date of death is given as 22nd June 1916, even though he was known to be alive on the 23rd. Conversely, William Hackett is commemorated on the Ploegsteert Memorial and his date of death is given as 27th June 1916, although he could not possibly have survived that long after the tunnel collapsed on 23rd June. Neither Memorial seems to fit the geographical limits fixed by the CWGC. The Loos Memorial appears to be a much more appropriate place to commemorate both men. However, due to the expense and disruption involved, the CWGC takes the view that such errors will not be corrected and the two men will continue to be commemorated where they are.

25th June 1916

120 Capt Arthur Batten-Pooll, 3rd (att'd 2nd) Battalion, The Royal Munster Fusiliers (3rd Brigade, 1st Division)

121 Pte John William Jackson, 17th Battalion, Australian Imperial Force (5th Australian Brigade, 1st Australian Division)

Near Calonne, France

As the Somme offensive drew nearer, Sir Douglas Haig wished to keep the enemy guessing where the blow would fall. On 14th June, instructions were issued to launch a series of heavy and well-planned raids in other areas in the period 20th–25th June. The dates were modified the following day to 20th–30th June. As a guide, each corps was expected to carry out a raid every night.

One of these raids was launched by D Company, 2nd Royal Munster Fusiliers near Cité Calonne, north of Liévin on 25th June 1916. The 160 strong raiding party rehearsed the operation on replica trenches at Bully Grenay. Brigadier General HR Davies, commanding 3rd Brigade, and Major General EP Strickland, commanding 1st Division, watched the rehearsals on 22nd June. On the 24th, trench mortars cut lanes through the wire and that night they were subjected to heavy small arms and artillery fire to dissuade the Germans from making repairs. That night, 2nd Royal Munster Fusiliers, less one company, relieved 8th Royal Berkshire in the left sub-section of the Calonne section, where the Battalion came under the command of 1st Brigade.

The plan for the raid was for two equal sized parties to enter the enemy lines independently through two saps (northern and southern), 300m from the British lines and 200m apart. Each party was subdivided into four groups consisting of:

- Riflemen with fixed bayonets to secure the flanks of each section of trench.
- Bombers to work outwards for about 60m from where the saps joined the German front line.

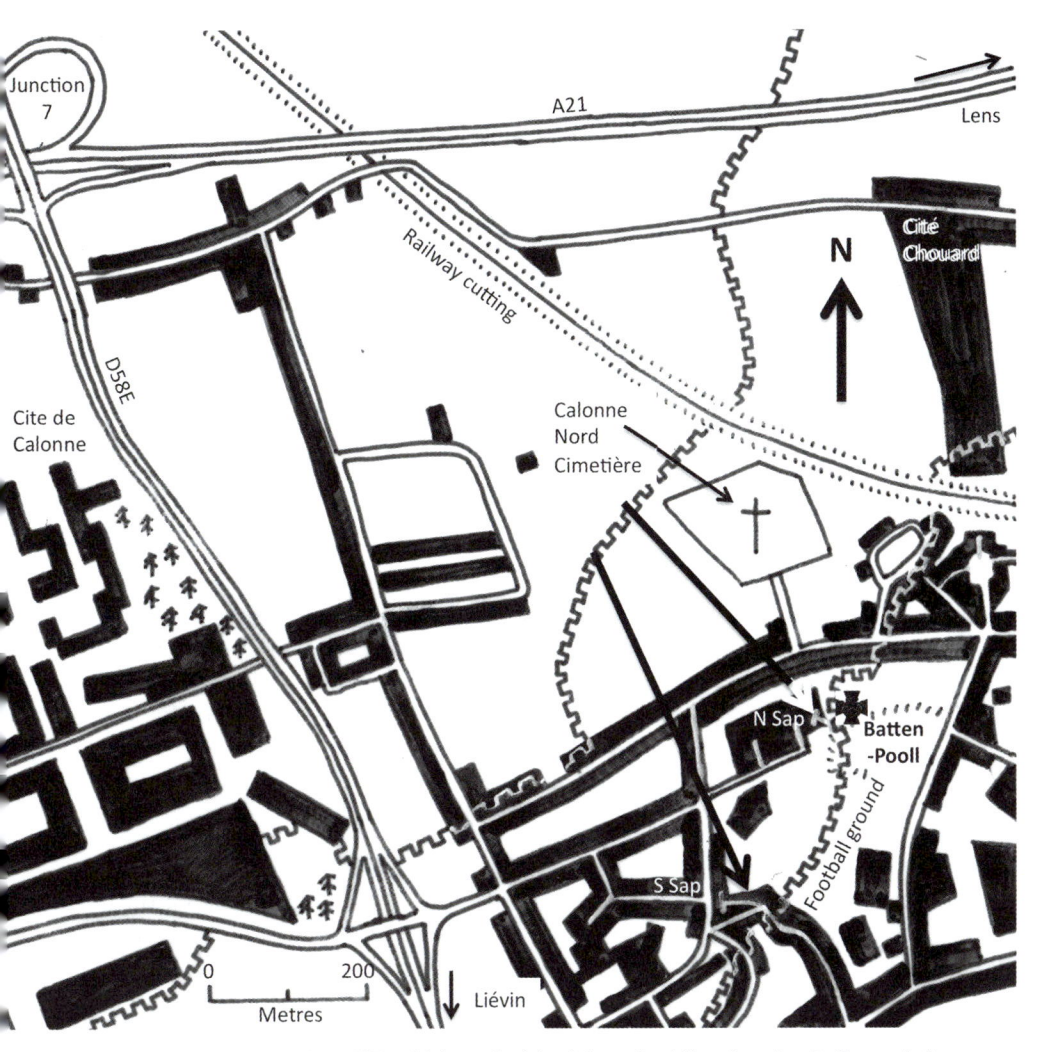

Approach from the north on the D58E, which can be joined from the A21 at Junction 7. Go south for a kilometre and come off signed 'ZAC des Marichelles' and 'ZI des Allouettes'. From the slip road turn left over the bridge and at the crossroads go left. After 100m turn right. Follow this road eastwards for 250m and turn right signed for 'Institut Medico-Educatif'. Take the next left, a dead end (Rue Hans Christian Andersen). At the far end is a clump of trees beyond the fence, this is where the northern sap was in 1916. Return by turning right and right again and continue east, passing the turning to 'Calonne Nord Cimètiere' on the left. Turn right after 350m and go on 150m to park at the football ground on the right. This is the site of a former mine shaft (Puits 16 bis) and spoil dump. The northern sap was at the base of the spoil dump, west of the football pitch near the clump of trees. It is difficult to find a vantage point from which to see the whole of the raid area because of the encroachment of housing. The southern sap was about 300m to the southwest and is now covered by houses. If the football grounds are open, walk to the far end to overlook the site of the northern sap. Look northeast to the cemetery, to the west of which the raid was launched. The northern end of Calonne Cimetière Nord, close to the railway, is on slightly higher ground and there is a view over the raid battlefield, although it is somewhat interrupted by houses.

- Two groups to return wounded and prisoners:
  - One group at the enemy parapet.
  - The other halfway across no man's land.

The southern party was led by Major Shildrick and the northern party by **Captain Arthur Batten-Pooll**. The aim was to seize prisoners, identify units, seize arms and equipment and inflict losses on the enemy.

During the evening of the 25th guide tapes were laid in no man's land and gaps were cut in the wire 20m either side of each saphead. The trench mortars had done most of the work and only a few strands remained to be cut. At 11.10 p.m., two red flares were put up from A Company's lines on the left. This was the German SOS signal and the ruse succeeded in drawing the enemy's attention to the railway cutting, which had previously been used as a covered approach for the raiders to reach the British trenches. The Germans immediately opened a furious barrage on A Company, but there were few casualties as the men were already sheltering in deep dugouts.

Covered by the commotion on the left, the raiders slipped into no man's land and took cover in a depression to await the end of the barrage. After five minutes, the British guns shifted their fire into a box barrage to seal off the raid area; this was most effective and after the raid the officers commented that it saved them from being overwhelmed. The two parties surged forward, covered by fire from 1st Brigade Machine-Gun Company just over their heads.

Shildrick's party encountered some hastily deployed wire and were illuminated by salvoes of flares. They were subjected to heavy small arms fire and rifle grenades, resulting in six casualties. The Germans had established bombing posts either side of the gap in the wire. Despite this the party entered the Southern Sap and reached the main trench. This was something of a surprise, because it was three metres deep, very narrow and had a high firestep. Each firebay had two grenade stores and the dugouts appeared to be about five metres deep. The floor was boarded, but the sides only in places. Sentries did not have fixed bayonets and abandoned their rifles (all new) as soon as the raiders were upon them. The sentries seemed automatically to revert to bombing instead.

The southern party split left and right. The party on the right headed south under 2nd Lieutenant WS Smith. It went for about 70m, passing through six firebays, each manned by five to seven Germans. As they progressed, they were bombed almost continuously from behind the parados. A large dugout after 30m put up some resistance and it was bombed, resulting in a great commotion being heard below. Another dugout was bombed 20m on, but Smith was killed (Loos British Cemetery – XVIII D 18) just south of the first communications trench junction. The leading NCO was wounded and many others became casualties. Bombs ran short and the party began to retire, bringing back their dead and wounded as best they could, while being closely pressed by the Germans. A piquet left at the communications trench junction had disappeared; all the men were posted missing.

They had fallen back to within 20m of the saphead, when the withdrawal signal was heard and it took a few minutes to recover the casualties. This party believed it accounted for thirty Germans and took four prisoners. One tried to push his escort into the entrance of a dugout and was promptly clubbed (presumably to death). The depth of the trench made it difficult to get out and as one group busied itself with the wounded another dispatched the prisoners prior to leaving.

The left party encountered only one bombing post prior to reaching its objective. Three Germans were accounted for and two escaped. They bombed a dugout and were subjected to rifle grenades throughout, but otherwise seem to have had an easier time than the party on the right.

Batten-Pooll's party at the northern sap found its section of trench fully manned by an enemy more than willing to fight it out. In the approach they encountered a patrol which fell back hastily before them. The northern sap was found to be full of wire, so they pressed on and entered the front line trench over the parapet. They came under the same rifle grenade barrage and bombing as the southern party and a trench mortar fired a few rounds from the north, killing two men.

As he reached the parapet, Batten-Pooll fell wounded by a grenade splinter, which shattered the fingers of his right hand. 2nd Lieutenant Beevor and two NCOs were also wounded before getting to the trench. Batten-Pooll got up and continued directing the battle, while also cheering his men on as if on a foxhunt. Although urged to retire, he continued walking along the parapet shouting encouragement, his voice carrying clearly over the din of the battle, *Tally Ho, lads, have at 'em lads!* The party split left and right and encountered heavy resistance. Bitter hand-to-hand fighting ensued; but because the area was isolated by the box barrage, the raiders soon gained the upper hand. The front line trench was found to be in remarkably good condition in spite of the bombardment. Showers of rifle grenades from the communications trenches in the rear caused major difficulties.

The right party, led by 2nd Lieutenant WS Clarke, made slow progress, but pressed on and bombed a dugout. It was halted after 40m. Such strong resistance had not been expected and, although the raiders maintained pressure, they ran short of bombs. Clarke and a few others attempted to climb the parados to engage the enemy bombers to the rear, but they were either shot or hit by grenade fragments.

Site of the northern sap from within the football ground. Calonne Nord Cimetière is beyond the houses on the left. In the centre is the end of the spoil heap where the northern sap extended from the German front line. The Double Crassiers at Loos are on the far right.

Clarke's body (Arras Memorial) and another had to be left on the parados where they fell. Three prisoners were taken and two were handed over to the parapet party. As the rather diminutive 2nd Lieutenant Jordeson was shoving one prisoner over the parapet, he was seen by one of his men, who thought he was in difficulties. He bludgeoned the prisoner's brains out. The other prisoner was being escorted back when he made an attempt to escape and was pursed and bayoneted by Pte P Rock, who was subsequently killed (Loos British Cemetery – XVIII C 23).

The left party drove back a bombing post to reach its objective. It was estimated about twenty-five Germans were accounted for, excluding an unknown number bombed in the dugouts. Casualties mounted steadily and Jordeson advised Batten-Pooll it was time to go. At about 11.35 p.m., Batten-Pooll sounded the horn signifying the first stage of the withdrawal back to the saps. It took seven to ten minutes to clear the trenches. The raiders pulled back along the front line, bringing as many wounded as could be evacuated.

The flank parties came under more pressure and the final withdrawal was signalled at 11.40 p.m. by klaxon horn and green Very light. The officers were the last out, but on the way back it was realised they had failed to capture a machine-gun, one of the specific aims of the raid. Some men went back, but the Germans were already regaining control of their trenches and resistance was growing stronger. Reluctantly they were forced to return empty handed. A group of covering riflemen was killed at this stage holding off the enemy while the rest fell back.

Batten-Pooll was wounded twice more in the dash back across no man's land. The survivors passed through the parapet and wire cutting party, which had suffered

From the northern end of Calonne Nord Cimetière looking over the raid area. The northern sap was at the trees on the left. The southern sap was just to the right of the large tree on the right. The football ground is between the two.

The eastern end of Rue Hans Christian Andersen. The northern sap was just beyond the fence on the left.

casualties from showers of grenades while the fighting had been going on in the trenches. A machine-gun on the right also caused some casualties. Men in this party made a number of hazardous trips over no man's land to bring back wounded and deliver information.

With 100m to go, Batten-Pooll collapsed and had to be carried the rest of the way. He was rushed to hospital, along with many other wounded. No prisoners made it back over no man's land, although limited quantities of identification material were gathered (rifles, caps, respirators, notice boards etc). In his report the CO explained, *Our parties suffered heavily on entering the saps. Consequently the men were in no temper to take prisoners and moreover the evacuation of the wounded occupied the attention of all ranks.*

It was estimated that fifty Germans were killed, in addition to casualties caused by bombing five or six dugouts. The raiders' casualties amounted to half the officers and a third of the other ranks. Only two of the wounded were not the result of bomb fragments. A quarter had leg and feet wounds, which complicated the evacuation, but everyone had been trained in carrying disabled men on their backs and this resulted in at least twenty-four stretcher cases being recovered and three dead. Total casualties recorded at the time were three killed, thirty-six or thirty-seven wounded and eleven or twelve missing. CWGC records show ten killed or died of wounds on 25th/26th June; most are buried in Loos British Cemetery or are recorded on the Arras Memorial.

Two MCs, three DCMs and nine MMs were awarded in addition to Batten-Pooll's VC. First Army Intelligence concluded that the enemy knew about the raid. The German trenches had been thinned out between the gaps cut in the wire, blocks had been established and rifle grenadiers were ready to counter the attack. In addition the saps had been filled with wire and bombing parties had been positioned to ambush the raiders. German machine-guns covered the gaps cut in the wire, but fortunately they fired high. Masses of flares illuminated the scene throughout and it was suspected these were launched through holes in the roofs of dugouts.

In his report, the CO (Lieutenant Colonel WB Lyons) concluded that revolvers had been very useful and the time spent training with them was amply rewarded; nearly every man so armed claimed hits. Rifles and bayonets were found to be less useful in the narrow trenches. Irish soldiers appeared to be fond of bludgeons and used them to great effect, but not enough bombs were taken. Identification marks, such as blackened faces, white patches and passwords worked well, but as the whole scene was well illuminated, recognition was fairly straightforward anyway. Just about every man had his legs torn by wire and some form of covering was recommended for future raids.

Near Bois Grenier, France

The same night another raid was carried out by 5th Australian Brigade, southeast of Bois Grenier. The aims were almost the same as for the Calonne raid. The raiding party was made up of volunteers from all units in the Brigade and consisted of eight officers and sixty-five other ranks (some accounts quote nine officers and seventy-three other ranks). It was organised as follows:

- Command – Major RJA Travers DSO, 17th Battalion and his deputy, Lieutenant RR Harper, 20th Battalion – to remain in the front line in telephone contact forwards with the Assault Party and rearwards with Advanced Brigade HQ, the artillery group, local batteries, Divisional Trench Mortar Officer and the trench mortar batteries involved.
- Scouts – 2nd Lieutenant C Wallach, 19th Battalion and five men.
- Assault Party – Captain Keith Heritage and his deputy, Lieutenant LB Heath, both 19th Battalion, with a telephonist, linesman and two runners positioned close to the point of entry:
    - Right and Left Parties – commanded by Lieutenant JJ Fay, 17th Battalion, and Lieutenant JB Lane, 18th Battalion respectively. Each consisting of:
        - Bombing Party – NCO and seven men (three bayonet men and four bombers) to enter and clear the enemy trench.
        - Parapet Party – NCO and two bayonet men to maintain contact with the Bombing Party and ensure the enemy did not interfere with it from the rear.
        - Blocking Party – NCO and three men (bayonet man and two bombers) to seal the trench where the Bombing Party reached.
        - Intelligence NCO – to collect ID disks, pay books, shoulder titles, letters, pocket books and small items of equipment.
        - Machine-gunner – to collect a machine-gun or mortar.
        - Engineer – to work with the machine-gunner and destroy whatever could not be brought back.
        - Stretcher Bearers – two men, who were not to enter the trenches, to bring back casualties passed to them.
        - Prisoner escorts – two men to bring back captives as quickly as possible.
- Covering Party – Captain EW Kirke, 18th Battalion, with two NCOs and ten men.

The Brigade had been engaged on fatigue work in and out of the line for the previous ten weeks and was considered to be stale. A progressive training programme was

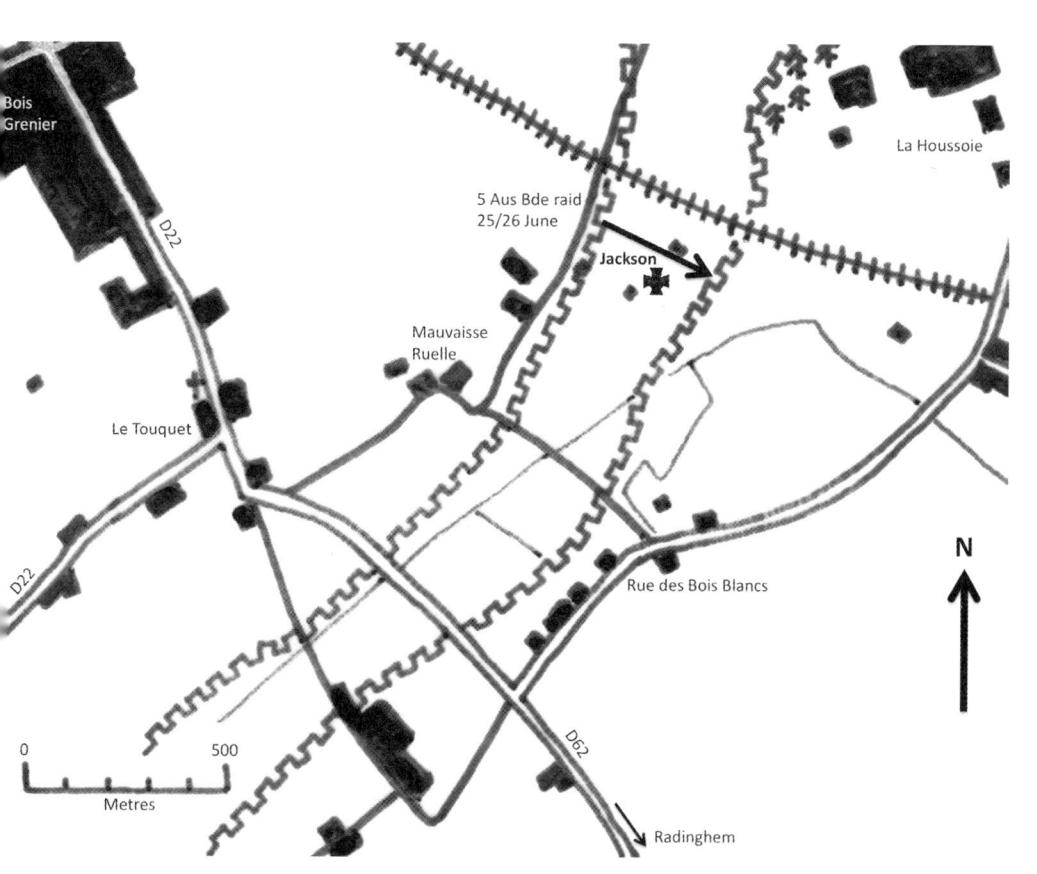

From the church in Bois Grenier drive south on the D22, which turns right after a kilometre, but continue straight on. Go round the next left bend and 75m on turn left into a minor road for access only. There is a large open area of hard standing at the junction and sometimes there are heaps of hard core on it, which give a better view over this flat area. Look along the road to the northeast beyond the houses at Mauvaisse Ruelle. Beyond where the power lines concentrate is the area of the raid on 25th/26th June 1916.

instituted for the raiders, starting with three days of physical training, sports and some bayonet fighting and grenade throwing. A noticeable brightening and quickening was noticed amongst them. 5th Field Company constructed practice trenches based on the area to be raided and a more intensive period of training followed – bayonet fighting, bombing, firing revolvers, trench clearing, 'nut cracking', night firing, aiming at sounds and the evacuation of wounded. Training was carried out with blank and live ammunition, day and night. To round off each day, the men went to the divisional baths for a cold plunge and a tot of rum. There were also lectures on intelligence, handling casualties and how to deal with a gas attack. Specialised training followed for each man to carry out his assigned role. Officers and NCOs went into no man's land at night to familiarise themselves with the raid area.

There were a number of innovations. Scouts were issued tomahawks and these proved useful in cutting exits from trenches. Bayonet men had torches bound to their rifles, which proved very effective at night in trenches. Three-inch wide bands of white tape were worn on each arm for identification. These were covered in khaki fabric until the trenches were entered. The message ordering the raid to take place on a particular night was, *Holmes leaves for Paris at …. p.m. tonight. Acknowledge.*

In the days before the raid the artillery and trench mortars bombarded the enemy trench and cut the wire. A known machine-gun post was also destroyed. Machine-gun fire at night prevented the Germans repairing their wire. During the 25th the artillery engaged various targets. During the afternoon the Germans bombarded the Australian trenches from where the raid was to be launched.

The raiders left the trenches before the protective barrage opened. The scouts led at 10.26 p.m. and came under heavy small arms fire. They discovered the Germans working on their wire, but got there without any casualties. At 10.48 p.m. the Assault Party crawled out along Ditch 22 to their forming up places. As the artillery lifted into a box around the raid area, the scouts dashed ahead to cut any remaining wire, followed by the Assault Party. Machine-guns isolated a communications trench leading to the front line and stood by to engage any German machine-guns causing the raiders problems.

At 11.30 p.m., the preparatory barrage opened on a diversionary target. By 11.33 p.m., the raiders were in position and at 11.40 p.m., the artillery engaged the raid area. Four minutes later, the Assault Party dashed forward. A deep ditch filled with barbed wire blocked the way unexpectedly, but they got over it using a footbridge leading to a German listening post. The Germans seemed to be ready for the attack and swept no man's land with a machine-gun, but by keeping low, the raiders managed to stay under its fire and there were no casualties. The Assault Party broke into the German trenches and cleared 30m either side of the entry point, meeting little opposition; the defenders appear to have taken shelter in their deep dugouts.

Looking northeast along the rear of the British front line. Billy Jackson's VC action was to the right of the houses (Mauvisse Ruelle) where there is a concentration of low pylons. Visibility in this area (and in many others on the Western Front) is severely restricted in the summer months, particularly where maize is grown.

Lieutenant Lane was knocked down by an exploding grenade, but the thrower and a man with him were shot by the Parapet Party. The Covering Party moved up to the enemy wire to sweep both flanks with fire. Listening posts in the enemy wire were dealt with by the scouts, who also laid white tape through the wire and cut gaps in the enemy parapet to assist the raiders during the withdrawal. Telephone communications were maintained with the Assault Party commander near the parapet throughout, with information being passed back using various codewords, e.g. 'Whisky' meant 'in enemy trench'. No machine-guns or trench mortars were found, but samples of bombs, gas helmets and rifle grenades were brought back. The sapper with the right assault party blew up a large bomb store and the left assault party destroyed another smaller store.

Withdrawal was signalled by codeword at 11.54 p.m. (flares were held as a backup). The men pulled back, following the white tape. The prisoners came in first at 12.03 a.m. As the raiders withdrew, the Germans retaliated with heavy artillery fire on the trenches and in no man's land. There were fourteen casualties at this time, including one man killed. The German guns ceased firing twenty-five minutes after the British barrage stopped. By 12.52 a.m. all parties were back in and the wire in front had been replaced. The Assault Party commander was the last man to return. The German counterattack came just too late; bombers were seen progressing towards the trench vacated by the raiders two minutes after they returned to their own lines.

Private Billy Jackson is described as a scout, but was with Captain Heritage's party. He brought back a captured enemy soldier under intense shell and machine-gun fire. He learned that wounded comrades were stuck out in no man's land and immediately went back to rescue them. He brought one man in and returned for a second. Jackson was assisted by Sergeant Hugh Alison Camden of 19th Battalion to recover the seriously wounded Private Alfred Robinson. A shell exploded among them; Camden was knocked unconscious, Jackson's right arm was shattered and Robinson sustained further injuries. Despite his wound, Jackson returned to the lines, where a tourniquet was applied to his arm using a piece of string and a stick.

Jackson believed Camden and others were still out in no man's land. Despite his own very serious injury, he went back and spent half-an-hour searching for them. Only when he was satisfied that no one had been left behind, did he return to his own lines.

The raiders had one man killed and thirteen wounded. CWGC records show two men from 5th Australian Brigade died on 25th/26th June – 963 Sergeant JL Mitchell, C Company, 17th Battalion, from Aberdeenshire is buried in Brewery Orchard Cemetery, Bois Grenier (IV D 26) and 1876B Lance Corporal EM Abercrombie, 18th Battalion is buried in Erquinghem-Lys Churchyard Extension (I K 7).

It was estimated that thirty Germans were killed, mainly during the bombardment, and four prisoners were brought back from 231st Regiment (50th Reserve Division).

A fifth prisoner caused trouble in no man's land and had to be killed there. 50th Reserve Division recorded its casualties as thirteen killed, twenty-five wounded and four missing, presumably the prisoners.

Jackson was sent to hospital and stated that he, *"did not feel much, just a numbing sensation"*. He was evacuated to England, where most of his arm was amputated. Both Camden and Jackson were awarded the DCM, but Jackson's was later replaced by the VC. Keith Heritage was killed on 26th July 1916 (Pozières British Cemetery – IV L 37).

Opposite Ficheux, France, 28th June 1916

> 122 Pte James Hutchinson, 2/5th Battalion The Lancashire Fusiliers (164th Brigade, 55th Division)

On 28th June 1916, 55th Division mounted six raids along a two-mile front as part of the deception plan for the forthcoming Somme offensive. One of these raids was launched by 2/5th Lancashire Fusiliers near Blairville, with another by 1/4th Loyal North Lancashire 200m to the west. The 2/5th Lancashire Fusiliers raiding party was divided into three groups; left, centre and right. Having gained entry to the enemy trenches, the left and right groups were to bomb outwards to the flanks, while the centre group pushed down a communications trench to the rear. For a fortnight before the raid the sixty-seven strong party rehearsed behind the lines under its commander, Captain Lawrence Henry Bloy, who was the Battalion's

From the middle of no man's land, with the German lines on the right along the tree line. The British trenches were on the far left. The 2/5th Lancashire Fusiliers raiding party crossed the track in the centre (it leads to the lone tree parking place) towards the far side of the trees. For a map of this action, see the account for Edward Baxter on 17/18th April 1916.

Adjutant. From 24th June onwards, the enemy lines were shelled and the wire cut, exactly as was happening in preparation for the Somme offensive to the south.

Once all preparations had been completed, there was a pause to wait for the right wind conditions. On the afternoon of 28th June, the wind was ideal and a discharge of gas commenced at 5 p.m., followed five minutes later by the artillery barrage. The gas should have been turned off at 5.25 p.m., but by then all the sappers were casualties and the cylinders continued to pour out their deadly contents for a further ten minutes. At 5.35 p.m., the artillery lifted onto the enemy support line and at the same time a smoke cloud began to develop.

The raiders left the British lines and moved forward using the smoke for cover. They had covered 160m before the Germans saw them and opened fire. All three groups suffered casualties crossing no man's land, but the gaps in the wire allowed them to close quickly with the enemy. The right and centre parties got into the front line trench and proceeded to bomb along it and the communications trench. The centre party was only five strong due to casualties, but managed to advance about 35m and bombed several dugouts. Both parties were eventually halted by blocks of wood and sandbags and forced back by German bombers.

The left party under Lieutenant MH Young was only nine strong when it reached the German trench. They failed to get their ladders into it and jumped down. Young shot a German officer before being mortally wounded (Fillievres British Cemetery – A 1) and **Private James Hutchinson**, the lead bayonet man, then led the way. He jumped into the trench and shot a man who was attempting to bring a machine-gun into action. He then bayoneted a second man and shot a third. Rounding the next traverse, he shot and bayoneted two more Germans and then carried on to the third traverse, where he dispatched three more. By the time he entered the fourth traverse, he had run out of ammunition, but the opposition was too shocked to take advantage. A block was reached, but the party scrambled over it and bombed several dugouts. It was noted that the German blocks corresponded exactly with the gaps cut in the wire by the artillery. They clearly knew the limits of the raid even before it commenced.

When the order to withdraw was given at 5.50 p.m., Hutchinson held the enemy at bay while the rest of the party got out and the wounded were evacuated. Throughout this period he was under constant close range rifle and machine-gun fire. On returning to the British lines, he helped bandage the wounded and assisted them back to the dressing station before taking a message from one end of the Battalion's lines to the other. Hutchinson was the only member of the raiding party to bring back any material; a cap.

Next day the raiding party was presented to the divisional commander, who told Hutchinson that he must have something to wear on his chest. In addition to his VC, a MC, a DCM and a MM were awarded for this raid. The casualties recorded at the time totalled thirty-nine, including seven dead and seventeen missing. The CWGC records reveal twenty deaths, so the majority of the missing had been killed.

From the German front line, which ran along the line of this fence. On the left is Blairville Wood (les Fosses). The simultaneous raid by 1/4th Loyal North Lancashire on 28th June 1916 was 100m on the other side of the tip of the Wood. Left of centre in the middle distance is Bois de Martinets. The 2/5th Lancashire Fusiliers' raid was launched from the dark area of vegetation right of centre.

Amongst the dead was Hutchinson's brother, Corporal Frank Hutchinson, who is commemorated with the majority of the dead from the raid on the Arras Memorial, and Captain Bloy (Fillievres British Cemetery – B 1). One of the missing was 2nd Lieutenant Harold Mason Ainscow, who was taken prisoner and repatriated on 4th October 1918.

The Boar's Head, Richebourg L'Avoue, France, 30th June 1916

> 123 CSM Nelson Carter, 12th Battalion, The Royal Sussex Regiment 116th Brigade, 39th Division)

On the morning of 30th June 1916, 116th Brigade attacked the enemy lines at the 'Boar's Head' near Richebourg L'Avoué. This was one of a number of diversions or large-scale raids across the British front designed to keep the Germans guessing where the forthcoming offensive on the Somme would fall. Other attacks took place at Loos and Ploegsteert. During the planning for the 'Boar's Head' attack, one of the battalion COs expressed concern that his relatively inexperienced men would be advancing over unfamiliar ground and it would end in disaster. He was replaced and his battalion consigned to a supporting role, leaving the attack to be launched by 13th Royal Sussex on the right and 12th Royal Sussex on the left.

Training for the attack took place behind the lines, but as the men moved up for the assault the Somme offensive was delayed for two days due to bad weather. The diversionary attacks were also delayed and the assault troops had to remain in the forward areas for two extra days, which did little to ensure they were in peak condition for the attack. The night before the attack, parties cut gaps through the wire and positioned bridges over a deep ditch in no man's land. Scaling ladders were fixed in place at 2.50 a.m. on 30th June. Five minutes later the artillery preparation commenced and at 3.50 a.m. the attack commenced.

The left companies of 13th Royal Sussex stalled in front of the wire, drifted to the right and exposed their flank to machine-gun fire. This, together with smoke used to mask the advance, caused considerable confusion and very few of 13th Royal Sussex reached the German lines, but some did and managed to get as far as the support line.

12th Royal Sussex advanced with its companies in line (from right to left – A, B, C and D), each on a frontage of one platoon. A Company's right was close to Vine Street and the left of D Company was on Hazara Street. The left was held up by uncut wire and the right by a ditch. Despite this and 13th Royal Sussex being checked on the right, 12th Royal Sussex reached the enemy support line and held it for half an hour and the front line for four hours. The attackers were forced to withdraw as their supply of bombs and ammunition dwindled and a heavy German barrage on the British front line and communication trenches prevented reinforcement.

During the attack, **CSM Nelson Carter** commanded a platoon of A Company in the fourth and final wave. As the officers became casualties it was left to the NCOs to take the lead. Carter took

The ditch just in front of 12th Royal Sussex' front line.

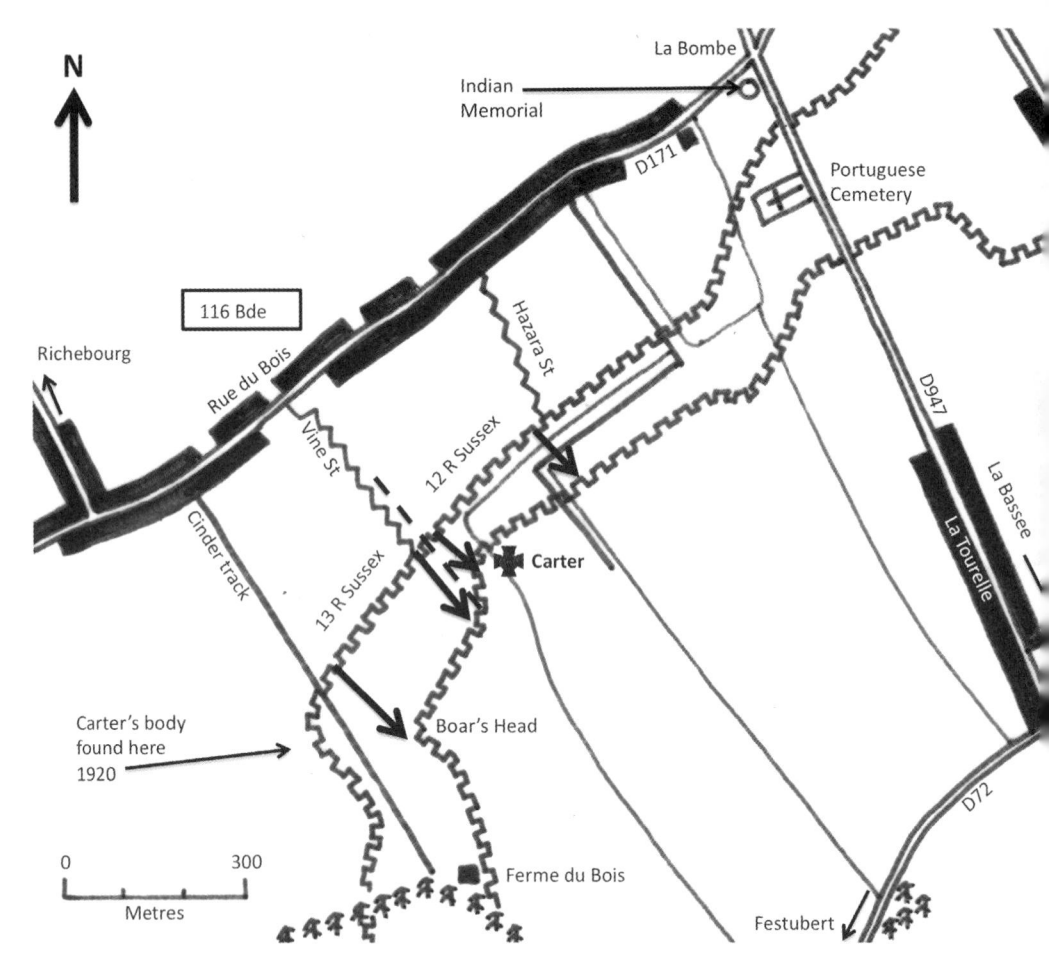

From the Indian Memorial at La Bombe crossroads drive southwest along the D171 Rue du Bois road. After 400m turn left onto a metalled minor road. It soon gives way to a farm track with a reasonable surface at first, but do not be tempted to drive further as it soon degenerates. Park and walk 350m to the right turn where a deep ditch runs across the track. The British front line was just behind it in June 1916. Continue to the right for 300m to the left turn and follow it for another 70m. This is the German front line. Nelson Carter's VC action was about 200m west of this point, close to a significant ditch.

From behind the German front line looking north into the British lines. Vine Street ran from the area of the house on the extreme left through the field out of view to the left. Nelson Carter and A Company, 12th Royal Sussex attacked astride the overgrown ditch in the left foreground towards the camera. The ditch bends round to the right and runs across the middle of the picture parallel with Rue du Bois in the distance. Part of the Portuguese Cemetery is just visible between the tall thin poplars on the right.

over when his company commander was killed. Despite heavy casualties, and armed only with a pistol, he pressed on over no man's land through the few gaps in the wire that were passable. With only four or five men he managed to reach the German second line. There his small party inflicted heavy casualties on the enemy, but with no support on either flank they were eventually forced back to the enemy front line. On the way back Carter captured a machine-gun, having shot the gunner with his revolver and returned to the British trenches. He then went back into no man's land repeatedly to rescue the wounded. Carrying men on his back for considerable distances demanded great physical strength as well as courage. As he was setting out to rescue the seventh or eighth man, he was shot through the chest and fell back into the trench. He died a few minutes later. The Battalion was relieved at 10 a.m., having suffered 429 casualties, including sixty-one killed and 125 missing.

Nelson Carter was buried within the trench system at map reference 36S16a12. His grave was not rediscovered until March 1920. There is no reason to doubt the accuracy of this reference, but it is 400m southwest of the closest point in 12th Royal Sussex' lines and may indicate that he returned via 13th Royal Sussex' lines. It may also be that there was an organized battlefield cemetery at that point and his body was taken there soon after the VC action.

These British .303 cartridges were found between the German front and support lines. This area is still fairly heavily littered with small items of battlefield debris.

Biographies

7709 LANCE CORPORAL WILLIAM ANGUS
8th (Lanark) Battalion, The Highland Light Infantry (att'd 8th Battalion, The Royal Scots (Lothian Regiment)

William Angus was born at 16 Polkemmet Road, Armadale, Linlithgow, West Lothian, Scotland on 28th February 1888. His father was George Angus (1862–1918), an iron miner. His mother, Margaret née Malloy (c.1862–1913) was a jelly worker in 1881. Both parents were Irish. The family moved to Carluke, Lanarkshire when he was very young. William had seven siblings:

- Margaret Angus (1886–1922).
- Daniel Angus (1890–94).
- Jane 'Jeannie' Angus (born 1892).
- Mary Angus (1896–1980), a hosiery worker, married James McNulty (c.1900–73), a public house barman, in 1921 at the Roman Catholic Chapel, Carluke. They had three children – James McNulty 1921, George Angus McNulty 1924 and Margaret McNulty 1930.
- Anne 'Annie' Angus (born 1900).
- George Angus (1902–74) was a haulage contractor. He married Jessie McIntosh (c.1894–1972) and they lived at The Cottage, Achnasheen, Ross & Cromarty.
- Violet Angus (1904–44), a hosiery worker, married Charles Floyd (c.1898–1958), a railway shunter, in 1927 at the Roman Catholic Chapel, Carluke and they lived at 21 Whitehill Crescent, Carluke.

William was educated at St Athanasius Roman Catholic School, Carluke until 1902 and was then employed as a miner. He played professionally for Glasgow Celtic in 1911 and later joined Wishaw Athletic as captain.

William Angus in Celtic strip (GD Fordyce).

Biographies 185

Armadale.

Carluke (Charles Reid).

During a recruiting campaign in Carluke in August 1914, Colour Sergeant George Cavan enlisted William Angus and James Martin into 8th HLI. Both men were keen to get into action and volunteered for attachment to 8th Royal Scots. William went to France on 17th February 1915. He received a gun shot wound to the leg at Festubert six weeks later and was in hospital in Boulogne for three weeks.

Awarded the VC for his actions at Givenchy, France on 12th June 1915, LG 29th June 1915. As a result of the forty wounds sustained during the VC action, he was blinded in his left eye and lost part of his foot and calf. He was hospitalised at Boulogne and moved to Fort Pitt Military Hospital, Chatham on 17th July, where Lieutenant James Martin visited him. Queen Mary sent William a white sleeping garment and a card wishing him good luck. His father was brought from Scotland to visit him in hospital on 26th July.

The VC was presented by the King at Buckingham Palace on 30th August, with William dressed in the wounded soldier's uniform. He was the first Scottish Territorial soldier to be awarded the VC. Hearing that William's father was outside the Palace, the King insisted he was brought in and congratulated him on having such a brave son. Receptions were held at Carluke and Celtic Park in September.

Fort Pitt Military Hospital (Keith Gulvin).

William being looked after in hospital, possibly at Fort Pitt Military Hospital, Chatham (Jim McNulty).

186 Victoria Crosses on the Western Front April 1915–June 1916

Every year on the anniversary of the VC action, James Martin sent his rescuer a telegram, *Congratulations on the 12th.*

William had to wear a surgical shoe to rectify the imbalance caused by damage to his foot. This prevented him returning to active duty, but he served as a sergeant (241464) in the Cameronians on recruiting duties. He was invalided out of the Army in 1917, but his service record has not survived and the precise date is not known.

William Angus married Mary Ann née Nugent (1893–1968), a preserve worker, on 12th January 1917 at St Athanasius Roman Catholic Church, Carluke. She was born to Irish parents from Co Tyrone, who moved to Carluke after they married. William was living at 22 Douglas Street, Carluke at the time. William and Mary had five children:

William being met at Carluke station. On the right is Lieutenant James Martin (Jim McNulty).

- George, born on 16th October 1917.
- Nugent, born on 22nd August 1919. He became an engineer and manufactured the VC on his father's headstone.
- Rose, born on 1st July 1921, married as Buxton.
- William, born on 25th February 1924.
- Henry, born on 21st May 1926.

Early in 1918, William joined the man who recruited him, George Cavan, by then a Company Sergeant Major, at an official function in the Lanarkshire Yeomanry Drill Hall. Cavan returned to the front with 9th HLI and died of wounds on 13th April 1918 (Ploegsteert Memorial).

William was presented with a cheque for £1,000 by Lord Newlands at Mauldslie Castle. He started a haulage business with his brother-in-law, Harry Nugent, which they sold when they went to Australia in November 1927. The business continued as Adamson's of Carluke. William coincidentally travelled out with Thomas

William Angus just after his investiture.

Biographies 187

William Angus with his wife and children about 1927 (Jim McNulty).

The Carluke VCs – William Angus with Thomas Caldwell in a post-war studio picture (Jim McNulty).

Caldwell VC on the *Moreton Bay*. He either went into an engineering firm or grew sugar in Northern Queensland, but he did not settle and the venture was not a success. He returned in 1928 and moved to England, where he was employed as master of works at the Racecourse Betting Control Board in Middlesex until 1949. He and his wife retired to Carluke, but their grown up children remained in England. William became a JP and was President of Carluke Rovers Football Club, where he was known simply as 'The VC'.

Mauldslie Castle during a Royal visit in 1914.

William Angus junior was killed on 30th May 1945 while serving as a pilot Flying Officer (164981) with the RAFVR in the Near East (Alamein Memorial, Egypt). With David Hunter VC, William led a protest march in Glasgow on 29th September 1957 against the amalgamation of the HLI and Royal Scots Fusiliers into the Royal Highland Fusiliers.

William Angus died at Law Hospital, Carluke on 14th June 1959 and is buried in Wilton Cemetery, Carluke (Lair 36, Section O). In addition to the VC, he was awarded the 1914–15 Star, British War Medal 1914–20, Victory Medal 1914–19, King George VI Coronation Medal 1937 and Queen Elizabeth II Coronation Medal 1953. His medals are held by the National War Museum of Scotland, Edinburgh Castle and are displayed alongside James Martin's medals. He is commemorated in a number of other places:

SS *Moreton Bay*.

- Angus Road, Carluke.
- Angus House, Crawforddyke Primary School, Eastfield Road, Carluke, opened in 1957.
- A memorial to fourteen Lanarkshire VCs, including William Angus, was dedicated at Hamilton, Lanarkshire on 19th April 2002.
- A memorial to famous Carluke men, unveiled in 2000 by the Rotary Club of Carluke to commemorate the Millennium, includes William Angus VC, Thomas Caldwell VC, Donald Cameron VC and the founder of the Ordnance Survey, Major General William Roy.
- A stained-glass window in Carluke's Lifestyle Centre, opened in October 2009, is a tribute to famous figures in the town's history, including Major General Roy and the three VCs.
- William's VC action featured in five issues of the *Victor* comic on 31st August 1963, 24th May 1975, 20th November 1976, 7th August 1982 and 29th June 1985.

3902 COMPANY SERGEANT MAJOR FREDERICK BARTER
1st Battalion, The Royal Welsh Fusiliers

Frederick Barter was born at 66 Minny Street, St John, Cardiff on 17th January 1891. His father, Samuel or Sam Barter (1864–1950), was born at Otterford, Somerset. He was a gravedigger when Frederick was born and at other times was employed as a general labourer. His mother, Emily Ann née Sage (1870–97), was born at Wells, Somerset. Sam and Emily married in Cardiff in the 2nd quarter of 1889. Emily died in the 3rd quarter of 1897, when Frederick was only six. By the time of the 1901 Census, Sam and his four children were living with his parents, John and Charlotte Barter, at 158 Woodville Road, Roath, Cardiff. Frederick had three siblings:

- John Thomas Barter (1890–1914) served as 9791 Private JT Barter in 1st Royal Welsh Fusiliers and was killed in action on 30th October 1914. He is commemorated on Panel 22 of the Ypres (Menin Gate) Memorial, Belgium.
- Robert Samuel Barter (born 1893) married May Dennett (1893–1973) in 1913 and had two sons – Ronald born 1914 and Frederick born 1915.
- Elizabeth Ann Barter (1896–1964).

Frederick was educated at Crwys Road Board School, Cardiff. He was employed in the Wagon Works in Cardiff, then as a collier and later as a porter on the Great Western Railway. His first attempt to join the Army was rejected because his chest measurement was below the minimum standard. He enlisted in 3rd (Reserve) Battalion, Royal Welsh Fusiliers, formerly Militia, on 4th December 1908 and rose to sergeant before transferring to the Royal Welsh Fusiliers Special Reserve.

Frederick was employed by the Cardiff Gas, Light & Coke Company as a stove repairer when he was recalled on 5th August 1914. Although the Battalion landed at Zeebrugge on 7th October, his medal card shows he arrived in France on 25th November. This is confirmed by him not being awarded the 'Mons' clasp to the 1914 Star, as qualification for it ended on 22nd November. Frederick was appointed Company Sergeant Major later in 1914.

Awarded the VC for his actions at Festubert, France on 16th May 1915, LG 29th June 1915. Frederick returned to Britain on 2nd July and visited 3rd (Reserve) Battalion at Litherland, near Liverpool on 8th July. A full battalion parade was followed by a smoking concert in the Sergeants' Mess in the evening. He was presented with a cheque for £20 by the sergeants, and a cheque for £30, a gold cigarette case, matchbox and sovereign case by the officers. He also travelled to Cardiff and was met at the railway station by the Lord Mayor and other dignitaries. An impromptu collection at the Cardiff Coal Exchange raised £11/4/- for the purchase of War Bonds, which were presented to him. His old school also contributed, as did the Cardiff Gas Light & Coke Company, which presented him with shares in the Company and the Cardiff Coal Exchange and £50 in War Bonds. The VC was presented by the King at Buckingham Palace on 12th July. Frederick did not enjoy adulation and, with other VC winners

Crwys Road Board School, Cardiff.

who had just been invested, he hailed a taxi and slipped away. **He was also awarded the Cross of the Order of St George, 3rd Class (Russia), LG 25th August 1915.**

Frederick was commissioned as a probationary 2nd lieutenant on 26th August and returned to France until he was posted to the Western Command Bombing School at Prees Heath, Shropshire as a temporary lieutenant instructor on 10th May 1916. On 29th December he returned to France and rejoined his Battalion at Louvencourt on 17th January 1917. On 16th March he was seconded to the Indian Army, appointed 2nd lieutenant Indian Army on 6th May (seniority from 26th May 1916), and joined 4/3rd Queen Alexandra's Own Gurkha Rifles at Kohat, Northwest Frontier on 18th May. At one time he was the Brigade Bombing Officer. Promoted lieutenant Indian Army 26th May. He joined 2/3rd Queen Alexandra's Own Gurkha Rifles at Kibbiah in Palestine as the Adjutant in December. Appointed Acting Captain 26th January 1918. **Awarded the MC for his actions at El Kefr, Egypt on 10th April 1918 while leading two platoons in a flank attack up a precipitous hill. He then placed one platoon with two Lewis guns to command the enemy line of retreat while he gallantly led an attack with the other platoon from the rear and a flank, killing or capturing almost the whole garrison, LG 26th July 1918.** Rifleman Karanbahudur Rana was awarded the VC for a separate incident in the same action.

Frederick relinquished his commission in the Royal Welsh Fusiliers on 6th May 1918 on being confirmed in the Indian Army. He was invalided home in January 1919 with fever. Promoted captain Indian Army 26th May 1920. Frederick retired on 8th September 1922. He joined the Associated Equipment Company Ltd, Windmill Lane, Southall, Middlesex in 1928 and remained with the Company as a labour manager until 1952.

Frederick married Catherine Mary Theresa, late McLaren, née Wright (1886–1944) on 13th May 1925. She owned the Heathfield Hotel, Heathfield, East Sussex,

Frederick Barter received an enthusiastic welcome when he visited 3rd (Reserve) Battalion at Litherland, near Liverpool on 8th July 1915.

Kohat Pass on the Northwest frontier.

Rifleman Karanbahudur Rana VC.

The AEC works at Windmill Lane, Southall opened in 1926 and closed in 1970. The famous Routemaster London bus was produced there.

close to the former Heathfield railway station. They did not have any children. Her previous marriage to John McLaren in 1902 at Reading, Berkshire ended in divorce. Frederick and Catherine lived at Chota Garh, Melbury Avenue, Norwood Green, Middlesex. She died of cancer in the 1st quarter of 1944 at Brentford, Middlesex. He was a major commanding 4/7th Company, 4th Middlesex Battalion, Home Guard from 1st February 1941 and transferred to 10th Middlesex Battalion on 24th June 1942.

Frederick Barter died at St Ann's Nursing Home, Canford Cliffs, Bournemouth on 15th May 1953. The cause of death was myocardial degeneration and failure, arteriosclerosis and chronic nephritis. He was cremated at Bournemouth and his ashes were scattered in the Rose Garden of the Garden of Remembrance. At the time of his death his address was recorded as 44 Dogfield Street, Cardiff. He is also commemorated at Barter Road and Barter Court, Hightown, Wrexham, Clwyd, Wales.

In addition to VC and MC, Fredrick Barter was awarded the 1914–15 Star, British War Medal 1914–20, Victory Medal 1914–19, George VI Coronation Medal 1937, Elizabeth II Coronation Medal 1953 and the Russian Cross of St George, 3rd Class. Barter's Regiment was keen to obtain his medal group when it came up for auction at Spink's from a private collection in the United States. It was feared that their interest would drive up the price, so rumours were circulated that the Regiment could not afford to buy the group. The Museum curator, Captain Bryan Finchett-Maddock, attended the auction on 27th March 1992 and maintained a low profile. As a result he was able to make the successful bid of £18,500. Barter's VC group is held at the Royal Welch Fusiliers Museum, The Castle, Caernarfon, Gwynedd, Wales.

The group includes the Russian Cross of the Order of St George, 4th Class, but Frederick was gazetted with the 3rd Class and it is not known what happened to the original. A Cross of St George formed part of Lot 1856 (Barter's miniatures and other memorabilia) sold by Gorringes of Lewes, East Sussex on 12th June 2008. It is not known if this was the one actually awarded to him.

Frederick died eighteen days before the coronation of Elizabeth II, but the Elizabeth II Coronation Medal 1953 forms part of his medal group. The medal was issued immediately after the Coronation and it is likely that the authorities were not aware of his death at the time of issue. His Victory Medal 1914–19 has a Mentioned-in-Despatches oakleaf on the ribbon, but there is no trace of it in the London Gazette.

CAPTAIN ARTHUR HUGH HENRY BATTEN-POOLL
3rd (attached 2nd) Battalion, The Royal Munster Fusiliers

Arthur Batten-Pooll was born at Rutland Lodge (now the Turkish Consulate), Rutland Gardens, Knightsbridge, London on 27th October 1891. His father's original surname was Langford, but under the terms of the Will of his great-uncle, Henry Batten-Pooll, he assumed the surname Pooll by Royal Licence on 12th June 1871. Subsequently, he adopted the additional names Henry Batten and became Robert Pooll Henry Batten-Pooll (1850–1939). He was commissioned in the North Somerset Yeomanry on 20th January 1875 and resigned as a Captain (Supernumerary) on 2nd June 1888. Robert was Deputy Lieutenant Somerset 16th January 1896, High Sheriff of Somerset for 1896 and Justice of the Peace in Somerset and Wiltshire. He was living at Northfield House, Rode, Somerset in 1875. Robert was Chairman of Frome United Breweries Co Ltd and a Director of the Frome Newspaper Printing and Publishing Company. When he died, his estate was valued at £98,804, with net personalty £93,506. Arthur's mother, Sophia Frederica Christina Hastings née MacRae (1853–1925), was born at Lucknow, India. Robert and Sophia were married on 13th November 1879 at St Paul's Episcopal Church, Rothesay, Bute. At the time of the 1881 Census the family was living at 25 & 26 George Street, Hanover Square, London. They had moved to Rode Manor, Somerset by 1889. Arthur had four siblings:

- Robert Duncan (Henry) Batten-Pooll (1881–94).
- Walter Stewart Batten-Pooll (1882–1953) succeeded his father as Lord of the Manors of Rode and Woolverton. He was commissioned in the North Somerset

Yeomanry (Territorial Force) on 1st April 1909, promoted lieutenant 29th November 1909 and captain 29th August 1914. Appointed Adjutant 31st October 1914 – 31st August 1915. He held a number of staff appointments 1st September 1915 – 15th May 1917 and was seconded to the Labour Corps 19th August 1917 – 25th January 1919. He was commissioned in the Defence Force as a Temporary Captain 11th April 1921 – 22nd May 1921, transferred to the Territorial Army Reserve of Officers (Class II) on 19th July 1922 and retired having attained the age limit on 16th July 1932. Justice of the Peace in Somerset 1919, Deputy Lieutenant Somerset on 30th September 1931 and High Sheriff for 1946. He also served on Frome Rural District Council. He lived at Rode Manor and Merfield House, Rode and never married.

Rutland Lodge in Knightsbridge, where Arthur Batten-Pooll was born. It is now the Turkish Consulate (S Ehran).

- John Alexander Batten-Pooll (1889–1965) was commissioned from the Royal Military College Sandhurst in 5th (Royal Irish) Lancers on 23rd February 1910. Promoted lieutenant 28th January 1911. MID, LG 22nd June 1915. MC, LG 23rd June 1915. Appointed Staff Captain Royal Artillery in France 13th January – 19th December 1916 and temporary captain 15th April – 19th December 1916. GSO3 Home Forces and in France 20th December 1916 – 24th February 1917. Acting captain 20th February – 6th March 1917. Promoted captain 7th March 1917. DSO, LG 26th July 1918 – for reconnoitering under heavy fire, driving the enemy back with bombs over a canal and organising a counterattack to restore the situation. Although wounded, he continued to direct his squadron, until he was wounded a second time. MID, LG 20th December 1918. Appointed Adjutant 4th November 1919 – 25th October 1921. Promoted major in 7th Queen's Own Hussars on 26th October 1921. Appointed GSO2 Northern Command, India 24th November 1924 – 8th March 1926. Appointed local lieutenant colonel while GSO2 Staff College 30th September 1926 – 30th September 1929. Appointed brevet lieutenant colonel 1st January 1929. Promoted lieutenant colonel on 23rd October 1931. CO 7th Queen's Own Hussars 23rd October 1931 – 1st July 1932.

One of Frome United Breweries' products about 1900 (Martin Hendry).

He retired and transferred to the Regular Army Reserve of Officers (6604) on 2nd July 1932 and ceased to belong to it on account of poor health on 19th November 1941. John married Gwendolen Augusta Shaw (1906–74) in 1930.

* Mary Margaret Batten-Pooll (1884–1959) lived at 'Le Vieux Clos', Saint-Buc, Le Minihic-sur-Rance, Ille et Vilaine, France and did not marry.

Rode Manor, Somerset.

Arthur's paternal grandfather, Joseph Langford (1815–73), married Ann Pooll née Britton (c.1817–51). He was a landed proprietor living at Vale House, Timsbury with 278 acres in 1861. By 1871 he had moved in with his mother at Huish House, Kilmersdon, Somerset.

His maternal grandfather, Duncan MacRae (1816–98) joined the Honourable East India Company in Bengal as Assistant Surgeon on 24th January 1839. He married Grace née Stewart (c.1830–1912) in 1852. Appointed Surgeon January 1853, Surgeon Major February 1859 and Deputy Inspector-General of Hospitals, Lahore September 1863. He retired from the Indian Medical Service in December 1868 having taken part in the Afghan War 1839–42, Sind Campaign 1842–43, Punjab War 1848–49 and the Indian Mutiny 1857–58. Appointed Justice of the Peace for Bute and Deputy Lieutenant Bute 21st June 1895. In addition to Sophia they had five children including:

* Stuart MacRae (1855–1927) was a master maltster and a member of the King's Body Guard for Scotland (Royal Company of Archers). He married Ethel Evelyn Martha Smith in 1891 and they had three children including:
  ◦ Kenneth Stuart MacRae (1892–1960) was commissioned from the Special Reserve in 10th Black Watch on 10th June 1914 and had been promoted to captain by December 1916. Appointed Aide de Camp 1st April 1915–19th June 1916. Awarded the Croix de Guerre and served as a member of The King's Bodyguard for Scotland (Royal Company of Archers) 1921.
  ◦ John Nigel MacRae (1894–1918) was commissioned in the Nottinghamshire (Sherwood Rangers) Yeomanry on 1st June 1911. Transferred to the Territorial Force Reserve on 16th December 1914.

A member of the Royal Company of Archers (J Moffat).

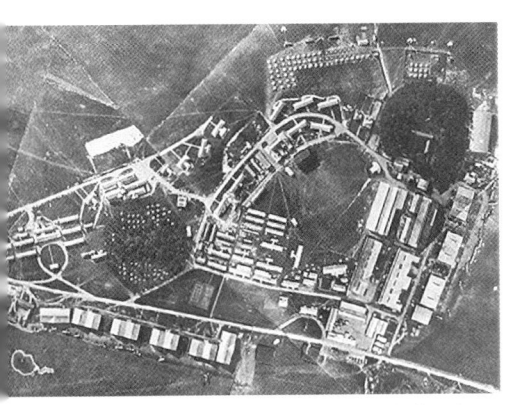

The Central Flying School at Upavon during the First World War.

John MacRae-Gilstrap and his wife Isabella. He was the 22nd Constable of Eilean Donan Castle, which he spent almost twenty years renovating.

Regular Commission 5th January 1915. Attended the Central Flying School from November. Posted to 38 Squadron in February 1916 and 15 Squadron in March. He was found guilty of failing to obey Squadron Routine Orders by Field General Court Martial on 9th June. His seniority as a flying officer was reduced, but it was meaningless as it was an appointment not a rank at that time. Posted to 76 Squadron, a home defence unit, in December and became a flight commander in January 1917. Served in 198, 199 and 119 Squadrons before returning to France in March 1918. Appointed temporary captain on 1st April and was killed in a flying accident on 11th April; buried in Lapugnoy Military Cemetery, France (VI C 10).

- John MacRae-Gilstrap (formerly MacRae) (1861–1937) was commissioned in the Antrim Militia (Queen's Royal Rifles) on 5th July 1880. Transferred to 6th Brigade, Scottish Division, Royal Artillery (Militia) 9th May 1883. Regular commission in 1st Black Watch as a lieutenant on 5th December 1883. He served in the Sudan Expedition 1884 and retired as a captain in August 1890. He married Isabella Mary Gilstrap DJStJ in 1889. Appointed captain in 3rd Black Watch (Militia) on 22nd October 1890 and retired as honorary major 27th April 1898. HM Honourable Corps of Gentlemen-at-Arms 1901. Appointed temporary major 24th August 1914 and temporary lieutenant colonel while CO 11th (Reserve) Battalion, Black Watch 2nd December 1914 – 31st May 1918 (the unit became 38 Training Reserve Battalion in September 1916 and 202 Graduated Battalion in May 1917). Honorary lieutenant colonel 1st June 1918. OStJ, LG 3rd January 1930. Deputy Lieutenant Argyll 1932. Justice of the Peace and County

Eilean Donan Castle.

Palace of Holyroodhouse.

Councillor for Argyll. Member of the King's Body Guard for Scotland (Royal Company of Archers). Deputy Keeper of the Palace of Holyroodhouse. He was the 22nd Constable of Eilean Donan Castle (one of the most famous Scottish island castles), which he rebuilt 1913–32. CStJ, LG 1st January 1937. John and Isabella had seven children including:

- John Duncan George MacRae (1896–1966), 23rd Constable of Eilean Donan, was commissioned in the Seaforth Highlanders on 17th February 1915. By December he was training with the RFC and served with 45 and 65 Squadrons. He was injured on 15th July 1916 in a flying accident. He returned to duty and was taken prisoner by the Turks on 5th October 1917. He returned to Alexandria on 24th November 1918 and was repatriated through Dover, Kent on 16th December.
- Margaret Helen MacRae married Brigadier Sir Bruce Atta Campbell KCB CBE in 1913. He was commissioned in the Scottish Horse on 16th May 1913. Appointed Adjutant 3rd November 1914. Appointed Brigade Major 7th May 1918. GSO1 Scottish Command, Army Cadet Force 4th October 1943. Chair & Military Member, Argyll Territorial Association as a colonel 24th August 1939. Honorary Colonel Territorial Army 21st July 1940. Lord Lieutenant Argyll 1949–54. President Argyll Territorial & Auxiliary Forces Association in the early 1950s as a Brigadier.
- Colin William MacRae (1869–1952) was commissioned in 4th Sherwood Foresters (Derbyshire Regiment) on 6th August 1887. Regular commission in the Black Watch 28th June 1890. He served in South Africa 1899–1902 and was seconded to 5th (Perthshire Highland) Volunteer Battalion as Adjutant December 1902 – January 1905. Promoted captain 3rd December 1904 and retired on 5th August 1905. He married Lady Margaret Crichton-Stuart DJStJ OBE JP in 1909. Major 29th January 1917 and Aide-de-Camp 14th February – 30 March 1918. KGStJ, LG 13th April 1920. CBE for services with the British Red Cross Society, LG 31st December 1921. KLStJ, LG 22nd June 1926. CVO, LG 2nd January 1933. Knight Bachelor, LG 26th July 1935. Honorary Colonel 13th (Highland) Light Brigade, Royal Artillery TA January 1935 (54th

(West Highland) Field Brigade from 1936). Honorary Colonel 51st Anti-Tank Regiment RA TA November 1938 – July 1939. HM Body Guard of the Yeomen of the Guard – Exon 4th May 1906 and lieutenant 17th June 1932 until his resignation on 30th August 1945. Member of the King's Body Guard for Scotland (Royal Company of Archers) 1909. Deputy Lieutenant Bute 1919 and Vice-Lieutenant 1935. Justice of the Peace for Buteshire and County Councillor for Bute and Argyll. Chamberlain to His Holiness the Pope; awarded the Order of the Holy Sepulchre (Vatican). Colin and Margaret had three children:

- John Donald Christopher Stuart MacRae (1912–1942) was commissioned in 2nd Scots Guards (53165) 1st September 1932. Adjutant 22nd June 1937. Captain 1st September 1940. He served in Palestine 1936–39. Awarded DSO, MC and MID, LG 1st April 1941. He was killed in action at El Alamein on 19th July 1942 and is buried in El Alamein War Cemetery, Egypt (XXIX B 21).
- Gwendolen Margaret Mary Grace MacRae (born 1910) married Captain Oswald James Battine RE in 1936. He was commissioned on 26th August 1924. Adjutant TA November 1930 – January 1935. He was killed on active service in India on 19th September 1938 and Gwendolen married again in 1939.
- Margaret Anne Mary MacRae married Lieutenant Colonel Richard Arundell Hugh Whatton MBE in 1933. Richard was commissioned as temporary lieutenant ASC 1st July 1917 and as war substantive lieutenant RASC 9th September 1939. Staff Captain Department of Adjutant General as temporary captain June 1940. Deputy Assistant Military Secretary October 1945 as temporary major. MBE, LG 9th June 1949. Local lieutenant colonel June 1950. Regular major Wiltshire Regiment 9th September 1952. He was killed accidentally on 17th December 1953.

Arthur was educated at Eton and then pursued his interests in science and fox hunting. He was commissioned in 3rd Somerset Light Infantry (Special Reserve) on 1st June 1911. Promoted lieutenant on 23rd March 1913 and resigned from the Special Reserve on 4th July 1914. He was commissioned into 5th (Royal Irish) Lancers Special Reserve on 22nd September 1914 and was attached to 6th Reserve Regiment of Cavalry in Dublin. He transferred to 3rd (Reserve) Battalion, Royal Munster Fusiliers at Aghada, Cork on 14th July 1915 with seniority from 22nd September 1914. Promoted lieutenant 24th July and attached to 2nd Battalion in France from 9th February

Eton College Quadrangle.

1916. Promoted captain after his VC action with seniority from 28th February 1916.

Awarded the VC for his actions near Calonne, France on 25th/26th June 1916, LG 5th August 1916. The VC was presented by the King at Buckingham Palace on 4th November 1916. Appointed ADC to Major General (later Sir) Richard P Lee KCB, GOC 18th Division, 4th March – 2nd August 1917. **Awarded the MC for his actions at Chérisy on 3rd May 1917 – when the advance seemed to be wavering he rallied and led all the men he could collect to the objective, which he held. By his example he kept the men together and inflicted heavy losses on the enemy, LG 26th July 1917.** Mentioned in Field Marshal Sir Douglas Haig's Despatch dated 7th November 1917, LG 11th December 1917.

Balliol College, Oxford.

Arthur returned to the 2nd Battalion on 3rd August 1917 to command C Company. He was taken prisoner at Passchendaele on 10th November and was transferred for internment in Switzerland on 27th December in a party of eighty-four officers and 854 other ranks. He was repatriated on 24th March 1918 and appointed Deputy Assistant Provost-Marshal 14th November 1918 – 26th May 1919. Appointed liaison officer to 2/6th North Russian Rifles in the North Russian Expeditionary Force July – October 1919. Relinquished his commission on 1st April 1920, retaining the rank of captain.

Arthur was at Balliol College, Oxford 1922–25, where he gaining Diplomas in Agriculture and Rural Economics. Fellow of the Linnean Society 1925. He travelled extensively in pursuit of his scientific interest in flora and fauna as well as angling. His travels included Dalmatia 1932, the Pacific islands, including Tahiti and Marquesas 1934, New Zealand 1934–35, South America, particularly the Amazon 1935, Persia 1936, Morocco 1934 and 1939, Bulgaria 1938, Malaysia 1939–40 and Nigeria 1946–47. When he reached Cairo in 1940, he could not get back to England or obtain service. He wrote *Some Globetrotting with a Rod* 1937 and *A West Country Potpourri* 1969. Vice-President of the Royal Humane Society 1961.

Arthur never married and died at his home, Ugborough House, near Ivybridge, Devon on 21st January 1971. He is buried at St Lawrence's Parish Churchyard, Rode, Somerset. He left £105,400 in his will.

Ugborough.

In addition to the VC and MC, he was awarded the British War Medal 1914–20, Victory Medal 1914–19 with Mentioned-in-Despatches Oakleaf, George VI Coronation Medal 1937 and Elizabeth II Coronation Medal 1953. He bequeathed his medals to the National Army Museum where they are held. Arthur is also commemorated:

* On the Eton College Cloisters For Valour Memorial. He is one of thirty-seven Eton VCs.
* By Lucuma batten-poollii Benoist, a variety of eggfruit-bearing tree discovered by Arthur in Brazil in 1935 and named in his honour in 1938 by the French botanist Raymond Benoist.

2ND LIEUTENANT EDWARD FELIX BAXTER
1/8th (Irish) Battalion, The King's (Liverpool Regiment)

Edward Baxter was born at 'Thornleigh', 35 Hagley Road, Old Swinford, Stourbridge, Worcestershire on 18th September 1885. His birthplace later became a YMCA Centre. His father was Charles Albert Baxter (1845–1922), a miller, maltster and corn merchant working at Lower High Street, Stourbridge. He was declared bankrupt several times, on the last occasion for £452/12/11 in January 1899. His mother was Beatrice Anita née Sparrow (1864–1935). They married on 2nd June 1881 at Himley, Staffordshire. The family moved to 'Ivy Cottage', Hind Lane, Hartlebury in 1891 and later to 'Mostyn', 2 Shrubbery Street, Kidderminster. Edward had four siblings:

* Kenneth Charles Baxter (1882–1959) married Frances Eliza Poole (born c.1882) in 1910. He was a bank clerk in 1911, living with his wife at 7 Comberton Terrace, Kidderminster. Kenneth was well known as a cricketer in the Birmingham League. He served as a lieutenant in 1/7th Worcestershire and later with the Special Brigade Royal Engineers. Promoted lieutenant 1st June 1916. He was gassed on 31st July 1918 and evacuated to England on 12th August, where he was treated at 3rd Southern General Hospital, Oxford and Mont Dore Hospital, Bournemouth until 31st October. He served at the Special Brigade Depot, South Raglan Barracks, Devonport until fully fit and was demobilised on 24 April 1919.
* Eric Hamilton Baxter (1889–1933) was an assistant master at a preparatory school at St Annes-on-the-Sea, Lancashire in 1911.

- Madeleine Anita Beatrice Baxter (1884–1963) married Edmund B Wood (born c.1880) in 1911.
- Nina Francis Baxter (1887–1958) married Douglas Gilbert Prentice (1891–1961) in 1914.

Edward's paternal grandfather, John Alexander Baxter MA (1805–49) graduated from St John's College, Cambridge in 1827 and became stipendiary curate at St Mary's Church, Kingswinford, Staffordshire 1828–31. He was curate at Holy Trinity Church, Wordsley, Worcestershire 1831–43 and perpetual curate at Christchurch, Coseley, Staffordshire 1843–49. He was admitted to Droitwich Lunatic Asylum, where he died on 21st June 1849. He had undertaken personal financial responsibility for the building of new schools and a bazaar was organised in Coseley after his death to pay off his debts. Amongst Edward's uncles were:

- John Henry Churchill Baxter MA (c.1843–1926) who also became a clergymen. He married twice and had five children.
- Edward Alexander Baxter (1847–1907) migrated to Natal, South Africa in 1875, where he married Martha Maria Christina Ries at Bishopstowe in 1878 and they had six children.

Edward was educated at Queen Elizabeth Grammar School, Hartlebury from 1894 and Christ's Hospital Horsham 1897–1901. Wilfrith Elstob VC attended Christ's from 1898 and Henry Pitcher VC was there in the 1840–50s. Edward was employed by United Counties Bank as a clerk and later became Chief Commercial Master at Skerry's College in Rodney Street, Liverpool.

Edward Baxter married Leonora Mary née Cornish (1886–1988) on 24th February 1906 at the West Derby Register Office, Liverpool. Leonora's brother, Henry Pountney Cornish (1899–1971), served as a private in 34th London (881072) in France from 1st August 1918. Edward and Leonora had a daughter, Leonora Francis Baxter, born on 11th June 1907 at 147 Faulker Street, Abercromby, Liverpool.

Edward and Leonora were keen motorcycle racing competitors. He had some successes in track racing and road trials in northern England, particularly around Liverpool. They were members of the Liverpool Auto Cycle Club and he raced many times at New Brighton. He competed in the Isle of Man Tourist Trophy Race in 1910, but lost control on the fourth of sixteen laps and bent the front forks. He was not injured, straightened the forks as best he could and continued

Queen Elizabeth Grammar School, Hartlebury.

The start of a race during the 1910 Isle of Man Tourist Trophy.

Rodney Street, Liverpool.

racing, but the bike would not steer properly and he was forced to retire on the fifth lap. Edward also worked on model aeroplanes as a hobby.

Edward enlisted in the Royal Engineers (32072) on 4th September 1914 and was promoted sergeant as a dispatch rider on the Headquarters Staff of the Mersey Defence Corps at Rodney Street, Liverpool the same day. He was described as 5′ 11¾″ tall, weighing 156 lbs, with sallow complexion, brown hair and eyes and his religious denomination was Church of England. He was commissioned into 3/8th King's on 17th September 1915 and went to France to join 1/8th King's in January 1916. He was appointed Bombing Officer.

Awarded the VC for his actions near Blairville, France on 17th – 18th April 1916, LG 26th September 1916. He was killed during the VC action and was buried by the Germans in the churchyard of Boiry St Rictrude and St Martin. He was reported missing in April 1916 and his death was not confirmed until 15th May through the US Embassy in Berlin. His remains were removed to Fillievres British Cemetery, near Hesdin, France (A 10) in 1925. The Germans preserved his personal effects (cigarette case, silver match box, two knives and two francs), which were returned to his wife via the War Office in August 1920. He left £212/8/5 to his widow. Edward is also commemorated by Baxter's House at Queen Elizabeth's Grammar School, Hartlebury, now King Charles I Comprehensive School.

The VC was presented to his widow by the King at Buckingham Palace on 29th November 1916. They were living at 5 Blantyre Road, Sefton Park, Liverpool at the time of his death. Leonora moved back to Kidderminster to be near her family and lived at 3 Roden Avenue with her daughter. The War Office wrote to her about the VC pension and wearing her husband's ribbons at Garage, Royal Aircraft Factory, South Farnborough, Hampshire on 12th April 1919. By May 1919 her address was c/o Mrs Cornish, Hales Park, Bewdley, Worcestershire.

Leonora married Alexander Gray (1896–1980) in October 1922 and they lived at 10 Bungalow, RAF Uxbridge, Middlesex. Leonora and Alexander had two daughters – Jean M Gray 1924 and Nina R Gray 1925. He enlisted as a private in the Highland Light Infantry at the outbreak of the Great War, was commissioned in the Argyll and Sutherland Highlanders and transferred to the Royal Flying Corps in early 1916. He served with 55 Squadron and was twice wounded – shell splinter right hand on 14th January 1917 and gunshot wound right hand 1st March 1917. MC, LG 27th October 1917. Appointed flight commander December 1917. Posted to 12 Squadron 1918. Posted to Malta November 1928, testing aircraft for the Fleet Air Arm at Hal Far and the seaplane base. Promoted group captain 1939 and appointed to command RAF Manston. Promoted air commodore and posted to India in 1942. Awarded CB, LG 8th June 1944. Promoted air vice marshal and appointed Air-Officer Commanding Air Headquarters at Habbaniyah, Iraq April 1947. He retired from the RAF in 1949.

In addition to the VC, he was awarded the British War Medal 1914–20 and Victory Medal 1914–19. His VC was donated to the Imperial War Museum by his family in August 1988. His British War Medal and Victory Medal plus other memorabilia were sold at a Spink's auction in London on 6th September 2012 in aid of 'The Bentley Priory Battle of Britain Trust Appeal' for an estimated £5–7,000. Also sold were the No.1 Uniform of Air Vice Marshal Alexander Gray CB MC and other memorabilia of his for an estimated £3–500.

9539 LANCE SERGEANT DOUGLAS WALTER BELCHER
1/5th (City of London) Battalion, The London Regiment (London Rifle Brigade)

Douglas Belcher was born at 2 Park Villas, Arlington Road, Surbiton, Surrey on 15th July 1889. His father was Walter Harry Belcher (1857–1916) a draper. His mother was Emily née Taylor (1853–1927) a cook working for a surgeon, Edward Cook, in 1881. Walter and Emily's marriage was registered during the 4th quarter of 1884 at Kingston upon Thames, Surrey. They were living at 2 Park Villas, Arlington Road in 1891, 17 Brighton Road in 1901 and 101 Brighton Road in 1911. His brother, Cecil George Belcher (1891–1975), a commercial clerk joined the Royal Navy (F11789), enlisting on 14th February 1916 and served at the Crystal Palace and Earl's Court until transferring to the RAF on 1st April 1918.

Douglas was educated at Tiffin Boy's School, Kingston-upon-Thames from 1900. He was very fit, regularly swimming in the Thames and was also keen on rowing, cycling, cricket and tennis. He was a member of the Surbiton United

Tiffin's Boys School, Kingston on Thames.

Waring and Gillow, 164–182 Oxford Street, London (English Heritage).

and Ditton Hill Cricket Clubs, St Mark's Company, Church Lads' Brigade and sang in the choir at St Mary's, Surbiton. He worked in his father's drapery business before being employed as a clerk by Joseph Randall Porter of Surbiton and later by the antiques department of Waring & Gillow's, Oxford Street, London.

Douglas enlisted in 26th Middlesex (Cyclist) Volunteer Rifle Corps in 1906 and transferred to 25th (County of London) Cyclist Battalion on 23rd April 1908 (129) following the creation of the Territorial Force on 1st April. He was discharged on

SS *Chyebassa*, launched in 1907 for the British India Steam Navigation Company, which was taken over by The Peninsular and Oriental Steam Navigation Company in 1914. On 7th August 1914 she became an Expeditionary Force transport and her crew had to be replaced because the Indian crew refused further duty. She was torpedoed in December 1917 by UC25 south of Malta and collided with the *City of Marseilles*. *Chyebassa* was beached and repaired, but the following March she struck and sank the minesweeper trawler *Adrian* in fog off Orfordness. She was broken up in Italy in 1939.

31st March 1909 and later served in 9th (County of London) Battalion, London Regiment (Queen Victoria's Rifles), winning a silver cup for shooting in 1912. In April 1913, he enlisted in 5th (City of London) Battalion, London Regiment (London Rifle Brigade). A year later on 19th/20th April 1914, he was one of sixty officers, NCOs and men of the Battalion who marched the fifty-two and a half miles from London to Brighton, carrying forty pounds, in the impressive time of fourteen hours and twenty-three minutes. This established a new record for the distance within 1st London Infantry Brigade. Douglas embarked for France from Southampton on SS *Chyebassa* as a lance-sergeant on 4th November 1914. The Battalion arrived at Le Havre and No.1 Rest Camp on 5th November, moved to St Omer two days later and by 22nd November the Battalion had moved to Ploegsteert, Belgium attached to 11th Brigade, 4th Division.

Awarded the VC for his actions south of Wieltje to St Julien Road, near Ypres, Belgium on 13th May 1915, LG 23rd June 1915. He was the first Territorial Force other rank to receive it. The VC was presented by the King at Buckingham Palace on 12th July 1915. Next day he was received at Tiffin Boys' School and presented with a black marble clock. On 17th July, Waring & Gillow presented him with a silver rose bowl and a purse of gold at a ceremony at the firm's premises at White City, London attended by over 3,000 employees. On 21st July, the last day of his leave, at Victoria recreation ground in Balaclava Road, he was formally received by Surbiton and presented with a purse of money and an inscribed service revolver.

Douglas was commissioned into 3/9th (County of London) Battalion, The London Regiment (Queen Victoria's Rifles) on 10th February 1916. He was promoted lieutenant on 10th August 1917 and demobilised from the TF on 29th October 1918. The following day he was seconded for service in the Indian Army on probation and attached to 1/6th Gurkha Rifles from 2nd November 1918 at Abbottabad, with seniority as lieutenant Indian Army from 10th November 1917. He was promoted captain Indian Army on 10th November 1920 and served as a company commander in Mesopotamia in 1921 following the Arab Rising. Later in 1921 he was attached to 5th Battalion, 70th Burma Rifles at Meiktila as a company commander and retired on 19th July 1922 due to poor health.

Douglas married Emily Frances née Luxford (1st July 1896 – 1963) on 31st January 1917 at St Mark's, Surbiton. They had two sons:

* Francis Douglas 'Bill' Belcher was born on 31st December 1917. He

Mount Ephraim, Tunbridge Wells.

married his cousin, Avis Mary née Luxford (born 1917), registered during the 4th quarter of 1941 at Surrey North West. They had three children. Francis served in the Royal Army Service Corps (61672) and the Royal Electrical and Mechanical Engineers. As a staff sergeant, he was awarded the British Empire Medal (Military Division), LG 14th June 1945. He was a WO2 serving at Parsons Barracks, Aldershot, Hampshire in 1956.

Calverley Road, Tunbridge Wells.

- Brian Wynn Belcher was born on 15th February 1926. His marriage to Betty Fenetta née Wordley was registered at Bury St Edmunds in the 3rd quarter of 1948. They had two children. Brian became director of Belcher Engineering Ltd, specialising in precision engineering and restoration of Ford cars, and Michael Belcher Ltd, a construction company in Norfolk.

Douglas and Emily initially lived at 6 St Andrews Road, Surbiton. He worked for a cigar merchant before returning to Waring and Gillow's, but suffered from neurasthenia from 1926 and was forced to seek other employment. They moved to Mount Ephraim Road, Tunbridge Wells, Kent in 1926 and ran a greengrocer's shop at 69 Calverley Road from 1928. He was active with ex-servicemen's associations in Tunbridge Wells. In 1927, he became Chairman of the local British Legion and in 1932 founded, and was later President of, the local branch of the Old Contemptibles Association, which was named 'Belcher VC Branch' in his honour.

The shop was supplied with produce by Reginald Larkin (1893–1963). Reginald and his brother, Ernest Archibald Larkin, moved to Australia, but the brother drowned in 1913. Reginald returned to work on his father's farm at Tunbridge Wells growing vegetables for markets. He served during the war and was evacuated to Haslar Hospital, Gosport, Hampshire with a gunshot wound to his knee, which resulted in a permanent limp and being discharged from the Army (Silver War Badge 325204). His brother, G/13656 Private Cyril Larkin, 12th Royal Sussex, was killed on 31st

St Ethelburga's Church, Bishopgate, London (HR Allenam).

July 1917 and is commemorated on the Ypres (Menin Gate) Memorial. Emily appears to have had a relationship with Reginald. The shop was sold in October 1933 and the family, including Emily's mother, Louisa, and Larkin, moved to a poultry farm at Westhorpe Old Rectory, Suffolk, which is understood to have been purchased by Larkin. Over time Douglas was treated more like a lodger, but he was in poor health and could do little about it. Later he moved out with his mother-in-law, Louisa, possibly to 34 Woodbines Avenue, Kingston-upon-Thames. When Douglas' health improved, he filed for divorce in February 1935 – decree nisi granted by Mr Justice Bucknill on 7th October 1935. The case was uncontested and Douglas was granted custody of their two sons. Emily married Reginald Larkin at Hartismere, Suffolk, registered in the 1st quarter of 1941. She ran a business, buying and selling properties, renovated by her son Brian's building company. By October 1937, Douglas was a clerk-commissionaire working for a city firm of chartered accountants, living in Villiers Avenue, Surbiton.

In April 1939, Douglas attended the 25th Anniversary Dinner of the Brighton March at Brigade HQ, Bunhill Row, London. Although many had been lost in the war, forty former members of the pre-war marching teams were there, including three lieutenant colonels, six majors, seventeen captains and nine subalterns. Between them they held a VC, two DSOs and six MCs.

On 24th May 1939, Douglas relinquished the rank of captain retired Indian Army on enlistment into the ranks of the London Rifle Brigade, The Rifle Brigade (Prince Consort's Own) (TA). He was promoted sergeant in 1940 and served with the National Defence Company, The Rifle Brigade. He returned to the London Rifle Brigade, retitled 7th Battalion, The Rifle Brigade and was medically discharged on 2nd May 1940 following a fall at Woolwich and was granted the rank of captain. He was then employed with the Royal Army Pay Corps (188583) and at his own request reverted to lieutenant on 26th August 1941. He was employed on PoW duties and was restored to captain on 12th August 1943 on ceasing to be employed. He worked as a civil servant thereafter.

On 5th August 1941, Douglas married Gertrude Elizabeth née Brine (1888–1967) at St Ethelburga's Church, Bishopgate, London. They had no children. They were living at Villiers Avenue, Surbiton in 1941, 11 Alwyne Mansions, Alwyne Road, Wimbledon in 1949 and 'Tera', 16 Rythe Road, Claygate, Surrey in 1953. The last property was bought for them by Emily's mother, Louisa Luxford, and they moved there after he suffered a stroke. One of Gertude's brothers, William Thomas Brine (1887–1918), died on 24th November 1918 while serving as a sergeant major in 309th Home Service Field Ambulance RAMC (504001) and is buried in Kingston on Thames Cemetery (C 3614).

Douglas became a Freemason on 4th March 1916 when he was Initiated into the Arts and Crafts Lodge No.3387, meeting at Freemasons' Hall, London. He was Passed on 5th April and Raised on 6th May. He was a Petitioner (Founder Member) of Hazara Lodge No.4159 Punjab, India, when it was founded on 13th July 1920 and served as Junior Warden until he resigned on 31st October 1922. In November 1937 he joined the London Rifle Brigade Lodge No.1962, meeting in Mark Masons' Hall, London. On 27th April 1945 he became a joining member of Lodge of Amity No.171, Freemasons' Hall, London and resigned on 13th November 1949. Because of Indian independence, Hazara Lodge No.4159 transferred on 6th November 1947 from the District Grand Lodge of the Punjab to Freemasons' Hall, London. Douglas rejoined the Lodge in April 1948 and was Worshipful Master from June 1948. In March 1951 he was elected an Honorary Member.

Douglas Belcher died at his home 'Tera', 16 Rythe Road, Claygate, Surrey on 3rd June 1953 and is buried in Holy Trinity Churchyard, Claygate. He left £1,702. Douglasis commemorated in a number of other places:

- Belcher Branch, Tunbridge Wells Old Comrades Association, Tunbridge Wells, Kent.
- The Victoria Cross Grove Memorial, Dunorlan Park, Tunbridge Wells commemorates the 400th anniversary of Royal Tunbridge Wells and the 150th anniversary of the Victoria Cross. Tunbridge Borough Council commissioned Andrew Motion, Poet Laureate, to write the poem 'Remembrance' and the artist Charles Gurrey to create a memorial sculpture. The Memorial is dedicated to the ten VCs associated with the Borough – Charles Lucas, Matthew Dixon, William Temple, John Duncan Grant, Douglas Belcher, William Addison, Eric Dougall, William Clarke-Kennedy, Lionel Queripel and John Brunt. It was unveiled by HRH The Princess Royal on 13th October 2006.
- Twenty two Berberis shrubs represent the 22 members of the Church Lads' Brigade who were awarded the VC at the Church Lads & Church Girls Brigade Memorial Plot at the National Memorial Arboretum, Alrewas, Staffordshire.
- The Rifle Brigade's Roll of Fame in Winchester Cathedral.

In addition to the VC, Douglas Belcher was awarded the 1914 Star, British War Medal 1914–20, Victory Medal 1914–19, War Medal 1939–45, George VI Coronation Medal 1937 and Elizabeth II Coronation Medal 1953. It is not known if the War Medal 1939–45 and Elizabeth II Coronation Medal 1953 were ever claimed or received. His son, Francis, presented the medals to the Royal Green Jackets Museum, Peninsular Barracks, Romsey Road, Winchester. The Museum is now the Royal Green Jackets (Rifles) Museum incorporating The Rifle Brigade (Prince Consort's Own), Oxfordshire & Buckinghamshire Light Infantry and King's Royal Rifle Corps.

LIEUTENANT EDWARD DONALD BELLEW
7th Battalion (1st British Columbia), Canadian Expeditionary Force

Edward Bellew was born on 28th October 1882 at Malabar Hill, Bombay, India. However, when he enlisted, his place of birth was given as, on the high seas. His father was Surgeon Major Patrick Francis Bellew (1832–1909). He studied medicine at Plymouth St Andrew, Devon (MRCS 1854, LCA). He was commissioned as Assistant Surgeon in the Bengal Medical Department on 6th September 1854 and served during the Sonthal Insurrection 1855–56. Patrick was appointed Surgeon on 6th September 1866, Surgeon Major on 1st July 1873 and retired from the Indian Medical Service on 1st December 1882. He also held a number of civil appointments – Deputy Assay-Master of the Calcutta Mint 1868, Officiating Commissioner of Paper Currency at Madras 1870, Deputy Assay-Master of the Bombay Mint 1870 until after 1877, when he was Assay-Master until his retirement. Edward's mother was Sophia Elizabeth née Fordyce (1844–85). Patrick and Sophia married on 15th May 1862 at St Peter's, Bayswater, London. They were living at 87 Talbot Road, Bayswater, London in 1881. After Sophia died, Patrick married Letitia Louise Box (1857–1912) in 1885 at Paddington, London. She was a singing and dancing teacher. They were living at Colley House, Tedburn St Mary, Devon in 1891. Edward had a sibling from each marriage:

- Anna Lorna Bellew (1884–1958). In 1907 she married Hans Andreas Dahl (1881–1919) from Düsseldorf, Germany and had two sons. Hans Francis John Bellew Dahl (1910–42) was commissioned (145161) on 17th August 1940 and promoted lieutenant on 17th February 1942. He was killed in action serving with 7th Green Howards on 7th June 1942 and is buried in Knightsbridge War Cemetery, Acroma, Libya (1 F 18). Eric Anthony Bellew Dahl (1915–89) was also commissioned in the Green Howards (143542) on 17th August 1940. Promoted lieutenant 17th February 1942 and captain 20th February 1946. By June 1947 he had been released to the Reserve. He transferred to the Intelligence Corps, Regular Army Reserve of Officers as lieutenant and honorary captain on 1st January 1949. Anna married for the second time Walter Normann (c.1880–1951) in 1921.
- Henry Esmonde Bellew (1886–1917) was commissioned in 4th Battalion, Devonshire Regiment (Militia) on 19th March 1906. He transferred to the Army Service Corps as 2nd lieutenant on 28th May 1910 and served with the West African Frontier Force. He resigned his commission on 26th June 1912 and

married Henrietta Thorne (c.1880–1957) the same year. Henry died on 11th August 1917 at Katensa Allah, Nigeria leaving £192/17/1 to his widow. Henrietta married George William Skardon (1884–1951) in 1920.

Edward's paternal grandfather was Major Henry Walter Bellew (1802–42), whose brother, Captain Francis John Bellew (1799–1870), was the maternal grandfather of Major General Sir Robert Bellew Adams VC KCB (1856–1928). Edward was commissioned in the Bengal Army as a lieutenant in 56th Bengal Native Infantry on 1st January 1821. He married Anna née Jeremie (1810–1905) from St Peter's, Guernsey on 17th August 1831 at Agra, India where her father, Captain Peter Jeremie (1786–1831), was assistant opium agent. As a brevet major from 23rd November 1841, Edward was appointed Assistant Quartermaster General attached to the Kabul Army. He was hacked to death on 13th January 1842 during the disastrous retreat from Kabul. In addition to Patrick, Edward and Anna also had:

- Henry Walter Bellew (1834–92) was educated at St George's Hospital, London (MRCS & LSA 1854). He entered the Army Medical Department as Acting Assistant Surgeon on 24th November 1854, served in the Crimean War during the winter of 1854–55 and resigned on 6th October 1855. He was commissioned as Assistant Surgeon in the Bengal Medical Establishment on 14th November 1855 and arrived in India in March 1856 to be appointed to the Corps of Guides. He accompanied Major Henry Lumsden's mission to Kandahar 1857, served with the Yusafzai Field Force and at Umbeyla 1863–64. He was appointed Surgeon on 14th November 1867 and civil surgeon at Peshawar on 10th January 1868. In Kashmir in 1869 he was employed by Lord Mayo as interpreter to the Amir, Sher Ali, during the durbar at Ambala. He accompanied Major General FR Pollock's mission in Sistan 1871 (Companion of the Star of India, LG 14th February 1873). He married Isabel Jane née MacGregor (c.1851–1912), daughter of Major Robert Guthrie MacGregor RA and sister of General Sir George MacGregor. They had four children. Appointed Surgeon Major 1st July 1873, he was attached to Sir Douglas Forsyth's embassy to Kashgar and Yarkand 1873–74, followed by Residency Surgeon Nepal 1876 and Sanitary Commissioner for the Punjab 1877. He was Chief Political Officer in Kabul and served with the Kurram Field Force 1878–79 (MID, LG 4th May 1880). Appointed Deputy Surgeon General (as colonel) on 14th November 1881 and retired as

Edward Bellew was distantly related to Major General Sir Robert Bellew Adams VC KCB (1856–1928). He was awarded the VC for his actions on the North West Frontier during the Tirah Campaign on 17th August 1897.

honorary Surgeon General on 14th November 1886. He published a number of books including: *Journal of a Political Mission to Afghanistan in 1857*; *A Grammar and Dictionary of the Pukkhto or Pukshto Language*; *The Mission to Seistan under General Pollock*; *From the Indus to the Tigris: a Narrative of a journey through the countries of Balochistan, Afghanistan, Khorassan and Iran in 1872*; *A History of Kashgaria*; *Kashmir and Kashgar: a narrative of the journey of the embassy to Kashgar in 1873–74*; *Afghanistan and the Afghans*; and *The History of Cholera in India from 1862 to 1881*.

- Anna Claire Bellew (1835–87) married Archibald Tisdall (1822–96) in 1856 at Calcutta, India. They had five children. His great uncle was the great-great grandfather of Sub-Lieutenant Arthur Walderne St Clair Tisdall VC (1890–1915). Archibald was commissioned in the 64th Foot on 26th June 1840 and transferred to 35th Foot on 3rd July. He served during the Indian Mutiny and rose to lieutenant colonel on 30th June 1873 and brevet colonel on 1st October 1877. He commanded the Brigade Depot at Aberdeen from 13th February 1878 and 75th Regimental District (Gordon Highlanders) until he retired as honorary major general on 1st April 1882. He was a member of the Irish Land Commission in the 1880s.
- Sarah Sophia Bellew (born 1836) married Charles Edward Lance (1827–1916) in Bengal in 1857. He served in the Bengal Civil Service 1848–75 and his final appointment was Judge of Midnapur. Sarah died in India in 1866 or before. Charles married Mary Elizabeth née Portman (1841–1928) on 5th November 1866 at Calcutta. She was the daughter of the Reverend Fitzhardinge Berkeley Portman (1811–93).
- Maria Adelaide Bellew (1839–1910) married Thomas Edward Bristow Judge (born 1831) in 1857 at Calcutta. He was an attorney-at-law in Calcutta. They had three sons. Thomas died before 1871, by when she was living with her mother in Kensington, London.

Edward's maternal grandfather was Lieutenant General Sir John Fordyce KCB (1806–77), who was commissioned in the Bengal Artillery on 10th May 1822. His first wife, Sophia Clarke (Mrs Barnett), died in 1830 aboard *Warrior* on passage from Calcutta. His second wife, Maria Louisa née Alleyne (1812–45), was Edward's grandmother. She was born in Barbados, married John on 16th March 1842 and died on 2nd September 1845. John commanded a battery at Ferozeshah and Sobraon in the Sutlej campaign 1845–46, 9th Troop, Bengal Horse Artillery at Chillianwallah and Goojerat in the Punjab campaign 1848–49, the artillery in Colonel Bradshaw's force sent into Enzufzai country in late 1849 and in Sir Charles Napier's force in the Kohat Pass 1850. He was on the staff of Allahabad Brigade 1860 and Commandant of Bengal Artillery & Commander of Meerut Brigade later that year. Promoted major general on 29th April 1861 and transferred to the Royal Artillery as a colonel on 29th April 1862. In 1867 he was Temporary Commander of Presidency Division and Commander in January 1868. Having commanded the Sirhind Division in 1870 he returned to Britain in 1871. Promoted lieutenant general on 21st January 1872 and appointed Colonel Commandant Royal Artillery on 5th April 1873. KCB, LG 24th May 1873. John's third wife was Phoebe née Graham (1827–98). They married on 14th April 1847 in India and had eight children including:

- John Fraser Dingwall Fordyce (1850–1924) was commissioned into 21st Hussars on 4th February 1869 and promoted lieutenant on 28th October 1871. He was admitted to the Bengal Staff Corps on 10th January 1872 and took part in the Afghan War 1878–79. John married Alice Margaret née O'Brien (c.1860–1948) on 27th December 1880 at Mooltan, Bengal. He rose to lieutenant colonel 4th February 1895, brevet colonel 3rd April 1902 and retired on 10th August 1902.
- Arthur Lawrence Dingwall Fordyce (1852–86) was commissioned in the 81st Foot on 23rd September 1871. He transferred to 56th Foot on 14th October and was promoted lieutenant 28th October. He joined the Bombay Staff Corps as a lieutenant on 18th December 1874, serving with 11th Bombay Native Infantry with seniority from 28th October 1871. Appointed Assistant Political Officer at Sandra in 1877. Promoted captain 23rd September 1883 and appointed Wing Officer, 8th Bombay Native Infantry. Appointed Assistant to Political Agent at Kathiawar until his death in Bombay of remittent fever.
- Sidney Agnes Dingwall Fordyce (1857–1934) married Colonel Eden Moyle Baker (born 1851) in 1917. Sidney was Eden's second wife. Eden was commissioned as lieutenant in the Royal Artillery on 15th December 1871. He went to India in February 1873. During the Afghan War 1878–80, he took part in the advance on Kandahar and Kelati-Ghilzai, the march from Kabul to relieve Kandahar and the Battle of 1st September. Promoted captain 2nd July 1881. He was Adjutant Tynemouth Artillery Volunteer Corps on 18th September 1881, Adjutant 2nd Kent Artillery Volunteer Corps 30th June 1883 – 30th April 1886, Instructor at the Artillery College from 1st May 1886. Promoted major 12th October 1887 and lieutenant colonel 12th October 1892. Appointed Professor of Artillery at the Artillery College 2nd June – 30th September 1897. Half Pay from 30th November 1897. Promoted colonel 6th March 1900 and appointed Assistant Adjutant General Dublin District until 12th May 1902, then Half Pay until he retired on 3rd September 1902.
- Alexander Dingwall Fordyce (1860–1925) was commissioned in the 19th Foot on 22nd January 1879, transferred to 16th Foot on 15th March and promoted lieutenant Bedfordshire Regiment 2nd July. Admitted to the Bombay Staff Corps on 16th August 1880 and served in the Burma War 1886–87. Promoted captain 22nd January 1890, major 22nd January 1899 and retired on 11th February 1899.
- Henry Lawrence Dingwall Fordyce (1867–1932) was commissioned in the Royal Artillery on 16th February 1887. He went to India in December 1887 and transferred to the Indian Staff Corps as a lieutenant on 17th April 1891. He served

in the Burma War 1892–93 in the Chin Hills, Chitral Relief Force 1895 and Tirah Expeditionary Force 1897–98. Henry married Carlotta Blanche née Burdett (born 1869) in 1894 at Blean, Kent. They had a son. He became the Base Supply Officer on North West Frontier of India 1908 and took part in operations in the Zakka Khel country. He was later appointed to the Indian Supply & Transport Corps. Promoted lieutenant colonel 16th February 1913. Appointed Deputy Director of Supplies and Transport 16th April 1915. Appointed Brevet Colonel 29th October 1915 and retired on 16th February 1919. MID, LG 5th April 1916 and 18th May 1918. He was a partner in the Weir Engineering Company at Hamble, Hampshire until it was dissolved in 1929.

Edward was educated at Blundell's School, Tiverton, Devon 1894–96 and Clifton College, Bristol, Somerset 1897–1900. He joined the Royal Military College Sandhurst as a Gentleman Cadet in 1900 and won the Heavyweight Boxing and Rugby Football Cups. He was commissioned into 2nd Battalion, The Royal Irish Regiment on 8th May 1901 and served in India and Afghanistan until resigning his commission on 26th August 1903.

Edward married Charlotte Muriel née Rees (1878–1961) on 24th August 1901 at Fulham, London. They migrated to Canada in 1907. Edward spent three years in northern British Columbia as a prospector and explorer, prior to joining the Provincial Forestry Service. In 1912 he joined the Dominion Civil Service as Assistant to the District Engineer of Public Works, employed on harbour construction at New Westminster, British Columbia.

On 10th August 1914, Edward was commissioned into 11th Irish Fusiliers of Canada as Machine-gun Officer. He was described as 6'2" tall, weighing 205lbs, with fair complexion, black hair and brown eyes. He transferred to 7th Battalion CEF at Valcartier on the creation of the Canadian Expeditionary Force. He sailed for England aboard the *Virginian* on 3rd October 1914, disembarking at Plymouth, Devon on 16th October. The Battalion trained on Salisbury Plain, Wiltshire before going to France on 10th February 1915 aboard the *Cardiganshire*, arriving at St Nazaire on 15th February.

Awarded the VC for his actions at Gravenstafel Ridge near Keerselaere on 24th April 1915, LG 15th May 1919. Having been captured, he was taken to Staden and tried for a breach of the laws of war, as he continued firing after part of his unit had been forced to surrender. He was found guilty and sentenced to death. He was against the wall of Staden Church with a firing party formed up when he protested to the commander that word of this crime would become known and reprisals would follow. The officer returned Bellew to custody. A retrial took place at Roulers and Bellew was acquitted and sent to a prison camp in Saxony with a large party of wounded Canadians. They were crowded into fourth-class Belgian railway carriages with wounded and gassed French colonial soldiers.

Edward spent two years and eight months as a prisoner in six different camps at Bischofswerda, Krefeld, Schwalmstadt, Holzminden, Freiburg and Heidelberg. A Swiss medical commission assessed the condition of the prisoners on 27th December 1917 and Bellew was selected for internment in neutral Switzerland at Chateux d'Oex and the Hotel de l'Europe at Montreux. On 20th July 1918 he was promoted captain, backdated to 12th January 1916. Having spent eleven months regaining his strength in Switzerland, he was repatriated to England on 10th December 1918 and was admitted to Prince of Wales Hospital, Marylebone, suffering from neurasthenia, bronchitis and sciatic neuritis. His wife joined him to assist in his care and was living at 91 Borough Road, London. He was also treated at Grove Military Hospital, Tooting, 19–25th February 1919, for scabies. They returned to Canada, leaving Britain on 28th March 1919. He was released from service on 13th April and demobilised on 5th November 1919.

Details of his actions were known during his imprisonment, but it was decided not to announce the award of his Victoria Cross until he had been released. He received the VC from General Ross, Area Commandant Vancouver, British Columbia in 1919; Ross stood in for the Lieutenant Governor of British Columbia who fell ill before the ceremony and died soon afterwards.

Edward returned to the Public Works Department until 1922 as an Inspector of Dredging on the Fraser River. He retired to a ranch at Monte Creek, British Columbia to pursue his interests in fly-fishing, youth welfare and gardening. He was a committee member of the Victoria Cross and George Cross Association, Honorary Member of the Royal Society of St George and a life member of the Royal Canadian Military Institute.

When he was invited to attend the 1960 VC & GC Association Reunion he was in poor health and his doctor advised against the trip as the strain could kill him. Edward accepted the risk and was a lively participant in the reunion. He told Brigadier Sir John Smyth VC, Chairman of the VC and GC Association, that the risk had been well worthwhile. However, as predicted, soon after his return to Canada, he died following a stroke at the Royal Inland Hospital, Shaughnessy, Kamloops, British Columbia on 1st February 1961. He is buried at Hillside Cemetery, Kamloops (Section Z, Row 5, Lot 11, Sub Lot E). Edward is commemorated in a number of other places:

- Bellew Gate, Scarborough, Toronto, Ontario is a housing development built in 2006.
- Bronze plaque on a wall opposite the Canadian Expeditionary Forces Memorial at Vancouver Corner, St Julien, Belgium unveiled on 8th September 2008.
- Bronze plaque on a stone monolith pedestal in Riverside Park, Lorne Street, Kamloops erected by the British Columbia Regiment Association on 23rd October 2004.

- Captain Edward D Bellew VC Memorial Bursary awarded annually by the British Columbia Regiment (Duke of Connaught's Own) Association to a serving member of the Regiment for academic achievement and loyalty to the Regiment.
- The Victoria Cross obelisk to all Canadian VCs at Military Heritage Park, Barrie, Ontario dedicated by HRH The Princess Royal on 22nd October 2013.
- His VC action was featured in Issues No. 742 and 1274 of the *Victor* comic dated 10th May 1975 and 20th July 1985.

In addition to the VC, Edward was awarded the 1914–15 Star, British War Medal 1914–20, Victory Medal 1914–19, George VI Coronation Medal 1937 and Elizabeth II Coronation Medal 1953. His medals passed to his brother-in-law, Mr SE Crossman, of Hendon, London, and were sold at Sotheby's for £6,000 on 5th July 1974, which at the time was a record price. Missing was the George VI Coronation Medal 1937, but it is understood that the missing medal has since been reunited with the group. Spink's bought the medals, acting for the Stephen B Roman Foundation of Canada, who presented them to the British Columbia Regiment. The group was transferred to the Royal Canadian Military Institute, 426 University Avenue, Toronto, Ontario, from where the VC was stolen sometime between January 1975 and 22nd July 1977. It has not been recovered. The Institute still holds Edward's other medals.

2ND LIEUTENANT GEORGE ARTHUR BOYD-ROCHFORT
1st Battalion, Scots Guards

George Boyd-Rochfort was born at Middleton Park, Castletown, Co Westmeath, Ireland on 1st January 1880. His father was Major Rochfort Hamilton Boyd (1844–91), who added Rochfort to his surname by Royal Licence in 1888 on succeeding to the estates left by his paternal grandmother. He served as a captain in 15th Hussars from 7th August 1867 and later as a major in the West Kent Yeomanry. He appears in the Army List as Rochfort H Rochfort-Boyd. He was appointed High Sheriff of Co Westmeath in 1876 and was also a JP. In his will he decreed that his sons would also be named Boyd-Rochfort. George became a ward of Chancery following his father's death. His mother was Florence Louisa née Hemming (1855–1944). Rochfort and Florence married on 1st May 1875, registered at St George, Hanover Square, London. In 1911 she was living at 1 Kilhugh, Middleton, Co Westmeath, Ireland. George had six siblings:

- Ethel Victoria Boyd-Rochfort (1876–1961) married John Richard Mordred Henry L'Estrange Malone on 13th August 1898, son of Colonel John Richard Malone of Baronston, Co. Westmeath. Their son, 37556 Sergeant Reginald John Malone, was serving with 46th Training Squadron RFC when he died on 30th August 1917; he is buried in Catterick Cemetery, Yorkshire (E15).

A contemporary sketch of Middleton Park House built by George Boyd-Rochfort in 1850. It is now a hotel.

- Alice Eleanor Boyd-Rochfort (1878–1931) married Percy Philip O'Reilly on 18th January 1900, of Colamber, Co Westmeath. They had three sons and three daughters.
- Harold Boyd-Rochfort (1882–1960) served during the Boer War. He was wounded and Mentioned in Lord Roberts' despatch of 4th September 1901 (LG 10th September) while serving as a 2nd lieutenant with 4th Scottish Rifles and 1st Royal Munster Fusiliers. He went on to serve as a brevet lieutenant colonel in 21st Lancers during the Great War and commanded a tank battalion in 1918; DSO (LG 4th June 1917), MC (LG 3rd June 1918) and was Mentioned in Despatches three times (LG 1st January 1916, 15th June 1916 & 5th July 1919). During the Second World War he served on the staff 1940–45; MBE (LG 13th June 1946). Harold married Winifred née Akroyd (1887–1925) of Birdingbury Hall, Rugby, Warwickshire on 7th January 1909. They had a daughter, Diana Nancy Boyd-Rochfort (1910–67), who married Brigadier John Pell Archer-Shee MC on 22nd July 1953, son of Lieutenant Colonel Sir Martin Archer-Shee CMG DSO of Ashurst Lodge, Sunninghill, Berkshire. Harold and Winifred divorced in 1922 and she married Reginald Seymour later that year. Harold married Dorothea Iris Taylor from South Africa on 24th April 1935 at Westminster, London. She died in 1973.
- Winifred Florence Boyd-Rochfort (1883–1941) was Matron of St Dunstan's, Brighton, Sussex; OBE posthumously 1942. She never married.
- Cecil Charles Boyd-Rochfort (1887–1983) served as a 2nd lieutenant in 4th Scottish Rifles 1904–06 before becoming a pupil trainer with Henry Seymour Persse at Grateley, Wiltshire. In 1908 he became assistant trainer to Captain RH Dewhurst at Newmarket and in 1912 was racing manager to Sir Ernest Cassel. He was commissioned in the Scots Guards on 15th August 1914 and went to France, where he fractured his ankle falling into a trench on 5th May 1915. He was declared fit for General Service on 2nd November and returned to France, but contracted influenza and was evacuated to England on 23rd March 1916. A Medical Board at King George V Hospital, Dublin on 10th June found him fit for General Service and he rejoined the Scots Guards on 12th June. He was

awarded the French Croix de Guerre avec Palme (LG 18th April 1918) and became a brigade major with the RFC until being demobilised as a temporary major on 12th September 1919. Returning to Newmarket to manage Cassel's racing interests at Moulton Paddocks, he also managed Marshall Field's horses and bought Freemason Lodge at Newmarket in 1923 after Cassel's death. His first winner of a listed race was with *Royal Minstrel* in the Eclipse Stakes in 1929. Americans William Woodward and Joseph Widener became the new owners in 1930 and this marked a turning point in Cecil's career. The first classic success came in 1933, when Woodward's *Brown Betty* won the Epsom Oaks and in 1936 *Boswell* won the St Leger. Cecil was the leading flat racing trainer in 1937, 1938, 1954, 1955 and 1958. In 1943, he commenced training King George VI's private horses and Queen Elizabeth II continued to keep her home-bred horses at Freemason Lodge. The 1950s and 1960s were the stable's golden years. He won the King George VI and Queen Elizabeth Stakes with *Aureole* in 1954, the 1,000 Guineas with *Hypericum* in 1956, the 2,000 Guineas with *Pall Mall* in 1958 and the Eclipse Stakes with *Canisbay* in 1965. He also won the Oaks with *Meld* in 1955, the Epsom Derby in 1959 with *Parthia* and the Ascot Gold Cup with *Precipitation* in 1937 and *Zarathustra* in 1957, the latter ridden by Lester Piggott. Cecil won the Goodwood Cup four times between 1962 and 1966. In total he won thirteen classic races and 1,156 others, earning total prize money of £1,651,514. Cecil was appointed CVO (LG 5th June 1952) and KCVO when he retired (LG 1st January 1968). He married Elizabeth Rohays Mary Cecil in 1944, daughter of Major General Sir James Lauderdale Gilbert Burnett of Leys and widow of Captain Hon Henry Cecil. As a result he became stepfather to Henry (later Sir Henry) Cecil (1943– 2013), who is regarded as one of the greatest flat racing trainers of all time; he was Champion Trainer ten times and trained twenty-five Classic winners.

* Muriel Boyd-Rochfort (born 1888) married John Oloff McCall of Ballyhooly, Co Cork on 5th August 1909. They had three sons and a daughter.

Some of George's uncles had military careers:

* Charles Augustus Rochfort Rochfort-Boyd (1850–1940) was commissioned in the Royal Engineers as a lieutenant on 23rd July 1870. He served during the Second Boer War and was Mentioned in Lord Roberts' Despatch of 2nd April 1901. He rose to brevet colonel on 5th August 1900 and was awarded the CMG on 29th November. He retired on half pay on 5th September 1902.

George's brother, Sir Cecil Charles Boyd-Rochfort, who trained thirteen classic race winners and 1,156 others in a career spanning sixty years.

Biographies 217

- George Warren Woods Rochfort-Boyd (1854–91) was commissioned as a lieutenant in 96th Foot from the Militia on 2nd December 1874. He was Adjutant of 2nd Manchester 1879–1886 and Adjutant of 4th Volunteer Battalion, Manchester Regiment from 1st November 1889. He was promoted major 31st May 1890 and retired in October 1901.
- Francis Richard Hemming (1851–89) was a Militia officer.

His aunt, Beatrice Sophia Hemming (1857–1933), married Lieutenant Colonel Hugh Sutlej Gough CB CMG (1848–1920) in 1886. He was commissioned in 10th Hussars on 2nd May 1868 and was Adjutant 21st December 1873 – 22nd June 1875. Following promotion to captain on 23rd June 1875, he became ADC to Commander-in-Chief East Indies on 21st November 1876 until 7 April 1881. Awarded CMG 27th January 1886. Rose to colonel 21st May 1888 (substantive 8th July 1893) and was appointed Assistant Adjutant General under the Inspector General of Cavalry 8th July 1893–7th July 1898. Placed on half pay 8th July 1898. Awarded CB 3rd June 1899. Promoted major general 1st January 1900. Appointed Lieutenant Governor and Commander Troops, Jersey 1st October 1904 until his retirement in June 1910.

Another aunt, Edith Sarah Hamilton Rochfort-Boyd (c.1848–1930), married Sir Thomas Robert Tighe Chapman (1846–1919) in 1873. Thomas left Edith for the children's governess, Sarah Junner (1861–1959), and moved to Oxford, where they lived as Mr and Mrs Lawrence (Sarah's father's surname). They had a son, Thomas Edward Lawrence (1888–1935), better known as Lawrence of Arabia.

George was educated at Eton and Trinity College Cambridge (BA 1901), where he was Master of Beagles. He travelled extensively, hunted big game, played polo for the All-Ireland team and raced horses; he rode winners in the Westmeath Gold Cup and National Hunt Cup. On 9th June 1901, he married Olivia Ellen née Ussher (1875–1958) at Woolwich, London. They lived at Middleton Park, Castletown, Co Westmeath, Ireland. There were no children. Her brother, William Arland Ussher (born 1876), served as a 2nd lieutenant in 3rd Connaught Rangers from 25th September 1915 and was later attached to the 6th Battalion. He last appears in the Army List in July 1917.

George was High Sheriff of Co Westmeath in 1904 and also Deputy

Eton College, attended by George Boyd-Rochfort. Thirty-six other former pupils have been awarded the VC. The first was Lieutenant Colonel (later General Lord Henry Percy) Henry Hugh Manvers Percy, 3rd Grenadier Guards, at the Battle of Inkerman in the Crimean War in 1854. The latest being Lieutenant Colonel H Jones, in the 1982 Falklands War.

Lieutenant. He was badly hurt in a polo match in late August 1914, which delayed him from volunteering. He was initially rejected medically, but following an operation for varicose veins he enlisted on 1st March 1915 and was commissioned on 3rd April in the Special Reserve Scots Guards. His butler, Private Thorowgood, a Boer War veteran, served with him. He went to France on 13th June and was promoted lieutenant on 16th June.

Awarded the VC for his actions between Cambrin and La Bassée, France on 3rd August 1915, LG 1st September 1915. He was the first Guards officer to be awarded the VC since the Crimean War. He returned to Co Westmeath on 3rd September for a few days. On 6th September the King presented the VC to him at Windsor Castle.

Having returned to France, he was wounded in an incident in which he silenced one German with a blow from his pistol butt and another with his fist. He returned to Middleton Park to convalesce. Appointed acting captain and Adjutant of the Guards Divisional Base Depot until 20th April 1918. He was demobilised on 20th April 1919, although he appears in the Army List until July 1920.

After the war he bred racehorses. His stud at Middleton Park produced the winners of the 1936 St Leger (*Boswell*) and the 1937 Ascot Gold Cup (*Precipitation*); both horses were trained by his brother Cecil. He received an Honorary MA from Oxford University. Appointments included Director of Westmeath Race Co Ltd, Senior Steward of the Irish National Hunt Steeplechase Committee and the Irish Turf Club.

George died at Dublin, Ireland on 7th August 1940 following an operation and is buried at Castletown Church of Ireland Old Churchyard, Geohegan, Co Westmeath. He is also commemorated on a plaque in Castletown Church of Ireland Old Churchyard and on a memorial in Tyrellspass Church of Ireland Church.

In addition to the VC, he was awarded the 1914–15 Star, British War Medal 1914–20, Victory Medal 1914–19 and King George VI Coronation Medal 1937. The VC is held by the Scots Guards Regimental Headquarters, Wellington Barracks, London.

Three of George's cousins were killed during the war:

- Henry Charles Rochfort-Boyd RHA & RFA from September 1897, served in South Africa 1899–1900. At Modder River he was noted for his reliability and ability to act without orders and was Mentioned in Lord Methuen's Despatch of 1st December 1899 (LG 26th January 1900) and in Lord Roberts' Despatch of 4th September 1901 (10th September). Awarded the DSO for his actions at Ypres 21st-23rd October 1915 (LG 18th February 1916). Mention in Despatches in November 1914 while serving with 9th Brigade RFA, November 1916 and April & November 1917 (LG 17th February 1915 and 4th January, 18th May and 14th December 1917). He was wounded three times (August 1914 and January & February 1915) and died of wounds on 4th December 1917 at Rouen while serving with XVI Brigade RHA (St Sever Cemetery, Rouen – Officers B 5 17).

- Lieutenant Colonel Hugh Annesley Gray-Cheape DSO and Bar, Worcestershire Yeomanry, had previous service with 4th Argyll & Sutherland Highlanders. He drowned on 27th May 1918 when SS *Leasowe Castle* was torpedoed off Alexandria (Alexandria (Chatby) Memorial, Egypt). His daughter, Barbara, married Lieutenant Colonel Alexander William Henry James Montgomery Cuninghame DSO, Royal Scots Fusiliers attached to the Colonial Office, who died on active service on 3rd July 1944. He was the grandson of William James Montgomery Cuninghame VC.
- Captain Leslie St Clair Cheape served with 1st (King's) Dragoon Guards, Household Cavalry and other cavalry units, including the Yeomanry and Imperial Camel Corps. He was killed in action on 23rd April 1916, serving as Adjutant of the Worcester Yeomanry (Jerusalem Memorial, Israel).

6738 LANCE SERGEANT OLIVER BROOKS
3rd Battalion, Coldstream Guards

Oliver Brooks was born at Paulton, near Midsomer Norton, Somerset on 31st May 1889. His father was Joseph Henry Brooks (1852–1925) a butcher running his own shop in 1881. In 1891 he was boarding at 31 St James Parade, Bath and by 1901 was a pit labourer at Norton Hill Colliery, Somerset. His mother was Mercy Jane née Snelling (1855–92). Joseph and Mercy's marriage was registered in the 2nd quarter of 1874 at Clutton. The family lived at Bloomfield, Paulton, but by 1891 Mercy was living with her children at Gladstone Street, Midsomer Norton. In 1906 the family was living at Bellevue, Welton. By 1913 Joseph was living at 3 Burlington Road, Midsomer Norton. Oliver had six siblings:

- Joseph William Brooks (1875–1959). He married Ruth née Matthews (1873–1954) in 1896 and they had five children – Alfred Charles Brooks 1897–98, Stanley Brooks 1900, Mildred Annie Brooks 1901, George William James Stuart Brooks 1902 and Mabel Brooks 1903. He was on the morning shift on 10th April 1908 at Norton Colliery and volunteered to help the rescue teams following an explosion. He found his brother Andrew's body on his back beside a wagon with no apparent marks on him. Joseph was awarded a certificate in recognition of his bravery during the rescue attempt.
- Alfred James Brooks (1877–1970) was a coal miner. He married Elizabeth 'Eliza' née Vranch (1876–1954) at Lambeth Registry office in 1898. He enlisted in 1st Coldstream Guards (130) at Taunton on 22nd June 1895, giving his age as eighteen years and one month. He was serving with 4th Somerset Light

Postcard commemorating the disaster at Norton Hill Colliery on 9th April 1908 in which Oliver Brooks' brother, Andrew, was killed.

infantry at the time. He was described as 5' 8¼" tall, weighed 147 lbs with fresh complexion, grey eyes, brown hair and his religious denomination was Church of England. He served in Gibraltar from 10th March 1899 and went to South Africa on 28th October. Alfred returned to Britain on 5th October 1902 and was discharged to the Reserve on 17th October 1902. He was awarded the Queen's South Africa Medal with six clasps (Belmont, Modder River, Driefontein, Johannesburg, Diamond Hill & Belfast) and the King's South Africa Medal with two clasps (South Africa 1901 and South Africa 1902). His character was assessed as Exemplary and he was awarded Good Conduct Pay on 22nd June 1897 and 22nd June 1901. Having been discharged from the Reserve on 21st June 1907, having completed twelve years service, he re-enlisted in the Section D

Norton Hill Colliery, Midsomer Norton, where Oliver Brooks worked before joining the Army in 1906.

Victoria Barracks, Windsor, demolished in the 1980s.

SS *Cawdor Castle* ferried 3rd Coldstream Guards to France and later carried Territorial Force troops to India.

Reserve on 5th July. Alfred was awarded a certificate for conspicuous bravery in an underground rescue at Norton Hill Colliery on 9th April 1908 following a gas explosion, which killed his brother Andrew and nine others. Alfred and Elizabeth had four children – Stella Gertrude 'Gertie' Annie Brooks 1899, Ethel Brooks 1903, Alfred Rowland Brooks 1905 and Leonard Brooks 1907.
- Bertie Brooks (born 1879).
- Andrew Brooks (1881–1908) married Caroline née Rhymer (1883–1962) in 1905. He was a Sunday School teacher at the Baptist Church and worked as a coal miner at Norton Hill Colliery. He was killed in an underground gas explosion on 9th April 1908. An inquest held at the town hall in Midsomer Norton from 24th

Chateau de la Jumelle at Aire-sur-la-Lys, where King George V lived during his visit to the front in October-November 1915.

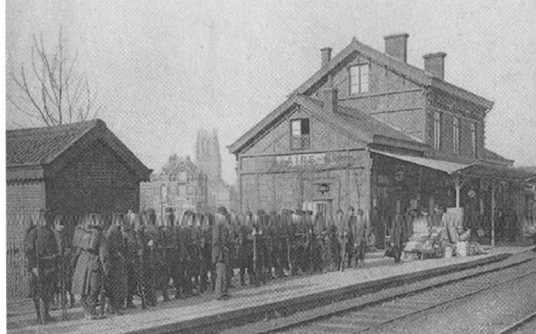

Aire Station, where Oliver Brooks' VC investiture took place.

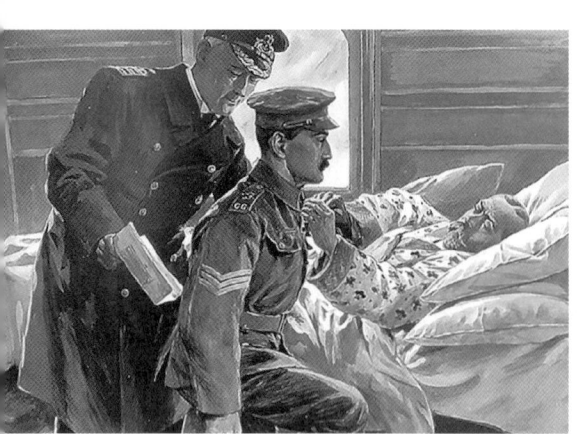

The Illustrated London News' portrayal of the scene aboard a train at Aire Station on 1st November 1915, as the King pinned the VC on Oliver Brooks, assisted by the King's Equerry, Captain Sir Charles Cust RN.

Aldbourne, in Wiltshire, where Oliver Brooks married Marion Loveday in August 1918.

April to 4th June, found the ten men had died as a result of an explosion of coal dust ignited by a shot fired by Chares Burge in the Slyving Vein Incline. Andrew and Caroline had two children – Florence Mercy Brooks 1906 and Ivy Brooks 1907. Caroline married another miner, David James Gay (1876–1947), in 1910 and they had two children – John C Gay 1912 and Elsie I Gay 1914.

- Ernest Brooks (born c.1884) was a coal miner.
- Stella Gertrude Annie Brooks (1887–88).

Oliver was educated at Midsomer Norton Church of England Infant and Primary Schools and was then employed at Norton Hill Colliery as a carting boy. He enlisted at Bath on 17th April 1906, adding two years to his age. He was described as 5' 7½" tall, weighing 134 lbs and his religious denomination was Baptist. He trained at Caterham and served at Victoria Barracks, Windsor. In December 1906 he extended his service to complete seven years. On 22nd June 1907, he was posted to the Depot. During his service he had numerous health problems and was in hospital for nine days with inflamed glands, thirteen days with tonsillitis and fifteen days with cowpox. He was

3rd Coldstream Guards leaving Chelsea Barracks on 12th August 1914. Oliver Brooks had rejoined the Battalion from the Reserve only five days before.

transferred to the 1st Class Army Reserve on 17th April 1913.

Oliver returned to the mines for a while and then became manager of the Palladium Theatre in Peasedown, near his home. On 7th August 1914 he was recalled and went to France on 12th August on the Union Castle Mail Steamship Company's SS *Cawdor Castle*. Promoted lance corporal 25th November and corporal and lance sergeant 12th July 1915.

Awarded the VC for his actions near Loos, France on 8th October 1915, LG 28th October 1915. He was promoted sergeant on 9th October. On 28th October, the King was reviewing troops of I Corps at Hesdigneul on a chestnut mare lent by General Sir Douglas Haig. The horse, frightened by sudden cheering from a Wing of the RFC, reared, dismounted the King and landed on him. He suffered a fractured pelvis and other injuries and was taken to Chateau de la Jumelle, Aire-sur-la-

Oliver Brooks when he was doorman at the Dorchester Hotel on Park Lane, London (Carol Scott).

Thames Street, Windsor, looking towards High Street. The White Hart (now Harte and Garter) Hotel is the building with the tower on the right of the street.

A group of Foot Guards VC winners from the First World War outside the Guards Chapel at Wellington Barracks, London. There were twenty-four Foot Guards VCs during the war but many did not survive. Back row left to right – J Moyney, GA Boyd-Rochfort, CH Frisby, WD Fuller, J McAulay, G Evans. Front row left to right – GH Wyatt, O Brooks, JV Campbell, Viscount Gort, R Bye, F McNess.

Lys before boarding a hospital train for the journey back to England. Brooks' VC was gazetted the same day and the King wished to decorate him in person before leaving. Brooks was summoned to the hospital train at Aire Station on 1st November, accompanied by his CO. A private investiture was held at the King's bedside. Brooks knelt beside the bed, bending over the King, who was lying on his back, propped up with pillows. Captain Sir Charles Cust RN KCVO CB CMG, the King's Equerry, read the citation. The King was in considerable pain and needed assistance to push the VC pin through Brooks' tunic.

Oliver returned to Midsomer Norton in November, where he was presented with an illuminated address by the Urban District Council. He became a bombing instructor at the Guards Division HQ in France, where he trained the Prince of Wales in the use of grenades. He was wounded in the head and left shoulder at Ginchy on 15th September 1916 in the same action that his CO, Lieutenant Colonel JV Campbell, won the VC. Oliver was evacuated to England and spent three months in the King George Hospital, London. He never returned to France because of his injuries and spent the rest of the war at Victoria Barracks, Windsor and as a bombing instructor at Aldershot. He was discharged on 27th February 1919 and remained on the Reserve until 31st March 1920.

Oliver Brooks married Marion née Loveday (1894–1972) on 17th August 1918 at the parish church in Aldbourne, Wiltshire. They lived at 17 Alexandra Road, Windsor, Berkshire before moving to 47 Clewer Avenue in 1925. Oliver and Marion had four children:

- Oliver Victor Loos Brooks (18th June 1919 – February 1985) served in the Oxford & Buckinghamshire Light Infantry during the Second World War. His marriage to Pearl C née Yolland (born 1922) was registered in the 3rd quarter of 1941 at Newton Abbott, Devon. He was the standard bearer for the Ashburton Royal British Legion before they moved to Berkshire in 1958. Oliver and Pearl had two children – David R Brooks 1943–45 and Carol Brooks 1947.
- Diana May Brooks (2nd March 1921 – 2004). Her marriage to James A Lucas-Carter was registered in the 3rd quarter of 1941 at Windsor. Diana and James had five children – Barry M Lucas-Carter 1942, Brian Lucas-Carter 1948, who was serving in the Coldstream Guards in 1967, Valrie A Lucas-Carter 1949, Lynn Lucas-Carter 1950 and Diana P Lucas-Carter 1952.
- Douglas William Brooks (29th May 1923–1971) served in the Coldstream Guards. His marriage to Nancy L née Meyer was registered in the 3rd quarter of 1944 at Newton Abbott. Douglas and Nancy had two sons – Peter DW Brooks 1945 and Graham J Brooks 1947.
- Dorothy Brooks (born 31st October 1929–2014). Her marriage to Derek W Mole (born 1927) was registered in the 2nd quarter of 1950 at Windsor. They lived at Bournemouth, Dorset and had a daughter – Anne E Mole 1954.

Oliver was a member of the VC Guard at the interment of the Unknown Warrior on 11th November 1920. He became the doorman at the White Hart Hotel (now Harte and Garter Hotel) in Windsor and later at the Dorchester Hotel, Park Lane, London. At the VC Garden Party at Buckingham Palace on 26th June 1920, the King remembered him as the commissionaire at the White Hart, *Ah, you have not your usual uniform on today*. The Prince of Wales was a frequent visitor to the White Hart and would stop to chat to his former bombing instructor. At the Dorchester in April 1933, Oliver's hand was shaken by the Kaiser's grandson who said, *Every nation can recognise a brave man*.

On 31st October 1929, Oliver carried the wreath laid by Field Marshal Lord Plumer, President of the Ypres League, at its commemoration ceremony at the Cenotaph. He was present with Michael O'Leary VC at the Ypres Day service at Horse Guards Parade on 30th October 1933, where he was photographed chatting to the Reverend Tubby Clayton, founder of Toc H in Poperinghe. Oliver attended the funerals of King George V at Windsor on 28th January 1936 and Arthur P Sullivan VC in the Guard's Chapel, Wellington Barracks, London on 13th April 1937.

Oliver Brooks died of neoplasm of the mediastinium at Windsor, Berkshire on 25th October 1940 and is buried in Windsor Borough Cemetery (Section GN 352:2 down, 5 across). He is also commemorated at:

- Holy Trinity Church (Garrison Church), Windsor where a plaque was dedicated by the Windsor Branch of the Coldstream Guards Association on 24th April 1988.

- His home at 47 Clewer Avenue, Windsor where a Blue Plaque was dedicated on 27th May 1998. The ceremony was attended by his daughter, Diana Lucas-Carter, granddaughter Carol Scott, grandson Peter Brooks, Lieutenant Colonel James Bucknall, CO 1st Coldstream Guards, RSM David Hall CG and the Mayor of Windsor and Maidenhead, Councillor Kathy Newbound.
- St John's School, Midsomer Norton, Somerset.
- Oliver Brooks Road, Midsomer Norton, a housing development built in 2003.
- In June 2015 the Royal Borough of Windsor & Maidenhead created a Rememberance Garden in Kidwell Park, Maidenhead. A display board gives information about the part played by the town during the First World War and brief details of the VC recipients connected with Maidenhead, including Oliver Brooks, Charles Doughty-Wylie, William Thomas Forshaw, Francis Grenfell, Harry Greenwood, Thomas Tannatt Pryce and Ferdinand West.

In addition to the VC, he was awarded the 1914 Star with 'Mons' clasp, British War Medal 1914–20, Victory Medal 1914–19 and George VI Coronation Medal 1937. The VC is owned by the Coldstream Guards at the Guards Museum in Wellington Barracks, London.

1665 CORPORAL ALFRED ALEXANDER BURT
1/1st Battalion, The Hertfordshire Regiment

Alfred Burt was born at Port Vale, Hertford on 3rd March 1895. His father was Thomas Richard Burt (1859–1936) a railway porter. His mother was Martha née Dear (1863–1942). Thomas and Martha married on 11th October 1880 at All Saints, Battle Bridge, Islington, London. They were living at 179 Copenhagen Street, Islington in 1881, at Brown's Terrace, Portland Street, Arnold, Nottinghamshire in 1891 and moved to 19 Nelson Street, Hertford in 1895. Alfred had six siblings:

- William Thomas Burt (1885–1964) was a butcher's boy before he enlisted in the Royal Navy for twelve years as a signalman on 17th October 1902. He served on numerous ships and shore establishments, including *Impregnable, Lion, Victory, Cressy, Glory, Firequeen, Pandora, Pioneer, Psyche, Crescent, Maine, Iphigenia, Dreadnought, Exmouth* and *Zealandia*. He was promoted leading signalman 14th April 1906 and yeoman of signals 1st September 1910. He passed the education for petty officer on 3rd March 1908 and became chief yeoman of signals on 30th January 1913 and signals boatswain on 9th March 1914. When war broke out, he volunteered to continue serving on 17th October 1914. William married Harriet M West (1899–1979), his brother Alfred's sister-in-law, in 1918 and they had two children – Harry WV West 1918 and Norman L West (1927–2002) who served in the Royal Navy as a CERA. William was commissioned on 10th February 1925 and was promoted signals lieutenant 15th May 1931 and signals lieutenant commander 15th May 1939. During the inter-war years he served on *Swiftsure, Campania, New Zealand, Dido, Centaur, Cardiff, Argus, Queen Elizabeth, Coventry, Victory* and *President*. He was awarded the MBE (LG 4th June 1934) and retired on 17th October. William was recalled on 4th September 1939 and served until 13th May 1945.

- Francis Burt (1889–1933) married Agnes M McLellan (born 1900) in 1922 and they had a son, Francis JV Burt in 1923.
- Ellen Martha May Burt (1881–1970) was a general servant. She married Robert Akers (1888–1918), a cattle stockman, in 1908 and they had two children – May Matilda Akers 1908 and Edith Lilian Akers 1910. Ellen married George Wallis in 1925.
- Edith Lilian E Burt (1883–1945) married Charles John Aird (1882–1960) in 1909.
- Ellen Margery Burt (born 1897).
- Thomas Lionel Burt (1902–54) was an engineering millwright's mate. He married Dorothy Mary Jane Drew (1902–53) in 1925 and they had a son, Leslie George Lionel Burt 1930.

Alfred was educated at Cowbridge Road School, Hertford and was employed by Hertford Gas Company as a toolboy and later became a fitter. He enlisted in 1st Hertfordshire underage on 15th February 1911 and was only 5′ 3″ tall. He joined because his future wife's older brother, 2746 Private Harry West (1889–1914), someone young Alfred looked up to, was serving. Alfred gained a new job in Basingstoke a few days before war broke out, but was mobilised on 5th August 1914.

The VC Guard at the interment of the Unknown Warrior on 11th November 1920.

Promoted corporal on 18th September, he went to France on 6th November with 1/1st Battalion. Harry West was killed at Alfred's side on 19th November and was buried by him. Harry's remains were not identified after the war and he is commemorated on the Ypres (Menin Gate) Memorial, Belgium.

Awarded the VC for his actions at Cuinchy, France on 27th September 1915, LG 22nd January 1916. He was admitted to 19th Field Ambulance with myalgia on 11th November 1915. It developed into influenza and he was transferred to No.11 Stationary Hospital at Rouen. He went to No.1 Infantry Base Depot on 30th November and did not return to his unit until 23rd January 1916. He was evacuated to England, having been gassed, on 2nd February and was put on the strength of the Administrative Centre, Hertford. He was granted leave to 1st March and during this time he was presented with an illuminated address at Hertford. The VC was presented by the King at Buckingham Palace on 4th March 1916. Alfred was discharged on 31st March as no longer fit for service due to gas injury; he was 5' 5½" tall and weighted 140 lbs at the time.

Alfred Burt in later life.

Alfred Burt married Jane Elizabeth née West (1893–1964) on 23rd December 1916 at Hertford. News that his wife's younger brother, 10978 Private William Horace West, 8th Bedfordshire (born 1897), had died of wounds on 21st December 1916 arrived as they left the church. He is buried in Béthune Town Cemetery, France (VI A 31). Alfred and Jane had two children:

- Jenny May Burt (14th November 1917 – April 2002). Her marriage to Leslie John Newton (1918–98) was registered in the 1st quarter of 1941 at Amersham, Buckinghamshire. They had a son, David J Newton, in 1942.
- Alfred Victor Charles Burt (18th May 1920 – 4th April 1973) was a garage hand. He married Joan Evelyn Peck (1924–2007) on 16th October 1954 at Chesham Registry Office.

The family was living at Priors Wood Cottages, Hertford Heath, Hertford in 1922 and at 175 Chartridge Lane, Chesham in 1939. Alfred returned to fitting for the Hertford Gas Company and was a member of the VC Guard at the interment of the Unknown Warrior on 11th November 1920. He rejoined 1st Hertfordshire as a private (5987897) on 12th April 1922 and was appointed unpaid lance corporal on 29th July. He won a major shooting competition, but was discharged at his own request on 26th August 1925 when he moved to Chesham and became landlord of the New Inn. Just before the Second World War he returned to fitting and during the war worked for Arthur Lyon's in Chesham, producing searchlights and generators. He was also an ARP Warden for a time. The years took their toll and he was an invalid from the early 1950s and in a wheelchair by 1956.

Alfred Burt died of carcinomatosis and carcinoma right bronchus at Tindal General Hospital, Chesham, Buckinghamshire on 9th June 1962. He was described as a drawing office clerk in heavy engineering. He was cremated at West Hertfordshire Crematorium, Watford, where his ashes were interred (Plot AR-48). Alfred is also commemorated at Alfred Burt Close, Chesham, a development of two and three bedroom homes built in 2013–14; the Mayor of Chesham, Mark Shaw, unveiled a commemorative stone on 11th December 2013.

In addition to the VC, he was awarded the 1914 Star with 'Mons' clasp, British War Medal 1914–20, Victory Medal 1914–19, George VI Coronation Medal 1937 and Elizabeth II Coronation Medal 1953. The medals were gifted to the Bedfordshire and Hertfordshire Regimental Museum by his daughter in 1979 and are held at the Hertfordshire Regiment Museum, Hertford Museum.

9730 PRIVATE JOHN JOSEPH CAFFREY
2nd Battalion, The York and Lancaster Regiment

John Caffery was born at Crinkle, Parsonstown, King's County (later Offaly), Ireland on 1st November 1891 (also seen as 23rd October). His surname was originally Caffery, but he became Caffrey on enlistment. Other members of the family are variously recorded as Caffery and Caffrey.

His father was John Caffery (1850–1914), a bricklayer's labourer born in Nottingham, whose parents, Patrick Caffery (born c.1797) and Bridget née Feely (c.1819–66), were born in Ireland. He served in the Nottingham Militia before enlisting in the 65th Foot (later 1st York & Lancaster) at Leicester on 11th February 1873 (2295). He was described as 5′ 7¾″ tall, with sallow complexion, hazel eyes, brown hair and his religion was Roman Catholic. He reported to the

(F Smith)

Curragh on 21st February, was attested on the 24th and posted to Jersey on 23rd July. He went with the Battalion to the East Indies on 27th January 1874, landing on 2nd March and marching to Lucknow on the 18th. John extended his service to complete twelve years on 9th September 1878 at Simla. The Battalion went to Aden on 1st August 1882, where it was held in reserve for the Egyptian Campaign. It embarked on HMS *Serapis*, landing at Trinkitat, Sudan on 28th February 1884 and took part in the Battle of El Teb. On 29th March the Battalion embarked on HMS *Jumna* and arrived at Dover on 22nd April. He extended his service again to complete twenty-one years on 29th April. Postings throughout the north of England followed – Sheffield in 1885, Tynemouth September 1887, Sheffield April 1888, Strensall June, York September, Strensall May 1889 and York again in July. On 14th December the Battalion went to Birr, King's County (later Co Offaly), Ireland. John moved to Portumma, Co Galway in September 1890 and returned to Birr in September 1891. His last move was to Cork on 12th September 1892, from where he was discharged on 14th February 1894; his character on discharge was described as "latterly good" (see below). During his twenty-one years service, John was treated in hospital numerous times for:

Simla in the foothills of the Himalayas was the seat of British government in India during the summer months.

- Rheumatism – July 1873.
- Primary syphilis – March-May 1874, December 1877 – February 1878, April-May 1878 and January 1879.
- Secondary syphilis – November-December 1885.
- Syphilitic ulcer – January-February 1886.
- Ague – September-November 1874, May 1875, November-December 1879, September-October 1881.
- Gonorrhoea – June 1876, July-August 1884 and March 1887.
- Contusion – February-March 1882.
- Synovitis – October 1884.
- 'Itch' – April 1887.
- Accidental wound – May 1887.

Aden.

Hillsborough Barracks, Sheffield.

He also had numerous brushes with authority, being awarded and forfeiting Good Conduct Pay on a number of occasions:

- Awarded Good Conduct Pay on 2nd May 1876, 2nd January 1881, 2nd January 1883, 21st February 1885, 14th June 1888, 14th June 1889 and 14th June 1891.
- Forfeited Good Conduct Pay on 8th November 1876, 19th May and 14th June 1887.

He was awarded the Egypt and Sudan Medal 1882–89 with clasps 'El-Teb' and 'Tamaai' and the Khedive's Star 1884 (Egypt). From 1887 onwards he appears to have been a reformed character, putting disciplinary problems and sexually transmitted diseases behind him. He was a Nottingham Corporation road labourer in 1901, living with his family at 4 Wood Court, Nottingham and in 1911 at 8 George Yard, Nottingham.

John Joseph's mother was Hannah née Cowan (c.1865–1948) born at Cork, Ireland. John and Hannah were married at St George's Roman Catholic Church, York on 10th December 1889. She was a charwoman in 1911. John had eight siblings:

- Florence Caffery (twin with Nora) born and died in the 3rd quarter of 1893 at Nottingham.
- Nora Caffery (twin with Florence) birth registered in the 3rd quarter of 1893 at Nottingham and her death was registered there in the 4th quarter.
- James Bartholemew Caffery (7th February 1894–1959), whose birth was registered as Bartholomew Caffery. He was a stout bottler in 1911. James married Charlotte Odina Armstrong (born 1892, registered as Charlotte Ordoyno Armstrong) in 1915 and they had a son, James, in 1916. They lived at 3 Amber Terrace, King's Meadow Road, Nottingham. In 1916 he was serving in the Sherwood Foresters on the staff of the local Territorial HQ. He enlisted in 60th North Midlands Brigade RFA (TA) on 12th July 1921 at Nottingham (743228). He was described as 6′ 1″ tall, weighing 170 lbs, with sallow complexion, hazel eyes and dark brown hair. He was a motor driver by trade and passed an MT Driving Course with the RASC in York 6th-19th March 1933. He served until 6th February 1939, having reached the age limit.
- Margaret 'Maggie' Caffery (born 1897) was an errand girl for a lace manufacturer in 1911.
- Joseph 'Joe' Caffery (born 1900) married Edith Green in 1924 and had a daughter, Eileen E Caffrey in 1926.
- Kate Caffery (born 1907).
- Mary Caffery (1907–12).
- Beatrice Caffery, born in the 3rd quarter of 1909 at Nottingham and her death was registered there in the 1st quarter of 1910.

SS *Minneapolis*, first of four Minne class ships ordered for the Atlantic Transport Line, made her first trans-Atlantic voyage in 1900. On 9 October 1913, she was one of eleven ships that went to assist the burning Italian vessel *Volturno*, resulting in twenty-two members of the crew receiving Sea Gallantry Medals from the Board of Trade. *Minneapolis* was torpedoed by U-35 in the Mediterranean on 23rd March 1916. She was towed by various other vessels, but sank on 25th March.

John was educated at St Mary's Catholic School, Derby Road, Nottingham and was a member of 12th Nottingham Company, Boys' Brigade. He enlisted in 7th Sherwood Foresters (Nottinghamshire and Derbyshire Regiment) in May 1910, but in July enlisted for regular service in 2nd York and Lancaster, the Regiment in which his father had served. He went to Ireland, where he won two medals for Army cross-country championships and another for the Aldershot cross-country championship.

John's Battalion was mobilised on 4th August 1914 and moved from Limerick to Queenstown. It embarked on the London and North Western Railway TSS *Slieve Bawn* on 14th August, bound for Holyhead, Anglesey and sailed for France on the Atlantic Transport Line SS *Minneapolis* on 8th September, arriving at St Nazaire early the next day. **Awarded the Russian Cross of the Order of St George 4th Class for rescuing an injured officer under fire, LG 25th August 1915. Awarded the VC for his actions near La Brique, Belgium on 16th November 1915, LG 22nd January 1916.** The VC was presented by the King at Buckingham Palace on 23rd February 1916. Promoted corporal and later sergeant. John was discharged on 8th February 1922, and was issued Silver War Badge 187425.

John Caffrey married Florence Annie Avey (4th June 1889 – 1977) on 24th March 1917 at St Barnabus Church,

St Barnabus Church, Cambridge, where John Caffrey married Florence Avey in March 1917.

Shakespeare Street, Nottingham.

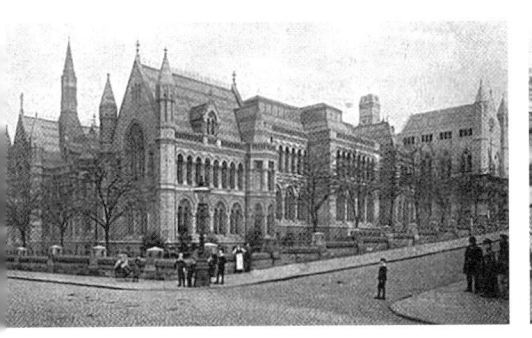

Butlin's Holiday Camp at Filey. It closed in the 1980s.

Cambridge. They lived at 41 Wilmot Street, Derby. There were no children. Florence's father, Charles William Avey, was born c.1865 at Delhi, India.

John was a member of the VC Guard at the Interment of the Unknown Warrior on 11th November 1920. He served as a constable with the River Wear Watch. He then worked for Messrs Cammell Laird at their 'Metropolitan Carriage and Wagon Company' works until 26th June 1931, when it closed and he was on the dole. He was employed by Mr Norman Birkett KC, Liberal candidate for East Nottingham, for the duration of the 1931 election campaign at Shakespeare Street. Alderman Green then found him a job as an assistant public administrator at the council offices. On 2nd April 1936, he attended the funeral of his friend, RSM Frank Parr MC DCM, at Wilford Hill Cemetery, Nottingham.

John became a member of the National Defence Companies in 1937. He is reputed to have served as a company sergeant major in the Sherwood Foresters from November 1939. In September 1939, National Defence Companies were called up, attached to regular regiments and became the basis of home service battalions to guard vulnerable points and prison camps. The Sherwood Foresters formed two Home Defence Battalions, the 10th in 1939 and the 15th in 1940 (both disbanded

John Caffrey meeting Billy Butlin at Filey (Butlin's).

An older John Caffrey.

1941). His age seemed to preclude him from regular service and the Local Defence Volunteers/Home Guard did not form until May 1940. It seems likely that he served in one of the Sherwood Foresters Home Defence Battalions and possibly the Home Guard thereafter.

After the Second World War he became a 'sergeant' at Butlin's Holiday Camp, Filey, Yorkshire. Harry Nicholls VC was also employed there as the boxing instructor.

John Caffrey died at Derbyshire Royal Infirmary on 26th February 1953 and is buried in Wilford Hill (Southern) Cemetery, Nottingham (R 23 – 8). His name was not included on the original headstone. Ron Booth, a descendant of Anthony Booth VC, and the local Western Front Association organised a new headstone, which was dedicated on 23rd May 2007.

In addition to the VC, he was awarded the 1914 Star with 'Mons' clasp, British War Medal 1914–20, Victory Medal 1914–19, George VI Coronation Medal 1937 and the Russian Cross of St George 4th Class. The George VI Coronation Medal 1937 was not included with his group. The VC is held by the York & Lancaster Regiment Museum, Clifton Park Museum, Rotherham.

LIEUTENANT FREDERICK WILLIAM CAMPBELL
1st Battalion (Ontario Regiment), Canadian Expeditionary Force

Frederick Campbell was born on 15th June 1867 at Mount Forest, Oxford County, Ontario, Canada, although his year of birth appears as 1869 on his Attestation Papers. His father was Ephraim B Campbell (1829–1917) a servant in 1851 and later a farmer living at Gleneden, Grey County, Ontario. He subsequently settled at Normanby, Mount Forest, Oxford County, Ontario. His mother was Esther Hunt née McLaughlin (born 1837). She was of Irish origin and pre-deceased her husband. Frederick had three sisters:

- Jeannie born on 23rd February 1863. She was single and living with her parents in the 1901 Census.
- Ella born in December 1864. She was widowed by the time of the 1911 Census and living with her parents. She had a daughter, Harrie [sic], born in December 1901.
- Cora born on 25th January 1874. She was single in the 1911 Census and living with her parents.

A distant relative on his father's side was Captain Ames, who served under Sir Isaac Brock, helping to repel United States invaders from Canada in the War of 1812. Frederick was educated at Mount Forest School before farming at Normanby, Ontario.

He also bred horses, was appointed Public School Trustee of No.15 State School at Normanby and later became a director of the Mount Forest Agricultural Society. Before 1911 it is understood he spent eighteen months in the United States.

Frederick's military career commenced in 1885 when he joined 30th Wellington Battalion of Rifles, a Militia unit. About 1894 he enlisted in 5 Company, 13th Battalion Volunteer Militia (Infantry) at London, Ontario. When was broke out in South Africa he served there with 2nd (Special Service) Battalion, Royal Canadian Regiment in a Maxim machine-gun team. He was in action in Cape Colony from 11th October 1899, at Paardeberg 17th-26th February 1900, Driefontein 10th March and Johannesburg 31st May. At Modder River he repaired one of the wheels of his gun carriage, using legs from a table taken from a Boer house. The wheel is in the Citadel Museum in Quebec. He was Mentioned in Despatches, possibly for this action. Frederick was promoted to sergeant and returned to Canada later in 1900, where he continued serving in the Militia. He was commissioned as a lieutenant in 1902 and was later promoted captain.

Mount Forest, Ontario.

Frederick married Margaret Ann 'Annie' née MacGillivray (1872–1934) on 25th November 1903 at Mount Forest. They had three children:

- Arthur Clive Campbell born 1st August 1904. He later lived in Detroit, Michigan, USA.
- Jean Margaret Campbell born August 1905.
- Freda MacGillivray Campbell.

One of the daughters married as de Gore. Frederick was a member of the Canadian Contingent at the coronation of HM King George V in 1911.

On the outbreak of the First World War, Frederick recruited in his local area before travelling to Valcartier Camp, Quebec on 17th August 1914 with a dozen volunteers. He enlisted in 1st Battalion at Valcartier on 23rd September with the rank of lieutenant. He was 5′ 9″ tall, with dark complexion, hazel eyes, grey hair and his religious denomination was Methodist. The Battalion, 1,166 strong, sailed on the White Star Line SS *Laurentic* on 3rd October, arriving at Plymouth, Devon on 18th October. It moved to Bustard Camp, Larkhill, on Salisbury Plain, Wiltshire to carry out basic training. The weather during that winter was particularly wet and cold. The Battalion sailed for France from Avonmouth on 8th February 1915, arriving at Merris near Hazebrouck on 14th February. Frederick commanded a Machine-Gun Section.

1st Battalion incurred heavy losses in a counterattack northeast of Ypres on 23rd April. Over the next few weeks, Frederick was twice recommended for promotion

SS *Laurentic*, 14,900 tons, started life with the Dominion Line in 1908 as SS *Alberta*, but changed name when taken over by the White Star Line in 1909. Her first voyage was between Liverpool and Quebec commencing on 29th April 1909. When the murderer Dr Hawley Harvey Crippen escaped from Britain on SS *Montrose*, he was recognised by the Captain who radioed back his suspicions. Chief Inspector Walter Dew of the Metropolitan Police boarded the faster SS *Laurentic* and reached Canada ahead of Crippen to effect his arrest on 31st July 1910 and brought him back to Britain for trial and subsequent hanging. She was in Montréal when war broke out and was immediately commissioned as a troop ship for the CEF and in 1915 was converted into an armed merchant cruiser. *Laurentic* was sunk by two U-boat laid mines off Ireland on 25th January 1917; 354 passengers and crew were lost. The ship was carrying 43 tons of gold (valued in 2014 at £380M). All but one percent of this was recovered by RN divers between 1917 and 1924.

and a decoration by his CO, Lieutenant Colonel FW Hill. **Awarded the VC for his actions at Givenchy, France on 15th June 1915, LG 23rd August 1915.** He was admitted to a Casualty Clearing Station, from where he was transferred to No.7 Stationary Hospital, Boulogne on 17th June. Following surgery, his wound began to heal, but infection set in and he fell into a coma at midday on 19th June. Frederick died of heart failure three hours later. He is buried in Boulogne Eastern Cemetery (II A 24). Belatedly, his appointment to temporary captain from 23rd April appeared in the London Gazette on 5th January 1916.

King George V inspecting Canadian troops at Bustard Camp, Larkhill on Salisbury Plain during the dreadfully wet winter of 1914–15.

The VC was sent to Canada by the War Office on 28th August 1915 and was subsequently presented to his widow at Mount Forest, Oxford County, Ontario. Its current location is unknown. In addition to the VC, he was awarded the Queen's South Africa Medal 1899–1902 with four clasps ('Cape Colony', 'Paardeberg', 'Driefontein' & 'Johannesburg'), 1914–15 Star, British War Medal 1914–20, Victory Medal 1914–19 and King George V Coronation Medal 1911. Frederick is also commemorated at:

- Frederick Campbell Elementary School, Canadian Forces Base Borden, Ontario closed in June 2010.
- Victoria Cross Public School, Mount Forest, Ontario, formerly Forest Park Public School, was relocated in November 2005 and renamed on 22nd March 2006 to honour Mount Forest's two VCs – FW Campbell and L Honey.
- Captain Fred Campbell VC Branch No.134, Royal Canadian Legion, 140 King Street West, Mount Forest, Ontario. A memorial plaque in the grounds was unveiled by his daughter, Mrs VS de Gore, on 20th June 1965.
- 895 (Fred Campbell VC) Squadron, Royal Canadian Air Training Corps at Mount Forest formed on 1st January 1983, supported by Captain Fred Campbell VC Royal Canadian Legion Branch No.134.
- Campbell Platoon, Canadian Forces Leadership and Recruit School, Saint-Jean Garrison, St-Jean-sur-Richelieu, Quebec.
- Lieutenant FW Campbell VC Trophy donated to 4th Battalion, Royal Canadian Regiment by Lieutenant Colonel MEK Campbell CD on 3rd June 2005 when he relinquished command, awarded annually to the best junior officer in the Battalion.
- Canadian Forces College, Toronto – a wooden plaque bearing fifty-six maple leaves, each inscribed with the name of a Canadian-born VC holder, was dedicated in November 1999.
- An obelisk commemorating all Canadian VCs at Military Heritage Park, Barrie, Ontario was dedicated by HRH The Princess Royal on 22nd October 2013.
- His VC action featured in the *Victor* comic dated 21st March 1970.

SD/4 COMPANY SERGEANT MAJOR NELSON VICTOR CARTER
12th Battalion, The Royal Sussex Regiment

Nelson Carter was born at 3 Hybridge Terrace, Latimer Drive, East Eastbourne, Sussex on 6th April 1887. The family moved to Hailsham when he was six. His father, Richard Carter (1857–1925), was a fisherman in 1881, a bricklayer's labourer in 1901 and a general labourer at the Water Works in 1911. His mother was Harriet née Goldsmith (1857–1917). She was a charwoman in 1891. Richard and Harriet were married on 22nd January 1881 at St Mary's Church, Hailsham, Sussex. The family lived at 9 Carlton Road, Eastbourne and had moved to 3 Hydridge Terrace, Latimer Road, Eastbourne by 1891. In 1901 they were living at Battle Road, Harebeating, Hailsham. Nelson had eight siblings:

- Winnifred 'Winney' Blanche Margaret Carter (1878–1927) married Edward Medhurst (1878–1958) in 1898. He was a platelayer and they were living at 33 Back Fort Pitt Street, Chatham, Kent in 1901. Winnifred and Edward had six children:
  - Edward Medhurst 1896.
  - Edwin Charles Medhurst c. 1898.
  - Phoebe Elizabeth Medhurst (1899–1965) married Oswald Horace Goode in 1924 and had seven children.
  - Henry 'Harry' Thomas Medhurst (1900–59) married Clara Elizabeth Sparkes (1902–93) in 1922 and they had seventeen children between 1922 and 1946. Clara was the sister of Ivy Louise Sparkes who married Robert Downie VC. Clara had a daughter, Lydia A Sparkes, in 1920 and she had a daughter Jean in 1937, possibly making Clara the youngest grandmother in Britain at the time.
  - Winifred 'Winnie' Mary A Medhurst (born 1902) married Walter J Milner in 1922 and had nine children.
  - Ernest Medhurst 1912–13.
- Martin Luther Carter (1881–1956), a brick maker, enlisted in the Royal Sussex Regiment on 5th January 1899. He was posted to Malta on 1st December and returned to Britain on 23rd August 1900. He saw active service in South Africa in Cape Colony and the Orange Free State (Queen's & King's South Africa Medals), before being posted to India in 1902 for nine months and returned to Britain again. Promoted lance corporal 7th July 1903 and corporal 21st July. Postings to Malta, Crete and India followed. In India he was promoted sergeant and returned to Britain on 9th January 1911 to be discharged next day after twelve years and five day's service. He also served in the Militia, bringing his total service to eighteen years. Martin was a postman in Canterbury when he re-enlisted in 5th (Reserve) Battalion, East Kent Regiment on 11th December 1915 (G13432). His address was The Green, Derringstone, Barham, Canterbury. He was transferred to the Reserve next day until mobilised on 15th June 1916 and was promoted corporal next day. He served with 6th East Kent in France from 30th December. Martin was wounded in the right knee and foot on 2nd May 1917 and was admitted to 3rd Canadian General Hospital, Boulogne on the 5th. He moved to 7th Convalescence Depot on 10th May and 38 Infantry Base Depot, Étaples on 6th June, before rejoining his unit on 1st August. He received a bayonet wound in the right thigh on 21st November and was admitted to 37th Field Ambulance. He transferred to No.10 General Hospital, Rouen before being evacuated to Britain on 23rd November on HMHS *Essequibo*. He

Hailsham Market Place.

was at Eastern Command Depot at Shoreham-on-Sea 28th December 1917 – 12th March 1918. Martin was wounded by a bullet in the right heel on 25th August and admitted to No.5 General Hospital, Rouen before being evacuated to Britain on SS *Gloucester Castle* on 4th September. He was treated at Graylingwell War Hospital at Chichester from 5th September until posted to Eastern Command Depot 4th October – 2nd December. Martin was demobilised on 6th February 1919 from Crystal Palace and transferred to the Class Z Reserve on 6th March 1919. He married Susan Marsh (born 1882) at Bridge Parish Church near Canterbury on 25th December 1903. They had seven children – Frederick Martin Carter 1905; Winifred Maud Carter 1911; Ernest Richard Carter 1913; Queenie May Carter 1915; Ivy I Carter 1921, who married Mark E Wilkinson in 1942 and had at least three children; Alfred C Carter 1923; and Robert R Carter 1925.

- Edwin Richard Carter (1883–1957) joined the Sussex Artillery (Militia) c.1899 before enlisting in the Royal Garrison Artillery for service in Bermuda and Jamaica. He was discharged on 26th December 1912 and became a gardener and caretaker at Herstmonceux Castle, Sussex. He served again in the RGA and was medically discharged before September 1916. Edwin had a daughter, Winnifred (1902–84), who married Robin G Burleton in 1922 and had five children. Edwin married Ada Mary Lucy Jenkins (1891–1973) on 2nd August 1913 at St Anne's Church, Eastbourne. They lived in Buckinghamshire and later Somerset, where he worked as a cowman on an estate owned by Lord Carnarvon. The family moved to Weybridge, Surrey before migrating to Canada, travelling on the Canadian Pacific liner SS *Melita*, leaving Southampton for Saint John, New Brunswick on 3rd April 1926. They settled in British Columbia. Edwin and Ada had four children – Betty Florence Carter (1914–93) married Carl William Bjorkquist (1905–76) in 1933 in Saskatchewan and had eleven children; twins Philip Richard Carter and Constance Amy Carter 1918; and Anthony Lawrence Carter (1920–92). Betty was not aware of her half-sister, Winnifred, until 1957 and they did not meet until 4th October 1975, when Winnifred travelled to England.
- Joseph Thomas Carter (born 1885) served as a driver in the Army Service Corps (T/28337) and went to France on 10th April 1915. He was medically discharged before September 1916. He married a lady known in the family as 'Scottish Granny' and had three children – Florence, Mary and Robert. Joseph made a living travelling throughout the country carrying out demolition work.
- Gordon Victor Carter (1891–1970) was a general building labourer in 1911. He drove a horse drawn dustcart at one time and served in the Army Service Corps as a driver (DM2/165241) in France after 31st December 1915. He married Ada Maria 'Daisy' Sporne (1892–1964) in 1914. They had eight children – Nelson R Carter 1914; Jesse V Carter 1916, who married Irene L Pateman in 1935 and had two daughters; William J Carter 1927; Ronald F Carter 1929; Richard A Carter 1931; Maisie Madeline Alexine Carter (1924–78), who married Leonard Albert

Knightly (1923–87) in 1943 and they had five children; Ernest A Carter 1934, who married Shirley Tarrant in 1955; and John B Carter 1936.

- Ernest Alfred Carter (1893–1973) was a kennel lad at the local harriers in Harebeating in 1911. He joined the Home Counties RFA at Hailsham and served in France after 31st December 1915 as a bombardier (102564). He married Galina Shiller (1898–1942) from Warsaw, Poland and they had a son, Alfred Ernest Carter 1924. Ernest married a second time in 1943; it is understood his wife was Elsie L Forge (born 1916). Ernest was a policeman in Leyland, Lancashire (No.494) and joined the Corps of Military Police on 19th October 1937 at Chorley, Lancashire. He was an acting sergeant 1941–43 and returned to the civilian police until retiring in 1953.
- Jesse 'Jess' Carter (1895–1953) was a baker's boy in 1911. He married Winifred Louise George (born 1886) in 1915 as George F Carter; the reason for the change of name is not known. Jesse was in the Special Reserve and was called up to serve in France from 23rd August 1914 in the RFA as a gunner/acting bombardier with 32nd Brigade RFA (13178). He was employed by Mr White, a wine merchant, and worked at Haddon Hall, Devonshire Place and the Sussex Hotel, Eastbourne. Jess and Winifred had a son, Noel J Carter, in 1919.
- Florence Carter (born 1900) married Robert W Webb in 1926 and had a son, Harold Webb.

His maternal grandfather, Thomas Goldsmith (c. 1829–1901) enlisted in 7th Regiment of Foot (Royal Fusiliers) and served during the Crimean War. He was wounded at the Battle of the Alma on 20th September 1854 and slightly wounded in the first attack on the Redan on 18th June 1855. On 11th August 1855, he was dangerously wounded at Sebastopol, losing a leg. He was an out-pensioner of Chelsea Hospital in 1861, living with his family at Cacklebury, Halisham, Sussex. Three of Nelson's uncles also had military service:

- George William Goldsmith (1873–1950) served in No.5 Company, 2nd Sussex Artillery Volunteers in the 1890s while living at Hailsham.
- Charlie Richard Goldsmith (1877–1956) served in 2nd Sussex Artillery Volunteers 1896–1900. He enlisted in the Army Veterinary Corps at Brighton on 10th November 1914 as a horse keeper (1024). He was described as 5'7" tall, with fresh complexion, blue eyes and brown hair. He was discharged on 25th March 1919.
- Thomas Inkerman Goldsmith (born 1881) was a spinner when he enlisted

The Old Town Cinema on High Street, Eastbourne where Nelson Carter worked before the war (Margaret Smith).

in the Militia as Inkerman Sebastopol Goldsmith on 21st November 1899 at Eastbourne (3494). He was living at 3 Battle Road, Hailsham and described as 5'9" tall, weighing 148lbs, with fresh complexion, blue eyes, light brown hair and his religious denomination was Church of England. He was embodied in the Sussex Artillery on 1st May 1900 and disembodied on 17th October. He enlisted in the Royal Garrison Artillery as Inkerman Sebastopol Goldsmith on 24th October at Eastbourne (6268), joining at Dover, Kent the following day. He served in 22 Company RGA from 22nd December and 32 Company RGA from 1st September 1901. On 8th October he went to India and served with 104 Company RGA (formerly 32 Company) at Rawalpindi and Deolali. Having been posted to No. 2 Depot on 15th March 1902, he returned to Britain on 6th April. The tendon in a hammer toe had contracted but he refused surgery and was consequently discharged unfit for further service on medical grounds on 6th May 1902 from Netley, Hampshire. Thomas re-enlisted in the RGA as Charles Thomas Ryan (19157) on 7th April 1904 at Portsmouth, Hampshire, stating he had never previously served in the armed forces. He joined at Fort Rowner, Gosport on 11th April, but the false statements on enlistment were discovered. He was charged and appeared before the Police Court at Portsmouth on 26th April, sentenced to one month in jail and was discharged on 9th May.

Nelson was educated at Hailsham Board School and left aged twelve in 1899 to work for Charles Goldsmith (probably his uncle) as a carter and then on Mr Simmonds farm as a general labourer. After four years he ran away and enlisted in the RFA on 18th November 1902 (28771) under the name Nelson Smith. He served in 53rd Brigade RFA from 16th December. Appointed acting bombardier 5th February 1903, but was discharged on 17th August being medically unfit due to a hammertoe. He re-enlisted on 23rd August 1906 (25672) and was posted to Dover on 14th September, 27th Brigade RFA on 16th November and 22nd Brigade RFA on 1st August 1907. He joined 78th Brigade RFA in Singapore on 30th October. Nelson returned to England on 17th February 1909 and was admitted to Princess Alice Memorial Hospital, Eastbourne where he underwent an operation, possibly for a hernia. He contracted a bladder infection and was declared unfit for further service in the Army, or even the police, and discharged on 15th June 1909 from Woolwich.

He worked for Charles Goldsmith again before settling in Eastbourne, where he originally lived at the Soldier's and Sailor's Home. There he worked at Eversley Court, Endcliffe School, Burlington Hotel

St Mary's Church, Old Town, Eastbourne, where Nelson Carter married Kathleen Camfield in October 1911.

and finally as a doorman at the Old Town Cinema when it opened in December 1913.

Nelson Carter married Kathleen Camfield (1881–1934) at St Mary's Church, Old Town, Eastbourne, Sussex on 13th October 1911. She was born at the Union Workhouse, Uckfield and was a cook working at 12 Upperton Road, Eastbourne in 1901 and at 'Engedi', St Leonard's Road, Eastbourne in 1911. She was recorded as Catherine on the marriage certificate, Kathleen on her children's birth certificates, Katie on other documents and was known as Kitty within the family. At the time of their marriage, Nelson was living at 27 Uppertown Road, Eastbourne and Kitty at 32 Broomfield Road, Eastbourne. They subsequently lived at 33 Greys Road, Old Town, Eastbourne. Nelson and Kitty had two children:

- Richard Francis Carter was born on 27th February 1912 at 32 Broomfield Street, Eastbourne and died there on 19th May of acute eczema pharyngitis.
- Jessie Olive Carter (2nd January 1916 – 2001). She married Stephen William Baker (1905–79) on 23rd March 1935 at Eastbourne and they lived at 78 St Philip's Avenue. Jessie attended many VC/GC Association reunions wearing her father's medals, including the 1956 Centenary Celebrations with her daughter Gillian. Jessie visited her father's grave for the first time on the 70th anniversary of his death in 1986. Jessie and Stephen had at least five children – Gillian C Baker 1936; Jacqueline Baker; Richard Baker born and died 1944; Stephanie Baker 1947; and Geoffrey VM Baker 1955. Jessie was unaware of the existence of her deceased brother Richard until she was sent an old postcard from a family member in Canada in 1993. The postcard had been sent by Harriet Carter (Jessie's grandmother) to her son Edwin (Jessie's uncle) in 1912, wishing him a happy birthday and asking him if he had been to see his new nephew Richard. Jessie died in 2001 and some of her ashes were scattered on her father's grave in France.

When he re-enlisted, this time in 11th Royal Sussex on 5th September 1914, he had a number of tattoos, including Buffalo Bill on his left forearm, a Japanese Lady on his upper right arm and Buffalo Bill on his back. He was described as 6' 1" tall, with fresh complexion, grey eyes and brown hair. He was promoted corporal the same day. The prefix of his number 'SD', stood for Southdowns, of which there were three battalions (11th, 12th and 13th) in the Royal Sussex Regiment, known as 'Lowther's Lambs', as they were raised by Lieutenant Colonel Claude

CSM Nelson Carter in an A Company photograph (Geoffrey and Mairi Baker).

Lowther MP. The Battalion trained at Maidstone, Cooden near Bexhill-on-Sea and Witley. Promoted sergeant 29th September and colour sergeant 10th November. He transferred to the 12th Battalion on 11th November and was appointed CSM of A Company on 28th January 1915. He was RSM temporarily 20th August–16th October. Nelson was a noted athlete and boxer. He won a medal in the Regimental Championship and the cup for the heavyweight champion in 1915.

Nelson went to France with the Battalion on 4th March 1916. He was recommended for the MC in May 1916, for carrying a wounded man 400m on his back over open ground, but it was not awarded, probably because it was overtaken by events the following month. On 28th June, he wrote what was to be his final letter home:

"My Darling Little Kitty
It does seem a long time since I had a letter from you. How are you & young Jessie getting along? I suppose that you are having just as rotten weather at home in England as we are out here…. One day its pouring with rain & the next its boiling hot, just the right sort of weather to lay the Lads up, but I suppose we shall get a rest shortly & some of the poor devils need it too. I had a letter from home the other day. It is the first one since I left England. I have not the time at present so I am going to drop them a card.

I am sorry that I can't get those cards yet, but will send them on to you as soon as I can get some. Did you see my letter to Mr Hollebone in the Eastbourne Gazette that you sent me last week.

Well Duck I have a devil of a lot to do before we move off tonight, so I suppose that I must draw to a close.
With fondest love & Kisses
Your Loving Husband
Nelson

Awarded the VC for his actions at the Boar's Head, Richebourg L'Avoue, France on 30th June 1916, LG 9th September 1916. He was killed in the same action and was originally buried within the trench system (Map reference 36S16a12). His grave was lost, but rediscovered in March 1920 and his remains were identified from his identity disk. He is buried in Royal Irish Rifles Graveyard, Laventie (VI C 17). Nelson is also commemorated in a number of other places:

- Regimental Memorial in Chichester Cathedral, Sussex.
- War Memorial, Hailsham, Sussex.
- Blue Plaque on his former home at 33 Greys Road, Old Town, Eastbourne, unveiled on 31st July 2007 by

Despite the pressures of training there was time for relaxation. Here Nelson Carter plays the part of a woman in a theatrical production (Geoffrey and Mairi Baker).

Nelson Carter on the right in another theatrical production (Geoffrey and Mairi Baker).

Nelson Carter's grave in Royal Irish Rifles Graveyard, Laventie.

the Lord Lieutenant of West Sussex, Mr Hugh Wyatt. Also present were family members and Nigel Waterson MP.
- The former Royal Sussex Regiment Depot, Roussillon Barracks at Chichester, was redeveloped for housing and six roads were named after Royal Sussex VCs, including Carter Road.

The VC was presented to his widow by the King at Buckingham Palace on 2nd May 1917. In addition to the VC, he was awarded the British War Medal 1914–20 and Victory Medal 1914–19. His daughter, Jessie, left instructions in her will that the Royal Sussex Regiment should have first refusal on the VC. It was handed over to the Regiment at a ceremony on 28th June 2003 by her son, Geoffrey Baker. The VC is held by The Royal Sussex Regiment Museum, Eastbourne.

Kitty received a small pension of £1/3/9 per week. An appeal by his company officer, Captain Harold Robinson, an Eastbourne resident, raised £90 and the town's Emergency Fund was asked for support, but it was unable to help due to the large number of other deserving cases. The 'Carter VC Fund' was set up by Mrs Rupert Gwynne, wife of the local MP. The aim was to raise £500 to invest in War Loans to help bring up and educate Nelson's only surviving child.

Hailsham War Memorial.

Biographies 245

Nelson Carter's VC (Phil and Anthony Carter).

The Old Town Cinema and Hailsham Electric Theatre held screenings with the proceeds going to the Fund. By the end of July 1918, the Fund had raised over £400. Kitty died on 22nd November 1934 at Eastbourne and is buried in Ocklynge Cemetery.

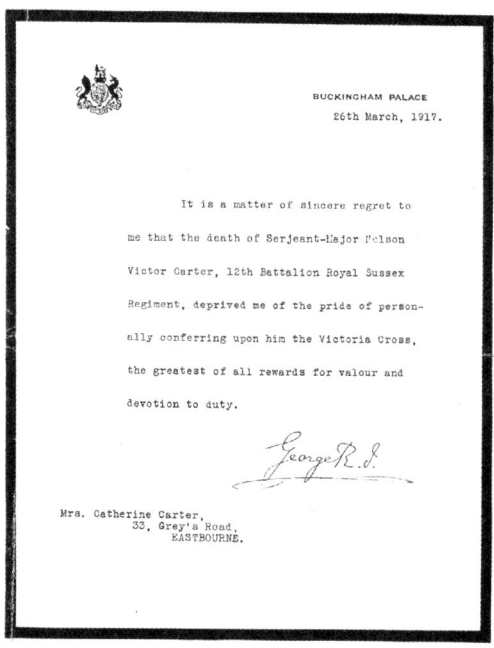

The letter from the King to the next of kin of a posthumous VC winner (Margaret Smith).

Nelson Carter is distantly linked with Robert Downie VC MM. Nelson's sister Winnifred's son, Henry, married Clara Elizabeth Sparkes, who was Robert Downie's sister-in-law. Nelson's VC action featured in Issue 146 of the *Victor* comic on 7th December 1963.

19384 PRIVATE GEORGE WILLIAM CHAFER
1st Battalion, The East Yorkshire Regiment

George Chafer was born at 77 Mill Lane, Bowling, Bradford, Yorkshire on 16th April 1894. His father is unknown. He was the illegitimate son of Lucy Chafer (born 1873), possibly by the son of her employer in Bradford. She was a domestic servant at the home of Reverend Robert Lickes, a Wesleyan Minister at Queen Street, Epworth in 1891 and had a similar position with a family in Bradford by 1894. By 1901 she had moved in with her parents at Studcross, Epworth, Lincolnshire. She was working as a servant for William Robert Lane (1860–1943) at Station Terrace, Cotherstone, near Barnard Castle,

Durham in 1911. William Lane, a railway clerk, had married Alice Moore (1870–1905), a grocer, in 1897 at Newcastle upon Tyne and they had a son, Victor Lane in 1898. In 1901 they were living at 1 Treville Street, West Hartlepool, Durham. William and Lucy married on 4th April 1916 at Thorne and settled at Cotherstone.

Willie, as George was known in the family, was brought up at Skyers Farm and Studcross, Epworth, Lincolnshire by his grandparents, William Chafer (c.1821–1904) and Amelia née Glew (c.1832–1908). Later he lived with his aunt, Mrs Leah Elizabeth Whitley (1866–1956) (née Chafer later Whitley and Brooke), at 23 Lord Street, Sowerby Bridge, Yorkshire and later at Ravenfield Common, Rotherham. Willie was educated at Epworth Church of England School 1899–1908. He was employed as a woollen spinner at Sowerby Bridge until moving to Rotherham, where he was employed as a weigh clerk at Silverwood Colliery.

He enlisted on 2nd June 1915 and went to France on 21st December. **Awarded the VC for his actions east of Meulte, France on 3rd/4th June 1916, LG 5th August 1916.** He was evacuated to hospital where his injured leg was amputated and was later treated at Stobhill Hospital, Glasgow. The VC was presented by the King at Buckingham Palace on 4th November 1916. **Awarded the Russian Cross of St George 3rd Class, LG 15th February 1917.** He was discharged on 2nd December 1916 and was a member of VC Guard at the interment of the Unknown Warrior 11th November 1920.

Willie lived in Bramley, near Rotherham, at various times with Mr and Mrs Read of 15 Silverwood Cottages and Bill and Clara France in Flanderwell Lane. He had a milk delivery business, which failed and started a poultry farm in 1929. Then he worked for the Ministry of Labour and National Service in Rotherham and Lincolnshire for thirty-five years. He was a local councillor and Chairman of Bramley Parish Council until he retired in April 1959. He was a founder member of the Fellowship of the Services, a long time member of the British Legion and

Silverwood Colliery.

King George V visited Silverwood Colliery in 1912.

one-time President of the Wickersley Branch.

During the Second World War, Willie served in the Home Guard as a platoon sergeant, because his duties could be carried out in spite of his missing leg. In June 1956, £189 was raised locally to allow him to go to London for the VC Centenary celebrations. He retained links with his old Regiment and travelled to West Germany as its guest when new Colours were presented.

Stobhill Hospital, Glasgow. During the First World War it housed 3rd and 4th Scottish General Hospitals.

Willie never married. He died at Rotherham General Hospital on 1st March 1966 and was cremated at Rotherham. His ashes were buried in the yard of Bramley Youth and Community Centre, which he was largely responsible for creating. He left £3,062 (£2,786 net), including £1,000 to Captain David Anderson of Edinburgh, who served with him in France.

In addition to the VC, he was awarded the 1914–15 Star, British War Medal 1914–20, Victory Medal 1914–19, George VI Coronation Medal 1937, Elizabeth II Coronation Medal 1953 and the Russian Cross of St George 3rd Class. The VC is held by the Prince of Wales's Own Regiment of Yorkshire Museum, York.

Willie is commemorated on a memorial stone in the Garden of Remembrance behind Bradford Cenotaph dedicated on 26th July 1999 to men associated with Bradford who were awarded the VC. Also named are Mathew Hughes, William Napier, Samuel Meekosha, Thomas Maufe, Eric Anderson and James Magennis.

Bradford Cenotaph.

10210 PRIVATE HARRY CHRISTIAN
2nd Battalion, The King's Own (Royal Lancaster Regiment)

Harry Christian was born at Walthwaite Farm, Pennington, near Ulverston, Lancashire on 17th January 1892. His father was William Christian (1868–1947), an ironstone miner. His mother was Mary Jane née Glessal (1870–1950). William and Mary's marriage was registered during the 4th quarter of 1890 at Ulverston, Lancashire. The family was living at Harrison Cottages in 1891, Farn Close, Osmotherley, Lancashire in 1901 and at 16 Low Mill, Egremont, Cumberland in 1911. Harry had six siblings:

- George Henry Glessal (1889–1958) whose natural father is unknown, but may have been William Christian. He was living with his grandmother, Catherine Glessal, as William H Glessal in 1891 and changed his name to William Henry George Christian by 1901. He was a limestone quarryman in 1911. George enlisted in 4th King's Own on 27th August 1914 and transferred to 8th King's Own on 12th November 1916. He married Bertha Rusling (1900–82) as William HG Christian in 1921. They had a daughter, Ethel Christian in 1922.
- Maggie Ann Christian (born 1893) was a domestic servant in 1911.
- John Thomas Christian (1896–1986) married Sylvia Husdan (born 1902) in 1919 and they had three children – Lionel S Christian 1922, Vera Christian 1924 and Harry Christian 1927.
- Martha Christian (1899–1929) married John Sydney Amor (1900–60) in 1919 at Whitehaven, Cumberland. They had four children – Marjorie Amor 1920–74, Walter William Amor 1924–2004, Olive E Amor 1926–2005 and John Amor 1929. John senior married Eleanor Carruthers McKee (1907–31) in 1930. She died giving birth to Eleanor Amor in 1931. John married Jennie Riley (c.1913–38) in 1933.
- James Christian (born 1901) married Eleanor Violet Margaret Graham (born 1900) in 1930 and they had a son, Brian C Christian, in 1931.
- Walter Christian (1905–84) married Winifred Salmond (1897–1991) in 1942.

Harry was educated at the National School, Ulverston. He worked on several farms including his uncle's and may also have been an iron ore miner at some stage. He enlisted in the King's Own (Special Reserve) at Lancaster on 10th November 1909 (1525) and was described as 5′ 4″ tall, weighing 110 lbs. He enlisted as a Regular on 5th April 1910 (10210) and was posted to the 2nd Battalion in Jersey, Channel Islands on 7th April. His disciplinary record throughout his career was poor. On 16th June he was charged with being drunk in barracks at St Peter, Jersey and was confined to barracks for four days. On 18th August 1911 he was charged with being drunk at Charing Cross, St Helier, fined 2/6d and confined to barracks for eight days. On 14th September, he sailed for India aboard HMT *Rewa* to join the 1st Battalion at Lucknow on 7th October. The Battalion moved to Calcutta on 3rd December 1912.

Harry went back to the 2nd Battalion on 19th December when the 1st Battalion left for Dover. He was admitted to hospital in Calcutta 26th January – 2nd April 1913 with gonorrhoea. The Battalion moved to Lebong, where he was charged with using obscene language to an NCO on 4th July and was confined to barracks for ten

2nd King's Own (Royal Lancaster Regiment) disembarking at St Helier, Jersey on 5th November 1908.

Charing Cross, St Helier, with Fort Regent, where 2nd King's Own (Royal Lancaster Regiment) was based, dominating the town in the background.

days. He was charged with striking his superior officer on 29th November and awarded ninety-one days detention on 2nd January 1914 at Lucknow Detention Barracks; he was released on 18th March with fifteen days remission. The bad behaviour continued. On 30th April he was charged with wilful damage when he kicked over a native tea seller's can, used obscene language to an NCO, was drunk in barracks and used obscene and threatening language to an NCO on duty – he was ordered to pay for the damage, fined five shillings and awarded fourteen days detention. The Battalion moved to Barrackpore on 23rd May. He was out of bounds in a canteen on 5th June and created a disturbance for which he was confined to barracks for eight days. On 4th July 1914 he used threatening language to an NCO, violently resisted an escort and was drunk in barracks, for which he was fined ten shillings and confined to barracks for ten days.

Harry returned to England on HMT *Kenilworth Castle* on 16th November. He was absent from Reveille at Winchester, Hampshire on 24th December until apprehended by the Military Police at 10.16 p.m. in a drunken state in the High Street. He was charged with disorderly conduct and using obscene language, fined 7/6d and confined to barracks for ten days. Almost as soon as he was allowed to walk out again, he was charged with assaulting a police constable on 12th January 1915 at Walworth, Surrey and sentenced to one month's imprisonment with hard labour. He was transferred to the 3rd Battalion on 15th January. Soon after completing his sentence, he was posted back to the 2nd Battalion and sailed for France on 24th February.

Harry received a gunshot wound to the head on 22nd April and was taken to No.14 General Hospital at Wimereux and No.9 General Hospital at Rouen on 29th April, before being discharged on the same day. **Awarded the VC for his actions at Cuinchy, France on 18th October 1915, LG 3rd March 1916.** The Battalion left for Egypt on 25th October before moving to Salonika. He contracted malaria in

HMT *Rewa* was launched on 14 Feb 1906 for the British India Steam Navigation Company. She operated for two years before becoming a permanent troop transport and was later converted to a hospital ship. She was sunk by a U-boat in the Bristol Channel on 4th January 1918 with the loss of three lives.

Barrackpore (Francis Frith).

December 1916 and was admitted to 4th Canadian General Hospital. He returned to England on leave in September 1917.

The VC was presented by the King at Ibrox Park, Glasgow on 18th September 1917. He had to be carried to the investiture due to a recurrence of malaria. He returned to Salonika, where he failed to comply with a direct order in the field on 6th June 1918 and was awarded fourteen days Field Punishment No.1. He was drunk on duty in the field on 20th September and underwent twenty-eight days Field Punishment No.1. When the war ended, he was stationed at Lake Doiran in Macedonia and in November was posted to Turkey.

He transferred to the 9th Battalion on 13th March 1919 and contracted malaria again on 12th April at Chanak. Harry transferred to the Section B Army Reserve on demobilisation on 10th June to live at 16 Low Mill, Egremont, Cumberland. He was discharged from the Army Reserve on 4th April 1922.

Harry Christian's marriage to Ellen Simm (19th June 1889 – 4th October 1970), a cotton spinner, was registered during the 3rd quarter of 1920 at Whitehaven, Cumberland. Her birth was registered as Edith Ellen Simm. They lived at 1 Dent Road, Thornhill, near Egremont, Cumberland. There were no children.

HMT *Kenilworth Castle*. On 4th June 1918, she collided with HMS *Rival* in mid-Channel and cut off the latter's stern. Several depth charges from *Rival* exploded under *Kenilworth* Castle causing a large hole in the hull. The bulkheads held, but through a misunderstanding some boats were lowered and two were swamped, resulting in fifteen people being drowned. She limped into Plymouth for repairs.

Harry became landlord of the Park Head Inn, Egremont, Cumberland for forty years. He died at West Cumberland Hospital, Cumbria on 2nd September 1974

Four King's Own (Royal Lancaster Regiment) VCs at a reunion at Bowerham Barracks, Lancaster in 1932. From the left – Albert Halton, James Hewitson and Tom Mayson with Harry Christian seated (King's Own Royal Regiment).

High Street, Winchester.

and is buried in Egremont Cemetery. He is also commemorated on a plaque at the entrance to Ulverston Coronation Hall, unveiled on the 50th anniversary of VE Day on 8th May 1995. His VC action was featured in Issue 1057 of the *Victor* comic on 23rd May 1981.

In addition to the VC, he was awarded the 1914–15 Star, British War Medal 1914–20, Victory Medal 1914–19, George VI Coronation Medal 1937 and Elizabeth II Coronation Medal 1953. The VC is held by the King's Own (Royal Lancaster) Regiment Museum, Lancaster.

The King received an enthusiastic welcome at Ibrox Park, Glasgow on 18th September 1917 prior to the investiture.

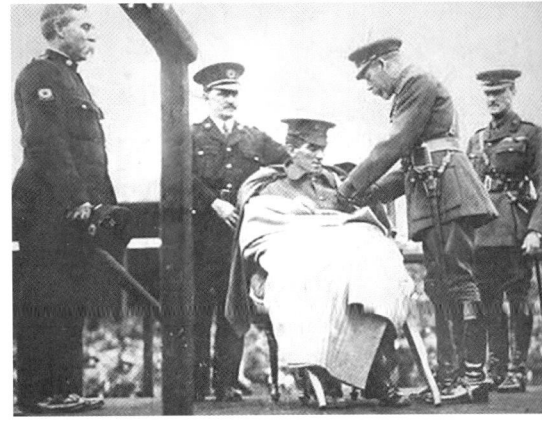

Harry Christian, covered in blankets because of a bout of malaria, receives his VC from the King (King's Own Royal Regiment).

L/6707 ACTING CORPORAL WILLIAM RICHARD COTTER
6th Battalion, The Buffs (East Kent Regiment)

William Cotter was born at 38 Sidney Street, Folkestone, Kent on 5th February 1882. His father was Richard Cotter (c.1851–1927) from Bantry Bay, Cork, Ireland. He served with the 24th Regiment in South Africa during the 1870s. He was a general labourer in 1881 and a plasterer's labourer in 1891. His mother was Amy née Richards (1860–1929). Richard and Amy's marriage was registered in the 2nd quarter of 1880 at Elham, Kent. The family lived at various times at Cheriton, at 43 Walton Road and Young's Road in Folkestone and 2 Barton Cottage, Wilberforce Road, Sandgate. William had eight siblings:

(Marilyn Harris)

- Edith Cotter (born 1881) married Edward Saunders (1879–1950) in 1900 and they had four children – Frederick Edward Saunders 1909–55 (moved to Dover, Piscataquis, Maine, USA), William Richard Bernard Saunders 1917–96 (moved to Australia), Winifred E Saunders 1919 and Stephen Saunders 1921–24.
- Frederick Edward M Cotter (born 1884) was a plasterer's labourer before enlisting in 2nd Battalion, The Buffs (East Kent Regiment). He died of fever while on service in South Africa. He does not appear in the South African War casualty lists and probably died there after the war; 2nd Buffs was in South Africa 1900–07.
- Stephen J Cotter (c.1886–1914) was a draper's shop boy before enlisting in the Royal Field Artillery. He died on 9th February 1914 in South Africa.
- Thomas Lawrence Cotter (1888–1973) was a fireman living at 20 Cannon Street, London in 1911. He served with 2nd Battalion, The Buffs (East Kent Regiment) (2/8287) in France from 17th January 1915 and Salonika from November. He transferred to the Class Z Reserve on 6th October 1919. He married Amy Elizabeth Taylor (1900–62) in 1922 and they had four children – Edith Amy Cotter 1922–82 (served in the WAAF during the Second World War), Eileen Cotter 1926–2007, William Frederick Cotter 1928–2002 (served in the Royal Navy) and Maurice Donald Cotter 1933–37.
- Bernard Alfred Cotter (1890–1914) lived at Sandgate, Kent. He enlisted as a private in The Rifle Brigade (2664) on 7th February 1908 at Canterbury and trained at Winchester. He transferred to The Buffs (East Kent Regiment) (L/8881) on 16th March 1908 to serve with his brother William in the 1st Battalion. He attended a Regimental Transport Duties course in February 1912 and committed a string of military offences, mainly drunkenness, in Aldershot and Dublin, for which he was

confined to barracks for various periods and also fined on occasions up to 7/6. He was assessed in September 1913 as being slovenly, irregular and addicted to drink, but hard working. Bernard was admitted to hospital in Dublin in May 1913 for a serious contusion to the right arm, having been struck by the wheel of a wagon at Fermoy. He went to France on 17th September 1914 and died of wounds at Bois Grenier on 19th October. He is commemorated on the Ploegsteert Memorial, Belgium.
- Maurice George Cotter (born 1892 as Morris) was a labourer in 1911. He served in the Royal Navy as a Stoker 1st Class.

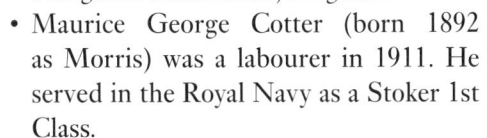

Barton Cottage, one time home of the Cotter family, in March 1893, following a massive landslide in the area (Folkestone Herald).

- Alfred Lloyd Cotter born and died in 1896 (twin with Ellen).
- Ellen 'Nelly' Kathleen Cotter (born 1896), a twin with Alfred, married Pierson GW Le Cornu (c.1895–1963) in 1917. He was born at St Peter, Jersey. They had a daughter, Kathleen Y Le Cornu, in 1918.

One of William's uncles, Lance Corporal Alfred Richards, West Riding Regiment, was held prisoner in Germany. Three of his cousins were killed in the war:

- K/17488 Stoker 1st Class Frederick Henry Holmes drowned when HMS *Pathfinder* was sunk by *U-21* off the east coast of Scotland on 5th September 1914; the first warship sunk by a submarine launched torpedo. *Pathfinder* was commanded by Francis Martin-Leake, brother of the first double VC. Frederick is commemorated on the Chatham Naval Memorial.
- G/793 Private Herbert Horace Holmes, 6th Buffs, was killed on 13th October 1915 and is commemorated on the Loos Memorial.
- 6837 Bandsman William Richards, 2nd Suffolks, died of wounds on 6th September 1915 and is buried in Lijssenthoek Military Cemetery, Poperinghe, Belgium (III B 31).

William was educated at Folkestone Roman Catholic School (now Stella Maris Catholic Primary School). He had a variety of jobs, including in the building trade, selling newspapers and as a steward on a Union Castle liner.

William enlisted in the Militia on 23rd August 1901 and transferred to Regular service in the Buffs on 11th October 1901, giving his mother as his next-of-kin. On 23rd November, walking along Military Road, Canterbury with three companions

HMS *Pathfinder* has the dubious honour of being the first warship sunk by a submarine launched torpedo on 5th September 1914. One of the dead was William Cotter's cousin, Frederick Henry Holmes. *Pathfinder's* Captain, Francis Martin-Leake, survived. He was the brother of Arthur Martin-Leake, the first VC and Bar.

he was pushed violently by a civilian. William pushed back and the civilian threw a bottle, injuring Cotter on the right forearm. A Court of Inquiry at Station Hospital, Canterbury convened on 13th December, concluded that the injury was not likely to affect his efficiency as a soldier. He was admitted to hospital at Shorncliffe with conjunctivitis 15th–22nd April. He was admonished for being absent from duty and drunk on 12th May 1902. William joined the 1st Battalion in India and served there 15th October 1902–13th October 1903. Appointed unpaid lance corporal 8th August. Reprimanded, having been absent from a butchery examination on 15th September. He served with the Battalion in Aden from 14th October. He extended his service to complete eight years on 9th April 1904, but reverted to private for an irregularity while on canteen duty at Crater, Aden on 13th May. Admitted to hospital in Aden with ague 16th–21st April. The Battalion returned to Britain on 9th December and was based at Dover.

On the night of 28th October 1905, William was in the 'Lion' public house in Dover with some of his comrades when he was accosted by some drunken civilians. He ignored their taunts, but was knocked to the ground and as he got up a glass was thrown, striking him in the left eye. He was admitted to Dover Military Hospital next day and the eye was removed surgically. A Court of Inquiry convened at Dover on 6th November found he was not to blame for the incident. He was confined to barracks for five days on 31st March 1906 for being drunk at Lydd. Appointed unpaid lance corporal 14th May 1907. He extended his service to complete twelve years on 21st May 1908 and was promoted lance corporal on 22nd August, but reverted to private for misconduct on 15th May 1911. He was provided with an artificial eye on 10th May 1911. William extended his service to complete twenty-one years on 10th December 1912. He was confined to barracks for five days and fined 5/- on 31st October 1913 for being drunk in barracks. He transferred to the Reserve on 13th March 1914 from Fermoy and joined the Section D Reserve from 2nd April 1914. During his service he was granted or restored Good Conduct Pay on four occasions and these were forfeited on three occasions.

William worked for Sandgate Council as a labourer until he was recalled to the 1st Battalion on 5th August 1914 and went to France on 7th September. He reported sick with myopia on 16th January 1915 and was treated at 16 Field Ambulance. He was transferred to No.2 Casualty Clearing Station at Bailleul on 18th January and No.5 General Hospital at Rouen next day until moved to 6th Infantry Base Depot on 23rd January. The strain on his good eye caused him to be sent back to England on 29th May for an operation, followed by garrison duties in Dover. He joined the 6th Battalion in France on 20th October and was promoted lance corporal on 14th November. He distinguished himself on several occasions as a bayonet fighter and in December was recommended for the Distinguished Conduct Medal, but did not receive it. Appointed acting corporal 12th February 1916.

Awarded the VC for his actions at the Hohenzollern Redoubt, near Loos, France on 6th March 1916, LG 30th March 1916. He was taken to a Casualty Clearing Station at Lillers, where he suffered a severe haemorrhage and was so dangerously ill that the doctors felt it unwise to administer an anaesthetic. His gangrenous leg was amputated through the knee while he was unconscious. He was visited by the Corps Commander, Lieutenant General Hubert Gough, to be

Military Road, Canterbury (Canterbury Collection).

Shorncliffe.

The Crater district of Aden in 1903 (JM Coutinho).

There were at least five pubs in Dover with 'Lion' in their title at this time (Golden Lion, Red Lion etc), but the 'Lion' in Dover's Elizabeth Street in the Western Docks area seems the most likely scene of the fracas in October 1905 in which William Cotter lost an eye. Dover Castle's ramparts are in the background.

The Military Hospital in Dover, below the western heights (Dover Museum).

Sandgate War Memorial.

Grand Shaft was one of a number of barracks in Dover at that time. It has since been demolished. Note the profusion of pubs along the harbour front to service thirsty sailors and soldiers.

told he had been recommended for the VC. William lapsed into unconsciousness and died at 8 p.m. on 14th March 1916. He is buried in Lillers Communal Cemetery (IV E 45).

As William never married, the VC was presented to his parents by the King at Buckingham Palace on 29th November 1916. In addition to the VC, he was awarded the 1914–15 Star, British War Medal 1914–20 and Victory Medal 1914–19. The VC was held for some time by the Buffs Museum. In July 2003, the Trustees of the Buffs Regimental Museum Trust donated the entire Buffs Museum Collection to the National Army Museum. Included were three VCs, including William Cotter's, which is now displayed at the National Army Museum, Royal Hospital Road, Chelsea. William is also commemorated on:

Biographies 257

A floral tribute at the Leas, Folkestone, to mark the 100th anniversary of the inauguration of the VC in 1956. Five Buffs VCs are commemorated – Frederick Maude, John Connors, James Smith, Anders Lassen (later Commandos and SAS) and William Cotter.

William Cotter's grave in Lillers Communal Cemetery.

- A plaque at the entrance to Chichester Memorial Hall, High Street, Sandgate, Kent unveiled by Colonel FGA Wiehe on 5th May 1917.
- The Sandgate War Memorial, unveiled on 11th May 1921 by the Countess of Rocksavage.
- A memorial plaque at Stella Maris Roman Catholic School, Folkestone.

91608 CORPORAL JAMES LENNOX DAWSON
187th (Special) Company, Royal Engineers

James Dawson was born at 1 Hill Street, Tillicoultry, Clackmannanshire, Scotland on 25th December 1891. His father was John Dawson (born 1861), a mechanic of 16 Preston Street, Glasgow, Lanarkshire. His mother, Janet née Lennox (born 1864), was a warper originally from Alva, Clackmannanshire. John and Janet were married on 15th March 1889 at her home at 29 Ochil Street, Tillicoultry, Clackmannanshire. By 1891 the family was living at Greig's Block, Hill Street, Tillicoultry and in 1911 were at 11 Kellie Place, Alloa. James had three brothers:

- John Dawson born 26th January 1890, was an assistant chemist in 1911.
- William George Lennox Dawson born 13th October 1894, was a law clerk in 1911. He joined the Royal Navy (JS4719) on 14th June 1916, giving his occupation as wireless student, and trained at Devonport at the shore establishment, HMS *Vivid I*. Having served on the pre-Dreadnought battleship HMS *Caesar* for five weeks, he returned to HMS *Vivid I* and was discharged due to epilepsy on 7th March 1917. He emigrated to Australia aboard SS *Osterley* (HMAT *Osterley* during the war), leaving London on 24th November 1928 for Freemantle. He was a farmer in 1931 at Robinson, Kalgan River, Forrest, Albany, Western Australia. By 1936 he was a cleaner at the White Star Hotel in Forrest, a porter at the People's Palace, Perth in 1943 and a cleaner, living at 119 Murray Street, Perth, 1949–58.
- Peter McLaren Dawson (24th April 1898–1970).

James was educated at Sunnyside Primary School Alloa, Alloa Academy (also attended by John Crawford Buchan VC) and the Royal Technical College Glasgow (now University of Strathclyde). He was a member of the Alloa YMCA. James enrolled at the University of Glasgow in 1909 to read Mathematics and Physics and passed the First Year examinations, but experienced difficulties later and left in 1913 after several unsuccessful resits. In 1911 he was a boarder at 28 West End Park Street, Glasgow as a student teacher. He was employed as a science teacher at Abraham Hill's Trust School, Govan and retook his Chemistry degree examination in 1914, but was unsuccessful again.

James enlisted in 5th Cameronians on 28th November 1914 (7793) and trained with 2/5th Battalion until he went to France on 11th March 1915 to serve with 1/5th Battalion. He was promoted

The Royal Technical College Glasgow, attended by James Dawson and John Crawford Buchan VC (Glasgow City Council).

Alloa Academy.

Kellie Place, Alloa, where James Dawson's family was living in 1911.

corporal, but against his will was transferred to the Special Brigade Royal Engineers on 19th July as a sergeant.

Awarded the VC for his actions at the Hohenzollern Redoubt, near Loos, France on 13th October 1915, LG 7th December 1915. His second cousin, Corporal JD Pollock, won the VC in the Hohenzollern Redoubt a few weeks previously on 27th September 1915. James was promoted WO2 (Company Sergeant Major) on 7th November. The VC was presented by the King at Buckingham Palace on 15th December. James left France on 29th January 1916 and was commissioned on 27th February. He returned to France and was wounded in the hand prior to the Somme offensive on 27th June. Posted to London District Anti-Gas School in November and was appointed acting captain while officer in charge from 26th April 1917. Posted as officer in charge No.2 Anti-Gas School, Humber Garrison in July and appointed temporary lieutenant on 27th August. On 9th October he was appointed to the British Military Mission to the USA. Temporary major graded Instructor (Class EE) 14th November 1917–4th September 1918 in charge of Camp Training Group. Returned to France on 13th July and to England 4th September. Appointed officer in charge of troops at HM Factory, Ellesmere Port, Cheshire in November. James was demobilised on 1st February 1919 and appears in the Army List until June 1920.

On 4th October 1919, James was presented with a gold watch by Magistrate Bailie Boyle at Partick Police Court. The watch had been purchased at auction at a special constables' concert in Partick for £42 by Sir Thomas Dunlop GBE, Lord Provost of Glasgow, who stipulated it should be presented to the first Partick man to gain the VC. On handing the watch to James Dawson, Magistrate Boyle explained that although Dawson was not a native of Partick he was an esteemed citizen prior to enlistment when he taught at Govan.

James Dawson married Margaret Maxwell née Nicoll on 8th October 1917. She was born on 29th July 1890 at 6 Cumberland Street, Glasgow and died at Eastbourne, Sussex in 1968. They did not have any children. He returned to Glasgow University in the summer of 1919 and passed the Chemistry Laboratory class in October, but fell short of the range of

Abraham Hill's Trust School, Govan (Glasgow City Council).

James Dawson being welcomed back to Abraham Hill's Trust School, Govan.

University of Glasgow (T & R Annan).

subjects required for a BSc degree. He appealed to the University's Clerk of Senate on 17th February 1920 to be awarded a BSc in Pure Science under war service regulations, avoiding the need to sit the outstanding examinations. He was awarded a special pass in Geography and graduated BSc on 23rd June 1920.

James was commissioned as a probationary lieutenant in the Army Educational Corps on 11th December 1920, with seniority from 15th June 1920 (confirmed in rank and seniority 1st July 1921). He was a Temporary Instructor (Class FF) at the School of Education, Newmarket, 19th November 1920–31st March 1921. Promoted Captain 1st April 1921. He transferred to the Indian Army on 30th May 1921 with seniority as lieutenant from 7th October 1919. Appointed Staff Captain 1st October 1924 and was District Education Officer, Peshawar in the Indian Army List of January 1925. His next appointment was Instructor (Class B) at the Army School of Education (British Wing), Belgaum, India 20th March 1926–9th June 1929. The following day he was employed in the Indian Army Ordnance Corps on probation at Kirkee and transferred to the IAOC on 30th May 1931 with seniority as lieutenant from 7th October 1919 and as captain from 1st October 1924.

His first appointment in the IAOC was Staff Captain, Directorate of Ordnance Services India, Provision Section 31st January 1933–1st January 1936, followed by Deputy Assistant Director of Ordnance Services, HQ India 2nd January 1936–23rd April 1937. Promoted major 1st October 1936 and attended the Staff College at Quetta in 1938. He was appointed Assistant Director Ordnance Services, HQ India 17th October 1940 to 31st July 1941 as acting lieutenant colonel 17th

Peshawar in the 1920s.

October 1940–17th January 1941, when he was appointed temporary lieutenant colonel until 30th September 1943. James was a Vehicle Liaison Officer with the India Supply Commission in North America 1st August 1941–1946. During this time he was local colonel 5th October 1942, acting colonel 1st April–30th September 1943, War substantive lieutenant colonel and temporary colonel 1st October 1943 and lieutenant colonel 1st October 1944. He transferred from the Indian Army to the Special List (14040), but remained in India for some time after independence in 1947 to assist the Indian Army. On retirement on 26th March 1948, he was granted the rank of honorary colonel.

James Dawson died at his home at 9 Hartfield Road, Eastbourne, Sussex on 15th February 1967. He was cremated at Eastbourne Crematorium and his ashes were scattered in the Garden of Remembrance (Section AL–4).

In addition to the VC, he was awarded 1914–15 Star, British War Medal 1914–20, Victory Medal 1914–19, Defence Medal 1939–45, War Medal 1939–45, George V Jubilee Medal 1935, George VI Coronation Medal 1937 and Elizabeth II Coronation Medal 1953. The VC is held by the Hunterian Library, Glasgow University.

Indian Army Staff College at Quetta, now in Pakistan.

James Dawson with his wife in the 1960s.

LIEUTENANT COLONEL ANGUS FALCONER DOUGLAS-HAMILTON
6th Battalion, The Queen's Own Cameron Highlanders

Angus Douglas-Hamilton was reputedly born at Brighton, Sussex on 20th August 1863. However, in the 1881 Census he and his siblings were recorded as being born in India and no trace of his birth could be found in the England and Wales records. The family surname was changed to Douglas-Hamilton on 23rd November 1875. His father was Major General Octavius Douglas-Hamilton (1821–1904). He was commissioned on 24th January 1839 in 2nd Bengal European Cavalry. Promoted lieutenant 23rd September 1841, captain 20th December 1851, major 19th January 1858, lieutenant colonel Bengal Staff Corps 21st April 1863 and colonel 24th January 1870. He retired on 1st August 1875 and was granted the honorary rank of major general from 23rd October 1875. By 1881 the family was living at 'Nottimar', Ellerdale Road, Hampstead and in 1891 at 46 Marylands Road, Paddington, London. Angus' mother was Katherine Augusta Westenra née MacLeod (1823–1902). Octavius and Katherine married on 29th June 1852 at Charlton Parish Church, Kent. She was living with her children at 12 Marine Square, Brighton, Sussex in 1861. Angus had six siblings:

* Hamilton Anne Douglas-Hamilton (1853–1929) was a double Blue for cricket and rugby at Trinity College, Cambridge, where he was chiefly responsible for arranging the first rugby match between Oxford and Cambridge (Varsity Match) in 1872; Oxford won. He was ordained by the Bishop of Salisbury in 1876 and held a variety of appointments: Vicar of East Witton Within, Yorkshire 1878; Vicar of Winslow, Buckinghamshire 1882; Vicar of Latimer, Buckinghamshire and Chaplain to Lord Chesham; Vicar of Holy Trinity, Halifax; Vicar of Charlton, Kent: Archdeacon of Kimberley, South Africa 1902; Canon of Bloemfontein Cathedral; Vicar in Pretoria; Domestic Chaplain to Lord Cadogan at Culford 1907; Vicar of All Saints', Newmarket 1910; Rector of St Mary-le-Tower, Ipswich 1915; Honorary Canon of St Edmundsbury; Honorary Chaplain to the Bishop of St Edmundsbury 1924; Rector of Marlesford, Suffolk 1925; Honorary Secretary for the Society for the Propagation of the Gospel. He married Lillie née Bowles (c.1856–1918) in 1875 at Geneva, Switzerland and Hon Agnes Rosamund Hanbury-Bateman in 1922. With Lillie he had four children:

- Basil Sholto Anne Douglas-Hamilton (1876–1920) was commissioned in the Army Service Corps 1st April 1901 and served during the Boer War.
- Ilta Douglas-Hamilton (1879–1957) married Captain Henry Laing Russell Watt (1874–1940), 10th Seaforth Highlanders, in 1915.
- Mary Hamilton Douglas-Hamilton (1885–1977) married Major Christopher Martin Ingoldby RAMC (1887–1927) in 1915. He was commissioned as a lieutenant 26th January 1912 and served in Mesopotamia 3rd June 1916–3rd June 1918 and Persia and Persian Gulf 4th June 1918–13th April 1919 (MID, LG 12th March 1918). He was acting lieutenant colonel 4th December 1919–19th March 1921 while serving in Waziristan (MID 1st June 1923). Promoted major 26th January 1924 and was employed under the Colonial Office in the Gold Coast from 8th October 1924, where he died on 26th June 1927.
- James Angus Douglas-Hamilton (born 1890) served as a commander in the Royal Navy in both World Wars. He married Joan Mary née MacCormack in 1938, daughter of Surgeon-Lieutenant JSD MacCormack RN.

- Augustus Maynard Douglas-Hamilton (1854–1928) served as a captain in 4th Battalion (Militia), East Surrey Regiment. He married Frances Wilhelmina née Cloete (c.1864–1938) in 1909.
- Charles Reginald Sydney Douglas-Hamilton (1856–1935) (known as Sydney) was commissioned in 6th Dragoon Guards (Carabiniers) on 5th September 1877 from the Militia. Promoted lieutenant 5th October 1878 and captain 4th December 1886. He transferred to the Gordon Highlanders on 13th April 1887 and was Adjutant Volunteers 1st November 1890–31st October 1895. He retired from 2nd Gordon Highlanders 17th February 1897. Charles married Mary Isabel Hammond née Whitla (1860–1948) in 1890.
- Camilla Alexandrina Lucy Douglas-Hamilton (1859–1906).
- Katherine Seymour Douglas-Hamilton (c.1860–1944).
- Basil Sholto Douglas-Hamilton (born 1866).

Angus' paternal grandfather, Augustus Barrington Price Anne Powell Hamilton (1781–1849), served as a lieutenant in the Royal Navy. Amongst Angus' uncles and aunts were:

- Charles Henry Douglas-Hamilton (1808–73) served as a captain in the Royal Navy. He married three times.
- Douglas Ryves Douglas-Hamilton (1814–94) served as a captain in the Royal Lanarkshire Militia.
- Frederic Douglas-Hamilton (1815–87) was Attaché at Buenos Ayres 1834, Rio de Janeiro 1836 with Mr Hamilton Hamilton's special mission, Montevideo 1852 as Secretary to Sir Henry Ellis's mission, Secretary of Legation at Stuttgart as Chargé d'Affaires to the Germanic Confederation 1853, Secretary of Legation

to Stockholm 1862, accredited to the Central American Republic as Chargé d'Affaires and Consul-General Quito 1867, Minister Resident and Consul-General to Ecuador 1872.
* Adolphus Douglas-Hamilton (1816–93) was a clergyman who married Henrietta Charlotte Carew (c.1823–1901) in 1847, daughter of Admiral Sir Benjamin Hallowell-Carew GCB.
* Alexandrina Idonia Charlotte Susan Douglas-Hamilton (1824–95) married Lieutenant Robert Peel (born 1828), 13th (Prince Albert's) Light Infantry in 1851. He served in the Crimea from 10th June 1855 and was present at the Battle of the Tchernaya and the siege and fall of Sebastopol. He also served during the Indian Mutiny, commanding the Rear Guard in the retreat from Jugdispore and was in action at Bootwul and Toolsepore.

Angus' maternal grandfather was Captain Donald MacLeod CB RN (c.1802–93).

Angus was educated at Foster's Naval Preparatory School, privately by army tutors and at the Royal Military College Sandhurst. He was commissioned in the Dorsetshire Regiment on 23rd August 1884 and was promoted lieutenant in the Cameron Highlanders 15th November 1884. Angus was involved in the latter part of the Sudan Expedition 1885 and was in the Sudan Frontier Field Force 1885–6. Promoted captain 7th December 1892 and appointed Adjutant 6th Gordon Highlanders 1st February 1894–30th April 1899.

Angus married Anna Watson née Mackenzie (1866–1945) on 1st August 1894. His brother Hamilton was the officiating minister at the wedding. Angus and Anna had a daughter, Camilla Beatrice, born on 9th August 1895. Anna's father was Captain Alexander Watson Mackenzie (1827–99), 8th Mackenzie of Ord, Ross & Cromarty, who served in 91st Highlanders 1848–54. Her brother, Alexander Francis Mackenzie (1861–1935), was commissioned in 76th Foot on 22nd January 1881, transferred to 93rd Foot on 19th February 1881, lieutenant 1st July 1881, acting captain with 1st Ross Highland Volunteer Battalion at Dingwall 6th June 1888, captain 31st March 1890, returned to 2nd Battalion 31st January 1890, Adjutant Militia 23rd February 1898–22nd February 1903, Deputy Lieutenant Ross and Cromarty 18th October 1898, major 3rd July 1901; awarded MVO. He transferred to the Reserve of Officers on retired pay as a lieutenant colonel on 12th August 1911. He served during the Great War on the strength of 3rd Reserve Battalion, Seaforth Highlanders, as a lieutenant colonel commanding 10th Argyll & Sutherland Highlanders from 12th August 1914; CMG 1st January 1916 (LG 14th January 1916). Brevet colonel

British troops in Sudan, 1885.

Gibraltar in 1900.

Special Reserves and lieutenant colonel 16th February 1920. Vice Lieutenant Ross and Cromarty 2nd July 1930. He married Olive Jane L née Holdsworth in 1898.

Angus' military career continued with his appointment as Acting DAAG in Gibraltar 1900 and then service with 2nd Cameron Highlanders in Gibraltar, Malta, South Africa, North China and India. Promoted major 9th March 1901 and retired on 24th August 1912. He was recalled from the Reserve of Officers as Railway Transport Officer in Southampton 5th August 1914. Appointed temporary lieutenant colonel and CO 6th Cameron Highlanders 1st October 1914 and went to France in July 1915. **Awarded the VC for his actions at Loos, France on 25th/26th September 1915, LG 18th November 1915.** He was killed during his VC action and is commemorated on the Loos Memorial. In January 2013 it was reported that his remains had been identified, possibly from his whistle. However, the MoD confirmed the story was incorrect and he would continue to be commemorated on the Loos Memorial.

His VC was originally sent to his widow by post in January 1916, but was later presented formally by the King at Buckingham Palace on 29th November 1916. She settled in Ord, Forest Hill, Muir of Ord, Ross-shire. She was presented with a bronze statue of a Cameron Highlander by former 1914–18 prisoners of war in appreciation of her work on their behalf.

In addition to the VC, he was awarded the Egypt Medal 1882–1889 with clasp 'The Nile 1884–85', 1914–15 Star, British War Medal 1914–20, Victory Medal 1914–19 and Khedive's Star 1884–6 (Egypt). The medals were left by his widow to her only daughter for the duration of her lifetime. In April 1965, the medal group and his death plaque were presented to the Queen's Own Highlanders' Museum, Fort George, Inverness-shire, which is now the Highlanders' Museum.

Angus' mother-in-law's sister, Ellen Georgiana Babington Peile, married Charles Theophilus Metcalfe, whose mother was Felicité Anne Browne, sister of Samuel James Browne VC.

S/107 CORPORAL ALFRED GEORGE DRAKE
8th Battalion, The Rifle Brigade (The Prince Consort's Own)

Alfred Drake was born at Copley Street, Stepney, London on 10th December 1893 and was baptised on 18th December 1898 at St Dunstan's, Stepney. His father was Robert Drake (1864–1927), a rope maker in 1881, lodging at Tower Hamlets, Mile End Old Town, London. In 1890 he was lodging at 12 Ernest Street, Stepney. By 1891 he was a plasterer's labourer and in 1898 a dock labourer. His mother was Mary Ann née Potter (1864–1940). Alfred and Mary married on 1st June 1890 at St Simon Zelotes, Bethnal Green, London. The family was living at 3 Trafalgar Square, Mile End Old Town in 1891 and 42 Bale Street, Mile End Old Town In 1898. Alfred had three sisters (two other children did not survive infancy):

- Lilian 'Lily' Drake (born 28th October 1892) was a tailoress in 1911. She married Samuel McAdams (1894–1981) in 1920 at St Thomas, Stepney. She was living at 62 Copley Street, Stepney at the time. He was living at No.64 and was a dock labourer. They had two children – Iris L McAdams 1922 and Alfred S McAdams 1927.
- Ellen Louisa Drake (18th November 1898–1959). She is understood to have married Joseph Fox (born 1898) in 1920 at Fulham. They had three children – Ellen M Fox 1923, William J Fox 1929 and Christopher EB Fox 1935.
- Caroline Drake (born 1901) is understood to have married William G Tanner in 1924 at Islington.

Two of Alfred's uncles served in the Royal Navy:

- William Henry Drake (1843–87) was a sailor in 1861. He married Mary Matilda Ticehurst (1856–1931) in 1880 and had a daughter, Rose, in 1886.
- George Drake (born 11th May 1845) enlisted as a Boy 2nd Class on 14th May 1859, serving on HMS *Wellesley*, the receiving ship at Chatham. He continued his service for ten years' adult service from 11th May 1863 (17581A & 72958). He was described as 5' 5" tall, with dark hair, grey eyes and ruddy complexion.

St. Dunstan's Church, Stepney, where Alfred Drake was baptised.

Part of the Rifle Brigade Memorial in Winchester Cathedral. Alfred Drake's name is at the top of the left panel (Paul Goodwin).

Alfred Drake's headstone in La Brique Military Cemetery No.2.

He served on HMS *Adventure* from 1st January 1873 and HMS *Duke of Wellington* 29th May–2nd June 1873.

Alfred was educated at Ben Jonson London County Council School, Stepney before being employed as a messenger by the Port of London Authority. He enlisted on 3rd September 1914 and went to France on 20th May 1915.

Awarded the VC for his actions near La Brique, Belgium on 23rd November 1915, LG 22nd January 1916. He was killed during his VC action and is buried in La Brique Military Cemetery No.2 (I C 2). Alfred is also commemorated:

- At Ben Jonson School, Stepney, where a memorial was dedicated on 23rd April 1923 by FM the Earl of Cavan. Major GC Tryon MP, cousin of Lieutenant Tryon, whose life Drake had saved, attended (Grenadier Guards 1890–1916, Conservative MP for Brighton 1910–40, Privy Counsellor, Minister of Pensions 1922–29 and 1931–35, Postmaster General 1935–40, Baron Tryon 1940).
- On the Rifle Brigade Memorial, Winchester Cathedral, Hampshire.

Alfred never married and the VC was presented to his father by the King at Buckingham Palace on 16th November 1916. In addition to the VC, he was awarded the 1914–15 Star, British War Medal 1914–20 and Victory Medal 1914–19. The VC was purchased privately by Michael Ashcroft's VC Trust in 2001 and is part of the Lord Ashcroft VC Collection in the Imperial War Museum.

His cousin, Charles Frederick Potter (1896–1915), served as a private in 2nd Hampshire (16281). He was killed in action at Gallipoli on 13th August 1915 and is commemorated on the Helles Memorial.

18274 PRIVATE ROBERT ANDERSON DUNSIRE
13th Battalion, The Royal Scots (Lothian Regiment)

Robert Dunsire was born at East Wemyss, Buckhaven, Fife, Scotland on 26th November 1891. His father was Thomas Dunsire (1856–1934), a coal miner and by 1891 an underground coal manager. His first marriage was to Elizabeth née Lonie (c.1856–75) on 6th March 1874 at Donibristle Colliery, Aberdour, Fife. She died on 3rd January 1875. Robert's mother was Elizabeth Anderson née Warrender (1857–1932), a mill worker. Thomas and Elizabeth married on 10th January 1876 at Buckhaven, Fife. They were living at Methilhill, Wemyss at the time. The family was living at 112 East End, Buckhaven in 1881, 95 Station Road, Buckhaven in 1891, 19 Overton Road, Dysart, Fife in 1901 and 84 Commercial Street, Kirckaldy in 1915. Robert had twelve siblings:

- Thomas Dunsire (1876–1960), a coal miner. He married Margaret Brodie in 1889 and had a son.
- Margaret Taylor Dunsire (1878–82).
- Alexander Warrender Dunsire (1880–82).
- Catherine 'Katie' Anderson Dunsire (1882–1959).
- Peter Dunsire (1884–85).
- Elizabeth 'Lizzie' Jemima Warrender Dunsire (1886–1927).
- Isabella 'Bella' Mitchell Dunsire (born 1887) married Alexander Hitchin in 1911.
- Grace Warrender Dunsire (1889–1971) married Lawrence Taylor Gibb (1887–1938) in 1908 and had a son.
- Margaret 'Maggie' Warrender Dunsire (born 1893).
- John Anderson Dunsire (1897–1980) married Mary Christie in 1919 and had two children.
- William Isaac Joy Dunsire (1900–54) married Jessie Crombie in 1921.
- Marshall Dunsire (1901–12).

Robert was educated at Pathhead Public School, Kirkcaldy and was then employed as a miner at Rannie Pit of the Dunnikier Colliery, Kirkcaldy and later at Rosie Pit, Buckhaven of the Wemyss Coal Company. He was a talented musician, playing solo cornet and violin with the Dunnikier Colliery Band. Robert married Catherine née Pitt (1895–1959) on 22nd July 1914. There were no children. They lived at 84 Commercial Road, Pathhead, Kirkaldy, before moving to 210 Denbeath, Methil (later Dee Street).

Pathhead, Kirkcaldy.

East Wemyss.

He enlisted on 6th January 1915 and was described as 5′ 5½″ tall, weighing 134 lbs. He went to France on 9th July. **Awarded the VC for his actions at Hill 70, Loos, France on 25th/26th September 1915, LG 18th November 1915.** He returned to Britain and received the Freedom of Kirkcaldy on 29th November. The VC was presented by the King at Buckingham Palace on 7th December. A song was composed in his honour by Mr F Slevin of the Balfe Music Company, Shaftesbury Avenue, London. Robert returned to France mid-January 1916 and went into the trenches at Hulluch with his unit on 23rd January. His leg was blown off when his dugout was hit by a trench mortar bomb on 29th January. He was taken to 46th Field Ambulance at Mazingarbe, but died of wounds a few hours later on 30th January. He is buried in Mazingarbe Communal Cemetery Extension (18).

Robert Dunsire's grave in Mazingarbe Communal Cemetery Extension.

In addition to the VC, Robert was awarded the 1914–15 Star, British War Medal 1914–20 and Victory Medal 1914–19. His VC is held by the Royal Scots Museum, Edinburgh Castle. Robert is commemorated in a number of other places in Fife.

- Dunsire Streets in Kirkaldy and Methil.
- War Memorials at Kirkaldy, Buckhaven, Methil and Innerleven.

His wife was awarded a pension of 10/- per week from 14th August 1916. She married Robert James Stewart on 24th September 1921 at Edinburgh, Midlothian and lived in Methilhill.

200476 SERGEANT JOHN MACLAREN ERSKINE
5th/6th Battalion, The Cameronians (Scottish Rifles)

John Erskine was born at 30 Bridge Street, Dunfermline, Fife, Scotland on 13th January 1894. His father was William Erskine (1850–1908), a master draper and senior partner in Messrs W & J McLaren & Co drapers of 26–30 Bridge Street, Dunfermline. William was an Elder/President of the United Free Church, Chalmers Street, Dunfermline. His mother, Elizabeth 'Bella' or 'Bessie' née Dick (1868–1953), was a teacher at Bathgate Academy, Dunfermline, living as a lodger at High Road, Cairneyhill, Carnock, Fife in 1891 before moving to Mill Cottage, Bathgate, West Lothian. William and Elizabeth married on 29th March 1893 at The Bath Hotel, Bath Street, Glasgow. They lived at Park Avenue, Dunfermline and at 32 Bridge Street, Dunfermline. She moved to 1 East Saville Road, Edinburgh and died there on 24th February 1953. John had six siblings:

- William McLaren Erskine (6th May 1895–18th November 1916) enlisted in the Highland Cyclist Battalion (1409) at Kirkcaldy, Fife. He transferred as a lance corporal to B Company, 16th Highland Light Infantry (43245) and went to France on 28th July 1916. He was killed in action on 18th November 1916 and is buried in New Munich Trench Cemetery, Beaumont-Hamel, France (F 3). He is also commemorated on the family grave at Cairneyhill and the Cairneyhill and Dunfermline War Memorials.

Bridge Street, Dunfermline.

Chalmers Street, Dunfermline, with the church half way up on the right.

Princes Street, Edinburgh.

Pettigrew & Stephens department store on Sauchiehall Street, Glasgow. The cupola was designed by Charles Rennie Mackintosh.

- Elizabeth 'Bessie' Tennant Erskine born 3rd December 1897.
- David Dick Erskine born 7th January 1902.
- Gilmour Erskine born 30th July 1903.
- Stewart Erskine born 18th January 1906.
- Harold Erskine born 25th June 1908.

John was educated at Dunfermerline High School. Following an apprenticeship with Messrs Robert Maule & Son of Princes Street, Edinburgh, he was employed as a draper with Messrs Pettigrew & Stephens of Glasgow. His father intended he would eventually take over his position at Messrs W & J McLaren & Co.

Private Thomas Hughes, Connaught Rangers, receives his VC from the King during the investiture in Hyde Park on 2nd June 1917. John Erskine's mother was also there to receive her son's VC (Bridgeman Art Library).

Robert Maule's department store in Edinburgh (Yerbury).

John enlisted on 10th August 1914 (original number 7064) and carried out basic training at Glasgow, Falkirk and Larbert. He was stationed at Broughty Ferry, near Dundee, Angus in September and sailed with the Battalion from Southampton for France, arriving at Le Havre on 5th November. Promoted lance corporal, corporal and appointed acting sergeant. **Awarded the VC for his actions at Givenchy, France on 22nd June 1916, LG 5th August 1916.** Promoted sergeant July 1916 and was wounded in action on the Somme in the same month. He was posted to Fourth Army School of Instruction before returning to active duty. John was decorated with the VC ribbon by GOC 33rd Division, Major General RJ Pinney at Bellancourt, France on 1st January 1917. He was killed in action near Fontaine-les-Croisilles, Arras, France on 14th April 1917 and is commemorated on the Arras Memorial. He is also commemorated in a number of other places:

- Dunfermline High School Roll of Honour.
- War Memorials at Dunfermline and Cairneyhill.
- On the family grave at Cairneyhill.
- The 'J Erskine VC Memorial Award', conferred annually by Dunfermline High School for excellence in the arts and sciences; the prize includes the 'Erskine Memorial Medal'.

As he never married, the VC was presented to his mother by the King at Hyde Park, London on 2nd June 1917. In addition to the VC, he was awarded the 1914 Star with 'Mons' clasp, British War Medal 1914–20 and Victory Medal 1914–19. His sister and brothers presented the VC to the Cameronians in June 1965. It is held by the Cameronians Museum, Hamilton. A number of commemorative presentations were made to his mother:

- An illuminated address and gold watch and chain by the people of Dunfermline.
- A silver rose by the staff and pupils of Dunfermline High School.
- A bound Bible by the Chalmers Street Congregation.
- A silver cup by his former employer, Messrs Pettigrew & Stephens of Glasgow.

1780 LANCE CORPORAL DAVID FINLAY
2nd Battalion, The Black Watch (Royal Highlanders)

David Finlay was born at Guardbridge, Leuchars, Fife on 29th January 1893. His surname has been seen as Findlay. His father was George Finlay (1869–1956), a shepherd working for George Dun at Woodmill, Falkland, Fife and living at Todhall, Dairsie in 1892. His mother was Susan née Small (1871–1939), a paper mill worker. George and Susan married on 25th November 1892 at Guardbridge, Leuchars. By

1901 the family was living at Threefords Farmhouse, Cameron, East Fife and in 1915 at Letham, Glenfarg. David had ten siblings:

- James Small Finlay (1895–1984) married Jessie McLean.
- Susan Finlay (1896–1968) married David Oliphant.
- George Finlay (c.1897–98).
- John Finlay (born 1899) married twice, the second time to Orient McDonald Wylie.
- William Finlay (1900–76) married twice, the second time to Mary Valentine.
- Elizabeth Small Finlay (1901–84) married Harold Wallace.
- Georgina Finlay (1903–89) married James Millar.
- Helen Finlay (born 1905) married James Forbes (1904–82) and had two children.
- Albert Finlay (born 1908).
- Annie Finlay (born 1913).

As a shepherd, his father moved frequently and consequently David attended a number of schools. It is known he attended Forgan, Gauldry and Balmullo Schools and possibly Glenfarg School as well as a number of others before he left aged fourteen. He was then employed as a ploughman.

On 5th February 1910, David enlisted in the Black Watch, giving his age as eighteen years and one month. He served in Britain for two years and then went to India with the 2nd Battalion. The Battalion departed Karachi and arrived at Marseilles on 12th October 1914. **Awarded the VC for his actions near Rue du Bois, France on 9th May 1915, LG 29th June 1915.** David was promoted corporal on 23rd May and sergeant on 27th June.

David Finlay married Christina née Cunningham (c.1894–1967) on 27th July 1915 at 34 Crossgate, Cupar, Fife by declaration. They had no children. The VC was presented by the King at Windsor Castle on 30th July. The 2nd Battalion arrived at Basra, Mesopotamia on 31st December. It was involved in the First Attack on Hanna during the fighting to relieve Kut. On 20th January 1916, Sergeants Mitchell and Finlay found good positions and dug in about 300m from the Turkish line at Hanna. On the morning of the 21st, the Battalion launched a bayonet charge on the enemy after an artillery bombardment. David Finlay was killed during the attack, one of 163 casualties suffered by the 2nd Battalion. He has no known grave and is commemorated on the Basra Memorial, Iraq. He is also commemorated on the Leuchars Parish War Memorial.

Crossgate, Cupar.

This is understood to be David Finlay's medals being handed over to the Black Watch in 1967.

In addition to the VC, he was also awarded the 1914 Star with 'Mons' clasp, British War Medal 1914–20 and Victory Medal 1914–19. His family presented the medals to the Black Watch on 17th May 1967. They are held at The Black Watch Regimental Museum (The Royal Highland Regiment), Balhousie Castle, Hay Street, Perth.

On 26th March 1920, Christina Finlay married Peter Wilson (born 1885) and they lived at The Anchorage, St Abb's, Coldingham, Berwickshire. They had six children including: Robert Thorburn Wilson, born on 13th January 1921. He served in the Merchant Navy and died on 21st September 1941 when MV *Walmer Castle* was sunk by enemy aircraft while escorting a convoy from Gibraltar to Britain. Robert was one of fourteen crew lost, including the Captain, and is commemorated on the Tower Hill Memorial, London (Panel 116).

David Finlay was impersonated for forty-four years by a man who claimed he had won the VC in 1915, rose to the rank of colonel, served in the occupation of Germany and in India for seventeen years. In the Second World War he claimed he served in France until Dunkirk, after which he went to Australia in 1942 to set up a business. It was only when obituary notices were placed in newspapers that the VC & GC Association investigated and discovered the imposter, albeit too late for any action to be taken against him.

24066 LANCE CORPORAL FRED FISHER
13th Battalion (Royal Highlanders of Canada), Canadian Expeditionary Force

Fred Fisher was born at Church Street, St Catherine's, Ontario, Canada on 3rd August 1894 (1895 on his attestation paper). His father, William Henry Fisher (born c.1860–64), a bank clerk from Pitlochry, Perthshire, Scotland, emigrated to Canada where he was an accountant for the Canadian Bank of Commerce and later manager of Sovereign Bank, Niagara-on-the-Lake, Ontario. His mother was Alice S Fisher née McGibbon (c.1866/69–1946). The family lived at 197 Church Street, St Catherine's before moving to Dunnville, Ontario by the time of the March 1901 Census. They were living at Niagara-on-the-Lake by 1904 and moved to Montreal, Quebec in October 1905. When Fred enlisted, his fathers address was 576 Lansdowne Avenue, Westmount, Quebec and he later moved to 1004 Dorchester Street, Montreal. Fred had three siblings:

- Donald Alexander Fisher (1889–1959) was a mechanic who served in 7th Field Battery CFA at St Catherine's for two years. He enlisted in 1st Canadian Motor Machine-Gun Brigade on 28th August 1914 (45560). He was described as 5'10" tall with medium complexion, dark grey eyes, dark brown hair and his religious denomination was Church of England. He was later commissioned into 60th Battalion (Victoria Rifles of Canada), CEF. Donald was wounded on 4th October 1916 and discharged unfit on 30th September 1917.
- William Henry Fisher (1892–1937) was a clerk when he enlisted in 2nd Highland Battery CFA on 14th November 1914. He was described as 5'9" tall with healthy complexion, light blue eyes, light brown hair and his religious denomination was Church of England. He served with Montreal Heavy Artillery/6th Siege Battery CGA and was awarded the MC for forward reconnaissance work on 27th September 1918 during operations leading to the capture of Cambrai – he went forward with the infantry under heavy machine-gun fire to select battery positions east of the Canal du Nord. A few days later he went forward into Sancourt, Blécourt, Raillencourt and St Olle under fire and brought back valuable information (LG 9th December 1919). Discharged unfit 6th May 1919.
- Alice Mary Fisher (born 1898) married Lieutenant Colonel George Ross Robertson (1892–1939). He served in the infantry in the First World War and was awarded the MC as a captain (LG 1st January 1917) and VD.

Fred's paternal grandfather, Donald Fisher (1825–1908), served as an officer in the Black Watch. He later farmed shorthorn cattle and was also a hotel-keeper, acquiring Fisher's Hotel in Pitlochry around 1853, which still exists. Robert Louis Stevenson and his wife lived at the hotel until Kinnaird Cottage was prepared for them in the summer of 1881. William Gladstone also stayed there in 1864 and 1887. Donald later moved to the Royal Hotel, Pitlochry and extended his farm to 710 acres.

Fred's maternal grandfather, Alexander McGibbon (1829–1904), spent his early years on the family farm until employed by Neil McIntosh, a Montreal merchant.

In 1856, Alexander opened his own business selling tea, coffee, wines, liquors and choice groceries. He became President of the St Andrew's and Caledonian Societies, governor of Montreal General Hospital and House of Refuge, a member of the City Council 1863–66 and a supporter of the Conservative party. In the spring of 1885, the North-West Rebellion broke out and he was appointed quartermaster general and chief transport officer to the forces under Major General Thomas Bland Strange. Based at Calgary, he distributed supplies to the Alberta Field Force. In the aftermath, the Department of Indian Affairs was expanded to prevent further trouble and in May 1886 Alexander became a travelling inspector, overseeing the Department's agents in the North-West Territories. He was assigned to Qu'Appelle, covering what is now southern Saskatchewan. In 1902 he transferred to Calgary. He gained a reputation for reliability and attention to detail, but constantly travelling over rugged terrain in all weathers took its toll. In November 1903 his doctor ordered him to rest for two months and he went to Montreal to be with friends. He soon felt better and returned to Calgary, but on 24th February 1904 died of appendicitis. His obituary in the 'Calgary Herald' said that he was, … *a man of a kindly and generous disposition, who never lost a friend or made an enemy.*" Fred was educated at:

- Dunnville.
- Niagara Public School September 1900–1905 (now the Bran Cliff Inn).
- Westmount Academy, Montreal until June 1912 (later Westmount High School, attended by the singer-songwriter Leonard Cohen). Fred captained the football team in 1912, played in the senior hockey team and was editor of the Academy Bulletin.
- McGill University, Montreal from September 1912, where he studied Engineering and joined the Alpha Psi Chapter of the Zeta Psi Fraternity. He was a talented athlete, a member of the championship track team in 1914 and a reserve for the championship football team.

McGill University, Montreal.

Camp Valcartier.

SS *Alaunia* carried 13th Canadian Battalion from Gaspé Basin, eastern Quebec to Plymouth in October 1914. She was sunk by a mine off Hastings on 19th October 1916.

Fred joined the Montreal Amateur Athletic Association and was involved in tennis, swimming and shooting. He also spent two years in the Toronto Public Schools Battalion Cadet Corps. He abandoned his university studies and enlisted in 5th Regiment (Royal Highlanders of Canada) on 16th August 1914. He was described as 5′ 9½″ tall, weighed 142 lbs with fair complexion, hazel eyes, light brown hair and his religious denomination was Church of England. He trained at Bleury Street Armoury before being posted to 13th Battalion CEF at Camp Valcartier on 24th August, where he was attested on 23rd September.

On 25th September the 1st Canadian Contingent began moving to Quebec. The 13th Battalion embarked on SS *Alaunia* at Gaspé Basin, eastern Quebec, sailing on 3rd October and arriving at Plymouth on 14th October. The Battalion moved to Larkhill on Salisbury Plain, Wiltshire for further training. The weather that winter in Britain was atrocious, with double the usual rainfall, turning the ground into a sea of mud. Fred was promoted lance corporal on 22nd December and joined the Battalion Machine-Gun Section.

Gaspé Basin, from where the First Canadian Contingent sailed for Europe.

Canadian troops march past Stonehenge near Larkhill on Salisbury Plain.

With double the usual rainfall, the winter of 1914/15 was atrocious. Conditions for the Canadians, most living under canvas, were extremely demanding.

Fred and his brother visited the old family home near Dundee, Angus while on leave and are reputed to have dined with the officers of the Black Watch. This would have been an unusual honour for ordinary soldiers and an indication of the respect still held for their grandfather.

The Battalion embarked on SS *Novian* at Avonmouth on 11th February 1915, disembarking at St Nazaire on 14th February. The Canadians initially went to the Armentières area to gain experience in the trenches under instruction until the Division took over a section of the line on 3rd March near Fleurbaix. In mid-April it moved to the Ypres area in Belgium. On 9th April, Fred was admitted to No.2 Canadian Field Ambulance Rest Hospital with orchites (inflammation of the testes) and was discharged from No.10 Canadian Casualty Clearing Station on the 13th.

Awarded the VC for his actions at St Julien, Belgium 22nd–24th April 1915, LG 23rd June 1915. He was the first Canadian-born man to be awarded the VC while serving in the Canadian Army. The VC was sent to his parents by post on 5th August and was followed by a letter from King George V on 5th October. When his mother died in 1946, Fred's sister presented the VC to the Black Watch and it is held by the Canadian Black Watch Museum, Montreal. In addition to the

The Canadian Memorial Cross.

An early photograph of the Ypres (Menin Gate) Memorial to the Missing, where Fred Fisher is commemorated.

VC, Fred Fisher was awarded the 1914–15 Star, British War Medal 1914–20 and Victory Medal 1914–19. In July 1920 his mother received the Memorial Cross, a gift from Canada to the mothers or widows of all Canadian servicemen killed during the War.

Fred Fisher was killed during his VC action and was buried in the trench where he fell by Lieutenant JG Ross and others. The grave was subsequently lost and he is commemorated on the Ypres (Menin Gate) Memorial, Belgium. He is also commemorated in a number of other places:

St James the Apostle Church, St Catherine Street West, Montreal where Fred Fisher is commemorated on a memorial plaque.

- Book of Remembrance at the Peace Tower, Parliament Buildings, Ottawa.
- Memorial plaque at Memorial Park, St Paul Street West, St Catherine's, Ontario, dedicated on 28th June 1970.
- Plaque on the doors of St Catherine's City Hall.
- A street in St Catherine's is named after him.
- Memorial plaque at St James the Apostle Church, St Catherine Street West, Montreal.
- Life sized picture by George Horne Russell, gifted to Westmount High School by his mother. It was loaned to the Black Watch of Canada Museum in 2012 for a year and was subsequently transferred to the Museum permanently.
- Memorial plaque in the Museum of the Black Watch (Royal Highland Regiment) of Canada, Rue de Bleury, Montreal.
- Wooden plaque bearing fifty six maple leaves each inscribed with the name of a Canadian-born VC holder at the Canadian Forces College, Toronto.
- Painting by the Australian portrait painter George James Coates, held by the Canadian War Museum.
- McGill University Honour Roll and portrait at McGill Union dated 25th April 1916.
- A Victoria Cross obelisk to all Canadian VCs at Military Heritage Park, Barrie, Ontario dedicated by HRH The Princess Royal on 22nd October 2013.
- His VC action was featured in the *Victor* comic dated 27th March 1982.

Dr Michael Smith purchased a silver box in a charity shop in Ontario engraved, *'Victoria Rifles (V.R.A.) 1931 to Colonel Ross Robertson MC VD'* for CAN$600. It contained an unnamed MC, the British War and Victory Medals to Lieutenant RWS Robertson (Fred Fisher's nephew), British War Medal to Lieutenant Donald A Fisher and the 1914–15 Star and Victory Medal to Fred Fisher. In 2006, the VC was loaned to St Catherine's Museum for an exhibition. When negotiating the loan of Fred Fisher's 1914–15 Star and Victory Medal to the exhibition, Dr Smith indicated he might auction the medals (valued at more than CAN$20,000). They were offered to the Canadian Black Watch Museum, but the price was considered excessive and the sale did not take place. The location of his British War Medal is not known. However, other sources say that his British War Medal and Victory Medal are in a private collection and the 1914–1915 Star is missing.

Two cousins also served during the First World War:

- Gilbert Donald McGibbon (1885–1916) joined the 13th Battalion as a captain on 22nd September 1914 and became the Signals Officer. As a major he was killed on 20th April 1916 (Vlamertinghe Military Cemetery – I A 29).
- His brother, Roy Hosmer McGibbon (1886–1961), was a doctor serving with 1st Field Ambulance, Canadian Army Medical Corps. On 30th November 1939 he was appointed Deputy District Medical Officer for Military District 4 and on 31st August 1940 became District Medical Officer. He was promoted acting colonel on 20th November 1941 and colonel on 12th January 1943. Roy carried out a six-month tour of overseas duty and on 12th January 1946 became a serving brother of the Most Venerable Order of the Hospital of Saint John of Jerusalem. He was also made an Officer of the Order of the British Empire, LG 13th June 1946. During the Second World War his son, Lieutenant Robert L McGibbon, served with 2nd Battalion, The Leicestershire Regiment and became a PoW in Germany. Another son, Sub Lt Gordon McGibbon RCNVR, was an engineer officer serving with the Royal Navy.

2ND LIEUTENANT ALFRED JAMES TERENCE FLEMING-SANDES
2nd Battalion, The East Surrey Regiment

Alfred Fleming-Sandes was born as Northstead Road, Tulse Hill Park, London on 24th June 1894. He was known to his colleagues as 'Sandy'. His name is often seen as Arthur rather than Alfred. It is understood that this error started with the London Gazette entry for his VC on 18th November 1915. However, it was corrected to Alfred in the London Gazette a few days later on 26th November. His father, Alfred Francis Fleming Sandes (1870–98), was born at Rathfarnham, Dublin, Ireland. The hyphenated surname is a combination of his parent's surnames (father Sandes and mother Fleming) and was changed by deed poll. Alfred's mother was Grace Emily née Routh (1866–1931). Alfred and Grace were married on 29th March 1893 at St Augustine's, Honor Oak Park, London. The family lived at 38 Stockwell Road, Lambeth. Grace was living with her widowed mother at Heath Bank, Trinity Road, Wandsworth in 1881, at 1 Westhill Villas, Ryde, Isle of Wight in 1901, 34 Queen's Road, Beckenham, Kent in 1911 and later at 'Thornedene', South Eden Park Road, Beckenham. Alfred had a sister, Eileen Doris Fleming-Sandes (1896–74), who married John F Poole (c.1878–1961) in 1935.

Alfred was educated at Dulwich College Preparatory School and King's School Canterbury 1907–13, where he was a member of the Cadet Force; William John Vousden VC was a former pupil. He enlisted in 1/28th London Regiment (Artists' Rifles) (1482) on 5th August 1914 and went to France on 26th October. He was commissioned into 2nd East Surrey on 9th May 1915 while serving in France.

King's School Canterbury.

Awarded the VC for his actions at the Hohenzollern Redoubt, France on 29th September 1915, LG 18th November 1915. He was badly wounded in the VC action and spent a long time convalescing. The VC was presented by the King at Buckingham Palace on 15th January 1916. Alfred became an instructor with No.5 Officer Cadet Battalion at Trinity College, Cambridge and was then employed by the War Office. Promoted lieutenant 1st July 1917 and acting captain 14th November 1918–4th January 1919. He returned to France in October 1918 and was to be demobilized in January 1919, but insisted on serving on and worked at the War Office until he was discharged on 7th September 1919 (he appears in the Army List until November 1919).

Alfred was a master at Copthorne School, Sussex in 1919 before moving to the Sudan, where he joined the Education Department of the Sudanese Government. He was back in Britain for a time in 1922 as a guest at the wedding of Benjamin Handley Geary VC, as was George Roupell VC. He attended Gordon College in Khartoum to study law. He was seconded to the Political Service in 1924 and became Assistant

Cadets of No.5 Officer Cadet Battalion dining at Trinity College, Cambridge.

Gordon College, Khartoum.

District Commissioner at El Nahud. Appointed District Judge Sudan in 1926 and was called to the Bar (Gray's Inn) on 17th November 1927. He was District Judge Red Sea Province in 1929. Alfred became fluent in Arabic and conducted hearings in the vernacular to be fair to the accused and avoid misinterpretation. In 1932 he became a Provincial Judge. **Awarded the Order of the Nile 4th Class, LG 10th June 1932**. Much of his work at this time involved settling disputes over White Nile lands and registering titles in preparation for the opening of the Jebel Aulia Dam in 1937 (at the time the largest dam in the world).

All Saints' Church, Newchurch, Isle of Wight.

Alfred married Dorothea May née Weeks (born 1888) at All Saints' Church, Newchurch, Isle of Wight on 27th August 1932. She was the Matron of a large boarding school at Montreux, Switzerland. They did not have any children. Alfred became a Judge of the Sudan High Court in 1935, initially in Gezira Province and then in Khartoum. Occasionally he acted as Chief Justice. He was commissioned as a bimbashi (major) in the Sudan Auxiliary Defence Force on 23rd July 1941 and was Judge Advocate General, Sudan Defence Force 1942–44. Alfred was a Freemason (Khartoum Lodge No.2877 and Red Sea Lodge No.4570).

When he retired in 1944, he returned to Britain and became Chairman of the Pensions Appeal Tribunal of England and Wales 1945–58. He and Dorothea settled at 'Redway', Dawlish Road, Teignmouth, Devon. Alfred died unexpectedly at the White Horse Hotel, Romsey, Hampshire on 24th May 1961. He was cremated at Torquay Crematorium, Devon, where his ashes were scattered. He left £29,344/19/4 to his widow, £50 to the Colonel of the Regiment's Fund of The Queen's Royal Surrey Regiment, £50 to the Victoria Cross Association, £500 to the Old King's Scholars Bursarship Society, £250 to Dr Barnado's and £50 to the People's Dispensary for Sick Animals. During the Second World War, 2nd East Surrey had a Universal Carrier Mark II named 'Fleming Sandes'.

In addition to the VC and Order of the Nile, he was awarded the 1914 Star with 'Mons' clasp, British War Medal 1914–20, Victory Medal 1914–19, War Medal 1939–45, George VI Coronation Medal 1937 and Elizabeth II Coronation Medal 1953. His medals were stolen from his bungalow in Sudan, but the case in which they were kept was recovered still containing the VC. The thief evidently discarded it as being of no value. The other medals were replaced. Alfred left his medals to his wife for her lifetime. They were to be offered to the Queen's Royal Surrey Regiment (amalgamation of Queen's Royal West Surrey and East Surrey Regiments in 1959) after her death. The medals are held by the Surrey Infantry Museum, Clandon Park, Guildford and survived the fire that severely damaged the building on 30th April 2015 as they were held in a bank.

136414 SAPPER WILLIAM HACKETT
254th Tunnelling Company, Royal Engineers

William Hackett was born at Patriot Street, Sneinton, near Nottingham, on 11th June 1873. His father was John Hackett (c.1836–99) a bricklayer's labourer in 1881. He was a travelling brewer in 1900 and did good business with country inns. His mother was Harriet née Ward (1841–1913). John and Harriet's marriage was registered in the 3rd quarter of 1859 in Nottingham. The family was living at Speedwell Terrace, Staveley, Derbyshire in 1861. By 1871 it was at 16 Patriot Street, Nottingham and had moved to Sneinton, Nottingham by 1881. William had six siblings:

- Walter John Hackett (1860–1915) was a trimmer in hosiery in 1881. He was living with his mother and sister Ellen at 12 Finch Street, Nottingham in 1911, by which time he was a labourer.
- Harriet Hackett (1863–1917) was a lace clipper in 1881. She married Frederick William Leeming (1858–1939) in 1889. He was a framework knitter. They were living at 8 Villa Place, Nottingham in 1901 and 20 Alfred Street South, Nottingham in 1911, at which time he was a hosiery hand. Harriet and Frederick had five children – Clara Leeming 1893, who married William H Hunt in 1913 and had a daughter; Elizabeth Ann Leeming 1894 was a blouse machinist in 1911; Helen Leeming 1895–1956 was a frilling machinist in 1911, who married Harold Scott in 1916 and had three children; Kate Leeming 1896; and possibly Frederick Leeming, born and died 1898.
- Arthur Hackett (1865–1929) was a lace dresser in 1881. He married Susan Sarah née Morgan (1865–1909) in 1884. He was a gas stoker working for Nottingham Corporation by 1911, living at 3 Fountain Place, Woolpack Lane. Arthur and Susan had twelve children, three of whom died in infancy. The known children are – Mary Ann Elizabeth Hackett (1886–1965), who married Arthur Richards in 1915 and had three children; Harriet Hackett 1888; Thomas William Hackett (1890–1950), who married Louisa Jerram (1888–1928) in 1914; Albert Hackett (1892–1945) married Susan A Gunn in 1914 and had seven children; Christopher Hackett 1893; Walter Hackett 1895; Kate Hackett 1897 and Samuel Frederick Hackett 1899.
- Anna Hackett (born 1867).
- Elizabeth Hackett (born 1871).
- Ellen Hackett (1879–1925) married William Hastings in 1898.

It is understood that William never went to school; he certainly could not read or write, as comrades in France had to write letters home for him. He was employed in factories in Nottingham until aged eighteen, when he became a miner in the Mexborough area of Yorkshire. He worked at Denaby Main for twenty-three years filling mine tubs and then at Manvers Main as a dataller, laying and repairing tracks. He was known as 'Youthey' because he called all youngsters 'youth'. In his free time he frequently walked the ninety miles round trip to Nottingham to visit his parents.

Finch Street, Nottingham.

William Hackett married Alice née Tooby (1874–1948) on 16th April 1900 at Conisbrough Parish Church. At the time he was living at 33 Shafforth Terrace and she at 30 Shafforth Terrace. They lived at 22 Cusworth Street, Denaby and later moved to 49 Cross Gate, Mexborough, near Doncaster. By 1911 they were living at 10 Herbert Street, Mexborough. William and Alice had two children:

Denaby Main Colliery.

- Arthur Hackett (18th November 1901–1962). He lost his right leg in a mining accident at Manvers Main in January 1916 when a train of tubs came off the rails only four weeks after he started working there. His mother arranged a shorthand course for him at Mexborough Secondary School, commencing on 2nd April 1917. On completion he transferred to the clerical branch at Manvers Mine.
- Mary Winifred Hackett (29th December 1903–1974). She married Albert Hopkin (1904–96) in 1928 and they had a daughter, Winifred Hopkin, in 1930.

Alice's brother, Frederick Christopher Gill Tooby (1881–1965), served with 2nd West Riding Field Ambulance RAMC (403644) from 10th April 1914 until discharged on 10th April 1918.

William tried to enlist in the York and Lancaster Regiment three times, but was rejected with suspected heart trouble and because of his age. He was accepted by the Royal Engineers and enlisted on 1st November 1915. His training lasted only two weeks at Chatham, because he was already a skilled miner. He went to France on 21st November 1915 and joined 172 Tunnelling Company, but transferred to 254 Tunnelling Company on its formation on 15th May 1916.

Field Marshal Sir Evelyn Wood VC – *The most divine-like act of self-sacrifice...*

Conisbrough Parish Church (Harrison Series).

Awarded the VC for his actions at Shaftesbury Avenue Mine, near Givenchy, France on 22nd/23rd June 1916, LG 5th August 1916. He died officially at Givenchy, France, on 27th June 1916 and is commemorated on the Ploegsteert Memorial, Belgium. However, he could not have survived that long after the tunnel collapsed on 23rd June. The man with him, Thomas Collins, is commemorated on the Thiepval Memorial and his date of death is given as 22nd June 1916, although he was known to be alive on the 23rd. It seems unusual that two men lying side by side are commemorated on different memorials. In addition, neither appears to be commemorated on the correct Memorial. The geographical limits fixed by the CWGC would suggest that the Loos Memorial is more appropriate. Field Marshal Sir Evelyn Wood VC, described Hackett's actions as, *The most divine-like act of self-sacrifice of which I have read...*

Alice was living at 53 Cross Gate, Mexborough in 1916. She received a cheque for £67 from the officers and men of her husband's Company. His VC was presented to his widow by the King at Buckingham Palace on 29th November 1916. She was awarded a pension of £1/1/- per week from 15th January 1917 and used most of the money collected in his memory to educate her children. She married Harry Flinders (1874–1934) in 1919 at Doncaster and continued living in Mexborough.

William Hackett's family soon after he died.

In addition to the VC, he was awarded the 1914–15 Star, British War Medal 1914–20 and Victory Medal 1914–19. The VC was purchased from one of his sisters in 1965 and is held by the Royal Engineers Museum, Gillingham, Kent. William is commemorated in a number of other places:

- A memorial in Castle Hills Park, Mexborough was originally mounted on the wall of the Market Hall, Mexborough, but when it became a bingo hall the local Royal British Legion branch considered it inappropriate and it was moved in 1997.
- A memorial on the site of Manvers Colliery, Mexborough.
- The War Memorial in Castle Hills Park, Mexborough.
- A memorial in the grounds of Nottingham Castle dedicated on 7th May 2010 to commemorate the twenty men born or buried in Nottingham and Nottinghamshire who have been awarded the VC.
- A memorial unveiled at Givenchy, France on 19th June 2010 to William Hackett and other tunnellers who lost their lives during the war.

The memorial to William Hackett in Castle Hills Park, Mexborough which was originally mounted on the wall of the Market Hall (*Bob Wood*)

1539 COLOUR SERGEANT FREDERICK WILLIAM HALL
8th Battalion (Winnipeg Rifles), Canadian Expeditionary Force

Frederick Hall was born on 21st February 1885 at Kilkenny, Co Kilkenny, Ireland. His father, Frederick Matticott Hall (1856–1905), enlisted in the 104th Regiment (Bengal Fusiliers, later Royal Munster Fusiliers) on 14th December 1869 at Westminster, London (792 and later 3980). He was described as 4′ 6″ tall, with hazel eyes, brown hair and fresh complexion. He served at Shorncliffe, Gosport, Aldershot, Portsmouth and Dover in Britain and Birr, Belfast, Dublin, Curragh and Enniskillen in Ireland. He became a Bandsman on 6th July 1871 and a private on 1st April 1875. He attained the 2nd Class Army Certificate of Education on 3rd May 1875 and by 15th December 1878 had qualified for two allocations of Good Conduct Pay. Promoted corporal on 14th February 1879, lance sergeant on 19th February 1879 and sergeant on 18th June 1879. He transferred to 4th Battalion, Essex Regiment Militia on 14th November 1881 and re-engaged in the Royal Munster Fusiliers at

Warley on 1st December to complete twenty-one years service. He transferred to 5th Battalion, Royal Irish Regiment (1345) on 3rd August 1883 and 4th Battalion, Border Regiment on 15th February 1887 (2051). Having been discharged at his own request with exemplary character on 22nd February 1888, he became Bandmaster of 2nd Volunteer Battalion, South Lancashire Regiment. The family lived at 81 Ormskirk Street, Windle, St Helens, Lancashire and by 1901 had moved to 56 Dentons Green Lane, St Helens.

His mother was Mary Ann 'Marianne' Ellen Hall née Finn (1862–1956). She married Frederick senior at St Ann's Church, Belfast on 12th October 1880. She was living at 260 Young Street, Winnipeg, Manitoba in September 1914, but by April 1915 was at 43 Union Road, Leytonstone, London. By December 1916 she was living at 30 Hargrave Street, Winnipeg and later at 115 Kennedy Street. Fred had six siblings:

- Ada Hall (c.1882–1970) was a music teacher.
- Louisa Emily Hall (born 1883) was a teacher and married Ernest Atkinson in Kensington in 1910. The family was living in Manhattan in 1920.
- Edmund Alexander Hall (1887–1928) served as a lance corporal in 2nd Cameronians (Scottish Rifles). He married and was living in Chicago, Illinois when he died.
- Augusta May Hall (born 1889) married Charles Manning.
- Percy Albert Hall (c.1892–c.1970).
- Henry 'Harry' Cecil Hall (born 1894) was a clerk before serving as a sergeant (19805) in 10th Battalion CEF from 28th September 1914. He married Ann Smart Reid in Winnipeg in 1924.

Fred enlisted in the Cameronians (Scottish Rifles) Special Reserve at Warrington (SR/7040) on 4th February 1901, giving his trade as musician. He claimed previous service with 2nd Volunteer Battalion, South Lancashire Regiment. He was described as 5′ 2″ tall, weighing 88 lbs, with sallow complexion, grey eyes, reddish brown hair and his religious denomination was Church of England. He requested to serve with 2nd Battalion to work with his uncle, Lieutenant and Quartermaster Thomas Finn, commissioned 6th July 1898, who served in the Gaika War 1878, Zulu War 1879 and South African War. He joined at Chatham, Kent on 5th February, gained 3rd Class Certificate of Education on 3rd April and 2nd Class on 28th September. On 27th November 1902 he was appointed Bandsman and was posted to South Africa on 6th January 1903 to join 2nd Battalion. He was granted Good Conduct Pay of 1d a day on 4th February. Having reverted to private at his own request on 18th April 1905, he returned to Britain on 28th May, was appointed lance corporal on 26th August and posted to 1st Battalion in India on 6th October. He was granted Good Conduct Pay of 2d per day on 4th February 1906 and promoted paid lance corporal on 28th February. Fred passed Class of Instruction in Telegraphy on 24th May 1907. Promoted Corporal on 3rd February 1909. He qualified in the use and care of field telephones at Roorkee on 19th March, 1st Class Certificate of Education 30th March and was posted to South Africa on 15th December.

Fred's rise through the ranks continued. He qualified for promotion to sergeant on 5th July 1910 and was appointed unpaid lance sergeant on 25th August 1911. He qualified at the School of Musketry, South Africa on the Ordinary Course on 30th October (Distinguished) and the Machine-Gun Course on 2nd December. Having re-engaged at Tempe, Orange Free State, to complete twenty-one years service on 12th February 1912, he returned to Britain on 12th March. Promoted paid lance sergeant on 15th May and qualified in the use of the 'Mekometer', a device to measure distance accurately, at the School of Musketry, Hythe, Kent on 13th September. Fred was promoted sergeant on 14th March 1913 and was discharged on 20th May after twelve years and 106 days service.

He migrated to Canada and worked as a clerk in Winnipeg, Manitoba. He served in 106th Regiment (Winnipeg Light Infantry) before the First World War. Fred enlisted in 8th Battalion (Winnipeg Rifles), CEF (known as the 'Little Black Devils') in September 1914. He was described as 5′ 8″ tall, with ruddy complexion, brown eyes, auburn hair, a tattooed scorpion on his right arm and his religious denomination was Church of England. The Battalion embarked on SS *Franconia* on 3rd October and arrived at Plymouth, Devon on 15th/16th October. It went

The entrance to the School of Musketry at Hythe, about ten years before Frederick Hall was there.

Larkhill Camp, looking west along the Packway, with the south camps on the left, behind the theatre.

SS *Archimedes*, built in 1911 as SS *Ben of Airlie*, renamed *Archimedes* in 1912 and *Benmacdhui* in 1932. She survived a bombing attack on 10th February 1941, but was lost to a mine off Spurn Head on 21st December 1941 with the loss of two crewmen.

to Larkhill South Camp on Salisbury Plain and trained there for four months in appallingly wet weather.

Frederick was promoted acting sergeant on 22nd October and colour sergeant on 1st December. The Battalion sailed for France on SS *Archimedes* from Avonmouth on 10th February 1915 and disembarked at St Nazaire on 13th February. The Battalion moved into the front line late on 15th April, taking over positions from the French.

Awarded the VC for his actions at Gravenstafel near St Julien, Belgium 22nd–24th April 1915, LG 23rd June 1915. The VC was posted to Canada by the War Office on 5th August and was later presented to his mother in Winnipeg, Manitoba. In addition to the VC, Frederick Hall was awarded the 1914–15 Star, British War Medal 1914–20 and Victory Medal. His VC was acquired by the Canadian War Museum, 1 Vimy Place, Ottawa, Ontario on 8th November 2012.

Frederick Hall was killed during his VC action on 24th April 1915. He is commemorated on the Ypres (Menin Gate) Memorial, Belgium. He never married and had no children. He is also commemorated in a number of other places:

- Valour Road (formerly Pine Street), Winnipeg was named in 1925 to honour three VCs who lived in the 700 block – Frederick Hall at 733, Leo Clarke at 785 and Robert Shankland at 778.
- A bronze plaque on the corner of Portage Avenue and Valour Road was erected by the Women's Canadian Club of Winnipeg in 1925. It was moved on 5th November 2005 to Valour Plaza, which features monuments in the shape of the Victoria Cross and sculptures portraying three soldiers in No Man's Land.
- A Victoria Cross obelisk to all Canadian VCs at Military Heritage Park, Barrie, Ontario dedicated by HRH The Princess Royal on 22nd October 2013.
- Frederick's VC action featured in Issue No.1329 of the *Victor* comic dated 9th August 1986.

2ND LIEUTENANT RUPERT PRICE HALLOWES
4th Battalion, The Duke of Cambridge's Own (Middlesex Regiment)

Rupert Hallowes was born at Checkley House, Station Road, Redhill, Surrey on 6th May 1881. His father was Dr Frederick Blackwood Hallowes FRCS LSA (c.1835–96), a surgeon educated at King's School in Canterbury, Kent & Canterbury Hospital and St Bartholomew's Hospital, London (MRCS 1858 & LSA 1860). He was also a Fellow of the Obstetric Society, Member of the Pathological Society, Member of the Council of Epsom College, President of the South-Eastern Branch of the BMA, medical officer of the Redhill Reformatory and St Ann's Royal Asylum Schools. Frederick later became a general practitioner in partnership with Messrs Martin and Holman at Redhill. Rupert's mother was Mary Ann Taylor née Hutchinson (1843–1941) daughter of Reverend William Hutchinson of Checkley, Staffordshire. Frederick and Mary married on 18th June 1868 at the Parish Church, Checkley, Staffordshire. In 1911 she was living at 9 Cyril Mansions, Prince of Wales Road, Battersea Park, London. Rupert had three siblings:

* Mary Blackwood Hallowes (1871–1915) married Dr Arthur Leopold Tatham MRCS (1868–1936) in 1903 at Chelsea, London. Arthur was a First Class cricketer, playing for Abergavenny Cricket Club and Monmouthshire in the Minor Counties Championship 1901–08. They were living at 52 Castle Street, Abergavenny, Glamorgan in 1911. They had a daughter, Margaret Rose Tatham, in 1905, who married twice.
* William Brabazon Hallowes (1874–1953) was managing director of Robert Byass & Co, Port Talbot and Glamorgan and District Commissioner of the Port Talbot Boy Scouts Association. He married Constance Eva née Carnegy (1878–1961) in 1907, daughter of Major James Ogilvy Carnegy. He was an ensign in 63rd Regiment from 3rd August 1855 without purchase and served in the Crimea from 28th February 1856. He was then commissioned as a lieutenant in 21st (Royal North British Fusilier) Regiment of Foot on 10th September 1858. On 25th May 1861 he became

Station Road, Redhill.

Adjutant of 2nd Monmouthshire Rifle Volunteer Corps (South Wales Borderers) based at Pontypool. Temporary captain 25th February 1874 and honorary major 22nd September 1879. He retired from 3rd Volunteer Battalion, South Wales Borderers on 18th January 1891. They were living at Craigavon House, Port Talbot, Glamorgan in 1911. Their son, Frederick Carnegy Hallowes (born 1910), served in 1st Welch and rose to major on 1st July 1946. He served as second in command in Korea 1st October 1951–30th September 1952; he last appears in the Army List in 1957. He married Diana Barbara née Marriott (born 1914) in 1944 at the Parish Church, Bovey Tracey, Devon. She was the daughter of Major Richard George Armine Marriott DSO (1867–1924) and was serving as a subaltern in the Auxiliary Territorial Service at the time.

- Frederic Chaworth Hallowes (1877–1967) was a mining engineer, known in the family as 'Chang'. He lost two fingers on his right hand in 1907 and could not enlist. After working in Northumberland he went to Spain during the Depression and took an engineering appointment with Rio Tinto Zinc at Villiablino, returning to England in 1935. At other times he was Colliery Manager at Burradon & Cox Coal Co and Managing Director of Robert Byass & Co Ltd. He married Elizabeth née Reah (1882–1970) in 1908. They were living at High Gosforth House, High Gosforth Park, Newcastle on Tyne, Northumberland in 1911. They had three children including, Rupert Blackwood Hallowes (born 1920), who served as a lieutenant commander in the Royal Navy.

Rupert was educated at Conyngham House School in Ramsgate and Haileybury College. He shot for the school in the Ashburton Shield at Bisley in 1896 and 1897 and was also a member of the Officers' Training Corps.

He was working as a coal contractor's clerk at Staines, Middlesex in 1901 and was then employed by Hull, Blythe and Co in London until 1909. He moved to Wales to be Assistant Works Manager of Robert Byass & Co Ltd, Mansel Tin Plate Works at Aberavon, Port Talbot, Glamorgan, where his elder brother William was the manager. Rupert lived at Pen-Y-Cae, Port Talbot, where he was a boy

Haileybury College.

Public Schools shooting for the Ashburton Shield at Bisley.

scout instructor with St Peter's Troop and Assistant Secretary of the Boy Scouts Association. At other times he worked in London with the firm of Harold Flower in Gracechurch Street and a metal brokers' company owned by Sidney H Byass JP. Rupert was a freemason, a member of Roscacy Lodge No.2851 from 1908.

Rupert enlisted into 28th London Regiment (Artists' Rifles) about 1900. He had risen to sergeant when he was commissioned on 26th October 1909. He resigned on 24th April 1910 when he moved to Wales. He re-enlisted in the Artists' Rifles on 5th August 1914 (1422) and was promoted corporal and lance sergeant on 7th August and sergeant on 26th September. Rupert went to France on 29th December. A GHQ Cadet School had been established as part of 1/28th London Regiment at Bailleul at the end of November and it moved to Blendecques later. Rupert reverted to private at his own request on 7th February 1915, probably as a prerequisite to undergo officer training. He was commissioned into 4th Middlesex on 5th April, following training at the Cadet School at Blendecques, St Omer. He joined the Battalion on 12th April.

During an enemy attack down a communications trench at Hooge, Belgium on 19th/20th July, the defenders were short of bombs. Rupert climbed out of the trench in order to fire at the enemy and hit several of them, although very exposed himself. He also assisted in constructing a block, dug out a communications trench under heavy shellfire and rebuilt a blown in parapet. Throughout the night he assisted in keeping touch and supplying bombs. **For this action he was awarded the MC, LG 6th September 1915. He was also Mentioned in Sir John French's Despatch dated 30th November (LG 1st January 1916).**

Awarded the VC for his actions at Hooge, Belgium on 25th-30th September 1915, LG 18th November 1915. He died of his wounds early on 1st October at Hooge and was buried in Sanctuary Wood. After the war his remains were moved to Bedford House Cemetery Enclosure No.4 (XIV B 36).

Rupert did not marry and his will was administered by his brother William. The VC was originally sent to his mother on 25th February 1916, but was presented to her formally by the King at Buckingham Palace on 29th November. In addition to the VC and MC, he was awarded the 1914–15 Star, British War Medal 1914–20 and Victory Medal 1914–19 with Mentioned-in-Despatches oak-leaf. The medals were presented to the Middlesex Regiment Museum, Bruce Castle, Tottenham, by his nephew and godson, Major FC Hallowes, Welch Regiment. When the Museum closed in 1992, the medals were transferred to the National Army Museum, Chelsea, London.

Rupert Hallowes is commemorated in a number of other places:

- Royal Antediluvian Order of Buffaloes, Rupert Hallowes VC Lodge, Port Talbot, Glamorgan.
- A ward and X-Ray department at Aberavon General Hospital, Port Talbot, West Glamorgan were named after him having been paid for by the staff of Robert Byass & Co Ltd and the Port Talbot Boy Scouts Association.

Geoffrey Macleod Hallowes.

Odette Hallowes (née Brailly, formerly Sansom and Churchill) GC MBE.

Odette and Peter Churchill on their wedding day in 1947 (Keystone Press Agency).

- The gateway to Talbot Memorial Park, Taibach, Port Talbot, Glamorgan was dedicated to him.
- Memorial at Haileybury College Chapel.
- Plaque at North East Surrey Hospital, Redhill.
- Portrait in St Theadore's Mission Room, Port Talbot, Glamorgan.

Rupert's cousin, Edward Price Hallowes (1886–2004), was commissioned into 18th Royal Fusiliers (Public Schools Battalion) on 1st January 1915 and later served in the Machine Gun Corps. After the war he joined the family wine business, Hallowes and Tosetti, becoming sole partner in 1925. He merged with Twiss & Brownings, to become Twiss & Brownings & Hallowes. In the Second World War he was commissioned in the Pioneer Corps on 9th September 1940, appointed Adjutant 2nd July 1941 and temporary captain 2nd October. He was Middle Warden of the Worshipful Company of Distillers in 1944 and Master in 1930 and 1946. He was also Master of the Worshipful Company of Loriners in 1948. In 1952, Twiss & Browning & Hallowes merged with Justerini and Brooks to form United Wine Traders. Edward became Vice Chairman until retiring in 1959. He married Bessie Aileen Macleod in 1916 and they had a son, Geoffrey Macleod Hallowes (1918–2006), who married Odette Churchill in 1956. Odette was born Marie Celine Brailly at Amiens, France in 1912. She married Roy Sansom in 1932 and they moved

Rupert Hallowes' grave in Bedford House Cemetery Enclosure No.4

to England, where they had three children. In 1942 she volunteered for special duties, joining the Special Operations Executive through the First Aid Nursing Yeomanry. In France she worked with Captain Peter Churchill DSO. On 16th April 1943 they were arrested by the Abwehr, but by claiming that they were husband and wife and related to Winston Churchill, hoped to receive better treatment. Odette was sent to Fresnes Prison, Paris and was tortured by the Gestapo; her back was seared with a red-hot iron, but she refused to give her companions away. On 13th May 1944, she and seven other female SOE agents were taken to Ravensbrück Concentration Camp. With the Red Army closing in early in 1945, she persuaded the commandant, Fritz Suhren, to drive her to the Allied lines in the west. Odette and Roy Sansom were divorced in 1946 and she married Peter Churchill in 1947. They divorced in 1956 and later that year she married Geoffrey Hallowes. Odette was awarded the MBE (LG 30th October 1945), George Cross (LG 20th August 1946) and the Legion d'Honneur in 1950. Her wartime exploits were the subject of the film *Odette* starring Anna Neagle, in 1950. She died in 1995.

Another cousin, Geoffrey Blackwood Hallowes (1887–1916) enlisted in 18th Royal Fusiliers as a private (1577) on 2nd September 1914. He was in the Military Hospital at Fort Pitt, Chatham 19th April–5th May 1915 with an impacted fracture of the left humerus, resulting from a fall from a motorcycle on duty. A medical board at Rochester found him fit for general service on 21st June and he was commissioned on 31st July 1915 in 3rd (Reserve) Battalion, Queen's Own (Royal West Kent Regiment) at Fort Darland, Chatham. He went to France on 1st August 1916 and joined 1st Battalion on 4th August, but was killed in action on 4th September 1916 and is buried in Guillemont Road Cemetery, France (III F 6).

8273 PRIVATE SAMUEL HARVEY
1st Battalion, The York and Lancaster Regiment

Samuel Harvey was born at 3 Annesley Place, Basford, Bulwell, Nottinghamshire on 17th September 1881, a twin with sister Mahala. He was known as 'Monkey' because of his sense of humour and practical jokes. His father was William Harvey (c.1841–1908), a farm labourer. His mother was Mary Ann née Calver (1854–1929), a charwoman. The family lived at various addresses in Ipswich – Vernon Street, 27 Upper Orwell Cottages at St Margaret and 74 Albion Street. Mary was living with her children Ellen, Frederic and George at 8 Vernon Street in 1911. Samuel had eight siblings:

- Emily Harvey (born 1873).
- Rose 'Rosanna' Anna Harvey (1876–1904). Her marriage to George William Brown (1874–1960), a former soldier, was registered in the 1st quarter of 1900 at Ipswich.
- William Harvey (born 1879) was a quay labourer in 1901. He enlisted as 3/10233 Private William Harvey in 10th Suffolk on 9th October 1914 and was discharged on 20th or 26th July 1916. No medals are recorded, so it is assumed he did not serve abroad.
- Mahala Harvey (1881–1908) was Samuel's twin. She was a sack worker in 1901.
- George Harvey (1888–1931) was a general labourer in 1911, who appears to have called himself Henry George. He served in the Royal Field Artillery. He married Elizabeth B née Gurr in 1913 and they had nine children – Mary F Harvey 1915, Henry G Harvey 1918, Walter F Harvey 1920, Rose A Harvey 1922, Annie L Harvey 1924–25, Annie L Harvey 1926, George H Harvey 1928, William Harvey 1930 and James R Harvey 1931. George died in an accident at Ipswich Docks in 1931.
- Frederic Harvey (born 1886) was an iron founder in 1911. He served in 3/4th Suffolk.
- Ellen 'Nellie' Harvey (1891–1961) was a puncher in a corset factory in 1911. Her marriage to Reuben J Gosling (1889–1946) was registered in the 4th quarter of 1912 at Ipswich. They had six children – Phyllis M E Gosling 1914, Eric J H Gosling 1919, Frederick G Gosling 1921, Donald E Gosling 1923, Doris E Gosling 1924 and Edna L Gosling 1926.
- Walter Charles Harvey (1895–1904).

Upper Orwell Street, Ipswich.

Great White Horse Hotel, Ipswich.

The courtyard of the Great White Horse Hotel, Ipswich.

Samuel was educated at the village school and employed as a farm labourer. He enlisted in 1905 and served for seven years in India before transferring to the Reserve in 1912. He was recalled on the outbreak of war and went to France on 9th September 1914. **Awarded the VC for his actions at Big Willie Trench, Hohenzollern Redoubt, near Loos, France on 29th September 1915, LG 18th November 1915.** The VC was presented by the King at Buckingham Palace on 24th January 1917. He is alleged to have winked at the Queen after the VC was pinned on his chest and said in a loud voice, *Mine's a pint*. Samuel was wounded three times and transferred to 3rd (Home Service) Garrison Battalion, Northumberland Fusiliers (31198) in Sunderland on 7th October 1916. The Battalion served in Ireland 1917–18. He was discharged on 15th May 1918.

Sam Harvey's gravestone (John Greenacre).

He found it hard to get a steady job due to his wounds and at various times was an odd-jobber, a gardener and then an ostler at the Great White Horse Hotel, Ipswich. He married Georgina Brown (c.1875–1948) in Ipswich in August 1944, widow of George Brown (c.1867–1940) of Georgiana Villas, St Olave's Road, Kesgrave, near Ipswich. Samuel and Georgina lived at 10 Adelphi Place and did not have any children. She was a diabetic and died in the 2nd quarter of 1948 at Ipswich. She is buried in Old Ipswich Cemetery.

After his wife died, Samuel fell on hard times and lived in the Salvation Army Hostel, Fore Street, Ipswich for many years. He narrowly escaped serious injury when some guttering fell near him in 1953. In 1955 he injured his hip in a fall and was unable to walk. Eventually there was a public outcry and funds were raised to have him cared for in Heathfields Old Persons Home, Ipswich. He was taken to the VC Centenary Celebrations in 1956 in a wheelchair. Canon Lummis, who knew him when he was a curate in Ipswich and vicar in Kesgrave, said, *He was an Ipswich man – a rough diamond. I met him on one or two occasions… Sam was quite a good looking young man; but a hard-bitten looking fellow when I met him. He had always to be escorted up to London when going to any function in case he over-celebrated.*

Samuel died of myocardial degeneration and senility at Stow Lodge Hospital, Onehouse, Stowmarket, Suffolk on 23rd September 1960. He was buried in an unmarked grave in Ipswich Old Cemetery (X 21 3). A headstone was erected on 29th September 2000. Samuel is also commemorated:

- On the 'Nottingham and Nottinghamshire Victoria Cross Memorial' dedicated at Nottingham Castle on 7th May 2010 to commemorate twenty VCs born in Nottingham and Nottinghamshire or who are laid to rest there.
- By a tree planted in Ipswich Old Cemetery by the Mayor of Ipswich, Councillor Hamil Clarke, in February 2014, following fund raising by staff and residents of Park View Care Home and Sprites School.

In addition to the VC, he was awarded the 1914 Star with 'Mons' clasp, British War Medal 1914–20, Victory Medal 1914–19, George VI Coronation Medal 1937 and Queen Elizabeth II Coronation Medal 1953. It has been claimed he was also awarded the Legion d'Honneur and Order of St George, but there is no provenance for these awards. Samuel claimed he lost his VC while sleeping in a wood near Ipswich after a drinking session. Miniatures of the VC and other medals were found under his pillow after he died. Various theories on the fate of the VC have been provided – he may have traded it for beer in a public house, lost it as described above or sold it privately. It was once believed the VC was with a private collector, Jack Stenabaugh of Ontario, Canada, but he owned the VC of FMW Harvey of Lord Strathcona's Horse, which is now in the Lord Strathcona's Horse Museum in Calgary.

2579 PRIVATE JAMES HUTCHINSON
2/5th Battalion, The Lancashire Fusiliers

James Hutchinson was born at 18 Bank Top, Radcliffe, Lancashire on 9th July 1895. His father was Samuel Lord Hutchinson, born as Samuel Lord (1856–1922). Samuel's mother, Phoebe née Lord (c.1836–1914), married James Hutchinson (c.1836–1903) in 1857; he may have been Samuel's father. Samuel was a coal miner in 1881 and a soft wood labourer in a paper mill in 1901. James' mother was Ann née Nuttall (1858–1930), a cotton weaver in 1881. Samuel and Ann were married on 8th February 1879 at Radcliffe Parish Church. They were living with her parents in 1881 at 29 Bank Top, Radcliffe; at 18 Bank Top, Radcliffe in 1901; and at High Bank, Woos Nab, Radcliffe in 1911. James had six siblings:

- Alice Hutchinson (1879–1943) was a calico weaver in 1901. She married John William Fowler (1879–1912) in April 1904 at St Mary's, Bury. They had two sons. Norman Fowler (1906–96) married Doris Hemmings (1906–90), had four children

and was the Town Hall Keeper and Mace Bearer for Bury. Herbert Fowler (born 1909). Alice is believed to have married Albert F Stephenson in 1922 and had a daughter, Clara Stephenson, in 1923.
* Arthur Hutchinson (born 1881) was a calico weaver in 1901 and a milk dealer in 1911. He married Emily Cartlidge in 1912 and had two children – Jack Hutchinson 1913 and Harry Hutchinson 1914. He served as a private in 1st York and Lancaster (3/4753), was killed in action on 8th May 1915 and is commemorated on the Ypres (Menin Gate) Memorial, Belgium. Emily married Edwin Smith in 1916 and had four children. She was living at 9 Elizabeth Street, Goldthorpe, West Yorkshire in the early 1920s.

Radcliffe.

* Alfred Hutchinson (1884–1917) was a calico weaver in 1901 and 1911. His marriage to Hannah Buckley (1881–1956) was registered in the 1st quarter of 1913 at Bury. She was living at 4 Radcliffe Road, Warth Fold, Bury. Alfred served as a private in 15th Lancashire Fusiliers (242829) and went to France after 31st December 1915. He was killed in action on 8th July 1917 and is buried at Ramscappelle Road Military Cemetery, Nieuwpoort, Belgium (IV D 10).
* Frank Hutchinson (1887–1916) was a calico weaver in 1901 and 1911. His marriage to Alice Ann Harrison was registered in the 4th quarter of 1915 at Bury. He served as a corporal in 2/5th Lancashire Fusiliers (201206) and went to France after 31st December 1915. He was killed during the raid in which his brother won the VC on 28th June 1916 and is commemorated on the Arras Memorial, France. He is also commemorated on the Lancashire Fusiliers Memorial at Wellington Barracks, Bury. Alice married Stephen Evans in 1927.
* Phoebe Hutchinson (1892–1969) was a calico weaver in 1911. Her marriage to George R Hedges was registered in the 3rd quarter of 1920 at Bury.
* Lena Hutchinson (1898–1964) married Harry Howson (1895–1954) in the 3rd quarter of 1923 at Bury and had two sons – Alfred 1924 and George 1927.

James was educated at Radcliffe Hall Parish Church School (now Radcliffe Hall Church of England/Methodist Primary School) and was a member of the Radcliffe Company, Church Lads' Brigade. He attended Bank Top Sunday School, played for its football team and became a teacher there. He was employed as a piecer at Mellor Mill, Warth Fold, Bury.

2nd London General Hospital, Chelsea.

A ward at 2nd London General Hospital.

James enlisted on 28th September 1914, trained at Southport and went to France on 3rd May 1915. **Awarded the VC for his actions near Ficheux, France on 28th June 1916, LG 9th September 1916.** He lost the sight in his right eye to a shell splinter on the Somme three weeks later. As a result he was treated at Rouen and 2nd London General Hospital at St Mark's College, Chelsea. The VC was presented by the King at Buckingham Palace on 2nd December 1916. He became a bombing instructor and did not return to the front. Later he was a corporal in the Labour Corps (532895) and was discharged on 17th December 1918.

James Hutchinson married Laura Fogg (1898–1971) on 8th February 1919 at St Peter's, Bury. She was living at 42 Buckley Wells, Bury at the time. They had a son, James J Hutchinson, in 1924. He married Noreen Morgan at Sodbury, Gloucestershire and was later living in Bristol, Avon. They had two daughters – Sandra M Hutchinson 1952 and Janice 1953. Laura's date of birth recorded with her death registration is 24th April 1897, but her birth was registered in the 2nd quarter of 1898.

James and Laura settled in Bury for a while and he worked in the building trade as an electrician. He found the VC hampered him on occasions. In 'The Sunday Times' of 26th June 1966, he commented, *Trying to get back into the building trade after the war, I often lost the chance of a job I wanted because it was not considered 'good enough' for me.* They moved to Torquay, Devon and ran the 'Ellerslie' private hotel in Falkland Road. They were members of the Torquay Social Club and Torquay Royal British Legion. He ran a poultry farmer at Newton Abbott around 1956.

James suffered from chronic bronchitis and was cared for by Mrs Strode for nine months following the

James Hutchinson towards the end of his life.

death of his wife in 1971. He died at his home 'Barnshill', Zion Road, Torquay, Devon on 21st January 1972. The cause of death was recorded as myocardial infarction, arteriosclerosis, bronchial asthma and emphysema. The funeral was conducted by the Reverend Harold Mason Ainscrow. He had been on the raid in which James won his VC and was taken prisoner, remaining in captivity for two and a half years. The funeral was followed by cremation at Torquay Crematorium, where his ashes were scattered in the Gardens of Remembrance.

In addition to the VC, he was awarded the 1914–15 Star, British War Medal 1914–20, Victory Medal 1914–19, George VI Coronation Medal 1937 and Elizabeth II Coronation Medal 1953. The VC is held privately. James is commemorated:

- On the Roll of Honour of Radcliffe and Bury Parish Churches.
- Twenty-two Berberis shrubs represent the twenty-two members of the Church Lads' Brigade who were awarded the VC at the Church Lads & Church Girls Brigade Memorial Plot at the National Memorial Arboretum, Alrewas, Staffordshire.

588 PRIVATE JOHN WILLIAM ALEXANDER JACKSON
17th Australian Infantry Battalion AIF

Billy Jackson was born on 13th September 1897 at 'Glengower' Station, Gunbar, near Hay, New South Wales, Australia. He was known as Billy to his family and Jacko to his friends. His father was John Gale Jackson (c.1868–1920), born at Paddington, Sydney, New South Wales. He was a farm labourer and moved with his family to Merriwa, New South Wales and later to 68 Green Street, Ivanhoe, Victoria. His mother was Adelaide Ann née McFarlane (c.1873–1905). Her father, John McFarlane, was born in 1836 in Aberdeen, Scotland. He established a carrying business in the Yass area of New South Wales before moving to Gunbar, where he carted wool to Sydney with a team of Clydesdales. John Jackson and Adelaide McFarlane married at Seaton Farm, Gunbar Station, New South Wales in 1890. She died on 16th November 1905. Billy had seven siblings:

- Eliza Jackson 1891–94.
- Alice NAE Jackson 1893. She died in a shooting accident on 29th June 1903.
- Elizabeth MJ Jackson birth registered in 1896.

HMAT *Themistocles* leaves from Sydney on 12th May 1915.

Alexandria Harbour, Egypt.

- Catherine M Jackson birth registered in 1901.
- Albert Gale Jackson birth registered in 1903. He died in 1967.
- Adelaide May Jackson 1904–81 married Leslie Norman McLeod (1900–64) at Carlton, Victoria and had four children.
- Leslie Joseph Jackson (16th November 1905–c.1978). He married Hazel Joyce Bennett (1913–2000) in c.1976. She married firstly Frank Craven (1895–1973) in 1948 and had five children.

Helipolis.

Following the death of their mother, the children were cared for by their grandparents, John and Elizabeth McFarlane. Their father continued to work on Gunbar Station. Billy was employed as a labourer by William Gibson of 'Carlowrie', New South Wales until February 1915.

HMHS *Assaye* (Australian War Memorial).

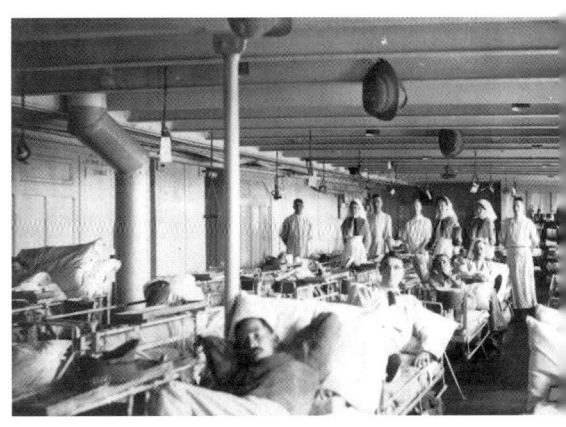

A ward aboard HMHS *Essequibo*.

He enlisted in the Australian Imperial Force at Hay on 20th February 1915 and was posted to Liverpool, New South Wales. He was described as 5′ 10″ tall, weighing 167 lbs with fair complexion, grey eyes and fair hair. He embarked with B Company, 17th Battalion AIF on HMAT *Themistocles* from Sydney on 12th May. He disembarked at Alexandria, Egypt and was stationed at Heliopolis until taking part in operations at Gallipoli from 20th August. He took part in the initial attack on Kalajik Aghyl (Hill 60) the following day. Diarrhoea and a problem with his teeth on 3rd October resulted in him being evacuated on HMHS *Assaye*, arriving at Malta on 10th October, where he was treated at St Patrick's Hospital. He boarded HMHS *Essequibo* on 7th January 1916 suffering from dysentery and was admitted to 1st Auxiliary Hospital in Cairo, Egypt on 10th January. Having been discharged from hospital on 12th February, he rejoined his unit at Moascar Garrison on 8th March.

The port of Marseilles, France.

Billy embarked at Alexandria on 16th March, landing at Marseilles, France on 23rd March. 1st Australian Division took over a forward position in the Armentières area on 10th April. **Awarded the VC for his actions south of Armentières, France on the night of 25th/26th June 1916, LG 9th September 1916.** He was the youngest Australian VC recipient and the first VC Australian on the Western Front. He was originally recommended for the DCM and unusually it was gazetted on 22nd September, almost two weeks after the VC. The DCM was cancelled by a correction in the London Gazette on 20th October. The VC was presented by the King at Buckingham Palace on 18th November 1916.

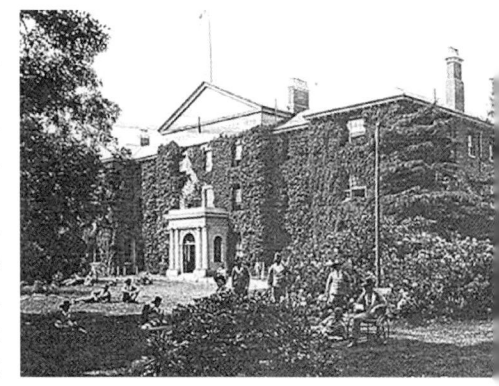

No.1 Australian Auxiliary Hospital, Harefield Park.

Billy was admitted to 2nd Canadian Stationery Hospital and was evacuated aboard HMHS *St Patrick* from Boulogne

3rd London General Hospital, now the Royal Victoria Patriotic Building.

to 3rd London General Hospital on 30th June. He was transferred to No.1 Australian Auxiliary Hospital, Harefield Park, Middlesex on 20th July where the upper part of his arm was amputated. He was treated at a number of other medical facilities – Auxiliary Military Hospital, Southall (Maypole Institute in Margarine Road) on 3rd September; Queen Mary's General Hospital on 26th October; and 2nd Australian Auxiliary Hospital (St Marylebone School, South Road, Southall) on 5th December. He was granted leave on 23rd January 1917 and was finally discharged from hospital on 5th April.

On 4th May, Billy embarked at Devonport, Devon aboard HMAT *Themistocles* and disembarked at Sydney, New South Wales on 5th July. He visited Hay, New South Wales accompanied by Sergeant Camden DCM on 26th July. They were met at the station by a large crowd before being conveyed to the Post Office square. After a welcoming speech by the Deputy Mayor, Sergeant Camden told the crowd, *Bill had gone out looking for him without his arm. Not looking for a VC but for a cobber*. Billy was discharged from the Army on 15th September.

He was offered a farm property by the people of Gunbar during a visit, but had to decline because he did not feel able to handle a farm with one arm. He lived at 'Yuletide', Duke Street, Kensington, New South Wales initially and moved to Merriwa in 1919/20, where he lived in Bettington Street and later at the Fitzroy Hotel, before building a home in Flags Road, despite his disability. He became a dealer, buying and selling horses and skins and is understood to have acquired a property at Merriwa, but was dogged by six droughts in seven years.

Billy's home burned down in 1926 and he lost his military documents. The military authorities replaced them on 14th November 1930 and also sent him

2nd Canadian Stationery Hospital, Le Touquet.

Hay, New South Wales.

Royal Exhibition Building, Melbourne.

Sir Dudley de Chair.

Royal Prince Alfred Hospital, Sydney.

belatedly his Victory Medal. He left Merriwa in 1927 to become licensee of the Figtree Hotel, Wollongong, New South Wales, for eighteen months. He took part in the ANZAC Commemoration Service on 25th April 1927 at the Royal Exhibition Building, Melbourne, Victoria in the presence of HRH The Duke of York. In the march past the twenty-three VCs conceded pride of place to blinded soldiers who insisted on marching.

In November 1929, he and thirteen other VCs were entertained at a luncheon at Government House by the Governor of New South Wales, Sir Dudley de Chair. That September Billy met Ivy Muriel Alma Morris (born c.1909), a dressmaker at the Royal Prince Alfred Hospital, Missenden Road, Camperdown, Sydney, where Billy and Ivy's relatives were patients. In 1930, Billy was living at the Peoples Palace, King Street, Melbourne. Billy and Ivy were married at St Paul's Anglican Church, Kogarah, New South Wales on 12th January 1932. The wedding party consisted only of the bride, groom, bride's mother and Billy's cattle dog, Jackie. The best man

Peoples Palace, Melbourne.

King Street, Melbourne.

was to be John Joseph Clasby, but he fell ill. The two men served together during the war. Clasby was wounded, gassed and invalided home in 1917. He was elected as the United Australia Party Member of the House of Representatives for East Sydney in the general election on 19th December 1931, but died on 15th January 1932 before being sworn in. Billy Jackson wrote a tribute in 'Reveille' magazine on 31st January 1932, *Jack Clasby was the best pal I ever had*. He later commented that Jackie, the dog, had been his best man. Billy and Ivy had a daughter, Dorathea Anne Helen Jackson, in 1932. The family was living at 91 St George Parade, Hurstville, New South Wales in August 1935 and moved to 54 Vine Street, Hurstville around 1939.

John Joseph Clasby.

Billy enlisted again at Paddington, New South Wales (N107906) at the outbreak of the Second World War and served as a corporal/acting sergeant. He was posted to Eastern Command Provost Company on 31st March 1941. Back in 1919, his father was asked to return the official notification of the award of the DCM to his son, but had already passed it to Billy, who was asked in December 1941 why he was wearing the DCM ribbon. He produced the official notification and denied any knowledge of the cancellation. He also had the medal, the official gazette, an entry in his pay book and it was on his discharge certificate. He was asked to return the DCM and replied he would continue to wear it and would apply for discharge rather than surrender it. He was discharged at his own request. There was no question that the DCM had been cancelled officially, but it was felt inappropriate to take further steps to recover it. Billy enlisted again less than three weeks later in 2nd Australian Labour Company as a corporal (N391402), but opted for voluntary discharge on 14th September 1942.

In 1946 he was managing a greengrocery business, selling fruit and vegetables from a stall in King Street, Sydney. He was also a clerk with the Metropolitan Water, Sewerage & Drainage Board in Sydney at some time. Returning from a skin buying trip to Wollongong on 5th October 1946, he was driving a truck through fog and light rain at Waterfall, south of Sydney when he was involved in a four vehicle accident. He suffered minor injuries, but two people were killed and he was charged with manslaughter, driving in a dangerous manner and negligent driving. He appeared before Wollongong Court of Quarter Sessions on 13th May

Melbourne Town Hall.

Field Marshal Sir William Slim.

The Anzac Memorial in Hyde Park, Sydney.

1947. Billy had been driving the truck for five months and it had been fitted in accordance with the restricted license that he held. It was also his first accident in thirty years and the poor weather had been a factor. Judge Nield had served in the same Battalion as Billy, albeit after he was wounded. He told the jury this caused him some embarrassment and instructed it to return its verdict on the facts of the case alone. Billy was found not guilty and discharged.

Billy was appointed Commissionaire and Enquiry Attendant at Melbourne Town Hall on 1st June 1953. His duties included driving dignitaries to civic receptions. In August 1953 his passenger was the Governor-General, Field Marshal Sir William Slim, who noticed the crimson VC ribbon. Slim ignored the accompanying civic dignitaries and engaged Billy in a lengthy conversation.

RMS *Orcades* at Port Said.

Boronia House, where Billy Jackson's ashes were scattered, is now a tea room.

Billy was a member of the Merriwa, NSW and Carlton, Victoria sub-branches of the Returned Services League. During the 1954 Royal Tour, he was chosen to unfurl the Royal Standard as the Queen stepped from her car on arrival at Melbourne Town Hall. He was a guest at the State Dinner given for the Royal couple in Sydney and met them again when they visited the Anzac Memorial in Hyde Park, Sydney.

Billy's marriage ended in divorce on 23rd May 1955. Against his doctor's advice, he sailed aboard RMS *Orcades* with thirty-four other Australian VCs to attend the 1956 Victoria Cross Centenary Celebrations. He suffered a heart attack on the voyage and spent six weeks in hospital in England. He recovered and was able to attend a garden party at Marlborough House before being flown home to Australia.

Billy was admitted to Austin Repatriation Hospital, Heidelberg, Melbourne, Victoria suffering from cardiac failure and died there on 5th August 1959. His funeral with full military honours was followed by cremation at Springvale Botanical Cemetery, Melbourne. His ashes were placed in Boronia House Gardens (now Boronia Tea Rooms). He is commemorated in a number of places:

- The Members Bar at the Merriwa Returned Services League Club was named in his honour.
- The 'William Jackson VC Memorial Park', constructed by the Merriwa RSL as a Rest Area/Park on the Golden Highway at Gungal, south of Merriwa, was dedicated on 4th October 2003.
- Jackson Street, Albury, Victoria.
- A plaque unveiled on Balmain, Sydney, War Memorial on 11th November 2001.
- The Victoria Cross Memorial, Campbell, Canberra dedicated on 24th July 2000.
- The Victoria Cross Memorial, Queen Victoria Building, George Street, Sydney, New South Wales.
- A plaque at the Sailors, Soldiers & Airmen's Club, Leichardt, New South Wales.

In addition to the VC, he was awarded the 1914–15 Star, British War Medal 1914–20, Victory Medal 1914–19, War Medal 1939–45, Australia Service Medal 1939–45, George VI Coronation Medal 1937 and Elizabeth II Coronation Medal 1953. The VC group was offered for sale by Bonham & Goodman in Sydney in November 2007 and by Noble Auctions on 8th-11th April 2008, but attracted no bids. The group was sold later to Barry Hibbard, a New South Wales coin collector, for $650,000. Its current location is not known.

2ND LIEUTENANT FREDERICK HENRY JOHNSON
73rd Field Company, Royal Engineers

Frederick Johnson was born at 13 Bedford Row, (later High Street), Streatham, London on 15th August 1890. His father was Samuel Rogers Johnson (1859–1917), a confectioner's traveller in 1891, living with his family at 8 High Road, Streatham, London. By 1901, he was a baker and confectioner with his own shop, living with his family at 61 High Street, Croydon, Surrey. In 1911 he was a commercial traveller in the confectionary business, living with his family at 4 Hanover Gardens, Kensington, London. Frederick's mother was Emily née White (born 1857). Samuel's and Emily's marriage was registered during the second quarter of 1884 at Camberwell, London.

Frederick had a brother, Benjamin Bertie Johnson, born on 28th December 1884, although his year of birth has been seen as 1883 and 1885 in official documents. He was an engineer who worked for Croydon Corporation Electricity Department 1901, Nalder Bros and Thompson & Elliott Bros 1902, the National Telephone Company in London 1903-08, the Anglo-Portuguese Telephone Company in Lisbon 1908-15 (fluent in Portuguese) and the Relay Automatic Telephone Company at Marconi House, Strand, London 1915–16. He married Laura Lydia King (1885–1960), registered at Lambeth in the third quarter of 1911. Benjamin enlisted at Battersea

Bedford Row (later High Street), Streatham (London Borough of Lambeth).

St Dunstan's College, Catford.

Battersea Polytechnic (RW Thomas).

Town Hall on 19th May 1916. He was 5′3½″ tall, weighed 132lbs and was living at 100 Norroy Road, Putney and later at 24 Cranworth Gardens, Brixton. Having been provisionally selected for employment in the Royal Engineers, he was not required immediately and was released to the Army Reserve next day. He was commissioned on probation in the Royal Flying Corps on 9th February 1917 and reported initially to the School of Military Aeronautics, Reading, becoming an Equipment Officer 3rd Class on 11th April. Appointed temporary captain on 1st August, acting captain on 9th August 1918 and transferred to the Unemployed List on 22nd February 1919. He rejoined the Relay Automatic Telephone Company and took out a patent relating to improvements to telephone systems on 21st September 1926. He also applied for a patent for an automatic telephone exchange system on 22nd March 1955. His death was registered in the 2nd quarter of 1969 at Wandsworth, London, giving his date of birth as 28th December 1883.

Frederick was educated at Whitgift Middle School, Croydon and St Dunstan's College, Catford September 1902–March 1907. He was employed as an engineer apprentice and improver 1907–11 and then attended Battersea Polytechnic 1911–14 (BSc(Eng) Hons 1914 – University of London).

Frederick joined London University OTC in August 1914 and was living in Cranworth Gardens, Brixton Road, London at the time. He was commissioned on 24th October 1914 and went to France between 7th and 13th July 1915. **Awarded the VC for his actions at Hill 70, Loos, France on 25th September 1915, LG 18th November 1915.** He was evacuated to England and promoted to lieutenant on 8th December. The VC was presented by the King at Buckingham Palace on 22nd December. He returned to France in January 1916, but was back in Britain on 12th May, when Battersea Polytechnic gave him a hero's welcome and he was presented with a portrait painting by Canon Curtis. A duplicate was presented to Battersea Polytechnic later in 1916. He was appointed temporary captain on 15th January and acting major on 30th November. Promoted captain 18th September 1917. Later he commanded 231st Field Company RE.

While conducting a reconnaissance with two other officers in Bourlon Wood on 26th November 1917, they came under fire and one of the officers went missing. While looking for him, Johnson was shot and died of wounds later the same day at Graincourt Dressing Station. He was buried near Bourlon Wood, but the grave was not found after the war and he is commemorated on the Cambrai Memorial. His VC action was featured in the *Victor* comic dated 8th June 1968.

Frederick never married. His will was administered by his mother and Edgar Thomas Eiseman, a civil servant; estate valued at £806/7/11. His VC was unsold at a Glendining's auction on 1st March 1989. However, the VC was reportedly purchased at the time for £9,000 by the former British Trade Minister, Alan Clark MP. Its current location is unknown and it is assumed it is held in a private collection.

LIEUTENANT RICHARD BASIL BRANDRAM JONES
8th Battalion, The Loyal North Lancashire Regiment

Richard Jones was born at 7 Honor Oak Rise, Camberwell, London on 30th April 1897. His father was Henry Thomas Brandram Jones (1867–1946), manager director of Brandram Bros of London, manufacturers of white lead, saltpetre and sulphuric acid. The company started by manufacturing gunpowder and occupied a twenty-one acres site at Rotherhithe, stretching to the river at Brandram's Wharf. After his death, the surviving family members already had their own careers and it was decided to sell the company, including some of its patents, to a large paint manufacturer. Richard's mother was Caroline Emma née Gray (1865–1950). Henry and Caroline were married on 4th September 1894 at the Parish Church, Hove, Sussex. The family was living at 2 Thicket Road, Anerley, London in 1911. Richard had three siblings:

• Humphrey Francis Brandram Jones (1904–70) married Jeannie Mary Lamond (born 1905) in 1928 and had four sons including – Richard Brandram Jones 1929 and Robert A Brandram Jones 1932.

Dulwich College (S Phillips).

Cadets shooting for the Ashburton Shield in the Public School's Competition at Bisley (Gale & Polden).

- Margaret Gray Jones (born 1896) became a doctor.
- Ursula Mary Jones (born 1907) served in the Royal Army Medical Corps.

One of his uncles, Richard Charles Stuart Jones (1866–1941), was a Clerk in Holy Orders in 1891 and subsequently became Canon of Gloucester. Richard's maternal grandfather, French Gray (1813–74), worked for the Ceylon Civil Service as a collector of Customs. He married his first wife, Susan Jane Warburton, on 3rd December 1840 at St James Church, Nellore, Jaffna, Ceylon and they had ten children. Amongst them were: William Cosby Gray (1844–1912), a tea planter; Cosby Warburton Gray (1853–86), who was killed by Dacoits near Mandalay, Burma on 9th January 1886; and James Patrick Gray (1855–1930), also a tea planter. French married his second wife, Caroline née Pointing (1826–1909), on 29th May 1862. She was the Principal of the Female Seminary at Colombo, Ceylon. In addition to Caroline they also had Elizabeth Susan Gray (1864–1937). French died on 25th April 1874 off the coast of Aden aboard the *Eldorado*.

Thicket Road, Anerley.

Richard was educated at Dulwich College Preparatory School and Dulwich College 1909–14. He was captain of the Dulwich Gymnastics Team and a keen member of the OTC. He won the Lane Challenge Cup for the highest score in the Dulwich shooting team in the Ashburton Shield competition at Bisley and also won the Lady Hamilton Challenge Cup and the Mrs Grey Cup.

Richard was commissioned on 17th October 1914 and promoted lieutenant on 26th November. He became the Battalion Sniping Officer, having been a Bisley shot. He went to France on 16th September 1915 and was slightly wounded on 12th December. **Awarded the VC for his actions at Broadmarsh Crater, Vimy, France on 21st May 1916, LG 5th August 1916.** He was killed in the VC action and is commemorated on the Arras Memorial, France. As he never married, the VC was presented to his parents by the King at Buckingham Palace on 20th December 1916.

In addition to the VC, he was awarded the 1914–15 Star, British War Medal 1914–20 and Victory Medal 1914–19. The VC is held by Dulwich College. He is named on the Dulwich College Memorial. The Howard-Jones Challenge Cup for rifle shooting is awarded by Dulwich College and is dedicated to Old Alleynians, Richard Jones and 2nd Lieutenant Cecil Cunningham Howard, who also served in 8th Loyal North Lancashire and was killed on 23rd May 1916, two days after Jones.

8655 PRIVATE HENRY EDWARD KENNY
1st Battalion, The Loyal North Lancashire Regiment

Henry Kenny was born at 34 Upper Market Street, Woolwich, London on 27th July 1888; his birth was registered as Harry Edward Kenny. His father was John Kenny (1863–1914), a carman born in Leeds, but both his parents came from Co Limerick, Ireland. His mother was Susan née Brown (1886–1938). John and Susan were married on 3rd July 1882 at Shoreditch, London. The family was living at 6 Glenmohr Place, Woolwich in 1891, at 6 Dagnal Place, Bethnal Green in 1901 and by 1911 had moved to his mother-in-law's house at 16 Margaret Street, Hackney. Henry had seven siblings:

- John James Kenny (1886–1953) was a van guard in 1901. His marriage to Elizabeth Louisa Paul (born 1891) was registered in the 3rd quarter of 1913 at Hackney. They had four children – Lilian C Kenny 1914, John A Kenny 1916–20, Leonard H Kenny 1919 and Florence E Kenny 1921.
- Ethel Honora Kenny (1890–1967) was a box maker in 1911. She married Percy George Wiles (1883–1940) on 24th December 1911 at Hackney. They had six children – John P Wiles 1912, Eileen N Wiles 1915, Ethel HL Wiles 1916–17, Harry Wiles 1918, George Wiles 1920–22 and James F Wiles 1925–58.
- Clara Amelia Kenny (born 1892) was a pipe polisher in 1911. She married Alfred Frederick Barton (1890–1971) on 25th December 1915 at St John of Jerusalem, South Hackney.
- Leonard Alfred Kenny (1895–1973) was an apprentice printer in 1911.
- Horace William Kenny (born 1896) enlisted as L26090 Driver HW Kenny in C/173rd (East Ham) Brigade RFA on 25th May 1915; he was only 5′ 4½″ tall. Promoted bombardier 16th July, but overstayed his leave 7th–9th November and was reprimanded. He went to France on 28th November. Admitted to 13 General Hospital, Boulogne on 3rd August 1917 with a slight gun shot wound to the right shoulder. Posted to A/174 Brigade RFA on 26th August. Promoted corporal on 19th September 1918. On 23rd January 1919 he was reduced to bombardier and forfeited seven days pay for absence. He returned to Britain on 6th June 1919 via Dunkirk and was processed through the Disposal Centre at Crystal Palace. Demobilised on 31st March 1920. He married Ada ER Reynolds (born 1906) in 1927 at Hackney. They had two sons – John W Kenny 1928 and Terry G Kenny 1937.

Beresford Square in Woolwich, close to Market Street where Henry Kenny was born.

- Eileen Nellie Kenny (1899–1901).
- Florence Emily Kenny (born 1902) married George HT Roberts (1905–71) in 1933 and they had two children – Thomas P Roberts 1934 and Patricia E Roberts 1937.

Henry was educated at St John's Certified Industrial School, Walthamstow. He enlisted on 29th October 1906 and transferred to the Reserve in 1911. He was employed by Messrs Abdulla, the cigarette manufacturers of London, until recalled and went to France on 12th August 1914. Henry was in the Retreat from Mons and the Battles of the Marne and the Aisne, followed by First Ypres in October and Festubert in December. In 1915 he took part in fighting at La Bassée and Neuve Chapelle.

Awarded the VC for his actions near Loos, France on 25th September 1915, LG 30th March 1916. He was wounded in the same action and was treated at No.1 British Red Cross Society Hospital (Duchess of Westminster's Hospital), Le Touquet and later at Lady Astor's Hospital at Taplow, Buckinghamshire. Having recovered from his wounds, he went to 3rd Battalion in Felixstowe as an instructor. After ten days he requested and was granted a transfer back to 1st Battalion in France before Christmas 1915.

The VC was presented by the King at Buckingham Palace on 20th May 1916. Henry was later promoted sergeant and was discharged in March 1919. He was a member of the VC Guard at the interment of the Unknown Warrior on 11th November 1920. Post-war he was employed as a checker by Spencer Press Ltd in London, a subsidiary of Abdulla's in the tobacco trade.

Henry Kenny married Edith Maud née Holford in the 2nd quarter of 1921 at Hackney. They had two daughters:

* Vera FA Kenny (1922–63) married William E Grimwood (died 1979) in 1948 and had two children – Alan M Grimwood 1955 and Susan J Grimwood 1959.
* Audrey D Kenny (born 1925).

In October 1921, Henry took part in the unveiling of the War Memorial at Hackney, accompanied by Issy Smith VC. Henry also attended the funeral of AP Sullivan VC in the Guard's Chapel, Wellington Barracks, London on 13th April 1937. During the Second World War, Henry served in the Local Defence Volunteers and Home Guard at Highams Park, London. He challenged the King when he inspected 2,000 LDVs at their headquarters at Woodford, Essex. When he was introduced to the King later the same day, the King recalled meeting Henry at the Hackney Empire in 1920 when, as Duke of York, he attended a special performance for a discharged soldiers' organisation.

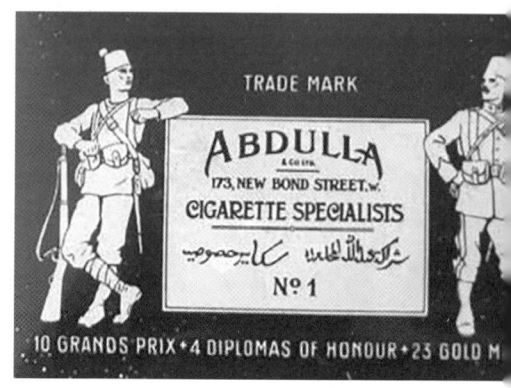

Abdulla cigarettes.

Henry Kenny died at St Peter's Hospital, Chertsey on 6th May 1979 and was cremated at St John's Crematorium, Woking. His ashes are interred at St Mark's Churchyard (Plot 109), Whiteley Village, Hersham, Surrey. He is also named in the Book of Remembrance at Whiteley Village Church.

In addition to the VC, he was awarded the 1914 Star with 'Mons' clasp, British War Medal 1914–20, Victory Medal 1914–19, Defence Medal 1939–45, George VI Coronation Medal 1937, Elizabeth II Coronation Medal 1953 and Elizabeth II Silver Jubilee Medal 1977. His VC was sold by Glendining's for £12,500 on 24th June 1992. It was purchased by Michael Ashcroft and is displayed in the Lord Ashcroft VC Collection in the Lord Ashcroft Gallery of the Imperial War Museum.

No.1 British Red Cross Society Hospital (Duchess of Westminster's Hospital), Le Touquet.

17424 PRIVATE THOMAS KENNY
13th Battalion, The Durham Light Infantry

Thomas Kenny was born at Hartbushes, Hutton Henry, South Wingate, Co Durham on 4th April 1882. The family name also appears as Kenney in various official documents and other variations have been seen. His father was Dermot (also seen as Darby, Derby or even Deriment) Kenny (1856–1920), a navvy drainer in 1881 and a brickyard labourer in 1901, whose parents came from Ireland. His mother was Mary 'Polly' née McGuire (also seen as McGuins and McQuin) (1865–1951). Her father was also Irish. Dermot and Mary's marriage was registered in the 3rd quarter of 1880 at Easington, Durham. The family lived at various times at Hutton Henry, South Wingate and Pond Row, South Wingate. Thomas had six siblings:

- Annie Kenny (born 1884) married Thomas Woodward (1880–1955), a police constable in 1909. They had two children – John Kenny Woodward 1911 and Elizabeth Woodward 1917.
- John Kenny (born 1887).
- Winifred Kenny (1890–1947), a dressmaker, married Hugh Condren (1890–1922), a miner, in 1915 and they had a son Hugh in 1922.
- Dermot Kenny (1894–1931) married Margaret Horner in 1928.
- Mary Catherine Kenny (1898–1906).
- Hugh James Kenny (1899–1918) served as a private in 8th Lincolnshire (49809) and was killed in action on 25th August 1918 (Vis-en-Artois Memorial, France).

Thomas was educated at St Mary's Roman Catholic School in Wingate and was then employed as a brickyard labourer and later as a miner at Wheatley Hill Colliery. He married Isabella Applegarth (1881–1956) at Easington in the 2nd quarter of 1903 and they were living at Walker's Buildings, South Wingate, Co Durham in 1911. They had twelve children, plus two more who did not survive infancy prior to 1911:

- Olive Mary Kenny (born 1905) married Charles Matthews in 1933. He is understood to have died in 1940 at Ashford, Kent, but there are no civil deaths registered that match his description. However, 3954360 Sergeant Charles Matthews, Welch Regiment, died on 18th July 1940 and is buried in Englefield Green Cemetery, Surrey (Plot 15, Grave 410). It is not known if this was Oliver's

husband, but it is known that he was born in Glamorgan and Sergeant Matthews was serving in a Welsh regiment.
* Isabell Kenny (born c.1906).
* Annie Kenny (born 1909) married William Barber in 1927 and they had five children – Monica 1928, William 1929, Thomas 1933, John 1935 and Kathleen 1942.
* John George Kenny (1911–20).
* Thomas Kenny (born 1912) married Evelyn Horan (born 1915) in 1935 and they had two sons – James 1937 and Thomas 1942.
* Catherine 'Kitty' Kenny (born 1914) married Richard Bell in 1936 and they had a son, Brian, in 1940.
* Margaret 'Maggie' Kenny (born 1915) married Charles R Nicholls in 1941 and they had a child.
* Norah Kenny (born 1919) married Stephen R Fairbairn in 1947.
* Veronica 'Ron' Kenny (born 1922) married Thomas Beresford in 1946 and they had four daughters – Maureen 1949, Norma 1952, Janice 1956 and Margaret 1958.
* Hugh Kenny (born 1923) married Georgina 'Jeanna' B Atkinson (1928–67) in 1951 and they had two children – David 1952 and Gwendoline 1956.
* Elizabeth 'Belle' Kenny (born 1924).
* James Kenny (born 1925) married Joan Crangle in 1947 and they had two children – Eileen 1949 and Terence 1951.

Thomas enlisted in August 1914. On 16th September, the Battalion moved by train from Newcastle to Bullswater Camp, Surrey to join 68th Brigade, 23rd Division. It was also based in Aldershot, Ashford and Bramshott before crossing to France on 25th August 1915. **Awarded the VC for his actions near La Houssoie, France on 4th November 1915, LG 7th December 1915.** He came home on leave in December 1915.

Wheatley Hill Colliery.

The VC was presented by the King at Buckingham Palace on 4th March 1916. When he came out of the Palace, Thomas was met by Lieutenant Brown's mother, who took him to her home in Beckenham. From then until her death in 1945 she corresponded regularly with Thomas and his wife. One of his daughters went into domestic service with Lieutenant Brown's brother. Every year, on the anniversary of his VC action, Thomas received a gift of money from Mrs Brown and her daughter continued this after her death. While on leave for the investiture, he visited his old school on 11th March and was presented with a clock by the staff and pupils.

Wingate Colliery in 1927.

During the Battle of the Somme, on 17th July 1916, Thomas saved 19368 Private Frank Moody's life by carrying him to safety after he had received a serious gunshot wound to his leg; it was subsequently amputated and he was discharged in May 1917. They met again at 13th Battalion's first annual dinner and reunion in December 1929. Thomas was wounded in October 1916, but returned to the front and was eventually promoted to CSM. The Division moved to Italy in November 1917 and remained there for the rest of the war, but Thomas returned to the Western Front in March or September 1918. He was demobilised in 1919.

Post-war he worked at Wingate Colliery until 1927 and then returned to Wheatley Colliery as a stoneman and drifter. During the Second World War he served in the Home Guard. After an underground accident in 1944, he became a surface worker.

Philip Brown (Northern Echo).

Thomas Kenny and his wife, Isabel, visiting his old school on 11th March 1916, where he was presented with a clock by the staff and pupils.

Thomas Kenny died at South Wingate, Co Durham on 29th November 1948. He was living at 13 Darlington Street, Wheatley Hill at the time. He was buried in an unmarked grave at Wheatley Hill Cemetery. An appeal was launched by members of 'The Faithful Inkerman Dinner Club' and a headstone was added in August 1994, unveiled by Captain Richard Annand VC.

In addition to the VC, he was awarded the 1914–15 Star, British War Medal 1914–20, Victory Medal 1914–19 and George VI Coronation Medal 1937. His VC is held privately. Thomas is also commemorated with ten other DLI VCs on a commemorative stone in the grounds of the Durham Light Infantry Museum,

Aykley Heads, Durham. It was unveiled on 8th September 2001 and the ceremony was attended by the Regiment's sole surviving VC holder, Richard Annand. Kenny House at Durham Johnson Comprehensive School, Crossgate Moor, Durham was named after him.

3026 LANCE CORPORAL LEONARD JAMES KEYWORTH
1/24th (County of London) Battalion, The London Regiment (The Queen's)

Leonard Keyworth was born at 22 Coningsby Street, Lincoln on 12th April 1893. His father was James Keyworth (1854–1924), a tailor. His mother was Emma née Taylor (1859–1921). James' and Emma's marriage was registered in the 4th quarter of 1880 at Lincoln. Leonard had a sister, Lillie Milly Keyworth (1884–1961), a millinery manageress, lodging with the Sayles family in Rotherham in 1911. She married William Perkins (c. 1882–1956) in the 4th quarter of 1921 at Lincoln and they had a son, Leonard James Keyworth Perkins in 1923.

Leonard was educated at Rosemary Lane Wesleyan School and Municipal Technical School, Lincoln. He was a keen sportsman, playing football and cricket, the latter with the Silver Street Cricket Club and the Rechabites Cricket Club, with whom he won two medals. He sang in the choir of the United Methodist Church in Silver Street and was also a member of the YMCA. After school, he was initially an apprentice tailor before becoming a clerk with Messrs William Foster & Co Engineers and was later an insurance clerk in the Lindsey insurance department of Messrs Burton, Scorers and White Solicitors.

Leonard tried to enlist in the Lincolnshire Regiment at the outbreak of war, but was rejected. He travelled to London and enlisted in 2/24th (County of London) Battalion, The London Regiment (The Queen's) on 16th September 1914. Early on he transferred to 1/24th London and was initially stationed at St Albans, Hertfordshire where he was billeted at Culver Road Hall and then at 63 Heath Road. The Battalion moved to Hatfield in January 1915 and on 16th March 1915 crossed to France where it was initially based near Béthune.

The Battalion suffered over 100 casualties during the Battle of Aubers Ridge on 9th May. **Awarded the VC for his actions at Givenchy, France on 25th/26th May 1915, LG 3rd July 1915.** He returned to England on 11th July and the following day the VC was presented to him by the King at Buckingham Palace. Leonard then

Leonard Keyworth with 2/24th London at Bishop Stortford on 20th July 1915.

Another picture from his visit to 2/24th London.

took part in recruiting rallies. One was at the Old Vic Theatre, Waterloo Road, London during which one of the French artistes, Gaby Deslys, gave him her lapel watch. On 17th July, he visited Lincoln including his old school, the Municipal Technical School. After his speech he passed the VC around for the masters and boys to see. During the same visit, he was presented with an illuminated address and a purse of £26. Later he and Corporal James Upton VC, were entertained by the Mayor at the Albion Hotel. During his visit to Lincoln, he was presented with a gold watch and chain by the Lincoln Young Liberals and the Lincoln Liberal Club. He received another illuminated address from the Lincoln Young Men's Christian Association, a purse of four gold guineas, a khaki testament and one year's membership of the YMCA. Lincoln Silver Street Church and Sunday School presented him with a clock inscribed from the Salford Unity of the Lincolnshire Independent Order of Rechabites. A third illuminated address and an inscribed wrist-watch were presented by his employers, Messrs Burton, Scorers and White. On 20th July, he visited his old unit, 2/24th London, at Bishops Stortford. On his return to London on 21st July, he was paraded through the streets of Southwark with the Deputy Mayor and received another illuminated address and a pair of binoculars. He returned to France towards the end of July.

Leonard was also awarded the Russian Medal of St George, 2nd Class, LG 25th August 1915. The Battalion was involved in an attempt to capture Hulluch on 15th October, during which he was wounded in the head and taken to 5th Field Ambulance near Noeux-les-Mines. He was moved to No.5 Stationary Hospital at 5 Rue des Capucins, Abbeville, but died of his wounds around 8.45 p.m. on 19th October without regaining consciousness. His death was registered at Abbeville at 11.30am on 20th October by Charles Stone and Stanley Hobbs, military nurses. Leonard Keyworth is buried in Abbeville Communal Cemetery (III C 2). Leonard is commemorated in a number of other places:

- 'Keyworth VC 1915 Memorial Prize', established by London County Council using £112/16/- raised by the Borough of Southwark, to provide book prizes for schoolchildren in the Borough. Later, the 'Keyworth VC 1915 Memorial Prize Fund' provided two prizes annually for the five schools in the Borough – Faunce Street, Crampton Street and Rockingham Street Schools in Newington, Victory Place School in Walworth and Charles Dickens' School in Southwark.
- Keyworth Primary School, formerly Faunce Street School, Southwark, renamed in 1951.
- Keyworth Street, formerly Danzig Street, was renamed on 4th November 1919. Keyworth Place, formerly Providence Place off Keyworth Street, was also renamed in his honour.
- City of London War Memorial.
- Named on a memorial at All Saints' Church, Lincoln originally in Silver Street Methodist Church, which was demolished in the 1960s. The memorial was buried in a garden in Cherry Willingham, Lincolnshire and was identified by the daughter of one of the sixteen men named on it. The Lincoln Royal Lincolnshire & Royal Anglian Regimental Association arranged for it to be erected in All Saints' Church and it was rededicated on 25th November 2007.
- A commemorative stone at the endtrance to the Drill Hall, Free School Lane, Lincoln was dedicated on 4th June 2015 to mark the centenary of his award.

A commemorative serviette from the Southwark reception on 21st July 1915.

In addition to the VC, he was also awarded the 1914–15 Star, British War Medal 1914–20, Victory Medal 1914–19 and Russian Medal of St George, 2nd Class. Leonard never married and the VC eventually passed to his sister Lillie, who died in 1961. The VC and other medals were purchased by John Tamplin in March 1963 for £460. He was a former member of the London Regiment and because of this it was assumed that the Regiment had purchased the medals. Tamplin created a museum in the Drill Hall, London for his collection of militaria and Keyworth's VC group. When the Drill Hall closed, he donated Keyworth's VC and campaign medals to the Queen's Royal Surrey Regiment Museum, Clandon Park, Guildford, Surrey in March 2005. The Museum was renamed the Surrey Infantry Museum following the merger of the collections of the East Surrey Regiment and Queen's Royal Surrey Regiment. The medals survived the fire that severely damaged the building on 30th April 2015, as they were held in a bank. A copy of the illuminated address presented to Leonard in Southwark in July 1915 was presented to the Museum by Mrs Patricia White on 16th March 2014.

CAPTAIN ARTHUR FORBES GORDON KILBY
2nd Battalion, The South Staffordshire Regiment

Arthur Kilby was born at East Hayes, Cheltenham, Gloucestershire on 3rd February 1885. No Christian names were recorded when his birth was registered. His family provided two Lord Mayors of York – Thomas Kilby in 1784 and John Kilby in 1804, both were brewers. His father, Sandford James Kilby (c.1847–1922), was born at sea in Algoa Bay, South Africa. He served in the Bengal Police, Customs Preventative Service and Salt Department and took out several patents in regard to his work in 1886–87, including 'Kilby's Automatic Counter'. By 1901 he had returned to Britain and the family was living at Penywern, Hope, Flintshire. He became a straw-hat manufacturer and moved to Skelton House, Leamington Spa, Warwickshire. When he died on 27th August 1922, his effects were valued at £16,510/1/9 and he left £11,902, net personalty £9,714 to his widow. Arthur's mother was Alice Flora née Scott (1856–1938). Sandford and Alice married on 24th December 1878 at Calcutta, Bengal, India. When she died on 19th November 1938 at The Abbey, Portishead, Somerset, her effects were valued at £3,347/8/8. Arthur had four siblings:

- Reginald George Kilby (born c.1874–1949) was born at Moynffopore, India and became a civil servant. His marriage to Hazel Ermyntrude Miles née Pollard (1887–1926) was registered in the fourth quarter of 1908. She died on 11th July 1926 at Nerbuddah Estate, Turbo, Kenya Colony, British East Africa.
- Dorothy Alice Kilby (1881–1971) was born at Calcutta, India. She married George Hewlett MA (1874–1962) on 6th April 1910 at St Mary Magdalene, Lillington, Warwickshire. He was a master at Rugby School. From 1921 to 1961 they lived at The Abbey, Portishead, Somerset. They had two sons – George HK Hewlett 1913 and Arthur J Hewlett 1920.
- Sylvia Mary Kilby (1882–83) was born and died at Calcutta.
- Winifred Rosa Kilby (1890–1907) died on 31st January 1907 at Girton House, Torquay, Devon following an appendix operation.

Arthur's paternal grandfather, George Henry Kilby (born c.1820), was the son of John Kilby, Lord Mayor of York. He married Ann née Worrier on 29th June 1840 at the Native Mission Chapel, Burdwan, India. In addition to Sandford, they had three other children – George Charles Kilby (1841–1923) became a barrister, Emily Ann Kilby 1843 and William John Kilby (1845–1902), all born at Fort William, Calcutta.

His maternal grandfather, Henry Emmanuel Scott (c.1805–60), a civil engineer, was born in Bengal, son of Lieutenant Colonel William Scott. He married Mary Ann née Kilby (born c.1822) on 9th December 1841 at Wakefield, Yorkshire. She was Principal of a ladies' school at East Hayes, Cheltenham, Gloucestershire in 1881. In addition to Alice, they had nine other children – Henry George Scott 1843, Francis Kilby Scott 1845–48, Arthur Percy Hall Scott 1847, Elizabeth Frances Scott 1848, Caroline Mary Scott 1850, Laura Blanche Scott 1852–1920, Rosamond Scott 1853, Charles Thomas Scott 1855–1926 and Lawrence Scott 1858–1922. Henry died on 10th April 1860 at Karachi, India.

Arthur was educated at Bilton Grange Preparatory School at Dunchurch, near Rugby, Winchester College (Southgate House) 1898–1902 and privately by Mr Geidt of Frankfurt-am-Main. After being trained at the Royal Military College Sandhurst he was commissioned into 1st South Staffordshire on 16th August 1905. Promoted lieutenant 31st October 1907 and captain 1st April 1910. He transferred to the 2nd Battalion in December 1910 to command E Company. Arthur was a talented linguist, being an interpreter in German and Hungarian (the only officer in the Army with this qualification) and was also fluent in Spanish and French. He was at No.6 Regimental District, Whittington Barracks, Lichfield, Staffordshire in 1911.

When war broke out, Arthur went to France with the Battalion on 13th August 1914. He was badly concussed by shellfire and exhaustion on 25th/26th August and was evacuated to the Base, returning to the Battalion on 24th September 1914. He carried out valuable solo reconnaissance work and sniping forays behind enemy lines on the Aisne front. The Battalion moved to the Ypres area in October. At Becelaere on 1st November, he led a counterattack, earning praise from his CO. **Awarded the MC for his actions in the Becelaere/Moorsleede area on 12th/13th November 1914; a critical situation arose when the French retreated on the Brigade's left flank and the South Staffordshires filled the gap, supervised by Captains Kilby and SG Johnson (also awarded the MC), LG 18th February 1915.** Arthur was wounded in the right arm and lung

Winchester College.

Whittington Barracks, Lichfield.

and evacuated to hospital in England. While recovering he was attached to the 8th Battalion in March 1915, but never fully regained the use of his right hand. He was presented with the MC by the King at Buckingham Palace on 10th May. The King was interested to see the bullet hole in his uniform. Lieutenant John Dimmer VC also received his MC in the same investiture.

Arthur rejoined the Battalion in France later in May. On the night of 5th/6th September, he and Lieutenant Thompson, 1st King's, carried out a dangerous reconnaissance towards Embankment Redoubt, south of the La Bassée Canal. He came back with valuable information about the German defences and was recommended for the Distinguished Service Order, but this was overtaken by events later in the month. **Awarded the VC for his actions south of the La Bassée Canal, near Auchy, France on 25th September 1915, LG 30th March 1916.** He was also Mentioned in Sir John French's Despatches of 14th January and 30th November 1915, LG 17th February 1915 and 27th January 1916 respectively.

Arthur Kilby was killed during his VC action. The Germans buried him with great respect and marked his grave with a cross, but his remains were not identified until 19th February 1929 and now lie in Arras Road Military Cemetery, Roclincourt (III N 27).

As he never married, his VC was sent to his father by post, as was the practice for posthumous awards at that time. It was previously understood that Kilby's father received the VC from the King at Buckingham Palace on 11th July 1916. However, there is no record of the presentation in the Court Circular on that day or any other in the period 1916–21. The first confirmed presentation to a next of kin by the King was to the widow of Captain John Green on 7th October 1916. Arthur's will was administered by his father, effects £849/10/5.

In addition to the VC and MC, he was awarded the 1914 Star with 'Mons' clasp, British War Medal 1914–20 and Victory Medal 1914–19 with Mentioned-in-Despatches oak-leaf. His medals and death plaque were sold at a Spink's auction on 19th July 2012 for £240,000 and form part of the Lord Ashcroft VC Collection in the Imperial War Museum. His portrait and the bullet-holed tunic he wore when

York and the Minster, where Arthur Kilby spent many hours while based at nearby Strensall.

Leamington Spa War Memorial (Martin Edwards).

wounded at Ypres passed from his father to his mother and then to his sister Dorothy. They are now held by the Regimental Museum. Arthur is also commemorated on memorials at:

- St Nicholas's Chapel, York Minster – a memorial bust and family coat-of-arms designed by Sir WJ Tapper was dedicated in 1919. Arthur often visited the Minster when he was based at Strensall nearby.
- Garrison Church, Whittington Barracks, Lichfield, Staffordshire.
- Royal Leamington Spa War Memorial, Warwickshire.

2129 RIFLEMAN KULBIR THAPA
2nd Battalion, 3rd Queen Alexandra's Own Gurkha Rifles

Kulbir Thapa was born on 15th December 1889 at Nigalpani village, Palpa District, Nepal. His year of birth has also been seen as 1888. He was a Thapa of the Magar people. His father was Haria Gulte, but there are few other details about his family. It is known that he was married and had at least one son.

Kulbir enlisted as a Rifleman on 15th December 1907 in 1st Battalion, 3rd Queen Alexandra's Own Gurkha Rifles. He transferred to 2nd Battalion at the outbreak of war and sailed for France, arriving in September 1914. He was in action at Givenchy later that year and at Neuve Chapelle and Festubert in 1915.

Awarded the VC for his actions at Fauquissart, south of Mauquissart, France on 25th-26th September 1915, LG 18th November 1915. He was wounded during the VC action and admitted to hospital. Kulbir rejoined his Battalion in Egypt on 4th January 1916. He was promoted naik (corporal) next day and havildar (sergeant) later. While serving in Palestine, Rifleman Karanbahadur Rana of the same Battalion was also awarded the VC and the two were photographed together at the Gurkha Memorial at Gorakhpur c.1937. Kulbir Thapa was discharged from the Army in 1929.

There does not appear to have been a formal investiture. This is probably because Kulbir's unit departed for Egypt before the VC was gazetted. Volume 3 of the Victoria Cross Register in the National Archives (WO98/3) simply says, *No record of presentation*. It is reputed that the King expressed a desire to see Kulbir Thapa, who was ushered into Buckingham Palace, where the King presented him with the VC. However, there is no record of such a meeting.

In addition to the VC, he was awarded the 1914–15 Star, British War Medal 1914–20, Victory Medal 1914–19, George V Jubilee Medal 1935, George VI Coronation Medal 1937 and Elizabeth II Coronation Medal 1953. His VC is held by the Gurkha Museum, Peninsular Barracks, Romsey Road, Winchester, Hampshire.

Kulbir Thapa died at Nigalpani on 3rd October 1956 and is buried in Nigalpani Cemetery, but the precise location is not known. He is also commemorated at:

* 'Kulbir Thapa VC Residential Home', Kaski at Ram Ghat, Ward 10, Pokhara, Kaski, Nepal opened by Lieutenant General Sir Philip Trousdell in July 2010. The home was the first of its kind for British Gurkhas and their widows and was built by the Gurkha Welfare Trust.
* A special panel in the Royal Leicestershire Regiment Museum at Newarke Houses Museum, Leicester.

15851 PIPER DANIEL LOGAN LAIDLAW
7th Battalion, The King's Own Scottish Borderers

Daniel Laidlaw was born at Little Swinton, near Berwick-upon-Tweed, Northumberland on 26th July 1875. His father was Robert Laidlaw (1845–1918). He was a cattleman in 1867, an agricultural labourer living with his family at Crooks, Coldstream, Berwickshire in 1871, by 1875 a ferryman and in 1881 he was a stone-quarryman living with his family at 11 College Place, Berwick-upon-Tweed, Northumberland. By 1891 he was an engineman living at Bilton, near Alnwick, Berwickshire and in 1901 was living at Lesbury, Northumberland. Daniel's mother was Margaret née Logan (c.1852–1927) a field worker at the time of her marriage to Robert on 13th December 1867 at Swinton Mill, Northumberland. Daniel had seven siblings:

* William Robert Laidlaw (born 1868). He served in the KOSB for twenty-one years.
* Isabella Janet Laidlaw (1873–1906). She married John Cunningham Turnbull (born c.1874) in 1898.
* Alice Laidlaw (1877–1953). She married William John Quince (1879–1969) in 1900 and they had four children. In 1911 they were living 14 Limber Hill, Melton Mowbray, Leicestershire.
* Mary Anderson Laidlaw (1883–1956).

- James Laidlaw (born 1885), an agricultural labourer in 1901. He served in the RFA during the Great War.
- George Laidlaw (born 1887). He served in the RE during the Great War.
- Margaret Laidlaw (born 1893).

Daniel was educated at Berwick National and Lesbury Schools. He was a Boy Scout and by 1891 was an apprentice miller. He enlisted in 2nd Durham Light Infantry on 11th April 1896 and served in India, including on plague duties 22nd March–1st May 1898. Daniel was claimed by his eldest brother in June 1898 and transferred to the King's Own Scottish Borderers as a Piper.

Lesbury School, now the village hall.

Daniel married Georgina Mary née Harvie (1882–1947) on 11th April 1906 at the Baptist Church, Alnwick, Northumberland and they lived at East Kirk Newton, Northumberland. Daniel and Georgina had five children:

- Andrew Robert Laidlaw born 3rd February 1906. He married Agnes Ewart in 1928 and had three sons – Daniel and David 1928 and Joseph 1931.
- John Hume HH Laidlaw born 26th July 1909. He married Andrina W Hodge in 1934 and had two sons – Arthur 1934 and David 1940.
- Georgina M Laidlaw born 10th December 1912. She married David H Law in 1931 and had a son, Jeffrey, in 1931.
- Margaret E Laidlaw born 21st August 1913.
- Victor Loos Laidlaw (1920–82) enlisted in the King's Own Scottish Borderers in 1940. He married Isabella A Crosby in 1942 and had two sons – Victor 1943 and Robert 1947.

The family was living at Pottergate Place, New Row, Alnwick in 1911. Daniel was discharged to the Reserve on 11th April 1912 and was engaged in various civilian employments, including canteen manager at Alnwick Co-operative Stores at Alexandria and as a groom at D and DH Porter's horse breeding centre at South Doddington, Northumberland. He was also Assistant Scout Master of 1st Alnwick Troop.

Pottergate, Alnwick (English Heritage).

Daniel re-enlisted on 7th September 1914. He was described as 5′6″ tall, weighing 122 lbs, with hazel eyes, dark brown hair and his religious denomination was Presbyterian. Appointed acting corporal 26th September and went to France on 9th February 1915. He was found drunk in his billet on 19th February and reverted to private on 22nd February.

Awarded the VC for his actions near Loos and Hill 70, France on 25th September 1915, LG 18th November 1915. He was also awarded the Croix de Guerre (France), LG 1st May 1917. He was evacuated to Britain and treated at Lord Derby's Hospital, Warrington. While in hospital he was on the strength of the Depot from 2nd October and proceeded on sick leave 16th–25th December. He transferred to 9th (Reserve) Battalion at Catterick and later at Kinghorn on 19th January 1916.

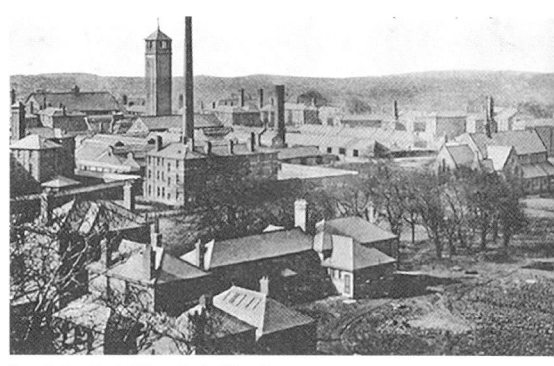

Lord Derby's Hospital, Warrington.

The VC was presented by the King at Buckingham Palace on 3rd February. Promoted corporal 16th June. 9th (Reserve) Battalion became 53rd Training Reserve Battalion on 1st September and Daniel received a new number (TR/2/4242). Promoted lance sergeant 17th October 1917 and transferred to 3rd (Reserve) Battalion at Claremorris on 4th November 1918 and the Depot on 11th November. He was demobilised on 3rd April 1919 and transferred to the Class Z Reserve on 30th April. From 29th July, he was granted 6d per day disablement pension.

Daniel was a member of the VC Guard at the Interment of the Unknown Warrior on 11th November 1920, during which he played the pipes. He spent many years moving to find work in industry or on the land around Berwickshire, Northumberland and Durham. He was out of work for eight years following the slump in the shipyards. Daniel played himself, 'The Piper of Loos', in the films, *The Guns of Loos* 1928 and *Forgotten Men* 1934. He was also interviewed on one of the earliest BBC television programmes. He tried chicken farming to escape unemployment and became sub-postmaster in Shoresdean, near Berwick, in 1938.

Daniel Laidlaw died at Shoresdean on 2nd June 1950 and was buried in an unmarked grave in Norham Churchyard, Northumberland. Among the mourners was Mr AG Lindsay Young,

Daniel Laidlaw in 1934 (Getty Images).

brother of Daniel's platoon commander at Loos. Daniel believed that the Army would provide a headstone, but as he died in peacetime he was not entitled to one. A headstone was finally dedicated on 2nd June 2001. He is also commemorated on a plaque in Norham Church.

In addition to the VC, he was awarded the 1914–15 Star, British War Medal 1914–20, Victory Medal 1914–19 with MID Oakleaf, George VI Coronation Medal 1937, Defence Medal and French Croix de Guerre with Bronze Palme. Although the Victory Medal carries the MID oakleaf, no trace of a Mention was found in the London Gazette. His VC is held by the National War Museum of Scotland, Edinburgh Castle having been presented by his son, Victor, and grandson (also a piper) on the field of the Battle of Loos on 25th September 2005. The King's Own Scottish Borderers could not accept it because of the cost of insurance.

1272 PRIVATE JOHN LYNN
2nd Battalion, The Lancashire Fusiliers

John Lynn was born at 6 Helvetia Street, Perry Hill, Catford. London on 21st April 1888. His birth was registered at Lewisham by his foster parents as John Walter Harrison Lynn, but he was generally known as John Harrison until he joined the Army. His father is unknown and beyond her name, Lily Lynn, nothing is known of his mother. John was fostered by Philip (or John) and Elizabeth J Harrison (born c.1861) when he was three days old. At the time of the 1891 Census, he was a visitor at the home of Robert and Emma Hodder at 33 Bradford Road, Lewisham.

(Lancashire Fusiliers)

North Surrey District School, Anerley, Upper Norwood, Surrey, where John Lynn was sent in September 1899. The School was founded in 1849 to cover the Poor Law Unions of Richmond, Croydon, Kingston, Lewisham, Wandsworth and Clapham, Chelsea and Kensington. Behind the School on the right is the Crystal Palace (www.workhouses.org.uk).

Training Ship *Exmouth*. She was launched in 1854 and in 1877 was loaned to the Metropolitan Asylums Board as a training ship.

John Lynn as a young bandsman (Lancashire Fusiliers).

He was educated at Christ Church School (now Christ Church, Church of England Primary School), Forest Hill, where he was known as John Harrison. He was sent to North Surrey District School, Anerley, Upper Norwood, Surrey, from 1st September 1899, but ran away during the short period he was there. The School was founded in 1849 to cover the Poor Law Unions of Richmond, Croydon, Kingston, Lewisham, Wandsworth and Clapham, Chelsea and Kensington, as an industrial school for 500 children. It closed in 1937.

John was admitted as a boy sailor (Entrant 7135) on the Training Ship *Exmouth* on 18th October 1899 from the Lewisham Poor Law Union. He was registered as J H Lynn, aged ten and a half. *Exmouth* was launched in 1854, armed with 90 guns and in 1877 was loaned to the Metropolitan Asylums Board as a training ship until she was broken up in 1905. John was discharged from *Exmouth* on 12th January 1901 and enlisted as a bandsman in 3rd Lancashire Fusiliers under his real name.

He served with 2nd Battalion in Malta, India and at Wellington Barracks in Bury, Lancashire. John transferred to the Reserve early in 1914 and took a job in the armour plate grinding department of Messrs Armstrong-Whitworth in Openshaw. He lodged at 56 Queens's Road, Gorton, Manchester and became engaged to the daughter, Miss Alice Mason (born 1887). Alice planned a double wedding with her sister for November 1914, but it was postponed to April 1915 because of the outbreak of war.

John was recalled in August 1914 and went to France on the 26th. Alice was on holiday in Blackpool when war broke out and her efforts to say farewell to John

John Lynn, second from left in the front row in 1912 (Lancashire Fusiliers).

Vlamertinghe Church, where John Lynn was buried. His grave was lost in later shelling and he is commemorated on the Vlamertinghe Churchyard Memorial in Grootebeek British Cemetery, Reninghelst. His remains may still be here somewhere.

before he left the Depot were thwarted by trains crammed with soldiers. **John was awarded the DCM for his actions at Le Touquet in the Battle of Armentiéres on 21st October 1914;** he took charge of an isolated machine-gun when his sergeant (actually 1421 Corporal Edgar M Parkinson) was killed, brought it out of action when it jammed and returned to the firing line with fresh ammunition when it was repaired and brought it back into action, **LG 17th December 1914.** He took part in the Christmas Truce 1914, during which the Battalion won a soccer match against the Saxons 3–2.

John was unable to get leave for his wedding in April 1915. **Awarded the VC for his actions near Ypres, Belgium on 2nd May 1915, LG 29th June 1915.** John had told a comrade that in the event of his death, his possessions were to go to his fiancée, Alice Mason. As a result the VC was sent to her by post at 56 Queen's Road, Gorton on 29th March 1916. Her distress at losing John was compounded when her handbag containing his letters from the front was lost. **Also awarded the Russian Cross of the Order of St George 4th Class, LG 25th August 1915.**

John Lynn died of gas poisoning at St Julian, Belgium on 2nd May 1915 and was buried in Vlamertinghe Churchyard. His grave was later destroyed by shellfire and he is commemorated on the Vlamertinghe Churchyard Memorial in Grootebeek British Cemetery, Reninghelst. He is also commemorated:

- On a plaque in the shopping centre at Lewisham, London.
- On a memorial at the church of St Mary the Virgin, Bury, Lancashire.
- His VC action was featured in Issue No. 1148 of the *Victor* comic dated 19th February 1983.

In addition to the VC and DCM, John Lynn was awarded the 1914 Star with 'Mons' clasp, British War Medal 1914–20, Victory Medal 1914–19 and the Russian Cross of St George, 4th Class. His medals were presented to the Lancashire Fusiliers Regimental Museum in 1955 and are held by The Fusiliers' Museum Lancashire, Moss Street, Bury, Lancashire.

LIEUTENANT GEORGE ALLAN MALING
61st Field Ambulance, Royal Army Medical Corps (att'd 12th Battalion, The Rifle Brigade)

George Maling was born at Bishopwearmouth, Sunderland, Co Durham on 6th October 1888. His father was Edwin Allan Maling JP MRCS (1838–1920), a surgeon. His mother was Maria (or Mary) Jane née Hartley (1846–1932). Edwin and Maria married on 30th April 1868 at St George, Hanover Square, London. The family was living at 48 John Street, Bishopwearmouth in 1881, Mowbray Road, Bishopwearmouth in 1891, Middleton Tyas, Yorkshire in 1901 and Blackwell House, Darlington, Co Durham in 1920. His paternal grandmother, Joanna Mary Maling née Allan, was related to Henry Havelock VC. George had eight siblings:

(Dr J Maling)

- Eleanor Maud Maling (1870–1950) never married.
- Allan Hartley Maling (1871–79).
- Arthur Freville Maling (1872–1838) graduated from Oxford University and became a solicitor. He was commissioned on the General List, Territorial Force Reserve during the Great War. Promoted lieutenant 7th September 1916. Appointed temporary captain and employed by the Ministry of National Service as Chief Registration Officer of an Area on 29th June 1917. He relinquished his commission on 15th January 1919. He married Maud Victoria née Nichol in 1920.
- William Allan Maling (1874–86).
- Edwin Mulgrave Maling (1877–1954) was deaf from infancy. He married Winifred née Whiting in 1924 and they had two children.
- Florence Mary Maling (1879–87).
- Winifred Hartley Maling (1880–1948) married Walter Carless Harrild in 1908.
- Amy Louise Maling (1883–1962) never married.

Amongst his uncles were:

- William Haygarth Maling (1861–1923) served as a temporary captain from 1st May 1917 at Sunderland War Hospital, relinquishing his commission on 3rd November 1919. He married Evelyn Stafford née Robinson (1881–1955) in 1907 and they had two children.
- Frederick Maude Maling (1868–1938) married Caroline Jane née Hodgson (1873–1937) in 1898 and they had two sons and two daughters. He was a Merchant Navy captain with the Nautilus Steam Shipping Co Ltd. During the war he was commissioned as a lieutenant in the Royal Naval Reserve aboard the unarmed munitions ship SS *Palm Branch* (Nautilus Steam Shipping Co Ltd). On 21st November 1916, she was sailing for America when a U-boat opened fire on her. Maling ordered full speed ahead and plotted a weaving course. Although several shells holed the lifeboats and damaged the superstructure, the distance increased and the U-boat commander called off the attack. Maling called in to port for repairs and arrived safely at his destination. He was awarded the Distinguished Service Order (LG 12th May 1917). SS *Palm Branch* was fitted with a 13 Pounder gun and was carrying a cargo of high explosives and poison gas bound for North Russia when a U-boat was spotted off the Murmansk coast on 4th May 1917. Its torpedo passed underneath the hull and she surfaced. Maling ordered fire to be opened. It is alleged U-*75* was sunk, but she was not lost until December 1917 and there are no records of a U-boat being lost in that area at that time. It is more likely the U-boat submerged and withdrew. A second U-boat surfaced and opened fire but SS *Palm Branch* disabled her guns with two shots and she also made her escape. Maling was awarded a Bar to the DSO (LG 22nd June 1917). He was placed on the Retired List on 6th July 1920.
- James Hartley (1838–1908) was a captain in the Northumberland Fusiliers.

George was educated at Oatlands College in Harrogate, Uppingham School 1903–07, Exeter College Oxford 1907–14 (BA Hons Natural Sciences & MA 1914) and St Thomas's Hospital, London (MB BCh 1914, MRCS & LRCP 1915). He was commissioned in the RAMC as a lieutenant on 18th January 1915 and went to France on 20th July. **Awarded the VC for his actions near Fauquissart, France on 25th September 1915, LG 18th November 1915.** The VC was presented by the King at Buckingham Palace on 15th January 1916. George was appointed temporary captain on 18th January and served at the Military Hospital Grantham until returning to the front in 1917 to join 34th Field Ambulance in 11th Division until the end of the war. He relinquished his commission on 8th April 1919.

George married Daisy Mabel née Wolmer (born c.1890) from Winnipeg, Canada on 5th May 1917. She was a Queen Alexandra's Imperial Military Nursing Service Reserve ward sister and they met at Belton Military Hospital, Grantham. As a staff nurse she was awarded the Royal Red Cross Decoration 2nd Class for valuable services in connection with the war (LG 3rd June 1916). George and Daisy had four children:

- John Allan Maling (1920–2012) joined 6th Queen's Own (Royal West Kent Regiment) (164818). On his first night in barracks he was so appalled to discover that none of the soldiers wore pyjamas, that he resolved to gain a commission as soon as possible. He was granted a Regular Army Emergency Commission on 21st December 1940 and in November 1942 landed at Bougie, Algeria and joined the advance on Tunis. On 17th November, his unit marched twenty miles, during which they were continuously strafed. The Battalion arrived at Djebel Abiod at 4 a.m. and Maling's platoon was ordered to defend an important road junction. Eighteen Mark IV Panzers followed by several vehicles carrying infantry advanced towards his position. Maling held his fire until the leading tanks had driven over his slit trenches and then gave the order. His platoon killed 40–50 enemy paratroopers, for the loss of only one man. He led his men through enemy territory after dusk and got them back to his own lines at dawn. For this action

Uppingham School Chapel.

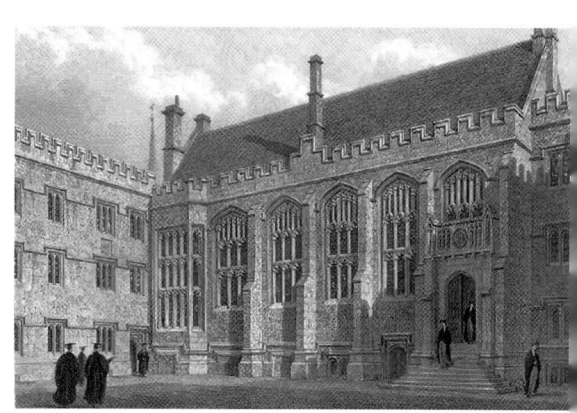

Exeter College (F Mackenzie/JH Le Keux).

St Thomas's Hospital, London (Henry Taunt).

he was awarded the Military Cross (LG 11th February 1943). He took part in the capture of Tunis, the invasion of Sicily and Italy and finished the war in Austria. Promoted captain and temporary major on 19th June 1946. After demobilization he studied medicine at St Thomas's Hospital and went into general practice at Tonbridge Wells, Kent. John married Daphne Judith 'Judy' née Haines in 1952 and they had three children, one of whom died very young. John retired in 1980 and moved to Burwash, Etchingham, East Sussex where he enjoyed fishing, gardening and reading military history.

- Edwin Lambton Maling (twin with Phyllis) (1922–41) joined the Royal Navy as an ordinary seaman (JX/301909). He died of meningitis at HMS *Ganges*, a shore based training establishment, on 18th October 1941, just a few weeks after enlisting. He is buried in Shotley Royal Naval Cemetery, Suffolk (1 E 7).
- Phyllis Mary Maling (twin with Edwin) (1922–2008) married Richard David Mortlock (1923–76) in 1951 at Tonbridge, Kent and they had three children.
- Barbara Maling (1927–49).

George became resident medical officer at Victoria Hospital for Children in Chelsea. He was later outpatients surgeon at St John's Hospital, Lewisham before going into partnership practicing in Lee, South London. He was a keen fisherman and tennis player.

George Maling died at his home, 'St Monica's', Lee, London on 9th July 1929 and is buried in Chislehurst (Town) Cemetery, Kent (A2017). He left £15,579 in his will. He is also commemorated on memorials at:

- St George's Memorial Church, Ypres, Belgium.
- Millbank, London.
- Uppingham School, Rutland.
- Royal Army Medical Corps Memorial Grove at the National Memorial Arboretum at Alrewas, Staffordshire.

Victoria Hospital for Children, Chelsea. During the First World War two wards were used by 2nd London General Hospital for a period. In the Second World War it was hit by bombs a number of times. It closed in 1964.

In addition to the VC, he was awarded the 1914–15 Star, British War Medal 1914–20 and Victory Medal 1914–19. The VC is held by the Army Medical Services Museum, Mytchett, Surrey.

A/2052 RIFLEMAN WILLIAM MARINER
2nd Battalion, The King's Royal Rifle Corps

William Mariner was born at 12 Wellington Street, Chorley, Lancashire on 29th May 1882. He was registered at birth as John William Mariner. The family name was recorded as Marriner or Mariner in various census returns and registry office entries. William's father is unknown. His mother was Alice Ann Marriner (1865–1935), a cotton weaver in 1881, lodging at 15 Wellington Street with the Wilkinson family (probably her uncle on her mother's side). Alice's mother, Nancy Marriner née Wilkinson (c.1838–1900), was living at 12 Wellington Street at the time with her son George (born 1869). Alice had another child illegitimately, Frederick Mariner, in 1884. She married John Wignall (1870–99) in the 4th quarter of 1888. They had a daughter, Mary Elizabeth Wignall (born 1889) and a son, Harold Wignall (1896–1957). At the time of the 1891 Census, they were living with Alice's parents, William (c.1838–93) and Nancy Marriner at 11 Wellington Street. The VC was recorded as William Mariner's son, as was Frederick, rather than his grandsons. This may have been an enumerator's mistake, but it could have been deliberate for the sake of appearances.

John Wignall died in 1899 and at the time of the 1901 Census, Alice was living at 13 Wellington Street, the address William gave when he enlisted. In 1904, Alice had another son illegitimately, Dennis Wignall, but no record of the birth or details of the father could be identified. By 1911 she had moved to 18 Fletcher Street, Lower Broughton, Salford, Lancashire.

William was educated at St Laurence Parochial School Chorley, following which he was employed as a weaver by Mr Felder of Chorley and later as a miner. When he enlisted in 3rd Loyal North Lancashire (6159) on 28th February 1899, he was described as 5′ 2½″ tall, weighing 108 lbs, with fresh complexion, grey eyes and brown hair. His religious denomination was Church of England. Having purchased his discharge on 17th June, he enlisted again on 3rd January 1900 (2519) at Gosport, this time in the King's Royal Rifle Corps. He gave his occupation as labourer and was posted to the Depot the same day. He had grown an inch and put on nine pounds in just under a year, but was still under 5′ 5″ and weighed less that eight and a half stones. Having been posted to 4th Battalion on 30th March and 2nd Battalion on 2nd November, he served in India from 2nd November 1901 to 27th December 1907. While there he became a lightweight wrestling champion.

He was granted Good Conduct Pay on 3rd January 1902, but forfeited it on 7th February 1903. On 6th June he was sentenced by a District Court Martial to eighty-four days imprisonment with hard labour for using violence and threatening language to a superior officer. He extended his service to complete eight years on 1st April 1904 and was upgraded to Class 2 the same day. He achieved 3rd Class Education on 4th October, but his progress did not last for long. On 9th June 1906, he was tried again by District Court Martial for using threatening language to a superior officer and was imprisoned for fifty-six days with hard labour. On 20th May 1907 he was upgraded to Class 2 again and Good Conduct Pay was restored on 30th July. Having been upgraded to Class 1 on 22nd August, he transferred to the Army Reserve on 2nd January 1908, from which he was discharged on 2nd January 1912.

He found work as a brick-setter, but was convicted for breaking and entering and served a year in jail in Manchester. He did not marry and is not thought to have had any children.

William re-enlisted on 26th August 1914 and went to France on 29th November. **Awarded the VC for his actions near Cambrin, France on 22nd May 1915, LG 23rd June 1915.** He returned to Salford on leave in early August 1915 and left home one day without telling his mother. She suspected he was going to receive his VC and travelled to Windsor with her daughter, but on arrival discovered the investiture was to take place in London. The VC was presented by the King

Peninsula Barracks, Winchester, Depot of the King's Royal Rifle Corps and Rifle Brigade.

William Mariner watches as preparations are made for his civic reception in Salford in August 1915.

The reception at Salford Town Hall.

outside Buckingham Palace on 12th August 1915. Alice and Mary joined hundreds of other spectators and saw William as he left the investiture. The crowd was so large that William and fellow VCs, Henry May and Joseph Tombs, left immediately in a taxi, unaware that his mother and sister were in the crowd. Back in Salford he received a civic reception from the Mayor and Corporation and was presented with an illuminated address and a gold watch. He was also given a reception at Chorley, accompanied by Sergeant Williams, the first member of the Australian contingent to be awarded the DCM. On the way to Chorley, William called to see Mrs Peddie, a former mistress at his school. He was received at the Town Hall by Sir Henry Hibbert and the Mayor, Councillor Kellick.

William returned to the front, where he was wounded and evacuated to England on 24th August. He was charged with absence at Clerkenwell on 5th October for being two days overdue from leave. He claimed, *I have been messing about with Jack Johnson and doing a bit of recruiting.* He returned to France on 12th October.

William Mariner took part in a raid on the night of 30th June/1st July 1916 at the Railway Triangle near Double Crassier, southeast of Loos, France. A witness, Giles Eyre, recorded what happened, *And then Marriner loses his remaining senses ... and runs down in pursuit of the retreating enemy. And as I round the corner and glimpse Marriner in the very act of bayoneting a prone German – a whistling swish seems to fill the world – Marriner, caught full tilt by a shell, has been blown to fragments.* No remains were recovered and he is, strangely, commemorated on the Thiepval Memorial.

In addition to the VC, William was awarded the 1914–15 Star, British War Medal 1914–20 and Victory Medal 1914–19. He is also commemorated on a memorial plaque at

William Mariner's name on the Thiepval Memorial.

The much enlarged Double Crassier at Loos, near which William Mariner was killed on the night of 30th June/1st July 1916.

Chorley, dedicated in 2002. His VC action featured in Issue 554 of the *Victor* comic on 2nd October 1971.

The whereabouts of the VC was unknown for many years until in late 2005 the home of William Wignall (probably the son of the VC's half-brother Dennis), near High Peak, Derbyshire was being cleared after his death. During the clearance the VC was found in a drawer, where it had probably been since 1946. The owners insisted on anonymity, so their relationship to William Mariner it is not known. The VC was auctioned by Spink's on 23rd November 2006 (Sale 6025, Lot 222). Lord Ashcroft learned that the Civic Museum, Astley Hall, Chorley was interested in purchasing it, so did not bid. Unfortunately the Civic Museum failed to secure the VC and it was sold to a private collector for the hammer price of £105,000. The location of William's other medals is not known.

LIEUTENANT ERIC ARCHIBALD McNAIR
9th Battalion, The Royal Sussex Regiment

Eric McNair was born at 5 Harrington Street, Calcutta, India on 16th June 1894. He was known to his friends as 'Fuzzy'. His father was George Burgh McNair, born at Monghyr, West Bengal in 1852. He was senior partner in the firm of Morgan and Co, Solicitors of Calcutta and died there in 1932. His mother was Isabella Frederica née Gow-Smith, born at Jessore, West Bengal in 1851. George and Isabella's marriage was registered in the 3rd quarter of 1882 at Kensington, London. The family also lived at 1 Hastings Street, Calcutta. Isabella died at Calcutta in 1940. Eric had three siblings:

- George Douglas McNair (1887–1967) was born at Calcutta. He was called to the Bar, Middle Temple in 1911. His marriage to Primrose Garth (1891–1968) was registered in the 4th quarter of 1914 at Amersham, Buckinghamshire and they had three children – Erica McNair 1920, Richard D McNair 1925 and Philip GG McNair 1929. He served in the Indian Army in Mesopotamia 1916–19; MID twice and MBE, LG 3rd June 1919.

Old Court House Street, Calcutta.

He held various appointments – Puisne Judge of the High Court of Judicature, Calcutta 1934; Chairman of the Dacca Riots Enquiry Committee 1941–42; Puisne Judge of the High Court of Judicature at Fort William, Bengal, during which he was Knighted, LG 1st January 1943; Legal Chairman of the Pensions Appeals Tribunals 1946–47; JP Devon 1950; Chairman Standing Joint Committee 1956–58; Deputy Chairman Quarter Sessions 1954 and Chairman from 1956. They lived at Morden, Cockington Lane, Torquay, Devon.
- Frederica Annie Lillian McNair (born 1884) married Oswald Alan Geoghegan (1879–1961) in 1906 in Calcutta and they had a son, Peter Burgh Geoghegan, in 1909. Oswald was commissioned in the South Staffordshire Regiment on 12th August 1899. Promoted lieutenant 1901, captain 1908, major 1915, lieutenant colonel 1925 and colonel 12th August 1929 (1st February 1930). He was appointed Superintendent Gymnasia India 1904–06 and transferred to the Supply and Transport Corps, Indian Army, in 1909. Appointed Assistant Director Supply & Transport Aden as temporary lieutenant Colonel March–October 1917; Assistant Director Supply & Transport India 1926–29; Deputy Director, Supply & Transport India February 1930; HQ Staff Army of India, Directorate of Supply & Transport as Deputy Director of Personnel June 1932.
- Violet Isabelle McNair (1885–86).

Eric was educated at Mr Sylvester's School, Branksome Hall, Godalming and then at Charterhouse 1907–13, where he was a member of the OTC and head of school. In 1913 he went to Magdalen College, Oxford, intending to take an Indian Civil Service post on graduation.

While at Oxford, he became a Freemason, being Initiated into Apollo University Lodge (No.357) November 1913, Passed to the Second Degree January 1914 and Raised on 6th December 1914. Lieutenant John Norwood VC and Lieutenant Colonel John Collings-Wells VC were also members of Apollo University Lodge.

Eric was commissioned in 10th Royal Sussex on 8th October 1914 and promoted lieutenant on 22nd December. He transferred to 9th Battalion in August 1915,

Charterhouse School, Godalming.

went to France on 8th October and was promoted captain on 14th October. **Awarded the VC for his actions near Hooge, Belgium on 14th February 1916, LG 30th March 1916.** The VC was presented by the King at Buckingham Palace on 20th May 1916. Eric was severely wounded at Guillemont on the Somme on 18th August with gun shot wounds to shoulder and back. He attended a staff course in early 1917 and was appointed GSO3 on 20th August.

Magdalen College, Oxford.

He returned to active duty in Italy early in 1918. Appointed GSO3 18th April–17th July. He was evacuated to Genoa Base Hospital (either 11th General or 38th and 51st Stationary Hospitals) with chronic dysentery and died there on 12th August 1918. He is buried in Staglieno Cemetery, Genoa, Italy (I B 32). He never married.

In addition to the VC, he was awarded the 1914–15 Star, British War Medal 1914–20 and Victory Medal 1914–19. His brother, Sir George Douglas McNair, left the VC to the Royal Sussex Regiment when he died in 1967. It is held by the Royal Sussex Regiment Museum, Eastbourne, East Sussex. Eric is also commemorated:

- On the Regimental Memorial, Chichester Cathedral.
- On a memorial outside the chapel at Magdalen College, Oxford – also commemorated is JF Russell VC DSO MC.
- The former Royal Sussex Regiment Depot, Roussillon Barracks at Chichester, was redeveloped for housing and six roads were named after Royal Sussex VCs, including McNair Way.
- His VC action featured in Issues 219 and 853 of the *Victor* comic dated 1st May 1965 and 25th June 1977.

1147 (LATER 240048) CORPORAL SAMUEL MEEKOSHA
1/6th Battalion, The Prince of Wales's Own (West Yorkshire Regiment)

Samuel Meekosha was born at 3 High Street, Leeds, Yorkshire on 16th September 1893. The family moved to 91 Tennant Street, West Bowling, Bradford in 1895. His father was Alexander Mikosza (c.1865–1948) a Russian/Polish tailor from Suwalki, Poland, who anglicised his surname to Meekosha and settled in Bradford. One of his uncles, Colonel Vladislor Mikosza, served in the Russian Imperial Cavalry in the late 19th Century and during the Russo-Japanese War.

(GA Wilkinson)

Tennant Street, Bradford where the Meekosha family lived in the 1890s.

Suwalki, Poland in the late 19th Century.

Samuel's mother was Mary Catherine Cunningham née Mason (1866–1936), a tailoress. Her first marriage was to Martin Cunningham (c.1864–c.1890) in 1886. Mary was living as a widow with her widowed mother and brother at 82 High Street, Leeds in 1891. Alexander and Mary's marriage was registered in the 4th quarter of 1892 at Leeds. In 1901 the family was living at 57 Longcroft Place, Bradford. In 1911 Mary was living as head of household with her children at 7 Bramley Street, Bradford. Alexander married Charlotte 'Lottie' L Dore (1888–1962) in the 1st quarter of 1936 at Leeds North. Charlotte married Thomas Weir in 1951. Samuel had six siblings:

- Martin Meekosha (born 1895) was a weaver in 1911 and was training to be ordained as a Catholic priest in Holland when the war broke out. In 1937 he married Madeleine Glynn (1895–1949) at Manchester North.
- Joseph Meekosha (born 1898) enlisted in 18th West Yorkshire (2nd Bradford Pals) on 11th April 1915 (18/738), adding two years to his age. He was described as a warehouseman, 5′ 4¾″ tall and weighed just 99 lbs. He gave his next of kin as his mother at 91 Tennant Street, West Bowling, Bradford. At Clipstone on 9th March 1916 he was absent and confined to barracks for four days. On 22nd April he was promoted lance corporal in 20th West Yorkshire and transferred to 89 Training Reserve Battalion on 1st September. On 22nd October he failed to report to the guardroom when leaving camp and was reduced to private. On 25th November he was absent and confined to barracks for three days and later that month he failed to report again. He transferred to the RGA Reserve Brigade on 30th December (142032–10760 also appears in his record). Posted to 47 Company, RGA Signal Training Depot on 27th January 1917. He was absent at Catterick in March, but qualified as a Signaller Class 1 on 19th April. Posted to A Siege Depot, Hipswell Camp, Catterick on 26th June. He was with 401 Siege Battery at Bedford when ordered overseas on 28th July and went to France on the 30th, joining 307 Siege Battery on 10th August. Admitted to 35 Field Ambulance with myalgia on 15th

342 Victoria Crosses on the Western Front April 1915–June 1916

September and to No.14 General Hospital on 12th October. On 20th September 1918, he was granted sixteen days leave from 59th Brigade. He was attached to B Siege Park Workshops 9th–23rd November. On 19th February 1919 he was charged with absence and neglect and lost seven days' pay. Joseph left France on 9th June, reported to Ripon next day and was demobilised from there to the Class Z Reserve on 9th July. The address he gave for his medals to be delivered was 9 Norton Gate, Little Horton, Bradford. Joseph married Lillian Hodges in 1920. They adopted a son, George, who served in the Royal Navy before living in Iceland. Joseph served in the Army again in the Second World War.

- Bernard Meekosha (1906–07).
- Elizabeth Meekosha (1896–97).
- Mary Meekosha (born 1899) married Fred Watson in 1925 and they had four children – Eleanor Watson 1926, Alfred Watson 1930 and twins Kathleen and Kenneth Watson 1932.
- Eleanor Meekosha (1904–63) married James W Howard (1899–1968) in 1942 and they had two children – Sylvia Howard 1943 and James E Howard 1948.

Samuel was educated at St Joseph's Roman Catholic School, Bradford and was a member of Sedburgh Boys Club there. He was employed as an office worker by Messrs J Emsley & Co of Parkside Mills, West Bowling, Bradford and later by the Ivel Boot Company, Manchester Road, Bradford.

He enlisted into 6th West Yorkshire (Territorial Force) on 20th February 1911 and was mobilised on 5th August 1914. Promoted corporal 13th February 1915. Undertook defence duties on the Lincolnshire Coast until 9th April, when the Battalion moved to Gainsborough in preparation for service overseas. He went to France on 16th April and was promoted srgeant on 15th November.

Awarded the VC for his actions near the Yser, Belgium on 19th November 1915, LG 22nd January 1916. He was originally decorated with the DCM ribbon by General Sir Herbert Plumer at Ypres in December 1915. The VC was presented by the King at Buckingham Palace on 4th March 1916. Samuel left France on 5th November 1916 and was commissioned in 1/5th West Yorkshire on 27th June 1917. He served in France 15th August–19th December and was wounded in the right wrist and left temple in October. Promoted lieutenant 27th December 1918 and appointed Station Accountant Officer and temporary captain on 15th May 1919. Temporary Accountant Grade 2, 1st August–18th November 1919 when he

Samuel and Bertha on their wedding day, 16th November 1916 (Mary Booth).

was demobilised. He transferred to the Corps of Military Accountants as a captain and Accounts Officer 6th Class on 31st January 1920 with seniority from 19th November 1919. He retired on 17th March 1926 as a captain Regular Army Reserve of Officers with seniority from 15th January 1919.

Samuel Meekosha married Bertha Elizabeth Charlotte née Duval (1889–1945) on 16th November 1916 at Bradford. Bertha's father, Georg Felix Duval (c.1862–1934), was born in Alsace in France, migrated to England and was manager of a wool business in 1901, living at 1 Ann Place, Bradford. He married Sarah Jane née Whitehead (1856–1908) in 1884 at Bradford. Samuel and Bertha had three children:

- Felix Samuel Meekosha (13th January 1919–November 2000) served in the Royal Engineers during the Second World War in North Africa and Italy. He married Clarissa J Clarke in 1945 at Nottingham, where they settled and had three children – Mark Meekosha 1947, Helen Meekosha 1951 and Clare Meekosha 1956.
- Sidney Alexander Meekosha (later Ingham) born 29th December 1920 served in the RAF before moving to the USA about 1951.
- Mary Cecilia Meekosha (later Ingham) (30th June 1922–c.2001) served in the ATS during the Second World War. She married Clifford Booth in 1945 and they had at least one daughter, Pauline.

Samuel bought a wholesale tobacco business in Bradford with financial assistance from Bertha. The business started well but, when rental costs proved too heavy, she

Family photograph at the wedding of Samuel's daughter, Mary. Standing on the left in Royal Navy uniform is George, adopted son of Joseph Meekosha, Samuel's brother. Second from the left is Samuel's son, Sidney, in RAF uniform. In the centre are Clifford Booth and Mary, who is standing next to her father. Second from the right is Joseph Meekosha (Mary Booth).

had to turn the family home into a place of business. Bad luck and bad debts forced them to sell in April 1929. He left his family at 288 Great Horton Road, Bradford and moved to 21 Beaufort Road, Edgbaston, Birmingham in September 1929, where he worked on a commission basis. He found employment in early 1930 as a sales representative with John Player & Sons, covering South Wales. He lived for a time in Penarth, Glamorgan and later at 2 Penrhiw Villas, Oakdale, Monmouthshire.

After the 1929 VC Reunion Dinner, he felt that Bradford cared little for his circumstances, in contrast with nearby Leeds, where there was much more popular support for its VCs. He was not offered a post in Bradford following the collapse of his family business, but was offered positions in London from total strangers. Later in 1929, he attended the funeral of John Crawshaw Raynes VC on 16th November.

With the outbreak of the Second World War, he was recalled on 24th August 1939 and on 15th January 1940 transferred from the General List, Miscellaneous to the West Yorkshire Regiment in the rank of captain, retaining his seniority (22077). He transferred to the Royal Army Ordnance Corps on 26th October, retaining his seniority and was appointed acting major on 29th October 1941. He transferred to the Regular Army Reserve of Officers on 6th October 1944 and returned to the tobacco business. He was discharged from the Reserve as Captain S Ingham on 6th October 1948, having exceeded the age limit of liability to recall. He was granted the rank of honorary major.

In contrast to being almost ignored in 1929, by 1941 Samuel was unhappy with the attention he received due to his distinctive surname. The outbreak of the Second World War brought renewed interest. In 1941, he changed his name by deed poll to Ingham, including his wife and most of the children, but the eldest son, Felix, chose to retain Meekosha. One theory why he chose Ingham is because it was the last part of his mother's former married name, but it was also his second wife's maiden name.

Bertha died on 5th August 1945, having been in a mental institution for some time, and Samuel married Constance Emily Ingham (c.1903–c.1981) on 16th September 1945 at Leeds Registry Office.

Samuel Meekosha during the Second World War (Mary Booth).

Samuel died at home at 2 Penrhiw Villas, Oakdale, near Blackwood, Monmouthshire on 8th December 1950 after suffering a heart attack while attempting to start his car. He was cremated at Glyntaff Crematorium, Pontypridd and his ashes were scattered somewhere on Ilkley Moor. He is commemorated on:

- A plaque to Leeds VC winners at Victoria Gardens, Leeds Garden of Rest, The Headrow, Leeds.

- A memorial stone in the Garden of Remembrance behind Bradford Cenotaph was dedicated on 26th July 1999 to men associated with Bradford who were awarded the VC. Also named are Mathew Hughes, William Napier, George Chafer, Thomas Maufe, Eric Anderson and James Magennis.

In addition to the VC, he was awarded the 1914–15 Star, British War Medal 1914–20, Victory Medal 1914–19, King George VI Coronation Medal 1937, War Medal 1939–45 and Defence Medal. He did not claim the last two, but after his death his daughter Mary did claim them. After his son Felix died in 2000, his widow sold the VC at auction at Sotheby's on 3rd May 2001. It went to a private buyer for £101,000 (hammer price £92,000).

CAPTAIN THE REVEREND EDWARD NOEL MELLISH
Army Chaplains Department att'd 4th Battalion, The Royal Fusiliers (City of London Regiment)

Edward Mellish was born at Oakleigh Park, Friern Barnet, Hertfordshire on 24th December 1880. His second name, Noel, was because he was born on Christmas Eve. His father was Edward Mellish (1834–1916) a banker and businessman. His first marriage was to Ellen Borrowes (c.1831–1863), an Irishwoman, in 1855 in Victoria, Australia. His second marriage was to Sarah Waterworth in 1863 in Hong Kong, a former missionary with the Church Missionary Society. She died in 1875 at Honiton, Devon. His third marriage to the VC's mother, Mary 'Minnie' née Coppin (1852–1931), was on 28th August 1878 at St John's, Holloway, London. The family spent much time abroad in Mauritius and Hong Kong in the 1860s and 1870s, but were living at Tenable House, Oakleigh Road, Friern Barnet, Middlesex by 1881. Edward senior moved to Launceston in Cornwall with the intention of retiring, but his partner's gambling habits led to bankruptcy and he was forced to return to London. By 1891 the family was living at 24 Breakspear Road, Deptford and in 1901 at 261 Lewisham High Road. By 1906 they were at 8 Lewisham Road and were still there in 1911. Edward junior had fourteen siblings from his father's three marriages:

- Thomas Cotton Mellish, was born in 1857 in Australia and lived in India for a time before becoming a solicitor in Launceston, Cornwall. On 3rd August 1893, he, his half-sister Amy, a friend from India, Dr Hugh Leslie Anstead, and his sister Maud, were on the rocks near Backpit, Boscastle, Cornwall. Thomas slipped and cut his forehead. As he bent at the water's edge to bathe the wound, a large wave dragged him into the water. Anstead tried to rescue him and was dragged in by another wave. Amy, who could not swim, tried to reach them with her umbrella, but she was also washed off the rocks. Maud raised the alarm. PC Richards, Mr S Langdon, Mr Richard Bath and Mr R Pickard heard the screams and rushed over. Langdon went for a rope while Bath plunged in after the two men and Pickard tried to reach Amy, but the sea was too rough. Bath tied the rope around himself and was able to reach Amy, but she had already drowned. Thomas Mellish and Hugh Anstead were recovered later, but attempts to resuscitate them failed. At the inquest on 4th August, the jury returned a verdict of Accidental Death. Bath and Pickard were highly commended for their courage.

Oakleigh Park, Friern Barnet.

Lewisham High Road, later Lewisham Way.

- Ellen Mellish born and died in 1858.
- Edward Claude Mellish (c.1859–c.1861).
- Edith Mary Mellish (1861–1922) was born at Pailles, Moka, Mauritius. She was ordained Deaconess at St Andrew's Deaconess Community in London on 13th April 1891 and established the Community of the Sisters of Bethany (its name changed in 1912 to the Community of the Sacred Name to avoid confusion with an English community) in Christchurch, New Zealand, where she arrived in August 1893. She was New Zealand's first resident Anglican Deaconess. Edith was involved with rescue work among unmarried women and provided accommodation and assistance at St Mary's Home in Christchurch, which closed in 1910 after the establishment of a similar government institution. She then ran St Saviour's Home for orphaned children at Shirley and established St Agnes' Hostel for girls at Hokitika.
- Arthur Herbert Mellish (born c.1862) migrated to America, married Judith Sedora Stimson (born c.1864) and had two children – John Edward Mellish (c.1886–c.1970) and May Edith Mellish, born c.1889.

- Agnes Muriel Mellish (1865–1957) was born in Hong Kong. She married Robert Benson Sidgwick (1851–1934), a coffee-planter and they lived at Kingston, Jamaica. They had several children including – John Benson Sidgwick 1891, Agnes Muriel Sidgwick 1894–1951 and Henry Mellish Sidgwick 1907–66, who migrated to Brisbane, Queensland, Australia in 1928 and worked for the airline Qantas.
- Alice Louisa Mellish (1867–1954) was born in Hong Kong. She was Headmistress of Guernsey Ladies College and Jerusalem College, living at Grange Road, St Peter Port, Guernsey in 1911.
- Amy Adelaide Mellish (1869–93) drowned with her half-brother Thomas at Boscastle, Cornwall on 3rd August 1893.
- Lilian Emma Mellish (c.1871–1900) married Francis Tom Collins (1860–1939) in 1896. After Caius College, Cambridge 1877–81, he taught at Nuneaton School and Tonbridge School 1892–99. He was headmaster of Central Foundation School, Cowper Street, London 1899–1903 and headmaster of Alleyn's School, London 1903–20.
- Cecil Everard Mellish (c.1872–1949) was born in Hong Kong. He entered the Civil Service and was Assistant Clerk at St James in 1892. He moved to Jamaica, where he lived for twenty-five years, serving as a magistrate at Montego Bay. He was Commissioner for the Cayman Islands 1916–19.
- Mary Kathleen Mellish (1879–1952) married Walter John Hodson (1879–1961) in 1903 and had a daughter, Cicely M Hodson, in 1914. He was the son of the Rector of St Paul's, Deptford and worked at the Bank of England before going into property development. He married Margaret E Harris in 1952.
- Margaret Sara Mellish (1883–1912) contracted typhoid as a child, which left her frail for the rest of her life.
- Charles Gordon I Mellish (1885–86) died of typhoid fever.
- Richard Coppin Mellish (1890–1915) was born at Brockley, Kent. He was a bank clerk in 1911 and migrated to Canada. He returned to fight in the war as a 2nd lieutenant in 1st Middlesex and was killed in action on 25th September 1915 during the Battle of Loos. He is buried in Cambrin Churchyard Extension, Pas de Calais, France (K 26).

Edward was educated at King Edward VII Grammar School, Saffron Waldon, Essex 1893–95 and was a member of the Church Lads' Brigade. He was employed as a clerk in his father's business, but had an argument with his father's partner, who refused to release him early one Saturday to attend an important long-range shoot at Runnymede. He resigned and worked as a junior clerk in the Big Tree Wine Company, Waterloo Bridge, London for £1 per week.

Edward enlisted into the Artists' Rifles in 1899. He embarked on SS *Idaho* on 15th December 1900, landing at Cape Town on 9th January 1901. He enlisted in Baden Powell's Police (E505) at Bloemfontein. The unit was renamed the South African

Constabulary from 20th July 1902 and he was promoted to Trooper 2nd Class. While trapped in a farmhouse, he rode out through the Boers to seek assistance, returning immediately to assure his comrades that help was on its way. He was recommended for, but did not receive, the DCM for this action. At one time he was very ill with jaundice, dysentery and enteric fever and nearly died. When he was discharged from No.9 General Hospital at Bloemfontein, he chose to rejoin his Troop rather than transfer to a unit under his mother's cousin, Major Hicks. This involved marching sixty miles and his features were described as skeletal when he arrived. He re-engaged for two years in February 1903 and was granted three months leave in England. Having returned to South Africa to rejoin his unit at Fauresmith, he was discharged by purchase at Bethulie on 10th October.

No.9 General Hospital at Bloemfontein (Underwood & Underwood).

After the war he worked on the South African Railways before working at De Beers Diamond Mines at Jagersfontein, Orange Free State, as a supervisor for seven years. He was also involved in lay mission work 1907–10 and believed he should go into the church. He returned to England, where he discussed this with the Vicar of Lewisham, Canon RP Roseveare, who advised him to return to South Africa for a while and, if he still felt the same, he should then return to England for formal training and ordination. He studied Afrikaans at night and was licensed as a Lay Reader by the Bishop of Bloemfontein in March 1907. He passed the Central Entrance Examination in 1909, resigned his job in South Africa in 1910 and returned to England to enroll at King's College, London, where he studied Theology. He became an Associate in 1912, gained a 1st Class Pass and was ordained deacon at Southwark Cathedral,

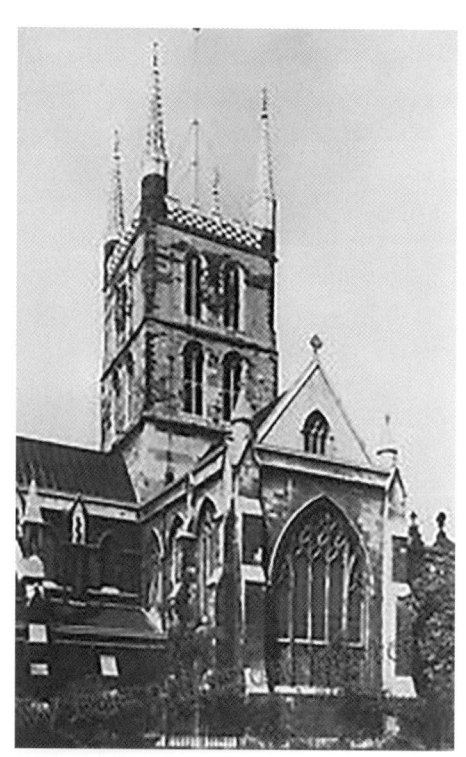

Southwark Cathedral, where Edward Mellish was ordained deacon on 29th September 1912.

London on 29th September 1912. Edward was appointed curate of St Paul's Deptford, where he was a captain in the Church Lads' Brigade (eventually commanding officer of St Paul's Brigade) and was ordained priest in December 1913. He took over an old public house behind the Deptford Empire Music Hall in New Cross Road and converted it into a boys' club, which they named 'The Noel Club'.

The Deptford Empire Music Hall in New Cross Road close to where Edward Mellish converted a disused pub into 'The Noel Club'.

On the outbreak of war Edward volunteered to serve as a chaplain, but the Bishop of London initially refused to release him. He later relented and Edward went to France on 4th May 1915, being commissioned as Chaplain 4th Class the same day. He served at 27th/28th Infantry Base Depot in Rouen, then with 142nd Field Ambulance in 3rd Division and then 4th Royal Fusiliers in September. He attended the execution of a deserter in March 1916.

Awarded the VC for his actions at St Eloi, Belgium on 27th–29th March 1916, LG 20th April 1916. Captain (later Major) William La Touche Congreve, who was later awarded the VC, received the DSO for his part in this action. The VC ribbon was presented by Major General JAL Haldane CB DSO, GOC 3rd Division on 24th April outside Flêtre church, near Bailleul, France. The VC was presented by the King at Buckingham Palace on 12th June 1916. Edward was made an Honorary Fellow of King's College London.

Edward was evacuated to No.45 Casualty Clearing Station at Daours and then to No.2 Red Cross Hospital at Rouen on 10th August, probably with trench fever, before being moved to England. While on sick leave at Saighton Camp, Chester on 2nd September, he fell, fractured his skull and was unconscious for two weeks. He returned to France on 4th December to serve with XIII Corps Heavy Artillery. He suffered attacks of aphasia (loss of speech and understanding) from January 1917, caused by the fall the previous year. He was admitted to hospital on 17th June and declared unfit for active service. A medical board at Edinburgh Military Hospital found him fit again on 16th August and he rejoined 4th Royal Fusiliers in France in September. He was attached to HQ 3rd Division July–August 1918 and sprained an ankle while taking cover from shellfire on 31st August.

On one occasion in the trenches, he overheard a soldier complaining about the clergy. Mellish said, *I will not allow such language to be used to my cloth. In the second place, kindly remember you are addressing an officer.* The soldier raised his arm threateningly and Mellish struck him squarely on the jaw, to the cheers of the other men.

Edward was Mentioned in Sir Douglas Haig's Despatch of 16th March 1919, LG 10th July 1919. Awarded the MC for his gallantry during the last two months of the war, LG 12th December 1919. He was demobilised on 17th February 1919 and relinquished his commission on 4th May. He received the MC from the King at Buckingham Palace on 25th June 1920.

No.2 Red Cross Hospital at Rouen.

Edward Mellish married Elizabeth Wallace née Molesworth (6th October 1894–27th December 1982) at St Paul's, Deptford on 3rd December 1918; the ceremony was conducted by Canon Roseveare. Elizabeth was born in Texas, USA. She was matron of a house at Wycombe Abbey School. They were living at 8 Lewisham Hill, South East London in 1919. Edward and Elizabeth had five children:

- Martin Molesworth Mellish born July 1920 and died a month later.
- Patrick Molesworth Mellish (9th December 1921–1st September 2009) was commissioned into 2nd Royal Fusiliers on 28th June 1941 (193692). Promoted war substantive lieutenant 1st October 1942. He lost a leg in North Africa and relinquished his commission on 19th June 1944, being granted the honorary rank of lieutenant. He lived at Flaxlands Farm, Merriot, Crewkerne, Somerset.
- Richard Wallace Paul Mellish (15th January 1923–10th December 2008) qualified as a doctor (MB, BS) and was commissioned as a Flying Officer in the Medical Branch RAFVR on 16th May 1946 (202757). He served on the Isle of Man and in India from January 1946 to May 1948. Promoted flight lieutenant 16th May

St Paul's Deptford where Edward was appointed curate in 1912 and where he married Elizabeth Molesworth in December 1918 (Friends of St Paul's).

Wycombe Abbey School, where Edward's wife Elizabeth was a house matron.

1947. He married Finetta Veronica Angell Bagot (born 1933) on 27th October 1956 at Wells, Somerset. Her father was Colonel Charles Edward Kirwan Bagot MC, commissioned Connaught Rangers 1915, transferred to Gloucestershire Regiment 1922, commanded 1st Battalion in Burma 1942 and retired in 1947. They migrated to the USA, where he became a paediatrician and they lived at Kiawah Island, South Carolina and Chittenden, Vermont. Richard and Finetta had three children – Martin Christopher Bagot Mellish 1957, Nicholas Charles Mellish 1961 and Fiona Molesworth Mellish 1964.

- Robin Hugh Mellish (21st May 1924–5th March 2004) was educated at Trinity Hall Cambridge. He was commissioned on 25th February 1944 (311318) and served in 2nd Royal Fusiliers. Promoted war substantive lieutenant 25th August 1944 and attached to 5th Battalion, Parachute Regiment in Greece and Palestine. He transferred to 1st Royal Fusiliers and served in Germany. He married Leonie Maria Petronella Knibbeler (1924–92) on 12th September 1954 at Folkestone. They ran a small farm and Robin was a land agent on various estates before working for Lord Pembroke at the Wilton Estate, Salisbury, Wiltshire. Robin and Leonie had two children – Elizabeth Leonie A Mellish 1956 and Nicholas Noel Mellish 1960. Robin married Kythe Plesance 'Penny' Hayne (née Peyps) on 20th December 1997 at Burcombe, Wiltshire.
- Margaret Elizabeth Claire Mellish, born on 4th December 1935, was known as Claire. She worked as a house matron and lived in Bath, Somerset.

Edward was offered the Parish of St Mark's, Lewisham by Canon Roseveare in November 1918 and took over as Vicar in March 1919. He was Vicar of Wangford-cum-Henham and Reydon near Southwold, Suffolk from September 1925 and Honorary Chaplain to St Felix School for Girls, Southwold. He was a member of the Mission of Help to India October 1922–March 1923, organised by the Archbishop of Canterbury. From 8th June 1928 he was Vicar of Great Dunmow in Essex. On 29th December 1929, a candle was blown against a casement curtain in the Lady Chapel following evensong. Edward raised the alarm, grabbed a fire extinguisher from his house and extinguished the flames, but the curtains and altar rails were badly damaged. In 1932, he appeared on the floor during a dance adjacent to the church, dressed only in pyjamas and ordered it to cease at midnight, although it was licensed to continue to 1 a.m. In 1933, he was left £500 by an admirer, *in grateful remembrance of his share in the Great War*. On 2nd May 1936, thieves broke in through a back window of Dunmow vicarage and dragged away an iron safe weighing about 80 Kgs from his study. It was smashed open with a pickaxe and his VC and MC were taken. Edward made an appeal for their safe return in The Times on 4th May and, on 21st May, he discovered the medals in an envelope under some papers on his desk.

Edward was a firm believer in preventing another war and supported the League of Nations rather than rearmament to secure peace. He volunteered to serve as a British Legion policeman in the Sudetenland in October 1938 and, although

St Mary's, Great Dunmow (Essex Churches).

St Mark's, Lewisham; the church was demolished in 1965.

released by his Bishop, he was never deployed. During the Second World War, Edward served as an ARP Warden and ran a forces canteen in a vacant public house on Dunmow High Street (St Martin's Club for Soldiers, Sailors and Airmen).

Edward was appointed DL Essex 22nd June 1946–1947. He was Perpetual Curate of Baltonsborough, near Street, Somerset from 1948 until he retired in 1953 to a farmhouse near Castle Cary, Somerset, moving to 'Court House', South Petherton in 1959. He conducted occasional services even though retired. In June 1950, he officiated at the rededication of the Royal Fusiliers' Regimental Chapel and took part in the 250th regimental birthday celebrations. On 25th June 1956, Edward joined four other clergymen VCs (Keith Elliott, John Foote, Arthur Procter and Geoffrey Woolley) at the Royal Army Chaplains' Department annual dinner at the Hotel Rembrandt, London on the evening before the VC Centenary Celebrations at Hyde Park.

Edward loved gardening and kept a donkey, a goat, a black sow, hens, ducks and beehives. In Somerset his bees suffered a disease, which he treated with a new American solution. A Ministry of Agriculture official instructed him to destroy the hives. Edward asked for time to see if the treatment was effective, but the official refused. Edward was summoned to appear in court and pleaded guilty, but in his defence said, *Yes. I refused to obey because it was a stupid order. If you ordered me to kick this policeman beside me I would refuse that too because it would be a stupid order. If my treatment does not work, then I will comply but I should be given time to try out a remedy which has been proved in America.* He was found guilty and

Dunmow High Street (Willott).

ordered to pay £25, but stated he would not pay and was prepared to go to prison, but only after Harvest Festival! He was inundated with letters of goodwill, many containing cheques, which he returned with thanks. He eventually decided to pay the fine, but at the court he was informed it had already been paid anonymously. The bees recovered and there was no follow up visit from the Ministry.

Edward Mellish died at his home, 'Court House', South Petherton, Somerset on 8th July 1962. He was cremated at Weymouth Crematorium and his ashes were scattered in the churchyard of St Mary the Virgin at Dunmow in Essex. Elizabeth moved to a smaller house in South Petherton, where she was cared for by her daughter Claire. Edward is commemorated on plaques at:

Edward Mellish in retirement.

- St Mary the Virgin's Church, Great Dunmow, Essex, recording all incumbents.
- Lewisham Civic Centre, dedicated in May 1995, bearing the names of eight VCs – Harold Auten, George Evans, Philip Gardner, Sidney Godley, Alan Jerrard, George Knowland, Noel Mellish and John Pattison. It was unveiled by the only survivor, Captain Philip Gardner VC.
- The Royal Regiment of Fusiliers Church, Holborn, London, dedicated on Remembrance Sunday, 2004.
- High Street in Great Dunmow opposite the War Memorial, unveiled by his daughter, Miss Claire Mellish, on 19th June 2008. Nine members of the Mellish family attended, including his great niece, Sophie, Countess of Wessex. The service was conducted by the Reverend Canon David Ainge assisted by the Venerable Stephen Robbins, Chaplain General to the Armed Forces.
- Twenty-two Berberis shrubs represent the twenty-two members of the Church Lads' Brigade who were awarded the VC at the Church Lads & Church Girls Brigade Memorial Plot at the National Memorial Arboretum, Alrewas, Staffordshire.

In addition to the VC and MC, he was awarded the Queen's South Africa Medal 1901–02 with clasps 'Cape Colony' and 'Orange Free State', 1914–15 Star, British War Medal 1914–20, Victory Medal 1914–19 with Mentioned-in-Despatches Oakleaf, George VI Coronation Medal 1937 and Elizabeth II Coronation Medal 1953. His VC and other medals were presented to the Royal Fusiliers Museum at the Tower of London in 1966.

JEMADAR MIR DAST
55th Coke's Rifles (Frontier Force) attached 57th Wilde's Rifles

Mir Dast (name also seen as Mir Dost) was born on 3rd December 1874 at Landai, Tirah Province, India. He was a Kambar Khel Afridi. His father was Madha Mir, an Afridi Pathan from Maidan, Tirah, India, now in the tribal areas of Pakistan.

A brother, Mir Mast, served as a Jemadar in 58th Vaughan's Rifles (Frontier Force) (now 10th Battalion, Frontier Force Regiment, Pakistani Army) during the First World War. He saw action in the Ypres Sector in 1914 and was commanding a section of line near Neuve Chapelle when he deserted on the night of 2nd/3rd March 1915, taking with him a number of other soldiers, mainly Afridis (depending on source, the number varies from six to twenty-four). As a Muslim it seems likely that he was offended by the British being at war with Ottoman Turkey, at that time the world's leading Islamic power. Mir Mast was reputedly awarded the Iron Cross by Kaiser Wilhelm II. The award of the Indian Distinguished Service Medal to Jemadar Mir Mast and 3097 Sepoy Azam Khan, 58th Vaughan's Rifles, which appeared in the London Gazette on 10th March 1915, was cancelled on 1st April; it is likely Azam Khan was also a deserter. Mir Mast made his way to Kabul, Afghanistan and joined a small German-Turkish military mission, headed by Captain Oskar Von Niedermayer and including Khired Bey, a staff colonel, and Mohammad Abid (alias Abidin), an Arab drill instructor at Kabul. Mir Mast fermented anti-British sympathies in Tirah and by the middle of 1916 the mission had recruited about 400 Afridis to serve in the Turkish Army, including some deserters from the British Army.

Mir Dast enlisted on 3rd December 1894, into 1st Regiment of Infantry, Punjab Frontier Force (836). He served on operations on the North West Frontier 1897–98 in the Tochi Valley. His Regiment became 1st Punjab Infantry in 1901 and he was promoted naik (corporal) on 15th September. He continued on operations on the North West Frontier in Waziristan. The Regiment became 1/55th Coke's Rifles (Frontier Force) after a former commander in 1903. Promoted havildar (sergeant) on 29th September 1904 and served on the North West Frontier until 1908. He was in action as part of the Mohmand Field Force on 18th May 1908 at Khan Khor Beg. With 1780 Sepoy Kalandar and another man, he found himself close to a group of enemy holding a position behind a low wall among bushes above a small nullah. The three men rushed the position, shooting two of the enemy and bayoneting a third. During the action Mir Dast was severely wounded with a gunshot to the right thigh. **Awarded the Indian Order of Merit, 3rd Class, General Order 526/1908 dated 26th June 1908.** On 3rd March 1909, Mir Dast was commissioned as jemadar (lieutenant). He was one of twelve representatives of the Regiment to attend the Coronation Durbar for the proclamation of King George V as Emperor.

When the First World War broke out, 55th Coke's Rifles remained in India, but during the first year it reinforced 57th Wilde's Rifles with eight officers, forty-three NCOs and 330 Sepoys. One of the reinforcements was Mir Dast, who went to France and served on the Western Front from 19th January 1915. He saw action at Neuve Chapelle.

Mir Dast chatting with Field Marshal Lord Kitchener when he visited the Royal Pavilion Military Hospital at Brighton in July 1915.

Awarded the VC for his actions at Wieltje, Belgium on 26th April 1915, LG 29th June 1915. He was the first Indian officer to receive the VC; Indians only became eligible in 1912. Promoted subadar (captain) 27th April. He was gassed, but continued to carry out his duties until wounded in June. He was then evacuated to England and admitted to the Royal Pavilion Military Hospital, Brighton, Sussex, where he was visited by Lord Kitchener in July. The VC was presented by King George V at the Royal Pavilion Military Hospital, Brighton on 25th August. During convalescence, the effects of gas became more marked and he was sent back to India on 19th October, where he rejoined his Regiment. He later remarked, *The gas has done for me ... I had rather not have been gassed than get the Victoria Cross.*

Mir Dast's investiture at the Royal Pavilion, Brighton, on 25th August 1915.

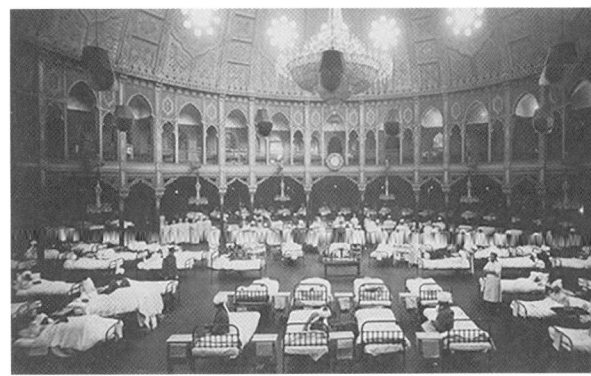

The Royal Pavilion, Brighton was used as a military hospital for Indian troops during the First World War.

Awarded the Russian Cross of St George, 3rd Class, LG 25th August 1915. Awarded the Order of British India, 2nd Class (entitling him to the title 'Bahadur') on 17th December 1915, Gazette of India 3rd June 1916. Mir Dast never fully recovered and was transferred to the Indian Army Reserve on pension on 22nd September 1917. In addition to the VC, he was awarded the Indian Order of Merit 3rd Class, Order of British India 2nd Class, India Medal 1895–1902 with clasps 'Punjab Frontier 1897–98' and 'Waziristan 1901–2', India General Service 1908–35 with clasp 'North West Frontier 1908', 1914–15 Star, British War Medal 1914–20, Victory Medal 1914–19, George VI Coronation Medal 1937 and Russian Cross of St George 3rd Class. The location of his VC is not known.

Mir Dast died at Shagi Landi Kyan Village, Tehsil District, Peshawar, India (now Pakistan) on 19th January 1945. He is buried in Warsak Road Cemetery, Shagi Landi Kyan Village. A monument at the Memorial Gates, Hyde Park Corner, London commemorates VCs of Indian heritage, including Mir Dast.

His grandson, Dr Shakil Afridi, assisted the US Central Intelligence Agency to locate the compound where Osama Bin Laden, leader of the terrorist group Al Qaeda, was living in Abbottabad, Pakistan. He set up a vaccination programme, which managed to obtain DNA samples to confirm Bin Laden was there. Following the raid that resulted in the death of Bin Laden on 2nd May 2011, Shakil Afridi was arrested by the Pakistani authorities while trying to flee the country. In May 2012, he was sentenced to thirty-three years imprisonment for conspiring against the state and alleged ties with a militant group, Lashkar-e-Islam. In August 2013, a retrial was ordered, but he remained in Peshawar Prison and in November 2013 was also charged with killing a teenage boy when he operated on him for appendicitis in 2006.

Dr Shakil Afridi, grandson of Mir Dast, who assisted the US Central Intelligence Agency to locate Osama Bin Laden in 2011 (UNewsTV).

R11941 PRIVATE GEORGE STANLEY PEACHMENT
2nd Battalion, The King's Royal Rifle Corps

George Peachment was born at Parkhills, Fishpool, Bury, Lancashire on 5th May 1897. His father was George Henry Peachment (1859–1920) from Swanton Morley, Norfolk. He was a hairdresser and newsagent. George's mother was Mary née Barnes (1869–1959) an elementary schoolmistress from Newmarket, Cambridgeshire. George and Mary were married in the second quarter of 1891

at Downham, Cambridgeshire. The family lived at 209 Manchester Road, Bury. George had three siblings:
- Charles Henry Peachment (1892–1950) was a pupil teacher in 1911 and was living at 71 Bootham, York in 1915. He married Alice Higham in 1918 at Bury and they had two children – Vyvienne 1920 and Audrey 1922. By 1940 he was an Inspector of Schools. Alice died in 1976.
- David Algernon Peachment (1895–1940) was a junior clerk in 1911. He enlisted in 6th East Lancashire (9583) and served as an acting sergeant at Gallipoli. He was wounded and discharged on 8th August 1916 as unfit for further service. He married Mary Hargraves Heap (born 1899) in 1924 and they had two sons – Geoffrey 1926 and Stanley 1929.
- Mabel Lois M Peachment (1906–68) married Cecil W Lloyd in 1936 and they had two children – David 1937 and Ann 1943.

Amongst his cousins were:

- Reginald Ernest Amos Garwood (1899–1917) was an office boy before he joined HMS *Impregnable* as a Boy 2nd Class on 3rd May 15; he was a bugler. Appointed boy 1st class on 14th August and was drafted to HMS *King Alfred* on 16th September. Appointed ordinary seaman (J/38114) on 8th April 1917 on his 18th birthday and entry into man service. He was described as 5′ 2¾″ tall with dark brown hair, brown eyes and fresh complexion. Drafted to HMS *Pembroke I* on 9th August and HMS *Diligence* for HMS *Strongbow* on 12th September. He was killed on 17th October 1917 in an action against the German light cruisers *Brummer* and *Bremse* off Lerwick and is commemorated on the Chatham Memorial.
- Henry Charles Leggett (1888–1917) was a sergeant serving with 18th Lancashire Fusiliers (26417) when he died on 29th November 1917. He is buried in Haringhe

Parkhills Road, Bury

HMS *Strongbow* lost in an action off Lerwick on 17th October 1917, in which George Peachment's cousin, Reginald Garwood, was lost.

(Bandaghem) Military Cemetery (I B 19). He married WAV Weeks in Kensington earlier in 1917.
- Arthur Leggett (1890–1916) served with 2nd Norfolk as a Lance Corporal. He died as a prisoner of war on 5th October 1916 and is buried in Baghdad (North Gate) War Cemetery (XXI M 10).

George was educated at Parkhills United Methodist Church School, St Chad's Junior School and Bury Technical School, where he studied engineering. He was an apprentice fitter engineer at Ashworth & Parker of Elton, Bury and later with JH Riley. His first attempt to enlist was unsuccessful as he was underage, but he succeeded on 18th April 1915, giving his age as nineteen years and one month. He was posted to A Company, 5th KRRC. He absented himself from 7.30 p.m. on 2nd July until 8.10 a.m. on 5th July and was fined seven days' pay. George transferred to 2nd Battalion on being sent to France on 27th July. He was confined to barracks for three days on 19th September for having a dirty sword (KRRC parlance for a bayonet) on guard mount parade.

Bury Technical School.

Awarded the VC for his actions near Hulluch, France on 25th September 1915, LG 18th November 1915. He was killed during his VC action and is commemorated on the Loos Memorial. The initial recommendation was made by the man whose life he saved, Captain Guy Rattray Dubs. A memorial service was held on 17th October at Parkhills United Methodist Church, Bury.

George never married and the VC was presented to his mother by the King at Buckingham Palace on 29th November 1916. In addition to the VC, he was awarded the 1914–15 Star, British War Medal 1914–20 and Victory Medal 1914–19. The medal group, a letter of condolence from Captain GR Dubs to his mother, George's death plaque and other documents were purchased for £31,050 by medal specialist Michael Naxton on behalf of Lord Ashcroft at a Spink auction on 6th November 1996. The VC is held by the Lord Ashcroft Victoria Cross Collection and is displayed in the Imperial War Museum's Lord Ashcroft Gallery.

S/12087 CORPORAL JAMES DALGLEISH POLLOCK
5th Battalion, The Queen's Own Cameron Highlanders

James Pollock was born at 24 Ochil Street, Tillicoultry, Clackmannanshire, Scotland on 3rd June 1890; his second name was registered as Dalglish. His father was Hugh Pollock (1862–1900), a wool sorter in 1881 and a journeyman dyer in 1885. His mother was Margaret 'Maggie' Helen née Dalgleish (1860–1924), a factory worker. Her surname has also been seen as Dalglish and Dalgliesh. She was living at 32 Ochil Street, Tillicoultry in 1881 and 26 Ochil Street at the time of her marriage. Hugh and Margaret married on 11th September 1885 at 36 Albert Place, Stirling. The family lived at 24 Ochil Street for a while, before moving to Montgomeryshire in Wales, where four of the children were born 1892–99. After Hugh died, Margaret returned to Tillycoultry and was living at Hill Street in 1901 and at 28 Ochil Street in 1924. James had six siblings:

- Richard Pollock (born 23rd July 1885 illegitimately) was a printer and compositor in 1901.
- Mary Wylie Pollock (26th February 1888–3rd January 1961) was a clerk, living at 28 Ochil Street, Tillicoultry at the time of her marriage to James Faill (c.1876–1925) in 1923. He was a postman.
- Hugh Montgomery Pollock (1892–1979) was a colliery clerk. He served during the Great War as a trooper in the Fife & Forfar Yeomanry. He was living at 121 Union Street, Cowdenbeath, Fife at the time of his marriage to Agnes Beveridge Gibb (1891–1973) in 1914. She was a shop assistant. They were living at 161 Stenhouse Street, Cowdenbeath in 1924. They had at least two children – Janet Allan Kinneil Pollock (1916–88) married Henry Byers Tulloch in 1941; and Duncan Beveridge Pollock (born 1920) married Agnes Arnott Cousin in 1956.
- Janetta 'Jessie' Sophie Dalgleish Pollock (1894–1932) was Assistant Matron at the Royal Scottish National Institution, Larbert, Stirlingshire.
- George Pollock (1896–1918) served during the Great War as D/12307 Trooper G Pollock, B Squadron, 5th Dragoon Guards (previous number

Ochil Street, Tillicoultry.

GS/3519). He went to France on 22nd October 1915 and died of wounds on 26th March 1918. He is buried in St Sever Cemetery Extension, Rouen (P VII F 9A).
* Maggie Helen D Pollock (born 1899).

James was educated at Tillycoultry Public School and served an apprenticeship with Messrs J & D Paton, textile manufacturers of Tillycoultry. He moved to Glasgow in 1910, where he worked for Messrs Stewart & McDonald. In 1912, he moved to Paris to work for Messrs Porter & Co of London. While there he was a member of the Anglo/American Branch of the Paris YMCA. He travelled extensively in France, Belgium and Holland and, although an excellent linguist, failed to gain employment as an interpreter when war broke out.

James enlisted in Glasgow on 5th September 1914, declaring two and a half years previous service with 5th Cameronians, a Territorial Force unit, presumably during his time working in Glasgow 1910–12. He was promoted lance corporal 24th October and corporal 18th November and went to France on 10th May 1915. **Awarded the VC for his actions at Hohenzollern Redoubt, near Loos, France on 27th September 1915, LG 18th November 1915.** A second cousin, Corporal JL Dawson, was awarded the VC for his actions at the Hohenzollern Redoubt just sixteen days later, on 13th October 1915; James' paternal grandmother's brother was Dawson's paternal grandfather.

While recovering from his wounds at the Royal Victoria Hospital in Belfast, he was held on the strength of the Depot from 2nd October and transferred to 3rd (Reserve) Battalion at Invergordon on 17th November. The VC was presented by the King at Buckingham Palace on 4th December 1915. Having recovered from his wounds, he attended either No.9 or No.10 Officer Cadet Battalion at Gailes in Ayrshire. He was commissioned into 8th Reserve Battalion on 7th July 1916 and served in 6th Battalion. Appointed a Regular 2nd lieutenant on 6th April 1917, retaining his previous seniority. James lost his left eye when a rifle grenade exploded prematurely in April 1917. Promoted lieutenant 7th January 1918 and was attached to the War Office in the Army List May 1918–September 1919. Relinquished his commission on 12th July 1919, retaining the rank of lieutenant.

James Pollock married Margaret née Bennett (21st May 1896–12th November 1957) on 26th February 1919 at St Andrew's Church, Ayr. They met while he was at the Officer Cadet Battalion, Gailes, Ayrshire in 1916. They had one daughter, Clara H Pollock, whose birth was registered in the 3rd quarter of 1928 at Hampstead, London. She married Basil Rider Cottam (1920–86) in 1948 at Ayr. Basil joined the Rotherham branch of the family steel firm, Edwin

Royal Victoria Hospital, Belfast.

James Pollock carrying the ROC Ensign on parade at RAF North Weald on 24th June 1945 (ROC Association).

Ballochmyle Hospital (Billy Frew).

Cottam & Co Ltd, in the 1940s and ran the factory with his brother Geoffrey in the 1950s. The firm went into voluntary liquidation in 1972. Basil's brother, Lieutenant Edwin Cottam RE (153764), was attached to 55 Squadron, Indian Observer Corps when he was killed in action on 7th May 1944. He is buried at Taukkyan War Cemetery, Myanmar (12 C 5).

James paraded at Inverness when the Duke of York (future King GeorgeVI) presented Colours to 7th and 9th Cameron Highlanders at the Regimental Depot in September 1920. He worked for the Ministry of Munitions for a period then returned to France with the body responsible for disposing of war stock. He moved to Ayr and then to London in 1923, becoming a director of an importing company. He returned to Ayr in 1940 and around 1950 moved to Leicester, where he was secretary and director of Midland Hosiery Mills. He was a freemason, a member of St Mary's Caledonian Operative Lodge No.339.

During the Second World War, he served in the Royal Observer Corps as an observer lieutenant and was appointed Duty Controller in No.33 Aberdeen (Ayr) Group. He is understood to be the only ROC Officer to have held the Victoria Cross. James carried the ROC Ensign at its dedication parade organised by the Air Ministry at RAF North Weald on 24th June 1945.

James Pollock died suddenly at Ballochmyle Hospital, Ayrshire, Scotland on 10th May 1958, just three weeks after returning from a biannual business trip to Canada. He is buried in the Bennett family grave in Ayr Cemetery (Wall Section, Lair 103).

In addition to the VC, he was awarded the 1914–15 Star, British War Medal 1914–20, Victory Medal 1914–19, Defence Medal 1939–45, George VI Coronation Medal 1937 and Elizabeth II Coronation Medal 1953. When he died, the medals passed to his daughter, Mrs Clare Cottam, for her lifetime and then went to the Regiment. They are held by the Highlanders Museum, Fort George, Inverness-shire.

3156 PRIVATE ARTHUR HERBERT PROCTER
1/5th Battalion, The King's (Liverpool Regiment)

Arthur Procter was born at 55 Church Street, Derby Road, Bootle, Lancashire on 11th August 1890. His surname is often seen incorrectly as Proctor. His father was Arthur Richard Procter (1864–1939), a clerk working for Parr's Bank, Liverpool, later acquired by the London County and Westminster Bank. By 1901 he was a shipping clerk. Arthur junior's mother was Sarah Ellen née Cumpsty (born 1862). Arthur and Sarah's marriage was registered in the 2nd quarter of 1886 at West Derby, Lancashire. The family was living at 55 Church Street, Derby Road, Bootle in 1891 and 8 Boundary Road, Wirral in 1901. Arthur had four siblings:

- Ethel Mary Procter (born 1886). She was manageress at a bakery in 1911, visiting the Thomas family at 50 Clifton Street, Garston, Lancashire. She married Dr Robert W Kelly in 1915 at Brighton, Sussex. He served with the Indian Army in Mesopotamia during the war.
- Clarence Procter (born 1891) was a gardener in 1911, living at 18 Rodney Street, Birkenhead.
- Ernest Procter (born 1897) was boarding with his brother Arthur at the home of Thomas and Sarah Fisher at 10 Wellington Terrace, Tranmere, Cheshire in 1911.
- Cecil Frederick Procter (1903–77) was living with his aunt, Edith Field, in 1911. He married Dorothy I Bird (1905–92) in 1928 and they had two daughters – Sheila H Procter 1929 and Maureen Procter 1935.

Arthur was educated at St Mary's Church of England School, Church Street, Bootle. His father lost his job, drank heavily and became aggressive towards Sarah and Arthur. By the time of the 1901 Census, Arthur junior was living with his uncle, Herbert Griffith Procter, and great aunt, Mary Tyerman, at 3 Elm Grove Terrace, Exeter. His mother's health deteriorated after the birth of Cecil in 1903 and her whereabouts at the time of the 1911 Census are unknown. The death of a Sarah Ellen Procter aged 86 was registered in Liverpool North in the 3rd quarter of 1949. Arthur returned to the Liverpool area, where he finished his education at Port Sunlight School until 1904. He lived with his aunt, Edith Field, and also lodged with the Codd family at 68 Derby Road, Tranmere and this is how he met his future wife, Hilda. In 1911 he was boarding with his brother Arthur with the Fisher family at 10 Wellington Terrace, Tranmere. Arthur was a member of the St Luke's Church Lad's Brigade in Tranmere and later became its chaplain. He was also a Sunday School teacher at St Paul's Presbyterian Mission, Stuart Road, Tranmere.

Port Sunlight Village Schools.

He was employed as a clerk by Wilson & Co in the wholesale provision and produce trade at Liverpool Produce Exchange 1904–14. He was a member of the Voluntary Aid Detachment of the Red Cross and gained the St John's Ambulance First Aid proficiency certificate.

Arthur enlisted on 26th November 1914 and went to France in February 1915. He was wounded in the arm by shrapnel on 16th May in the Béthune area and treated at 2nd Canadian Field Hospital at Le Touquet before returning to his unit in June. **Awarded the VC for his actions near Ficheux, France on 4th June 1916, LG 5th August 1916.** The VC was presented by the King at HQ Fourth Army, Querrieu, near Amiens, France on 9th August 1916. When he returned home on leave after his investiture, he received an enthusiastic reception at the Territorial Headquarters in Liverpool. He was congratulated by the Mayor and paraded through the streets to the Corn Exchange where he was employed before the war. There he was presented with a gold watch and chain, a cheque for 100 guineas and £100 in War Loans from the Liverpool Provision Trade Association Ltd. Arthur's number later changed to 200996. He was promoted corporal in 1918. Although recommended for a commission, he did not pass the medical due to his wounds and was discharged on 14th October 1918.

Arthur Procter married Hilda May née Codd (1898–1983) on 23rd May 1917 at St Paul's Presbyterian Church, North Road, Tranmere. They had four sons:

- Arthur Reginald Procter (3rd February 1919–19th August 2000). He was commissioned in the King's Own Royal Regiment (Lancaster) on 25th May 1941 and promoted war substantive lieutenant on 1st October 1942. He was taken prisoner by Vichy French forces in Iraq. Appointed temporary captain on 10th August 1944 and last appears in the Army List in March 1946. He became a teacher in Shrewsbury and married Gwendoline M Stephens in 1946. They had two daughters – Elizabeth I Procter 1950 and Hilary C Procter 1957.
- Cecil Charles Procter (born 1921) served in the RAF as a aergeant wireless operator/air gunner (990753) in 86 Squadron based at RAF North Coates. He was killed in a Beaufort on mine laying operations off the Friesian Islands on 21st July 1941 and is commemorated on the Runnymede Memorial.
- Herbert F Procter 1923–25.
- John Peter Procter, born on 22nd October 1927 was an epileptic and died in 1979.

Arthur was a member of the VC Guard at the Interment of the Unknown Warrior on 11th November 1920. He went back to being a salesman in the provisions trade, this time with George Wall & Co Ltd, until 1925. The family lived at 42 Kingfield Road, Walton on the Hill and moved to 24 Blomfield Road, Garston in 1925. On 19th July 1924, King George V and Queen Mary visited Liverpool for the consecration of the new Anglican Cathedral. During the afternoon the King reviewed the 55th (West Lancashire) Territorial Division at Wavertree Playground and Arthur was one of nine VCs presented. The others included Cyril Gourley, William Heaton, Arthur Richardson, Ronald Stuart, John Molyneux and John Davies. The Cathedral was started under Bishop Francis Chavasse, who resigned in 1923; he was the father of Noel Chavasse VC and Bar.

Arthur studied for a career in the clergy at St Aidan's College, Birkenhead in 1926 and was ordained deacon at Liverpool Cathedral on 18th December 1927. He held a number of appointments:

St Mary the Virgin, Prescot.

- Curate of St Mary the Virgin, Prescot, Lancashire.
- Vicar of St Mary the Virgin, Bosley, Cheshire 1931–33.
- Vicar of St Stephen's, Bennett Street, Flowery Field, Hyde, Cheshire 1933–41.
- Rector of St Mary's, Droylsden, Manchester 1946–51.
- Vicar of St Peter's, Claybrooke and Wibtoft, Rugby, Warwickshire 1951–63.
- Vicar of St John the Baptist, Bradworthy with Pancraswyke, near Holsworthy, North Devon 1963–65.

During the Second World War, Arthur served as a RAF squadron leader chaplain (63054) from 4th March 1941 until November 1944. In April 1954, he assisted at the funeral of Arthur Hutt VC in Coventry. Arthur retired to Shrewsbury in 1965 and lived at Clover Dell, 53 Mytton Oak Road. He was one of '10 VCs on a VC10' on the inaugural flight of the Super Vickers VC10 from London to Nairobi by East African Airlines on 6th April 1970. The ten VCs were guests of the company for a nine-day holiday in East Africa. They were

St John the Baptist, Bradworthy.

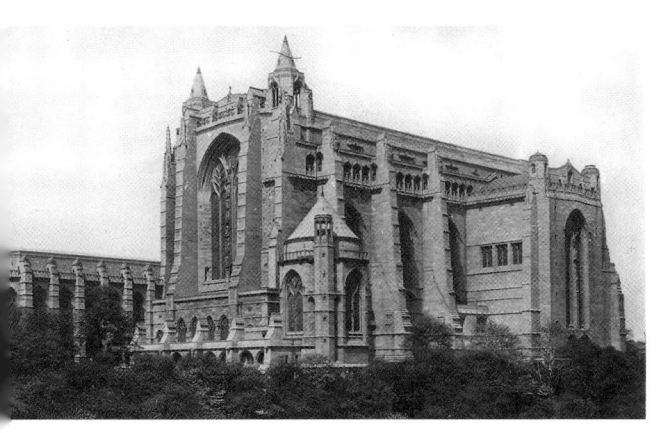

Liverpool's Anglican Cathedral was dedicated in July 1924, but it was not completed until 1978. It appears here without its tower.

Arthur Proctor while serving as a RAF chaplain in the Second World War.

selected, five each from WW1 and WW2, by drawing names out of a hat. The others were Tom Adlam, Richard Annand, Donald Dean, Philip Gardner, Norman Jackson, Anthony Miers, Bill Reid, Vic Turner and William White. In Kampala, Uganda they were hosted by General Idi Amin and on the final day visited State House to meet President Kenyatta of Kenya. In 1971, he and Hilda moved to 1 Cherry Tree Close, Netheredge, Sheffield.

Arthur Procter died at Winter Street Hospital, Sheffield, Yorkshire on 26th January 1973. His funeral was held in the Chapel of St George, Sheffield Cathedral, on 1st February, followed by cremation at City Road Crematorium. His ashes were interred in All Saint's Chapel, Sheffield Cathedral. Hilda died in 1983 after returning to Shrewsbury. Arthur is commemorated in a number of other places:

- Blue Plaques at St Mary's Church, Droylsden and St Stephen's Church Hyde, Cheshire.
- Blue Plaque to all Tameside VCs at the entrance to Ashton Town Hall, dedicated on 20th April 1995. The other VCs are – John Buckley, William Thomas Forshaw, Albert Hill, James Kirk, Andrew Moynihan, Harry Norton Schofield and Ernest Sykes.
- Memorial tablet in Sheffield Cathedral.
- Twenty-two Berberis shrubs represent the twenty-two members of the Church Lads' Brigade who were awarded the VC at the Church Lads & Church Girls Brigade Memorial Plot at the National Memorial Arboretum, Alrewas, Staffordshire.
- Book of Remembrance of the Manchester and King's Regiments in Manchester Cathedral.

In addition to the VC, he was awarded the 1914–15 Star, British War Medal 1914–20, Victory Medal 1914–19, Defence Medal, War Medal 1939–45, George VI Coronation Medal 1937 and Elizabeth II Coronation Medal 1953. His medals sold for £18,700 at a Glendinings auction on 19th September 1990. They are held by the King's Regiment Collection, Museum of Liverpool Life, Mann Island, Pierhead, Liverpool.

36830 ACTING SERGEANT JOHN CRAWSHAW RAYNES
A Battery, LXXI Brigade, Royal Field Artillery

John Raynes was born at Longley, Ecclesall, Sheffield, Yorkshire on 28th April 1887. His father was Stephen Henry Raynes (1862–1915), a railway clerk from Liverpool who in 1881 was boarding at 3 Offa Terrace, Bersham, Denbigh, Wales with the Thelwall family. He was the innkeeper of the 'Sheaf View Hotel', 25 Gleadless Road, Heeley, Sheffield in 1886 and was also an auctioneer's clerk. He was also at the Hotel in 1891 and 1901, but by 1911 he was a painter, living with his family at 843 Abbeydale Road, Sheffield. His mother was Hannah Elizabeth née Crawshaw (1859–1917). Stephen and Hannah's marriage was registered in the 1st quarter of 1886 at Wortley. John had three siblings:

- Francis 'Frank' Crawshaw Raynes (1895–1918) served as 285138 Lance Corporal FC Raynes, 11th Northumberland Fusiliers. He died on 27th October 1918 and is buried in Tezze British Cemetery, Italy (5 C 10).
- Mary Hannah Raynes (1889–1918). Her marriage to William Ratcliffe was registered in the 4th quarter of 1913 in Sheffield and they had a daughter, Marion, the same year.
- Elizabeth Winifred Raynes (born 1891) was a shop assistant in a Post Office in 1911. Her marriage to Samuel W James was registered in the 2nd quarter of 1916 in Sheffield.

John was educated at Heeley Church School, Sheffield and was a member of the Boys' Brigade. He worked for Mr TW Wood, a coal merchant, and also for his father as a decorator until he enlisted in the RGA on 10th October 1904 (20953). He transferred to the RFA on 1st June 1905 and was posted to 42nd Battery on 19th July. He extended his service to complete six years on 29th September 1906 and was

Sheaf View Hotel, Gleadless Road, Sheffield, where John Raynes' father was the innkeeper.

Leeds Registry Office in Leeds Town Hall is where John Raynes married Mabel Dawson in April 1907.

awarded a Good Conduct Badge on 10th October. It was forfeited on 5th July 1907, later restored and lost again on 1st January 1909. Promoted acting bombardier 31st May 1907 and bombardier 24th March 1910. Having transferred to the Section B Reserve on 10th October 1910, he became a policeman in Leeds.

John Raynes married Mabel née Dawson (1886–16th January 1971) on 24th April 1907 at Leeds Registry Office. They had four children:

- Two children, names unknown, were born and died before the 1911 Census. One may have been Hilda Raynes 1906–10.
- John Kenneth 'Ken' Raynes (30th January 1912–19th March 1972) was a policeman and volunteered for flying duties in the RAF in the Second World War. His marriage to Margaret née Fergusson was registered in the 4th quarter of 1941 at Scarborough. He is buried in the family grave at Harehills Cemetery, Chapeltown, Leeds.
- Tom Crawshaw Raynes (6th February 1920–22nd August 1945) worked in the motor trade. He married Joan Collins (born 1920) on 3rd August 1940 at Leeds and they had a daughter, Pamela Ann Raynes, born in 1941. They lived at Benson Street, Leeds. He served as 969128 leading aircraftman in the RAF, spending two years on the Gold Coast, where he contracted malaria. On 22nd August 1945, a month before he was due to be demobilised, Tom was hitch-hiking home on leave in a jeep driven by Private Ivor James Marshall of Gloucester, with another passenger, LAC Tom Norton, also from Leeds. The jeep was involved in an accident at Blisworth, near Northampton in which Tom was killed. Norton suffered serious back injuries and Marshall sustained leg injuries, but both recovered. Tom was cremated at Leeds (Lawnswood) Crematorium. Joan married George A Bowman in 1947.

John was recalled on 5th August 1914. Promoted acting corporal 10th October and acting sergeant 31st March 1915. He was an instructor at No.2 Depot RFA at Preston and was offered a commission, which he refused. He volunteered five times for active service before being posted to A/LXXI Brigade on 19th June and went to France as a corporal on 27th July.

Awarded the VC for his actions at Fosse 7 de Béthune, France on 11th and 12th October 1915, LG 18th November 1915. The VC was presented by the King at Buckingham Palace on 4th December 1915. Appointed acting battery sergeant major 13th October–7th December 1915 and returned to Britain on 1st January 1916. A number of postings followed – 5B Reserve Brigade in Edinburgh 1st February (appointed battery sergeant major 12th May), 393 Independent Battery RFA at Canterbury in Southern Army 10th February 1917, Recruiting Training Centre in Southern Army 19th July, No.2 RFA Officer Cadet School at Topsham Barracks in Exeter 28th November and 6th Reserve Brigade at Biscot near Luton 4th November 1918. He was discharged on 11th December 1918 as no longer fit for service and was issued the Silver War Badge (B.61327) on 3rd January 1919. During his service, he was Initiated into Freemasonry at Saint James's Operative Lodge, No.97, Edinburgh on 24th January 1916.

Yorkshire Evening Post article on 24th August 1945 about the death of Tom Raynes.

He returned to the Leeds Police as a sergeant, but his health deteriorated and he was transferred to work in the Aliens' Registration Office. In March 1924 worsening spinal problems forced him to give up work and the Leeds Watch Committee recommended an annual pension of £63/7/6. They were living at 52 Lofthouse Road, Blackness Lane, where the stairs proved too much for him. John refused to use his previous record to bring his plight to public attention. However, Sir Gervase Beckett MP initiated the 'Sergeant Raynes Fund' through The Yorkshire Post, which raised £700 by 8th November. It was used to purchase a new bungalow at 10 Grange Crescent, Chapeltown Road, Leeds.

John suffered paralysis for the last three years of his life, during which his wife nursed him. He was unable to attend the VC Dinner at the House of Lords on 9th November 1929. The other Yorkshire VCs sent him a telegram expressing their regret and promising him a memento of the occasion. John became very depressed over his inability to attend the Dinner, suffered a relapse and died at his home on 12th November 1929. He left £750/6/6 to his widow.

His funeral was held on 16th November 1929 at St Clement's, attended by the Lord Mayor and Lady Mayoress of Leeds and the Chief Constable, with a squad of police in attendance. Eleven VCs were present, of whom eight from Yorkshire (G Sanders, W Edwards, F McNess, C Hull, A Mountain, F Dobson, A Poulter and W Butler) acted as pallbearers. The other VCs, S Meekosha, AE Shepherd and JW Ormsby, followed the cortege. The coffin was carried on a gun-carriage from LXXI Field Brigade RA, followed by the Chairman of the Leeds 'Old Contemptibles Association', Captain WE Gage, carrying John's medals on a purple cushion. Lieutenant Wilfrid Edwards VC carried a wreath of Flanders poppies and evergreen in the shape of the Victoria Cross, brought from the VC Dinner as a present for John, not knowing it would be used at his funeral. It bore the message, *In affectionate memory from brother VCs of Leeds, who sorely missed their comrade at the Prince of Wales's dinner, whence this emblem was brought for him.* He was buried at Harehills Cemetery, Leeds (Section H, Grave 11). A firing party was provided by the West Yorkshire Regiment and the Last Post was sounded. The cemetery gates had to be closed because up to 30,000 people came to pay their respects. The Prince of Wales sent a letter of sympathy to Mrs Raynes. The grave was renovated and rededicated on 13th November 2008, with PC Anthony Child of West Yorkshire Police playing a significant role in the restoration. John is also commemorated on the Royal Artillery VC Memorial in the ruins of St George's Chapel, the former Garrison Church at Woolwich, which was reduced to a roofless shell by a V1 in 1944.

On the day of the VC Dinner in 1929, the 'Sheffield Telegraph' launched an appeal to raise £600 to purchase a new bungalow for John and his family. The fund raised £300, which was handed to his widow on 14th November 1929.

In addition to the VC, he was awarded the 1914–15 Star, British War Medal 1914–20 and Victory Medal 1914–19. On 26th September 1973, the medals were presented by his daughter-in-law, Mrs Margaret Raynes, to Major General Geoffrey Collin, GOC North East District, on behalf of the Royal Artillery at a ceremony in York. The medals are held by the Royal Artillery Historical Trust at the Royal Regiment of Artillery Museum 'Firepower' at Woolwich.

CAPTAIN ANKETELL MOUTRAY READ
1st Battalion, The Northamptonshire Regiment

Anketell Read was born at Beaumont House (now a hotel), 56 Shurdington Road, Cheltenham on 27th October 1884. His father was John Moutray Read (c.1840–1909) from Co Down, Ireland. He was commissioned as a lieutenant in the Queen's Royal Antrim Rifle Regiment of Militia on 20th September 1859 and became an ensign by purchase in 13th Foot on 21st December 1860. He was promoted by purchase to lieutenant 30th June 1865 and captain 24th September 1870. John does not appear in the Army List after 1874 until 14th April 1883, when he was appointed captain in 4th Cheshire at Stockport, Cheshire. He was granted the honorary rank of major on 22nd March 1884 and promoted major 12th May 1888 and lieutenant colonel and CO 23rd December 1893. He retired as a colonel on 12th May 1894.

Anketell's mother was Edith Isabella née Johnson, born c.1849 at Mussoorie, near Dehra Dun, India. John and Edith's marriage was registered in the 4th quarter of 1870 at South Stoneham, Hampshire. The family was living at 'The Orchards', Ham Lane, Charlton King's, Gloucester in 1881; Beaumont House, 56 Shurdington Road, Leckhampton, Gloucestershire in 1884; Sandford Dene, Bath Road, Cheltenham in 1891; 19 Earls Avenue, Hythe, Folkestone, Kent in 1901 and later at Little Beauchamp, Washfield, Devon. Edith was living at Castle Grove, Bampton, Devon in 1911; 17 Albany Road, St Leonard's-on-Sea, Sussex in 1915; and Salem, Co Wicklow, Ireland in 1917.

His paternal grandfather was Captain John Moutray Read of Union Park, Queen's County and Tullychin, Co Down. His maternal grandfather was Lieutenant Colonel Hugh Johnson (1805–74), 26th Bengal Native Infantry. Anketell had five siblings:

- Rose Hamilton Read (1871–1947) was an authoress living at 14 Avonmore Gardens, West Kensington, London in 1911. She never married.
- Beresford Moutray Read (1874–1936) was commissioned in 4th Cheshire on 25th February 1893. He served in the West African Frontier Force from 13th November 1997. Promoted captain Cheshire Regiment 24th November 1897, but was only a local captain from 31st January 1903 while employed with the West African Frontier Force. He was seconded for service with the Colonial Office as District Commissioner at Tamale, Northern Territories, Gold Coast from 1st January 1907 and last appears in the Army List in March 1908. Beresford married Henrietta Elliot Taylor (c.1885–1953) in 1911. They had a daughter, Henrietta Desirée Moutray Read (1917–79), who married Sir Christopher William Gerald Henry Codrington (1894–1979) in 1963. He served in the 19th Hussars in the Great War and was wounded. Henrietta was his second wife.
- Hugh Arthur Moutray Read (1876–1959) became a reporter in Auckland, New Zealand. He enlisted as a private in the New Zealand Mounted Rifles (529), part of the 2nd New Zealand Contingent and sailed for South Africa on SS *Waiwera* on 20th January 1900. Superintendent in the Transvaal Mounted Constabulary and Chief of Pretoria Fire Services 1900–03. He enlisted as a trooper in 2nd King Edward's Horse 1914. Commissioned as a lieutenant in the Army Service Corps 1915 and served in France. Staff captain War Office and Chief Inspector of Fire Services 1916–19. Appointed temporary captain 9th August 1917. His marriage to Florence Jane Islip (born 1880) was registered in the 2nd quarter of 1907 at Lambeth and they had at least two children. Hugh became an auctioneer and company director at 32 Fenchurch Street, London. He attended a bankruptcy hearing at the Bankruptcy Buildings, Carey Street, London on 25th November 1930 and later traded as Puzzo Company at 22 Hortus Road, Southall, Middlesex.

- Edith Susan A Read (1880–1960) married Frank William R Hill (1875–1942) in 1904.
- Ina 'Pearlie' Isabella Moutray Read (1884–1950), Anketell's twin, married Frederick Rufane St Lawrence Tyrrell (1869–1931) in 1909 and they had a son. Frederick joined the Royal Irish Constabulary in 1891 and was Adjutant of the RIC Depot, Phoenix Park, Co Galway in 1908. He was presented to King George V during the royal visit to Dublin on 8th July 1911 and accompanied the King to Dublin Castle. He transferred to the Royal Ulster Constabulary in 1922 and was serving at Portrush in 1929. He retired as a county inspector.

Anketell was educated at Glengarth Preparatory School in Cheltenham and the United Services College at Westward Ho! 1898–1902, where he was an officer in the Cadet Corps. The College was attended earlier by Rudyard Kipling; his 'Stalky & Co' stories are based on his experiences there. The College was also attended by Bruce Bairnfather, the famous cartoonist of the First World War and creator of 'Old Bill', and five fellow VCs, including George William St George Grogan, who was awarded his Cross for actions in May 1918.

The United Services College at Westward Ho.

He trained at the Royal Military College Sandhurst 1901–03 and was commissioned in the Gloucestershire Regiment on 21st November 1903. He served in India for eight years and was promoted lieutenant on 21st February 1906. He transferred to 7th Hariana Lancers on 12th July 1907 and served at Quetta until November 1908, then at Jacobabad and from February 1911 at Ferozepore. He transferred to the Northamptonshire Regiment on 7th September 1911. Having gained the Royal Aero Club Aviators' Certificate (No 336) on 22nd October 1912, he was attached to the RFC 17th April 1913–17th September 1914.

Quetta at around the time Anketell Read served there.

In India he was the Army heavyweight boxing champion eight times and middleweight twice. He was also the Army and Navy Heavyweight Champion in 1909 and 1911 and the Light Heavyweight Champion in 1912. When home on leave, he sparred with the captain of the local football club, John Salisbury, who later served as a private with 4th Devons at Ferozepore. In 1909, two noted Trinity College, Dublin men, Mick Leahy and William Patrick Heffernan, drew in the final of the Amateur Heavyweight Championship of Ireland. Anketell later fought

Leahy over four rounds, with Leahy winning narrowly on points. In October, Anketell fought Heffernan and knocked him out – 2nd Lieutenant William Patrick Heffernan, 3rd Royal Irish, attached 1st Gloucestershire, was killed in action on 9th May 1915 (Le Touret Memorial, France).

Anketell went to France on 12th August 1914 and was attached to 9th Lancers. Having been wounded on the Aisne in September 1914, he was promoted captain on 14th March 1915 and returned to 1st Northamptonshire in France on 29th May. Anketell was noted for his courage on a number of occasions. On the night of 29th/30th July 1915, he rescued a mortally wounded officer under very heavy rifle and grenade fire. He also showed conspicuous bravery during digging operations on 29th-31st August.

Awarded the VC for his actions near Hulluch, France on 25th September 1915, LG 18th November 1915. He was killed during his VC action and is buried in Dud Corner Cemetery, Loos (VII F 19). His will was administered by Arthur Fisher, attorney to his brother, Beresford; estate valued at £498/19/4 resworn £598/19/4. He is also commemorated on:

- Blue Plaque (No 4692) on his birthplace at 56 Shurdington Road, Cheltenham, Gloucestershire, dedicated on 11th September 2009.
- Plaque in St Michael and All Angels Church, Bampton, Devon.
- Cheltenham War Memorial.
- Haileybury College – United Services College memorial panel, stone memorial in the library and a brass memorial in the chapel.

As he never married, the VC was presented to his mother by the King at Buckingham Palace on 29th November 1916. In addition to the VC, he was awarded the 1914 Star with 'Mons' clasp, British War Medal 1914–20 and Victory Medal 1914–19. The VC is held by the Northamptonshire Regiment Museum, Abington Park, Northampton.

Anketell Read's grave in Dud Corner Cemetery, Loos.

3/2832 CORPORAL JOHN RIPLEY
1st Battalion, The Black Watch (Royal Highlanders)

John Ripley was born at Land Street, Keith, Banffshire, Scotland on 30th August 1867. His name has also been seen as Ripply. His father was Joseph Ripley (c.1833–1900), a railway and general labourer. His mother was Margaret née Cassells (c.1837–83), a domestic servant. Joseph and Margaret married on 24th January 1857 at Keith and lived at Land Street. By 1881 they were living at 225 Cross Street. Joseph was living at 167c Mid Street in 1891 and at 145 Land Street when he died. John had seven siblings:

- Margaret Ripley (1857–1936), a dressmaker. She married William Elder Seath (c.1837–94) in 1887. After William's death, Margaret married Alexander Seath (born 1841) in 1895. Alexander, the son of a Royal Artillery sergeant major, was a boy soldier for four years and 212 days before serving in the ranks for sixteen years. On 8th September 1875 he was appointed Quartermaster and retired on 8th September 1896 with the honorary rank of captain and seniority from 8th September 1885.
- Joseph Ripley (1860–1938), a school janitor and drill instructor in 1901. He married Elizabeth Walker (died 1948) in 1883 and they had five children between 1884 and 1894, including William Elder Seath Ripley (1894–1917). William served as a lance corporal (6535 & 292690) in 1/7th Black Watch and was killed in action on 23rd April 1917. He is buried in Brown's Copse Cemetery, Roeux, France (III B 3). Another son, John Ripley (born 1886), was twice champion of Montrose Golf Club.
- James Ripley (born 1862).
- Jessie Fordyce Ripley (born 1865).
- William Stewart Ripley (1870–1948) was a journeyman slater and also served as a chief gunnery instructor in the Royal Navy. He married Mary Ann McMillan (1870–1956) in 1894 and had seven children including:
  ○ David Ripley (c.1891–1966) served as a stoker on HMS *Lurcher* (K24392). His year of birth was recorded as 1895 on enlisting on 17th July 1915. He was previously a heating engineer and was demobilised on 28th February 1919.
  ○ Margaret Ripley (born 1897) married Robert Hills in 1918, a lance corporal in the Cameron Highlanders (9511), who went to France with the original BEF on 14th August 1914.
- Mary Ann Ripley (born 1873).
- Alice Ripley (1876–94).

John was initially employed as a wool spinner. By 1891 he was a railway porter, boarding at 264 Dulrait Road, Balloch, Bonhill, Jamestown and later became a slater. He enlisted in G Company, 6th (Fifeshire) Volunteer Battalion, The Black Watch based at St Andrew's in 1884 and was one of the best shots in the Company. He was promoted colour sergeant in 1909 and discharged in 1912.

John Ripley married Jane née Laing (1866–1913), a general domestic servant, on 21st June 1895 at New Gilston, Largo, Fife. They lived at various times at 9 College

Market Street, St Andrew's.

John Ripley with CSM Frederick Barter VC outside Buckingham Palace, having received their VCs from the King on 12th July 1915.

A studio portrait of John Ripley.

Street, 3 Market Street and 3 College Street, St Andrews and St Leonards, Fife. They had a son, Alexander Laing Ripley, born on 12th February 1896 at 9 College Street. He served in 1/7th Black Watch (1436 & 290072), landing in France on 2nd May 1915 and was disembodied on 9th March 1919. He migrated to the United States, where he married and had a daughter, June.

When war broke out, John volunteered as a recruiting sergeant, but enlisted for active service with the Black Watch as a corporal on 25th September 1914. He trained with the 3rd Reserve Battalion at Nigg, Ross-shire until allocated to the 1st Battalion in January 1915 and went to France on 18th February.

Awarded the VC for his actions at Rue du Bois, France on 9th May 1915, LG 29th June 1915. Having been wounded in the head during his VC action, he returned to the Depot on 11th May. He attended a civic reception at St Andrew's Town Hall on 29th June and was appointed Acting Sergeant in 3rd Reserve Battalion for recruiting duties in Edinburgh on 2nd July. The VC was presented by the King at Buckingham Palace on 12th July. He received a silver casket containing a War Loan and a purse of sovereigns from Provost Cheape on his return to St Andrews on 30th October.

While recovering from his wounds he was out walking with a friend, Willie Greig, when they were greeted by Brigadier General Grogan, *Hello Ripley! What are you doing here? Invalided home from France, sir*, replied John. When Grogan enquired how he got there, John responded, *Oh the pen must have slipped when I put my age in*. John was discharged to the Class Z Reserve on 28th March 1919.

He returned to work as a slater. He also swept chimneys and served in the town's fire brigade. John was a Freeman of St Andrew's, a member of the United Services Association, Black Watch Association and British Legion and became Chairman of the St Andrews Branch of the Black Watch Old Comrades Association. On 14th August 1933 he was examining the drains at Castlecliffe, The Scores, one of the residence houses of St Leonard's School for Girls, St Andrews. While climbing an 18' ladder, he fell and sustained serious spinal injuries. He was rushed to St Andrews Memorial Cottage Hospital, but died shortly after admission. He is buried in Upper Largo Churchyard near Leven, Fife (Lair 1124). The grave was renovated by Stuart Mackie, who had served in the Black Watch, and was rededicated in October 2001.

In addition to the VC he was awarded the 1914–15 Star, British War Medal 1914–20, Victory Medal 1914–19 and the Volunteer Long Service Medal. His medals are held privately and their location is not known.

John Ripley in later life.

A commemorative stone was laid in his honour at Keith War Memorial on 9th May 2015 to mark the centenary of his VC action. The ceremony was led by Lieutenant General Sir Alastair Irwin KCB CBE with the Vice Lord Lieutenant of Banffshire, David Goodyear. Descendants of the Ripley family attended.

3/10133 SERGEANT ARTHUR FREDERICK SAUNDERS
9th Battalion, The Suffolk Regiment

Arthur Saunders was born at Cauldhall Road, Ipswich, Suffolk on 24th April 1878. His father was Thomas Saunders (c.1835–1910), a saddle and harness maker. His mother was Anne Victoria née Clarke (1838–1914). Thomas and Anne's marriage was registered in the 2nd quarter of 1856 at Ipswich. The family was living at Cauldwell Hall Road in 1861, St Giles Terrace, Spring Road in 1871, 62 Spring Road in 1881, Holly Cottage, Ringham Road in 1891 and 14 Argyle Street in 1901; all addresses in Ipswich. Arthur had ten siblings:

- Thomas Sanders Soans Saunders (1859–1928) was a blacksmith.
- Alice Maude Saunders (1861–1920) married Thomas Brockwell (born 1854) in 1879 and had three children – Thomas Charles Brockwell 1879, Eva Alice Brockwell 1881–1963 and Arthur Brockwell c.1882.
- Samuel Chandler Saunders (1863–73).
- Harry Adolphus Vane Saunders (1865–1937) was an iron fitter and trimmer. He married Jessie Willis (née Siggers) (1876–1961) in 1900. She had previously married William Willis in 1895 and he died the following year. Harry and Jessie had eleven children – Florence Ada Saunders 1901, Daisy Eleanor Saunders

1902, Harry Sherrell Saunders 1904–69, Jessie Victoria Saunders 1905, Lily May Saunders 1907, Gertrude Phyllis Saunders 1908, Kate Mary Saunders 1910, Winifred M Saunders 1912, Arthur C Saunders 1913, Grace M Saunders 1915 and Alice M Saunders 1917.
* Kate Maria Saunders (1867–1927), an upholsterer, married Sidney Cowdell (1866–1928), a brass finisher, in 1888. They had a daughter, Kate Cowdell 1888.
* Florence 'Flora' Mary Saunders (born 1872) was a cook.
* Albert Edward Saunders (1869–98).
* Robert Clarke Lurk Saunders (1873–1939) was a harness and saddle maker. He married Letitia Georgina Foster (1877–1957) in 1899 at Wandsworth, London. They had five children – Robert Thomas F Saunders 1900–66, George Cecil M Saunders 1902, Letitia Marie L Saunders 1904, Christabel Victoria May Saunders 1907–89 and Alti Ruby E Saunders 1910.
* Walter Saunders (born c.1875) was a carpenter's boy in 1891.
* Eleanor 'Nelly' Elizabeth Saunders (1880–1961), a school-teacher, married Frederic Shaw (c.1880–1948), a carpenter and joiner, in 1904. They had three children – Norah Florence Shaw 1907, Frederic T Shaw 1915–17 and Harold F Shaw 1918.

Arthur was educated at St John's Church of England Primary and California Schools in Ipswich. He trained for the Merchant Navy on the former HMS *Warspite*, the Marine Society training ship November 1893–February 1894, before enlisting in the Royal Navy as a Boy on 25th February 1894. Training was carried out on the hulk *Boscawen*; the former HMS *Trafalgar* launched in 1841 and renamed HMS *Boscawen* in 1873. He later served at HMS *Pembroke*, a shore establishment at Chatham in 1901 as an able seaman and at HMS *Vernon*, the torpedo training school as a petty officer Class II. He received a certificate for 'Wounds and Hurts' on 22nd June 1905 and was discharged on 21st April 1908 from HMS *Pembroke*.

Arthur Saunders married Edith Muriel née Everitt (born 11th February 1890) on 6th December 1908. They were living in Ipswich at 2 Notre Dame Terrace,

HMS *Warspite*.

Boy trainees on one of HMS *Warspite*'s messdecks.

Hutland Road in 1911 and later at 180 Cauldwell Hall Road. He purchased 354 Foxhall Road with money donated to him after his VC action. Arthur and Edith had three children:

- Thomas Everitt Frederick Saunders (17th September 1909–16th July 1992) trained as a boy sailor at HMS *Ganges* from 23rd January 1925 and served there four times in his career. As a chief petty officer (C/J112916) he was Mentioned in Despatches, LG 1st January 1941, while serving aboard the armed merchant cruiser HMS *Circassia*. He served on HMS *Kempenfelt* from August 1943 (destroyer and flagship) as a gunnery instructor and retired on 16th March 1953. His marriage to Edith Durrell (born 1907) was registered in the 3rd quarter of 1931 at Ipswich. They had four children – Maureen N Saunders 1934, Barry D Saunders 1937, Judith A Saunders 1940 and Ian T Saunders 1947.
- Edward Stanley Charles Saunders (22nd June 1912–2002) joined the RAF in January 1928 at RAF Halton and retired as a warrant officer (562289) in February 1962. He was Mentioned in Despatches, LG 8th June 1944 and awarded the MBE, LG 1st January 1955. His marriage to Ellen ER Kelly (née Colthorpe) was registered in the 4th quarter of 1940 at Ipswich. She had been married previously to William J Kelly in 1933.
- Nina Madge Saunders born on 15th October 1922 worked as a Red Cross section leader dispenser at Ipswich Borough Hospital during the Second World War and afterwards trained as a teacher, retiring in 1981. Her marriage to Clive Brooks was registered in the 2nd quarter of 1953 at Ipswich.

Arthur was employed as an engine fitter's assistant by Ransomes, Sims and Jeffries Ltd, an engineering firm in Ipswich. He enlisted on 19th September 1914 from the

Ransomes, Sims and Jeffries Ltd factory in Ipswich.

A Ransome's advertisement from the period when Arthur Saunders worked for the company.

Ipswich Town Hall on the right.

Arthur Saunders while serving in the Home Guard 1940–44.

Special Reserve and was promoted sergeant within a month. He went to France with 9th Battalion on 30th August 1915. **Awarded the VC for his actions near Loos, France on 26th September 1915, LG 30th March 1916.** His was the first VC awarded to the Suffolk Regiment. Wounded in his VC action, he was evacuated to Beaulieu Hospital, Harrogate, Yorkshire and was also treated at St Thomas's Hospital in London and St George's Hospital, Harrogate for long periods. His leg was severely damaged, but it was saved, although he suffered the effects of his wounds for the rest of his life.

He received a public welcome on 22nd June 1916 at Ipswich Town Hall, where he was met by the Mayor and Corporation, officers of the Suffolk Regiment and his Commanding Officer, Lieutenant Colonel Bretell. He was later presented with

Sir (Alexander Frank) Philip Christison GBE CB DSO MC & Bar (1893–1993) was commissioned in the Cameron Highlanders in 1914. He was awarded the MC for the same action in which Arthur Saunders was awarded the VC and was assistant manager of the British Olympic team in Paris in 1924. After attending the Staff College, he was Brigade Major of 3rd Infantry Brigade in 1931. In 1937 he took command of 2nd Duke of Wellington's on the Northwest Frontier and later a brigade in India before becoming Commandant of the Staff College at Quetta. Command of 15th (Scottish) Division in Britain was followed in late 1942 by XXXIII Corps and XV Corps in 1943, both in Burma. He was knighted for his part in the Arakan Offensive in 1944. Christison commanded Fourteenth Army while deputising for General William Slim. He also deputised for Mountbatten, taking the surrender of the Japanese in Singapore on 3rd September 1945. His last appointment was GOC-in-C Scottish Command and Governor of Edinburgh Castle.

£365 from the residents of Ipswich and his Regiment, which he used to purchase 354 Foxhall Road, Ipswich, where he spent the rest of his life with his wife and family.

The VC was presented by the King at Buckingham Palace on 27th June 1916. Arthur was discharged on 13th November and returned to Ransomes, where he worked until retirement as a storekeeper. He was granted the Freedom of the Borough of Ipswich in April 1920 and on 6th October was in the Guard of Honour for Field Marshal Lord Allenby when he received the Freedom of the Borough of Bury St Edmunds. Arthur was appointed Justice of the Peace for Ipswich in January 1923. When the Prince of Wales visited HMS *Warspite* at Greenhithe that July, Arthur was presented as an 'old boy'. He met the Prince again on 4th July 1934, when he formed part of the Guard of Honour at the Royal Show. He served as a RQMS in the Home Guard 1940–44.

On 15th February 1947, Arthur was invited to Glasgow by Lieutenant-General Sir AFP Christison KBE CB DSO MC, GOC Scottish Command, who was with him during his VC action, to attend a gathering of the survivors of 6th Cameron Highlanders who were at Loos in September 1915. Arthur was made a member of the Battalion.

Arthur died of acute retention of urine and prostatic hyperplasia at Ipswich Borough Hospital, Suffolk on 30th July 1947 and was cremated at Ipswich Borough Crematorium. His ashes were scattered in the Garden of Rest in the New Cemetery and he is commemorated on Panel 64, Room D of the Temple of Remembrance at the New Cemetery. On 26th September 2010, a blue plaque was dedicated at 180 Cauldwell Hall Road, Ipswich, where Arthur was living when he was awarded the VC.

In addition to the VC, he was awarded the 1914–15 Star, British War Medal 1914–20, Victory Medal 1914–19, Defence Medal 1939–45 and George VI Coronation Medal 1937. His widow presented his medals to the Suffolk Regiment on her 99th birthday on 11th February 1989 at Howard House Retirement Home. They are held by the Suffolk Regiment Museum, Bury St Edmunds.

CAPTAIN FRANCIS ALEXANDER CARRON SCRIMGER
Canadian Army Medical Corps, attached 14th Battalion, Royal Montreal Regiment, Canadian Expeditionary Force

Francis Scrimger was born on 8th February 1880 at 83 Redpath Crescent, Montreal, Quebec. He was known as Frank, Scrim or Scrimy. His attestation paper records his birth as 10th February 1881. His father was the Reverend John Scrimger (1849–1915). He attended Knox College at the University of Toronto (BA 1869, MA 1871, DD 1873) and was ordained Pastor of Calvin Church, Montreal and lecturer in both the Old and the New Testament at the Presbyterian College. In

1882 he joined the College's permanent staff. He became one of the leading clergymen in Canada and a strong advocate of Church Union. He was appointed Principal of the Presbyterian College in 1904. Frank's mother was Catherine Charlotte née Gairdner (c.1851–1921). She was known as Charlotte. John and Charlotte married on 23rd April 1874 at Huron, Montreal. She was living at 69 McTavish Street, Montreal in 1914 and moved in with her son Frank in 1919.

A distant ancestor, Alexander Carron, took part in the Battle at the Spey in 1106, fighting for King Alexander I of Scotland, during which he caught the falling royal standard, rallied the troops and saved the day. He was knighted on the spot and the King granted him the right to bear the Scottish arms in reverse colours (gold lion rampant bearing a scimitar in its paw, set on a red background with the word 'Dissipate'). He was standard-bearer of Scotland until 1124 and the appointment became hereditary thereafter. The title later included the post of Constable of the Castle and town of Dundee. Alexander was also granted the right to add 'Skirmisheour' to his name. Over the years this became Scrymgeour and when the family emigrated it was simplified to Scrimger. Frank had four siblings:

- John Tudor Scrymgeour (1875–1945) adopted the old Scottish spelling of his surname. He served in France during the First World War as a chaplain and YMCA worker. He later migrated to Scotland.
- Anna Marks Scrimger (1877–1956) married Walter Ernest Lyman (born 1861) in 1901 and had four children.
- Ethel Scrimger (1883–1915) was a twin with Muriel. She died of whooping cough on 6th August 1915.
- Muriel E Scrimger (1883–1966) married Charles Harold Shelton (1878–1931) in 1911 and had a daughter.

Frank's paternal grandfather, John Scrimger (1812–90), was born in New York; his father was Scottish. John moved to Canada, married Janet née McKenzie (1823–1900) in 1844 and settled at Galt, Ontario. Frank's maternal grandfather was James Archibald Gairdner (died 1899), a Scot who migrated to Canada. He married Mary Jane née Marks (died 1908), whose family came from Wales.

Frank was educated at Montreal High School, McGill University Medical School in Montreal (BA 1901, MD 1905) and carried out postgraduate studies in Dresden, Vienna and Berlin. On 3rd March 1912 he joined the Canadian Army Medical Corps Militia and on 13th April, he was commissioned in the CAMC to serve with the Montreal Heavy Brigade, Canadian Garrison Artillery. He was described as

Montreal High School, attended by Frank Scrimger before studying at McGill Univeristy (McCord Museum).

SS *Andania* under construction alongside HMS *Ajax* in 1912 at Scott's shipyard, Greenock. She later transported troops to the landings at Suvla Bay, Gallipoli and on 26th January 1918 was sunk by *U-46* off Rathlin, County Antrim, Ireland (www.clydesite.co.uk).

5' 7½" tall with fair complexion, grey eyes, brown hair and his religious denomination was Presbyterian.

He attested in the Canadian Expeditionary Force on 9th August 1914 as a captain. On 22nd September 1914 he was appointed Medical Officer of 14th Battalion CEF and went with it to Valcartier Camp. The Battalion departed Quebec on 30th September aboard SS *Andania*, arriving at Plymouth, Devon on 13th October. The Battalion trained on Salisbury Plain, Wiltshire. Frank was detached to No.1 Canadian General Hospital, in the Netheravon, Larkhill and Bulford areas on 21st January 1915 suffering from bronchopneumonia. The Battalion sailed for France on 10th February, but Frank remained in England until 12th April, when he went to France with No.1 Canadian General Hospital. He was attached to the Advanced Dressing Station of 2nd Canadian Field Ambulance at Mouse (Shell) Trap Farm, north of Wieltje, Belgium on 19th April. One of the stretcher-bearers was Henry Norman Béthune (1890–1939), who as a frontline surgeon supported Republican forces during the Spanish Civil War with a mobile blood transfusion service. He later assisted Communist Chinese forces during the Second Sino-Japanese War, bringing modern medicine to rural China.

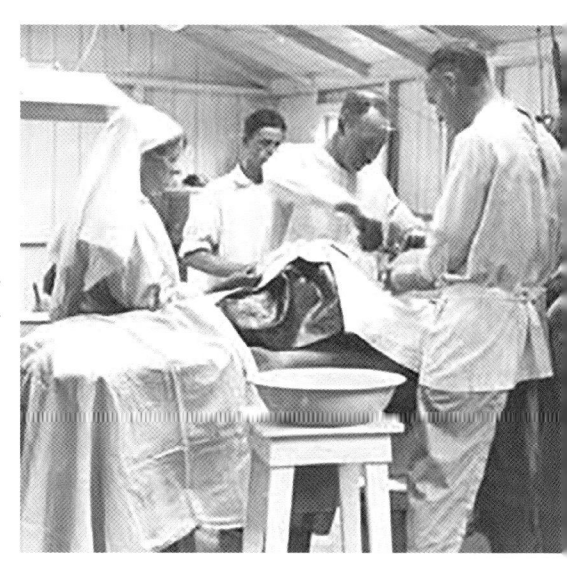

Army surgeons operating in a hutted hospital in France.

Awarded the VC for his actions near St Julien, Belgium 22nd–25th April 1915, LG 23rd June 1915. He was recalled to serve with 14th Battalion CEF on 23rd April, but did not join until 7th May, vice Captain Boyd, who had been wounded. Frank received the VC from King George V at Windsor Castle on 21st July. He was admitted to 1st Canadian Field Ambulance on 16th September with boils on his neck, transferred to No.3 General Hospital on the 19th and the convalescent home at Dieppe on 25th September until 2nd October. He spent a few days at the Canadian Base Depot before returning to 14th Battalion on 5th October.

On 31st December, Frank was posted to No.1 Canadian General Hospital, Étaples. While performing an operation there on 29th January 1916 the scalpel was knocked out of his hand by a patient. It inflicted a cut on the ring finger of his left hand, which became infected and he was admitted to No.6 British Red Cross Hospital at Étaples the following day. He was evacuated to England aboard HMHS *Jan Breydel* on 26th February and admitted to the Baroness de Goldsmid Hospital, 35 Chesham Place, London. The finger was amputated at the second joint and it was feared he might lose his arm. He was transferred to the Granville Canadian Special Hospital at Ramsgate, Kent on 9th March. While in England, Frank was visited by his mother, who had sailed from Canada following the death of her husband.

Frank's hand had recovered sufficiently for him to be granted one month's sick leave from 2nd June, following a medical board at 86 Strand, London. He joined the staff of Granville Canadian Special Hospital on 5th July, having been passed fit for duty by a medical board the previous day. He spent a few months attached to a number of organisations – Assistant Director Medical Services, Canadian Troops London Area from 31st October, Assistant Director Medical Services, Canadians Brighton Area from 19th November and Assistant Director Medical Services, Hastings from 28th November. Frank was appointed temporary major on 5th December and returned to London on 30th December.

On 1st March 1917, Frank returned to France to serve with No.3 Canadian Casualty Clearing Station at Remy Siding, Lijssenthoek. He was granted fourteen days leave on 24th November. During the German Spring Offensive he led a team to reinforce No.50 Casualty Clearing Station at Roye on 21st March 1918. He was accompanied by Nursing Sister Ellen Carpenter, anaesthetist Captain WG Lyall, two operating room orderlies and a batman. Scrimger reduced his staff to a minimum as the

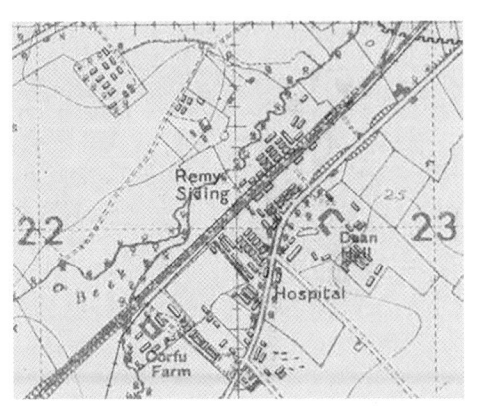

Extract from a military map showing Remy Sidings at Lijssenthoek, Belgium. The cemetery marked expanded massively and is now Lijssenthoek Military Cemetery containing 9,877 burials; second only to Tyne Cot in size. There is an excellent visitor centre.

German advance closed, including a reluctant Ellen Carpenter. They were evacuated to Montdidier. Being so far forward, the unit effectively became an Advanced Dressing Station. Eventually evacuation became inevitable. Frank remained with a skeleton staff to care for 200 patients who were unfit to travel immediately by train. They were evacuated using ambulances and any other means of transport available. Frank was the last to leave, walking about twenty miles with his team, pushing wheeled stretchers loaded with medical equipment to rejoin the rest of the team at Montdidier. On 29th March, the team was attached to No.3 Canadian General Hospital and returned to No.3 Canadian Casualty Clearing Station on 4th April.

Frank was granted fourteen days leave from 4th September, extended to 2nd October, during which he married. He was posted to No.3 Canadian General Hospital, Boulogne on 3rd October. He was appointed acting lieutenant colonel on 21st October 1918 to command the Hospital (commanded by John McRae, author of *'In Flanders Fields'* 1st June 1915–28th January 1918), but this was amended a few days later to command the surgical team of No.3 Canadian General Hospital. Frank remained in France after the Armistice, dealing with the backlog of surgical cases and the influenza epidemic. He was granted leave 3rd–17th January 1919. He became ill with influenza, but survived and was transferred to the CAMC Casualty Company, Shorncliffe, Kent 14th March–24th April. While there a Medical Board on 21st March decided a myopic astigmatism was not caused by his military service. Appointed temporary lieutenant colonel on 21st April. Frank sailed for Canada aboard SS *Baltic* from Liverpool on 29th April, arriving at Halifax on 7th May. He was demobilised on 16th May.

The family believe Frank was a colleague of Lieutenant Colonel John McCrae. They believe the two knew each other from school days, but as McRae was eight years older than Frank, they do not appear to have overlapped at any educational establishment. It is possible McRae tutored Frank while he was training at McGill University Medical School. The two certainly knew each other and met in France during this period. The family believe McCrae threw away *In Flanders Fields* following rejection by 'The Spectator'. Frank retrieved it and advised McCrae to send it to 'Punch' magazine, which published it on 8th December 1915.

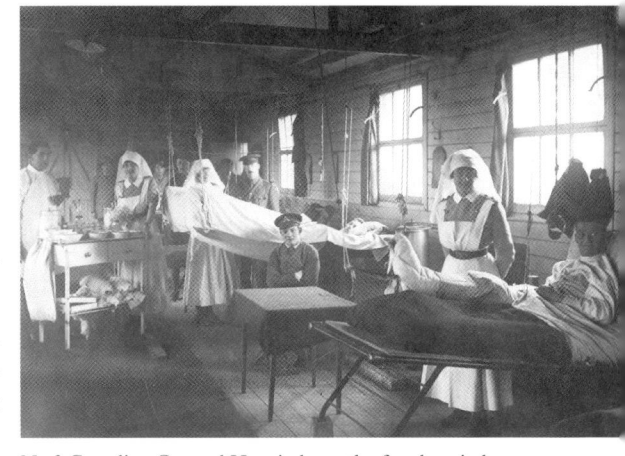

No.3 Canadian General Hospital was the first hospital unit operated by a University (McGill) during the war. It mobilised in Montreal on 5th March 1915 under Colonel HS Birkett, McGill's Dean of Medicine 1914–21 and, after a short period in England, moved to France on 16th June and opened at Dannes-Camiers on 19th June. From 6th January 1916 onwards it was in the old Jesuit college at Boulogne. Lieutenant Colonel John McCrae, who wrote 'In Flanders Fields', was involved in setting it up (McGill University).

However, other evidence suggests McRae threw the poem away before he sent it to 'The Spectator' and it was Cyril Allinson, Edward Morrison or J M Elder who persuaded him to persevere.

Frank met Nursing Sister Ellen Emerson Carpenter (1889–1973) while serving with No.3 Canadian Casualty Clearing Station at Remy Siding. Ellen was born Ellen Eason Emmerson on 14th December 1889 in Rome, Italy. Her father, John Emmerson, was half Italian, half English and her mother was Fanny Eason, who was English. Ellen grew up in Italy, but when her father died she moved with her mother to Germany, where she attended school. When her mother married Colonel Carpenter, Ellen took his surname. The family moved to the United States and lived in Chicago for some time. When her stepfather died, Ellen and her mother moved to Montreal, where she trained as a nurse at the Royal Victoria Hospital. She served in the Canadian Army Medical Corps as a nursing sister during most of the war until she resigned on 31st August 1918. Frank was granted fourteen days leave from 4th September, extended to 2nd October, and he and Ellen were married on 5th September 1918 at St Columba's Church (Church of Scotland), Pont Street, London. She was Mentioned in Sir Douglas Haig's Despatch of 7th April 1918, LG 28th May 1918. They lived on Metcalfe Street and later at 1389 Redpath Crescent, Montreal. They had four children, all born in Montreal:

- Jean Ligny Scrimger (23rd June 1919–22nd March 2010) married Tom Alexis Wootton in 1940 and had a son, John Charles Scrimger Wootton, who became a doctor and editor of the Canadian Journal of Rural Medicine.
- Alexander Carron Scrimger (11th December 1921–28th October 1944) served as a captain with 29th Armoured Reconnaissance Regiment, South Alberta Regiment, Royal Canadian Armoured Corps and was killed in action. He is buried at Bergen-Op-Zoom Canadian War Cemetery, Noord Brabant, Netherlands (4 G 6). Alexander visited the site of his father's VC action before he died.
- Charlotte Anna Scrimger born 14th August 1925, married as Corbett-Thompson.
- Elizabeth Ellen Scrimger (18th June 1929–2007) married as Fraser.

Frank was Assistant Surgeon at the Royal Victoria Hospital, Montreal January 1919–1931. He was also appointed Director of the Department of Experimental Medicine in 1919, carrying out research into Paget's Disease and the treatment of intractable duodenal and gastric ulcers. He was appointed to the McGill University staff as a lecturer in Clinical Surgery in 1921, while also managing a private consulting practice. In 1936 he was appointed Director of the Department of Surgery and Associate Professor in Surgery at McGill University Medical School. He qualified as a Master of Surgery, became a Fellow of the Royal College of Surgeons, a Fellow of the American College of Surgeons and a Member of the Association of Surgeons of America in 1930. He was also a Member of the Thoracic Surgeons of America, the Interurban Association of Surgeons of America, the Surgical Research Association of America and was appointed Chairman of the Canadian Pension Committee in Ottawa.

Frank Scrimger died of a heart attack at his home in Montreal on 13th February 1937 and is buried in the family plot at Mount Royal Cemetery, Montreal (M 727). He is commemorated in a number of other places:

- Mount Scrimger (2755m) in the High Rock Range, Kananaskis Park on the Alberta/British Columbia border in the Canadian Rockies, was named after him in 1918.
- Canadian Forces College, Toronto – a wooden plaque bearing fifty-six maple leaves, each inscribed with the name of a Canadian-born VC holder, was dedicated in November 1999.
- An obelisk commemorating all Canadian VCs at Military Heritage Park, Barrie, Ontario dedicated by HRH The Princess Royal on 22nd October 2013.
- Francis Scrimger VC Avenue – National Field of Honour, Donegani Avenue, Pointe-Claire, Quebec.
- Scrimger Room at the National Defence Medical Centre, 1745 Alta Vista Drive, Ottawa, Ontario was named in 1986 to commemorate the Centre's Silver Jubilee.
- 'Captain FAC Scrimger VC Trophy' awarded annually by the Royal Montreal Regiment to the 'best soldier'.
- Lac Caron-Scrimger, Lac-au-Brochet, La Haute-Côte-Nord, Quebec was named after him on 7th June 1996.

The Royal Victoria Hospital, Montreal in about 1895.

In addition to the VC, he was awarded the 1914–15 Star, British War Medal 1914–20 and Victory Medal 1914–19. His grandson, Dr John Charles Scrimger Wooton, presented the medals to the Canadian War Museum, 1 Vimy Place, Ottawa, Ontario on 17th October 2005. The 1914–15 Star is inexplicably missing from the group.

7942 CORPORAL CHARLES RICHARD SHARPE
2nd Battalion, The Lincolnshire Regiment

Charles Sharpe was born at Pickworth, near Folkingham, Lincolnshire on 2nd April 1890. His father was Robert Sharpe (1852–1935), a farm labourer. His mother was Charlotte Ann née Norris (c.1859–1923). Robert and Charlotte married at Frodingham, Lincolnshire on 12th December 1877. The family was living at Burton Coggles in 1881, Sapperton Road, Pickworth in 1901 and Haceby near Pickworth in 1912. Robert came from a family of thirteen children and Charlotte was one of nine. Charles had fourteen siblings:

- Robert Sharpe (twin with Charlotte) born 20th March 1878 and died the following day.
- Charlotte Sharpe (twin with Robert) born and died 20th March 1878.
- Elizabeth Sharpe (born 1879).
- Annie Sharpe (born 1881).
- Edith Sharpe (born 1882) married George Simpson (born c.1879) in 1905. He was a lime stone quarryman in 1911.
- Arthur Sharpe (1883–1952) enlisted at Lincoln in the King's Own Yorkshire Light Infantry (6497) on 1st March 1900. He was a labourer also serving in 4th Battalion, The Lincolnshire Regiment (Militia) at the time and gave his age at nineteen years and four months. He was 5′ 5½″ tall, weighed 124 lbs, with fresh complexion, blue eyes, light brown hair and his religious denomination was Church of England. He joined the Depot at Pontefract on 3rd March and was posted to the 1st Battalion on 4th May. On 19th January 1901 he was posted to the 2nd Battalion in South Africa, having been appointed lance corporal the previous day, but reverted to private on 1st April. Awarded the Queen's South Africa Medal with clasps 'Cape Colony', 'Orange Free State', 'Transvaal' and 'South Africa 1902'. He was granted Good Conduct Pay at 1d per day on 28th April 1902 and moved with the Battalion to Malta on 8th October. He was again appointed lance corporal on 16th June 1903 and gained 3rd Class Education on 24th August and 2nd Class on 16th December. On 24th December he passed for promotion to Corporal. He extended his service to complete eight years on 1st April 1904 and the same day his service pay was increased to Class 2 at 6d per day. On 30th April he qualified for Mounted Infantry. His lance corporal rank was removed on 24th December and his service pay was reduced on 1st March 1905 to Class 2 at 4d per day for failure in musketry. However, his records show his Service Pay was increased to 5d per day on the same date as well as being awarded a second Good Conduct Badge. On 11th March he returned to the 1st Battalion in Gibraltar. He forfeited one Good Conduct Badge on 31st October, but his Service Pay was increased to Class 1 at 7d per day on qualifying at musketry on 5th April 1906. He moved with the Battalion to South Africa on 5th September. On 31st October he regained the Good Conduct Badge and on 12th December was once again appointed lance corporal. It did not last long as he was reduced to private on 22nd March 1907. He returned to Britain on 24th January 1908, transferred to the Army Reserve on 29th February and was discharged to the Section B Reserve on 29th February 1912. Despite being reduced in rank a number of times, he was noted as a willing and hard worker and was thoroughly honest. He was accustomed to working with horses and was a good signaller. Arthur went to live in Ireland. He married Mary née Kilbride (c.1886–1959) and had two daughters.

- William Sharpe (born 1885).
- George Sharpe (born c.1887) was a carter working for Charles Beckett at Farm House, Pickworth in 1901.
- Ruth Sharpe (born 1888) married William Simpson (born c.1883), an ironstone labourer in 1907. They had five children.
- Emily Mary 'Betty' Sharpe (born 1892).
- Frank Norris Sharpe (born 1895). He was serving as a sergeant instructor in the Coldstream Guards when his brother was awarded the VC.
- Nellie Sharpe (born 1896).
- John Henry Sharpe (born 1901 as Sharp). His second name has been seen as Robert. He was employed by Mr Amyan in 1915.
- Wilfred Henry Sharpe (born 1904) married Bertha Louisa née Cox (1898–1969) in 1932.

Charles was educated at Newton School, Haceby, near Pickworth until 1905 and was employed in service at Messrs Langham and Garner's at Stroxton. He then worked on Mr William Knight's farm, a local landowner and also the churchwarden. He enlisted in 4th Battalion, Lincolnshire Regiment (Militia) (4574) on 3rd January 1907, giving his age as eighteen years and four months. He was 5′ 4″ tall, weighed 109 lbs, with fresh complexion, blue eyes, brown hair and his religious denomination was Church of England. He transferred to the Depot on 21st April for regular service with the 2nd Battalion and was known as 'Shadder'. Promoted Lance Corporal in 1908. Charles served at Portsmouth and Gibraltar and was stationed with his Battalion in Bermuda when war broke out. The Battalion returned to Britain and Charles had forty-eight hours leave before he went to France on 6th November 1914.

Awarded the VC for his actions at Rouges Bancs, France on 9th May 1915, LG 29th June 1915. The VC was presented by the King at Windsor Castle on 24th July 1915. Charles was allocated different numbers later in his service – 64567 and 4793702. He was involved in a recruiting drive, visiting many places in Lincolnshire, including Spalding and Bourne. He later returned to France and was seriously injured by a bomb. As a result he did not serve overseas again and carried shrapnel in his body for the remainder of his life. He later served in India and became master sergeant cook before being discharged in 1928.

Charles Sharpe married Rose Ivy Sibley née Cutting (1899–1959) in the 2nd quarter of 1936 at Bourne. Rose had married George A Sibley in 1920 and had four children – Dorothy 1921, George Albert 1923–46, Rose 1925 and Kathleen 1928–2002. George Albert Sibley was serving in the Royal Navy as an able seaman (C/JX 335813) on HMS *Zest* when he died on 10th April 1946; he is buried in Bourne Cemetery (37 A 31). Charles and Rose had three more children:

- Elizabeth Ann Sharpe (born 1933). Her birth was registered in the 4th quarter of 1933 and again in the 3rd quarter of 1936. She married Arthur Gregory in 1953 and had two sons.
- Charles Norris Sharpe (1935–41).
- John William Sharpe (born 1935) whose birth was not registered until the 4th quarter of 1936. He served in the Royal Navy as an engineer mechanic.

Bourne market place.

Charles returned to farm work with his father, but was later a gardener and physical education trainer at Hereward School Remand Home at Bourne. He served in the Home Guard in the Second World War and also at the town recruiting office. He was injured by a splinter when a bomb fell on the school. After the school closed, he worked as a council refuse collector and as a labourer and cleaner at the British Racing Motors firm in Bourne. His final job was gardener for the Bourne United Charities, where one of his duties was to tend the flowerbeds in the Garden of Remembrance.

Charles Sharpe died on 17th February 1963 at Workington Infirmary, Cumberland from cerebral thrombosis as a result of a fall in his step-daughter's (Mrs Dorothy Foster) garden at 17 Stainbank, Stairburn. He is buried in Newport Cemetery, Lincoln (H 354). Charles was the last surviving VC winner of the Lincolnshire Regiment. He is also commemorated at:

- Sharpe's Close, off Beech Avenue, Bourne, Lincolnshire.
- A Royal Lincolnshire Regimental Museum display depicting his VC action opened in April 2000 by the Duke of York.
- His VC action was featured in Issue No.341 of the *Victor* comic, dated 2nd September 1967.

In addition to the VC he was also awarded the 1914 Star with 'Mons' clasp, British War Medal 1914–20, Victory Medal 1914–19, War Medal 1939–45, George VI Coronation Medal 1937, Elizabeth II Coronation Medal 1953 and the Army Long Service & Good Conduct Medal. His medals were purchased at a Christie's auction on 21st November 1989 by Chris Farmer, treasurer of South Kesteven District Council, for £17,000 on behalf of the community. They are held by South Kesteven District Council, The Mayor's Parlour, Council Offices, St Peter's Hill, Grantham, Lincolnshire.

168 CORPORAL ISSY SMITH
1st Battalion, The Manchester Regiment

Issy Smith was born in Alexandria, Egypt on 16th September 1886 as Israel Smilovitch. He gave his place of birth as Cable Street, St George's-in-the-East, East London, when he enlisted, but this may have been to obscure the means by which he came to England. A number of different dates for his birth are known, with the latest being 18th September 1890 on his Russian birth certificate. However, the balance of evidence points to 1886 in Alexandria. There are also many versions of his original names – Israel, Ishroulch or Isroulch and Schmulovitch, Schmulevitch, Shmilovitch or Shmeilowitz. His father, Moses Smilovitch, was born at Berdichev, about 150 kms west of Kiev, Ukraine (then Russia) and became a French citizen, working for the French Consular Service as a clerk. He is understood to have worked in Paris, Alexandria and Constantinople at various times. Issy's mother was Eva née Tchukov, also French of Russian extraction. Issy had ten siblings, including:

- Olga (born c.1865) lived in Egypt, where she died in 1965 aged 100.
- Joseph (born c.1879) became a gas fitter and plumber in London with brother Mayer. He was boarding at 4 Providence Street, St George's-in-the-East, London with the Fetbroad family in 1901. In 1904 he was living at 481 Commercial Road and later migrated to America.
- Mayer (born c.1881) was known as Morris/Maurice. He became a gas fitter and plumber in London with brother Joseph. He was also boarding at 4 Providence Street, St George's-in-the-East, London in 1901. In 1904 he was living at 7 Church Lane, Whitechapel and later migrated to America, where he lived at San Diego, California. He had a son, Sam, born c.1924.
- Bernard, of whom nothing is known.
- Rosa moved to Brazil.
- Jeannette lived in Istanbul and had five children.
- Fanny (born before 1886) lived in Paris.
- Rachel married Lieutenant Colonel George Wall (c.1869–1952), who joined the New South Wales Lancers in 1892, was commissioned in 1894, served on the Nile Expedition 1898 and in the South African War. He was placed on the Retired List in December 1904. He was employed as a railway clerk until 13th September 1914, when he was appointed lieutenant & quartermaster in the Australian Imperial

Berner Street (now Henriques Street), Whitechapel, at the junction with Fairclough Street in 1909. The cartwheel marks the entrance to Dutfield's Yard, where the body of Elizabeth Stride, one of Jack the Ripper's victims, was found in 1888.

A similar view along Henriques Street (formerly Berner Street) in 2004, looking at the same corner as in the previous picture. The junction with Fairclough Street is in the foreground. The wall on the left surrounds Harry Gosling Primary School and the entrance to Dutfield's Yard was opposite the first parked car. On the right is the former Berner Street Board School attended by Issy Smith. In 1929 the school was taken over by a Jewish organisation, the 'Oxford and St George Club', founded by Basil Henriques, after whom the street is now named. Bernhard Baron donated the money to purchase the old school building and it became the 'Bernhard Baron Settlement'. The building has since been converted into flats (Bernhard Baron House).

Force and served in Egypt at the Training and Combined Base Depots at Tel el Kebir (MID). From 1st January 1917 he was Assistant Quartermaster General at HQ AIF in Britain with the rank of lieutenant colonel from 1st April. CMG, LG 1st June 1917 and CBE, LG 3rd June 1919. He returned to Australia in March 1920 on the Retired List. He married Rachel in 1922 at Randwick, New South Wales. His previous marriage to Ruby Caroline Ann Cutbush in 1902 ended in divorce in 1921 on the grounds of his misconduct.

It is believed that Issy ran away from home, stowed away on a ship and reached London alone in about 1898. He spoke no English, but did speak French, German and Turkish. He added an Indian dialect and some Swahili during his Army service. As a result, in later life he was used as a court interpreter on occasions. As a youngster he earned money delivering fish while also attending Berner Street London County Council School, Whitechapel, close to where Elizabeth Stride, one of Jack the Ripper's victims, was murdered in 1888. Issy was employed by a second hand furniture dealer in Commercial Road before becoming a plumber.

Issy enlisted in 6th Manchester (Militia) on 21st April 1904 as 9946 Private Issy Smith. At the time he was living at 5 Mazeppa Street, New Bury Road, Manchester and was working as a plumber for Mr Glasser of 57 Morton Street, Manchester. He was described as just over 5′ 2″ tall, weighing 112 lbs with a 33″ chest, fresh complexion, brown eyes and black hair. He had flags and clasped hands tattooed on his left forearm and his religion was stated to be Jewish. He was discharged from the Militia on 2nd September 1904 and enlisted the same day as a regular soldier in the Manchester Regiment under his anglicised name, giving his employment as plumber's mate. He gave no details of his father and his mother's address was unknown. Issy was posted to the 2nd Battalion on 18th September 1904. He was in detention for forty-two days from 17th April 1905 for using insubordinate language. He was posted to the 3rd Battalion at St George's Barracks, London on 15th March 1906 and extended his service to eight years on 11th May. On 28th October 1906, he was posted to the 1st Battalion in South Africa. He was in detention again for thirty-five days from 30th March 1907 for using insubordinate language. Awarded the 3rd Class Certificate of Education on 28th August 1909. He served in India from 11th October 1911, including during the Dehli Durbar.

Issy was the regimental middleweight boxing champion while in India. He was appointed unpaid lance corporal on 8th June 1912. Having transferred to the Reserve on 15th October 1912, he went to Australia, where he was given a job by his sponsor, Mr Tallent, with the Melbourne Metropolitan Gas Company. Issy continued boxing under the name Jack Daniels.

Issy was mobilised in Melbourne on 5th August 1914 and mustered at Broadmeadows Army Camp prior to being sent back to England. The claim that he served with Australian forces when they overran the German territories in New Guinea is believed to be untrue. Issy returned to the Regimental Depot at Ashton-under-Lyne on 9th December 1914. He was appointed acting lance corporal on 19th December and joined the 3rd Battalion on 6th January 1915. On 23rd February he went to France to join the 2nd Battalion. He was wounded at Neuve Chapelle on 11th March.

Awarded the VC for his actions at St Julien, Belgium on 26th April 1915, LG 23rd August 1915. He was also awarded the Russian Cross of the Order of St George, 4th Class for the same action, LG 25th August 1915. He was the first Jewish NCO to be awarded the VC. Issy was gassed in May 1915 and returned to England on the strength of the Depot on 7th August. He was hospitalised at Mount Joy (Dublin University VAD

Broadmeadows Camp was established in August 1914 at Mornington Park, Broadmeadows, Melbourne. At that time it was mainly tented and conditions were somewhat basic.

The Mansion House in Dublin, built in 1710, is the official residence of the Lord Mayor.

Auxiliary) Hospital in Dublin. While there he was besieged by Jews offering their congratulations and was carried by a crowd to be entertained at a restaurant in Sackville Street. The Jewish community in Dublin also presented him with a purse of gold at a reception at Dublin's Mansion House. On 4 September he was presented with a gold watch and chain by the Mayor of Stepney, from fellow members of 'Berners Old Boys Club'.

Having been appointed unpaid lance sergeant on 5th October, he was posted to the 3rd Battalion on 15th December. His VC was presented by King George V at Buckingham Palace on 3rd February 1916.

Issy was promoted sergeant on 7th March and was involved in recruiting in the north of England while recovering from his wounds. He left England on 4th September and rejoined the 1st Battalion on 16th September at Basra, Mesopotamia, where it had been since 8th January. On the journey out, Issy survived his ship being torpedoed. He was wounded at Baghdad in March 1917 and may have been present at the fall of Jerusalem. He transferred to the Royal Engineers as a sergeant in the Inland Water Transport on 1st April 1917 (WR/303001 & 271171).

Issy was wounded five times during the war. He departed Port Said on leave on 17th January 1919 and arrived in England on 11th February, according to his service record. This is understood to be incorrect, as he married Elsie Porteous Collingwood née McKechnie (1892–1955) at Camberwell Registry Office on 8th February. He gave his name as Israel Shimlovitz-Smith. The story that his parents disowned him for marrying a gentile, even though he also went through a Jewish wedding ceremony (performed by Major Sadler DSO, Senior Jewish Chaplain) at Hallam Street Synagogue on 24th March 1919, is not believed to be true. He was

Issy Smith at an ANZAC Day ceremony in 1927.

introduced to Elsie by his brother Maurice when he returned from India. He was discharged on 30th April and was a member of the VC Guard at the Interment of the Unknown Warrior on 11th November 1920.

Elsie and Issy had two children – Olive Hannah (1920–2000) born in Hackney, London and Maurice born at Essendon, Australia on 8th November 1932. Issy worked as an actor, music hall manager, bookmaker and cycle accessory salesman. He fell on hard times, returned to Britain and pawned his medals for £20 in 1924. They were recovered by Mrs Hertz, wife of the Chief Rabbi, who with eleven others gave Issy £10 each. The medals were placed in Mocatta Library, University of London by the Jewish Historical Society. Issy recovered them for £20 in 1925 and returned to Australia the same year on SS *Orsova*. He was manager of 'British International Pictures' Melbourne in 1928 and became a JP there in 1930. In 1931 he unsuccessfully contested a Melbourne seat for the United Australia Party. He became a commercial traveller for Dunlop Rubber Company in 1934 and was Control Officer of the Civil Aviation Department at Essendon Airport, Melbourne from 1937 until his death. The family was living at 54 Derby Street, Moonee Ponds, Essendon, Victoria in 1932 and 45 Bulla Road, North Essendon 6, Melbourne in 1940.

Issy Smith refused to accept discrimination due to his religion. On one occasion the family was dining in a Melbourne hotel. At an adjacent table a man was loudly denigrating Jews. Issy walked over to the man, picked up his meal and tipped it over his head. He then sat down and continued eating without saying a word. On another occasion, Joseph Aloysius Lyons (Prime Minister of Australia 1933–39) was to speak at a meeting in Melbourne. A crowd of disaffected men hooted, cat called, hurled insults and whistled so loudly the speakers were unable to make themselves heard. A number of speakers tried to calm the crowd without success. Issy Smith agreed to try. Despite his popularity he spoke only a few words before the clamour broke out again. A man near the centre of the hall raised his hand until the crowd simmered down. Then he spoke with loathing, *Who killed Christ?* A gasp swept through the hall. On the stage Issy stood for half a minute before saying, *Well, if you're a fair specimen of a Christian, thank God I am a Jew.* Not another word was spoken and the meeting ended.

Issy Smith died of a coronary thrombosis at his home at 45 Bulla Road, Moonee Ponds, Melbourne, Australia on 11th September 1940. His wife, Elsie, was under sedation when members of the local synagogue arrived. They sang and prayed before placing the body into a simple pine coffin and left without speaking to Elsie. Shortly afterwards members of the military arrived with a more elaborate casket and transferred the body to it. They also ignored Elsie and made arrangements to move the coffin to a funeral home. Word reached the synagogue and members of the Jewish community rushed back. An argument followed concerning the format of the funeral until a compromise was agreed, but without consulting Elsie. The funeral procession was subjected to a mixture of cheering and jeering from various groups.

Issy was buried in the Hebrew section of Fawkner Crematorium and Memorial Park, Melbourne (A 563). The day after the funeral, Elsie went to the grave on her own and was overcome with grief when she found it had been vandalised and the wreath stripped of flowers.

In addition to the VC and Cross of St George, he was awarded the Dehli Durbar Medal 1911, 1914–15 Star, British War Medal 1914–20, Victory Medal 1914–19 and King George VI Coronation Medal 1937. His medals were sold at auction in Australia for $A27,000 on 29th April 1992 and in London on 10th October 1995 for £35,288. The latter purchaser was a Manchester medal dealer. It is understood they are now held privately in Australia. Issy was seen wearing the Croix de Guerre, but there is no trace of the award in the London Gazette.

LIEUTENANT JOHN GEORGE SMYTH
15th Ludhiana Sikhs

John 'Jackie' Smyth was born at 'Greenmount', Ferndale Road, East Teignmouth, Devon on 24th October 1893. His father was William John Smyth (born 1869), a Double First from Balliol College, Oxford before joining the Indian Civil Service in Burma, where he died later. He was a talented cricketer and keen yachtsman. Jackie hardly knew his father, who was abroad for most of his childhood. He was cared for by his mother and a family friend, Mr HC Hapgood, an auctioneer at Witney, Oxfordshire, who became a second father. His mother was Lillian May née Clifford (c.1869–1956). William and Lillian were married on 25th February 1893 at Paddington, London. He was living at 30 Leinster Gardens, London and she at Witney, Oxfordshire. She lived at 177 Banbury Road, Oxford while her husband served in India and eventually moved to a flat at Southsea, Hampshire.

Military service went back a long way in the family. Jackie's paternal grandfather, Henry Smyth CB (1816–91), commanded 68th (Durham) Regiment of Foot (Light Infantry) during the Crimean War 1854–55, including at the Battles of the Alma, Inkerman (where his horse was killed) and the siege and fall of Sebastopol. He exchanged to the 76th Foot, held the Devonport command 1874–77, rose to general in 1878 and retired in 1879. In addition to the VC's father, Henry and his wife, Rebecca Mary née Peirce (1842–89), had three other sons:

- Henry Smyth (1866–1943) was commissioned in the Cheshire Regiment 1886 and took part in the Chin Lushai Expedition in Burma 1889–90 and the Tirah Expedition 1897–98. He was promoted lieutenant colonel in May 1915; DSO (LG 1st January 1918,) MID, Greek Medal of Military Merit, French Croix de Guerre (LG 1st May 1917) and Greek War Cross. He served in North West Persia and commanded 22nd (Wessex & Welsh) Battalion, The Rifle Brigade 1917–19 on mainly garrison duties in Salonika, attached to 228th Brigade. He married Alice Mary Caroline née Goodwin (1882–1949) in 1905 and they had two children.
- Thomas Charles Smyth (1868–1929) was appointed midshipman in the Royal Navy on 14th August 1883 rising to commander on 31st December 1907. He transferred to the Retired List at his own request as acting captain on 7th July 1908, following a period of ill health and periods at Osborne Convalescent Home. He returned to duty on 14th April 1915, but was unable to continue and left on 16th June. He married Leonora Lucy Farley née Pitts (1864–1949) in 1911. Leonora had two daughters prior to the marriage.
- George Abraham Smyth (1871–1939) was commissioned in the Royal Field Artillery 1891 and seconded for service with the Hyderabad Contingent 1895. During the First World War he was promoted lieutenant colonel; DSO (LG 1st January 1918). He settled in South Africa.

Jackie's godfather, Malcolm Jardine (1869–1947), was the father of Douglas Jardine (1900–58), England's cricket captain during the controversial 'Bodyline' test series of 1932–33. Malcolm Jardine and William John Smyth played cricket together at Oxford. Jackie's two brothers also had careers in the Army:

- Herbert 'Billy' Edward FitzRoy Smyth MC (born 1896) was commissioned in the Oxfordshire & Buckinghamshire Light Infantry in June 1915. He served in Mesopotamia 1916–18, North Russia 1919 and Palestine 1936–39. He attended the Staff College, Camberley in the early 1930s and was instructed by his brother Jackie (the second instance of VC brother instructing VC brother at the Staff College – the first being Hubert and Johnnie Gough VC in 1904). In 1938 he was promoted lieutenant colonel and transferred to the King's Own Yorkshire Light Infantry in August 1939. During the Second World War he served in France, Norway, Middle East and Burma; wounded twice. Appointed acting brigadier July 1940 and retired as honorary brigadier on 23rd January 1948. Herbert married Peggy Warren née Meade, daughter of Colonel Guy Warren Meade DSO MC in 1938 and they had a daughter.
- Henry Malcolm Smyth OBE (1898–1963) was commissioned from the Royal Military College, Quetta in October 1917 and joined 1st Battalion, 9th Gurkha Rifles on the North West Frontier. He served in the Third Afghan War 1919 and in Waziristan 1923; MID (LG 18th November 1924). In 1929 he went to Riga in Latvia to study Russian. In 1932 he was attached to the Shanghai Municipal Police

as an assistant commissioner and transferred in 1934. When hostilities between China and Japan broke out in 1937, the Japanese occupied the International Settlement and invited senior officials to remain. Henry was awarded the Shanghai Municipal Council Emergency Medal and OBE (LG June 1938) for his work in this period, during which he was promoted Deputy Commissioner. In August 1941, the Commissioner departed, leaving Henry as Acting Commissioner. When war with Japan broke out, the Japanese Consul-General asked senior officials to carry on. In February 1942, a Japanese was appointed to head the Police, but Henry was retained as an adviser. In August, he was one of 906 British diplomats, senior officials and others repatriated via Mozambique in exchange for Japanese citizens. Henry joined MI6 with the rank of lieutenant colonel and was based in a liberated area behind Japanese lines. He served as a member of the Berlin Military Government 1945–46 and with the Special Police Corps 1946–49. Henry never married.

Jackie was educated at Dragon Preparatory School, Oxford 1901–07, also attended by VCs William Leefe Robinson, Leonard Cheshire and John Randle. Other famous pupils include: Hugh Gaitskell, leader of the Labour Party; the author Nevil Shute; Ronnie Poulton-Palmer, England rugby captain; Lady Antonia Fraser and Sir John Betjeman, Poet Laureate. He suffered from dropsy and Bright's disease, resulting in him being confined to bed for two years, but he recovered and later excelled at sports. Jackie moved to Repton School in Derbyshire 1907–11, also attended by actor Basil Rathbone, author Roald Dahl, TV presenter Jeremy Clarkson, and Harold Abrahams, 1924 Olympics 100m Gold medallist. One of the headmasters, William Temple (1900–14), became Archbishop of Canterbury 1942–44, which started a trend. Temple was replaced at Repton by Geoffrey Fisher (1914–32), who went on to replace Temple as Archbishop of Canterbury 1945–61. Michael Ramsay, also a Reptonian, replaced Fisher as Archbishop 1961–74.

After Repton, Jackie trained at the Royal Military College, Sandhurst 1911–12 and played regularly for the Hockey and Soccer XIs and received his 'Blue' for revolver shooting. He also shot for the Army Eight. He won the Military History Prize, three volumes of 'Clausewitz on War', which went with him everywhere, but he admitted he never read them. He was commissioned on 24th August 1912 and sailed for India on the troopship *Plassy* in September, where he was attached to 1st Yorkshire

Repton School, Derbyshire, also attended by Basil Rathbone, Roald Dahl, Jeremy Clarkson and Harold Abrahams, as well as three 20th Century Archbishops of Canterbury.

The Royal Military College, Sandhurst.

(Green Howards) at Sialkot. He transferred to 15th Ludhiana Sikhs on 5th November 1913 at Loralai, Baluchistan.

When war broke out, the Battalion faced a march of eighty miles to the railhead, then on to Karachi, before sailing for Europe, arriving at Marseilles, France in September 1914. During the march, the temperature rose to 120°F. Every man was keen to go, but Jackie decided that Sepoy Harnam Singh, who was suffering from malaria, must be left behind. Three days later, he saw Harnam Singh, stepping out jauntily on the march. Jackie asked an Indian officer to explain. Harnam Singh had fallen in with the others and the officer had not the heart to turn him back. Jackie accepted that, but wanted to know how he marched all that way in his condition. *Oh, opium, Sahib. He is a non-opium eater and the effect of opium on him is therefore very great. We gave him a little opium before the march and put him to bed as soon as we got into camp and then did the same again the next day.* Harnam Singh reached Karachi, recovered on the voyage and served for a year in the trenches in France.

Jackie was promoted lieutenant on 24th November. The Battalion trained and acclimatised at Orléans before moving into the line in the Richebourg, Festubert and Givenchy areas. The Battalion was visited in the trenches by the Maharajah of Tikari. Early next morning, dressed in blue silk pyjamas, he asked Jackie if he could have a place to snipe from and was put somewhere out of the way. Jackie started his rounds and shortly afterwards heard some dull clangs, followed by roars of rage from the German trenches. Peering cautiously over the top, he saw six of their steel loopholes had been flattened, which seemed odd, as .303 bullets ricocheted off them. The Maharajah, still in pyjamas, was highly amused as he knocked out

HMTS *Plassy* (Martin Edwards).

Maharajah Gopal Saran Narain Singh of Tekari (1886–1958) was the first Indian prince to motor race in Europe, including several early Grand Prix races. He was a big game hunter and volunteered at the outbreak of the war as a special dispatch officer. After the war he joined the Indian National Congress Party.

every German loophole with an elephant rifle; the soft-nosed bullets were actually against the Geneva Convention. The Germans responded with a heavy mortar barrage, ending probably the most bizarre big game shoot the Maharajah ever experienced.

Life in the trenches had plenty of dark moments as well. Jackie was buried by an exploding minenwerfer, but his soldiers managed to dig him out before he suffocated. It left him with a hearing problem; when he was an MP he had to have the division bell installed in his room in Parliament. He also had a cigarette shot from his lips at Windy Corner and a piece of shrapnel cut his neck on another occasion.

Early in 1915 he was appointed Aide de Camp to Brigadier General EP Strickland, commanding the Jullundur Brigade, but requested to return to his Battalion when the Adjutant became a casualty. Strickland initially reprimanded him for his impertinence, but when Jackie asked the General what he would have done, Strickland smiled and bade him farewell. He was appointed Adjutant before the Battle of Neuve Chapelle in March 1915.

Awarded the VC for his actions at Richebourg L'Avoué, France during the Battle of Festubert on 17th May 1915, LG 29th June 1915. The VC was presented by King George V at Buckingham Palace on 12th July 1915. **Mentioned in Sir John French's Despatch dated 31st May 1915, LG 22nd June 1915. Awarded the Russian Order of St George, 4th Class, LG 25th August 1915.**

Jackie came to Sir Douglas Haig's attention for the wrong reasons, but it may explain why he received the Russian decoration. Jackie was asleep in the back of a staff car going to Béthune while Haig was visiting recently arrived troops. The Indian driver drove past, showering Haig's polished boots with mud. Jackie awoke to find Haig asking what he thought he was doing and his name. He explained the driver was young and inexperienced. On the return journey, Jackie selected an alternate route, but Haig was reviewing troops in a new location. The driver showered Haig again with Jackie once more asleep on the back seat. Waking to Haig's irate face, he muttered profuse apologies and hoped never to encounter him again. Proceeding on leave to England, he arrived as the boat cast off. The quay was higher than the deck and he was a good jumper, so tucked his kitbag under his arm, jammed his cap down and set off at a sprint when someone shouted to stop; it was Haig. Jackie's legs shot from under him and he watched the leave boat pull away. On the return boat, Haig saw him and sent his ADC with a note, *Sir Douglas Haig presents his compliments to*

Lieutenant Smyth and is sorry to have done him out of a day's leave but is sure he would have landed in the water. Jackie thanked Sir Douglas for his kind message, but was quite sure he would have reached the boat. A few weeks later Haig chose him from a number of other VCs to receive the Russian Order of St George, 4th Class. It came with a letter from the Tsar, telling him that the Order entitled him to become an inspector of girl's schools in Russia and to free travel on public transport. Jackie regretted never having the opportunity to avail himself of either privilege.

The Battalion moved to Egypt, landing at Ismailia in August 1915. In November it moved to Mersah Matruh by armed trawlers to take part in the Senussi Campaign in the Western Desert. With armoured cars and artillery support, the Battalion held the Senussi until the main force arrived. The Battalion returned to India in February 1916 for duty on the North West Frontier.

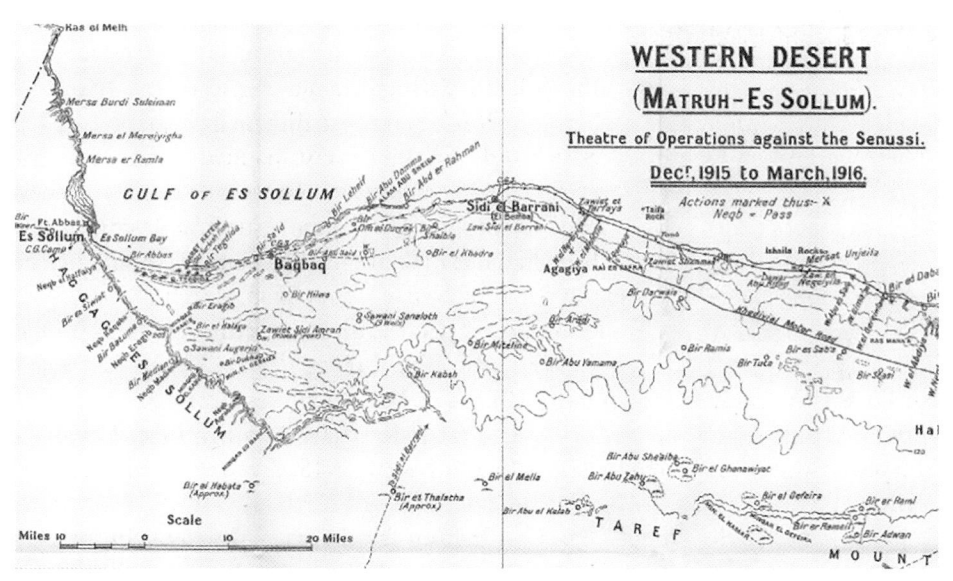

The Senussi Campaign was fought in an area of the Western Desert that would become very familiar to the British Eight Army in the Second World War.

Jackie was promoted captain on 24th August 1916 and took part in the Mohmand Blockade on the North West Frontier October–December 1916. He was granted leave in Kashmir to stay with Jack Manners-Smith VC, the Resident, but was recalled to continue the Mohmand campaign.

When not engaged on operations, Jackie was a keen rider and hunted with the Peshawar Vale Foxhounds. In late 1916, he was given a well-known racing pony, 'Lady Honor', by a British cavalry regiment ordered abroad. He had her trained for polo and became a skilled player. He was invited to join 17th Cavalry, but chose to remain with 15th Sikhs.

A blockhouse manned by 2/4th Border during the Mohmand Blockade.

Passing out top of the Staff School at Saugor in January 1918, Jackie was appointed acting major on 20th June 1918 and Brigade Major of the Bombay-Deolali Brigade. Later he was Brigade Major of 43rd Indian Brigade at Lahore. When the Punjab Disturbances broke out in April 1919, he was driving with his general to view the unrest when they heard shots and saw an angry mob of 10,000. The small police force was unable to hold them and a number of European women, nurses and children were in the path of the mob. Jackie ordered 17th Cavalry to disperse it and the mob withdrew.

The Wazirs and Mahsuds in Waziristan became increasingly troublesome after the Third Afghan War. Two columns were sent to deal with them – the Tochi Column against the Wazirs and the Derajat Column to deal with the Mahsuds. The Tochi Column consisted of 67th and 43rd Brigades under General Sir Andrew Skeen. On 21st October 1919 a convoy was attacked by a party of Mahsuds. Jackie Smyth set off with 300 men of 9th Jats in Ford vans, supported by two armoured cars. They arrived within two hours. While the infantry got behind the Mahsuds, Jackie drove the armoured cars straight at them. The Mahsuds retreated. **Awarded the MC for this action, LG 27th September 1920. Mentioned in Sir Charles Monro's Despatch dated 1st November 1919, LG 3rd August 1920.** Captain Henry Andrews, Indian Medical Service was awarded the VC posthumously for this action. During the rest of the Waziristan Campaign, Jackie took part in some of the fiercest fighting he ever encountered. The Mahsuds were defeated on 7th May 1920.

Waziristan in 1919.

While on leave in England for the first time in eight years, he was invested with the MC by The Duke of York at Buckingham Palace on 21st July; the King was ill. His brother, Herbert, received his MC on the same occasion. Next day, Jackie Smyth married Margaret née Dundas (born 1899) at the Brompton Oratory, London. She was given away by her great uncle, the Marquess of Zetland, as her father was with the Indian Civil Service. They had four children:

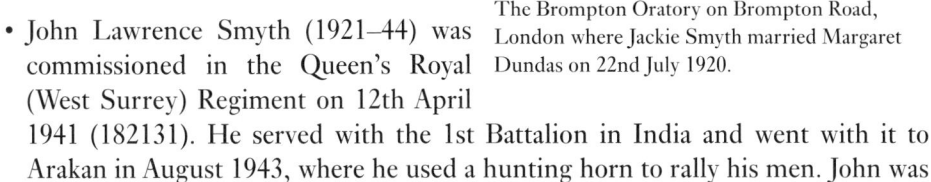

The Brompton Oratory on Brompton Road, London where Jackie Smyth married Margaret Dundas on 22nd July 1920.

- John Lawrence Smyth (1921–44) was commissioned in the Queen's Royal (West Surrey) Regiment on 12th April 1941 (182131). He served with the 1st Battalion in India and went with it to Arakan in August 1943, where he used a hunting horn to rally his men. John was killed in action leading his company in an attack on Jail Hill at Kohima, Assam on 7th May 1944 (Rangoon Memorial, Myanmar, Burma).
- Julian Smyth (1923–74) enlisted in the Royal Navy as an ordinary seaman. He emigrated to Australia and was employed in the Defence Department at Canberra. He married Phyllis Philomena Mary née Canon 1952 and they had seven children. Julian met his father at the 1968 VC/GC Reunion for the first time in fifteen years.
- Robin Smyth (1926–92) was commissioned in The Rifle Brigade on 1st September 1945 (14486788). He married Joan Harrison née Williams in 1961 and they had a son. He worked as Foreign Correspondent for the 'Observer' in Paris.
- Jillian Margaret Smyth (born 1929) married David George Firth in 1968 in a Quaker ceremony at Friend's House, Euston Road, London.

Jackie returned to India as Brigade Major of 74th Brigade and sailed for Basra, Mesopotamia in August 1920 to help put down the Arab Insurrection. **Mentioned in Sir Aylmer Haldane's Despatch dated 7th February 1921, LG 9th September 1921.** He spent the next two years in India, during which time he was appointed GSO3 from 13th January 1922 and transferred to 3/11th Sikh Regiment on 1st December.

In 1923, he played two first class cricket matches for the 'Europeans' in India. He returned to England to attend the Staff College later that year, having been nominated by Lord Rawlinson, Commander-in-Chief India. Two of his instructors were Philip Neame VC and Lord Gort VC. A fellow student was Arthur Percival, the ill-fated commander of British troops in Singapore in 1942.

While at the Staff College he was selected for the Army Hockey Team and captained the Combined Services Hockey XI in an English International trial. He also played lawn tennis and squash for the College, Army and Devon and was accepted for the Amateur Squash Championships. He finished in the top eight of the Staff Course and went back to India, where he was appointed GSO2 at Indian Army Headquarters, Delhi on 27th November 1925. Promoted brevet major on 1st January 1928, transferred back to 15th Sikhs (renamed 2/11th Sikh Regiment) on 26th May 1929 and was promoted major on 24th August.

Following leave in England, he returned to India and was posted to Peshawar. During the riots there, sparked by the arrest of Pathan leaders on 23rd April 1930, he was appointed City Commandant. On 31st May, at the guardroom at the Kabuli Gate, a lance corporal of the King's Own Yorkshire Light Infantry guard accidentally fired his rifle. The bullet passed within inches of Jackie's head, but killed an Indian woman and her two children passing in a trap. The city flared up into a riot, which required reinforcements and the Deputy Commissioner of Police handed the situation over to Jackie. He called the leading company of 15th Sikhs, under Captain Eustace, to clear the street. A brick struck Eustace in the face and Jackie ordered the assailant on a roof to be engaged with one round. It struck the wall close by, but had the effect of dispersing the rioters within minutes. **Mentioned in Sir William Birdwood's Despatch, LG 26th June 1931.**

In October 1930, Jackie returned to England as an instructor at the Staff College, Camberley, assuming the appointment on 16th January 1931. In 1933 he played tennis for the Army and was selected to play at Wimbledon in the Inter-Services Championship, but broke his wrist just before the Wimbledon fortnight. Appointed brevet lieutenant colonel on 1st July 1933 and returned to India as second-in-command of 3/11th Sikhs (45th Rattray's Sikhs) under Lieutenant Colonel KG Hyde-Cates at Rawalpindi on 25th November 1934. He took part in the Mohmand

Indian Army troops formed up during the Peshawar riots in April 1930.

Operations on the North West Frontier as temporary CO, arriving on 13th September 1935. **Mentioned in Sir Robert Cassels Despatch, LG 8th May 1936.**

Jackie was promoted lieutenant colonel on 16th July 1936 to command 3/11th Sikhs. Towards the end of the year, the unit joined the Chitral Relief Force, North West Frontier. As the senior officer, he was appointed Force Commander. While in Chitral in late 1936, he arranged for the cemeteries of Drosh and Chitral to be consecrated by Bishop Barne of Lahore. After the ceremony, Jackie and the Bishop attended a banquet hosted by the Mehtar of Chitral, Sir Shuja-ul-Mulk. Next morning, the Mehtar was ill and the Bishop and Jackie were also unwell. Arriving at the house of the Political Agent, Ian Scott, Jackie retired to bed, having been very sick. He was just getting into bed when Scott ran in to tell him the Mehtar was dead. Officially he died of heart failure, but Jackie believed he had been poisoned and he and the Bishop had been lucky.

He was posted to Allahabad on 9th October 1938, where he met his second wife, Frances, on the railway station. In anticipation of the war, he flew to England on 15th July 1939, having been promised a brigade by Lord Gort. He took a temporary position to assist with Civil Defence preparations and the Home Office refused to release him; the brigade was given to someone else. The War Office and Home Office reached an agreement resulting in Jackie being appointed GSO1, 2nd London Division. On 1st February 1940, he took command of 127th Infantry Brigade, 42nd East Lancashire Division, with headquarters at Rainscombe House, Marlborough, Wiltshire. It was clear on arrival that the Brigade was in a mess. The previous commander, brigade major and supply officer had been removed and a few days before he arrived the Inspector of Infantry had declared the Brigade unfit for service. Jackie selected a young Sapper subaltern, Charles Jones (later General Sir Charles Jones GCB OBE MC) as Brigade Major and Jackie Stevens as Supply Officer. Appointed temporary brigadier 5th February 1940–2nd April 1941.

Jackie's marriage to Margaret ended in divorce in 1940. He married Frances Mary Blair Read née Chambers (1908–89) on 12th April 1940 at Southsea, Hampshire. Her father was Lieutenant Colonel Robert Alexander Chambers OBE, Indian Medical Service. She worked at the War Office in 1943.

The Brigade sailed for France on 23rd April 1940 and was part of Macforce during the German invasion. After being withdrawn from Dunkirk on 31st May 1940, the Brigade reformed at Stokesley, Yorkshire, before moving to Barnsley on 8th July. **Mentioned in War Office Despatch, LG 20th December 1940.** Promoted colonel 23rd December 1940.

He sailed for India with his wife from Liverpool aboard *City of Venice* (sunk by *U-375* off Algeria in July 1943) on 13th April 1941, arriving at Bombay on 3rd June. Appointed acting brigadier 15th June 1941 and took command of 36th Indian Brigade at Baleli, near Quetta. He developed an anal fissure and contracted malaria and was admitted to Quetta Hospital. An earthquake struck the area, but he and

The Sittang Bridge, about seventy five miles from Rangoon in Burma, after being blown on Jackie Smyth's orders on 23rd February 1942. The bridge has been replaced by a new road bridge, but the supporting pillars remain.

his wife survived and he apparently made a full recovery. He was then appointed acting major general on 20th October 1941 to command 19th Indian Division at Secunderabad. He held a competition to select a divisional sign and his wife entered anonymously, submitting the Dagger symbol, which was subsequently adopted.

General Archibald Wavell, C-in-C India, appointed him to command 17th Indian Division in Burma during the Japanese invasion. He was still recovering from his operation and was criticised by Wavell later for not having a medical board before accepting the appointment.

Jackie flew to Rangoon from Calcutta on 9th January 1942. The Division tried to retreat over the Sittang, but the Japanese infiltrated behind, threatening the vital bridge over the river. Jackie was forced to order the bridge to be blown on 23rd February, but most of the Division was cut off on the enemy side. Wavell and Lieutenant-General Thomas Hutton (GOC Burma Command) blamed Jackie and he was sacked. However, ten days before, he had recommended to Hutton withdrawing to the west bank of Sittang where a strong defence line could be established; the recommendation was ignored.

Jackie flew back to India from Rangoon with Wavell on 2nd March, seated at the other end of the aircraft. At Calcutta, Wavell flew on to Dehli, leaving Jackie to arrange another flight. The only plane available was an antiquated two-seater Camel, flown by a Sikh pilot. It overshot the runway into thick bushes, lost a wing and ended up halfway up a tree, but neither pilot nor passenger was injured. In another Camel and with the same pilot, he arrived at Delhi safely.

Having reverted to brigadier, he was granted a month's leave by a medical board, but received no service medical treatment and his health deteriorated. Civilian doctors in Simla considered his condition so serious that his wife wrote to General Alan Hartley, Deputy C-in-C. As a result, Jackie was medically boarded on 6th June. He was suffering from the after effects of the operation plus paroxysmal tachycardia, acute dyspepsia and malaria. He was granted a further three months sick leave, after which he was boarded Category B, unsuitable for active service. On 17th September, Jackie had a final interview with Hartley, who had tried to change Wavell's mind to no avail. He sailed from Bombay on the troopship *Malaya* on 27th September and was granted the honorary rank of brigadier on retirement on 7th November 1942.

He became military correspondent for the 'Manchester Daily Despatch' and 'Glasgow Daily Herald' 1943–44 and the 'Daily Sketch' and 'Sunday Times' 1945–46. He was also lawn tennis correspondent for the 'Sunday Times' 1946–51 and correspondent for the 'News of the World' 1956–57. Jackie contested Wandsworth Central in 1945, losing to Ernest Bevin, but was elected Conservative MP for Norwood, London, 1950–66. He served as Parliamentary Secretary to the Minister of Pensions & National Insurance 1951–53 and was Joint Parliamentary Secretary for the Ministry of Pensions & National Insurance 1953–55. **Created 1st Baronet Teignmouth on 23rd January 1956.** Privy Councillor 1962.

Jackie was founder and first Chairman of the Victoria Cross & George Cross Association 1956–71 and Life President 1971–83. He attended every VC & GC Reunion 1958–81. In Parliament he championed the VC annuity, resulting in it being raised to £100 for all ranks on 30th September 1961, backdated to 1st August 1959. He was a Freeman of the City of London in the Worshipful Company of Farriers 1961–71, of which he was Master 1961–62. He was a member of many other organisations including:

- Councillor, East India Association.
- Chatham House.
- Royal Central Asian Society.
- Executive, Returned British PoW Association 1946–51.
- Governor or Comptroller of a number of schools 1947–66, including Dragon School Oxford 1953–66.
- Vice-President, Not Forgotten Association 1956.
- Vice-President, Distinguished Conduct Medal League 1957 and President 1958–70.
- Director, Creative Journals Ltd 1957–63.
- Trustee, Far East PoW and Internee Fund 1959–61.
- Honorary Vice-President, Far Eastern PoW Federation 1960.
- President, Old Reptonian Society 1960–61.
- Vice-President, Dunkirk Veterans Association 1963.
- International Lawn Tennis Club of Great Britain 1966.

Jackie was a prolific writer and his publications included:

Defence Is Our Business 1945, *Lawn Tennis* 1953, *The Game's the Same* 1956, *Before the Dawn* 1957, *The Only Enemy* 1959 (autobiography), *Sandhurst (History of the Military Cadet Colleges)* 1961, *The Story of the Victoria Cross* 1962, *Beloved Cats* 1963, *Blue Magnolia* 1964, *Behind the Scenes at Wimbledon* 1965, *Ming* 1966, *The Rebellious Rani* 1966, *Bolo Whistler* 1967, *The Story of the George Cross* 1968, *In This Sign Conquer* 1968, *The Valiant* 1969, *Will to Live: the story of Dame Margot Turner* 1970, *Percival and the Tragedy of Singapore* 1971, *Jean Borotra: the Bounding Basque* 1974, *Leadership in War 1939–1945,*

1974, *Leadership in Battle 1914–1918*, 1975, *Great Stories of the Victoria Cross* 1977 and *Milestones: a memoir* 1979.

He also wrote a series of three children's books – *Paradise Island* 1958, *Trouble in Paradise* 1959 and *Ann Goes Hunting* 1960 and two plays – *Burma Road* 1945 and *Until the Morning* 1950.

Jackie Smyth suffered a fall, breaking two ribs, and was admitted to King Edward VII Hospital for Officers, Marylebone, where he died on 26th April 1983. He was residing at Collingwood House, Dolphin Square, Pimlico at the time. He was cremated at Golders Green Crematorium, Hoop Lane on 29th April 1983 and his ashes were scattered in Section 2–L Garden of Remembrance (Ref 255870). He is also commemorated:

- On a board of Staff College instructors at the former Army Staff College, Camberley.
- On a plaque unveiled at Golders Green Crematorium on 7th April 2013 dedicated to fourteen VC recipients cremated there.
- His VC action featured in Issue 1158 of the *Victor* comic on 30th April 1983.

In addition to the VC, MC and Order of St George, he was awarded the 1914 Star with 'Mons' clasp, British War Medal 1914–20, Victory Medal 1914–19 with MID Oakleaf, India General Service Medal 1908 with five clasps ('Afghanistan NWF 1919', 'Mahsud 1919–20', 'Waziristan 1919–21', 'North West Frontier 1930–31' & 'North West Frontier 1935'), General Service Medal 1918–62 with clasp 'Iraq', 1939–45 Star, Burma Star, Defence Medal 1939–45, War Medal 1939–45 with MID Oakleaf, George V Silver Jubilee Medal 1935, George VI Coronation Medal 1937, Elizabeth II Coronation Medal 1953 and Elizabeth II Silver Jubilee Medal 1977. While serving in India, his medals, including the VC, were stolen and he was issued with official replacements. They are held by the Imperial War Museum, Lambeth Road, London.

Dolphin Square, Pimlico where Jackie Smyth lived until his death in 1983.

10073 LANCE CORPORAL JOSEPH HARCOURT TOMBS
1st Battalion, The King's (Liverpool) Regiment

Joseph Tombs was born as Frederick Griffith Tombs on 24th March 1887 at Pype Hayes, Chester Road, Erdington, Aston, Warwickshire, although in a newspaper article in October 1915, his father gave the place of birth as Turner Street, Sparkbrook. His father was Frederick Tombs (1856–1928), who was employed variously as a grocer, commercial traveller, Conservative Association Secretary, registration agent and political agent/officer. He was living at Grassmore House, Wigston Magna, Leicestershire in 1891 and at Casthorpe Road, Barrowby, near Grantham, Lincolnshire with his daughter Gertrude in 1901. At that time he was also a member of the Grantham Board of Guardians. He was living at 28 Industrial Road, Sowerby Bridge, Yorkshire in 1906 and at Vicarage Road, Chester in 1915. When Joseph enlisted in 1912 he did not know his father's address. His mother was Mary née Cole (born 1855) a domestic servant. Frederick and Mary's marriage was registered during the 4th quarter of 1882 at Islington. By 1901 she was living at West Cottage, Ramsdean, Langrish, near Southampton, Hampshire with her daughters Elizabeth and Nellie. When Joseph enlisted in 1912 he declared his mother was living at Deloraine, Tasmania. Joseph had three sisters:

* Annie Gertrude 'Gertie' Tombs (born 1883).
* Elizabeth Tombs (born 1884).
* Nellie Tombs (born 1889) married Leonard M Shaw in 1916 at Macclesfield, Cheshire and they had a son in 1924.

Joseph was educated at King Edward VI Five Ways School in Birmingham and King's School, Grantham 1901-03. The Admission Register for 21st January 1901 records him as, 'Tombs, Joseph' with 'Frederick' and 'Gruffydd' struck out. His date of birth is given as 23rd March, but with no year or age. His Parent/Guardian was 'Tombs, a Political Agent', whose address was given simply as Barrowby. At the time of the 1901 Census, Joseph was boarding with John Ely at 5 Redcross Street Grantham, adjacent to the School. John Ely's son, John B Ely, was also a pupil at King's School.

In 1906, Joseph was an apprentice electrical engineer working for JH Gath of Halifax. He enlisted in 3rd West Riding Regiment (Militia) for six years as Griffiths Tombs on 1st August 1906 (8518), giving his address as 90 Gibbet Street, Halifax. His age was recorded as seventeen years and five months. He was only 5' 2 3/8" tall, weighed 104 lbs with freckled complexion, grey eyes and red hair. His denomination was Wesleyan. Having completed forty-nine days drill, he was discharged on 9th May 1907 by purchase with Good Character. Joseph is alleged

King's School, Grantham. Isaac Newton was educated there 1655–60, as was William Cecil in 1530, later Lord Burghley, Chancellor and advisor to Elizabeth I. Albert Ball VC was a pupil 1906–7.

Church Street, Warrington.

to have run away to sea and possibly changed his name at this time. He may have spent some time in Cuba and worked as a mercenary in a border dispute in Peru. He travelled to Liverpool and settled in Warrington, where he was employed at Messrs Joseph Crosfield & Sons wharf in their soap works. He lodged at 17 Rowley Lane, off Church Street. Later he became a sheet roller with British Aluminium Company, Bank Quay, Warrington for eighteen months.

While living in Warrington, Joseph enlisted into 3rd (Reserve) Battalion, The King's Regiment on 5th March 1912. While undergoing training he attended the garrison school at Warrington to improve his education. Promoted lance corporal 2nd June 1913. Although he was mobilised on 8th August 1914, he was not sent to the front immediately, but spent some time in Scotland in a mixed King's and South Lancashire Regiment force. He eventually went to France to join the 1st Battalion on 23rd March 1915.

Awarded the VC for his actions near Rue du Bois, France on 16th May 1915, LG 24th July 1915. The original citation gave the date of the action incorrectly as 16th June. Promoted Corporal on 16th May 1915. The VC was presented by the King outside Buckingham Palace on 12th August 1915.

When news of Joseph's gallantry was published in the Warrington newspapers there was some doubt about his identity. Mr Stewart, an official of British Aluminium Company, corresponded with him twice to ensure he had the right man. Joseph returned to Warrington on 28th July. Accompanied by Mr Stewart, he visited the offices of the Warrington Guardian, British Aluminium Company and the Mayor before going away for a brief rest. He attended a public reception on 31st July, followed by a procession through the town to the cheers of a large crowd. He was later presented with an illuminated address and after a few days embarked on a recruiting campaign in Liverpool, St Helens and Bolton, which he continued after his investiture.

Joseph was also awarded the Russian Cross of the Order of St George, 4th Class, LG 25th August 1915. On 11th October, he visited King's School, Grantham while a patient at West Bridgford Military Hospital, Nottinghamshire.

He had a shrapnel wound in the shoulder and his ears had been affected by the close explosion of a shell. The OTC was formed up as a Guard of Honour and he was welcomed by the headmaster, Reverend CB Nichol. The ceremony was not prolonged and the public was not admitted in order not to cause him undue fatigue. He also received a wound that necessitated a toe being removed from his right foot. He was treated at 2nd Scottish General Hospital (Craigleith Hospital), Edinburgh at some time.

Probably on account of his wounds he did not return to the front, but was retained in the Army and employed on essential war work. This included being attached to the British Aluminium Company at Warrington from 16th March 1916, Brook Hoist Company Ltd in Chester from 11th November and munitions work from 7th January 1917. He attended a short electricians' course at the Ordnance School at Woolwich sometime in 1917 to become a maintenance mechanic.

Joseph Tombs married Ellen née Rowlands (c.1883-1921) at Toxteth Registry Office on 6th February 1917, giving their address as 159 High Park Street, Toxteth Park. They did not have any children. Joseph and Ellen lived at 17 Rowley Lane, off Church Street, Warrington.

Probably in late March 1917, Joseph transferred to 54th Anti Aircraft Company, Royal Garrison Artillery as a Corporal (2249) as part of the Firth of Forth Defences (Zone Z). He is reputed to have served as a gunner on the Canadian Pacific Railway Company's SS *Minnedosa*. However, her maiden voyage, during which she took Canadian soldiers home, was on 7th December 1918. Joseph was demobilised on 24th December 1919 to the Class Z Reserve and was formally discharged on 31st March 1920.

He joined the Merchant Navy (865718 changed to 113969 on 31st March 1920 and 142717 on 11th May) and was a steward on steamers along the west coast of South America. He was on the Glasgow United Shipping Company's SS *Kalimba* on 24th December 1919, the same day he was demobilised. He is reputed to have

Entrance to the Royal Arsenal, Woolwich.

SS *Minnedosa*.

The Sun Alliance Building in Montreal.

made his way to Philadelphia after working on the Panama Canal in a dredger. He also worked on several Canadian Pacific Railway ships, including SS *Minnedosa*. He joined the mailing department of Sun Life Assurance Company in Montreal from 4th July 1921 and became a special messenger in 1928. He lived at 589, 9th Avenue at some time.

Ellen died on 6th August 1921 while living at 159 High Park Street, Princes Park, Liverpool and is buried in Allerton Cemetery. Her sister, Alice Wilson, appears not to have known where Joseph was as she wrote to Army Records on 24th August in an attempt to locate him and reclaim the burial expenses. The War Office had previously written to Ellen seeking a photograph of Joseph to assist in identification in Canada. No reason was given. There are a number of examples of Joseph declaring false information, but the reasons for this are not known. For example:

- He stated his father was an Australian army officer, but in the 1901 Census and on the VC's wedding certificate in 1917, his father was listed as a political officer. No record could be found of an Australian army officer of that name.
- He claimed he attended the Naval College at Williamstown, Victoria, Australia as a boy, but no such establishment existed. The nearest establishment was the Naval Depot at Williamstown, but it was not a training establishment for boys.
- When he joined the Merchant Navy he gave his date and place of birth as 23rd March 1886 at Melbourne, Australia. In an article in the Birmingham Daily Mail on 5th October 1915, his father refuted this and confirmed he had been born in Birmingham.

Joseph married Minnie Sylvia Gooding McCarthy on 25th December 1925 in Montreal. They had no children. They lived in the suburb of Rosemount. Joseph served in No.4 Casualty Clearing Station, a Canadian volunteer reserve unit from the late 1920s until 15th May 1933 and then in the Royal Canadian Army Medical Corps until 1936. He was also a member of St John's Ambulance Brigade and was awarded the Association's Bronze Medallion.

The Canadian Pacific Railway arranged free return transport to England for him to attend the House of Lords VC Dinner in November 1929. He travelled on the *Minnedosa*, the ship he served on at the end of the Great War and afterwards as a steward. One of his sisters was waiting at the dock in Liverpool to welcome him. *Minnedosa* was commanded by Captain Ronald Niel Stuart VC until earlier in 1929, when he captained RMS *Duchess of York*, in which he brought a party of Canadian VCs to Britain for the VC Dinner. It is not known why Joseph did not join them.

RCAF Base Trenton.

Joseph enlisted in the Royal Canadian Air Force on 2nd December 1939 as an Aircraftsman 2nd Class (R54678). He volunteered for overseas service, but was retained in Canada on disciplinary duties. He was posted to the Flying School at Trenton on 13th June 1940 and promoted corporal. He was introduced to the Governor General, the Earl of Athlone, in July 1941 and to the Duke of Kent on 3rd August during their visits to the base. On 10th August 1941, he was posted to the Flight Training School at Brandon, Manitoba as a drill instructor. On 26th April 1942, he was posted to 12 Technical Services Detachment in Toronto, where he was promoted acting sergeant on 15th June. Joseph transferred to the Reserve on 8th December 1944.

Corporal Joseph Tombs VC RCAF meets the Duke of Kent on 3rd August 1941 during his visit to the Flying School at Trenton.

Joseph never fully recovered from an operation in 1952 to remove shrapnel from his stomach. He suffered a stroke in 1964 and was mainly confined to bed thereafter. He lodged with Mrs Frederica Johnson and her family on Second Avenue, Toronto for the last twenty years of his life and was known as Uncle Joe. Frederica Johnson's son, William Wheaton, was Joseph's distant nephew.

Joseph Tombs died at Toronto, Canada on 28th June 1966 and is buried in the War Veterans Plot, Pine Hill Cemetery, East Toronto (K 1056).

In addition to the VC he was awarded the 1914-15 Star, British War Medal 1914-20, Victory Medal 1914-19, George VI Coronation Medal 1937, Elizabeth II Coronation Medal 1953 and Cross of St George, 4th Class. He is reputed to have been awarded the Mercantile Marine War Medal 1914-18, but this seems unlikely as he was a soldier throughout the war. His VC and other medals were inherited by his nephew, William Wheaton, who donated them to the Royal Regiment of Canada on 27th October 1966. The King's Regiment and Royal Regiment of Canada are closely linked and agreed that the VC should be transferred back and forth between the Regiments, but remain the property of the Royal Regiment of Canada Foundation in Toronto. The George VI Coronation Medal 1937 and the Elizabeth II Coronation Medal 1953 do not form part of the group.

2ND LIEUTENANT ALEXANDER BULLER TURNER
3rd att'd 1st Battalion, Princess Charlotte of Wales's (Royal Berkshire Regiment)

Alexander Turner was born at 'Inversnaid', Southcote Road, Reading, Berkshire on 22nd May 1893. His father, Major Charles Turner (1862–1926), was commissioned as a lieutenant in 1st Battalion, Princess Charlotte of Wales's (Royal Berkshire

Regiment) from the Royal Military College, Sandhurst on 22nd October 1881. He served in the Anglo-Egyptian War 1882 (Egypt Medal 1882 and Khedive's Star 1882). Charles was promoted captain 23rd January 1889 and major 29th May 1901, serving as RTO at Aldershot Garrison until placed on Retired Pay and transferred to the Reserve of Officers on 15th January 1902. Appointed Justice of the Peace 1905, Berkshire County Councillor 1907 and Deputy Lieutenant Berkshire on 5th August 1922. Charles married Ella née Thornton (1863–87) on 16th March 1886 at St Helens, Isle of Wight. She was born at St Petersburg, Russia where her father was a merchant. She died of complications resulting from the birth of her son Charles in 1887.

Alexander's mother was Jane Elizabeth née Buller (1871–1953). She married Charles on 28th June 1892 at Plympton, Devon. When Charles died on 20th May 1926, he left £21,600 to his widow. She was an invalid for many years, cared for by her daughter, Milly. The family home was 'Thatcham House', Newbury, Berkshire until it was sold in 1948. Jane was distantly related to General Sir Redvers Buller, who was awarded the VC for his actions during the Zulu War at Inhlobana on 28th March 1879. Alexander had five siblings:

* Charles Walter Turner (born 1887), a half-brother from his father's first marriage, was commissioned in 1st Royal Dragoons from the Royal Military College, Sandhurst on 24th January 1906. He was promoted lieutenant 27th January 1909, captain 4th April 1914 and was appointed Adjutant Territorial Forces 7th November 1913–8th June 1915. He went to France on 1st July 1915 and was awarded the MC (LG 26th July 1918); commanding a squadron following the wounding of the commanding officer in support of a cavalry division which was being driven back, he took and held an isolated position, covering the retirement until almost surrounded, delaying the advance of a superior enemy force for at least an hour and avoided heavy losses. Appointed Company Officer of Gentlemen Cadets, Royal Military College on 10th September 1919 and Adjutant, Warwickshire Yeomanry on 20th March 1920. Charles retired on 9th July 1921.

* Jane Emily 'Mill' or 'Milly' Buller Turner (1894–1996) lived with her

The Turner family home, Thatcham House at Newbury, Berkshire.

brothers Cecil, Mark and Victor at Ditchingham Cottage, near Bungay, Norfolk, which they rented on the estate of Brigadier Bill Carr. Milly was the dominant figure in the close-knit family and was known for her kindness and strong faith. They were not well off, living on their pensions, but managed to do much good work in the community. Their one extravagance was shooting and any spare money was spent on cartridges. When invitations to shoots arrived, Milly sent whomever seemed most deserving on the day. When Cecil died in 1978, she moved into a cottage in Hedenham, Norfolk and then to various other homes. She remained fully alert until her last few months. At her 100th birthday party she was delighted that her favourite donkey was amongst the guests. Milly never married.

General Sir Redvers Buller VC, a distant relative of Alexander Turner.

- Cecil Buller Turner (1895–1978) entered the Royal Navy on 15th September 1908 and was appointed midshipman on 15th May 1913. He served aboard various ships – sweeping sloop HMS *Mimosa* from 14th September 1915, destroyer HMS *Radstock* from 15th September 1916, HMS *Cairo* from 14th January 1924 in the 4th Cruiser Squadron in the East Indies as Squadron Gunnery Officer, monitor HMS *Erebus* from 25th July 1927 and cruiser HMS *London* in the 1st Cruiser Squadron in the Mediterranean from 5th February 1929 as Squadron Gunnery Officer. He was promoted acting sub-lieutenant 15th May 1915, sub-lieutenant 15th December 1915, lieutenant with seniority from 15th March 1917 backdated from July 1919 having been acting since 15th June 1917, lieutenant commander 1st February 1927, commander 30th June 1930 and acting captain. He qualified as a gunnery officer on 1st May 1922. Cecil never married.
- Victor Buller Turner (1900–72) was commissioned in the Rifle Brigade on 20th December 1918 (17630) and served in Iraq 1919–20 (General Service Medal 1918–62 with clasp 'Iraq'). Promoted lieutenant 20th December 1920, captain 1st November 1932, major 1st August 1938, acting lieutenant colonel 8th July 1942, temporary lieutenant colonel 8th October 1942 and lieutenant colonel 15th March 1945. He was appointed Adjutant 5th June 1931–4th June 1934 and Adjutant Territorial Army 14th October 1934–31st October 1938. Victor took command of a company in June 1940 when 1st Battalion was reformed after the disaster at Calais. He became second-in-command of his Battalion and sailed for the Middle East in October 1941. He was taken prisoner, but turned on his captors and took them prisoner, bringing them back to his own lines with a convoy of enemy trucks. Victor was awarded the VC commanding 2nd Rifle Brigade at Kidney Ridge, Tel El Aqqaqir, Western Desert, Egypt on 27th October 1942; the only VC awarded for the Second Battle of El Alamein. He led the Battalion at

night for 4,000 yards through difficult country to their objective, capturing forty Germans. The Battalion was under continuous attack from 5.30 a.m. to 7 p.m. by ninety German tanks advancing in successive waves. Supported by 239 Anti-Tank Battery RA and the Battalion's 6 Pounder anti-tank guns, these tanks were repulsed. Thirty-five were destroyed completely and at least twenty more were immobilised. Throughout, Turner rallied his men and was always in the thick of the fighting. On one occasion he joined another officer and a sergeant manning a 6 Pounder and acted as loader; they helped in the destruction of five tanks. He was wounded in the head by a shell splinter, but refused medical attention until the last tank was defeated. He was on the critical list until 20th November and when recovered was appointed GSO1 Persia and Iraq 8th February–27th July 1943. Victor retired on 9th March 1949. He held various appointments in the King's/Queen's Bodyguard of the Yeomen of the Guard – Exon 27th February 1950, Ensign 31st August 1951, Clerk of the Cheque and Adjutant 15th April 1955 and Lieutenant 3rd November 1967, vice Major General Sir Allan Henry Shafto Adair KCVO CB DSO MC, until he retired in 1970; CVO, LG 1st January 1966. His VC action features in four issues of the *Victor* comic 1964–85 and he appears in a famous Terence Cuneo painting, *The Opening of the Minefields at El Alamein*. Victor was one of *10 VCs on a VC10* on the inaugural flight of the Super VC10 from London to Nairobi by East African Airlines on 6th April 1970. The ten VC recipients were guests of the company for a nine-day holiday in Kenya, Tanzania and Uganda. They were selected, five each from WW1 and WW2, by drawing names out of a hat. The others were Tom Adlam, Richard Annand, Donald Dean, Philip Gardner, Norman Jackson, Anthony Miers, Arthur Procter, Bill Reid and William White. During the trip they met General Idi Amin of Uganda and President Jomo Kenyatta of Kenya. Victor never married.

- Mark Buller Turner (1906–71) was commissioned in the Royal Artillery on 3rd February 1926 (34406). Promoted lieutenant 3rd February 1929, captain 1st November 1937, acting major 2nd September 1939, temporary major 2nd December 1939, war substantive major 23rd June 1942, acting lieutenant colonel 23rd March 1942, temporary lieutenant colonel 23rd June 1942, major 3rd February 1943, acting colonel 20th December 1944, acting brigadier 20th December 1944 and war substantive lieutenant colonel 20th June 1945. He retired as honorary brigadier on 22nd January 1949. Awarded the DSO (LG 29th March 1945) and OBE (LG 1st January 1949). Mark never married.

Victor Buller Turner, Alexander's younger brother, who was awarded the VC whilst commanding 2nd Rifle Brigade at Kidney Ridge on 27th October 1942 during the Second Battle of El Alamein.

Alexander's paternal grandfather, Robert Turner (c.1822–74), a merchant of Bishopsfield, Nottinghamshire, married Katherine née Timm (c.1835–1916) in 1861. After his death, she married Captain Legh Richmond Phillipps (c.1841–1901) in 1878. He was an ensign by purchase in 40th Foot on 6th January 1860, lieutenant by purchase 28th April 1863 and captain 15th March 1873. He was appointed Inspector of Musketry on 19th September 1868, transferred to 26th Foot on 24th January 1874 and went on to the Reserve on 1st October 1881.

Alexander's maternal grandfather, Admiral Sir Alexander Buller RN GCB (1834–1903), was the son of the Reverend Richard Buller (1804–83), Rector of Lanreath, Liskeard, Cornwall. His grandfather, James Buller, was a Lords Commissioner of the Admiralty 6th April 1807–17 June 1811 and Clerk to the Privy Council 19th August 1811–14th December 1830. Alexander Buller served as mate on HMS *Royal Albert* in the Black Sea during the Crimean War. He was commissioned lieutenant on 10th April 1855 and on HMS *Princess Royal* took part in the attacks on Kertch and Yenikale and in the capture of Kinburn. While serving aboard HMS *Edgar* at Queenstown, Ireland, he was awarded the Royal Humane Society's Bronze Medal for assisting in the rescue of two seamen who fell overboard from the main rigging on 12th August 1861 (Bronze Medals were also awarded for the same incident to Commander C Waddilove and R Mitchell of HMS *Edgar* and Boatswain's Mate J Cronion and Butcher J Daley of HMS *Sanspareil*). Promoted commander 10th June 1863 and captain 10th December 1869. He commanded the Naval Brigade during operations against the Malays in the Straits of Malacca 1875–76; CB. Appointed Naval Aide-de-Camp to Queen Victoria July 1884–January 1887. Appointed Admiral-Superintendent of Malta Dockyard January 1889–February 1892. Promoted vice-admiral in March 1892 and appointed Commander-in-Chief China Station 1895–97; KCB, LG 26th May 1896. He was promoted admiral in December 1897 and retired in 1899; GCB 26th June 1902. He married Emily Mary née Tritton (1840–1921) in 1870 and died on 3rd October 1903 while hunting with the Devon and Somerset staghounds near Exford. Alexander and Emily had five children in addition to Jane, including:

- Henry Tritton Buller (1873–1960) was a midshipman from 15th May 1889. Promoted sub-lieutenant 14th May 1893, lieutenant 30th June 1895, commander 31st August 1904, captain 22nd June 1911, rear-admiral 21st November 1921, vice-admiral 8th November 1926 and was placed on the Retired List as admiral on 1st April 1931. His appointments included – Commander, Royal Naval College, Dartmouth 1908–1911, command of the battleship HMS *Zealandia* November 1911, command of the cruiser HMS *Highflyer* 1st July 1913, command of the dreadnought HMS *Barham* as Flag Captain to Vice-Admiral Sir Hugh Evans-Thomas

Admiral Sir Alexander Buller RN GCB, who was awarded the Royal Humane Society's Bronze Medal for assisting in the rescue of two seamen in 1861.

HMS *Caroline* is the last remaining ship from the Battle of Jutland in 1916. She was decommissioned in 2011 and is being restored in Belfast.

April 1918, command of HMS *Valiant* 1st October 1918, command of the dreadnought HMS *Malaya* 14th May 1919, Chief of Staff to Sir Herbert Heath, C-in-C Coast of Scotland 17th May 1921 and command of HM Yacht *Victoria and Albert* 1922–31. Awarded CB (Edinburgh Gazette 2nd January 1919), GCVO (LG 15th August 1930) and the Belgian Grand Croix de l'Ordre de la Couronne 1934. He was appointed Groom in Waiting to King George V 1931–36 and Extra Equerry to George V, Edward VIII, George VI and Elizabeth II. He married Lady Hermione Stuart, only daughter of Morton Gray Stuart, 17th Earl of Moray, in 1919 and lived at Netherwood, Southwater, Horsham, Sussex. She died in 1989. They had four children including – Alexander John Stuart Buller (1920–40), who served in the RAF as a pilot officer (42391) with 101 Squadron and was killed on active service on 6th June 1940. He is buried in St Mary the Virgin Churchyard, Shipley, Sussex (C2).

- Francis Alexander Waddilove Buller (1879–1943) was appointed acting sub-lieutenant 15th July 1898. Promoted lieutenant 31st December 1900, commander 30th June 1913, captain 31st December 1917 and was placed on the Retired List as rear-admiral on 14th July 1922. Amongst his appointments were command of: destroyer HMS *Phoenix* 11th May 1912 (sunk by an Austrian submarine in May 1918, the only British warship ever sunk by the Austrian Navy); scout cruiser/minelayer HMS *Blanche* April 1918; and the light cruiser HMS *Caroline* 8th January 1919, but he was replaced the following month. Awarded the DSO (LG 4th June 1917) and was Mentioned-in-Despatches 20th July 1917. Francis married Mary Caroline Hammick (1893–1965) in 1916.
- Herbert Cecil Buller (1882–1915) was commissioned in The Rifle Brigade on 11th August 1900. Promoted lieutenant 18th January 1902, captain 22nd January 1910, temporary lieutenant colonel 21st March 1915 and major 1st September 1915. He was appointed Adjutant on 15th September 1907, Aide de Camp to Field Marshal HRH The Duke of Connaught on 6th October 1911, Adjutant PPCLI 1st September 1914 and CO PPCLI 21st March 1915; DSO (LG 23rd June 1915). He was killed in action on 2nd June 1916 and is buried at Voormezeele Enclosure No.3, Belgium (III A 7).

HM Yacht *Victoria and Albert*, commanded by Alexander Turner's uncle, Henry Tritton Buller, 1922–31.

Alexander was educated at Parkside Preparatory School, East Horsley and Wellington College until December 1908, where he was a member of the OTC. He

Alexander Turner's grave in Chocques Military Cemetery.

Wellington College, Crowthorne, Berkshire.

No.1 and No.2 Casualty Clearing Stations at Chocques in 1918.

was commissioned into 3rd (Reserve) Battalion, Royal Berkshire Regiment on 15th August 1914 and went to France on 9th June 1915, where he joined 1st Battalion on 22nd June. He was slightly wounded by a sniper on 12th August and returned to duty on 5th September.

Awarded the VC for his actions at Fosse 8, near Vermelles, France on 28th September 1915, LG 18th November 1915. Alexander was wounded fatally in the same action and died at No.1 Casualty Clearing Station at Chocques on 1st October. He is buried in Chocques Military Cemetery (I B 2) and is also commemorated on the Thatcham war memorial near Newbury, Berkshire.

As Alexander never married, the VC was posted to his father, but was presented formally by the King at Buckingham Palace on 16th November 1916. In addition to the VC, he was awarded the 1914–15 Star, British War Medal 1914–20 and Victory Medal 1914–19. After his brother Victor's death on 7th August 1972, the surviving siblings, Jane and Cecil, travelled to Newbury where they presented Alexander's VC to the Duke of Edinburgh's Royal Regiment (Berkshire and Wiltshire) and went on to Winchester, where they gave Victor's VC to the Royal Green Jackets Museum. Alexander's VC is now held by The Rifles (Berkshire & Wiltshire) Museum, The Close, Salisbury, Wiltshire.

10082 CORPORAL JAMES UPTON
1st Battalion, The Sherwood Foresters (Nottinghamshire and Derbyshire Regiment)

James Whitbread Upton was born at 5 Alexandra Cottages, Victoria Street (West Parade), Lincoln on 3rd May 1888. His father was James Whitbread (1845–1917). He married Eliza Tustino (born c.1844) in 1867 and at the time of the 1881 Census they were living at 9 Linton's Passage, St Peter-at-Gowts, Lincoln, close to where the VC's mother, Hannah, was living. In 1901 James was a lodger at 9 Sparrow Lane and in 1911 at 1 Cavill's Yard, Sheep Hill, Lincoln.

His mother was Hannah née Crane (1850–1935). She married Alfred Hemson Upton (born 1849), an iron driller of 47 King Street, St Peter-at-Gowts, Lincoln, in the 4th quarter of 1873. Hannah probably left Alfred around 1885. At the time of the 1891 Census she was housekeeper to James Whitbread of 5 Alexandra Cottages, Victoria Street (West Parade), Lincoln. Hannah separated from James Whitbread and moved to Nottingham between 1892 and 1895. At the time of the 1901 Census, Hannah was living at 4 St Martin's Hill, Lincoln with some of her family and was recorded as a widow living at 21 Hempshill Lane, Bulwell at the time of the 1911 Census. She later moved to Newmarket Road, Bulwell, Nottingham.

James had at least nine siblings:

- Mary Ann Crane (born 1866), also seen as Maria, married William Wilson (born 1859) in 1884. He was a railway platelayer in 1901 and a bricklayer's labourer in 1911. They were living at 57 Brierley Street, Nottingham in 1906. Mary and William adopted Irena Peel (1893–1954). She was recorded as Alice in the 1901 Census and Irena Peel Wilson in the 1911 Census, when she was a lace jennier and finisher.
- Martha (Pat) Crane (1869–1954) married John Thomas 'Tom' Gibson Mann (1869–1935) in 1891. She married again in 1937, George Frank Wallis (1871–1952). George had previously been married to Elizabeth Watson in 1893.
- John Henry Upton (c.1873–1951), a blacksmith's striker.
- Alfred Upton (born 1874), a moulder.
- Frank Upton (1877–1948) served in 8th Battalion, The London Regiment (Post Office Rifles) (3863 & 493575) and later in the Rifle Brigade (212818). He married Mary E Thompson in 1918.
- Herbert Upton (1879–1900) enlisted in 1st Lincolnshire (4602) on 16th October 1896, declaring previous service with 3rd Lincolnshire and giving his age as

eighteen years and eleven months. He died of cholera at Trimulgherry, India on 8th August 1900.
- Arthur Upton (born 1882).
- Florence Beatrice Upton (1885–1945) was a general domestic servant. She married Albert Dawson (c.1876–1921), a brewery labourer in 1908 and had three children between 1909 and 1917 (Joseph, Robert and Florence).
- Walter Whitbread Upton (1891–1950) served in 7th Sherwood Foresters in France in 1915. He married Louisa (born Lois) Cousins née Applewhite (1894–1974) in 1919 and they had eleven children between 1922 and 1938 (Aubrey, twins Beryl and Dulcie, David, Phyllis, Tessie, Gwendoline, Bernice, Terence, Muriel and Derek). She had previously married William H Cousins in 1914 and had a son, Harry, later that year. William H Cousins may have died in the First World War; two men in the CWGC database fit his profile. Walter and Lois had a daughter, Beryl Louise (1923–2008).

James was educated at St Peter-at-Gowts School, Lincoln and was a member of the Church Lads' Brigade. For part of his childhood he was brought up by his sister Martha 'Patricia' Mann of Ruston Lodge, Waterside, Lincoln, and her husband Tom, either when his mother went to Nottingham, or due to overcrowding in the cottage in Lincoln. He was employed as a labourer in Mr W Rigley's Wagon Works at Bulwell and may have lived with his mother at this time. When he enlisted in 1906 he was a general labourer, living with his sister, Mary Wilson, at 57 Brierley Street, Willingham, Nottingham.

James enlisted in 4th Sherwood Foresters (Militia) at Derby on 14th May 1906. His next of kin was his brother Frank Upton and sister Mary Wilson. He was described as 5′ 2⅛″ tall, weighing 122 lbs with fresh complexion, blue eyes, brown hair and his religious denomination was Church of England. He enlisted for regular service on 24th July 1906 and served in Ireland 1908–09 and then in India until war broke out. The Battalion sailed from Bombay on 3rd September 1914 and landed at Plymouth on 2nd October. James went to France on 4th November. **Awarded the VC for his actions at Rouges Bancs, France on 9th May 1915, LG 29th June 1915.** The VC ribbon was presented to him by Major General Sir Francis Davies, GOC 8th Division, near Sailly, France on 8th July. James returned to England on 14th July and his VC was presented by the King at Windsor Castle on 24th July. He was presented with an illuminated address and a purse of gold by the Mayor of Nottingham, but it is not known when this ceremony took place. James continued to serve in France until 7th February 1918 and is understood to have been engaged in recruiting in London thereafter. He was demobilized on 30th March 1919.

James Upton married Mary Jane née Chambers (1888–1949) on 20th July 1915. They had three sons:

- George Edward Chambers (23rd August 1909–1968), born before James and Mary married and a few months after he left for India. He married Mabel Stapleton (born 1907) in 1932 and they had five children (Janet, Marjorie, Doris, Anthony and John) between 1932 and 1945.
- Thomas Herbert Upton (10th May 1918–2000) was also brought up by Patricia Mann.
- Kenneth Victor Upton (18th December 1919–1995). He married Mary E Conway (died 1985) in 1943 and had two children – Joan in 1945 and David in 1954.

James deserted his wife in 1919 while she was pregnant with Kenneth and turned up in London some years later living at Victoria Lodge, Old Kenton Lane, Kingsbury, where he ran a social club in North London. He is believed to have married Ada Bennett bigamously at Chapel-en-le-Frith, Derbyshire in the 2nd quarter of 1927 and had a daughter, Rita M Upton, born and died in 1928 at Pancras, London. Mary Upton married Charles Harry Dove (1881–1946) in 1928.

In the Second World War, James was a captain in 12th Middlesex Battalion Home Guard from 1st February 1941 and was promoted major on 11th November 1942. He died at Edgware General Hospital on 10th August 1949 and was cremated at Golders Green Crematorium where his ashes were scattered. The cause of death was oedema of the lungs and paralytic ileus due to acute pacreatitis (usually but not exclusively associated with heavy drinking). A memorial plaque was unveiled at Golders Green Crematorium on 7th April 2013 to the fourteen recipients of the VC cremated there. James Upton is also commemorated at:

- The Church Lads & Church Girls Brigade Memorial Plot at the National Memorial Arboretum, Alrewas, Staffordshire includes 22 Berberis shrubs representing the 22 members of the Church Lads' Brigade who have been awarded the VC.
- The grounds of Nottingham Castle, where a memorial was dedicated on 7th May 2010 to the twenty men born or buried in Nottingham and Nottinghamshire who have been awarded the VC.

In addition to the VC he was awarded the 1914 Star with 'Mons' clasp, British War Medal 1914–20, Victory Medal 1914–19, George VI Coronation Medal 1937 and the Defence Medal. The VC was presented to the Regiment in 1962 by his sister-in-law, Mrs Louisa Upton (Walter's wife). It is held by the Sherwood Foresters Museum (Nottinghamshire & Derbyshire Regiment), Nottingham Castle. The First World War trio with the VC are named to J Ayers ASC. It is not known what became of the originals.

3719 PRIVATE ARTHUR VICKERS
2nd Battalion, The Royal Warwickshire Regiment

Arthur Vickers was born at 7 Court, Woodcock Street, Aston, Birmingham on 2nd February 1882. His father was John Vickers (1851–1908), a strip brass caster. His mother was Amy née Kennedy (1855–1911). John and Amy married on 4th April 1874 at St Laurence Church, Birmingham, Warwickshire. The family was living at 1 Back of 184 Francis Street, Aston in 1881; Court 4, House 12, 39 Dartmouth Street, Aston in 1891; and 26 Heneage Street, Birmingham in 1901. Amy was residing at St Barnabas, Aston Union Workhouse, Erdington in 1911. Arthur had six siblings:

- William 'Bill' Vickers (born c.1877) was a turner bicycle fitter.
- Richard Vickers (born 1878) was a brass caster.
- Thomas Vickers (born 1880) was a pen polisher.
- Alfred Vickers (1894–1901).
- Amy Vickers (1885–1936) was a machinist living as head of household with her brothers Richard and Arthur at 1 Upper Portland Street, Aston in 1911. She married Herbert Adkins (1885–1931) later in 1911. They were living at 145 Park Road, Aston in 1916 and had three children – Amy Adkins 1912, Herbert A Adkins 1918 and Leonard Adkins 1920.
- Elizabeth 'Eliza' Florence Vickers (1890–1973) married Arthur Ernest Walker (1885–1967) in 1907. He was a Gas Corporation stoker. They were living at 63 Yew Tree Road, Aston in 1911. Eliza and Ernest had twelve children, including – Arthur Ernest Walker (1908–97), Hilda Florence Walker (1910–2003), Leonard Walker 1912, Edna Alma Walker (1913–88), Norman W Walker (1915–34), Phyllis Elaine Walker (1917–99), Victor G Walker 1921, Vera Margaret Walker (1923–2002), Raymond Kenneth C Walker (1925–2005) and Nevil T Walker (1930–31).

A maternal aunt, Elizabeth Kennedy (1850–1924), became a nun of the Sisters of Mercy, living in various convents in Newcastle upon Tyne, Tynemouth, Westgate and Durham. Another aunt, Eliza Kennedy (1858–1949), moved to America where she married John J Dooley at Hartford, Connecticut. One of his cousins, John Joseph Kennedy (1896–1918), served as a fitter in the RFA (170644), died of wounds on 22nd March 1918 and is buried at Ham British Cemetery, Muille-Villette, France (I E 20).

Dartmouth Street, Aston.

Arthur was educated at Dartmouth Street School, Aston. He enlisted on 29th May 1902 and served for six years. He was then employed as a brass carter and later by General Electric Company at Witton, Birmingham 1908–14. It took him six attempts to re-enlist on 12th August 1914, having been rejected due to his height, which seems unusual given his previous service. He was known as Midge or Titch. Arthur went to France on 4th May 1915.

Awarded the VC for his actions at Hulluch, France on 25th September 1915, LG 18th November 1915. He was also awarded the Croix de Guerre (France), LG 24th February 1916. At the time his address was with his sister, Mrs Amy Atkins, in Park Road, Aston. The VC was presented by the King at Buckingham Palace on 15th January 1916. He was later promoted sergeant and served in the Territorial Force/Army post-war. He was a Member of the VC Guard at the interment of the Unknown Warrior on 11th November 1920.

Arthur Vickers married Lily Agnes née Price (1893–1944) on 29th April 1922 at St Peter & St Paul Church, Aston. He was still living at Park Road at the time. Lily was a warehouse girl in 1911, living with her parents at 26 Yew Tree Road, Aston and at 49 Beales Street at the time of her marriage. They were living at 6 House, 53 Court, Farm Street, Birmingham in 1927 and later moved to 6 Back, 232 Farm Street. They had one child – Arthur Herbert Vickers, whose birth was registered in the 3rd quarter of 1923 and his death in the following quarter. When Lily died on 21st August 1944, only a few weeks after Arthur, she left £129/8/4 to her sister, Jeannie Crisp.

Arthur was employed as a core builder when he married in 1922. From 1935 he was a millwright's mate at Messrs Lucas Ltd and later in life he collected glasses in a pub. He died of carcinoma of the stomach and pulmonary tuberculosis at City Hospital, West Heath, Birmingham on 27th July 1944. His death certificate describes him as an electrical works labourer. He was buried in an unmarked grave (Section 161 Grave 47760) in Witton Cemetery, Birmingham; it was

Aston Parish Church of St Peter & St Paul.

marked with a headstone by Birmingham City Council on 13th November 2000. Arthur is named on a memorial at Junction Industrial Park, Electric Avenue, Witton, Birmingham, dedicated on 11th November 1998, on the site of the old GEC factory where he worked.

In addition to the VC and Croix de Guerre, he was awarded the 1914–15 Star, British War Medal 1914–20, Victory Medal 1914–19 and George VI Coronation Medal 1937. His VC is held by the Royal Warwickshire Regiment Museum, Warwick.

Arthur Vickers in a post-war Territorial Army group photograph. He is seated front row, second from the right.

CAPTAIN CHARLES GEOFFREY VICKERS
1/7th (Robin Hood) Battalion, The Sherwood Foresters (Nottinghamshire and Derbyshire Regiment)

Charles Vickers was born in Nottingham on 13th October 1894. His father was Charles Henry Vickers (1851–1925), Director of Messrs Vickers & Hine, Lace Manufacturers. When he died on 23rd February 1925, he left £10,771/13/10 to his son Charles. His mother was Jessie Anna née Lomas (1858–1921). Charles and Jessie's marriage was registered in the 3rd quarter of 1882 at Leicester. When she died on 6th July 1921 at 6 Oxford Street, Nottingham, she left £2,426/0/5 to her surviving children, Jessie and Charles. The family lived at 4 Park Valley, Nottingham. Charles had two siblings:

- Jessie Margaret Vickers (1883) married the Reverend Walter M Browne in the 2nd quarter of 1914 at Nottingham. They had two daughters – Jessica 'Jessie' Margaret Browne 1917 and Sheila M Browne 1922.
- William Burnell Vickers (1890–1917) was in Norway at the outbreak of war. He returned and enlisted in the Royal Fusiliers (Public Schools Battalions) and was commissioned in 21st (4th Public Schools) Battalion, Royal Fusiliers on 17th March 1915. He went to France in November, returned to Britain in July 1916, transferred to the Royal Garrison Artillery on 8th July and returned to France

with a Siege Battery in October. William was killed in action on 21st June 1917 whilst serving with 184th Siege Battery RGA and is buried in Vlamertinghe New Military Cemetery, Belgium (II D 1).

Charles' paternal great grandfather was Alderman William Vickers JP (1798–1882), Mayor of Nottingham in 1843. Unusually, of Charles' twelve aunts and uncles on both sides of his family who survived to adulthood, only three uncles married.

Charles was educated at Oundle School (Sidney House) 1908–12, where he played rugby for the school and was a member of the OTC. From January to March 1913 he studied German in Germany. He went up to Merton College, Oxford in October, where he played rugby for the College and was also a member of the OTC.

Charles Vickers' great grandfather, Alderman William Vickers, Mayor of Nottingham in 1843.

Charles was commissioned on 2nd September 1914 and went to France on 28th February 1915. Appointed acting captain 29th August. **Awarded the VC for his actions at the Hohenzollern Redoubt, near Loos, France on 14th October 1915, LG 18th November 1915.** Having been wounded in the VC action, he was evacuated to England. The VC was presented by the King at Buckingham Palace on 15th January 1916. While recovering he served with a reserve battalion from 1st June and was appointed temporary captain on 30th July. He returned to 1/7th Battalion in France on 23rd September. Returned to England as an instructor and company commander at No.19 Officer Cadet Battalion, Pirbright on 20th February 1917 and was graded as a staff captain while commanding a company within the Officer Cadet Battalion 5th May 1917–6th January 1918.

Oundle School and its OTC contingent.

Christ and Merton Colleges, Oxford.

Charles Vickers married Helen Tregoning née Newton (born 8th June 1896 at Harpenden, Hertfordshire) on 21st March 1918 at St Andrew's Church, Malden Road, Haverstock Hill, London. She was living at 4 The Grange, Maitland Park, London, at the time, while he was living at Egremont, Derby Road, Nottingham. Helen's father was a director of Winsor and Newton, makers of watercolour paints and brushes; the company still exists. Charles and Helen had two children:

- Pamela Tregoning Vickers, born on 5th January 1921 at Leicester. Her marriage to Robert B Miller was registered in the 3rd quarter of 1955 at Chelsea, London. He was Director of Music at Oundle School.
- Douglas Burnell Horsey Vickers, born on 14th September 1922 at Leicester.

Charles returned to France as acting major and 2IC of 1st Lincolnshire 15th April–1st November 1918 and from 8th November 1918. He was wounded again. **Awarded the French Croix de Guerre while commanding a composite battalion at the defence of the Marne in June 1918, LG 6th November 1918. Mentioned in Sir Douglas Haig's Despatch of 8th November 1918, LG 28th December 1918.** He relinquished acting major on 15th March 1919.

While completing his degree in French, European History and Law at Oxford (BA & MA 1921), he also served in 4th Leicestershire (TF) from 14th July 1920. He transferred to 7th Nottinghamshire & Derbyshire on transfer to the TA Reserve on 29th April 1922 (the TF became the TA in October 1920). Charles qualified as a solicitor in 1923 and became a partner in Slaughter and May 1926–46. He enjoyed tennis and literary pursuits and was a keen sailor, coming second in the Fastnet Race shortly before the Second World War.

Charles' marriage to Helen was dissolved in 1934. He married Ethel Ellen née Tweed (born on 27th July 1902 at Billericay, Essex) on 25th June 1935 at Pancras, London. They had a son, Hugh Vickers, born on 24th June 1939 at Marylebone, London. Ethel died in 1972 at Oxford. His first wife, Helen, married John G Young in 1943 at Westminster and died in 1987 in Surrey.

Charles was granted a Regular Army Emergency Commission in the Sherwood Foresters and later the RAOC as a lieutenant (139890) on 27th June 1940. Promoted war substantive major 2nd November. He visited British communities in Venezuela, Brazil, Argentina, Uruguay, Chile, Peru, Colombia, Panama, Cuba and Portugal to produce a report on economic intelligence dated 16th December 1940. Appointed local colonel 13th January 1941 and Deputy Director-General of the Economic Intelligence Division of the Foreign Office 1941–44 and Director-General of the Economic Advisory Branch of the Foreign Office 1944–45. He was also a Member of the Joint Intelligence Committee 1941–45. He resigned his commission and was granted the rank of major from 27th September 1944.

Charles was knighted for his services as Director-General, Economic Intelligence Division, Foreign Office, LG 1st January 1946 (Intention),

conferred on 12th March and confirmed 15th March. Awarded the American Medal of Freedom with Gold Palm for his work in the Economic Advisory Branch of the Foreign Office, Ministry of Economic Warfare and as a member of the Joint Intelligence Sub Committee March 1942–June 1945 (War Department letter dated 6th September 1945).

Charles held numerous civil appointments:

- Member of the London Passenger Transport Board 1941–46.
- Member of the Council of the Law Society 1944–48.
- Legal Adviser to the National Coal Board 3rd June 1946–48.
- Member of the National Coal Board 1948–55 responsible for manpower, education, health and welfare.
- Chairman of the Research Committee of the Mental Health Research Fund 1951–67, which he helped to found.
- Member of the Medical Research Council 1952–60.
- Director of Parkinson Cowan Ltd 1955–65.
- Governor of the Royal Humane Society.
- Honorary Fellow of the Royal College of Physicians.

He was also a prolific author – *The Secret of Tarbury Tor* 1925, *Values and Decision Taking* 1956, *The Undirected Society* 1959, *The Impact of Automation on Society* 1964, *Industry, Human Relations and Mental Health* 1965, *The Art of Judgement* 1965, *Towards a Sociology of Management* 1967, *Value Systems and Social Processes* 1968, *Freedom in a Rocking Boat* 1970, *Science and the Regulation of Society* 1970, *Making Institutions Work* 1973, *Responsibility* 1980, *Human Systems are Different* 1983, *The Vickers Papers* 1984, *Policymaking, Communication and Social Learning* 1987, *Rethinking the Future* 1991 and *Moods and Tenses*, a collection of his poems 1983.

Charles Vickers' first of many books.

Charles Vickers died at The Grange, Goring-on-Thames, Oxfordshire on 16th March 1982 and was cremated at Oxford Crematorium, where his ashes were scattered. He is also remembered on the 'Nottingham and Nottinghamshire Victoria Cross Memorial', dedicated at Nottingham Castle on 7th May 2010 to commemorate twenty VCs born in Nottingham and Nottinghamshire or who are laid to rest there.

In addition to the VC and his knighthood, he was awarded the 1914–15 Star, British War Medal 1914–20, Victory Medal 1914–19 with Mentioned-in-Despatches

Charles Vickers in later life.

oakleaf, Defence Medal 1939–45, War Medal 1939–45, George VI Coronation Medal 1937, Elizabeth II Coronation Medal 1953, Elizabeth II Silver Jubilee Medal 1977, French Croix de Guerre and Medal of Freedom with Gold Palm (USA). His VC is held by the Sherwood Foresters Museum, Nottingham Castle.

7602 PRIVATE EDWARD WARNER
1st Battalion, The Bedfordshire Regiment

Edward Warner was born at 36 Cannon Street, St Alban's, Hertfordshire on 18th November 1883. His father was Mark Warner (1834–1912), a railway platelayer. His first marriage to Anne Bibby (1829–80) was childless. Edward's mother was Charlotte Maria Goodgame (1840–1922). Charlotte and Mark lived as husband and wife and are recorded as such on various Census returns, but no record of their marriage could be found. Edward had an older sister, Annie Maud Goodgame (1869–1939). The father was registered as Mark Goodgame, but as no trace of this man has been found and Mark Warner and Charlotte lived close to each other from at least 1861, it is assumed that Mark Warner was the father. One of Annie's sons, 204052 Lance Corporal Sidney Victor Catlin (born 1897), 1st West Yorkshire, was killed in action on 21st March 1918 and is commemorated on the Arras Memorial, France.

The family was living at Lattimore Road, St Alban's in 1891 and by 1901 Edward was employed as a straw hat stiffer and was boarding with the Cullin family at 38 Cannon Street, St Albans (next door to where he was born). He enlisted in the Bedfordshire Regiment late in 1903, served in India until the Battalion returned to Britain in 1908 and then transferred to the Reserve. He was employed by the Deep Well Boring Works, St Albans Council and the General Post Office Telephones Department. Edward was recalled from the Reserve when war broke out, joined 1st Bedfordshire and went to France on 16th August 1914. **Awarded**

The dedication of the Ypres (Menin Gate) Memorial on 24th July 1927.

the VC for his actions at Trench 46, Zwarteleen, near Ypres, Belgium on 1st May 1915, LG 29th June 1915. He died as a result of gas poisoning on 2nd May 1915 and is commemorated on the Ypres (Menin Gate) Memorial. He is also commemorated on St Peter's Green war memorial, St Albans.

His VC was sent to his mother by post on 20th July 1915, but was later presented to her formally by the King at Buckingham Palace on 16th November 1916. In addition to the VC, he was awarded the 1914 Star with 'Mons' clasp, British War Medal 1914–20 and Victory Medal 1914–19. Edward never married, but was engaged to Maud Amelia Burton (born 1882), a boot fitter, who was boarding with Edward and his parents in 1911.

St Alban's war memorial during the unveiling by the Earl of Cavan on 22nd May 1921.

When his mother died in 1939, the medals were bequeathed to his niece, Mrs Gwen Dixon (registered as Gladys at birth and marriage). She presented the medals to Lieutenant Colonel Norbury, CO Bedfordshire Regiment, and Lieutenant Colonel Young, Regimental Secretary, at a ceremony at her home at 114 Earlham Grove, Forest Gate, London on 20th June 1962. The VC is held at the Bedfordshire & Hertfordshire Regiment Museum, Wardown Park Museum, Luton, Bedfordshire.

L/8088 SERGEANT HARRY WELLS
2nd Battalion, The Royal Sussex Regiment

Harry Wells was born at Millbank, near Hoath, Herne Bay, Kent on 19th September 1888. His father was Samuel Wells (1849–1914), a bricklayer's labourer. His mother was Emma Elizabeth née Rose (1856–1941). Samuel and Emma married on 14th March 1885 at Herne Bay. They were living at In-the-Hole, Herne Bay in 1891 and King Bridge, Hoath, Kent in 1901. Emma had a daughter, Olive Gertrude Rose (born 1881), before she married Samuel. Harry had four other siblings:

- Harold Percy Wells (1895–1947) married Alice Sophia Hinchcliffe in 1919.
- Mabel Agatha Wells (1885–1966) married Alfred Frederick Judge (1884–1973) in 1906 and they had four children, including Henry 'Harry' William Frederick Judge (1907–33) who enlisted in the Royal Navy on 30th November 1924 (C/J107145) and died while serving on HMS *Brilliant* at Malta on 22nd December 1933.
- Mary Wells (1886–92).
- Ruth Wells (1891–1930) was a housekeeper in 1911 at 1 Ridley Villas, Herne Bay. She married Sidney A Harris in 1912 and they had three children. Sidney married Edith E Pilcher in 1939.

Harry was educated at Hoath School. He left aged twelve and was employed at Ridgeway Farm, Herne, where he lost two fingers in an accident with a haymaking machine. He worked later for Mrs Wootton at Herne Mill, before enlisting into 2nd Royal Sussex on 25th October 1904. He served most of his time as a battalion signaller and earned two Good Conduct Badges before transferring to the Reserve on 30th June 1911 from the Curragh. On 29th July 1911, Harry became a Kent County Constabulary policemen in Ashford, living at Ridley Villas, Herne Street, Herne Mill until he moved to Farningham. Having resigned on 13th December 1913, he worked and lived at the Beaver Inn in Ashford.

Harry was discharged from the Reserve on 30th June 1913, but was recalled on the outbreak of war and went to France on 12th August 1914. **Awarded the VC for his actions near Le Rutoire, Loos, France on 25th September 1915, LG 18th November 1915.** He was killed during his VC action and is buried in Dud Corner Cemetery, Loos (V E 2). He is also commemorated:

- On the Herne Bay War Memorial, Kent.
- At the Church of St Bartholomew, Herne Bay.

Marine Parade, Herne Bay.

Herne windmill.

- The former Royal Sussex Regiment Depot, Roussillon Barracks at Chichester, was redeveloped for housing and six roads or houses were named after Royal Sussex VCs, including Wells House.

As Harry never married, the VC was presented to his mother by the King at Buckingham Palace on 29th November 1916. In addition to the VC, he was awarded the 1914 Star with 'Mons' clasp, British War Medal 1914–20 and Victory Medal 1914–19. His medals were later presented to the Regiment by his sister-in-law and are held by the Royal Sussex Regiment Museum, Eastbourne, East Sussex.

Harry Wells is buried in Dud Corner Cemetery at Loos.

2ND LIEUTENANT SYDNEY CLAYTON WOODROFFE
8th Battalion, The Rifle Brigade (The Prince Consort's Own)

Sydney Woodroffe was born at High Field, St Johns, Lewes, East Sussex on 7th December 1895. His father, Henry Long Woodroffe (1856–1927), was commissioned as a lieutenant in 1st Sussex Volunteer Corps on 27th June 1883. He was a wine merchant in partnership with Frederick George Browning in the firm Browning & Woodroffe, trading from the Corn Exchange Buildings, Lewes. The partnership was dissolved by mutual consent on 16th February 1884 and Henry went into another with George Norman as brewers and maltsters at Cooksbridge, near Lewes, trading as George Norman and Co. This partnership was dissolved by mutual consent on 27th March 1899. Sydney's mother was Clara Eliza Alice née Clayton (1861–1951). Her birth was registered as Eliza Clara Alice. Henry and Clara married at St James' Church, Paddington on 10th October 1883. The family was living at King Henry's Road, Lewes, Sussex in 1891, at 20 Acusholt Branksome Wood Road, Bournemouth, Hampshire in 1911 and 'Woodmoor', Branksome Avenue, Bournemouth in 1915. Sydney's siblings were:

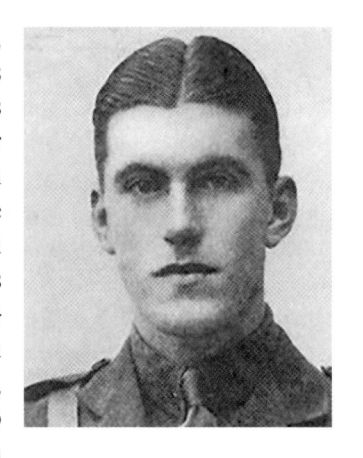

- Hugh Clayton Woodroffe (born 1884), a wine merchant who settled in Kuala Lumpur, Malaya. He married Norah Helen (maiden name unknown) (1884–1962) and they had two children, including Ivan Kenneth Woodroffe (born c.1915). He served as a sergeant in the RAFVR during the Second World War (914940) and was commissioned as a pilot officer (63416) on 25th March 1941 with seniority from 12th March. On 25th February 1954 he was appointed to a commission in the Secretarial Branch RAAF as a flying officer with five years in the Reserve and seniority from 19th January. It is understood Hugh married Nancy EN Cuthill in the 2nd quarter of 1964 at Bromley, Kent.

St Johns, Lewes, East Sussex.

- Leslie Woodroffe (1886–1916). At Marlborough College he was Head of the School and played in the Cricket XI and Rugby XV. After Oxford University he was an assistant schoolmaster and officer in Shrewsbury School Contingent, Junior OTC; promoted lieutenant 1st July 1910 and captain 10th June 1914. In 1911 he was living at 254 St James Court, Buckingham Gate, Westminster. He was appointed temporary captain in 8th Rifle Brigade on 27th December 1914. Leslie organised a dinner for Old Malburians at Rushmoor Camp on 18th April 1915; not one attendee survived the war. Leslie was severely wounded in the same action in which Sydney won the VC; MC, LG 14th January 1916. Leslie returned to the front to rejoin 8th Rifle Brigade on 1st June 1916 and was wounded the same day. He died at 6 Casualty Clearing Station on 4th June and is buried in Barlin Communal Cemetery Extension, Pas de Calais, France (I J 66). Mentioned in Despatches, LG 1st January 1916.
- An unnamed sister born and died in the 2nd quarter of 1891.
- Kenneth Herbert Clayton Woodroffe (1892–1915). He was Senior Prefect at Marlborough College, member of the Rugby XV and Hockey XI, Athletics Champion and Captain of the Cricket XI in 1912 against Rugby School at Lords. While at Pembroke College, Cambridge he took six wickets for Cambridge against Oxford at Lords in 1913. He was a fast bowler for Hampshire against the South Africans in 1912, taking five wickets, and for Sussex in 1913–14. Appointed 2nd lieutenant, Cambridge University Contingent, Senior Division, OTC on 27th December 1912. When war broke out, he was commissioned from the Unattached List, Territorial Force, OTC on 15th August 1914. He served with 6th and 3rd Battalions, Rifle Brigade and was Mentioned in Despatches, LG 22nd June 1915. Kenneth was shot through the head and killed in action at Neuve Chapelle on 9th May 1915 and is commemorated on the Le Touret Memorial, Pas de Calais, France (Panel 44). He left effects valued at £964/2/7, administered by his father.

Sydney was educated at Rose Hill School, Banstead then at Marlborough College, where he was Senior Prefect, Captain of the OTC and winner of the Curzon-Wyllie Medal awarded annually to the most efficient member of the OTC. He was also a member of the Rugby XV 1912–14, Hockey XI and Cricket XI. Sydney was

Rose Hill School, Banstead.

Marlborough College.

accepted for a classical scholarship at Pembroke College, Cambridge but did not take up the place due to the war.

Sydney was commissioned into the Rifle Brigade on 23rd December 1914. He went to France on 25th May 1915. **Awarded the VC for his actions at Hooge, Belgium on 30th July 1915, LG 6th September 1915.** The first VC awarded to a unit of the New Armies. He was killed during his VC action near 'Old Bond Street Trench', Zouave Wood, Hooge. Also killed nearby on the same day was Lieutenant Gilbert Talbot, after whom Talbot House in Poperinghe was named. Two days later his brother, Neville Talbot, crawled into no man's land and identified his brother's and Sydney's bodies. Neville managed to recover Gilbert a week later, but Sidney's body was not found after the war and he is commemorated on the Ypres (Menin Gate) Memorial. He never married and left effects valued at £968/16/10, administered by his father.

In addition to the VC, Sydney was also awarded the 1914–15 Star, British War Medal 1914–20 and Victory Medal 1914–19. The VC was sent to his father by post on 16th October 1916, but was presented formally to his parents by the King at Buckingham Palace on 29th November. The family sold the VC in the 1970s to

Lieutenant Gilbert Walbert Lyttelton Talbot, 7th Rifle Brigade, was born in Leeds in 1891. He was the son of Edward Stuart Talbot, Vicar of Leeds Parish Church (later Bishop of Winchester) and Lavinia Lyttleton, daughter of 4th Baron Lyttleton. Educated at Winchester and Christ Church Oxford, where he was President of the Union. He was killed in action at Hooge on 30th July 1915, the same day as Sidney Woodroffe. His body was recovered a week later and buried nearby. He now lies in Sanctuary Wood British Military Cemetery (I G 1). His brother, Reverend Neville Talbot and Reverend Tubby Clayton, named a soldier's club in his memory. Talbot House (Toc H) opened on 11th December 1915 at 43 Gasthuisstraat (at the time Rue de l'Hôpital) in Poperinghe. Toc H became a worldwide movement seeking to ease the burdens of others, promote reconciliation and bring disparate sections of society together.

Gilbert Talbot's brother, the Reverend Neville Stuart Talbot (1879–1943). What is now Talbot House in Poperinghe opened for the first time on 11th December 1915. It was run by the Reverend Philip 'Tubby' Clayton, who hung a notice at the front door, *All rank abandon, ye who enter here*. Initially it was going to be named Church House, but Neville Talbot said, *the staff of our Division saw a scarecrow in the name and smelt tracts*. It was thereafter known as Talbot House in memory of Gilbert Talbot. Neville Talbot was Bishop of Pretoria 1920–33.

The garden and rear of Talbot House, a haven of peace for thousands of troops out of the line. A visit cannot be recommended strongly enough.

Tubby Clayton.

a private collector. It was purchased privately by Michael Ashcroft in 2001 and is displayed in the Lord Ashcroft VC Collection in the Imperial War Museum.

Sydney is commemorated in a number of places:

- He and his brothers are named on a memorial in All Saints' Church, Branksome Park, Bournemouth, Dorset.
- Tablet outside 42 Trinity Square, Tulse Hill, London.

All Saints, Branksome.

- Rifle Brigade Memorial, Winchester, Hampshire.
- A poem by Charles Hamilton Sorley (1895–1915), a war poet who was at Marlborough with Sydney.

5938 PRIVATE WILLIAM YOUNG
8th Battalion, The East Lancashire Regiment

William Young was born at 74 Wynford Street, Maryhill, Glasgow on 15th January 1876. His father was Samuel Young (c.1849–95), a contractor's labourer. His mother was Mary née Tracey (c.1851–1910). Both were born in Ireland. Samuel and Mary were married on 22nd April 1872 at Girvan, Ayrshire. The family lived at various times at Longstone, Colinston, Edinburgh and Carrillis, Dalrymple, Ayrshire. Mary later married Joseph McIlroy and lived at 54 South Wellington Road, Glasgow. William had three siblings:

- Samuel Young born c.1882 at Greenock, Renfrewshire.
- Catherine Ann Young (1885–1982) married Daniel Herlihy in 1904 and they had a daughter, Mary Herlihy in 1906.
- Margaret Young born c.1892.

William was educated at St Mary's Roman Catholic School in Maryhill. He was employed as a labourer until he enlisted in the East Lancashire Regiment in May 1899. He was discharged to the Reserve in August 1902 and was an outdoor labourer at a sewage works in 1911. He then worked as a general labourer at Fulwood Barracks, Preston.

William Young married Mary Ellen Simmons (1881–1953) on 21st June 1902 at Preston. They were living at 7 Heysham Street, Preston in 1911. They had nine children:
- Catherine Young (1902–18) was dropped on her head accidentally as an infant and suffered brain damage. She was cared for thereafter in an institution.
- William H Young (born 1904) also served in the East Lancashire Regiment.
- John Young (born 1905).

Fulwood Barracks, Preston.

- Mary Ellen Young (born 1906) married Arthur Aloysius Salisbury (1904–95) in 1927. They had three children – Stella M Salisbury 1928, Frederick W Salisbury 1929 and Mary M Salisbury 1938.
- Margaret Ann Young (born 1907) married William Charnley in 1939.
- Elizabeth Alice Young (born 1910) married John Peet 1940 and they had three children – Patricia M Peet 1940, Anne C Peet 1942 and Madeline Peet 1944.
- Thomas Young (born 1912).
- Samuel Young (born 1913) married Agnes Kenny (born 1913) in 1937.
- Frederick Young (1915–25) died of pneumonia.

William and Mary Young.

William transferred to the Section D Reserve in May 1911. He was employed at Preston gas works when he was recalled on 5th August 1914 and went to France on 14th September to join the 1st Battalion. He was wounded by a bullet in the thigh at Ypres in November and was gassed in spring 1915. His eyesight was so badly affected he did not return to the front until December. **Awarded the VC for his actions at Trench 51, east of Fonquevillers, France on 22nd December 1915, LG 30th March 1916.** He was so modest he told nobody about his actions until it appeared in London Gazette.

As a result of the wounds he sustained during his VC action, he was evacuated to hospital at Rouen on 22nd December and then to England, where he was treated at Exeter, London and Aldershot. He underwent fourteen operations, including having most of his jaw replaced by silver. Released from hospital on leave on 19th April 1916, he arrived in Preston to a civic reception. The Mayor, Alderman Harry Cartmell, arranged for a horse and carriage to convey him to the Town Hall, but soldiers from the local volunteer force unhitched the horse and pulled the carriage. He was met by his children and Colonel Voyle, representing the East Lancashire Regiment, who called for three cheers before he was pulled home to Heysham Street. He watched a performance of *Kisses* that night from a private box at the Empire Theatre. The Hippodrome hosted him to a variety show in a private box on Saturday evening. A collection was organised during the interval and £15 was given to William and his wife as they left the theatre. He kicked-off a charity match at Deepdale Football Ground on 24th April in which Preston North End won 6 – 0 against munition workers from Dick, Kerr & Co.

William was re-admitted to Exeter Hospital on 25th April and returned home on leave again in late June for ten days. He was then admitted to Cambridge Hospital, Aldershot for a final operation, which was completed successfully on 26th August, but he had a reaction to the anaesthetic. His wife was notified by telegram that her

The Preston Hippodrome on the right side of Friargate.

William Young with his family at the reception at Preston Town Hall during his visit on 19th April 1916.

husband was dangerously ill and she arrived late that day. She remained at his bedside throughout the night and he died at 8.55 a.m. on 27th August without regaining consciousness. The doctor in charge of the operation, Captain HD Gillies RAMC, wrote to Mary Young:

Cambridge Military Hospital, Aldershot 1879–1996.

> *The operation in itself, was not difficult, neither was it particularly lengthy, and in advising him to have it done there was considerable advantage to be gained and no particular risk beyond the always present very slight risk of giving a patient an anaesthetic. He told me he was bad after his other anaesthetics, and undoubtedly the chloroform, this time, must have affected his heart. Everything that could be done was done for him, and five doctors saw him and did what was possible. Every precaution was taken during the operation and as little chloroform as possible was given, and that by an experienced doctor. It seems so terribly cruel to go through all he did, and so well, and then to die through the worst of bad luck.*

His body arrived at Preston on 29th August and the following morning was taken to his home in Heysham Street where it remained overnight. The coffin was carried on a gun carriage draped with the Union Flag and escorted by six sergeant pallbearers of the East Lancashire Regiment to the funeral service at the English Martyr's Roman Catholic Church in Garstang Road. Soldiers from the East Lancashire Regiment, Loyal North Lancashire Regiment and Royal Field Artillery provided an escort. Wounded soldiers from Cambridge Hospital, Aldershot formed a contingent at the rear. William was buried in Preston (New Hall Lane) Cemetery (Plot V Rc10). He is the only VC who died and was buried in Britain during the course of the war.

The VC was presented to his wife (mother according to the Court Circular) by the King at Buckingham Palace on 29th November 1916. Preston raised £522/8/11, which was invested to give Mary Young 10/- per week from the interest. She moved to 61 Lovat Road, Preston.

In addition to the VC, he was awarded the 1914 Star with 'Mons' clasp, British War Medal 1914–20 and Victory Medal 1914–19. His son, William, presented the medals to the Regiment on 7th July 1985. They are owned by the Queen's Lancashire Regiment Museum and are on loan to the Museum of Lancashire, Preston.

William Young's funeral procession leaves his home in Heysham Street, Preston.

The funeral procession at Preston Town Hall (Lancashire Lantern).

Sources

The following institutions, individuals and publications were consulted:

Regimental Museums

Buffs Regimental Museum, Canterbury; Hertford Regiment Museum, Hertford; Royal Army Medical Corps Historical Museum, Aldershot; King's Own Royal Lancaster Regiment Museum, Lancaster; Royal Warwickshire Regimental Museum, Warwick; RHQ The Royal Scots, Edinburgh; The Cameronians Regimental Museum, Hamilton; Royal Engineers Museum, Chatham; The Royal Gloucestershire, Berkshire and Wiltshire Regiment Museum, Salisbury; RHQ The Princess of Wales's Royal Regiment, Canterbury; Museum of Lincolnshire Life, Lincoln; Lancashire County and Regimental Museum, Preston; The Royal Army Chaplain's Department Association; Museum of the Manchesters, Ashton-under-Lyne; RHQ Worcestershire and Sherwood Foresters, Beeston; Museum of the Northamptonshire Regiment, Northampton; RHQ King's Own Scottish Borderers, Berwick-upon-Tweed; Royal Green Jackets Museum, Winchester; Regimental Headquarters Coldstream Guards, London; HQ Scots Guards, London; RHQ Queen's Lancashire Regiment, Preston; York & Lancaster Regiment Museum, Rotherham; RHQ Prince of Wales's Own Regiment of Yorkshire, York; Headquarters The Royal Anglian Regiment (Lincolnshire), Lincoln; Canadian War Museum, Ottawa; Royal Artillery Historical Trust; Lancashire HQ Royal Regiment of Fusiliers; The Black Watch (Royal Highland Regiment) of Canada Museum and Archives; The Royal Sussex Regiment Museum.

Individuals

Doug and Richard Arman, David Armstrong, Gaye Ashford, Geoffrey and Mairi Baker, Jessie Oliver Barber, Brian Belcher, John Belcher, Mary Booth, Sam Branson, Jackie Brittain, Peter Brook, Margaret Brown, Phillip and Anthony Carter, Richard Carter, Maj John Cotterill, Robert Elliston, Bill Finlay, Jacqueline Fowler-Roberts, Louise Graf, Elizabeth Gregory, Peta Hallowes, Richard Hallowes, Maisie Hankin, Marilyn Harris, Richard Hewlett, Terry Hissey, Pauline Hughes, Derek Hunt, Tom Johnson, Alan Jordan, Ian Kelshaw, Alasdair Macintyre, Dr J A Maling, George McNulty, Jim McNulty, Robin Mellish, Col Gerald Napier, Barbara Parker, Dennis Parker, Nathan Pearce, Alan Petcher, Joe and Conny Ripley, Carol Scott, Margaret Smith, Maurice Smith, John Starling, Iain Stewart, Vic Tambling, Jennifer Tombs, Dr Dave Upton, Maj Derrick Vernon, Freda Warren, Lt Col Les Wilson MBE, Enid Woodroffe, IK Woodroffe, Colin Yorke, John Young, Richard Young.

Record Offices, Libraries and Local Museums

London Metropolitan Archives, West Sussex Record Office.

Schools and Universities

Charterhouse, Godalming; Christ's Hospital, Horsham; King's School, Grantham; The King's School, Canterbury; Marlborough College; Uppingham School.

Divisional Histories

The Guards Division in the Great War. C Headlam. Murray 1929. Two volumes.
The History of the Second Division 1914–18. E Wyrell. Nelson 1921. Two volumes.
Iron Division, The History of the 3rd Division. R McNish. Allen 1976.
A Short History of the 6th Division August 1914–March 1919. Editor Maj Gen T O Marden. Rees 1920.
The Seventh Division 1914–18. C T Atkinson. Murray 1927.
The Eighth Division in War 1914–18. Lt Col J H Boraston and Capt C E O Bax. Medici Society 1926.
The History of the 9th (Scottish) Division 1914–19. J Ewing. Murray 1921.
History of the 12th (Eastern) Division in the Great War 1914–18. Editor Maj Gen Sir A B Scott. Compiler P M Brumwell. Nisbet 1927.
The Fifteenth (Scottish) Division 1914–19. Lt Col J Stewart and J Buchan. Blackwood 1926.
The History of the 20th (Light) Division. Capt V E Inglefield. Nisbet 1921.
The 23rd Division 1914–19. Lt Col H R Sandilands. Blackwood 1925.
The 25th Division in France and Flanders. Lt Col M Kincaid-Smith. Harrison 1919.
The 33rd Division in France and Flanders 1915–19. Lt Col G S Hutchinson. Waterlow 1921.
The 47th (London) Division 1914–19. Editor A H Maude. Amalgamated Press 1922.
A Short History of the 49th West Riding and Midlands Infantry Division (TA). Lt Col F K Hughes. Stellar 1958.
The Story of the 55th (West Lancashire) Division. Rev'd J O Coop. Liverpool Daily Post 1919.

Brigade Histories

A Short History of the 5th Infantry Brigade. Maj G D P Young. Forces Press 1965.

440 Victoria Crosses on the Western Front April 1915–June 1916

Regimental/Unit Histories

In order of precedence:
The Royal Artillery War Commemoration Book. Anon. G Bell 1970.
History of the Royal Regiment of Artillery, Western Front, 1914–18. Gen Sir M Farndale. Dorset Press 1986.
ARTYVICS – The Victoria Cross and The Royal Regiment of Artillery. Marc J Sherriff. Witherbys, Aylesbury St, London.
Tunnellers, The Story of the Tunnelling Companies Royal Engineers during the World War. Capt W Grant Grieve & B Newman. Herbert Jenkins 1936.
History of the Corps of Royal Engineers, Volume V, The Home Front, France, Flanders and Italy in the First World War. Anon. Institute of the Royal Engineers 1952.
The Coldstream Guards 1914–18. Lt Col Sir J Ross of Blankenburg. Oxford University Press 1928. Two volumes with a separate volume of maps.
A History of the Coldstream Guards Victoria and George Cross Holders. Sergeant L Pearce. RHQ Coldstream Guards 1995.
The Scots Guards in the Great War 1914–18. F Loraine Petre, W Ewart and Maj Gen Sir C Lowther. Murray 1925.
The Royal Scots 1914–19. Maj J Ewing. Oliver & Boyd 1925. Two volumes.
Historical Records of the Buffs, East Kent Regiment, Volume III 1914–19. Col R S H Moody. Medici Society 1922.
The King's Own, The Story of a Royal Regiment, Volume III 1914–50. Compiler Col J M Cowper. Gale & Polden 1957.
The Story of the Royal Warwickshire Regiment. C L Kingsford. Country Life 1921.
The Royal Fusiliers in the Great War. H C O'Neill. Heinemann 1922.
The History of the King's Regiment (Liverpool) 1914–19. E Wyrell. Arnold 1928–35. Three volumes.
History of the Lincolnshire Regiment 1914–18. Editor Maj Gen C R Simpson. Medici Society 1931.
The History of the Suffolk Regiment 1914–27. Lt Col C C R Murphy. Hutchinson 1928.
The West Yorkshire Regiment in the Great War 1914–18. E Wyrell. The Bodley Head 1924–27. Two volumes.
History of the Sixth Battalion West Yorkshire Regiment, Volume I 1/6th Battalion. Capt E V Tempest. Country Press 1921.
The East Yorkshire Regiment in the Great War 1914–19. E Wyrell. Harrison 1928.
The 16th Foot, A History of the Bedforshire and Hertfordshire Regiment. Maj Gen Sir F Maurice. Constable 1931.
The Story of the Bedfordshire and Hertfordshire Regiment Volume II – 1914–58. Compiled by Lt Col T J Barrow DSO, Maj V A French and J Seabrook Esq. Published privately 1986.
The History of the Lancashire Fusiliers 1914–18, Volumes I and II. Maj Gen J C Latter. Gale & Polden 1949.

The Lancashire Fusiliers Annual. No 26 – 1916 and No 28 – 1918. Editor Major B Smyth. Sackville Press 1917 and 1919
That Astonishing Infantry, The History of the Royal Welsh Fusiliers 1689–1989. M Glover.
Regimental Records of the Royal Welsh Fusiliers (23rd Foot), Volume III 1914–18 France & Flanders. Compiler Maj C H Dudley Ward. Forster Groon 1928.
The King's Own Scottish Borderers in the Great War. Capt Stair Gillon. Nelson 1930.
A Border Battalion, The History of the 7th/8th (Service) Battalion KOSB. Compiler Capt J Goss. Privately published 1920.
A Short History of the Cameronians (Scottish Rifles). Col H C Wylly. Gale & Polden 1924.
History of the Cameronians (Scottish Rifles), Volume II 1910–22. Col H H Story. Published unknown 1961.
The Fifth Battalion The Cameronians (Scottish Rifles) 1914–19. Anon. Jackson 1936.
History of the East Lancashire Regiment in the Great War 1914–18. Edited by Maj Gen Sir N Nicholson and Maj H T McMullen. Littlebury 1936.
History of the East Surrey Regiment, Volume II 1914–17 and Volume III 1917–19. Col H W Pearse & Brig Gen H S Sloman. Medici Society 1924.
A History of the Royal Sussex Regiment 1701–1953. G D Martineau. Moore & Tillyer 1955.
A Short History of the Royal Sussex Regiment 1701–1926. Anon. Gale & Polden 1927.
A History of the South Staffordshire Regiment 1705–1923. J P Jones. Whitehead Bros 1923.
History of the South Staffordshire Regiment. Col W L Vale. Gale & Polden 1969.
A History of the Black Watch (Royal Highlanders) in the Great War 1914–18, Volume I The Regular Army. Editor Maj Gen A G Wauchope. Medici Society 1925.
The 1st and 2nd Battalions The Sherwood Foresters (Nottinghamshire and Derbyshire Regiment) in the Great War. Col H C Wylly. Gale & Polden 1924.
The Robin Hoods (1/7, 2/7 and 3/7 Battalions Sherwood Foresters), Officers of the Battalions 1914–18. Bell 1921.
The Loyal North Lancashire Regiment, Volume II 1914–19. Col H C Wylly. Royal United Services Institute 1933.
The Northamptonshire Regiment 1914–18. Regimental Historical Committee. Gale & Polden.
The Royal Berkshire Regiment, Volume II 1914–18. F L Petre. Reading The Barracks 1935.
The Die Hards in the Great War, A History of the Duke of Cambridge's Own (Middlesex Regiment). F Wyrall. Harrison 1926–30. Two volumes (1911–16 and 1916–19).
The Annals of the King's Royal Rifle Corps, Volume V The Great War. Maj Gen Sir S Hare. John Murray 1932.
Somme Harvest. Giles E M Eyre. London Stamp Exchange 1991.
The King's Royal Rifle Corps Chronicles 1914, 1915, 1916 and 1917.
History of the Manchester Regiment, Volume II 1883–1922. Col H C Wylly. Forster Groom 1925.

The York and Lancaster Regiment 1758–1919. Col H C Wylly. Butler & Tanner 1930. Two volumes.
Faithful, The Story of the Durham Light Infantry. S G P Ward. Nelson 1962.
The Durham Forces in the Field 1914–18, Volume II The Service Battalions of the Durham light Infantry. Capt W Miles. Cassell 1920.
Officers of the Durham light Infantry 1758–1968 (Volume 1 – Regulars). M McGregor. Published privately 1989.
Proud Heritage, The Story of the Highland Light Infantry, Volume III 1882–1918. Lt Col L B Oates. House of Grant 1961.
Historical Records of the Queen's Own Cameron Highlanders, Volumes III and IV. Anon. Blackwood 1931.
The Fifth Camerons. Capt J H F McEwen. David McDonald.
History of the Royal Munster Fusiliers, Volume II 1861–1922. Capt S McCance. Gale & Polden 1927.
The History of the Rifle Brigade in the War 1914–18. Volume I August 1914–December 1916. R Berkley. Rifle Brigade Club 1927.
As above. Appendix – List of Officers and Other Ranks of the Rifle Brigade awarded Decorations or MID for services during the Great War. Compiled by Lt Col T R Eastwood and Maj H G Parkyn. Rifle Brigade Club 1936.
Rifle Brigade Chronicles 1915–1920. Editor Col W Verner. John Bale 1916–1921.
A Rifle Brigade Register 1905–63, Part 1 – A Roll of Officers who have served in the Regiment. Compiled by Col W P S Curtis. Culverlands Press 1964.
The History of the London Rifle Brigade 1959–1919. Anon. Constable 1921. Separate Maps Appendix.
In This Sign Conquer, The Story of the Army Chaplains. Brig Sir J Smyth. Mowbray 1968.
Not Least in the Crusade, A Short History of the Royal Army Medical Corps. P Lovegrove. Gale & Polden 1951.
History of the Great War, Medical Services, Volume IV General History. Maj Gen Sir W G MacPherson. HMSO 1924.
Medical Officers in the British Army, Volume II 1898–1960. Lt Gen Sir R Drew. Wellcome Historical Medical Library 1968.
The Royal Army Medical Corps. R Mclaughlin. Leo Cooper 1972.
The Medical Victoria Crosses. Col WEI Forsyth-Jauch. Arrow Press 1984.
The Army Medical Services Magazine.
Tales of Valour from The Royal New South Wales Regiment. Maj Gen GL Maitland 1992.
Canada in Flanders. Sir Max Aitken 1916.
The 13th Battalion Royal Highlanders of Canada 1914–1919. RC Fetherstonhaugh 1925.
With the Indians in France. Gen Sir James Willcocks 1920.
The Indian Corps in France. Lt Col JWB Merewether & Sir Frederick Smith 1919.
The Frontier Force Rifles. Brig WEH Condon 1953.
The History of Coke's Rifles. Col HC Wylly 1930.
The Regimental History of the 3rd Queen Alexandra's Own Gurkha Rifles. Edited by Maj Gen Nigel Woodyatt 1929.

General Works

A Bibliography of Regimental Histories of the British Army. Compiler A S White. Society for Army Historical Research 1965.
A Military Atlas of the First World War. A Banks & A Palmer. Purnell 1975.
The Battle of Loos. P Warner. William Kimber 1976.
The Times History of the Great War.
Gas! The Battle for Ypres, 1915. J McWilliams and R J Steel. Vanwell 1985.
Topography of Armageddon, A British Trench Map Atlas of the Western Front 1914–18. P Chasseaud. Mapbooks 1991.
The Battle Book of Ypres. B Brice. Murray 1927.
Before Endeavours Fade. R E B Coombs. Battle of Britain Prints 1976.
British Regiments 1914–18. Brig E A James. Samson 1978.
Orange, Green and Khaki, The Story of the Irish Regiments in the Great War 1914–18. T Johnstone. 1992.
The Ypres Salient, A Guide to the Cemeteries and Memorials of the Salient. M Scott. Gliddon Books 1992.
1915, The Death of Innocence. Lyn McDonald. Headline 1993.
Norfolk and Suffolk in the Great War. G Gliddon. Gliddon Books 1988.
Northamptonshire and the Great War 1914–1918. W H Holloway. The Northampton Independent 1923?
Leeds in the Great War 1914–1918. Leeds Libraries and Arts Committee 1923.
Cameos of the Western Front – Salient Points Four – Ypres & Picardy 1914–18. Tony Spagnoly and Ted Smith. Pen & Sword 2004.
A Serious Disappointment – the Battle for Aubers Ridge 1915 and the Munitions Scandal. Adrian Bristow.
The Battles of Neuve Chapelle, Aubers Ridge, Festubert 1915 – An Illustrated Pocket Guide. Michael Gavaghan. M&L Publications 1997.
So We Take Comfort. Dame Enid Lyons 1965.

Biographical

The Dictionary of National Biography 1901–85. Various Volumes. Oxford University Press.
The Cross of Sacrifice, Officers Who Died in the Service of the British, Indian and East African Regiments and Corps 1914–19. S D and D B Jarvis. Roberts Medals 1993.
Australian Dictionary of Biography.
Whitaker's Peerage, Baronetage, Knightage & Companionage 1913.
Our Heroes – Containing Photographs with Biographical Notes of Officers of Irish Regiments and of Irish Officers of British Regiments who have fallen or who have been mentioned for distinguished conduct from August 1914 to July 1916. Printed as supplements to Irish Life from 1914 to 1916.
The Bond of Sacrifice, A Biographical Record of all British Officers Who Fell in the Great War. Volume I Aug–Dec 1915, Volume II Jan–Jun 1915. Editor Col L A Clutterbuck. Pulman 1916 and 1919.

The Roll of Honour Parts 1–5, A Biographical Record of Members of His Majesty's Naval and Military Forces who fell in the Great War 1914–18. Marquis de Ruvigny. Standard Art Book Co 1917–19.
Birmingham Heroes. J P Lethbridge. Newgate Press 1993.
The Dictionary of Edwardian Biography – various volumes. Printed 1904–08, reprinted 1985–87 Peter Bell Edinburgh.

Specific Works on the Victoria Cross

The Register of the Victoria Cross. This England 1981 and 1988.
The Story of the Victoria Cross 1856–1963. Brig Sir J Smyth. Frederick Muller 1963.
The Evolution of the Victoria Cross, A study in Administrative History. M J Crook. Midas 1975.
The Victoria Cross and the George Cross. IWM 1970.
The Victoria Cross, The Empire's Roll of Valour. Lt Col R Stewart. Hutchinson 1928.
The Victoria Cross 1856–1920. Sir O'Moore Creagh and E M Humphris. Standard Art Book Company, London 1920.
Victoria Cross – Awards to Irish Servicemen. B Clark. Published in The Irish Sword summer 1986.
Heart of a Dragon, VC's of Wales and the Welsh Regiments. W Alister Williams. Bridge Books 2006.
The Seven VC's of Stonyhurst College. H L Kirby and R R Walsh. THCL Books 1987.
Devotion to Duty, Tributes to a Region's VCs. J W Bancroft. Aim High 1990.
For Conspicuous Gallantry, A Brief History of the recipients of the VC from Nottinghamshire and Derbyshire. N McCrery. J H Hall 1990.
For Valour, The Victoria Cross, Courage in Action. J Percival. Thames Methuen 1985.
VC Locator. D Pillinger and A Staunton. Highland Press, Queanbeyan, New South Wales, Australia 1991.
VCs of the First World War: The Western Front 1915. P F Batchelor & C Matson. Sutton 1997.
Black Country VCs. B Harry. Black Country Society 1985.
The VC Roll of Honour. J W Bancroft. Aim High 1989.
A Bibliography of the Victoria Cross. W James McDonald. W J Mcdonald, Nova Scotia 1994.
Canon Lummis VC Files held in the National Army Museum, Chelsea.
Recipients of the Victoria Cross in the Care of the Commonwealth War Graves Commission. CWGC 1997.
Victoria Cross Heroes. Michael Ashcroft. Headline Review 2006
Monuments to Courage. David Harvey. 1999.
The Sapper VCs. Gerald Napier. The Stationery Office, London 1998.
Liverpool Heroes – Book 1. Ann Clayton. Noel Chavasse VC Memorial Association.
Beyond the Five Points – Masonic Winners of The Victoria Cross and The George Cross. Phillip May GC, edited by Richard Cowley. Twin Pillars Books, Northamptonshire 2001.

Sources 445

Irish Winners of the Victoria Cross. Richard Doherty & David Truesdale. Four Courts Press, Dublin, Ireland 2000.
The Victoria Crosses and George Crosses of the Honourable East India Company & Indian Army 1856–1945. National Army Museum 1962.
Our Bravest and Our Best: The Stories of Canada's Victoria Cross Winners. Arthur Bishop 1995.
They Dared Mightily. Lionel Wigmore, Jeff Williams & Anthony Staunton 1986.
Francis Scrimger – Beyond the Call of Duty. Suzanne Kingsmill 1991.
For Valour – Lance Corporal Fred Fisher VC. Lt Col William A Smy 2010.
Nelson Carter VC – A Man of Valour. Margaret Smith 2007.
Private William Young VC. H L Kirby. THCL Books 1985.
Nottinghamshire Victoria Cross Holders, Nottingham & Nottinghamshire Victoria Cross Committee 2012.

Works on Other Honours and Awards

Distinguished Conduct Medal 1914–18, Citations of Recipients. London Stamp Exchange 1983.
Recipients of the Distinguished Conduct Medal 1914–1920. RW Walker.
The Distinguished Service Order 1886–1923 (in 2 volumes). Sir O'Moore Creagh and E M Humphris. J B Hayward 1978 (originally published 1924).
Orders and Medals Society Journal (various articles).
The Old Contemptibles Honours and Awards. First published 1915. Reprinted by J B Hayward & Son 1971.
Burke's Handbook to the Most Excellent Order of the British Empire. A Winton Thorpe (Editor). Burke Publishing Co Ltd, London 1921.
South African War – Honours and Awards 1899–1902.
Honours and Awards of the Indian Army: August 1914–August 1921. 1931.

University and Schools Publications

University of London OTC Roll of War Service 1914–19.
The Royal Technical College Glasgow, Sacrifice and Service in the Great War.
The OTC Roll – A Roll of Members and Ex-members of the OTC Gazetted to Commissions in the Army August 1914–March 1915. Tim Donovan 1989.

Official Publications and Sources

History of the Great War, Order of Battle of Divisions. Compiler Maj A F Becke. HMSO.
History of the Great War, Military Operations, France and Belgium. Compiler Brig Gen Sir J E Edmonds. HMSO. Published in 14 volumes of text, with 7 map volumes and 2 separate Appendices between 1923 and 1948.

Official History of Australia in the War of 1914–1918, Volume III – The Australian Imperial Force in France, 1916. 12th edition 1941.
Official History of the Canadian Army in the First World War – Canadian Expeditionary Force 1914–19. Col GWL Nicholson 1962.
Unit War Diaries in the Public Record Office under WO 95
Imperial Yeomanry Attestation Papers in the Public Record Office under WO 128/13
Military maps in the Public Record Office under WO 297.
Medal Cards and Medal Rolls in the Public Record Office under WO 329 and ADM 171.
Soldier's Service Records in the Public Record Office under WO 97, 363 and 364.
Officer's Records in the Public Record Office under WO 25, 76, 339 and 374.
RAF Officer's Records in the Public Record Office under Air 76.
Navy Lists
Army Lists – including Graduation Lists and Record of War Service.
Air Force Lists.
Home Guard Lists 1942–44.
Indian Army Lists 1897–1940.
India List 1923–40.
Location of Hospitals and Casualty Clearing Stations, BEF 1914–19. Ministry of Pensions 1923.
List of British Officers taken Prisoner in the Various Theatres of War between August 1914 and November 1918. Compiled from Official Records by Messrs Cox & Co, Charing Cross, London 1919.
London Gazettes
Census returns, particularly for 1881, 1891 and 1901.
Births, Marriages and Deaths records in the former Family Records Centre, Islington, London.
Service records from the Canadian Archives.
Officers and Soldiers Died in the Great War.

Reference Publications

Who's Who and Who Was Who.
The Times.
The Daily Telegraph.
Kelly's Handbook to the Titled, Landed and Official Classes.

Internet Websites

I hesitate to include websites because they change frequently, but the following were useful:

History of the Victoria Cross – www2.prestel.co.uk/stewart – Iain Stewart.
Victoria Cross Reference – www.chapter-one.com – Mike Chapman (no longer exists).
Trenches On The Web – www.worldwar1.com
Lanarkshire VCs – www.forvalour.com.
Commonwealth War Graves Commission – www.yard.ccta.gov.uk/cwgc.
Scottish General Registry Office – www.origins.net/GRO.
Free Births, Marriages and Deaths – www.freebmd.com

Periodicals

This England.
Coin and Medal News.
Journal of The Victoria Cross Society
The Contact – a newspaper serving 8 Wing/CFB Trenton – 25 March 2011.

Research for this book was spread over the years 1988–2014 and during this time it is inevitable that I will have omitted individuals and other sources. If so I apologise, it was not intentional.

Useful Information

Accommodation – there is a wide variety of accommodation available in southern Belgium and northern France. Search on-line for your requirements. There are also numerous campsites, but many close for the winter from late September.

Clothing and Kit – consider taking:
Waterproofs.
Headwear and gloves.
Walking shoes/boots.
Shades and sunscreen.
Binoculars and camera.
Snacks and drinks.

Customs/Behaviour – local people are generally tolerant of battlefield visitors but please respect their property and address them respectfully. The French are less inclined to switch to English than other Europeans. If you try some basic French it will be appreciated.

Driving – rules of the road are similar to UK, apart from having to drive on the right. If in doubt about priorities, give way to the right, particularly in France. Obey laws and road signs – police impose harsh on-the-spot fines. Penalties for drinking and driving are heavy and the legal limit is lower than UK (50mg rather than 80mg). Most autoroutes in France are toll roads.

Fuel – petrol stations are only open 24 hours on major routes. Some accept credit cards in automatic tellers. The cheapest fuel is at hypermarkets.

Mandatory Requirements – if taking your own car you need:
Full driving licence.
Vehicle registration document.
Comprehensive motor insurance valid in Europe (Green Card).
European breakdown and recovery cover.
Letter of authorisation from the owner if the vehicle is not yours.
Spare set of bulbs, headlight beam adjusters, warning triangle, GB sticker, high visibility vest and breathalyzer.

Emergency – keep details required in an emergency separate from wallet or handbag:
   Photocopy passport, insurance documents and EHIC (see Health below).
   Mobile phone details.
   Credit/debit card numbers and cancellation telephone contacts.
   Travel insurance company contact number.

Ferries – the closest ports are Boulogne, Calais and Dunkirk. The Shuttle is quicker, but usually more expensive.

Health

European Health Insurance Card – entitles the holder to medical treatment at local rates. Apply online at www.ehic.org.uk/Internet/startApplication.do. Issued free and valid for five years. You are only covered if you have the EHIC with you when you go for treatment.

Travel Insurance – you are strongly advised to also have travel insurance. If you receive treatment get a statement by the doctor (*feuille de soins*) and a receipt to make a claim on return.

Personal Medical Kit – treating minor ailments saves time and money. Pack sufficient prescription medicine for the trip.

Chemist (*Pharmacie*) – look for the green cross. They provide some treatment and if unable to help will direct you to a doctor. Most open 0900–1900 except Sun. Out of hours services (*pharmacie de garde*) are advertised in Pharmacie windows.

Doctor and Dentist – hotel receptions have details of local practices. Beware private doctors/hospitals, as extra charges cannot be reclaimed – the French national health service is known as *conventionné*.

Rabies – contact with infected animals is very rare, but if bitten by any animal, get the wound examined professionally immediately.

Money

ATMs – at most banks and post offices with instructions in English. Check your card can be used in France and what charges apply. Some banks limit how much can be withdrawn. Let your bank know you will be away, as some block cards if transactions take place unexpectedly.

Credit/Debit Cards – major cards are usually accepted, but some have different names – Visa is Carte Bleue and Mastercard is Eurocard.

Exchange – beware 0% commission, as the rate may be poor. The Post Office takes back unused currency at the same rate, which may or may not be advantageous. Since the Euro, currency exchange facilities are scarce.

Local Taxes – if you buy high value items you can reclaim tax. Get the forms completed by the shop, have them stamped by Customs, post them to the shop and they will refund about 12%.

Passport – a valid passport is required.

Post – postcard stamps are available from vendors, newsagents and tabacs.

Public Holidays – just about everything closes and banks can close early the day before. Transport may be affected, but tourist attractions in high season are unlikely to be. The following dates/days are public holidays:

1 January
Easter Monday
1 May
8 May (France only)
Ascension Day
Whit Monday
14 July (France only)
21 July (Belgium only)
15 August
1 & 11 November
25 December

In France many businesses and restaurants close for the majority of August.

Radio – if you want to pick up the news from home try BBC Radio 4 on 198 kHz long wave. BBC Five Live on 909 kHz medium wave can sometimes be received. There are numerous internet options for keeping up with the news.

Shops – in large towns and tourist areas they tend to open all day. In more remote places they may close for lunch. Some bakers open Sunday a.m. and during the week take later lunch breaks. In general shops do not open on Sundays.

Telephone
To UK – 0044, delete initial 0 then dial the rest of the number.
Local Calls – dial the full number even if within the same zone.
Mobiles – check yours will work in France and the charges. Beware roamer charges and/or disable before getting on the ferry.
Emergencies – dial 112 for medical, fire and police anywhere in Europe from any landline, pay phone or mobile. Calls are free.
British Embassy (Paris) – 01 44 51 31 00.
British Embassy (Brussels) – 02 287 62 11.

Time Zone – one hour ahead of UK.

Tipping – a small tip is expected by cloakroom and lavatory attendants and porters. Not required in restaurants when a service charge is included.

Toilets – the best are in museums and the main tourist attractions. Towns usually have public toilets where markets are held; some are coin operated.

Index

Notes
1. Not every person or location is included in the index. Most family members named in the biographies are not listed in the index.
2. Armed force's units, establishments, etc, are grouped under the respective country, except for Britain's, which appear under the three services.
3. Cemeteries/crematoria, churches, hospitals, schools, universities, Commonwealth War Graves Commission and other establishments appear under a group heading.
4. All orders, medals and decorations appear under orders.

1,000 Guineas, 216
2,000 Guineas, 216

Abbeville, 319
Abbottabad, 204, 356
Abdulla, Messrs, 313–14
Aberavon, 291
Abercrombie, LCpl E.M., 177
Abercromby, 200
Aberdeen, 210, 300
Aberdour, 268
Abergavenny, 290
Abrahams, Harold, 396
Abwehr, 294
Achnasheen, 184
Acroma, 208
Adair, Maj Gen Sir Allan, 414
Adams VC, Maj Gen Sir Robert, 209
Adamson's of Carluke, 186
Addison VC, Padre William, 207
Aden, 229–30, 254–5, 311, 339
Adlam VC, Tom, 365, 414
Admiralty, 415
Afghanistan & Afghan Wars, 194, 211–12, 354, 395, 400
Afridi, Dr Shakil, 356
Afridis, 354
Afrikaans, 348
Aghada, 198
Agra, 209
Ainscow, 2Lt Harold, 180, 300
Air Raid Precautions, 229, 352
Aire-sur-la-Lys, 221–4
Aisne, Battle of, 313, 322, 372
Albany, Western Australia, 258
Alberta, 385
Albrecht, Duke Gen Von Wurttemburg, 1, 3–4, 21
Albury, Victoria, 307
Aldbourne, 222–4
Aldershot, 224, 232, 252, 285, 316, 412, 435
Alderson, Lt Gen Edwin, 4, 8–10, 12, 17–18, 20, 68

Alexandria, 196, 219, 301–302, 326, 389
Algeria, 333, 403
Algoa Bay, South Africa, 321
Aliens Registration Office, 368
Allahabad, 403
Allen, Sgt, 140
Allenby, Gen Edmund, 379
Alloa, 257–9
Alma, Battle of, 240, 394
Alnwick, 325–6
Alnwick Cooperative Stores, 326
Al Qaeda, 356
Alrewas, 207, 300, 334, 353, 365, 420
Alsace, 343
Alva, 257
Amazon, 198
Amballa, 209
Amersham, 228, 338
Ames, Capt, 234
Amiens, 293, 363
Amir Sheri Ali, 209
Anderson, Capt David, 247
Anderson VC, Eric, 247, 345
Andrews VC, Capt Henry, 400
Anerley, 310, 329
Anglesey, 232
Anglo-Egyptian War, 412
Anglo-Portuguese Telephone Co, 308
Angus, 272, 278
Angus VC, LCpl William, 63, 66, 68, 184–8
Angus, William jnr, 187
Annand VC, Capt Richard, 317–18, 365, 414
Antrim, 381
Applegarth, Isabella, 316
Arab Rising/Insurrection, 204, 401
Arabic, 282
Arakan, 378, 401
Archer-Shee, Brig John, 215
Argentina, 425
Argyll, 196–7
Argyll Territorial & Auxiliary Forces Association, 196

Armadale, 184–5
Armentieres, 37, 132–3, 147, 278, 302, 330
Armstrong-Whitworth, 329
Arnold, 226
Arras, 37, 91, 272
Artois, 33, 91
Artois, Second Battle of, 65, 72, 131
Ascot Gold Cup, 216, 218
Ashburton Shield, 291, 310–11
Ashford, 315–16, 429
Ashton, 365
Ashton-under-Lyne, 391
Ashworth & Parker of Elton, 358
Asquith, Herbert, 65
Associated Equipment Co, 190–1
Aston, 407, 421–2
Atlantic Transport Line, 232
Aubers & Ridge, 33–4, 48, 80, 85
Aubers Ridge, Battle of, 37–48, 52, 318
Auchy-les-la-Bassee, 64, 323
Auchy-les-Mines, 104, 106–108, 116, 118, 120, 124
Auckland, 370
Austin, B.S.M., 126
Australia, 186, 205, 258, 300, 345, 347, 390–1, 393–4, 401, 410
Australian armed forces,
  Australian Imperial Force, 302, 389
  Defence Department, 401
  Divisions,
    1st Australian, 168, 302
  Brigades,
    5th Australian, 168, 174, 177
  Battalions AIF,
    17th, 168, 174, 177, 300, 302
    18th, 174, 177
    19th, 174, 177
    20th, 174
  Other units,
    2nd Australian Auxiliary Hospital Southall, 303
    2nd Australian Labour Coy, 305
    Eastern Command Provost Coy, 30

Index 453

New South Wales Lancers, 389
No.1 Australian Auxiliary
 Hospital, Harefield Park, 303
 Training & Combined Base
 Depot, Tel el Kebir, 390
Royal Australian Navy,
 HMAT *Osterley*, 258
 HMAT *Thermistocles*, 301–303
 Williamstown Naval Depot, 410
Australian Fromelles Memorial, 44
Australian House of Representatives, 305
Austria, 334
Austrian Navy, 416
Auten VC, Harold, 353
Avey, Florence, 232
Avon, 299
Avonmouth, 235, 278, 289
Ayr, 361
Ayres, Sgt John, 125–7
Ayrshire, 360–1, 434

Backus, Lt, 138
Baghdad, 392
Bagot-Chester, Lt, 83
Bailleul, 255, 292, 349
Bairnsfather, Bruce, 371
Baleli, 403
Balfe Music Co, 269
Balhousie Castle, 274
Ball VC, Albert, 408
Ballyhooly, 216
Balmain, Sydney, 307
Baluchistan, 397
Bampton, 370
Banffshire, 372
Bank of England, 347
Bantry Bay, 252
Barbados, 210
Barnard Castle, 245
Barne, Bishop, 403
Barnsley, 403
Baron Tryon, 267
Baronet Teignmouth, 405
Baronston, 215
Barrackpore, 249–50
Barrie, 214, 289, 385
Barrie, Ontario, 237, 279
Barrowby, 407
Barter, CSM Frederick, 48, 54–5, 188–92
Basford, 294
Basra, 273, 392, 401
Bath, 219, 222, 351
Bathgate, 270
Batten-Pool VC, Capt Arthur, 168, 170–3, 192–9
Battersea & Park, 290, 308
Baxter VC, 2Lt Edward, 151–5, 164, 178, 199–202
Bayswater, 208
Bean, Gnr Leonard, 127
Beaufort aircraft, 363
Baumetz, 163

Beaver Inn, Ashford, 429
Beazley, Rfn J.E., 138
Becelaere, 86, 322
Beckenham, 281, 316
Beckett MP, Sir Gervase, 368
Becourt, 162
Bedford, 341
Beevor, 2Lt, 171
Belcher, LSgt Douglas, 32–3, 35–6, 202–207
Belcher Engineering Ltd, 205
Belfast, 285, 416
Bellancourt, 272
Bellew VC, Lt Edward, 11, 13–15, 17–18, 208–14
Bellewaarde & Lake, 32, 34, 73, 85–6, 141–2
Bellewaarde, Second Attack on, 80, 85
Bengal, 210–11, 321–2
Bengal Civil Service, 210
Bengal Customs Preventative Service, 321
Bengal Police, 321
Bengal Salt Department, 321
Benoist, Raymond, 199
Bentley Priory, 202
Berberis shrub, 207, 300, 353, 365, 420
Berkshire, 191, 215, 224–5, 411, 417
Berlin, 2–3, 201, 380
Berlin Military Government, 396
Berlin Wood, 30, 32
Bermuda, 239, 387
Berthell, Sgt, 21
Berwickshire, 274, 325, 327
Berwick-upon-Tweed, 325, 327
Bethnal Green, 266, 312
Bethulie, 348
Bethune, 79–80, 107, 131, 318, 363, 398
Bethune, Henry, 381
Betjeman, Sir John, 396
Bevin, Ernest, 405
Bewdley, 201
Bexhill-on-Sea, 243
Big Bertha, 4–5, 7
Big Wine Tree Co, 347
Billericay, 425
Bills, Pte D., 47
Bilton, 325
Birdwood, FM Sir William, 402
Birkenhead, 362, 364
Birkett, Col H.S., 383
Birmingham, 199, 344, 410, 421–3
Birr, 230, 285
Bischofswerda, 213
Biscot, 368
Bishop Stortford, 319
Bishopsfield, 415
Bishopwearmouth, 331
Bisley, 291, 310–11
Black Sea, 415
Blackpool, 329
Blairville, 151–2, 154, 178, 180, 201
Blean, 212
Blecourt, 275

Blendecques, 292
Blisworth, 367
Bloemfontein & Cathedral, 262, 348
Bloy, Capt Lawrence, 178, 180
Bluff, 140–1
Boar's Head, 180, 243
Body Guard of the Yeoman of the Guard, 197
Bodyline Series, 395
Boer/South African War, 215–17, 235, 238, 252, 263, 287, 389
Boesinghe, 7, 12
Boetleer's Farm, 13, 16, 18–21
Boiry St Rictrude & St Martin, 201
Bois de Biez, 41
Bois de Martinets, 180
Boise de Sartel, 138
Bois Grenier, 132–3, 174–5, 177, 253
Bois Grenier, Action of, 80
Bois Hugo, 95, 97–8, 100, 112, 116–17
Bolimov, 2
Bolton, 408
Bombarded Cross Roads, 5
Bombay, 208, 403–404, 419
Bonham & Goodman, 307
Booth VC, Anthony, 234
Bootle, 362
Bootwul, 264
Borden, Ontario, 237
Boronia House, Melbourne, 306–307
Borstall, Brig Gen H.E., 68
Boscastle, 346–7
Bosch, Carl, 3
Bosley, 364
Bougie, Algeria, 333
Boulogne, 185, 236, 238, 302, 383
Bourlon Wood, 309
Bourne, 387–8
Bourne United Charities, 388
Bournemouth, 191, 225, 430, 433
Bovey Tracey, 291
Bowerham Barracks, Lancaster, 251
Boy Scouts, 290, 292, 326
Boyd-Rochfort VC, 2Lt George, 79, 214–19, 224
Boys' Brigade, 232, 362, 366
Bradford, 245, 247, 340–5
Bradshaw, Col, 210
Bradworthy with Pancraswyke, 364
Brakspear, Lt Col, 83
Bramley, 246–7
Bramshott, 316
Brandram Bros, 310
Brandram Wharf, 310
Brazil, 199, 425
Bretell, Lt Col, 378
Bretencourt, 151, 154
Brickstacks, 106
Brighton, 215, 240, 262, 267, 355, 362, 382
Bright's disease, 396
Brine, Gertrude Elizabeth, 206
Brisbane, Australia, 347
Bristol, 212, 299

Bristol Channel, 250
British Aluminium Co, 408–409
British Army (for Indian units *see* Indian Army),
  Army Certificate of Education, 286–8, 336, 386, 391
  Army Reserve, 250, 255, 296, 309, 326, 329, 336, 391, 415, 427, 429, 434
    1st Class, 223
    Class Z, 239, 252, 327, 342, 374, 409
    Regular Army Reserve of Officers, 193–4, 208, 343–4
    Reserve of Officers, 264–5, 412
    Section B, 250, 367, 386
    Section D, 220, 255, 435
    Special Reserve, 189, 194, 197, 240, 248, 265, 287
    Territorial Army Reserve of Officers, 193, 425
    Territorial Force Reserve, 194
  British Military Mission, 259
  Good Conduct Badge/Pay, 220, 231, 255, 285, 287, 336, 367, 386, 429
  Regular Army Emergency Commission, 333, 425
  Territorial Force/Army, 203–204, 221, 413, 422–3, 431
  Armies,
    First, 26, 37, 56–7, 59, 68, 72, 92, 108–109, 113, 127, 162, 173
    Second, 10, 23, 162
    Third, 162
    Fourth, 162, 363
    Eight, 399
    Fourteenth, 378
    Southern, 368
  Army Corps,
    Cavalry, 86–7, 94, 113
    I, 37, 39, 56, 68, 92, 103, 105, 223
    IV, 37, 42–3, 68, 92, 94, 99, 127
    V, 1, 3, 7, 10, 18, 21, 23, 26–7, 85
    VI, 85
    XI, 92, 108, 116, 127, 130
    XV, 378
    XXXIII, 378
  Commands,
    Burma, 404
    Eastern, 239
    Home Forces, 193
    Jersey, 217
    Northern, 193
    Persia & Iraq, 414
    Scottish, 196, 378–9
  Corps,
    Army Educational, 260
    Army Medical Department, 209, 311
    Army Service, 197, 208, 239, 263, 370
    Army Veterinary, 240
    Auxiliary Territorial Service, 291, 343
    Intelligence, 208
    Labour, 299
    Machine Gun, 293
    Military Accountants, 343
    Military Police, 240
    Pioneer, 293
    Queen Alexandra's Imperial Nursing Service Reserve, 145, 332
    Royal/Army Chaplains Department, 147, 345, 352
    Royal Army Medical Corps, 134, 263, 331–2, 334
    Royal Army Ordnance, 344, 425
    Royal Army Pay, 206
    Royal Army Service, 197, 205, 231–2
    Royal Electrical & Mechanical Engineers, 205
  Districts,
    Dublin, 211
    North East, 369
  Divisions,
    1st, 37, 48, 60, 79, 90, 92, 95, 99, 101, 103, 109, 112, 123, 127, 168
    1st Cavalry, 33–4
    1st London, 204
    2nd, 48, 50–3, 56–7, 60, 64, 90, 92, 106, 108, 113, 116–17
    2nd Cavalry, 26–7, 37
    2nd London, 403
    3rd, 85, 147, 349
    3rd Cavalry, 34, 108, 113
    4th, 13, 27–8, 30, 32–4, 204
    5th, 13, 27
    6th, 76, 78, 134
    7th, 27, 42, 48, 52–3, 56, 60, 66, 68, 71, 90, 92, 103, 105, 108, 120–1
    8th, 37, 42, 419
    9th, 92, 105, 108, 113
    11th, 332
    12th, 118, 127, 143
    14th, 72, 85, 137
    15th, 90, 92, 94–6, 99–100, 103, 108–109, 113, 125, 378
    18th, 86, 198
    19th, 82
    20th, 80
    21st, 92, 94, 108–109, 112–13, 118, 160
    23rd, 132, 316
    24th, 90, 94, 106, 108, 112–13, 118, 140
    25th, 155–6
    27th, 3, 9, 12–13, 18, 20, 27, 33–4
    28th, 3–4, 9–12, 18, 20–1, 27, 32, 34, 117, 119, 127
    33rd, 164, 272
    37th, 138
    39th, 180
    42nd, 403
    46th, 76, 78, 114–15, 118, 127, 131
    47th, 48, 56, 60–2, 92, 94, 97, 108, 116–18, 156
    49th, 76, 134, 136
    50th, 27
    51st, 60, 68, 71
    55th, 63, 69, 107, 151, 162, 165, 167, 178, 364
  Guards, 92, 113, 123, 127, 224
  Brigades,
    1st, 99–100, 103, 170
    1st Guards, 37–8, 40–1, 79, 123–
    2nd, 37, 40, 48, 60, 90, 95, 99–10
    2nd Cavalry, 34–5
    2nd Guards, 116–17, 124
    3rd, 37, 40–1, 100, 103, 168
    3rd Guards, 116
    4th Guards, 50, 60
    5th, 50–1, 57, 106
    6th, 48, 50–1, 56, 90, 106, 113
    6th Brigade, Scottish Militia, 195
    6th Cavalry, 112
    7th, 85, 87–8, 155–7
    7th Cavalry, 34
    8th, 85, 87–8
    8th Cavalry, 34
    9th, 85, 87–8, 147–8
    10th, 20–3, 26–8, 30–2
    11th, 21, 27, 32–3, 35, 204
    12th, 13, 28, 30–1, 34
    13th, 13, 20, 24, 27–8
    14th, 29
    15th, 13, 29
    16th, 78, 134
    17th, 140
    18th, 78
    19th, 106, 164
    20th, 53, 55–6, 103
    21st, 53, 57, 59–60, 103, 105
    22nd, 48, 53–4, 56, 66, 90, 103–105, 120
    23rd, 42, 46, 48
    24th, 37, 42–3, 109
    25th, 37, 42, 45, 47–8
    26th, 105, 113, 116, 119
    27th, 105, 119
    28th, 105
    36th, 143
    37th, 143
    41st, 72, 78, 137
    42nd, 78
    43rd, 76, 78
    44th, 94, 98–9
    45th, 90, 99, 109–10, 112
    46th, 90, 94–5, 99, 112
    60th, 80–1
    62nd, 109
    63rd, 109
    64th, 109, 160
    68th, 132, 316
    71st, 90, 109, 112–13
    72nd, 109, 112–13
    73rd, 106, 115, 119, 140–2
    80th, 32
    83rd, 32, 119, 121, 127, 131
    84th, 18, 20, 32, 123
    85th, 18, 21, 32, 117, 119, 123

Index 455

102nd, 160
112th, 138
116th, 180
127th, 403
137th, 128–9
138th, 128–9
139th, 127, 129–30
140th, 60, 156
141st, 156
142nd, 48
146th, 136
149th, 23, 26
150th, 17–18, 20
164th, 151, 178
165th, 162
228th, 395
Cavalry,
  1st (King's) Dragoon Guards, 219
  1st Royal Dragoons, 112, 412
  2nd King Edward's Horse, 370
  3rd Dragoon Guards, 112
  4th Hussars, 31
  5th Dragoon Guards, 359
  5th Lancers, 31, 193, 197
  6th Dragoon Guards, 263
  6th Reserve Cavalry, 197
  7th Hussars, 193
  9th Lancers, 372
  10th Hussars, 217
  15th Hussars, 214
  18th Hussars, 34
  19th Hussars, 370
  21st Hussars, 210
  21st Lancers, 215
  Fife & Forfar Yeomanry, 359
  Lanarkshire Yeomanry, 186
  North Somerset Yeomanry, 192–3
  Nottinghamshire Yeomanry, 194
  Scottish Horse, 196
  West Kent Yeomanry, 214
  Warwickshire Yeomanry, 412
  Worcestershire Yeomanry, 219
Home Guard, 234, 247, 314, 317, 378–9, 388
  4th Middlesex Battalion Home Guard, 191
  10th Middlesex Battalion Home Guard, 191
  12th Middlesex Home Guard, 420
Infantry,
  1st Sussex Volunteer Corps, 430
  5th (Perthshire Highland) Volunteer Battalion, 196
  7th Foot, 240
  13th Foot, 264, 369
  16th Foot, 211
  19th Foot, 211
  21st Foot, 290
  24th Regiment, 252
  26th Foot, 415
  26th Middlesex (Cyclist) Volunteer Rifle Corps, 203
  35th Foot, 210
  40th Foot, 415

56th Foot, 211
63rd Regt, 290
64th Foot, 210
65th Foot, 229
68th (Durham) Regt, 394
75th Regt, 210
76th Foot, 264, 394
81st Foot, 211
91st Highlanders, 264
93rd Foot, 264
104th Regiment, 286
Argyll & Sutherland Highlanders, 202
  4th Argyll & Sutherland Highlanders, 219
  7th Argyll & Sutherland Highlanders, 20, 31
  10th Argyll & Sutherland Highlanders, 264
  11th Argyll & Sutherland Highlanders, 110
Artists' Rifles, 347
Bedfordshire, 211, 427–8
  1st Bedfordshire, 13, 29, 427
  2nd Bedfordshire, 57
  8th Bedfordshire, 228
Black Watch, 196, 273–5, 278, 374
  1st Black Watch, 37–8, 40–1, 195, 372, 374
  2nd Black Watch, 37, 41–2, 272–3
  3rd Black Watch, 195, 374
  4th Black Watch, 41
  5th Black Watch, 43
  6th (Fifeshire) Volunteer Battalion, 373
  7th Black Watch, 373–4
  10th Black Watch, 194
  11th (Reserve) Black Watch, 195
Border,
  2nd Border, 53, 56
  4th Border, 287, 400
Cameron Highlanders, 264–5, 361, 373, 378
  1st Cameron Highlanders, 40–1
  2nd Cameron Highlanders, 265
  4th Cameron Highlanders, 57, 59
  5th Cameron Highlanders, 113, 115, 359
  5th/6th Cameron Highlanders, 164, 166, 270
  6th Cameron Highlanders, 90, 99, 110–11, 113, 262, 264–5, 358, 360, 379
  8th Cameron Highlanders, 360
  9th Cameron Highlanders, 361
Cameronians, 186, 272, 287
  1st Cameronians, 287
  2nd Cameronians, 46, 287
  3rd Cameronians, 360
  4th Cameronians, 215

5th, 1/5th & 2/5th Cameronians, 258, 360
10th Cameronians, 95
Cheshire, 370, 395
  2nd Cheshire, 20
  4th Cheshire, 370
  10th Cheshire, 157, 159
Coldstream Guards, 225–6, 387
  1st Coldstream Guards, 40, 226
  2nd Coldstream Guards, 124
  3rd Coldstream Guards, 123–4, 221–2
Connaught Rangers, 351
  1st Connaught Rangers, 23
  3rd Connaught Rangers, 217
  6th Connaught Rangers, 217
Devonshire,
  1st Devonshire, 29
  4th Devonshire, 371
  4th Devonshire (Militia), 208
Dorsetshire, 264
  1st Dorset, 29
Durham Light Infantry,
  2nd Durham Light Infantry, 326
  8th Durham Light Infantry, 21
  13th Durham Light Infantry, 132, 315–17
  15th Durham Light Infantry, 160
Duke of Cornwall's Light Infantry,
  2nd Duke of Cornwall's Light Infantry, 13
  6th Duke of Cornwall's Light Infantry, 78
East Kent, 238, 252–3
  1st East Kent, 252, 254–5
  2nd East Kent, 11–12, 15–16, 119–22, 252
  6th East Kent, 143, 145, 238, 252–3, 255
East Lancashire, 434, 436
  1st East Lancashire, 33, 435
  2nd East Lancashire, 43–4
  6th East Lancashire, 357
  8th East Lancashire, 138, 434
East Surrey, 282
  1st East Yorkshire, 160–1
  2nd East Surrey, 119–21, 281–2
  4th (Militia) East Surrey, 263
  7th East Surrey, 143
East Yorkshire,
  2nd East Yorkshire, 10, 32, 123
  4th East Yorkshire, 17, 19
Essex,
  2nd Essex, 34
  4th Essex Militia, 286
  11th Essex, 112
Gloucestershire, 351, 371
  1st Gloucestershire, 103, 351, 372

Gordon Highlanders, 210, 263
  1st Gordon Highlanders, 87–8
  2nd Gordon Highlanders, 263
  4th Gordon Highlanders, 87–8
  6th Gordon Highlanders, 56, 66
  10th Gordon Highlanders, 98–9
Grenadier Guards, 267
  1st Grenadier Guards, 56
  3rd Grenadier Guards, 124–5, 217, 219
Hampshire,
  1st Hampshire, 34
  2nd Hampshire, 267
Hertforshire,
  1/1st Hertfordshire, 113, 116–17, 226–8
Highland Cyclist Bn, 270
Highland Light Infantry,
  16th Highland Light Infantry, 270
Honourable Artillery Company,
  1st Honourable Artillery Company, 88
Highland Light Infantry, 187, 202
  1st Highland Light Infantry, 57
  2nd HLI, 56–7
  8th HLI, 66–7, 184–5
  9th HLI, 186
  12th HLI, 95
Irish Guards,
  1st Irish Guards, 125
  2nd Irish Guards, 117, 124
King's (Liverpool), 365, 408, 411
  1st King's, 48, 51–2, 56, 106, 108, 116, 323, 407–408
  4th King's, 57
  5th King's, 153, 162–4, 362
  6th King's (Liverpool), 164
  7th King's (Liverpool), 50–1
  8th King's, 151–4, 201
  9th King's (Liverpool), 100, 103, 199
  10th King's (Liverpool), 88, 141
  13th King's (Liverpool), 149
King's Own, 248, 363
  1st King's Own, 30–1, 34–5, 248
  2nd King's Own, 127, 131, 247–9, 251
  3rd (Reserve) King's, 408
  4th King's Own, 248
  5th King's Own, 32
  8th King's Own, 248
King's Own Scottish Borderers, 325–6, 328
  3rd King's Own Scottish Borderers, 327
  7th King's Own Scottish Borderers, 90, 95–7, 325
  9th (Reserve) King's Own Scottish Borderers, 327

King's Own Yorkshire Light Infantry, 386, 395, 402
  2nd King's Own Yorkshire Light Infantry, 20
  9th King's Own Yorkshire Light Infantry, 160
  10th King's Own Yorkshire Light Infantry, 160
King's Royal Rifle Corps, 335–6
  1st King's Royal Rifle Corps, 50
  2nd King's Royal Rifle Corps, 48, 60, 90, 101, 335, 356, 358
  4th King's Royal Rifle Corps, 32, 335
  5th King's Royal Rifle Corps, 358
  7th King's Royal Rifle Corps, 72, 75–6, 137
  8th King's Royal Rifle Corps, 75–6
  9th King's Royal Rifle Corps, 76, 78
  12th King's Royal Rifle Corps, 84
King's Shropshire Light Infantry,
  2nd King's Shropshire Light Infantry, 12
  6th King's Shropshire Light Infantry, 84
Lancashire Fusiliers, 298
  2nd Lancashire Fusiliers, 13, 30–1, 328–9
  3rd Lancashire Fusiliers, 329
  5th Lancashire Fusiliers, 152, 178, 180, 297–8
  15th Lancashire Fusiliers, 298
  18th Lancashire Fusiliers, 357
Leicestershire,
  2nd Leicestershire, 50, 82–4, 280
  4th Leicestershire, 425
Lincolnshire, 318, 388
  1st Lincolnshire, 386, 418, 425
  2nd Lincolnshire, 37, 45–6, 48, 385–6
  3rd Lincolnshire, 418
  4th Lincolnshire (Militia), 386–7
  8th Lincolnshire, 315
London, 320
  1st London, 45
  3rd London, 42, 50, 82
  5th London, 32–5, 202, 204, 206
  7th London, 56, 157, 159
  8th London, 418
  9th London, 20, 204
  12th London, 18, 20, 32
  13th London, 45–6
  14th London (London Scottish), 40, 100, 103
  20th London, 64, 112
  22nd London, 64

23rd London, 64
24th London, 48, 61–4, 318–19
25th London, 203
28th London, 281, 292
34th London, 200
Loyal North Lancashire, 436
  1st Loyal North Lancashire, 90, 101–102, 178, 312–13
  3rd Loyal North Lancashire, 313, 335
  4th Loyal North Lancashire, 178, 180
  8th Loyal North Lancashire, 155–7, 159, 310–11
Manchester, 83, 365, 391
  1st Manchester, 13, 22–5, 389, 391–2
  2nd Manchester, 217, 391
  3rd Manchester, 391
  4th Volunteer, Manchester, 217
  6th Manchester (Militia), 391
Middlesex,
  1st Middlesex, 347
  3rd Middlesex, 12–13, 120–1
  4th Middlesex, 85, 87–8, 290, 292
  8th Middlesex, 18, 20
  11th Middlesex, 143
  13th Middlesex, 142
Monmouthshire,
  1st Monmouthshire, 20
  2nd Monmouthshire, 34
  2nd Monmouthshire Rifle Volunteer Corps, 291
Norfolk,
  2nd Norfolk, 358
Northamptonshire, 371
  1st Northamptonshire, 90, 102, 369, 371
  2nd Northamptonshire, 43
Northumberland Fusiliers, 332
  1st Northumberland Fusiliers, 148–9
  2nd Northumberland Fusiliers, 20
  3rd (Home Service) Garrison Bn, Northumberland Fusiliers, 296
  11th Northumberland Fusiliers, 366
  13th Northumberland Fusiliers, 160
  21st Northumberland Fusiliers, 160
Nottingham Militia, 229
Oxfordshire & Buckinghamshire Light Infantry, 225, 395
  2nd Oxfordshire & Buckinghamshire LI, 50
Parachute,
  5th Parachute, 351
Queen's Lancashire, 437
Queen's Royal Antrim Rifle Reg of Militia, 369

Queen's Royal Surrey, 282
Queen's Royal West Surrey, 282, 401
   1st Queen's Royal West Surrey, 401
Rifle Brigade, 206–207, 252, 266, 336, 401, 413, 416, 418, 432, 434
   1st Rifle Brigade, 34, 413
   2nd Rifle Brigade, 43, 45–7, 413
   3rd Rifle Brigade, 431
   4th Rifle Brigade, 12
   6th Rifle Brigade, 431
   7th Rifle Brigade, 76–8, 155, 206, 432
   8th Rifle Brigade, 72, 75–8, 137, 266, 430–1
   9th Rifle Brigade, 76, 78
   12th Rifle Brigade, 80–1, 84–5, 331
   22nd Rifle Brigade, 395
Ross Highland Volunteers,
   1st Battalion, 264
   2nd Battalion, 264
Royal Anglian, 320
Royal Berkshire,
   1st Royal Berkshire; 50–2, 108, 113, 117, 411, 417
   2nd Royal Berkshire, 45
   3rd Royal Berkshire, 113, 411, 417
   8th Royal Berkshire, 168
Royal Dublin Fusiliers,
   2nd Royal Dublin Fusiliers, 20
Royal Fusiliers, 352, 423
   1st Royal Fusiliers, 351
   2nd Royal Fusiliers, 350–1
   3rd Royal Fusiliers, 119–21
   4th Royal Fusiliers, 147–9, 345, 349
   8th Royal Fusiliers, 143
   18th Royal Fusiliers, 293–4
   21st Royal Fusiliers, 423
Royal Highland Fusiliers, 187
Royal Inniskilling Fusiliers,
   2nd Royal Inniskilling Fusiliers, 50
Royal Irish Fusiliers,
   1st Royal Irish Fusiliers, 20
Royal Irish Regiment,
   1st Royal Irish Regiment, 17–20
   2nd Royal Irish Regiment, 212
   3rd Royal Irish Regiment, 372
   5th Royal Irish Regiment, 287
Royal Irish Rifles,
   1st Royal Irish Rfls, 45–7
Royal Lanarkshire Militia, 263
Royal Lincolnshire, 320
Royal Munster Fusiliers, 286
   1st Royal Munster Fusiliers, 215
   2nd Royal Munster Fusiliers, 103, 168, 192, 197

   3rd Royal Munster Fusiliers, 168, 192, 197
Royal Regiment of Fusiliers, 353
Royal Scots,
   2nd Royal Scots, 87–8, 149
   8th Royal Scots, 66–7, 184–5
   9th Royal Scots, 13
   13th Royal Scots, 90, 110–11, 267
Royal Scots Fusiliers, 187, 219
   2nd Royal Scots Fusiliers, 56–7
   7th Royal Scots Fusiliers, 110
Royal Sussex, 238, 244, 340, 430
   2nd Royal Sussex, 90, 100, 102, 428–9
   9th Royal Sussex, 140–2, 338–9
   10th Royal Sussex, 339
   11th Royal Sussex, 242
   12th Royal Sussex, 180–3, 205, 237, 242
   13th Royal Sussex, 180–1, 183, 242–3
Royal Warwickshire,
   2nd Royal Warwickshire, 53, 55, 90, 104–105, 421
Royal Welsh Fusiliers, 190
   1st Royal Welsh Fusiliers, 48, 53–6, 189
   2nd Royal Welsh Fusiliers, 165
   3rd Royal Welsh Fusiliers, 189–90
Royal West Kent (Queen's Own),
   1st Royal West Kent, 294
   3rd (Reserve) Royal West Kent, 294
   6th Royal West Kent, 333
Royal West Surrey,
   2nd Royal West Surrey, 55–6, 66
   6th Royal West Surrey, 146
Scots Guards, 113, 215, 218
   1st Scots Guards, 40, 79, 124, 214
   2nd Scots Guards, 53, 55–6, 197
Seaforth Highlanders, 196
   2nd Seaforth Highlanders, 20
   3rd (Reserve) Seaforth Highlanders, 264
   10th Seaforth Highlanders, 263
Sherwood Foresters, 231, 233–4, 423
   1st Sherwood Foresters, 37, 43–4, 418
   4th Sherwood Foresters, 196, 419
   5th Sherwood Foresters, 131
   7th Sherwood Foresters, 127, 129–1, 232, 418, 423–4
   8th Sherwood Foresters, 130
   10th Home Defence Battalion, Sherwood Foresters, 233
   15th Home Defence Battalion, Sherwood Foresters, 233

Somerset Light Infantry,
   1st Somerset Light Infantry, 34
   3rd Somerset Light Infantry, 197
   4th Somerset Light Infantry, 219
   6th Somerset Light Infantry, 76
South Lancashire, 408
   2nd Vol Bn, South Lancashire, 287
   5th South Lancashire, 31, 34
South Staffordshire, 322, 339
   1st South Staffordshire, 53–4, 56, 104, 322
   2nd South Staffordshire, 51, 55–6, 90, 106, 321
   8th South Staffordshire, 322
South Wales Borderers,
   3rd Volunteer Battalion, South Wales Borderers, 291
Suffolk, 378–9
   1st Suffolk, 18–20
   2nd Suffolk, 87–8, 150, 253
   3/4th Suffolk, 295
   4th Suffolk, 23, 25
   9th Suffolk, 90, 112–13, 375, 378
   10th Suffolk, 295
Welch/Welsh, 292, 315
   1st Welch, 291
   14th Welsh, 167
Welsh Guards, 131
West Riding (Duke of Wellington's), 253
   2nd West Riding, 378
   3rd West Riding, 407–408
West Yorkshire, 344, 369
   1st West Yorkshire, 427
   5th West Yorkshire, 137, 342
   6th West Yorkshire, 136, 340, 342
   8th West Yorkshire, 134, 136
   18th West Yorkshire, 341
Wiltshire, 197
   1st Wiltshire, 157
Worcestershire,
   1st Worcestershire, 43, 45
   2nd Worcestershire, 50
   3rd Worcestershire, 155
   7th Worcestershire, 199
York & Lancaster, 284
   1st York & Lancaster, 110, 131, 229, 294, 298
   2nd York & Lancaster, 134, 229, 232
Yorkshire, 208
   1st Yorkshire, 397
   2nd Yorkshire, 56
   4th Yorkshire, 17, 19
   7th Yorkshire, 208
Medical units,
   1 Auxiliary Hospital, Cairo, 302
   1 British Red Cross Hospital, Le Touquet, 313–14

1 Casualty Clearing Station, 118, 417
2 Casualty Clearing Station, 255, 417
2 London General, 299, 334
2 Red Cross Hospital, Rouen, 349–50
2 Scottish General Hospital, 409
2 West Riding Field Ambulance, 284
3 London General Hospital, 302–303
3 Scottish General Hospital, 247
3 Southern General Hospital, Oxford, 199
4 Scottish General Hospital, 247
5 Field Ambulance, 319
5 General Hospital, Rouen, 239, 255
6 British Red Cross Hospital, 382
6 Casualty Clearing Station, 431
7 Convalescence Depot, 238
7 Stationary Hospital, 236
9 General Hospital, Bloemfontaine, 348
9 General Hospital, Rouen, 249
10 General Hospital, Rouen, 238
11 General Hospital, 340
11 Stationary Hospital, 228
13 General Hospital, Boulogne, 312
14 General Hospital, Wimereux, 249, 342
16 Field Ambulance, 255
19 Field Ambulance, 228
34 Field Ambulance, 332
35 Field Ambulance, 341
37 Field Ambulance, 238
45 Casualty Clearing Station, 349
50 Field Ambulance, 382
51 Stationary Hospital, 340
61 Field Ambulance, 80, 331
142 Field Ambulance, 149, 349
309 Home Service Field Ambulance, 206
Auxiliary Military Hospital, Southall, 303
Belton Military Hospital, Grantham, 332
Cambridge Military Hospital, Aldershot, 436–7
Dover Military Hospital, 254, 256
Edinburgh Military Hospital, 349
First Aid Nursing Yeomanry, 294
Fort Pitt Military Hospital, 294
Genoa Base Hospital, 340
Graincourt Dressing Station, 309
Grantham Military Hospital, 332
Graylingwell War Hospital, 239
Grove Military Hospital, Tooting, 213
King George V Hospital, Dublin, 215
Mont Dore Hospital, Bournemouth, 199

Queen Mary's General Hospital, 303
Royal Pavilion Military Hospital, Brighton, 355
Sunderland War Hospital, 332
Miscellaneous units,
1st Brigade Machine-Gun Company, 170
2/6th North Russian Rifles, 198
1 Infantry Base Depot, 228
6 Infantry Base Depot, 255
27th/28th Infantry Base Depot, Rouen, 349
38 Infantry Base Depot, 238
Antrim Militia, 195
Carter Force, 113, 117
Commandos, 257
Defence Force, 193
Green's Force, 100, 103
Imperial Camel Corps, 219
London District Anti-Gas School, 258
Macforce, 403
Mersey Defence Corps, 201
National Defence Coys, 206, 233
No.1 Rest Camp, 204
No.2 Anti-Gas School, Humber Garrison, 259
No.6 Regimental District, 322
Seely's Detachment, 64
Special Air Service, 257
Royal Artillery, 193, 210–11, 218, 369, 373, 395, 414, 421
2nd London Battery RGA, 9
2nd Sussex Artillery Volunteers, 240
4th West Lancashire Battery, 163
5B Reserve Brigade, 368
6 Reserve Brigade, 368
7th Lancashire (Howitzer) Battery, 163
9th Brigade RFA, 218
13th (Highland) Light Brigade, 196
22nd Brigade RFA, 241
22 Company RGA, 241
27th Brigade RFA, 241
32 Company RGA, 241
42nd Battery, 366–7
47th Company, RGA Signal Training Depot, 341
51st Anti-Tank Regiment, 197
53rd Brigade RFA, 241
54th (West Highland) Field Brigade, 196–7
59th Brigade, 342
60th North Midlands Brigade RFA (TA), 231
78th Brigade RFA, 241
104 Company RGA, 241
122nd Heavy Battery RGA, 16
173rd (East Ham) Brigade RFA, 312
174th Brigade RFA, 312
184th Siege Battery RGA, 424

239 Anti-Tank Battery, 414
254th Anti-Aircraft Coy RGA, 409
307 Siege Battery, 341
393 Independent Battery RFA, 368
401 Siege Battery, 341
Artillery College, 211
A Siege Depot, 341
B Siege Park Workshops, 342
Home Counties RFA, 240
Kent Artillery Volunteer Corps, 211
LXXI Brigade, 125–6, 366, 368–9
No.2 Depot, RFA; 368
No.2 RFA Officer Cadet School, 368
Royal Field Artillery, 240–1, 252, 295, 326, 366, 436
Royal Garrison Artillery, 239, 241, 366, 423
RGA Reserve Brigade, 341
Sussex Artillery (Militia), 239, 241
Tynemouth Artillery Volunteer Corps, 211
XIII Corps Heavy Artillery, 349
XVI Brigade, 218
Royal Engineers, 197, 199, 201, 216, 284, 309, 326, 343, 392
3rd Field Company, 64
5th Field Company, 175
54th Field Company, 28
55th Field Company, 28
73rd Field Company, 90, 98, 308
170th Tunnelling Company, 106, 143
172nd Tunnelling Company, 284
173rd Tunnelling Company, 106
175th Tunnelling Company, 72
176th Tunnelling Company, 70
187th (Special) Company, 127, 257
189th Company, 81
231st Field Company, 309
254th Tunnelling Company, 164, 167, 283–4
Inland Waterways Transport, 392
Special Brigade, 199, 259
Royal Flying Corps, 196, 216, 223, 309, 371
6 Squadron, 3
12 Squadron, 202
15 Squadron, 195
38 Squadron, 195
45 Squadron, 196
46 Training Squadron, 215
55 Squadron, 202
65 Squadron, 196
76 Squadron, 195
119 Squadron, 195
198 Squadron, 195
199 Squadron, 195
Central Flying School, 195

Index 459

Training establishments/units,
   38th Training Reserve Battalion, 194
   53rd Training Reserve Battalion, 327
   89th Training Reserve Battalion, 341
   202 Graduated Battalion, 194
   Army Cadet Force, 196
   Cambridge University Officers' Training Corps, 78
   Fourth Army School of Instruction, 272
   GHQ Cadet School, 292
   London University Officers' Training Corps, 309
   No.5 Officer Cadet Battalion, 281
   No.9 Officer Cadet Battalion, 360
   No.10 Officer Cadet Battalion, 360
   No.19 Officer Cadet Battalion, 424
   Officers' Training Corps, 291, 311, 339
   Ordnance School, Woolwich, 409
   Oxford University Officers' Training Corps, 78
   Royal Military College/Academy Sandhurst, 193, 212, 264, 322, 371, 396–7, 412
   School of Education, Newmarket, 260
   School of Military Aeronautics, Reading, 309
   School of Musketry, 288
   Staff College, Camberley, 193, 378, 395, 401–402, 406, 411
   Western Command Bombing School, 190
British Columbia, 212–13, 239, 385
British East Africa, 321
British India Steam Navigation Co, 203, 250
British International Pictures, 393
British Legion/Royal British Legion, 205, 225, 246, 285, 299, 351, 374
British Medical Association, 290
British Racing Motors, 388
Brixton, 309
Broadmarsh Crater, 155–6, 158–9, 311
Broadmeadows Army Camp, Melbourne, 391
Brock, Sir Isaac, 234
Brockley, 347
Bromley, 431
Brook Hoist Co, 409
Brooks VC, LSgt Oliver, 120, 123–5, 219–26
Broughty Ferry, 272
Brown, Georgina, 296
Brown, Lt Philip, 132–4, 316–17
Browning & Woodroffe, 430
Bruce, Castle, 292
Brunt VC, John, 207
Buchan VC, John, 258
Buck, Rfm, 36

Buckhaven, 268–9
Buckinghamshire, 228–9, 239, 262, 313, 338
Buckingham Palace, 185, 189, 198, 201, 204, 225, 228, 232, 244, 246, 256, 259, 265, 267, 269, 271, 281, 285, 292, 296, 299, 302, 309, 311, 313, 316, 318, 323–4, 327, 332, 337, 340, 342, 349–50, 358, 360, 368, 372, 374, 379, 392, 398, 401, 408, 417, 424, 428, 430, 432, 437
Buckley, Capt, 122
Buckley VC, John, 365
Buenes Aires, 263
Bulfin, Maj Gen, 21
Bulford, 381
Bulgaria, 198
Buller, Adm Sir Alexander, 415
Buller, VAdm Sir Henry, 415–16
Buller, Herbert, 416
Buller VC, Gen Sir Redvers, 412–13
Bullswater Camp, Surrey, 316
Bully Grenay, 168
Bulwell, 294, 418–19
Bungay, 413
Burcombe, Wiltshire, 351
Burma, 311, 351, 378, 394–5, 404
Burma War, 211–12
Burradon & Cox Coal Co, 291
Burt VC, Pte Alfred, 107, 116–17, 226
Burton, Maud, 428
Burton, Scorers & White, 318–19
Bury, 297–9, 329–31, 356–8
Bury St Edmunds, 204, 379
Bush, Brig Gen, 18
Bustard Camp, 235–6
Bute, 192, 194, 197
Butler VC, William, 369
Butlin, Billy, 233
Butlin's Holiday Camp, 233–4
Bye VC, Robert, 224

Caernarfon, 191
Caffrey VC, Pte John, 134–5, 229–34
Cairneyhill, 270, 272
Cairo, 198
Calais, 413
Calcutta, 208, 210, 248, 321, 338–9, 404
Caldwell VC, Thomas, 186–8
Caledonian Society, 276
Calgary, 276, 297
Calonne, 168–9, 171–2, 174, 198
Camberwell, 308, 310, 392
Cambrai, 275
Cambridge, 262
Cambridgeshire, 356–7
Cambrin, 48, 60, 116, 218, 336
Camden, Sgt Hugh, 177–8, 303
Cameron, 273
Cameron VC, Donald, 188
Camfield, Kathleen, 241–2
Cammell Laird, 233
Campbell, Canberra, 307
Campbell VC, Lt Frederick, 66, 69–72, 234–7

Campbell VC, John, 224
Campbell, Lt Col M.E.K., 237
Canada, 212–13, 234, 236, 239, 274, 288–9, 297, 332, 347, 361, 380, 382–3, 410–11
Canadian Bank of Commerce, 274
Canadian Farm, 22, 24
Canadian Forces,
   Canadian Army,
      Canadian Expeditionary Force, 212–13, 236, 275, 379, 381
      Divisions,
         1st, 1, 4–5, 9–11, 13, 21, 66, 68
      Brigades,
         1st, 7, 10–11, 66, 68–70
         2nd, 3, 5, 9–10, 13, 16, 18–21, 60
         3rd, 1, 5, 8–11, 13, 16–18, 20–1, 57, 60, 70
         4th, 70
      Infantry,
         5th Regiment (Royal Highlanders of Canada), 277
         106th Regt (Winnipeg LI), 288
         British Columbia Regiment, 213–14
         Canadian Black Watch, 278
         Princess Patricia's Canadian Light Infantry, 32, 416
         Royal Montreal Regiment, 385
         Royal Regiment of Canada, 411
         South Alberta Regiment, 384
      Battalions,
         1st, 10, 12–13, 66, 69, 71–2, 234–5
         2nd, 10–12, 15, 18, 69–71
         2nd (Special Service), Royal Canadian Regiment, 235
         3rd, 10–12, 15, 18, 69, 71–2
         4th, 10, 12–13, 20
         4th Royal Canadian Regiment, 237
         5th, 5, 15–16, 18
         7th, 5, 9–10, 13, 15–19, 208, 212
         8th, 5, 10, 13–18, 21, 285, 288
         10th, 7, 9–12, 16, 19, 287
         11th Irish Fusiliers of Canada, 212
         13th, 1, 5, 8–10, 12, 15–16, 174, 177, 200
         13th Battalion Volunteer Militia, 235
         14th, 7–1, 13, 15–18, 21, 379, 381–2
         15th, 5, 10, 14–19, 21
         16th, 7, 9, 11, 16
         30th Battalion of Rifles, Militia, 235
         60th (Victoria Rifles), 275
      Artillery,
         1st Brigade CFA, 9
         2nd Battery CFA, 68

2nd Highland Battery CFA, 275
3rd Battery CFA, 15, 68
3rd Brigade CFA, 10–11
4th Battery CFA, 69
6th Battery CFA, 69
6th Siege Battery CGA, 275
7th Field Battery CFA, 275
9th Battery CFA, 10
10th Battery CFA, 6, 8, 10–11
11th Battery CFA, 10
12th Battery CFA, 10
Montreal Heavy Artillery, 275
Montreal Heavy Brigade CGA, 380
Engineers,
  1st Field Coy CE, 70
  3rd Field Coy CE, 8–9
Medical,
  1st Canadian Field Ambulance, 280, 382
  1st Canadian General Hospital, 381–2
  2nd Canadian Field Ambulance, 15, 21, 278, 381
  2nd Canadian Field Hospital, 363
  2nd Canadian Stationary Hospital, 302–303
  3rd Canadian Casualty Clearing Station, 382–4
  3d Canadian General Hosp, 238, 382–3
  4th Canadian Genewral Hosp, 250
  4 Casualty Clearing Station, 410
  10th Canadian Casualty Clearing Station, 278
  CAMC Casualty Coy, Shorncliffe, 383
  Royal/Canadian Army Medical Corps, 280, 379–80, 384, 410
  Canadian Army Medical Corps Militia, 380
  Granville Canadian Special Hospital, Ramsgate, 382
Other units,
  1st Canadian Motor Machine-Gun Brigade, 275
  3rd Canadian Brigade Grenade Coy, 8
  29th Armd Recce Regt, South Alberta Regt, 384
  Alberta Field Force, 276
  Camp Borden, Ontario, 237
  Canadian Base Depot, 382
  Canadian Forces College, Toronto, 279, 385
  Canadian Forces Leadership & Recruit School, 237
  Canadian Troops London Area, 382
  Canadians Brighton Area, 382

Lord Strathcona's Horse, 297
Royal Canadian Armoured Corps, 384
Royal Canadian Dragoons, 71
Toronto Public Schools Bn Cadet Corps, 277
Royal Canadian Air Force, 411
  12 Technical Services Department, 411
  895 (Fred Campbell VC) Sqn, Royal Canadian ATC, 237
  Flight Training School, Brandon, 411
  Flying School, Trenton, 411
  RCAF Base Trenton, 411
Royal Canadian Navy,
  Royal Canadian Naval Volunteer Reserve, 280
Canadian Orchard, 49, 53, 60
Canadian Pacific, 239, 409–10
Canal du Nord, 275
Canberra, 307, 401
Canterbury & Cathdral & Archbishop, 238–9, 252–4, 351, 368
Cape Colony, 235, 238
Cape Town, 347
Cardew, Capt, 99
Cardiff, 188–9, 191
Cardiff Coal Exchange, 189
Cardiff Gas, Light & Coke Co, 189
Carlton, Victoria, 301, 307
Carluke, 67, 184–5, 187–8
Carluke Rovers FC, 187
Carnock, 270
Carpenter, Sister Ellen, 382–4
Carrillis, 434
Carron, Alexander, 380
Carter VC, C.S.M. Nelson, 180–3, 237–45
Cassel, Sir Ernest, 215–16
Cassels, Sir Robert, 402
Castle Cary, 352
Castletown, 214, 217
Caterham, 222
Catford, 328
Catlin, LCpl Sidney, 427
Catterick, 327, 341
Cavan, CSgt George, 184, 186
Cayman Islands, 347
Cecil, Sir Henry, 216
Cemeteries & Crematoria,
  Allerton Cemetery, Liverpool, 410
  Ayr Cemetery, 361
  Bourne Cemetery, 387
  Bournemouth Crematorium, 191
  Castletown Church of Ireland Old Churchyard, Geohegan, 218
  Chislehurst (Town) Cemetery, 334
  City Road Crematorium, Sheffield, 365
  Eastbourne Crematorium, 261
  Egremont Cemetery, 251
  Englefield Green Cemetery, 315
  Fawkner Crematorium, Melbourne, 393

  Glyntaff Crematorium, Pontypridd, 344
  Golders Green Crematorium, 406, 420
  Harehills Cemetery, Chapeltown, Leeds, 367, 369
  Hillside Cemetery, Kamloops, 213
  Ipswich Borough Crematorium, 379
  Mount Royal Cemetery, 385
  New Cemetry, Ipswich, 379
  Newport Cemetery, 388
  Nigalpani Cemetery, Nepal, 325
  Norham Churchyard, 327
  Old Ipswich Cemetery, 296
  Oxford Crematorium, 426
  Pine Hill Cemetery, East Toronto, 411
  Preston (New Hall Lane) Cemetery, 437
  St John's Crematorium, Woking, 314
  St Mark's Churchyard, Whiteley Village, Hersham, 314
  St Mary the Virgin Churchyard, Shipley, 416
  Springvale Botanical Cemetery, Melbourne, 307
  Torquay Crematorium, 282, 300
  Upper Largo Churchyard, 375
  Warsak Road Cemetery, Shagi Landi Kyan, 356
  West Bridgford Military Hospital, 408
  West Hertfordshire Crematorium, Watford, 229
  Weymouth Crematorium, 353
  Wheatley Hill Cemetery, 317
  Wilford Hill (Southern) Cemetery, 234
  Wilton Cemetery, Carluke, 187
  Windsor Borough Cemetery, 225
  Witton Cemetery, Birmingham, 422
Cenotaph, 225
Central American Republic, 264
Central Intelligence Agency, 356
Ceylon, 311
Ceylon Civil Service, 311
Chafer VC, Pte George, 160–2, 245–7, 345
Chalet Wood, 95, 98–9, 110–12, 116
Chalk Pit Copse, 117
Chalk Pit Wood, 95, 99–100, 103, 111, 116–17, 123, 127
Chambers, Frances, 403
Chambers, Mary, 419
Champagne, 80, 91, 123
Chanak, 250
Chance, 2Lt Frank, 62
Channel Islands, 248
Chapel-en-le-Frith, 420
Chapelle St Roch, 49, 56, 60, 66, 68, 70
Chapeltown, Leeds, 367
Chapigny Farm, 81, 84–5
Charlton King's, 370
Chateau d'Oex, 213
Chatham, 238, 266, 284, 287, 294, 376

Index   461

Chatham House, 405
Chavasse, Bishop Francis, 364
Chavasse, Capt Noel, 141, 364
Checkley, 290
Chelsea, 222, 290, 292, 334, 425
Cheltenham, 321–2, 369–71
Cherisy, 198
Cheriton, 252
Cherry Willingham, 320
Chesham, 228–9
Cheshire, 259, 362, 364–5, 370, 407
Cheshire, Wg Cdr Leonard, 396
Chester, 349, 407, 409
Chicago, 287, 384
Chichester & Cathedral, 239, 243–4, 257, 340, 430
Child, PC Anthony, 369
Chile, 425
Chillianwallah, 210
Chin Hills, 212
Chin Lushai Expedition, 395
China, 265, 381, 396
Chitral Relief Force, 211, 403
Chittenden, Vermont, 351
Chlorine gas, 3, 15, 26
Chocolat Menier Corner, 37–8, 48–9, 52
Chocques, 118
Chorley, 335, 337–8
Christchurch, New Zealand, 346
Christian VC, Pte Harry, 93, 107, 116, 127, 131, 247–51
Christie's, 388
Christison, Lt A.F.P., 113, 378–9
Christmas Truce, 330
Churches,
    All Saints, Branksome Park, Bournemouth, 433
    All Saints, Islington, 226
    All Saints, Lincoln, 320
    All Saints, Newchurch, Isle of Wight, 282
    All Saints, Newmarket, 262
    Alnwick Baptist, 326
    Baltonsborough, Street, 352
    Bovey Tracey Parish, 291
    Bridge Parish, Canterbury, 239
    Brompton Oratory, 401
    Bury Parish, 300
    Calvin, Montreal, 379
    Charlton Parish, Kent, 262
    Checkley Parish, 290
    Christchurch, Coseley, 200
    Conisborough Parish, 284–5
    English Martyr's RC, Preston, 436
    Fletre, Bailleul, 349
    Holy Trinity, Halifax, 262
    Holy Trinity, Windsor, 225
    Holy Trinity, Wordsley, 200
    Hove Parish, 310
    Native Mission Chapel, Burdwan, India, 321
    Norham Church, 328
    Parkhills United Methodist, Bury, 358
    Radcliffe Parish, 297, 300
    Roman Catholic Chapel, Carluke, 184
    St Andrew's, Ayr, 360
    St Andrew's, Haverstock Hill, London, 425
    St Ann's, Belfast, 287
    St Anne's, Eastbourne, 239
    St Athanasius RC, Carluke, 186
    St Barnabus, Cambridge, 232
    St Bartholomew, Herne Bay, 429
    St Clement's, Leeds, 368
    St Columba's Church of Scotland, London, 384
    St Dunstan's, Stepney, 266
    St Ethelburga's, Bishopgate, London, 205–206
    St George's Chapel, Woolwich, 369
    St George's, Hanover Square, London, 214, 331
    St George's Memorial, Ypres, 334
    St George's RC, York, 231
    St James, Nellore, Jaffna, Ceylon, 311
    St James', Paddington, 430
    St James the Apostle, Montreal, 279
    St John of Jerusalem, South Hackney, 312
    St John's, Holloway, 345
    St John's, Lewes, 431
    St John the Baptist, Bradworthy with Pancaswyke, 364
    St Laurence, Birmingham, 421
    St Lawrence, Rode, 198
    St Luke's, Tranmere, 362
    St Mark's, Lewisham, 351–2
    St Mary-le-Tower, Ipswich, 262
    St Mary Magdalene, Lillington, 321
    St Mary's, Bury, 297, 330
    St Mary's, Droylesden, 364–5
    St Mary's, Eastbourne, 241–2
    St Mary's, Hailsham, 237
    St Mary's, Kingswinford, 200
    St Mary's, Surbiton, 203–204
    St Mary the Virgin, Bosley, 364
    St Mary the Virgin, Great Dunmow, 351–3
    St Mary the Virgin, Prescot, 364
    St Michael & All Angels, Bampton, 372
    St Paul's, Deptford, 347, 349–50
    St Paul's Anglican, Kogarah, New South Wales, 304
    St Paul's Presbyterian, Tranmere, 362–3
    St Peter & St Paul, Aston, 422
    St Peter's, Bayswater, 208
    St Peter's, Bury, 299
    St Peter's, Claybrooke & Wibtoft, 364
    St Peter's, St Albans, 428
    St Stephen's, Hyde, 364–5
    Silver Street Methodist, Lincoln, 319–20
    Tyrellspass Church of Ireland, 218
    United Free, Dunfermline, 270
    United Methodist, Lincoln, 318
    Wangford-cum-Henham & Reydon, 351
Church Lads & Church Girls Brigade, 203, 207, 298, 300, 347, 349, 353, 365, 420
Church Missionary Society, 345
Churchill, Capt Peter, 294
Churchill, Winston, 294
Cite Madagascar, 114–15, 120, 124, 128, 144
Cite St Auguste, 95, 97–8, 108
Cite St Elie, 103, 105, 109, 114
Cite St Laurent, 95, 97–8
Civil Service, 347
Clackmannanshire, 257, 359
Clandon Park, 282, 320
Claremorris, 327
Clark MP, Alan, 310
Clarke, 2Lt W.S., 171–2
Clarke VC, Leo, 289
Clarke-Kennedy VC, William, 207
Clarkson, Jeremy, 396
Clasby, John Joseph, 305
Claybrooke, 364
Claygate, 206–207
Clayton, Rev'd Tubby, 225, 432–3
Clerkenwell, 337
Clipstone, 341
Clwyd, 191
Coates, Cpl, 158–9
Codd, Hilda, 363
Cohen, Leonard, 276
Colamber, 215
Coldingham, 274
Coldstream, 325
Colinston, 434
Collin, Maj Gen Geoffrey, 369
Collings-Wells VC, Lt Col John, 339
Collins, Pte Thomas, 166–8, 285
Colombo, 311
Colonial Office, 219, 263, 370
Columbia, 425
Commonwealth War Graves Commission, 285
    Abbeville Communal Cemetery, 319
    Alamein Memorial, 187
    Alexandria (Chatby) Memorial, 219
    Arras Memorial, 172–3, 180, 272, 298, 311, 427
    Arras Road Military Cemetery, 323
    Authuille Military Cemetery, 137
    Avesnes-le-Comte Communal Cemetery Extension, 163–4
    Baghdad (North Gate) War Cemetery, 358
    Barlin Communal Cemetery Extension, 431
    Basra Memorial, 273
    Bedford House Cemetery, 292–3
    Bellacourt Military Cemetery, 164
    Bergen-Op-Zoom Canadian War Cemetery, 384
    Bethune Town Cemetery, 228

Beuvry Communal Cemetery, 71–2
Boulogne Eastern Cemetery, 236
Brewery Orchard Cemetery, 177
Brown's Copse Cemetery, 373
Cabaret-Rouge British Cemetery, Souchez, 108
Cambrai Memorial, 310
Cambrin Churchyard Extension, 347
Canadian Memorial, 156
Chatham Naval Memorial, 253, 357
Chocques Military Cemetery, 417
Dud Corner Cemetery, 96–7, 126, 371, 429–30
El Alamein War Cemetery, 197
Erquinghem-Lys Churchyard Extension, 177
Fillievres British Cemetery, 179–80, 201
Fosse 7 Military Cemetery, 126–7
Freetown (King Tom) Cemetery, 46
Fricourt New military Cemetery, 161
Gorre British & Indian Cemetery, 167
Grootebeek British Cemetery, 330
Guillemont Road Cemetery, 294
Ham British Cemetery, Muille-Villette, 421
Haringhe (Bandaghem) Military Cemetery, 358
Helles Memorial, 267
Hooge Crater Cemetery, 73–4, 78
Indian Memorial, Neuve Chapelle, 39, 42, 49, 182
Jerusalem Memorial, 219
Knightsbridge War Cemetery, 208
La Brique Military Cemetery No.2, 267
Lapugnoy Military Cemetery, 195
Le Touret Memorial, 55, 57, 62, 371, 431
Le Trou Aid Post Cemetery, 47
Leeds (Lawnswood) Crematorium, 367
Lijssenthoek Military Cemetery, 253, 382
Lillers Communal Cemetery, 256–7
Loos British Cemetery, 170, 172–3
Loos Memorial, 96–7, 168, 253, 265, 285, 358
Mazingarbe Communal Cemetery Extension, 269
Neuve Chapelle Memorial, 59
New Munich Trench Cemetery, 270
No Man's Cot Cemetery, 135–6
No.2 Canadian Cemetery, 156
Noeux-les-Mines Communal Cemetery, 95
Norfolk Cemetery, 160
Ploegsteert Memorial, 46, 168, 186, 253, 285
Pozieres British Cemetery, 178
Ramscapelle Road Military Cemetery, 298
Rangoon Memorial, 401

Ration Farm Military Cemetery, 132–4
RE Grave, 141–2
Royal Irish Graveyard, Laventie, 243–4
Runnymede Memorial, 363
Sanctuary Wood Cemetery, 72, 74, 78, 432
Seaforth Cemetery, 22, 33, 135
Shotley Royal Naval Cemetery, 334
St Mary's ADS Cemetery, 101
St Sever Cemetery, 218, 360
Staglieno Cemetery, Genoa, 340
Taukkyan War Cemetery, 361
Tezze British Cemetery, 366
Thiepval Memorial, 137, 168, 285, 337
Tower Hill Memorial, 274
Track A Cemetery, 136
Track X Cemetery, 135
Tyne Cot Cemetery, 12, 26, 382
VC Corner Australian Cemetery, 43–4, 47
Vermelles British Cemetery, 146
Vis-en-Artois Memorial, 315
Vlamertinghe Churchyard Memorial, 330
Vlamertinghe Military Cemetery, 280
Vlamertinghe New Military Cemetery, 424
Voormezeele Enclosure No.3, 416
Wailly Orchard Cemetery, 163
White House Cemetery, St Jean-les-Ypres, 25
Ypres (Menin Gate) Memorial, 10, 17, 77, 189, 205, 228, 278–9, 289, 298, 427–8, 432
Community of the Sacred Name, 346
Community of the Sisters of Bethany, 346
Congreve VC, Maj William, 349
Connecticut, 421
Connors VC, John, 257
Conservative Association, 407
Constantinople, 389
Contalmaison, 161
Cork, 197, 216, 230–1, 252
Cornish, Henry Pountney, 200
Cornish, Leonora Mary, 200
Cornwall, 345–7, 415
Coronation Durbar, 355
Corons de Maroc, 119
Corons de Rutoire, 108
Corville, Pte A., 150
Coseley, 200
Cotherstone, 246
Cotter VC, Pte William, 93, 143, 145, 252–7
Cour d'Avoue Farm, 51–2, 56–7, 60
Coventry, 364
Cowdenbeath, 359
Creative Journals Ltd, 405
Crete, 238
Crewkerne, 350

Crimean War, 209, 217–18, 240, 264, 290, 394, 415
Crinkle, 229
Crippen, Dr Hawley, 236
Crossgate Moor, 318
Croydon, 308
Croydon Corporation Electricty Department, 308
Crum, Maj F.M., 76
Crystal Palace, 202, 239, 312–13, 328
Cuba, 408, 425
Cuinchy, 60, 62, 79, 107, 113, 116–17, 127, 228, 249
Culford, 262
Cumberland, 247, 250
Cuneo, Terence, 414
Cuninghame, Lt Col Alexander, 219
Cuninghame VC, William, 219
Cunningham, Christina, 273
Cupar, 273
Curragh, 229, 285, 429
Currie, Brig Gen Arthur, 5, 16, 18–19, 21
Cust, Capt Sir Charles, 222, 224
Cutting, Rose, 387

D. and D.H. Porter, 326
Dacca Riots, 339
Dacoits, 311
Dahl, Roald, 396
Dairsie, 272
Dalmatia, 198
Dalrymple, 434
Dannes-Camiers, 383
Daours, 349
Darlington, 331
Dathan, Bdr Thomas, 127
Davies, 2Lt C.G., 64
Davies, Maj Gen Francis, 419
Davies, Brig Gen H.R., 168
Davies VC, John, 364
Dawson, Cpl James, 127–9, 257–61
Dawson, Mabel, 367
De Beers Diamond Mines, 348
De Chair, Sir Dudley, 304
Dean VC, Donald, 365, 414
Deedes, Lt, 25
Deep Well Boring Works, St Albans, 427
Dehli, 402, 404
Dehli Durbar, 391
Dehra Dun, 370
Delamere, Capt, 71
Deloraine, 407
Denaby, 284
Denaby Main, 284
Denbigh, 366
Deolali, 241
Department of Native Affairs, 276
Depression, 291
Deptford, 345, 349
Deptford Empire, 349
Deputy Lieutenant, 192–5, 197, 217, 264, 284, 352, 412
Derajat, 400

Index 463

Derby, 233
Derbyshire, 283, 338, 420
Desborough, Lord, 77
Deslys, Gaby, 319
Detroit, 235
Devon, 198, 208, 212, 225, 235, 282, 288, 291, 299–300, 303, 321, 339, 345, 364, 370–1, 381, 394, 402, 412
Devon and Somerset Draghounds, 156
Devonport, 199, 258, 303, 394
Dew, Ch Insp Walter, 236
Dewhurst, Capt R.H., 215
Dick, Kerr & Co, 435
Dieppe, 382
Dimmer VC, Lt John, 322
Distinguished Conduct Medal League, 405
Ditton Hill Cricket Club, 203
Dixon VC, Matthew, 207
Djebel Abiod, 333
Dobson, Pte Frederick, 369
Dominion Civil Service, 212
Dominion Line, 236
Doncaster, 284–5
Donibristle Colliery, 268
Dorchester Hotel, 223, 225
Dorset, 433
Double Crassier, 91, 94, 96, 102, 109, 120, 122, 127–8, 171, 337
Dougall VC, Eric, 207
Doughty-Wylie VC, Charles, 226
Douglas-Hamilton VC, Lt Col Angus, 90, 110, 262
Dover, Castle & Docks, 196, 230, 241, 248, 254–6, 285
Dover, Piscataquis, Maine, 252
Down, 369
Downham, 357
Dr Barnado's, 282
Drake VC, Cpl Alfred, 135–8, 266–7
Dresden, 380
Driefontein, 235
Droitwich Lunatic Asylum, 200
Drosh, 403
Droylesden, 364–5
Dublin, 197, 215, 218, 252–3, 280, 285, 371, 392
Dubs, Capt Guy, 101–102, 358
Duck's Bill, 68, 71, 80–2, 165
Duke of Connaught, 416
Duke of Kent, 411
Duke of York, 304, 314, 361, 388, 401
Dump, 92, 104–105, 114, 116–18, 120, 122, 124, 128–9
Dunchurch, 322
Dundas, Margaret, 401
Dundee & Castle, 272, 278, 380
Dunderdale, Pte W., 47
Dunfermline, 270, 272
Dunkirk, 274, 403
Dunkirk Veteran's Association, 405
Dunlop Rubber Co, 393
Dunlop, Sir Thomas, 259
Dunnikier Colliery, 268
Dunnville, 275

Dunsire VC, Pte Robert, 90, 109, 111–12, 268–9
Durham, 246, 315, 317–18, 327, 331, 421
Dusseldorf, 208
Duval, Bertha, 342–3
Dynamitiere, 95, 97–8
Dysart, 267

Earl of Athlone, 411
Earl of Cavan, 267
Earl's Court, 202
Easington, 315
East Africa, 364
East Fife, 273
East Horsley, 416
East India Association, 405
East Indies, 229, 413
East Kirk Newton, 326
East Sussex, 190, 192, 334, 340, 430
East Wemyss, 268–9
East Witton Within, Yorkshire, 262
Eastbourne, 237, 239–44, 259, 261, 340
Ecclesall, Sheffield, 366
Eclipse Stakes, 216
Economic Advisory Branch, 425–6
Economic Intelligence Division, 425
Ecuador, 264
Edgbaston, 344
Edinburgh & Castle, 269–71, 328, 368, 374, 378, 434
Edwards VC, Wilfrid, 369
Edwin Cottam & Co, 361
Egremont, 247, 250
Egypt, 84, 190, 249, 301–302, 324, 389–90, 399, 413
Egyptian Campaign, 229
Eilean Donan Castle, 195
El Alamein, 197, 413–14
El Kefr, 190
El Nahud, 282
El Teb, Battle of, 230
Elham, 252
Ellersmere Port, 259
Elliott VC, Keith, 352
Elliott-Cooper VC, Maj Neville, 143
Ellis, Sir Henry, 263
Embankment Redoubt, 106–108, 116, 323
Enniskillen, 286
Enzufzai, 210
Epsom Derby, 216
Epsom Oaks, 215
Epworth, 245, 246
Erskine VC, LCpl John, 164, 166, 270–2
Essendon, 393
Essex, 314, 347, 351–2, 425
Essex Farm, 33–4, 36
Estaires, 39, 57
Etaples, 382
Etchingham, 334
Eustace, Capt, 402
Evans VC, George, 224, 353

Evans-Thomas, VAdm Sir Hugh, 415–16
Everitt, Edith, 376
Exeter, 362, 368, 435
Eyre, Giles, 337

Falkirk, 272
Falkland, 272
Falklands War, 217
Far East PoW & Internee Fund, 405
Far Eastern PoW Association, 405
Farm Delaval, 38, 43–4
Farnborough, 201
Farningham, 429
Fastnet Race, 425
Fauquissart, 324, 332
Fauresmith, 348
Fay, Lt J.J., 174
Felixstowe, 313
Fellowship of the Services, 246
Ferme du Bois, 41, 50, 56–7, 59–60
Fermoy, 253, 255
Ferozepore, 371
Ferozeshah, 210
Ferry, Gen, 3
Festubert, 39, 66, 68, 107, 324, 397–8
Festubert, Battle of, 48–66, 185, 189, 313
Ficheux, 151–2, 162, 164, 178, 299, 363
Field Punishment No.1, 250
Fife, 268, 270, 272–3, 359, 373, 375
Figtree Hotel, Wollongong, New South Wales, 304
Filey, 233
Finchett-Maddock, Capt Bryan, 191
Finlay VC, LCpl David, 37, 39, 272–4
Finn, Lt Q.M. Thomas, 287
Firth of Forth, 409
Fisher VC, LCpl Fred, 1, 10–14, 274–80
Fisher, Archbishop Geoffrey, 396
Fisher's Hotel, Pitlochry, 275
Fleming-Sandes VC, Lt Arthur, 114–15, 119, 121, 128, 280–2
Fleurbaix, 81, 84, 278
Flintshire, 321
Foch, 27, 29, 64
Fogg, Laura, 299
Folkestone, 252, 257, 351, 370
Folkingham, 385
Foncquevillers, 138–40, 435
Fontaine-les-Croisilles, 272
Foote VC, John, 352
Ford vehicles, 103, 400
Fordyce, Lt Gen Sir John, 210
Foreign Office, 425–6
Forest Hill, 329
Forshaw VC, William, 226, 365
Forsyth, Sir Douglas, 209
Fort Darland, 294
Fort George, 265
Fort Glatz, 95–7, 100
Fort Pitt, 294
Fort Regent, 249
Fort William, Calcutta, 321, 339
Fortuin, 18–21

Fosse 7 de Bethune, 125–6, 368
Fosse 8, 105–106, 108, 112–14, 117, 123, 127, 417
Fournes, 37
Frankfurt-am-Main, 322
Fraser River, 213
Fraser, Lady Antonia, 396
Freemantle, 258
Freemasons, 206, 282, 292, 339, 361, 368
　Apollo University Lodge, 339
　Arts & Crafts Lodge, 206
　Freemasons Hall, London, 206–207
　Grand District Lodge of the Punjab, 207
　Hazara Lodge, 206
　Khartoum Lodge, 282
　Lodge of Amity, 207
　London Rifle Brigade Lodge, 207
　Mark Masons' Hall, London, 207
　Red Sea Lodge, 282
　Roscary Lodge, 292
　St James's Operative Lodge, 368
　St Mary's Caledonian Operative Lodge, 361
Freiburg, 213
French Army,
　Armies,
　　Tenth, 48, 91, 98, 117–18, 127
　Corps,
　　XXXVI, 78
　Divisions,
　　11th, 3
　　45th Algerian, 1, 4, 7–8, 11
　　58th, 79–80
　　87th Division, 7–8
　Regiments,
　　1st Tirailleurs, 8, 10
　　2nd Tirailleurs, 8
　　2nd bis Zouaves, 8
French Consular Service, 389
French, FM Sir John, 20, 23, 27, 65, 72, 108, 113, 323, 398
Fresnes Prison, Paris, 294
Frezenberg & Ridge, 16, 32, 36
Fricourt, 160–1
Fricourt German Cemetery, 161
Friern Barnet, 345–6
Friesian Islands, 363
Frisby VC, Cyril, 224
Frizeyell, Capt, 118
Frodingham, 385
Frome Newspaper Printing & Publishing Co, 192
Frome Rural District Council, 193
Frome United Breweries, 192
Fromelles, 42, 43–4, 46
Fulham, 212, 266
Fuller VC, William, 224
Fulwood Barracks, Preston, 434

Gaika War, 287
Gailes, 360
Gainsborough, 342
Gaitskell, Hugh, 396

Gallipoli, 34, 267, 302, 357, 381
Galt, Ontario, 380
Galway, 230, 371
Gardner VC, Capt Philip, 353, 365, 414
Garston, 362, 364
Gaspe Basin, 277
Geary VC, 2Lt Benjamin, 281
Geddes, Col A.D., 12–13, 23
General Electric Co, 422–3
General Post Office Telephones Department, 427
Geneva, 262–3
Geneva Convention, 398
George Norman & Co, 430
George Wall & Co, 364
German Forces,
　Army,
　　Armies,
　　　Fourth, 1
　　Corps,
　　　XXIII, 1, 5, 7, 12, 14
　　　XXVI, 1, 5, 8, 12, 14, 21
　　Divisions,
　　　39th, 34
　　　45th Reserve, 7
　　　46th Reserve, 7
　　　50th Reserve, 177–8
　　　51st Reserve, 3, 8–10, 14, 17
　　　52nd Reserve, 8–10
　　　53rd Reserve, 30
　　Brigades,
　　　2nd Ersatz, 14
　　Regiments,
　　　77th Landwehr, 154
　　　126th, 75
　　　134th Saxon, 68
　　　231st, 177
　　Other units,
　　　295 Pioneer Mining Company, 165
　　　Pioneer-Regiment 35
　German Navy,
　　Bremse, 357
　　Brummer, 357
　　U-21, 253
　　U-35, 232
　　U-46, 381
　　U-75, 332
　　U-375, 403
　　UC-25, 203
Germanic Confederation, 263–4
Germany, 208, 247, 253, 384, 424
Gestapo, 294
Gezira, 282
Ghent, 3
GHQ Line, 4, 8–10, 16–18, 20–1, 23, 26–7
Gibraltar, 219, 264, 274, 387
Gillies, Capt H.D., 436
Gillingham, Kent, 285
Ginchy, 224
Girvan, 434
Givenchy-les-le-Bassee, 48, 62–4, 69–70, 72, 107, 164–7, 236, 285, 318, 324, 397

Givenchy, Second Action of, 66–72, 185, 272
Gladstone, William, 275
Glamorgan, 290–3, 344
Glasgow, 250–1, 257, 258–9, 270–2, 360, 379, 434
Glasgow Celtic & Park, 184–5
Gledstanes, Capt, 29
Glendining's, 310, 314, 366
Glenfarg, 273
Gloucester, 311, 370
Gloucestershire, 321–2, 370–1
Godley VC, Pte Sidney, 353
Gold Coast, 263, 367, 370
Goldthorpe, 298
Gommecourt, 138–9
Goodwood Cup, 216
Goojerat, 210
Gorakhpur, 324
Gordon, Lt G.N., 71
Gorell-Barnes, Lt, 138
Goring-on-Thames, 426
Gort VC, Lord, 224, 401, 403
Gorton, 329–30
Gosport, 205, 285, 335
Gough VC, Lt Gen Hubert, 255, 395
Gough, Lt Col Hugh, 216
Gough VC, Johnnie, 395
Gourley VC, Bdr Cyril, 163, 364
Govan, 258–9
Grand Prix, 398
Grand Shaft Barracks, Dover, 256
Grant VC, John Duncan, 207
Grantham, 388, 407
Grateley, 215
Gravenstafel & Ridge, 1, 10, 13–14, 16, 17–20, 212, 289
Gray, AVM Alexander, 202
Gray's Inn, 282
Great Dunmow, 352–3
Great Western Railway, 189
Great White Horse Hotel, Ipswich, 295–6
Greece, 351
Green, Pte, 140
Green VC, Capt John, 323
Greenhithe, 379
Greenock, 381, 434
Greenwood VC, Harry, 226
Grenay, 57, 92, 96, 102, 109
Grenfell VC, Capt Francis, 77, 226
Grenfell, 2Lt Hon Gerald (Billy), 77
Grenfell, Hon Julien, 77
Grogan VC, Brig-Gen William, 371
Guardbridge, 272
Guards Chapel, 224–5, 314
Guernsey, 209, 347
Guildford, 282, 320
Guillemont, 340
Gunbar, New South Wales, 300–301, 303
Gunn, Lt K.G., 62
Gurkha Welfare Trust, 325
Gurrey, Charles, 207
Gwynedd, 191

Habbaniyah, 202
Haber, Fritz, 2–3
Hackett VC, Spr William, 164, 166–8, 283–6
Hackney, 312, 314, 393
Hague Conventions, 1
Haig, FM Sir Douglas, 37, 48, 65, 72, 92, 108–109, 116, 123, 131, 162, 168, 198, 223, 350, 384, 398, 425
Hailsham, 237, 238, 240–1, 243–5
Haines, 104, 106, 109, 118, 123, 125
Haldane, Sir Aylmer, 401
Haldane, Maj Gen J.A.L., 349
Hal Far, 202
Halifax, 407
Halifax, Nova Scotia, 383
Hall VC, CSM Frederick, 13, 16, 285–9
Hallam Street Synagogue, London, 392–3
Hallowes & Tosetti, 293
Hallowes, Geoffrey Blackwood, 294
Hallowes, Geoffrey Macleod, 293–4
Hallowes, GC Odette, 293–4
Hallowes VC, 2Lt Rupert, 85, 87–9, 290–4
Halton VC, Albert, 251
Hamble, 212
Hamilton, 188
Hamilton, Hamilton, 263
Hampshire, 201, 205, 212, 241, 249, 325, 370, 394, 403, 407, 430–1, 434
Hampshire Farm, 6, 8, 136
Hampstead, 262, 360
Hanebeek, 20–1
Hanna, First Attack on, 273
Hannescamp, 139
Hanover Square, London, 331
Hardy, Pte Thomas, 55, 57
Harebeating, 237, 240
Harefield Park, 303
Harmon, Spr, 71
Harpenden, 425
Harper, Lt R.R., 174
Harrogate, 378
Hartford, Connecticut, 421
Hartismere, 206
Hartlebury, 199
Hartley, Gen Alan, 404
Harvey VC, FMW, 297
Harvey VC, Pte Samuel, 119–20, 122, 294–7
Harvie, Georgina, 326
Hastings, 277, 382
Hatfield, 318
Haut Pommereau, 80
Haute Deule Canal, 99–100, 108
Hay, New South Wales, 300, 302–303
Hazebrouck, 235
Heath, Lt L.B., 174
Heathfield, 190–1
Heathfields Old Persons Home, Ipswich, 296
Heaton VC, William, 364
Hebuterne, 139
Hedenham, 413

Heeley, Sheffield, 366
Heffernam, 2Lt William, 371
Heidelberg, 213
Heidelberg, Melbourne, 307
Heliopolis, 301
Henriques, Basil, 390
Heritage, Capt Keith, 174, 177–8
Herne Bay & Mill, 428–9
Hersham, 314
Herstmonceux Castle, 239
Hertford, 226–9
Hertford Gas Co, 227–8
Hertfordshire, 318, 345, 425, 427
Hesdigneul, 223
Hesdin, 201
Het Sas, 12, 20, 23, 27
Hewitson VC, James, 251
Hibbard, Barry, 307
High Court of Judicature, Calcutta, 339
High Court of Judicature, Fort William, Bengal, 339
High Peak, 338
High Sherriff, 193, 214, 217
Hill 60, 4, 7, 10, 13, 28–9, 32
Hill 60, Gallipoli, 302
Hill 62, 72–3
Hill 70, 92, 95–9, 109–13, 116–18, 123, 269, 309, 327
Hill VC, Albert, 365
Hill, Lt Col F.W., 69, 236
Hill Top Ridge, 12, 22–5, 27–8
Hillsborough Barracks, Sheffield, 230
Himalayas, 230
Himley, 199
Hinges, 41
Hipswell Camp, Catterick, 341
Hitchins, Lt Col H.W.E., 25
Hobday, Cpl W., 138
Hohenzollern Redoubt & Actions of, 93, 103–105, 108, 113–16, 119–25, 127–31, 143–6, 255, 259, 281, 296, 360, 424
Hokitika, 346
Holborn, 353
Holland, 341
Holloway, London, 345
Holmes, Stkr Frederick, 253–4
Holmes, Pte Herbert, 253
Holsworthy, 364
Holyhead, 232
Holyroodhouse, 195
Holzminden, 213
Home Office, 405
Honey VC, Lewis, 237
Hong Kong, 345, 347
Honiton, 345
Honor Oak, 310
Honourable Corps of Gentlemen-at-Arms, 194
Honourable East India Company, 194
Hooge, 34, 36, 73–5, 85, 140, 292, 340, 432
Hooge, Action of, 72–8
Hope, Flintshire, 321
Horse Guards Parade, 225

Horsham, 416
Hospitals,
  Aberavon General, 292
  Austin Repatriation Hospital, Melbourne, 307
  Ballochmyle, Ayrshire, 361
  Baroness de Goldsmid, 382
  Beaulieu, Harrogate, 378
  Chelsea, London, 240
  City, West Heath, Birmingham, 422
  Craigleith, Edinburgh, 409
  Derbyshire Royal Infirmary, 234
  Edgware General, 420
  Exeter, 435
  Fort Pitt Military, Chatham, 185
  Ipswich Borough, 377, 379
  Kent & Canterbury, 290
  King Edward VII for Officers, 406
  King George's, London, 224
  Lady Astor's, Taplow, 313
  Law, Carluke, 187
  Lord Derby's, Warrington, 327
  Montreal General, 276
  Mount Joy (Dublin University VAD Auxiliary), 391
  North East Surrey, Redhill, 293
  Prince of Wales Hospital, Marylebone, 213
  Princess Alice Memorial, Eastbourne, 241
  Rotherham General, 247
  Royal Inland Hospital, Shaughnessy, Kamloops, BC, 213
  Royal Prince Alfred, Sydney, 304
  Royal Scottish National Institution, 359
  Royal Victoria, Belfast, 360
  Royal Victoria, Montreal, 384–5
  St Andrew's Memorial Cottage, 375
  St Ann's Nursing Home, Canford Cliffs, 191
  St Bartholomew's, London, 290
  St George's, London, 209
  St John's, Lewisham, 334
  St Patrick's, Malta, 302
  St Peter's, Chertsey, 314
  St Thomas's, London, 332–4, 378
  Stow Lodge, Stowmarket, 296
  Stobhill, Glasgow, 246–7
  Tindal General, Chesham, 229
  Victoria Hospital for Children, Chelsea, 334
  Winter Street Hospital, Sheffield, 365
  Workington Infirmary, 388
Houghton, Gnr Nicholas, 127
House of Lords, 368, 410
Houthulst, 4
Hove, 310
Howard, 2Lt Cecil, 311
Hughes VC, Mathew, 247, 345
Hughes VC, Pte Thomas, 271
Hull, Blythe & Co, 291
Hull, Brig Gen, 20
Hull VC, Charles, 369

Hulluch, 98–9, 101, 103–105, 108–10, 112, 127, 269, 319, 358, 371, 422
Humphreys, Gnr William, 127
Hunter VC, David, 187
Hunterian Library, Glasgow University, 261
Huron, Montreal, 380
Hurstville, New South Wales, 305
Hutchinson, Frank, 180
Hutchinson VC, James, 152, 178–80, 297–300
Hutt VC, Arthur, 364
Hutton Henry, 315
Hutton, Lt Gen Thomas, 404
Hyde, 364–5
Hyde-Cates, Capt, 57, 59
Hyde-Cates, Lt Col K.G., 402
Hyde Park, London, 271–2, 352, 356
Hyde Park, Sydney, 306–307
Hythe, 288

Ibrox Park, 250–1
Idi Amin, 365, 414
Ilkley Moor, 344
Ille et Vilaine, 194
Illinois, 287
Illustrated London News, 222
In Flanders Fields, 9
India, 192, 197, 202, 206, 208–209, 211–12, 220, 238, 241, 254, 260–2, 265, 296, 321–2, 329, 335, 338–9, 345, 350–1, 354–5, 370–1, 391, 393, 399, 401–402, 404, 406, 419, 427
Indian Army, 190, 204, 206, 260–1, 338, 362
 C-in-C India, 217
 Hyderabad Contingent, 395
 Indian Army HQ, 402
 Indian Army Reserve, 356
 Armies/Commands,
  Bengal Army, 209
  Kabul Army, 209
  Northern Command, 193
 Army Corps,
  Indian Corps, 37, 39–42, 57, 84
 Corps,
  Bengal Staff Corps, 210, 262
  Bombay Staff Corps, 210
  Corps of Guides, 209
  Indian Army Ordnance Corps, 260
  Indian Staff Corps, 211
  Indian Supply & Transport Corps, 212, 339
  Indian Medical Service, 193, 208, 400, 403
 Divisions,
  3rd (Lahore), 13, 21, 23–4, 26–7, 29, 48, 50, 82
  7th Meerut, 37, 41, 48, 50–1, 80, 82, 84
  17th Indian, 404
  19th Indian, 404
  Presidency, 210
  Sirhind, 211

Brigades,
 7th (Ferozepore), 13, 23–4, 26–7
 8th (Jullundur), 13, 23–4, 398
 9th (Sirhind), 26–9, 48, 50, 57, 60
 19th (Dehra Dun), 41, 50, 82–3
 20th (Garwhal), 41–2, 50, 80, 82
 21st (Bareilly), 37, 41–2, 82, 84
 36th Indian, 403
 43rd Indian, 400
 67th, 400
 74th, 401
 Allahabad, 210
 Bombay-Deolali, 400
 Meerut, 210
Cavalry,
 2nd Bengal European Cavalry, 262
 7th Hariana Lancers, 371
 17th Cavalry, 399–400
Infantry,
 1st Punjab Infantry, 354
 1st Regiment, Punjab Frontier Force, 354
 1/3rd Gurkhas, 324
 1/6th Gurkhas, 204
 1/9th Gurkhas, 395
 2/2nd Gurkhas, 41
 2/3rd Gurkhas, 190, 324
 2/8th Gurkhas, 82
 2/11th Sikhs, 402
 2/43rd Sikhs (Frontier Force), 55
 3/11th Sikhs, 401–403
 4/3rd Gurkhas, 190
 5th Battalion, 70th Burma Rifles, 204
 8th Bombay Native, 211
 9th Jats, 400
 11th Bombay Native, 211
 15th Ludhiana Sikhs, 48, 57, 59, 394, 397, 399, 402
 19th Punjabis, 59
 26th Bengal Native Infantry, 370
 39th Garwhal Rfls, 50, 82
 40th Pathans, 23
 41st Dogras, 41–2
 45th Sikhs, 59, 402
 47th Sikhs, 23
 55th Coke's Rifles, 13, 354–5
 56th Bengal Native Infantry, 209
 57th Wilde's Rfls, 13, 23, 25, 354–5
 58th Vaughan's Rifles, 41–2, 354
 59th Scinde Rfls, 23
 125th Napier's Rfls, 41
 129th Baluchis, 23
 Miscellaneous units,
 55 Sqn, Indian Observer Corps, 361
 Bengal Artillery, 210
 Bengal Medical Department, 208
 Bengal Medical Establishment, 209
 Directorate of Ordnance Services, 260

India Supply Commission in North America, 261
Training units,
 Royal Military College, Quetta, 395
 School of Education, Belgaum, 260
 Staff College, Quetta, 260–1, 378
 Staff School, Saugor, 400
Indian Civil Service, 339, 394, 401
Indian Mutiny, 194, 210, 264
Indian National Congress Party, 398
Indian Village, 53
Ingham, Constance, 344
Inhlobana, 412
Inkerman, Battle of, 217, 394
Innerleven, 269
International Lawn Tennis Club of Great Britain, 405
International Settlement, Shanghai, 396
Inverness, 361
Inverness-shire, 265
Ipswich, 295–6, 375, 377–9
Iraq, 202, 413
Ireland, 214, 218, 229–30, 232, 252, 280, 285, 296, 312, 315, 369–70, 386, 415, 419
Irish Land Commission, 210
Irish National Hunt, 218
Irish Turf Club, 218
Irwin, Lt Gen Sir Alastair, 375
Isle of Man, 200–201, 350
Isle of Wight, 280–1, 411
Islington, 226, 266, 407
Ismailia, 399
Italy, 203, 317, 334, 340, 343, 384
Ivanhoe, Victoria, 300
Ivel Boot Co, 342
Ivybridge, 198

Jack the Ripper, 390
Jackson VC, Pte John, 168, 176–8, 300–307
Jackson VC, Norman, 365, 414
Jacobabad, 371
Jaeger, Pte August, 3
Jaffna, 311
Jagersfontein, 348
Jamaica, 239, 347
James, Lt C.A., 71
Jamestown, 373
Japan/ese, 378, 396, 404
Jardine, Douglas, 395
J.D. Paton, Messrs, 360
J. Emsley & Co, Messrs, 342
Jebel Aulia Dam, 282
Jerrard VC, Alan, 353
Jersey, 248–9
Jerusalem, 392
Jessore, West Bengal, 338
Jesuits, 383
J.H. Gath, 407
J.H. Riley, 358
Joffre, Gen Joseph, 131
Johannesburg, 235

John Player & Sons, 344
Johnson, Pte E., 137
Johnson VC, 2Lt Frederick, 90, 98–9, 111, 308–10
Johnson, Capt S.G., 322
Joint Intelligence Committee, 425–6
Jones, Gen Sir Charles, 403
Jones VC, Lt Col H., 217
Jones VC, Lt Richard, 155–6, 158, 164, 310–11
Jordeson, 2Lt, 172
Joseph Crosfield & Sons, Messrs, 408
Joseph Randall Porter, 202
Judge, Henry, 429
Jugdispore, 264
Justerini & Brooks, 293
Justice of the Peace, 193–5, 197, 339, 379, 393, 412
Jutland, Battle of, 416

Kabul, 209, 211, 354
Kaiser Wilhelm II, 354
Kaiser Wilhelm Institute, 2–3
Kalandar, Sepoy, 354
Kamloops, 213
Kampala, 365
Kananaskis Park, Canada, 385
Kandahar, 209, 211
Karachi, 273, 322, 397
Karlsruhe, 3
Kashkar, 209
Kashmir, 209, 399
Katensa Allah, 209
Kathiawar, 211
Kattestraat, 33, 35–6
Keerselaere, 1, 7, 8, 10, 13, 15, 17–18, 212
Keith, 372–3, 375
Kelati-Ghilzai, 211
Kenny VC, Pte Henry, 90, 100–102, 312–14
Kenny, Pte James, 315
Kenny VC, Pte Thomas, 132–4, 315–18
Kensington, 210, 308, 338
Kensington, New South Wales, 303, 358
Kent, 186, 207, 212, 238, 252, 262, 281, 285, 287–8, 315, 334, 347, 370, 383, 428, 431
Kent County Constabulary, 429
Kent, Lt, 81
Kenya, 321, 365
Kenyatta, President Jomo, 365, 414
Kerr, Pte Thomas, 134
Kertch, 415
Kesgrave, 296
Keyworth, LCpl Leonard, 48, 61–3, 318–20
Khan Khor Beg, 354
Khan, Sep Azam, 354
Khartoum, 282
Khired Bey, Col, 354
Kiawah Island, South Carolina, 351
Kibbiah, 190
Kidderminster, 199, 201

Kidney Ridge, 413–14
Kiev, 389
Kilby VC, Capt Arthur, 90, 106–108, 116, 321–4
Kilby's Automatic Counter, 321
Kilkenny, 286
Kilmersdon, 194
Kimberley, 262
Kinburn, 415
King Alexander I, 380
King Edward VIII, 416
King George V, 204, 218, 221–2, 224–5, 228, 235–6, 244–6, 250–1, 256, 259, 265, 267, 269, 271–3, 278, 281, 285, 292, 296, 299, 302, 309, 311, 313, 316, 318, 323–4, 327, 332, 336, 340, 342, 349–50, 355, 358, 360, 364, 368, 371–2, 374, 379, 382, 387, 392, 398, 408, 416–17, 419, 424, 428, 430, 432, 437
King George VI, 216, 314, 416
King George VI and Queen Elizabeth Stakes, 216
King, Maj W.B.M., 10
King's/Queen's Body Guard for Scotland, 194–5, 197
King's/Queen's Body Guard of the Yeoman of the Guard, 414
King's County (Offaly), 229–30
Kinghorn, 327
Kingsbury, 420
Kingston-upon-Thames, 202, 206
Kingston, Jamaica, 347
Kingswinford, 200
Kipling, John, 101, 117
Kipling, Rudyard, 101, 117, 371
Kirk VC, James, 365
Kirkaldy, 268–9
Kirke, Capt E.W., 174
Kirkee, 260
Kitchener, FM Lord, 355
Kitcheners' Wood, 6, 8–9, 11–14, 16–21
Knightsbridge, 192–3
Knowland VC, George, 353
Kogarah, New South Wales, 304
Kohat & Pass, 190, 210
Kohima, 401
Krefeld, 213
Krupp, Bertha, 4
Krupps, 4
Kuala Lumpur, 430
Kurram Field Force, 209
Kut, 273

La Bassee, 37, 39, 79–80, 91, 103, 105, 109–10, 113, 116, 123, 127, 131, 164, 218, 313, 323
La Bassee Canal, 64, 68, 106–108, 116, 131
La Boiselle, 161
La Bombe, 39, 42, 182
La Brayelle Farm, 139
La Brique, 34, 134, 137, 232, 267
La Cliqueterie Farm, 37, 38, 41–2, 80
La Cordonnerie, 37–8

La Houssoie, 132, 316
La Quinque Rue, 48
La Russie, 38, 41
La Tourelle, 48–9
Lahore, 400, 403
Laidlaw VC, Ppr Daniel, 90, 96–7, 100, 325–8
Laing, Jane, 373
Lake Doiran, 250
Lambeth, 219, 280, 308, 370
Lanarkshire, 184, 188, 257
Lancashire, 199, 240, 247, 297, 330–1, 335, 356, 362, 364
Lancaster, 248
Landai, Tirah, 354
Lane, Lt J.B., 174, 177
Langemarck, 3, 6–9, 23, 27
Langham & Garner's, Messrs, 387
Langrish, 407
Larbert, 272
Largo, Fife, 373
Larkhill, 235–6, 277, 288–9, 381
Larkin, Reginald, 205–206
Lashkar-e-Islam, 356
Lassen VC, Anders, 257
Latimer, 262
Latvia, 395
Launceston, 345
Laventie, 244
Law Society, 426
Lawrence of Arabia, 217
Le Clercq Farm, 38
Le Havre, 204, 272
Le Rutoire, 103, 123, 125, 429
Le Touquet, 303, 313, 330, 363
League of Nations, 351
Leahy, Mick, 371
Leamington Spa, 321, 323–4
Lebong, 248
Leckhampton, 370
Lee, 334
Lee, Maj Gen Richard, 198
Leeds, 312, 340–1, 344, 367–8, 432
Leeds Police, 368
Leeds Watch Committee, 368
Leeman, Pte J.F., 47
Leggett, Arthur, 358
Leggett, Henry, 357
Leicester, 325, 361, 423, 425
Leicestershire, 325, 407
Leichardt, New South Wales, 307
Lekkerboterbeek, 9, 12
Lens, 91, 103, 108–10, 113, 123, 127
Lens Road Redoubt, 94–5, 126
L'Epinette, 23
Lesbury, 325
Leuchars, 272–4
Leven, 375
Lewes, 430
Lewisham, 280, 328, 330, 346, 353
Leyland, 240
Leytonstone, 287
Libya, 208
Lichfield, 322, 324
Lievin, 91

Ligny le Grand, 38, 41
Ligny le Petit, 38, 41
Lijssenthoek, 382
Lillers, 145, 255
Lillington, 321
Limerick, Lt, 151, 155, 232, 312
Lincoln, 318–20, 386, 418–19
Lincolnshire, 246, 320, 342, 385, 387–8, 407
Lindsey, 318
Linlithgow, 184
Linnean Society, 198
Lisbon, 308
Liskeard, 415
Litherland, 189–90
Little Swinton, 325
Liverpool & Cathedrals, 189–201, 236, 362–6, 383, 403, 408, 410
Liverpool Auto Cycle Club, 200
Liverpool, New South Wales, 302
Liverpool Produce Exchange, 363
Liverpool Provision Trade Association, 363
Lizerne, 12, 20, 23, 26–7
Lloyd-George, 65
Local Defence Volunteers, 234, 314
Locality C, 6, 10, 14–19
Lochnagar Crater, 160–2
London, 192, 202–206, 208–10, 212–13, 215, 217–18, 224–6, 252, 258, 262, 266, 269, 272, 280, 285, 287, 290–1, 296, 308–10, 312–14, 319–20, 328, 330–1, 334, 336, 338, 344–7, 349–50, 352–3, 360–1, 364, 370, 376, 378, 382, 384, 389–90, 393–4, 401, 405, 420, 425, 433, 435
London and North Western Railway, 232
London County and Westminster Bank, 362
London County Council, 320
London, Ontario, 235
London Passenger Transport Board, 426
Lone Tree, 99–103
Longstone, 434
Loos, 80, 85, 87, 255, 259, 296, 337, 424
Loos, Battle of, 90–131, 143, 180, 223, 265, 269, 309, 313, 328, 347, 360, 378–9, 429
Loos Road Redoubt, 94–6, 100
Loralai, Baluchistan, 397
Lord Ashcroft's VC Collection, Trust & Gallery, 267, 314, 323, 338, 358, 433
Lord Burghley, William Cecil, 408
Lord Cadogan, 262
Lord Carnarvon, 239
Lord Chesham, 262
Lord Lieutenant, 196, 244
Lord Methuen, 218
Lord Newlands, 186
Lord Mayo, 209
Lord Pembroke, 351
Lord Roberts, 215–16, 218
Lords cricket ground, 431

Louvencourt, 190
Loveday, Marion, 222, 224
Lowry Cole, Brig Gen Arthur, 46–7
Lowther MP, Lt Col Claude, 242–3
Lowther's Lambs, 242
Luard, Nursing Sister Katherine, 145
Lucas VC, Charles, 207
Lucas Ltd, Messrs, 422
Lucknow, 192, 229, 248–9
Lucuma batten-poollii Benoist, 199
Lummis, Canon, 296
Lumsden, Maj Henry, 209
Luton, 368, 428
Luxford, Emily Frances, 204
Lyall, 382
Lyle, Lt, 40
Lynn VC, Pte John, 13, 22, 30–1, 328–31
Lyon, Pte, 116
Lyons, Joseph Aloysius, 393
Lyons, Lt Col W.B., 173
Lys, River, 1

Macclesfield, 407
MacDonald, Capt Harold, 21–3
Macedonia, 250
MacGillvray, Margaret, 235
Mackenzie, Anna, 264
Mackintosh, Charles Rennie, 271
Madras, 208
Magars, 324
Magennis VC, James, 247, 345
Maharajah of Tikari, 397–8
Mahon, Capt, 25, 151
Mahsuds, 400
Maidenhead, 226
Maidstone, 243
Malabar Hill, 208
Maling VC, Lt George, 80–1, 85, 331–4
Malone, Sgt Reginald, 215
Malta, 202–203, 238, 265, 302, 329, 415, 429
Manchester & Cathedral, 329, 336, 341, 364–5, 391, 394
Mandalay, 311
Manhattan, 287
Manitoba, 287–9, 411
Manners-Smith VC, Jack, 399
Mansel Tin Plate Works, 291
Manvers Main, 284–5
Mariner VC, Rfn William, 48, 60–1, 116, 335–8
Marine Society, 376
Marlborough, 403
Marlborough House, London, 307
Marlesford, 262
Marne, Battle of, 313
Marquesas, 198
Marquess of Zetland, 401
Marseilles, 273, 302, 397
Marshall, Pte Ivor, 367
Martin, Lt James, 66–8, 185–7
Martin-Leake VC, Lt Arthur, 254

Martin-Leake, Francis, 253–4
Maryhill, 434
Marylebone, 406, 425
Mason, Alice, 329–30
Matthews, Sgt Charles, 315–16
Maude VC, Frederick, 257
Maufe VC, Thomas, 247, 345
Mauldslie Castle, 186
Maule, Messrs Robert & Son, 271
Mauquissart, 80–2, 324
Mauritius, 345–6
Mauser Ridge, 12–14, 22–7
May, Pte Henry, 337
Mayson VC, Tom, 251
Mazingarbe, 126, 269
McAulay VC, John, 224
McCarthy, Minnie, 410
McCrae, Maj John, 9
McCuaig, Maj D.R., 8, 10
McGibbon, Maj Gilbert, 280
McGibbon, Sub Lt Gordon, 280
McGibbon, Lt Robert, 280
McGibbon, Col Roy, 280
McKechnie, Elsie, 392
McLaren, Catherine Mary Theresa, 190
McLaren, Messrs W.J. & Co, 270
McLeod, Sgt, 12
McNair VC, Lt Eric, 140–2, 338–40
McNess VC, Fred, 224, 369
McRae, Lt Col John, 383
Meaulte, 160, 246
Medical Research Council, 426
Mediterranean, 232, 413
Meekosha, Pte Samuel, 135–7, 247, 340–5
Mehtar of Chitral, 403
Meiktila, 204
Mein MC, Lt, 25
Mekometer, 288
Melbourne, 303–307, 391, 393, 410
Melbourne Metropolitan Gas Co, 391
Mellish, Rev'd Edward, 147, 149–50, 345–53
Mellish, Richard, 347
Mellor Mill, Warth Fold, 298–9
Melton Mowbray, 325
Menin & Road, 85–6, 140–2
Mental Health Research Fund, 426
Merchant Navy, 274, 332, 376, 409–10
Merris, 235
Merriwa, 300, 303–304, 307
Mersah Matruh, 399
Mesopotamia, 204, 263, 273, 338, 362, 392, 395, 401
Messines, 147
Methil, 268–9
Methilhill, 268–9
Metropolitan Asylums Board, 329
Metropolitan Police, 236
Metropolitan Water, Sewerage & Drainage Board, Sydney, 305
Mexborough, 284–5
MI6, 396
Michael Belcher Ltd, 205
Michigan, 235

Middle East, 395, 413
Middle Temple, 338
Middlesex, 187, 190–1, 201, 291, 303, 345, 370
Middleton, 214
Middleton Tyas, 331
Midland Hosiery Mills, 361
Midlothian, 269
Midnapur, 210
Midsomer Norton, 219–21, 224, 226
Miers VC, Anthony, 365, 414
Mile End Old Town, 266
Millbank, 334
Minister of Pensions, 267
Ministry of Agriculture, 352
Ministry of Economic Warfare, 426
Ministry of Labour & National Service, 246, 331
Ministry of Munitions, 361
Ministry of Pensions & National Service, 405
Mir Dast VC, Jemadar, 13, 22, 25–6, 354–6
Mir Mast, Jemadar, 354
Mission of Help to India, 351
Mitchell, Sgt J.L., 177
Moascar Garrison, 302
Moated Grange (Ferme de Lestre), 82
Modder River, 218, 235
Mohammad Abid (Abidin), 354
Mohmand Field Force & Blockade, 354, 399–400, 402
Molyneux VC, John, 364
Monghyr, West Bengal, 338
Monmouthshire, 290, 344, 358
Monro, Gen, 56
Montdidier, 383
Monte Creek, 213
Montego Bay, 347
Montevideo, 263
Montreal, 236, 275–6, 278–9, 380, 383–5, 410
Montreal Amateur Athletic Association, 277
Montreux, 213, 282
Monro, Sir Charles, 400
Montrose, 373
Moody, Pte Frank, 317
Mooltan, 210
Moonee Ponds, Melbourne, 393
Moorsleede, 322
Morgan & Co, 338
Morland, 2Lt, 64
Morocco, 198
Morris, Ivy, 304
Morteldje, 134–5
Motion, Andrew, 207
Mound, 147
Mount Forest, 234–7
Mount Scrimger, 385
Mountain VC, Albert, 369
Mountbatten, Lord Louis, 378
Mouse (Shell) Trap Farm, 6, 8–11, 20–3, 30, 32, 34–6, 135, 381

Moyney VC, John, 224
Moynffopore, 321
Moynihan VC, Andrew, 365
Mozambique, 396
Muir of Ord, 265
Murmansk, 332
Museums,
    Army Medical Services, 334
    Bedfordshire & Hertfordshire Regiment, 229, 428
    Black Watch, 274
    Black Watch of Canada, 278–80
    Canadian War Museum, 279, 289, 385
    Citadel, Quebec, 235
    Durham Light Infantry, 317
    Duke of Edinburgh's Royal Regiment, 417
    East Surrey Regiment, 320
    Guards, 226
    Gurkha, 325
    Hertfordshire Regiment, 229
    Highlanders, 265, 361
    Imperial War, 202, 267, 314, 323, 358, 406, 433
    King's Own (Royal Lancaster) Regiment, 251
    King's Regiment, 366
    Lancashire Fusiliers, 331
    Liverpool Life, 366
    Lord Strathcona's Horse, 297
    Middlesex Regiment, 292
    Museum of Lancashire, 437
    National Army, 199, 256, 292
    National War Museum of Scotland, 187, 328
    Northamptonshire Regiment, 372
    Prince of Wales's Own Regiment, York, 247
    Queen's Own Highlanders, 265
    Queen's Royal Surrey Regiment, 282, 320
    Rifles (Berkshire & Wiltshire), 417
    Royal Artillery, 369
    Royal Engineers, 286
    Royal Fusiliers, 353
    Royal Green Jackets (Rifles), 207, 417
    Royal Leicestershire Regiment, 325
    Royal Scots, 269
    Royal Sussex Regiment, 244, 340, 430
    Royal Warwickshire, Regiment 423
    Royal Welch Fusiliers, 191
    St Catherine's, Ontario, 280
    Sherwood Foresters, 420
    Staffordshire Regiment, 324
    Suffolk Regiment, 379
    Surrey Infantry, 320
    York & Lancaster Regiment, 234
Mytchett, 334

Nairobi, 364
Nalder Bros, 308
Napier, Sir Charles, 210

Napier VC, William, 247, 345
Natal, 200
National Coal Board, 426
National Memorial Arboretum, 207, 300, 334, 353, 365, 420
National Telephone Co, 308
Nautilus Steam Shipping Co Ltd, 332
Naxton, Michael, 358
Neagle, Anna, 294
Neame VC, Lt Philip, 401
Nepal, 209, 324
Netheravon, 381
Netherlands, 384
Neuve Chapelle, 2, 23, 37–9, 49, 59, 80–1, 84, 313, 324, 354–5, 391, 398, 431
New Brighton, 200
New Guinea, 391
New South Wales, 300–301, 304–305, 307, 390
New Westminster, 212
New York, 380
New Zealand, 198, 346, 370
New Zealand Forces,
    2nd New Zealand Contingent, 370
    New Zealand Mounted Rifles, 370
Newbury, 412, 417
Newcastle-upon-Tyne, 161, 192–3, 246, 291, 316, 421
Newman, LCpl, 145
Newmarket, 215–16, 356
Newton Abbott, 225, 299
Newton, Helen, 425
Newton, Isaac, 408
Niagara-on-the-Lake, 275
Nichol, Rev'd C.B., 409
Nicholl, Margaret, 259
Nicholls VC, Harry, 234
Nigalpani, Palpa Distrcit, Nepal, 324–5
Nigeria, 198, 208
Nigg, Ross-shire, 374
Nile Expedition 1898, 389
Nobel Prize, 3
Noble Auctions, 307
Noel Club, 349
Noeux-les-Mines, 319
Norfolk, 205, 356, 413
Normanby, 234–5
Norsworthy, Maj E.C., 8, 12
North Africa, 343, 350
North Russian Expeditionary Force, 198, 395
North West Frontier, 190, 209, 212, 354, 378, 395, 399, 403
North West Persia, 395
North West Rebellion, 276
North West Territories, 276
Northampton, 367
Northern Queensland, 187
Northumberland, 291, 325–7
Norton, LAC Tom, 367
Norton Hill Colliery, 219–22
Norway, 395
Norwood, 405
Norwood Green, 191

Norwood VC, Lt John, 339
Not Forgotten Association, 405
Nottingham & Castle, 229, 231–4, 283–5, 297, 343, 419–20, 423–6
Nottinghamshire, 226, 285, 294–5, 297, 408–409, 415, 420, 426
Nugent, Brig Gen O., 78
Nugent, Mary Ann, 186

Oakdale, 344
Oaks, 216
Obstetric Society, 290
Odette, 294
Ogg, Pte Archibald, 166
Old Bill, 371
Old Comrades Association, 207
Old Contemptibles Association, 205, 369
Old Swinford, 199
Old Vic Theatre, London, 319
O'Leary VC, LCpl Michael, 107, 116, 225
Olympic Games, 378, 396
Ontario, 213–14, 234–7, 274–5, 279, 289, 297, 380, 385
Openshaw, 329
Orange Free State, 238, 288, 348
Order of Rechabites, 319, 355
Orders, Decorations & Medals,
    1914 Star, 189, 207, 226, 229, 234, 236, 272, 274, 282, 297, 314, 323, 372, 388, 406, 420, 428, 430, 437
    1914/15 Star, 187, 191, 214, 218, 247, 251, 256, 261, 265, 267, 269, 279–80, 285, 289, 292, 300, 307, 311, 317, 320, 325, 328, 334, 337, 340, 345, 353, 356, 358, 361, 366, 369, 375, 379, 385, 394, 411, 417, 423, 426, 432
    1939-45 Star, 406
    American Medal of Freedom, 426–7
    Army Long Service & Good Conduct Medal, 388
    Australia Service Medal, 307
    British Empire Medal, 204, 236
    British War Medal 1914-20, 187, 191, 199, 202, 207, 214, 218, 226, 229, 234, 244, 247, 251, 256, 261, 265, 267, 269, 272, 274, 279–80, 282, 285, 289, 292, 297, 300, 307, 311, 314, 317, 320, 323, 325, 328, 331, 334, 337, 340, 345, 356, 358, 361, 366, 369, 372, 375, 379, 385, 388, 394, 406, 411, 417, 420, 423, 426, 428, 430, 432, 437
    Burma Star, 406
    Canadian Forces Decoration, 237
    Canadian Memorial Cross, 278–9
    Croix de Guerre (France), 102, 194, 216, 327–8, 394–5, 422–3, 427
    Defence Medal 1939-45, 261, 314, 328, 345, 361, 366, 379, 406, 420, 425, 427
    Dehli Durbar Medal 1911, 394
    Distinguished Conduct Medal, 47, 71, 125, 134, 137–8, 140, 155, 159, 173, 178–9, 233, 255, 302–303, 330–1, 337, 342, 348, 395
    Distinguished Service Order, 46, 78, 197, 206, 215, 218–19, 294, 305, 323, 332, 349, 378–9, 392, 395, 414, 416
    Egypt & Sudan Medal 1882-89, 231, 265, 412
    General Service Medal 1918-62, 406, 413
    George Cross, 293–4
    Greek Medal of Military Merit, 395
    Greek War Cross, 395
    India General Service Medal 1908-35, 356, 406
    India Medal 1895-1902, 356
    Indian Distinguished Service Medal, 59, 354
    Indian Order of Merit, 26, 59, 356
    Iron Cross, 354
    Khedive's Sudan Medal, 231, 265, 412
    King George V Jubilee Medal 1935, 261, 325, 406
    King George VI Coronation Medal 1937, 187, 191, 199, 207, 214, 218, 226, 229, 234, 236, 247, 251, 261, 282, 297, 300, 307, 314, 317, 325, 328, 345, 353, 355, 361, 366, 379, 388, 394, 406, 411, 420, 423, 427
    King's South Africa Medal, 220, 238
    Legion d'Honneur (France), 46, 294, 297
    Mentioned in Despatches, 102, 134, 192–3, 197–9, 212, 215–16, 218, 235, 292, 323, 328, 338, 350, 353, 377, 384, 390, 395, 398, 400–403, 406, 416, 425–6, 431
    Mercantile Marine Medal, 411
    Military Cross, 77, 102, 143, 173, 179, 191, 193, 197–9, 202, 206, 215, 233, 243, 275, 279, 292, 322–4, 350–1, 378–9, 395, 400–401, 403, 406, 412, 414, 431
    Military Medal, 36, 134, 155, 159, 168, 173, 179, 245
    Order of British India, 356
    Order of St George (Russia), 190–2, 232, 234, 246–7, 297, 319–20, 330–1, 356, 391, 398–9, 406, 408, 411
    Order of St John of Jerusalem, 195, 280
    Order of St Michael & St George, 215, 217, 264, 390
    Order of the Bath, 196, 198, 202, 210, 217, 349, 378–9, 394, 403, 414–16
    Order of the British Empire, 196–7, 215, 227, 259, 280, 293–4, 338, 377–9, 390, 395–6, 403, 414
    Order of the Crown (Belgium), 416
    Order of the Holy Sepulchre (Vatican), 197
    Order of the Nile, 282
    Queen Elizabeth II Coronation Medal 1953, 187, 191–2, 199, 207, 214, 229, 247, 251, 261, 282, 297, 300, 307, 314, 325, 353, 361, 366, 388, 406, 411, 427
    Queen Elizabeth II Silver Jubilee Medal 1977, 314, 406, 427
    Queen's South Africa Medal, 220, 236, 238, 353, 386
    Royal Red Cross, 145, 332–3
    Royal Victorian Order, 216, 264, 414, 416
    Sea Gallantry Medal, 232
    Star of India, 209
    Victory Medal 1914-19, 187, 191–2, 199, 202, 207, 214, 218, 226, 229, 234, 236, 244, 247, 251, 256, 261, 265, 267, 269, 272, 274, 279–80, 282, 285, 289, 292, 297, 300, 304, 307, 311, 314, 317, 320, 323, 325, 328, 331, 334, 337, 340, 345, 353, 356, 358, 361, 366, 369, 372, 375, 379, 385, 388, 394, 406, 411, 417, 420, 423, 426, 428, 430, 432, 437
    Volunteer Long Service Medal, 375
    War Medal 1939-45, 207, 261, 307, 345, 366, 388, 406, 427
Orfordness, 203
Orleans, 397
Ormsby, Col, 83
Osama Bin Laden, 356
Osmotherley, 247
Otterford, 188
Ottawa, 279, 289, 384
Ottoman Empire, 354
Owen, CSM C., 71
Oxford, 217, 262, 394, 425
Oxford and St George Club, 390
Oxford County, 234, 236
Oxfordshire, 394, 426

Paardeberg, 235
Pacific, 198
Paddington, 208, 262, 394
Paddington, New South Wales, 300, 3[
Paget's Disease, 384
Pakistan, 261, 354, 356
Pakistani Army,
    10th Battalion, Frontier Force Regiment, 354
Palestine, 190, 197, 324, 351, 395
Palladium Theatre, Peasedown, 223
Palpa Distrcit, Nepal, 324
Panama & Canal, 420, 425
Pancras, 420, 425
Panzers, 333
Paris, 294, 378, 389, 401
Park Head Inn, Egremont, 250
Parkes, LCpl, 10
Parkinson Cowan Ltd, 426

Parkinson, Cpl Edgar, 330
Parkside Mills, West Bowling, 342
Parmenter, Pte S., 150
Parr, RSM Frank, 233
Parr's Bank, 362
Parsons Barracks, Aldershot, 205
Parsonstown, 229
Partick, 259
Passchendaele, 198
Pathans, 354, 402
Pathhead, 268–9
Pathological Society, 290
Pattison VC, John, 353
Paulton, 219
Payne, Cpl, 16
Peachment VC, Pte George, 90, 100–102, 356–8
Pearless DCM, Sgt Hugh, 17
Penarth, 344
Peninsular and Oriental Steam Navigation Co, 203
Peninsular Barracks, Winchester, 336
Pennington, 247
Pensions Appeal Tribunal, 282, 339
People's Palace, Melbourne, 304
Percival, Arthur, 401
Percy VC, Henry, 217
Persia, 198, 263
Persian Gulf, 263
Perth, 274
Perth, Western Australia, 258
Perthshire, 274
Peru, 408, 425
Peshawar, 260, 356, 399, 402
Peterson, Oberst, 3
Pettigrew & Stephens, 271–2
Philadelphia, 410
Pickworth, 385, 387
Pietre, Action of, 80–5
Pietre, Moulin du, 80–1, 84–5
Piggott, Lester, 216
Pilkem & Ridge, 1, 8–9, 11–12
Pimlico, 406
Pinney, Maj Gen R.J., 272
Pitlochry, 274–5
Pitt, Catherine, 268
Poegsteert, 180, 204
Plumer, Gen Sir Herbert, 1, 18, 20–1, 27–9, 225, 342
Plymouth, 212, 235, 250–1, 277, 288, 381, 419
Plymouth St Andrew, 208
Plympton, 412
Poelcapelle, 3–4, 6, 8–12, 18
Poet Laureate, 207
Pokhara, Kaski, Nepal, 325
Poland, 5, 240, 340–1
Pollock, Maj Gen F.R., 209
Pollock, George, 359
Pollock VC, Cpl James, 114–16, 128, 259, 359–61
Pont a Vendin, 118
Pont Moreau, 39, 41, 52
Pontefract, 386

Pontypool, 291
Pontypridd, 344
Pooley, Spr H., 167
Poor Law, 328–9
Pope, 197
Poperinghe, 4, 78, 137, 225, 432–3
Port Arthur, Neuve Chapelle, 48–9
Port of London Authority, 267
Port Said, 306, 392
Port Vale, 226
Port Talbot, 290–3
Porter & Co, Messrs, 360
Portishead, 321
Portrush, 371
Portsmouth, 241, 285, 387
Portugal, 425
Portuguese Cemetery, Neuve Chapelle, 39, 41–2, 49, 182
Portuma, 230
Postmaster-General, 267
Potijze, 20
Potter, Pte Charles, 267
Poulter VC, Arthur, 369
Poulton-Palmer, Ronnie, 396
Prees Heath, 190
Prescot, 364
Preston, 368, 433–7
Preston North End, 435
Pretoria, 262, 370
Price, Lily, 422
Prince of Wales, 224–5, 369, 379
Princes Road, 53
Princess Royal, 207, 214, 237, 279, 385
Privy Council/Counsellor, 267, 405, 415
Procter VC, Pte Arthur, 152, 162, 164, 352, 362–6, 414
Procter, Cecil, 363
Prowse, Brig Gen, 33–4
Pryce VC, Thomas, 226
Puits bis 14, 92, 95, 99–100, 110–11, 117, 123
Punjab, 206, 209, 400
Punjab Campaign, 210
Punjab War, 194
Putney, 309
Puzzo Co, 370

Qantas, 347
Quadrilateral, 49, 53, 56–7
Qu'Appelle, 276
Quarries, 105, 112–13, 115, 117, 120, 122–3, 127–8
Quebec, 235–7, 275, 277, 379, 385
Queen Elizabeth I, 408
Queen Elizabeth II, 192, 216, 416
Queen Mary, 185, 296, 364
Queen Victoria, 415
Queen Victoria Building, Sydney, 307
Queen's County, 370
Queensland, 347
Queenstown, 232, 415
Queripel VC, Lionel, 207
Querrieu, 363

Quetta, 260, 371, 403
Quito, 264

Racecourse Betting Control Board, 187
Radcliffe, 297
Raillencourt, 275
Railway Wood, 74, 140–1
Ramsay, Archbishop Michael, 396
Ramsgate, 382
Rana VC, Rfn Karanbahadur, 190–1, 324
Randle VC, John, 396
Randwick, New South Wales, 390
Rangoon, 404
Rannie Pit, 268
Ransomes, Sims & Jeffries Ltd, 377, 379
Rathbone, Basil, 396
Rathlin, 381
Ravensbruck Concentration Camp, 294
Rawalpindi, 241, 402
Rawlinson, Lord, 401
Raynes, LCpl Francis, 366
Raynes VC, Sgt John, 125–6, 344, 366–9
Raynes, Kenneth, 367
Raynes, Tom, 367–8
Read VC, Capt Anketell, 90, 101–102, 369–72
Read, Beresford, 370
Read, Hugh, 370
Reading, 191, 411
Rechabites Cricket Club, Lincoln, 318
Red Army, 294
Red Cross, 363, 377
Red Dragon Crater, 69, 165–7
Red Sea Province, 282
Redan, 240
Redhill, 290, 293
Reed, Pte G., 150
Rees, Charlotte Muriel, 212
Regan, Pte, 158
Reid VC, Bill, 365, 414
Relay Automatic Telephone Co, 308–309
Remy Siding, 382
Renfrewshire, 434
Reninghelst, 330
Returned British PoW Association, 405
Returned Services League, 307
Richards, Bdsm William, 253
Richardson VC, Arthur, 364
Richebourg l'Avoue, 48–9, 59, 69, 165, 180, 243, 397–8
Riddell, Brig Gen James, 26
Riga, 395
Rigley's Wagon Works, 419
Rio de Janeiro, 263
Rio Tinto Zinc, 291
Ripley VC, Cpl John, 37, 39–41, 52, 372–5
Ripley, Joseph, 373
Ripon, 342
River Wear Watch, 233
Riviere, 151–2, 154

Robert Byass & Co, 290–2
Robertson, Lt Gen Sir William, 27
Robins, Pte, 150
Robinson, Pte A., 177
Robinson, Capt F.W., 71
Robinson, Capt Harold, 244
Robinson VC, William, 396
Rochester, 294
Rock, Pte P., 172
Rocky Mountains, 385
Rode, 192–3
Roeux, 373
Rogerson, Pte, 16
Rome, 384
Rooke, Sgt, 24–5
Roorkee, 288
Rosemount, Montreal, 410
Rosie Pit, 268
Ross, Gen, 213
Ross, Lt J.G., 10–13, 279
Ross & Cromarty, 184, 264
Ross-shire, 265, 374
Rotherham, 234, 246–7, 318, 360
Rotherhithe, 310
Rothsay, 192
Rouen, 218, 299, 435
Rouge Bancs, 37–8, 42, 387, 419
Rouge de Bout, 45
Roulers, 212
Roussillon Barracks, Chichester, 244, 340, 430
Rowe, LCpl, 36
Rowlands, Ellen, 409
Roy, Maj Gen William, 188
Royal Aero Club, 371
Royal Air Force, 202, 343, 363, 365, 367, 377, 416
 86 Sqn, 363
 101 Sqn, 416
 Medical Branch, 350
 RAF Halton, 377
 RAF Manston, 202
 RAF North Coates, 363
 RAF North Weald, 361
 RAF Uxbridge, 201
 RAF Volunteer Reserve, 270, 301, 350, 431
 Royal Auxiliary Air Force, 431
  Secretarial Branch, 431
  Women's Auxiliary Air Force, 252
Royal Antediluvian Order of Buffaloes, 292
Royal Arsenal, 409
Royal Canadian Legion, 237
Royal Canadian Military Institute, 213–14
Royal Central Asian Society, 405
Royal College of Physicians, 426
Royal Company of Archers, 194–5, 197
Royal Exhibition Building, Melbourne, 303–304
Royal Hotel, Pitlochry, 275
Royal Humane Society, 198, 415, 426
Royal Irish Constabulary, 371
Royal Navy & Royal Marines, 202, 226, 236, 252–3, 258, 263, 266, 280, 291,
 334, 342, 373, 376, 387–8, 395, 401, 413
 1st Cruiser Squadron, 413
 4th Cruiser Squadron, 413
 Admiralty, 415
 China Station, 415
 Fleet Air Arm, 202
 HMHS *Assaye*, 301–302
 HMHS *Essequibo*, 238, 301–302
 HMHS *Jan Breydel*, 382
 HMHS *St Patrick*, 302
 HMS *Adventure*, 267
 HMS *Ajax*, 381
 HMS *Argus*, 227
 HMS *Barham*, 415
 HMS *Blanche*, 416
 HMS *Boscawen*, 376
 HMS *Brilliant*, 429
 HMS *Cairo*, 413
 HMS *Cardiff*, 227
 HMS *Caroline*, 416
 HMS *Centaur*, 227
 HMS *Circassia*, 377
 HMS *Coventry*, 227
 HMS *Crescent*, 226
 HMS *Cressy*, 226
 HMS *Dido*, 227
 HMS *Diligence*, 357
 HMS *Dreadnought*, 226
 HMS *Duke of Wellington*, 267
 HMS *Edgar*, 415
 HMS *Erebus*, 413
 HMS *Exmouth*, 226
 HMS *Firequeen*, 226
 HMS *Ganges*, 334, 377
 HMS *Glory*, 226
 HMS *Highflyer*, 415
 HMS *Impregnable*, 226, 357
 HMS *Iphigenia*, 226
 HMS *Jumna*, 230
 HMS *Kempenfelt*, 376
 HMS *King Alfred*, 357
 HMS *Lion*, 226
 HMS *London*, 413
 HMS *Lurcher*, 373
 HMS *Maine*, 226
 HMS *Malaya*, 416
 HMS *Mimosa*, 413
 HMS *New Zealand*, 227
 HMS *Pandora*, 226
 HMS *Pathfinder*, 253–4
 HMS *Pembroke I*, 357, 376
 HMS *Phoenix*, 416
 HMS *Pioneer*, 226
 HMS *President*, 227
 HMS *Princess Royal*, 415
 HMS *Psyche*, 226
 HMS *Queen Elizabeth*, 227
 HMS *Radstock*, 413
 HMS *Rival*, 250
 HMS *Royal Albert*, 415
 HMS *Sanspareil*, 415
 HMS *Serapis*, 229
 HMS *Swiftsure*, 227
 HMS *Trafalgar*, 376
 HMS *Valiant*, 416
 HMS *Vernon*, 376
 HMS *Victory*, 226–7
 HMS *Vivid I*, 258
 HMS *Warspite*, 376, 379
 HMS *Wellesley*, 266
 HMS *Zealandia*, 226–7, 415
 HMS *Zest*, 387
 HMT *Rewa*, 248, 250
 HMT *Kenilworth Castle*, 249–50
 HMTS *Malaya*, 404
 HMTS *Plassy*, 396–7
 HMY *Victoria and Albert*, 416
 Malta Dockyard, 415
 Minesweeper *Adrian*, 203
 Naval Brigade, 415
 Royal Naval College, Dartmouth, 415
 Royal Naval Reserve, 332
Royal Observer Corps, 361
Royal Show, 379
Royal Society of St George, 213
Royal Ulster Constabulary, 371
Royal Victoria Patriotic Building, 302
Roye, 382
Rue de Cailloux, 53
Rue d'Ouvert, 57, 68
Rue du Bois, 37–9, 48, 50, 52, 57, 59, 182, 273–4, 408
Rue Petillon, 46
Rugby, 215, 322, 364
Runnymede, 347
Rushmoor Camp, 431
Russell VC, J.F., 340
Russia, 1, 2, 332, 389, 398, 411
Russian Imperial Cavalry, 340
Russo-Japanese War, 340
Rutland, 334
Ryde, 280–1

Saffron Waldon, 347
Saighton Camp, Chester, 349
Sailly-sur-la-Lys, 42–3, 419
Salem, Co Wicklow, 370
Salford, 335–7
Salisbury, 262, 351, 417
Salisbury, Pte John, 371
Salisbury Plain, 212, 277, 289, 381
Salonika, 249–50, 252, 395
Salvation Army, 296
Sancourt, 275
Sanctuary Wood, 78, 85–6, 88–9, 140, 292
Sanders VC, George, 369
Sandgate, 252, 255–7
Sandra, 211
Saskatchewan, 239, 276
Saunders VC, Sgt Arthur, 90, 112–13, 375–9
Sayers, Pte J., 137
Scarborough, 267
Scarborough, Toronto, 213
Schofield VC, Harry, 365
Schools,
 Abraham Hill's Trust, 258–60

Index

Allcyn's, London, 347
Alloa Academy, 258
Bank Top Sunday, 298
Bathgate Academy, Dunfermline, 270
Ben Jonson County Council, 267
Berner Street Board, London, 390
Berwick National, 326
Bilton Grange Prep, Dunchurch, 322
Bury Technical, 358
California, Ipswich, 376
Central Foundation, London, 347
Charterhouse, 339
Christ Church, Forest Hill, 329
Christ's Hospital, Horsham, 200
Clifton College, 212
Conyngham House, Ramsgate, 291
Copthorne, 281
Cowbridge Road, Hertford, 227
Crawforddyke Primary, Carluke, 188
Crwys Road Board, Cardiff, 189
Dartmouth Street, Aston, 422
Dragon Prep, Oxford, 396, 405
Dulwich College & Prep, 281, 310–11
Dunfermline High, 271–2
Dunnville, 276
Durham Johnson Comprehensive, 318
Epsom College, 290
Epworth CofE, 246
Eton College, 197, 199, 217
Folkestone RC, 253
Forest Park Public, Ontario, 237
Forgan, 273
Foster's Naval Preparatory, 264
Frederick Campbell Elementary, Ontario, 237
Gauldry, 273
Glenfarg, 273
Glengarth Prep, Cheltenham, 371
Guernsey Ladies College, 347
Haileybury, 291, 293, 372
Hailsham Board, 241
Harry Gosling Primary, London, 390
Heeley Church, Sheffield, 366
Hereward Remand Home, 388
Hoath, Herne Bay, 429
Jerusalem College, Guernsey, 347
Keyworth Primary, Southwark, 320
King Charles I Comprehensive School, 201
King Edward VI Five Ways, 407
King Edward VII Grammar, 347
King's, Canterbury, 281, 290
King's, Grantham, 407–408
Lesbury, 326
Marlborough College, 431–2, 434
Mexborough Secondary, 284
Midsomer Norton CofE Infant & Primary, 222
Montreal High, 380–1
Mount Forest, 234

Mr Sylvester's, Godalming, 339
Municipal Technical, Lincoln, 318–19
National, Ulverston, 248
Newton, Haceby, 387
Niagara Public, 276
North Surrey District, Anerley, 328–9
Nuneaton, 347
Oatlands College, Harrogate, 332
Oundle, 424–5
Parkhills United Methodist Church, Bury, 358
Parkside Prep, East Horsley, 416
Pathhead Public, Kirkaldy, 268
Port Sunlight, 362–3
Queen Elizabeth Grammar School, Hartlebury, 200–201
Radcliffe Hall Parish Church, 298
Redhill Reformatory, 290
Repton, 396, 405
Rose Hill, Banstead, 431–2
Rosemary Lane Wesleyan, Lincoln, 318
Royal Technical College, Glasgow, 258
Rugby, 321, 431
St Ann's Royal Asylum, 290
St Athanasius RC, Carluke, 184
St Chad's Junior, Bury, 358
St Dunstan's College, Catford, 308–309
St Felix for Girls, Southwold, 351
St John's, Midsomer Norton, 226
St John's Certified Industrial, Walthamstow, 313
St John's CofE Primary, Ipswich, 376
St Joseph's RC, Bradford, 342
St Laurence Parochial, Chorley, 335
St Leonard's for Girls, St Andrew's, 375
St Mark's College, Chelsea, 299
St Marylebone, Southall, 303
St Mary's Catholic, Nottingham, 232
St Mary's CofE, Bootle, 362
St Mary's RC, Maryhill, 434
St Mary's RC, Wingate, 315
St Peter-at-Gowts, Lincoln, 419
Shrewsbury, 431
Skerry's College, Liverpool, 200
Stella Maris RC, Folkestone, 257
Sunnyside Primary, Alloa, 258
Tiffin Boy's, 202–204
Tillycoultry Public, 360
Tonbridge, 347
United Services College, 371–2
Uppingham, 332–4
Victoria Cross Public, Ontario, 237
Wellington College, 416–17
Westmount Academy, Montreal, 276
Westmount High, Montreal, 279
Winchester College, 322
Wycombe Abbey, 350
Scrimger VC, Capt Francis, 13, 15, 21–3, 379–85

Sebastopol, 13–14, 240, 264, 394
Second World War, 215, 225, 228, 247, 274, 280, 282, 293, 305, 314, 317, 334, 342–4, 352, 364–5, 367, 377, 388, 395, 399, 420, 425, 431
Secunderabad, 404
Sefton Park, 201
Senussi Campaign, 399
Shaftesbury Avenue Mine, 167, 285
Shagi Landi Kyan, Tehsil, Peshawar, India, 356
Shanghai, 396
Shanghai Municipal Police, 395
Shankland VC, Robert, 289
Sharpe, Arthur, 386
Sharpe VC, Cpl Charles, 37, 43, 46–7, 385–8
Sharpe, John, 388
Shaughnessy, 213
Sheaf View Hotel, Sheffield, 366–7
Sheffield & Cathedral, 230, 365–7
Shelley Farm, 147
Shildrick, Maj, 170
Shipley, 416
Ships,
 Eldorado, 311
 MV *Walmer Castle*, 274
 RMS *Duchess of York*, 410
 RMS *Orcades*, 306–7
 SS *Alaunia*, 277
 SS *Andania*, 381
 SS *Alberta*, 236
 SS *Archimedes*, 289
 SS *Baltic*, 383
 SS *Benmacdhui*, 289
 SS *Ben of Airlie*, 289
 SS *Cardiganshire*, 212
 SS *Cawdor Castle*, 221, 223
 SS *Chyebassa*, 203–4
 SS *City of Marseilles*, 203
 SS *City of Venice*, 403
 SS *Franconia*, 288
 SS *Gloucester Castle*, 239
 SS *Idaho*, 347
 SS *Kalimba*, 409
 SS *Laurentic*, 235–6
 SS *Leasowe Castle*, 219
 SS *Melita*, 239
 SS *Minneapolis*, 232
 SS *Minnedosa*, 409–10
 SS *Montrose*, 236
 SS *Morton Bay*, 187–8
 SS *Novian*, 278
 SS *Orsova*, 393
 SS *Osterley*, 258
 SS *Palm Beach*, 332
 SS *Virginian*, 212
 SS *Volturno*, 232
 SS *Waiwera*, 370
 TS *Exmouth*, 329
 TSS *Slieve Bawn*, 232
 Warrior, 210
Shipster, Lt, 25
Shoreditch, 312
Shoreham-on-Sea, 239

Shoresdean, 327
Shorncliffe, 254, 285, 383
Shrewsbury, 363
Shropshire, 190
Shute, Nevil, 396
Sialkot, 397
Sibley, A.B. George, 387
Sicily, 334
Silver War Badge, 135, 205, 232, 368
Silver Street Cricket Club, Lincoln, 318
Silverwood Colliery, Rotherham, 246
Simla, 229–30, 404
Simm, Ellen, 250
Sims, Lt T.C., 71
Sind Campaign, 194
Sing, Subadar Bhim, 83
Singapore, 241, 378, 401
Singh, Sepoy Fateh, 59
Singh, Sepoy Ganda, 59
Singh, Sepoy Harnam, 58–9, 397
Singh, Sepoy Ishar, 59
Singh, Sepoy Lal, 58
Singh, Havildar Mangal, 26
Singh, LNaik Mangal, 58–9
Singh, Sepoy Sapuram, 59
Singh, Sepoy Sarain, 59
Singh, Sepoy Sucha, 59
Singh, Sepoy Sundur, 59
Singh, Sepoy Ujagar, 59
Sino-Japanese War, 381
Sistan, 209
Sisters of Mercy, 421
Sittang, 404
Skeen, Gen Sir Andrew, 400
Slaughter & May, 425
Slevin, F., 269
Slim, FM Sir William, 306, 378
Smart, Capt Hugh, 55, 57
Smith, Pte, 71
Smith, Spr George, 168
Smith, Capt G.L., 70, 72
Smith VC, Cpl Issy, 13, 22–5, 314, 389–94
Smith, Spr James, 168
Smith VC, James, 257
Smith, 2Lt W.S. Smith, 170
Smith-Dorien, Gen Sir Horace, 10, 23, 27
Smyth VC, Lt John, 48, 57, 59, 213, 394–406
Smyth, John Lawrence, 401
Sneinton, 283
Snow, Maj Gen TD'O, 18
Sobraon, 210
Society for the Propogation of the Gospel, 262
Sodbury, 299
Somerset, 188, 192–4, 212, 219, 239, 321, 350–3
Somme, 6, 151, 160, 180, 259, 272, 299, 317, 340
Sonthal Insurrection, 208
Sophie, Countess of Wessex, 353
Sotheby's, 214, 345

South Africa, 196, 200, 215, 220, 252, 262, 265, 287–8, 321, 348, 370, 386, 391, 395, 431
South African Forces,
  Baden Powell's Police (South African Constabulary), 347
  Transvaal Mounted Constabulary, 370
South African Railways, 348
Southall, 190–1, 370
South America, 198, 409
Southampton, 239, 265, 272, 407
South Carolina, 351
South Doddington, 326
South Kesteven District Council, 388
South Petherton, 352–3
Southport, 299
South Raglan Barracks, Devonport, 199
Southsea, 394, 403
South Stoneham, 370
Southwark & Cathedral, 319–20, 348
South Wingate, 315, 317
Southwold, 351
Sovereign Bank, 275
Sowerby Bridge, 246, 407
Spain, 291
Spalding, 387
Spanish Civil War, 381
Sparkbrook, 407
Special Operations Executive, 294
Special Police Corps, 396
Spencer Press Ltd, 313
Spey, Battle of the, 380
Spink's, 191, 202, 214, 323, 338, 358
Spurn Head, 289
St Abb's, 274
St Albans, 318, 427–8
St Andrew's, 373–5
St Andrew's Deaconess Community, 346
St Andrew's Society, 276
St Anne's-on-the-Sea, 199
St Catherine's, Ontario, 274–5, 279
St Edmundsbury, 262
St Eloi, 1, 147, 150, 349
St George's Barracks, London, 391
St George's-in-the-East, 389
St Helens, 287, 408
St Helens, Isle of Wight, 412
St Helier, 248–9
St Jan/Jean, 7, 22, 33, 135
St-Jean-sur-Richelieu, 237
St John, New Brunswick, 239
St John's Ambulance, 363, 410
St Julien, 5–6, 8–23, 26, 30, 32–5, 135, 213, 278, 289, 330, 382, 391
St Leger, 216, 218
St Leonard's-on-Sea, 370
St Nazaire, 212, 232, 278, 289
St Olle, 275
St Omer, 204, 292
St Peter-at-Gowt's, 418
St Peter, Jersey, 248, 253
St Peter Port, Guernsey, 347
St Petersburg, 412

St Peter's, Guernsey, 209
Staden, 212
Stafford Corner, 49, 55
Staffordshire, 199–200, 207, 290, 300, 322, 324, 334, 353, 365, 419–20
Staines, 291
Stairs, Lt G.W., 10
Staveley, 283
Streatham, 308
Steenbeek, 18
Steenstraat, 1, 7–8, 12, 23, 27
Stenabaugh, Jack, 297
Stephen B. Roman Foundation of Canada, 214
Stephens, Lt Col R.B., 47
Stepney, 266–7, 392
Sterry, Pte W., 150
Stevenson, 2Lt David, 166–7
Stevenson, Robert Louis, 275
Stewart & McDonald, Messrs, 360
Stirk, Cpl Albert, 134
Stirling & Castle, 85, 359
Stockwell, Capt, 55
Stokesley, 403
Stonehenge, 277–8
Stourbridge, 199
Stowmarket, 296
Straits of Malacca, 415
Strand, London, 308
Strange, Maj Gen Thomas, 276
Strensall, 230, 323–4
Strickland, Maj Gen E.P., 168, 398
Stockholm, 264
Stockport, 370
Street, 352
Stroombeek, 15–16
Stroxton, 387
Stuart VC, Capt Ronald, 364, 410
Stuttgart, 263
Sudan, 229, 264, 281–2
Sudan Auxiliary Defence Force, 282
Sudan Expedition 1884, 195, 264
Sudan High Court, 282
Sudetenland, 351
Suffolk, 164, 182, 206, 262, 296, 334, 351, 375
Suhren, Fritz, 294
Sullivan VC, Arthur, 225, 314
Sun Alliance Assurance Co, 409–10
Sunderland, 296, 331
Surbiton, 202, 204–206
Surbiton United Cricket Club, 202
Surrey, 202, 205–207, 239, 249, 281, 290, 308, 314–16, 320, 328, 334, 425
Sussex, 215, 237, 239, 243–4, 259, 261–2, 310, 355, 362, 370, 416, 431
Sutlej Campaign, 210
Suvla, 381
Suwalki, Poland, 340–1
Swanton Morley, 356
Swinton Mill, 325
Switzerland, 198, 213, 262, 282
Sydney, 300–304, 307
Sykes VC, Ernest, 365

Tahiti, 198
Talbot, Lt Gilbert, 77–8, 432
Talbot, House, 77–8, 432–3
Talbot, Rev'd Neville, 432–3
Tamale, Gold Coast, 370
Tamplin, John, 320
Taplow, 313
Tasmania, 407
Taunton, 219
Tchernaya, Battle of, 264
Tedbury St Mary, 208
Tehsil, Peshawar, India, 356
Teignmouth, 282, 394
Tel el Kebir, 390
Tempe, 288
Temple VC, William, 207
Temple, Archbishop William, 396
Texas, 350
Thapa VC, Rfn Kulbir, 80–1, 84, 324–5
Thatcham & House, 412, 417
Thomas & Elliott Bros, 308
Thompson, Lt, 108
Thompson, Pte W., 150
Thornton, Spr Joseph, 168
Thorowgood, Pte, 218
Thruston, Capt B.J., 46
Tillicoultry, 257, 359
Timsbury, 194
Tirah Campaign, 209, 395
Tirah Expeditionary Force, 212
Tirah Province, 354
Tisdall VC, Sub Lt Arthur, 210
Titch, Pte M., 150
Tiverton, 212
Toc H., 225
Tochi & Valley, 354, 400
Tombs VC, LCpl Joseph, 48, 52–3, 337, 407–11
Tomlinson, Capt, 12
Tonbridge Wells, 334
Tooby, Alice, 284
Toolsepore, 264
Tooting, 213
Topsham Barracks, Exeter, 368
Toronto, 213–14, 411
Torquay, 299–300, 321, 339
Tottenham, 292
Tower Bridge, 92, 95, 98
Tower Hamlets, 266
Tower of London, 353
Toxteth & Park, 409
Tranmere, 362–3
Tranter, Lt, 71
Travers, Maj R.J.A., 174
Trench 46, 28–9, 428
Trimulgherry, 419
Trinkitat, 229
Trousdell, Lt Gen Sir Philip, 325
Tryon, Lt, 138, 267
Tsar, 399
Tulse Hill, 280, 433–4
Tunbridge Wells, 204–205, 207
Tunis, 333–4
Turbo, Kenya, 321

Turco Farm, 6, 12, 22, 25–6, 30, 32, 36, 135–6
Turkey, 250, 354
Turner VC, 2Lt Alexander, 118, 411–17
Turner VC, Brig Gen, 5, 8–9, 11, 13, 16–18
Turner VC, Victor, 365, 413–14, 417
Tuson, Lt Col, 13, 27
Tweed, Ethel, 425
Twiss & Brownings & Hallowes, 293
Tynemouth, 230, 421
Tyrone, 186

Uckfield, 242
Uganda, 365
Ugborough, 198
Ukraine, 389
Ulverston, 247, 251
Umbeyla, 209
Union Castle Mail Steamship Co, 223, 253
United Australia Party, 305, 393
United Counties Bank, 200
United Services Association, 374
United States of America, 201, 234–5, 259, 343, 346, 350–1, 374, 384, 389, 421
United Wine Traders, 293
Universal Carrier, 282
Universities,
  Bailliol College, Oxford, 198, 394
  Battersea Polytechnic, 309
  Caius College, Cambridge, 347
  Cambridge, 431
  Christ College, Oxford, 424
  Exeter College, Oxford, 332–3
  Glasgow, 258–9, 261
  Gordon College, Khartoum, 281
  King's College, London, 348–9
  Knox College, Toronto, 379
  Magdalen College, Oxford, 339–40
  McGill, Montreal, 276, 279, 380–1, 383–4
  Merton College, Oxford, 424
  Mocatta Library, London, 393
  Oxford, 425, 431
  Pembroke College, Cambridge, 431–2
  Presbyterian College, Montreal, 379–80
  Oxford, 331
  St Aidan's College, Birkenhead, 364
  St John's College, Cambridge, 200
  Strathclyde, 258
  Trinity College, Dublin, 371
  Trinity College, Cambridge, 217, 262, 281
  Trinity Hall, Cambridge, 351
Unknown Warrior, 225, 227–8, 233, 246, 313, 327, 364, 393, 422
Upper Norwood, 328–9
Upton VC, Pte James, 37, 43–5, 319, 418–20
Uruguay, 425

V1, 369
Valcartier Camp, Quebec, 235, 277, 381
Vancouver, 213
Vancouver Corner, 11, 14, 18, 213
Vanheule Farm, 21–2
Varsity Match, 262
VE Day, 251
Verdun, 140
Verlorenhoek Ridge, 33–4
Venezuela, 425
Vermelles, 99, 103, 105, 113, 116, 126–7, 417
Vermont, 351
Vice Lieutenant, 197
Vichy French, 363
Vickers & Hine, Messrs, 423
Vickers VC10, 364
Vickers, Alderman William, 424
Vickers VC, Pte Arthur, 90, 104–5, 421–3
Vickers VC, Capt Charles, 114–15, 127–8, 130–1, 423–7
Vickers, William Burnell, 423–4
Victor comic, 188, 214, 237, 245, 251, 279, 289, 310, 330, 338, 340, 388, 406, 414
Victoria, 300–301, 304, 307, 345, 393, 410
Victoria Barracks, Windsor, 220, 222, 224
Victoria Cross & George Cross Association, 213, 274, 405
Victoria Cross Centenary, 296, 307, 352
Vienna, 380
Villiablino, 291
Vimy & Ridge, 48, 64, 127, 155–6, 311
Vincent, Pte Harold, 71
Violaines, 60, 63, 68–70, 108, 165, 166
Vlamertinghe, 7, 14, 23
Voluntary Aid Detachments, 363
Von Falkenhayn, Gen Erich, 1–2
Von Niedermeyer, Capt Oskar, 354
Vousden VC, William, 281

Wailly, 152, 164
Wakefield, 322
Wallach, 2Lt, 174
Walthamstow, 313
Walton, Capt H.H., 130
Walton on the Hill, 363
Walworth, 249
Wandsworth, 280–1, 309, 376, 405
Wanless O'Gowan, Brig Gen R., 13
War Bonds, 189
Ward, Capt, 145
Warden, Capt, 15
Waring & Gillow, 203–205
Warley, 287
Warner VC, Pte Edward, 13, 28–9, 427–8
War of 1812, 234
War Office, 201, 236, 281, 289, 360, 370, 403, 410
Warren, Capt, 130

Warrington, 287, 408–409
Warsaw, 240
Warwick, 423
Warwickshire, 215, 321, 324, 364, 407, 421
Washfield, 370
Waterloo, London, 347
Watford, 229
Wavell, Gen Archibald, 404
Wavertree, 364
Waziristan, 263, 354, 395, 400
Wazirs, 400
Weeks, Dorothea, 282
Weeks, Sgt, 15, 17
Weir, Sgt, 166
Weir Engineering Co, 212
Wellington Barracks, Bury, 329
Wellington Barracks, London, 218, 224–6, 314
Wells, 188, 351
Wells VC, Sgt Harry, 90, 100–102, 428–30
Welton, 219
Wemyss Coal Co, 268
West African Frontier Force, 46, 208, 370
West Bengal, 338
West Derby, 200, 362
West VC, Ferdinand, 226
West, Pte Harry, 227–8
West Hartlepool, 246
West Heath, 422
West, Pte Horace, 228
West Kensington, 370
West Lothian, 184, 270
West Yorkshire, 298
West Yorkshire Police, 369
Western Australia, 258
Western Desert, 399, 413
Western Front Association, 234
Westgate, 421
Westmeath, 214, 217–18
Westmeath Gold Cup, 217
Westmeath Hunt Cup, 217
Westmeath Race Co Ltd, 218
Westminster, 215, 285, 425, 431
Westmount, 275
Weybridge, 239

Wheatley Hill, 317
Wheatley Hill Colliery, 315–17
White, Capt G., 134
White VC, William, 365, 414
White City, 204
White Hart (Harte & Garter) Hotel, Windsor, 223, 225
White Horse Hotel, Romsey, 282
White Star Line, 236
Whitehaven, 250
Whittington Barracks, Lichfield, 322, 324
Wibtoft, 364
Wicklow, 370
Wieltje & Farm, 3, 5, 8–9, 13, 17–18, 23, 26, 30–5, 355, 381
Wignall, William, 338
Wigston Magna, 407
Wilkinson, Pte E.J., 137
William Foster & Co, 318
Williams, Lt Marmaduke, 108
Williams DCM, Sgt, 337
Williamstown, Victoria, 410
Wilson & Co, 363
Wilton, Salisbury, 351
Wiltshire, 192, 212, 215, 224, 235, 277, 351, 381, 403, 417
Wimbledon, 206, 402
Winchester & Cathedral, 207, 249, 251–2, 266, 325, 336, 417, 432, 434
Windle, 287
Windsor & Castle, 218, 220, 222–6, 273, 336, 382, 387, 419
Windy Corner, 64, 398
Wingate Colliery, 317
Winnipeg, 287–9, 332
Winsor & Newton, 425
Wirral, 362
Wishaw Athletic, 184
Witley, 243
Witney, 394
Witton, 422–3
Wolmer, Daisy, 332
Wood, Lt, 83
Wood, FM Sir Evelyn, 285
Wood, Pte Robert, 145
Woodford, 314
Woodroffe, 2Lt Kenneth, 431

Woodroffe, Capt Leslie, 77, 431
Woodroffe VC, 2Lt Sydney, 72, 74–7, 430–4
Wollongong, New South Wales, 304–305
Woolley, 2Lt Geoffrey, 352
Woolverton, 192
Woolwich, 206, 217, 241, 312–13, 409
Worcestershire, 199–201
Wordsley, 200
Worshipful Company of Distillers, 293
Worshipful Company of Farriers, 405
Worshipful Company of Loriners, 293
Wortley, 366
Wrexham, 191
Wright, Catherine Mary Theresa, 190
Wyatt VC, George, 224

Yarkand, 209
Yass, New South Wales, 300
Yenikale, 415
YMCA, 199, 258, 319, 360, 380
York & Minster, 230, 321, 323–4, 357, 369
Yorkshire, 246, 262, 284, 322, 331, 365, 378, 403, 407
Young, Lt McdeB, 95
Young, Lt M.H., 179
Young VC, Pte William, 138–40, 434–7
Ypres, 37, 75, 85, 118, 134, 140–1, 147, 278, 322, 324, 330, 342, 428
Ypres, First Battle of, 1, 313, 354
Ypres, Second Battle of, 1–36, 235
Ypres, Third Battle of, 2, 36
Ypres League, 225
Yser Canal, 8, 11–14, 23, 27, 33–4, 136, 342
Yusafzai Field Force, 209

Zakka Khel, 212
Zeebrugge, 189
Zillebeke, 3, 28
Zonnebeke & Ridge, 14, 18
Zouave Wood, 73–8, 432
Zulu War, 287, 412
Zwarteleen, 13, 28, 428